DATE DUE

FEB 4 07			

DEMCO 38-296

THE LINGUISTIC TURN

THE LINGUISTIC TURN

ESSAYS IN PHILOSOPHICAL METHOD

Edited by
RICHARD M. RORTY

With two Retrospective Essays

THE UNIVERSITY OF CHICAGO PRESS

CHICAGO AND LONDON

The University of Chicago Press, Chicago 60637
The University of Chicago Press, Ltd., London
© 1967, 1992 by The University of Chicago
All rights reserved. Published 1992
Printed in the United States of America

01 00 99 98 97 96 95 94 93 92   1 2 3 4 5 6

Library of Congress Cataloging-in-Publication Data

The Linguistic turn : essays in philosophical method / edited by
    Richard M. Rorty ; with two retrospective essays.
        p.   cm.
    Includes bibliographical references.
    1. Semantics (Philosophy)   2. Language and languages—
Philosophy.   3. Analysis (Philosophy)   4. Methodology.
I. Rorty, Richard.
B840.L528   1992
149′.94—dc20   91-38851
                                                CIP
    ISBN: 0-226-72569-3 (pbk.)

PREFACE

This anthology provides materials which show various ways in which linguistic philosophers have viewed philosophy and philosophical method over the last thirty-five years. I have attempted to exhibit the reasons which originally led philosophers in England and America to adopt linguistic methods, the problems they faced in defending their conception of philosophical inquiry, alternative solutions to these problems, and the situation in which linguistic philosophers now find themselves. I have not attempted to cover all the methodological issues which have been raised by opponents of linguistic philosophy, or all the internecine quarrels about method among its proponents. I hope, however, that I have included the issues and quarrels which have been most important to the development of linguistic philosophy.

Part I of the anthology includes various "classic" essays on what philosophy should be. Much of the material included in subsequent parts consists of implicit or explicit comment on one or another of these essays. Some of them — notably Carnap's "Empiricism, Semantics and Ontology," Malcolm's "Moore and Ordinary Language," and Ryle's "Systematically Misleading Expressions" — have been frequently anthologized and are readily available. I have included them nonetheless, so that readers of, for example, Chisholm's and Passmore's criticisms of Malcolm, Shapere's criticism of Ryle, or Quine's and Corn-

man's comments on Carnap, will have the texts at hand.

Part II of the anthology is entitled "Metaphilosophical Problems of Ideal Language Philosophy." The pieces by Copi, Bergmann, and Black included in this part bear directly on the sort of philosophizing typical of Russell and of the early Carnap. The pieces by Ambrose, Chisholm, Cornman, and Quine, however, fit less easily under this title. I include them in this part because they bear in obvious ways on the metaphilosophical position which Carnap assumed in "Empiricism, Semantics, and Ontology." This latter position, with its celebrated turn in the direction of pragmatism, is quite different from the position which Carnap and his fellow logical positivists had adopted earlier. Nevertheless, its links with positivism are so close, and its differences from the metaphilosophical position characteristic of "Oxford philosophy" so sharp, that it seemed most natural to include discussions of it in Part II.

Part III begins with comments (by Chisholm, Passmore, Maxwell and Feigl, and Thompson) on the metaphilosophical position adopted by Malcolm in his "Moore and Ordinary Language." Then come two pieces (by Hare and Henle) on the question of how the ordinary-language philosopher finds out what we ordinarily say, and on the philosophical interest which this might have. The following two pieces (by Geach and Cornman) criticize certain overly simple moves made by ordinary-language philosophers in inferring philosophical conclusions from linguistic facts. Next are four pieces which attempt to characterize or criticize the work of the most influential (from a methodological point of view) of ordinary-language philosophers — J. L. Austin.[1] Part III concludes with an essay by Hampshire which, though clearly written with an eye to Austin's work, attempts a very general and radical criticism of certain positions frequently adopted by ordinary-language philosophers.

Part IV includes a number of broader and more sweeping discussions of the aims and methods of linguistic method in philosophy, as well as two forecasts about directions which linguistic philosophy might profitably take. The first of these forecasts is Strawson's discussion of "descriptive metaphysics" in his "Analysis, Science, and Metaphysics," and the second is Katz's "The Relevance to Philosophy of Linguistic Theory." I have tried to make Part IV a summary of the position in which linguistic philosophers now find themselves. The questions which are raised by

Shapere and Hampshire, those asked of Urmson and Strawson by their fellow participants in the Royaumont Colloquium, and those which Black raises about projects such as Katz's, seem to me to show where the crucial issues in metaphilosophy now lie. I have concluded this section, and the anthology as a whole, with a short essay by Bar-Hillel which, I think, states freshly and clearly the essential challenge which linguistic philosophy offers to the tradition.

Many people have generously taken time out to help me decide what should be included in this anthology. I should like to mention especially Gustav Bergmann, Roger Hancock, Carl G. Hempel, John Passmore, George Pitcher, Amélie Rorty, and Rulon Wells; they were all good enough to look over my first, tentative, table of contents. I owe a special debt to Vere Chappell, who has aided this project at every step. I am also grateful to my students in a seminar given at Princeton in 1964–65; their response to various readings helped me decide what to include, and their criticisms of various metaphilosophical theses which I put forward helped me decide what I wanted to say about many issues. Ronald de Sousa, Gilbert Harman, Klaus Hartmann, Alasdair MacIntyre, and George Pitcher read the penultimate draft of the introduction, and their comments led me to make many revisions.

I am grateful to P. F. Strawson and J. O. Urmson for looking over my translations of their papers (and of the ensuing discussions) given at the Royaumont colloquium. They detected many errors; those that remain are entirely my responsibility. Jerome Neu is mainly responsible for the bibliography; his thoroughness and precision have been extraordinary. Mrs. Laura Bell and Mrs. Araxy Foster typed the introduction and the bibliography with great care, and caught many mistakes which I had missed. Mrs. Barbara Oddone took many of the burdens of assembling the manuscript off my shoulders.

---

[1] I should concede that Wittgenstein has often been thought of as an ordinary-language philosopher, and that he has been more influential than Austin. But I would argue that his influence has consisted in bringing philosophers to adopt substantive philosophical theses rather than methodological attitudes and strategies. Austin's influence, on the other hand, has been almost entirely of the latter sort.

(A word about the omission of both Austin and Wittgenstein may be in point here. The only piece of Austin's that contains any sustained discussion of metaphilosophical issues is his "A Plea for Excuses." Apart from the fact that this long essay has been almost anthologized to death, only its initial section is relevant to the concerns of this anthology. Detaching this section from what follows would, I think, betray Austin's intentions. Omitting it has given me space for some essays about Austin which seem to me very valuable. As for Wittgenstein, I would have liked to include Sections 89–113 from Part I of the *Philosophical Investigations*; Wittgenstein's literary executors, however, have adopted a firm, and quite understandable, policy of not permitting this work to be excerpted.)

CONTENTS

INTRODUCTION

Metaphilosophical Difficulties
of Linguistic Philosophy

I. Introductory

The history of philosophy is punctuated by revolts against the practices of previous philosophers and by attempts to transform philosophy into a science — a discipline in which universally recognized decision-procedures are available for testing philosophical theses. In Descartes, in Kant, in Hegel, in Husserl, in Wittgenstein's *Tractatus*, and again in Wittgenstein's *Philosophical Investigations*, one finds the same disgust at the spectacle of philosophers quarreling endlessly over the same issues. The proposed remedy for this situation typically consists in adopting a new method: for example, the method of "clear and distinct ideas" outlined in Descartes' *Regulae*, Kant's "transcendental method," Husserl's "bracketing," the early Wittgenstein's attempt to exhibit the meaninglessness of traditional philosophical theses by due attention to logical form, and the later Wittgenstein's attempt to exhibit the pointlessness of these theses by diagnosing the causes of their having been propounded. In all of these revolts, the aim of the revolutionary is to replace opinion with knowledge, and to propose as the proper meaning of "philosophy" the accomplishment of some finite task by applying a certain set of methodological directions.

In the past, every such revolution has failed, and always for the same reason.

The revolutionaries were found to have presupposed, both in their criticisms of their predecessors and in their directives for the future, the truth of certain substantive and controversial philosophical theses. The new method which each proposed was one which, in good conscience, could be adopted only by those who subscribed to those theses. Every philosophical rebel has tried to be "presuppositionless," but none has succeeded. This is not surprising, for it would indeed be hard to know what methods a philosopher ought to follow without knowing something about the nature of the philosopher's subject matter, and about the nature of human knowledge. To know what method to adopt, one must already have arrived at some metaphysical and some epistemological conclusions. If one attempts to defend these conclusions by the use of one's chosen method, one is open to a charge of circularity. If one does not so defend them, maintaining that given these conclusions, the need to adopt the chosen method follows, one is open to the charge that the chosen method is inadequate, for it cannot be used to establish the crucial metaphysical and epistemological theses which are in dispute. Since philosophical method is in itself a philosophical topic (or, in other words, since different criteria for the satisfactory solution of a philosophical problem are adopted, and argued

1

for, by different schools of philosophers), every philosophical revolutionary is open to the charge of circularity or to the charge of having begged the question. Attempts to substitute knowledge for opinion are constantly thwarted by the fact that what *counts* as philosophical knowledge seems itself to be a matter of opinion. A philosopher who has idiosyncratic views on criteria for philosophical success does not thereby cease to be accounted a philosopher (as a physicist who refused to accept the relevance of empirical disconfirmation of his theories would cease to be accounted a scientist).

Confronted with this situation, one is tempted to *define* philosophy as that discipline in which knowledge is sought but only opinion can be had. If one grants that the arts do not seek knowledge, and that science not only seeks but finds it, one will thus have a rough-and-ready way of distinguishing philosophy from both. But such a definition would be misleading in that it fails to do justice to the progressive character of philosophy. Some philosophical opinions which were once popular are no longer held. Philosophers do argue with one another, and sometimes succeed in convincing each other. The fact that in principle a philosopher can always invoke some idiosyncratic criterion for a "satisfactory solution" to a philosophical problem (a criterion against which his opponent cannot find a non-circular argument) might lead one to think of philosophy as a futile battle between combatants clad in impenetrable armor. But philosophy is not really like this. Despite the failure of all philosophical revolutions to achieve their ends, no such revolution is in vain. If nothing else, the battles fought during the revolution cause the combatants on both sides to repair their armor, and these repairs eventually amount to a complete change of clothes. Those who today defend "Platonism" repudiate half of what Plato said, and contemporary empiricists spend much of their time apologizing for the unfortunate mistakes of Hume. Philosophers who

do not change (or at least re-tailor) their clothes to suit the times always have the option of saying that current philosophical assumptions are false and that the arguments for them are circular or question-begging. But if they do this too long, or retreat to their tents until the winds of doctrine change direction, they will be left out of the conversation. No philosopher can bear *that*, and this is why philosophy makes progress.

To say that philosophy makes progress, however, may itself seem to beg the question. For if we do not know what the goal is — and we do not, as long as we do not know what the criteria for a "satisfactory solution" to a philosophical problem are — then how do we know that we are going in the right direction? There is nothing to be said to this, except that in philosophy, as in politics and religion, we are naturally inclined to define "progress" as movement toward a contemporary consensus. To insist that we cannot know whether philosophy has been progressing since Anaximander, or whether (as Heidegger suggests) it has been steadily declining toward nihilism, is merely to repeat a point already conceded — that one's standards for philosophical success are dependent upon one's substantive philosophical views. If this point is pressed too hard, it merely becomes boring. It is more interesting to see, in detail, why philosophers *think* they have made progress, and what criteria of progress they employ. What is particularly interesting is to see why those philosophers who lead methodological revolts think that they have, at last, succeeded in becoming "presuppositionless," and why their opponents think that they have not. Uncovering the presuppositions of those who think they have none is one of the principal means by which philosophers find new issues to debate. If this is not progress, it is at least change, and to understand such changes is to understand why philosophy, though fated to fail in its quest for knowledge, is nevertheless not "a matter of opinion."

The purpose of the present volume is to provide materials for reflection on the most recent philosophical revolution, that of linguistic philosophy. I shall mean by "linguistic philosophy" the view that philosophical problems are problems which may be solved (or dissolved) either by reforming language, or by understanding more about the language we presently use. This view is considered by many of its proponents to be the most important philosophical discovery of our time, and, indeed, of the ages. By its opponents, it is interpreted as a sign of the sickness of our souls, a revolt against reason itself, and a self-deceptive attempt (in Russell's phrase) to procure by theft what one has failed to gain by honest toil.[1] Given the depth of feeling on both sides, one would expect to find a good deal of explicit discussion of whether it is in fact the case that philosophical problems can be solved in these ways. But one does not. A metaphilosophical question at so high a level of abstraction leaves both sides gasping for air. What one does find is: (a) linguistic philosophers arguing against any non-linguistic method of solving philosophical problems, on the basis of such substantive philosophical theses as "There are no synthetic a priori statements," "The linguistic form of some sentences misrepresents the logical form of the facts which they signify," "All meaningful empirical statements must be empirically disconfirmable," "Ordinary language is correct language," and the like; (b) other linguistic philosophers, as well as opponents of linguistic philosophy, arguing against these theses; (c) linguistic philosophers pointing with pride to their own linguistic reforms and/or descriptions of language, and saying "Look, no problems!"; (d) opponents of linguistic philosophy replying that the problems may have been disingenuously (or self-deceptively) evaded.

The situation is complicated by the fact,

noted in (b) above, that many of the substantive philosophical theses which for some linguistic philosophers count as reasons for adopting linguistic methods, are repudiated by other linguistic philosophers, who nevertheless persist in using these methods. There is a growing tendency among linguistic philosophers to abandon the sort of argument mentioned under (a), to fall back on (c), and to ask to be judged solely by their fruits. This tendency goes along with a tendency to say that either one *sees*, for example, that Wittgenstein has dissolved certain traditional problems, or one does not. Some linguistic philosophers who adopt this attitude are fond of the analogy with psychoanalysis: either one sees that one's actions are determined by unconscious impulses, or one does not.[2] (The psychoanalyst's claim that one's actions are so determined can always be countered by the patient's statements of his reasons for his actions. The psychoanalyst will insist that these reasons are merely rationalizations, but if the patient is good at rationalizing, the difference between rationalizations and reasons will remain invisible to him; he may therefore leave as sick as he came.) The irritation which this analogy creates in opponents of linguistic philosophy is intense and natural. Being told that one holds a certain philosophical position because one has been "bewitched by language" (Wittgenstein's phrase), and that one is unsuited for serious philosophical conversation until one has been "cured," results in attempts by such critics of linguistic philosophy as Gellner and Mure to turn the tables. These critics try to explain away linguistic philosophy as a psychologically or sociologically determined aberration.

A further source of confusion and complication is the tendency of more recent linguistic philosophers to drop the anti-philosophical slogans ("All philosophical

[1] See, for example, Blanshard [2], especially Chapters 1, 7, 8; Gellner [5]; Mure [1]; Adler [1], especially Chapters 1, 16.

[2] See Wisdom [9], [10]; Cavell [2] (especially the concluding pages), and also his "Aesthetic Problems of Modern Philosophy" in *Philosophy in America*, ed. Max Black (Ithaca, 1965).

questions are pseudo-questions!" and the like) of a somewhat earlier period, and to remark blandly that they are doing exactly what the philosophers of the past were doing — that is, trying to find out the nature of knowledge, freedom, meaning, and the like. Since these philosophers, however, tacitly equate "discovering the nature of X" with "finding out how we use (or should use) 'X' (and related words)," [3] opponents of linguistic philosophy remain infuriated. The linguistic philosopher's claim of continuity with the Great Tradition can be substantiated only by saying that insofar as the philosophers of the past attempted to find out the nature of X by doing something *other* than investigating the uses of words (postulating unfamiliar entities, for example), they were misguided. The opponents of linguistic philosophy therefore demand an account of *why* they were misguided, but they get little response save "Since they could never agree, they *must* have been misguided; a method which does not lead to a consensus cannot be a good method."

This is hardly a conclusive argument. One can always rejoin that the lack of consensus is a function of the difficulty of the subject matter, rather than the inapplicability of the methods. It is easy, though not really very plausible, to say that philosophers do not agree, while scientists do, simply because philosophers work on more difficult problems.[4] Conclusive or not, however, this argument has had a decisive historical importance. As a sociological generalization, one may say that what makes most philosophers in the English-speaking world linguistic philosophers is the same thing that makes most philosophers in continental Europe phenomenologists — namely, a sense of despair resulting from the inability of traditional

philosophers to make clear what could count as evidence for or against the truth of their views. The attraction of linguistic philosophy — an attraction so great that philosophers are, *faute de mieux*, willing to stoop even to the highly un-Socratic tactic of saying "Well, either you see it or you don't" is simply that linguistic analysis (like phenomenology) *does* seem to hold out hope for clarity on this methodological question, and thus for eventual agreement among philosophers. As long as this hope remains, there is little likelihood that linguistic philosophers will change their ways.

2. The Search for a Neutral Standpoint

These preliminary remarks suffice to show that two questions must be answered before one is in a position to evaluate the methodological revolution which linguistic philosophers have brought about: (1) Are the statements of linguistic philosophers about the nature of philosophy and about philosophical methods actually presuppositionless, in the sense of being dependent upon no substantive philosophical theses for their truth? (2) Do linguistic philosophers actually have criteria for philosophical success which are clear enough to permit rational agreement? The essays contained in this volume have been selected with these questions in mind. Directly or indirectly, each essay puts forward arguments for an answer to one or the other (or both). In the following discussion, I shall try to sketch various answers which have been given, indicating where (in the essays which follow, and elsewhere) arguments for and against these answers may be found. The present section will deal with answers to the first question; Section 3 with a topic which will emerge from comparing these answers — the contrast between "ideal language" and "ordinary language" philosophy; and Section 4 with answers to the second question.

The classic affirmative answer to the first question is given by Ayer. In distinguishing

---

[3] See, for example, the opening paragraphs of P. F. Strawson, "Truth," in *Philosophy and Analysis,* ed. M. MacDonald (Oxford, 1954), and J. L. Austin, "Truth," in *Philosophical Papers* (Oxford, 1961).

[4] See Adler [1], Chapter 10.

his own anti-metaphysical revolt from Kant's, Ayer quotes Bradley's suggestion that "the man who is ready to prove that metaphysics is impossible is a brother metaphysician with a rival theory of his own" and rejoins:

Whatever force these objections may have against the Kantian doctrine, they have none whatsoever against the thesis that I am about to set forth. It cannot here be said that the author is himself overstepping the barrier he maintains to be impassable. For the fruitlessness of attempting to transcend the limits of possible sense-experience will be deduced, not from a psychological hypothesis concerning the actual constitution of the human mind, but from the rule which determines the literal significance of language. Our charge against the metaphysician is not that he attempts to employ the understanding in a field where it cannot profitably venture, but that he produces sentences which fail to conform to conditions under which alone a sentence can be literally significant.[5]

How does Ayer know when a sentence is literally significant? The official answer to this question is implied in the following passage.

The propositions of philosophy are not factual, but linguistic in character — that is, they do not describe the behaviour of physical, or even mental, objects; they express definitions, or the formal consequences of definitions. Accordingly, we may say that philosophy is a department of logic.[6]

One would expect, from this latter passage, that the "rule which determines the literal significance of language" (Ayer's "verifiability criterion") would be a consequence of the definitions of such terms as "significance," "meaningful," "language," and the like. Whose definitions? Not, surely, definitions reached by the lexicographer's inspection of ordinary speech. In fact, Ayer simply made up his own definitions. His actual argument for his "rule of significance" was roughly as follows: we should not call "significant" (or, at least, "cognitively significant") any statement to which we cannot assign procedures for verification (or, at least, confirmation). The only such procedures we can discover are, roughly speaking, those used in mathematics and logic (derivation from definitions and axioms) and those used in empirical inquiry (confirmation by reference to sense-experience). Since the metaphysician uses neither procedure, his statements are not significant.

When the argument is put in this way, it can be seen that what Ayer is saying may be best put as a challenge to the metaphysician: "tell us what counts for or against what you are saying, and we shall listen; otherwise, we have a right to ignore you." More recent linguistic philosophers have tended to agree that it was unfortunate that Ayer disguised this eminently reasonable injunction under the guise of a discovery about the meaning of "meaningful." [7] For present purposes, however, it is important to see why he did so. Roughly speaking, it was because he had taken over from Carnap the thesis (cited above) that "philosophy is a department of logic." This thesis was itself a reflection of Carnap's conviction that philosophers said the odd things they did because they did not understand "the logical syntax of language." For instance, Carnap had suggested, Heidegger was led to ask questions like "Does the Nothing exist only because the Not, i.e., the Negation, exists?" because he did not realize that although the "historical-grammatical" syntax of "Nothing is outside" parallels that of "Rain is outside," the "logical syntax" (or, as Carnap sometimes revealingly put it, the syntax of a "logically correct language") of the latter was of the form "F(rain)" and of the former "-(Ex) Fx." Carnap and Ayer both held that the same sort of analysis which revealed Heidegger's confusion would show that certain sentences were (cognitively)

---

[5] Ayer [6], p. 35.
[6] *Ibid.*, p. 57.

[7] See, for example, M. White [8], pp. 108 ff., and Popper [1] and [2].

meaningful and others were not. What neither saw in this period (the middle thirties), was that Carnap's only procedure for deciding whether a given language was "logically correct" was whether or not its sentences were susceptible to verification (or confirmation) in one or the other of the two ways mentioned above. Consequently, neither realized that the question "Are there meaningful sentences which are not susceptible to verification (or confirmation) in any of the standard ways?" was not itself a question which could, without circularity, be answered by "logic." As was obvious to their contemporary opponents, and became obvious to Carnap and Ayer themselves later on, there is no such discipline as a philosophically neutral "logic" which leads to pejorative judgments about philosophical theses. The "logic" of *Language, Truth and Logic* and of *The Logical Syntax of Language* was far from presuppositionless. It appeared to be so only to those who were antecedently convinced of the results of its application, and thus were prepared to accept persuasively loaded definitions of "logic," "significance," and similar terms.

The realization that Carnap's (and Ryle's[8]) original attempt to conduct a philosophically neutral inquiry had failed did not, however, lead linguistic philosophers to abandon the effort which Carnap had initiated in *The Logical Syntax of Language* (and in such earlier works as *Der Logische Aufbau der Welt*). Rather, it led them to recast their descriptions of their activity. One such reformulation is offered by Bergmann, who holds that Carnap should have said that he was constructing a sketch of an "Ideal Language."

An improved language is called ideal if and only if it is thought to fulfill *three conditions*: (1) Every nonphilosophical descriptive prop-

osition can in principle be transcribed into it; (2) No unreconstructed philosophical one can; (3) All philosophical propositions can be reconstructed as statements about its syntax . . . and interpretation. . . .[9]

To see the importance of the suggestion that such a language might be constructed, one should note the implications of the first two conditions alone. Suppose that there were a language in which we could say everything else we wanted to say, but in which we could not express any philosophical thesis, nor ask any philosophical questions. This in itself would be sufficient to show that a certain traditional view of philosophy was false — namely, the view that common sense, and/or the sciences, *present* us with philosophical problems; according to this view, philosophical problems are *inescapable* because they *arise out of* reflection upon extra-philosophical subjects. To put the matter another way, this suggestion provides an interpretation for the cryptic slogan that "philosophical questions are questions of language" which is close to, and yet significantly different from, Carnap's original interpretation of this slogan. Carnap, at least when he spoke of the "logical syntax" of ordinary sentences (rather than of the reformulation of such sentences in a "logically correct" language), had suggested that philosophers said what they said because of the gap between "historico-grammatical syntax" and "logical syntax"; by "question of language" he meant a question raised as a result of ignorance of this "logical syntax." Given Bergmann's way of looking at the matter, we can throw away the notion that the expressions of our language have a hidden "logical syntax" lurking behind their surface "historico-grammatical syntax," and simply say that our language is unperspicuous, "unperspicuous" meaning simply "such as to make possible the formulation of philosophical questions and theses." On this view, to say that "philo-

---

[8] For a succinct account of the similarities between Carnap's metaphilosophical program in *The Logical Syntax of Language* and Ryle's in his "Systematically Misleading Expressions," together with a criticism of both, see Bar-Hillel [5].

[9] Gustav Bergmann [5], p. 43.

sophical questions are questions of language" is just to say that these are questions which we ask only because, as a matter of historical fact, we speak the language we do.

The fulfillment of Bergmann's first two conditions would show that we do not have to speak the language we do (unless we *want* to ask philosophical questions), and thus would quash the traditionalist rejoinder that we speak the language we do, and therefore must ask the philosophical questions we ask, because language reflects a reality which can be described or explained only if we are willing to philosophize. If a Bergmannian ideal language could be constructed, the philosopher would have to deny that it "adequately represented *reality*" on the *sole* ground that one could not philosophize in it. This, however, would be embarrassing. The usual defense of traditional philosophers, when confronted with complaints that they indulge in endless futile debate on esoteric matters, is to insist that they do not *want* to be esoteric, but that they are *forced* to be, because ordinary language and scientific descriptive discourse confront them with problems requiring esoteric solutions. Confronted with Bergmann's alternative language, and thus deprived of this defense, they would have to fall back on a moral or an aesthetic appeal, and insist that because philosophy is fun (or sublime, or character strengthening), Bergmann's language is inadequate — not because it fails to "represent reality," but because it makes impossible an activity which is intrinsically worthwhile. This position, though theoretically tenable, is rarely occupied. Few of the opponents of linguistic philosophy have been willing to characterize philosophy *simply* as an art form, or as an exercise of one's intellectual muscles.

Yet even if we grant Bergmann's point that we only philosophize because we speak the language we do, and that we need not speak this language, a sense of discomfort may remain. One feels that a language

might be adequate to represent reality if it did not permit us to philosophize, but that it would not be adequate unless it permitted us to discuss what philosophers want to discuss — philosophers are, for better or worse, real. (A language which would not permit us to speak as savages do might be adequate, but not a language which would not permit anthropologists to talk about the way savages talk.) It is this discomfort which Bergmann's third condition is designed to allay. If the ideal language is such that "all philosophical propositions can be reconstructed as statements about its syntax and interpretation," we are then given a way of talking about the history of philosophy. We view traditional philosophical theses as suggestions about what an ideal language would be like. We assume that the philosophers of the past were trying to find a language in which philosophical propositions could not be stated, and philosophical questions could not be asked. (If this seems too violent a "reconstruction" of, for example, Spinoza and Kant, it may help if we consider the analogy with the language of savages: we naturally tend to take a good many of the strange things savages say as awkward attempts to do science — to predict and explain phenomena. We therefore "translate" their statements into statements about entities which we know to exist — diseases, climatic changes, and the like. These translations, however, are better called "reconstructions," for we would make them even if we find that they have *no* words for diseases and the like, and cannot be made to grasp such concepts. *We* know what they are trying to do, even if they do not, and thus when we "translate," we do so in part by considering what we would say in a similar situation.) This attitude toward past philosophy may be condescending, but it can be supported by a variant of the same challenge to the philosophical tradition which we attributed above to Ayer: "If you were *not* making proposals for such an ideal language, what *were* you doing? Certainly you were not making empirical inquiries, nor deducing consequences from self-evident truths; so if not this, what?"

If there is a single crucial fact which explains the contemporary popularity of linguistic philosophy, it is the inability of its opponents (so far, at any rate) to give a satisfactory answer to this question. It is no good saying that the great philosophers of the past were not interested in anything so piffling as *language*, but were interested instead in the nature of *reality*, unless we can get some clear idea of what it was they wanted to know about reality, and of how they would know that they had this knowledge once they had it. If one construes, for example, Spinoza's "There is only one substance" as a proposal to stop talking about persons and physical objects in the ordinary (roughly, Aristotelian) way, and to start talking about them as dimly-seen aspects of a single atemporal being, a being which is both mental and physical, then one *will* have some criteria for evaluating his statement (which, unconstrued, strikes one as patently absurd). If one talks Spinozese, one will indeed be unable to state the propositions about minds and bodies which so worried the Cartesians, or the propositions about God's creation of the world which so worried the scholastics. Now it was precisely upon this that Spinoza prided himself — that the mind-body problem and problems about the relation between God and the world could not (or, at least, not very easily) be formulated in his system. It was this fact that made him confident that he had grasped the true nature of things. Using Bergmann's spectacles enables us to evaluate Spinoza in terms of criteria which do not seem far from his own; rather than the simple diagnosis of "confusion about logical syntax" which Carnap and Ryle offered us, we now have a much more sympathetic, and much more plausible, account of Spinoza's thought and of the history of philosophy in general.

This account of Bergmann's third condition has been something of an excursus from our main topic — the quest for presuppositionlessness. Let us now return to this topic, and ask what Bergmann presupposes. In what we have quoted from him so far, he has presupposed nothing; he has merely offered a stipulative definition of the term "ideal language," and, implicitly, a proposal for the future use of the term "philosophy." He is self-referentially consistent — that is, he himself abides by the rules he lays down for others (whereas Ayer, in laying down the verifiability principle, which was itself neither verifiable nor analytic, did not). Philosophy for Bergmann is linguistic recommendation, and that is all that he himself practices. If we are to look for presuppositions, we must look to his claim to have sketched an actual ideal language. If we do so, we will find him enunciating controversial philosophical theses — for example, the thesis that the primitive terms of the ideal language need include only the apparatus of an extensional logic, predicates referring to objects of direct acquaintance, and a few more. Fortunately, we need not consider such theses, since Bergmann does not use these theses to defend linguistic philosophy. His argument for the replacement of traditional methods by linguistic methods is complete without reference to such assumptions. This argument is summed up in the following passage.

All linguistic philosophers talk about the world by means of talking about a suitable language. This is the linguistic turn, the fundamental gambit as to method, on which ordinary and ideal language philosophers (OLP, ILP) agree. Equally fundamentally, they disagree on what is in this sense a "language" and what makes it "suitable." Clearly one may execute the turn. The question is why one should. Why is it not merely a tedious roundabout? I shall mention three reasons. . . .

First. Words are used either ordinarily (commonsensically) or philosophically. On this distinction, above all, the method rests. The prelinguistic philosophers did not make it. Yet they used words philosophically. *Prima facie* such uses are unintelligible. They require commonsensical explication. The method insists that we provide it. (The qualification, *prima facie*, is the mark of moderation.) The extremists of both camps hold that what the classical philosophers were above all anxious to express is irremediable nonsense.) *Second*. Much of the paradox, absurdity, and opacity of prelinguistic philosophy stems from failure to distinguish between speaking and speaking about speaking. Such failure, or confusion, is harder to avoid than one may think. The method is the safest way of avoiding it. *Third*. Some things any conceivable language merely shows. Not that these things are literally "ineffable"; rather, the proper (and safe) way of speaking about them is to speak about (the syntax and interpretation of a) language. . . .[10]

These arguments are *practical* arguments, not theoretical arguments based on theoretical considerations about the nature of language or the nature of philosophy.[11] They amount to saying to traditional philosophers: try doing it this way, and see if you don't achieve your purposes more efficiently. To attack these arguments, opponents of linguistic philosophy would have to hold (1) that their purposes and Bergmann's are different, or (2) that the philosophers of the past have not used terms "unintelligibly" and that prelinguistic philosophy is not marked by "paradox, absurdity, and opacity," or (3) that an ideal language which meets Bergmann's conditions cannot be constructed (holding that, though Bergmann has a good idea, it just won't work), or (4) that the linguistic turn is, in fact, a "tedious roundabout," because it forces us to attend to words alone, instead of the concepts or universals which words signify, and to which we must eventually return to check up on our words. Only the third and fourth alternatives hold any real promise, and these are, in fact, the

only alternatives which have been seriously developed by opponents of linguistic philosophy. That prelinguistic philosophy is marked by "paradox, obscurity, and opacity" is uncontroversial. To adopt a different set of purposes than Bergmann's would, as I suggested above, make philosophy either an art form or an exercise in character building.

Why might one hold (3)? Historically, suspicion of the possibility of constructing an Ideal Language is based on the fact that most linguistic philosophers have been empiricists (and also, often, behaviorists). They have assumed that the Ideal Language was one which took as primitives only the objects of "direct perceptual acquaintance" and that every descriptive proposition (specifically, propositions about consciousness, reason, knowledge, and the "underlying nature" of things) could be translated into propositions about these objects. Given this situation, all the usual arguments against empiricism and behaviorism have been trotted out to criticize the various sketches of ideal languages which have been proposed. But all these arguments are, as Bergmann takes pains to emphasize, irrelevant to the question of whether we should take the linguistic turn. It may well be that we cannot translate statements about consciousness and knowledge into statements about objects of direct perceptual acquaintance, but that would merely show that the ideal language is not an empiricist language. The linguistic turn may, for all we know now, lead us back to rationalism and to idealism.

Objection (4), though linked historically with (3), is not so obviously irrelevant. Empiricism and behaviorism have usually gone hand-in-hand with nominalism, the doctrine that there are no concepts and no universals. Many opponents of linguistic philosophy (notably Blanshard) have held that no one would have dreamed of taking the linguistic turn unless he were antecedently committed to nominalism. They have suspected that the linguistic turn is simply a sneaky move by which empiri-

---

[10] Bergmann [3], p. 177. The phrase "the linguistic turn" which Bergmann uses here and which I have used as the title of this anthology is, to the best of my knowledge, Bergmann's own coinage.

[11] For the importance of distinguishing between theoretical and practical arguments in this situation, see the debate between Copi and Bergmann (Copi [3], Bergmann [12], and Copi [4] — all reprinted below at pp. 127–35).

cists have silently inserted a commitment to nominalism into their methodology, in order to avoid having to argue for this commitment later on. Surely, they argue, in order to know whether the expressions of a language are adequate to say everything we want to say (outside of philosophy), we have to see whether these expressions adequately express our concepts (or, perhaps, the subsistent universals which our concepts themselves represent). Since traditional philosophy has been (so the argument goes) largely an attempt to burrow beneath language to that which language expresses, the adoption of the linguistic turn presupposes the substantive thesis that there is nothing to be found by such burrowing.

There are two ways in which one may reply to this objection. First, one may note that among the propositions which we would attempt to reconstruct in an ideal language are such propositions as "Words are often inadequate to express concepts," "There are concepts," "Concepts represent universals existing *ante rem*," and the like. If nominalism is false, we will find that it is false by attempting (and failing) to reconstruct such statements in an ideal language which does not admit, as primitive terms, words referring to such concepts and/or universals. The objector may well feel, however, that this procedure is circular, for the test determining whether "There are concepts" has been *adequately* reconstructed is unclear, and (he suspects) the linguistic philosopher will have assigned, in advance, a meaning to "concept" which will be adequately reconstructed in a nominalistic language, but which is not what *he* (the objector) means by "concept." This line of argument is important, but it takes us into the issues which are to be discussed in the next section — the question of whether linguistic philosophers have tests for such matters as "adequate reconstruction" which are themselves non-controversial. We shall therefore defer it until it may be considered in a broader perspective.

For the present, let us consider a second reply which can be made to this objection. The objection may be met directly, on its own ground, by saying that even if we grant the existence of concepts (and/or subsistent universals), the fact is that our only knowledge of these entities is gained by inspection of linguistic usage. Young philosophers, about to take the linguistic turn, are met by a little group of pickets holding signs saying "Don't waste your life on words — come to us, and we shall reason together about what these words *stand for!*" But if they have read Wittgenstein's *Philosophical Investigations*, they will have been struck by such remarks as:

"Imagine a person whose memory could not retain *what* the word 'pain' meant — so that he constantly called different things by that name — but nevertheless used the word in a way fitting in with the usual symptoms and presuppositions of pain" — in short he uses it as we all do. Here I should like to say: a wheel that can be turned though nothing else moves with it, is not part of the mechanism.[12]

You learned the *concept* 'pain' when you learned language.[13]

In order to get clear about the meaning of the word "think" we watch ourselves while we think; what we observe will be what the word means! — But this concept is not used like that. (It would be as if without knowing how to play chess, I were to try and make out what the word "mate" meant by close observation of the last move of some game of chess.)[14]

Neither these passages nor anything else in Wittgenstein's work provides a direct argument against the existence of concepts or universals, or against the view that we can inspect concepts or universals "directly" (that is, without looking at language) and then compare what we find with the way words are used. But they suggest reasons why we might be misled into thinking that we could do this, even though in fact we cannot. Largely because reading Wittgenstein takes away one's instinctive convic-

[12] Wittgenstein [1], Part I, Section 271.
[13] *Ibid.*, Section 384.
[14] *Ibid.*, Section 316.

tion that such inspection *must*, somehow, be possible (and suggests thought experiments in which one tries (and fails) to perform such inspections and such comparisons), what might be called "methodological nominalism" has become prevalent among linguistic philosophers. As I shall use this term, methodological nominalism is the view that all the questions which philosophers have asked about concepts, subsistent universals, or "natures" which (a) cannot be answered by empirical inquiry concerning the behavior or properties of particulars subsumed under such concepts, universals, or natures, and which (b) can be answered in *some* way, can be answered by answering questions about the use of linguistic expressions, and in no other way.

It is probably true that no one who was not a methodological nominalist would be a linguistic philosopher, and it is also true that methodological nominalism is a substantive philosophical thesis. Here, then, we have a presupposition of linguistic philosophy, one which is capable of being defended only by throwing the burden of proof on the opponent and asking for (a) a question about the nature of a particular concept which is not so answerable, and (b) criteria for judging answers to this question. Debates about the existence of concepts or universals, or about whether we possess faculties for inspecting them directly, are irrelevant to this issue. When choosing a philosophical method, it is not helpful to be told that one is capable of intuiting universals,[15] or that man's intellect is "a cognitive power . . . irreducible to all of his sensitive faculties."[16] One needs to know whether one has intuited universals correctly, or whether one's intellect is performing its irreducible function properly. Objection (4) has carried little weight

simply because no clear procedure has ever been put forward for determining whether or not a word did or did not adequately express a concept, or whether or not a sentence adequately expressed a thought.[17]

In offering this reply to objection (4), we have once again fallen back on the challenge to opponents of linguistic philosophy which we originally put in the mouth of Ayer: namely, tell us what other methods are available, and we shall use them. We can best see the force of this challenge by considering it a reply to a more general objection: what is the use of looking at our use of the word "X" if you want to know about X's, or things which are X? The most succinct form of the reply is given by Quine, in the course of a general account of "semantic ascent" ("shift from talk of objects to talk of words").

Semantic ascent, as I speak of it, applies anywhere. "There are wombats in Tasmania" might be paraphrased as " 'Wombat' is true of some creatures in Tasmania," if there were any point in it. But it does happen that semantic ascent is more useful in philosophical connections that in most, and I think I can explain why . . . The strategy of semantic ascent is that it carries the discussion into a domain where both parties are better agreed on the objects (*viz.*, words) and on the main terms concerning them. Words, or their inscriptions, unlike points, miles, classes, and the rest, are tangible objects of the size so popular in the marketplace, where men of unlike conceptual schemes communicate at their best. The strategy is one of ascending to a common part of two fundamentally disparate conceptual schemes, the better to discuss the disparate foundations. No wonder it helps in philosophy.[18]

If one tries to find substantive philosophical commitments lurking behind what Quine says here, all that one can find is (1) the principle that a statement about X's can often be paraphrased into one about the term "X," *and conversely*, so that to have found out something about "X" often

[15] For a critique of Wittgenstein's methodological nominalism employing this notion, see Blanshard [2], especially pp. 389 ff.; for a reply to Blanshard, see Rorty [3].

[16] Adler [1], p. 78. For a reply to the sort of diagnosis of linguistic philosophy which Adler offers, see Rorty [2].

[17] See Ambrose [5] and Pears [3].

[18] W. v. O. Quine, *Word and Object* (Cambridge, 1960), pp. 271–72. (See below, p. 169.)

tells you something about X's, and (2) the principle that a philosophical method which produces agreement among philosophers is, *ceteris paribus*, better than a method which does not. The latter principle is noncontroversial (unless one jumps on the *ceteris paribus* clause, and claims that what is lost by attaining agreement through looking to linguistic usage is more valuable than the agreement gained). The former principle is objectionable only if one claims that certain statements about "X" require knowledge of X's, and thus argues once again that the linguistic turn is a "tedious roundabout." But Ayer's and Carnap's original point, that empirical inspection of particular X's seems irrelevant to philosophical theses, together with the Wittgensteinian point that we cannot investigate *X*hood, nor the concept of X, except by investigating our use of words, is accepted by linguistic philosophers as a sufficient answer to this claim. If either point is challenged, all they can do is to shift, once again, the burden of proof to their opponents.

So much for the present about the Bergmannesque program of Ideal Language Philosophy. I now turn to an alternative attempt to reformulate (in a presuppositionless way) the original Ayer-Carnap thesis that philosophical questions are questions of language, an attempt which is the least common denominator of the metaphilosophical positions of those whom Bergmann calls "Ordinary Language Philosophers." This school of thought is celebrated for refusing to be considered a "school," and for systematically avoiding commitment to explicit methodological theses. Centered in Oxford (and therefore sometimes called simply "Oxford philosophy"), this school may be roughly defined as comprising those philosophers who would accept Bergmann's practical arguments as adequate reasons for taking the linguistic turn, but who refuse to construct an Ideal Language. Their refusal stems from the hunch that ordinary English (or, more precisely, ordinary English minus

philosophical discourse) may fulfill Bergmann's requirements for being an Ideal Language. As has often been (somewhat crudely, but fairly accurately) said, the only difference between Ideal Language Philosophers and Ordinary Language Philosophers is a disagreement about which language is Ideal.

From the traditional logical positivist point of view, the suggestion that ordinary English (or, indifferently, ordinary German, or Greek, or Tagalog) is Ideal sounds absurd, for was it not precisely the unperspicuous character of ordinary English which originally permitted the formulation of the traditional problems of philosophy? Positivists find it important to construct an alternative language (that is, one whose undefined descriptive terms refer only to objects of direct acquaintance, whose logic is extensional, etc.) in order to prevent the possibility of formulating such problems. To this, Ordinary Language Philosophy replies that philosophical problems arise not because English is unperspicuous (it is not), but rather because philosophers have not used English. They have formulated their problems in what *looks* like ordinary English, but have in fact misused the language by using terms jargonistically (while relying on the ordinary connotations of these terms), and similar devices. If Ordinary Language Philosophy had an explicit program (which it does not), it might run something like this: we shall show that any argument designed to demonstrate that common sense (or the conjunction of common sense and science) produces problems which it cannot answer by itself (and which therefore must be answered by philosophers, if by anyone), is an argument which uses terms in unusual ways. If philosophers would use words as the plain man uses them, they would not be able to raise such problems.

Much of the work of philosophers who (by their critics, at least) are classed as members of this school consists in just such analyses of typical philosophical problems. A paradigm of this sort of work is Austin's dissection of Ayer's "Argument from Illusion"[19] (an argument which was designed to show the utility of sketching an Ideal Language whose undefined descriptive predicates would refer to directly apprehended characteristics of postulated entities called "sense-data"). The existence of such paradigms has brought many contemporary philosophers to adopt tacitly the program sketched above. Explicit methodological remarks which suggest such a program are scattered throughout the recent literature. The most famous of these is perhaps the following passage from Wittgenstein:

When philosophers use a word — 'knowledge', 'being', 'object', 'I', 'proposition', 'name' — and try to grasp the *essence* of the thing, one must always ask oneself: is the word ever actually used in this way in the language-game which is its original home?

What *we* do is to bring words back from their metaphysical to their everyday use.[20]

As we shall see in more detail in Section 4, the interpretation of such programmatic remarks is vexing, for troublesome questions can be raised about the criteria for philosophical success which they implicitly invoke. (For example, what *is* the "language-game which is the original home" of the word "proposition," and how would one know that one had correctly identified it?) But for our present purposes, these questions can be postponed. What concerns us now is: does the program of Ordinary Language Philosophy, as sketched, presuppose any substantive philosophical theses? At first sight, it might seem that it obviously does, and a highly controversial one at that: namely, that ordinary language, plus science, is adequate to describe and explain everything that there is. We may best analyze this claim by viewing it as a form of another general objection to both types of linguistic philosophy: *viz.*, it is pointless to show that philosophers can no longer philosophize when deprived of

the necessary linguistic resources. It would seem that to show this merely puts off the real question: *should* we philosophize?[21]

Now, this latter question will receive different answers depending on how it is interpreted. If "Should we philosophize?" means (1) "Should we ask the sort of questions which traditional philosophers have raised? (for example, What is justice? Does God exist? Is man different in kind from the animals? Can we have objective knowledge of an external world?)," then it is rather silly. Having once read a sampling of traditional philosophy, we cannot choose *not* to ask such questions. But if "Should we philosophize?" means (2) "Should we attempt to find answers to these questions other than the answers which can be given by common sense and by science?" the answer is not so obvious. If it means (3) "Should we ask these questions as first-order questions about reality, rather than translating them into second-order questions about such words as 'justice', 'God', 'existence', 'kind', and 'objective'?" then, again, the answer is not obvious. The question "Should we philosophize?" is merely rhetorical if it is given the first of the above-mentioned interpretations. If it is given the third interpretation, it must then be taken as short for "*How* should we philosophize?" and *this* question cannot be answered rationally unless one knows whether an Ideal Language

---

[19] See Austin [3], especially Chapters 2, 3.
[20] Wittgenstein [1], Part I, Section 116.

[21] This general objection is particularly in point when raised against Ordinary Language Philosophy, for this school refuses to join Bergmann in regarding traditional philosophizing as a worthwhile activity. Part of Bergmann's advance over the early Carnap and the early Ryle was that he did not claim that traditional philosophers philosophized simply because they were "confused" about "logical form"; he claimed that, while they were doing something worthwhile, they were confused about what they were doing. The program of Ordinary Language Philosophy, viewed from this angle, is a throwback to the earlier charge of simple carelessness about language. The charge is now that traditional philosophers misused language, rather than that they were confused about its "logical syntax." For Ordinary Language Philosophy, as for Bergmann, there is no such thing as "logical syntax" hidden behind ordinary linguistic usage.

of Bergmann's type can be constructed (and, *a fortiori*, whether we already have such an Ideal Language in ordinary English). To say that linguistic philosophers have begged the question "Should we philosophize?" by insisting that we should philosophize by linguistic methods, would itself be question-begging. Most critics who claim that linguistic philosophers have begged this question would give the question the second interpretation. They would say that linguistic philosophers have assumed that common sense, science, and attention to the uses of words will suffice to give whatever answers can be given to these questions, and that if no further answers are forthcoming, it is because the questions are bad questions. They would argue that, in the absence of this assumption, the successful completion of the program of either Ideal or of Ordinary Language Philosophy would be of no interest, since all that such programs would show is that philosophers who are not permitted to introduce certain locutions into the language cannot say what they want to say. But since nobody would dream of trying to construct a language in which, for example, paleontologists or epigraphists could not say what they wanted to say, and since nothing about the value or significance of paleontological or epigraphical questions would be shown by constructing such a language, why should a similar project in philosophy have any interest, unless there is prior animus against philosophy?

In reply to this line of argument, linguistic philosophers can only fall back upon the challenges previously set forth, and thereby attempt to put the burden of proof back upon their opponents. If (they say) you think that there are questions which common sense and science cannot answer, it is up to you not just to state them, but to show how they *can* be answered. If you think that there is more to be described and explained than is described in, or explained by, common sense and science, tell us how you know whether you have described it accurately, or have

explained it correctly. If you cannot do either of these things, then we shall persist in regarding your questions (questions which could not be posed in an Ideal Language, or which could not be posed without misusing English) as bad questions. In showing that an Ideal Language can be constructed (or that Ordinary Language is Ideal), we shall not, indeed, have shown anything except that they are questions which are unnecessary to pose unless we wish to philosophize in the traditional manner. But the discovery that we are not *forced* to philosophize in the traditional manner is not a trivial discovery, simply because (to repeat an earlier point) traditional philosophers have insisted that common sense and science force such philosophizing upon us. To say that traditional philosophical questions are bad questions is, admittedly, to say more than that they are questions which employ ordinary expressions in unusual ways, or that they are questions which we are not forced to ask. It is to say that they are questions which, as they stand, are unanswerable. But the only presupposition which we must make is that if we have no criteria for evaluating answers to certain questions, then we should stop asking those questions until we do.

So far, I have been emphasizing the common ground shared by Ideal Language Philosophy and Ordinary Language Philosophy. I have tried to show that their programs are alternative means to the same ends, and that neither presupposes the sort of substantive philosophical theses to which their critics claim linguistic philosophy is committed. I have argued that those presuppositions which they do make boil down to a single, plausible claim: that we should not ask questions unless we can offer criteria for satisfactory answers to those questions. In so arguing, however, I have simplified many issues, and passed over many difficulties. In the next section, I shall discuss the issues which divide Ideal Language Philosophy from Ordinary Language Philosophy, and argue that they are not as relevant to questions about the value of linguistic philosophy as they have sometimes appeared. In Section 4, I shall discuss the difficulties which arise over the claim of linguistic philosophers to have formulated questions about which we *can* give criteria for satisfactory answers.

3. IDEAL LANGUAGE PHILOSOPHY VERSUS ORDINARY LANGUAGE PHILOSOPHY

Many of the essays included in the present volume are part of a continuing controversy between Ideal Language philosophers and Ordinary Language philosophers. From the lofty metaphilosophical standpoint we have adopted, it is not clear why such a controversy should exist, and many philosophers in fact regard it as factitious. (Thus we find Goodman remarking, and Carnap agreeing, that the "constructionalist" philosopher (one who constructs a Bergmann-like Ideal Language) "looks upon the verbal analyst as a valued and respected, if inexplicably hostile, ally.") [22] Any stick will do to beat the devil, and it would seem that offering an alternative to ordinary English might be effective in some cases, whereas demonstrating a misuse of English would be effective in others. In the present section, I shall outline the principal argument brought forward by Ordinary Language philosophers against "constructionalist" programs, and the replies typically made by Ideal Language philosophers. I shall then outline the principal argument brought by Ideal Language philosophers against their rivals, and the replies made to it. An analysis of these arguments, I shall suggest, shows that what is really in question between the two schools is the proper answer to the question "How can we find criteria for philosophical success which will permit rational agreement?" I hope to

show that the controversy, though not entirely factitious, has often been described in thoroughly misleading ways.

The *locus classicus* for the attitude of Ordinary Language philosophers toward constructionalism is in Strawson's criticism of Carnap and his followers. Strawson's central argument runs as follows:

> The [constructionalist's] claim to clarify will seem empty, unless the results achieved have some bearing on the typical philosophical problems and difficulties which arise concerning the concepts to be clarified. Now these problems and difficulties (it will be admitted) have their roots in ordinary, unconstructed concepts, in the elusive, deceptive modes of functioning of unformalised linguistic expressions . . . If the clear mode of functioning of the constructed concepts is to cast light on problems and difficulties rooted in the unclear mode of functioning of the unconstructed concepts, then precisely the ways in which the constructed concepts are connected with and depart from the unconstructed concepts must be plainly shown. And how can *this* result be achieved without accurately describing the modes of functioning of the unconstructed concepts? But this task is precisely the task of describing the logical behaviour of the linguistic expressions of natural languages; and may *by itself* achieve the sought-for resolution of the problems and difficulties rooted in the elusive, deceptive mode of functioning of unconstructed concepts. I should not want to deny that in the discharge of this task, the construction of a model object of linguistic comparison may sometimes be of great help. But I do want to deny that the construction and contemplation of such a model object can take the place of the discharge of this task. . . . [23]

To this line of argument, the constructionalist has two obvious replies: (1) If you know that talking in a certain way gets you into problems, and you have an alternative way of talking which does not get you into problems, who cares about examining the "logical behavior" involved in the first way

---

[22] Goodman [4], p. 554. For Carnap's agreement, see Carnap [7], p. 940. Compare the clerihew attributed (perhaps apocryphally) to Austin: "Everything done by Quine/ Is just fine/ All we want is to be left alone/ To potter about on our own."

[23] Strawson [1], pp. 512–13. See below, p. 316.

of talking? (Compare: if you can remove cancerous tissue and replace it with healthy tissue, there may be a certain morbid interest in the pathologist's report, but the cure is complete without that report.) The function of an Ideal Language is not to *clarify* ordinary concepts, but to *replace* them.[24] (2) "Describing the logical behavior of the linguistic expressions of natural language" *may* "by itself" bring about the desired result, but only practice will show, and the evidence so far is that it will not.[25]

Restricting our attention for the moment to the first rejoinder, we can see that Strawson will need to make certain further points to complete his critique of constructionalism. He might say first that a philosophical problem is more like a neurosis than a cancer. The neurotic is not cured unless he understands just why he was neurotic, whereas the cancerous patient is cured even if he knows nothing about how he acquired his disease. The man puzzled by philosophical problems is like the neurotic in the sense that it wouldn't count as "resolution of his problems" if we simply gave him a drug which caused him to stop worrying about the problems. Similarly, it would not count as a resolution of philosophical problems if one were to rear a new generation of men who spoke only a Bergmannian Ideal Language.

Alternatively, Strawson might argue in a different way. By Bergmann's and Goodman's own confession, he could point out, we are never going to get a language which can actually be used for everyday purposes and which is Ideal in the required sense. The analogy to the removal of a cancer is not in point — the actual situation is more like cruelly elaborating on the advantages of good health to the cancerous patient. The force of this rebuttal is strengthened by noting that Bergmann's original specification of the first requirement for calling a

language "Ideal" is that "Every nonphilosophical descriptive proposition can *in principle* be transcribed in it" (italics added). But how are we ever to know whether a given language is Ideal unless we actually do some transcribing? And what is the force of "in principle," if not to admit that in practice we cannot do any? To admit, as Bergmann seems to,[26] that no sentence in the Ideal Language will be materially equivalent to an unreconstructed sentence in ordinary use, seems to constitute an admission that the only function which Ideal Languages might serve *is* clarification, rather than replacement. For if such material equivalences are not available, then the Ideal Language can, at best, be what Goodman calls a "map" of the familiar terrain of ordinary discourse, rather than a passport into a new *Lebenswelt* in which philosophical problems are unknown. Suppose that Urmson is right in insisting that "reductive analysis" is impossible (because, roughly, the more interesting one's proposed reduction, the less plausible it is that any statement [even an indefinitely long one] in one's Ideal Language could be equivalent to a statement of ordinary discourse).[27] It then seems to follow that such an analysis could only direct our attention away from the problematic' aspects of our ordinary concepts by focusing on their unproblematic aspects.

This second sort of rebuttal, if it can be sustained, would seem to make the first unnecessary. If the analogy with curing cancer fails, then we need not worry about whether temptations to philosophize are more like neuroses than like cancers. To see whether it can be sustained we need to ask: what could be gained by noting, for example, that although no finite statement about sense-contents is (as phenomenal-

---

[24] Carnap makes this latter point in his reply to Strawson (Carnap [7], p. 938).

[25] See Feigl and Maxwell's criticism of Ryle's "misuse of language" dissolution of Zeno's paradoxes (pp. 195–96 below).

[26] I take this admission to be made in the course of Bergmann's reply to Urmson (Bergmann [5], pp. 60–62), but I am not sure what Bergmann believes that he has shown in this passage, and therefore I am not sure that the admission is actually made.

[27] See J. O. Urmson [3], Chapter 10, and pp. 296–97 below.

ists once mistakenly thought) materially equivalent to a commonsense statement about persons or physical objects, we could nevertheless cope with our environment (though very inefficiently) in a language which contained no names of persons or of physical objects? (Such a claim would result from paraphrasing Bergmann's phrase "could in principle be transcribed" as "could be replaced by, at no cost save inconvenience.") It seems safe to say that acknowledging this claim does nothing to clarify our ordinary concepts of "physical object" and "person." (To tell a scholarship student who is desperately attempting to get through college that if he drops out he can cope, though less efficiently, with his environment, does not clarify his concept of "education.") But may not acknowledging such a claim nevertheless dissolve a philosophical problem (in the way in which pointing out that the student does not *have* to finish college may relieve him of a neurotic compulsion)? Surely it may. The analyses of the notions of "the essential nature of substances" and of "the soul," which we find in Berkeley, Hume, and Kant, did in fact relieve philosophers of a host of problems which had tormented the scholastics and the seventeenth-century rationalists. If, taking the linguistic turn, we rewrite these analyses as claims about how we might be able to talk, then we retain the benefits of, for example, Kant's analyses, without their unfortunate side effects.[28]

If these benefits do in fact accrue, then Strawson's claim that "the construction and contemplation of such a model object" cannot "take the place of the discharge of this task" is beside the point, because his claim that the common aim of Ideal Language and Ordinary Language philosophers — the dissolution of philosophical

problems — requires the accurate description of "the modes of functioning of the unconstructed concepts," is simply false. The "reductive analyses" of the concepts of "substance" and "soul" offered by Kant do not provide such descriptions,[29] yet the discussion of these concepts has never been the same again. The problems concerning them, which post-Kantian philosophers have discussed, are radically different from those discussed by Kant's predecessors.[30] This historical retrospect suggests that the dichotomy of "clarification or replacement" is spurious. The Ideal Language philosopher, if he is wise, will freely grant that his Ideal Language is merely a sketch of a "form of life" that is logically possible, though pragmatically impossible, and thus

---

[28] The unfortunate side effects are due to the fact that if we accept Kant at face value (rather than reading him as a linguistic philosopher born before his time), we have to start worrying about his claim that physical objects are "appearances," about the status of the "transcendental standpoint," etc.

[29] See, respectively, the "First Analogy of Experience" and the "Paralogisms of Pure Reason" in the *Critique of Pure Reason.*

[30] Whatever Kant did, it cannot be interpreted as "clarification" via "description of linguistic behavior," any more than can, for example, his treatment of religion. Yet Kant and other writers of the Enlightenment brought men to a "post-religious" frame of mind — one in which they simply were not worried by questions which had worried their ancestors. They accomplished this more by providing what Stevenson has called "persuasive definitions" of ordinary terms than by offering the chance to play a new language-game, or by explicating the rules of the old one. In the same way, Ideal Language philosophers might suggest, a "post-philosophical" frame of mind may be induced in our descendents. (This suggestion is dealt with further below at pp. 34–35.)

One might object to this analogy that Kant's writing about religion was (unlike his analyses of "substance" and "soul") not philosophy, but prophecy or preaching. The issue cannot be discussed here, but I should argue that this objection stems from the dogma that changes in moral climate are "irrational," in contrast to that paradigm of rationality, changes in scientific theory, and from the further dogma that only the latter sort of change is a proper model for the changes which the linguistic philosopher hopes to bring about. I call these beliefs "dogmas" because I believe that recent work in the history and philosophy of science (notably the writings of Kuhn and Feyerabend) have undermined the distinctions which they presuppose. For an analysis of man's transition to a post-religious state of consciousness which avoids these dogmas, see Alasdair MacIntyre, "Is Understanding Religion Compatible with Believing?" in *Faith and the Philosophers,* ed. J. Hick (New York, 1964).

will give up his claim to literal *replacement of* ordinary discourse. But he will insist that contemplation of such sketches is an effective therapeutic method; that Strawson's tacit assumption that only "clarification" is effective is a *petitio principii*; and that Goodman's claim that the function of a constructional system is to "map experience"[31] is an injudicious and unnecessary concession to the notion that dissolution can be gained only through clarification.

Even when the dichotomy of "clarification or replacement" is discarded, however, difficulties remain for the Ideal Language philosopher. If he justifies the sketching of alternative ways of speaking by claiming that this is an effective therapy, he still needs to specify a test for determining whether a suggested Ideal Language does in fact fulfill the weakened form of Bergmann's first criterion suggested above: the criterion that the Ideal Language could replace a certain portion of ordinary discourse at no greater cost than inconvenience. He also needs to offer some reply to an argument which we previously put in Strawson's mouth — the argument, based on the analogy between philosophical problems and neurotic symptoms, that some methods of causing men to cease being bothered by philosophical problems do not count as "dissolutions" of these problems. These two difficulties are connected. If we do not have a criterion whose fulfillment can be tested, then it seems that we do not have *reasons* for saying that a philosophical problem is a pseudo-problem (or is "merely verbal," or need not be asked). It is not enough to *cause* someone to cease being preoccupied with, for example, the problem of the external world; this could, perhaps, be accomplished by drugs or torture.

Raising these problems brings into focus the real source of conflict between Ideal Language and Ordinary Language philosophers. In the early days of Ideal Language philosophy, the program presented by Car-

nap and Schlick seemed to be continuous with the earlier efforts of Moore and Russell[32] — both seemed to be offering "analyses" of sentences of ordinary discourse which told us what we really meant when we used these sentences. There seemed to be a test for such analyses — namely, that the analysans be a necessary and sufficient condition for the truth of the analysandum. As long as it was believed that interesting analyses of this sort could be presented, the problem of attaining agreement seemed to be solved. This belief gradually waned as many proposed analyses were found to fail the test; in addition, while simple material equivalence seemed too weak a test to support a claim to have analyzed "meaning," difficulties about analyticity had made philosophers dubious about the stronger test of "logical equivalence."[33] Thus, the problem about agreement was reopened. When philosophers like Bergmann and Goodman were forced to fall back on talk about

[31] See Goodman [4], p. 552.

[32] For an account of the similarities and differences between these two versions of "analysis" see Urmson, pp. 295–97 below, and also Black [14]. I should caution the reader that here, and in the pages that follow, I am not attempting to give a historically accurate account of the rise of "Ordinary Language" philosophy. In particular, it is not the case that the various (quite different) strategies employed by Ryle, Austin, and Wittgenstein were adopted because of difficulties encountered in the practice of Moore's and Russell's methods, nor because of dissatisfaction with the work of the "constructionalists." (In fact, Austin and Ryle were led to their respective strategies by such idiosyncratic factors as an admiration for Aristotle and, in Ryle's case, disenchantment with Husserlian phenomenology.) The story of the actual lines of influence which connect Moore, Russell, the early Wittgenstein, the Vienna Circle, Ryle, Austin, and the later Wittgenstein is extremely complicated, and for this story the reader is referred to Urmson [3], Warnock [3], and Ayer [16]. What I am presenting here is "dialectical" history, in which various "ideal types" (not perfectly exemplified by any single philosopher) are pictured as engaging in argument. I wish to account for the present situation in metaphilosophy by focusing on certain elements in the work of Austin, Carnap, Ryle, Wittgenstein, et al., while ignoring the actual genesis of these elements.

[33] For further discussion of various senses of "giving an analysis," see Section 4 below.

"sketches" and "maps." It became increasingly apparent that the linguistic turn might be leading us toward the same situation (*quot homines, tot sententiae*) as had prevailed in traditional philosophy. As the crucial word "transcribed" in Bergmann's first criterion became more and more difficult to interpret, the analogies between alternative proposals for Ideal Languages and alternative metaphysical systems became more obvious. In this situation, the Ordinary Language philosophers came forward to the rescue of the ideal of "philosophy as a strict science." Their chosen method — "description of the logical behavior of the linguistic expressions of ordinary language" — looked like a straightforward empirical enterprise. To show that a philosophical problem cannot be formulated in an Ideal language is interesting only if we know that that language is adequate for non-philosophical purposes. If we cannot test this adequacy, then we are in trouble. But we know already that English is adequate for non-philosophical purposes. We can test the claim that a philosophical problem cannot be formulated without misusing English if we can only determine the correct use of English expressions. Ordinary Language philosophers can argue that "constructionalists," if they are unable to answer the crucial question about a test of adequacy (which is, of course, simply another form of the question about the meaning of "can in principle be transcribed" in Bergmann's criterion), have lost precisely the advantage of "semantic ascent" which Quine cited. For the only sense in which it is true that philosophers are better agreed about words than about things is that philosophers who disagree about everything else can agree on how they use words in non-philosophical discourse. If we do not draw upon this agreement, then there is no point in taking the linguistic turn at all.

In this introduction, I cannot stop to take up the question of whether Ideal Language philosophers can resolve the difficulty of testing "capable of being transcribed in principle." Nor can I consider the usefulness, and the limitations, of Goodman's "map" analogy. Either task, if it were properly done, would involve examining the actual practice of Ideal Language philosophers, judging their methods by their fruits, and formulating a theory about why some of these fruits are better than others. It can only be noted that although both sides of the controversy tend to agree that the rudimentary sketches of languages constructed by Russell, Carnap, Goodman, Quine, and Bergmann are useful objects of study,[34] there exists no consensus about why they are useful, or any clear account of how we should choose among them.[35] Focusing our attention on the problem of finding a method which will produce agreement among philosophers, we must now turn to the complaint that Ordinary Language philosophers, despite their pretensions, do not offer us such a method. This complaint is made by Maxwell and Feigl in an article written in reaction to Strawson's criticism of Carnap. I quote their central arguments:

But will it not also be agreed, even insisted, that some philosophical problems do arise from failure to distinguish among the various meanings or uses of a term and that one of the tasks of the philosopher is to 'sort out' the various relevant meanings? But in what sense, if any, are these various *separate and distinct* meanings *already there* in ordinary language, waiting for the philosopher to unearth them? Surely the ordinary man (including ourselves) is not always conscious of their being there — otherwise, the 'philosophical problems' that rendered the 'sorting out' desirable would never have arisen. It might be retorted that by calling attention to the various uses of relevant terms we can often elicit agreement from the ordinary man (including ourselves) and in so doing remove his philosophical puzzlement. But how are we to decide whether this is the correct de-

[34] There are some who would deny even this. See Ryle [7].
[35] For an attempted resolution of this latter problem, see Bergmann [5], p. 56. Bergmann's discussion, however, turns on a notion of "isomorphism" which needs further explication.

scription of the situation, or whether we should say that we have persuaded the ordinary man to accept 'tightened up', perhaps modified — in short, *reformed* — meanings? . . . We strongly suspect that many cases of putative ordinary-usage analysis are, in fact, disguised reformations. Perhaps such activity differs only in degree from that of the avowed reconstructionist or system-builder.[36]

Surely this distinction (the analytic-synthetic distinction) is crucial for analytic philosophy; for the central concern of the analyst is the set of moves made according to the rules of the relevant language game. . . . Search ordinary usage of a particular linguistic move as much as we may, the most we are usually able to come up with is the fact that sometimes it seems to be made on the basis of an analytic premise, at other times on the basis of a factual premise; in most cases, ordinary use does not provide any definitive basis for placing it in either category. The ordinary-language analyst will, thus, in most cases, not be able to decide whether the move is within his province of certification or not. When he professes to do so, we contend, he is *actually indulging in tacit reformation and issuing a stipulation* as to what the terms in question *are to* mean.[37]

Maxwell and Feigl are saying, in effect, that Ordinary Language philosophers do not (and, if they are to accomplish anything, cannot) "leave everything as it is"[38] in ordinary language. When they distinguish senses of terms, or claim that "we would not use the expression '– – –' except in a situation in which . . . ," they are, so to speak, claiming that English *could easily be made* an Ideal Language, not discovering that it is one. The difference between them and their constructionist opponents thus amounts to the difference between pragmatic Burkeian reformers and revolutionaries, rather than

(as they themselves would like to believe), to the difference between tough-minded practitioners of an empirical discipline and disguised speculative metaphysicians. To Maxwell and Feigl the phrase "describing the logical behavior of the linguistic expressions of natural languages" looks at least as fuzzy as Bergmann's "every non-philosophical descriptive proposition can in principle be transcribed." Questions about criteria for "logical behavior" produce methodological problems that are just as difficult as questions about when "transcription" is possible "in principle."

A classic reply to this line of argument is given in Austin's discussion of "the snag of Loose (or Divergent or Alternative) Usage" and "the crux of the Last Word."[39] Austin cheerfully admits, on the first issue, that "*sometimes* we do ultimately disagree" (about what we should say in a given situation), but that such cases are rarer than one might think. In fact, we can find an astonishing amount of agreement, in a particular case, about what we would and would not say. On the "Last Word" question (the question of whether "ordinary language is the last word"), Austin held that there is little point in tightening up or reforming ordinary usage until we know what this usage is. If, he thought, we spent more time in observing how we ordinarily use certain words, our eyes would be opened to the difference between normal usage and philosophical usage, and we would see that philosophers make use of ordinary connotations of ordinary words, but nevertheless use these words in contexts in which they would never ordinarily be used. He offered no guarantee that realizing such facts would dissolve any or all philosophical problems, but merely asked that reform be postponed until our present linguistic resources are fully exploited.

The sweet reasonableness of Austin's position is so disarming that one may lose sight of the real issue which Maxwell and

---

[36] See below, p. 193
[37] See below, p. 197.
[38] The phrase is Wittgenstein's ([1], Part I, Section 124): "Philosophy may in no way interfere with the actual use of language; it can in the end only describe it. For it cannot give it any foundation either. It leaves everything as it is."

[39] See Austin [1], pp. 131–34.

Feigl raise. Granting, they may say, that one may get a surprising amount of agreement about what we say when, how do we get from such agreement to conclusions about the "logical behavior" of words, and thus to an empirically testable basis for the charge that a philosopher has "misused" an expression? This issue may be made more explicit by noting some distinctions drawn by Cavell between types of statements made about ordinary language:

(1) There are statements which produce *instances* of what is said in a language ('We do say . . . but we don't say ———'; 'We ask whether . . . but we do not ask whether ———'); (2) . . . statements which make explicit what is implied when we say what statements of the first type instance us as saying ('When we say . . . we imply (suggest, say) ———'; 'We don't say . . . unless we mean ———'). Such statements are checked by reference to statements of the first type. (3) Finally, there are *generalizations*, to be tested by reference to statements of the first two types.[40]

Statements of type (3) are those which provide Ordinary Language philosophers with weapons against their opponents. Cavell cites an example from Ryle, who says that "In their most ordinary employment, 'voluntary' and 'involuntary' are used . . . as adjectives applying to actions which ought not to be done." Ryle proceeds to argue that philosophers would not have been able to create the classic problem of the Freedom of the Will so easily had they not misused "voluntary" by letting it apply to *any* action, reprehensible or not. If we put to one side questions about how we verify statements of type (1) — questions which have been exhaustively discussed in the literature[41] — we may ask how, given a good stock of such statements, we would use them to ver-

ify statements about the misuse of language. Statements of type (3) may perhaps be regarded as the result of (rather complicated) inductive inferences from statements of type (1), but there seems to be a gap between "We do not ordinarily use . . . except when ———" and "Those who use . . . when it is not the case that ——— are misusing language." Except in a very unusual sense of "grammatical," a philosopher who says, for example, "All our actions save those performed under compulsion are voluntary," is not speaking ungrammatically. Except in very unusual senses of "logical" and "contradiction," he is not saying something which presupposes or entails a logical contradiction. About all we *can* say is that if Ryle is right, this philosopher is not using words as we ordinarily use them.

When we reach this point, it is tempting to say that we need not be too curious about how words are ordinarily used, since we can always ask the philosopher to define his terms (or, if he is unavailable, we can infer from his writings what definition he might have offered). To be sure, we must be careful that he does not give an ordinary word a technical sense in one premise and its ordinary sense in another. If we catch him doing so, we can simply charge him with arguing invalidly — a charge which antedates, and has nothing in particular to do with, the linguistic turn. It seems that the only value to philosophy of Austin's sensitivity to the ordinary use of ordinary expressions is to make us more sensitive to the possibility of such ambiguity, and thus to the possibility that a philosopher has committed the "fallacy of ambiguity." If this is so, it would then be just as well to drop Strawson's notion of "the logical behaviour of linguistic expressions of natural language" for roughly the same reasons that we dropped Carnap's notion of "logical syntax" and Ryle's notion of "logical form." As we noted, to find the "logical syntax" or the "logical form" of an expression is simply to find another expression which, if adopted in place of the origi-

---

[40] Cavell [4], p. 77.
[41] The question of whether our knowledge of what we would say when is empirical or a priori is discussed in Hare [1] and Henle [1] (both reprinted below at pp. 207–17 and 218–23 respectively) and in Mates [2], Cavell [2], Fodor and Katz [1], Henson [1], Tennessen [7] and [8].

nal, makes it harder to raise traditional philosophical problems. If we decide that the traditional philosophical use of an expression is not to count as part of its ordinary use (that is, if the type (1) statements we use as a basis for inferring type (3) statements do not contain statements made by philosophers), it would then seem that Strawson's "description of logical behavior" can be interpreted as "those generalizations about how we use words which are inferred from a sampling of uses, excluding philosophical discourse." (If we *do* include philosophical discourse in our sampling, it is hard to see how one could get what Strawson wants — a philosophically neutral basis for a charge that a philosopher has misused language.) Using this interpretation, philosophers need not worry (although lexicographers may) about how to tell the "logical" features of a word from those other, accidental, features which do not bear on questions of misuse. Instead of contrasting ordinary uses with misuses (as we once contrasted "historico-grammatical syntax" with "logical syntax," or "grammatical form" with "logical form"), we can simply contrast ordinary uses with special, philosophical, uses.

The preceding line of argument, however, should not blind us to the great importance of this contrast. It is important because (to repeat yet again a point we have noted twice before) the traditional view is that philosophical problems are created by internal inconsistency among, or the inexplicability of, the beliefs of ordinary "pre-philosophical" men. A philosopher who holds this view is committed to stating his problem in a form which does not use any word philosophically. This, as Austin's opponents discovered, is not easy to do. Whatever one's opinion of the notion of "misuse of language," one cannot question that many philosophers have lived by taking in each other's (and their predecessors') washing — taking it for granted that there is a Problem of the External World (or Truth, or Free Will, etc.),

and proceeding to criticize, or produce, solutions without asking whether the premises which produce the problem are actually accepted by ordinary men. Nor can one question that this carelessness is partially due to the fact that the putatively commonsensical premises invoked by those who formulate the problems are in fact premises in which a special, philosophical, sense has tacitly been given to an ordinary expression. This does not prejudice the suggestion that detection of this fact may lead to a dissolution of many, or perhaps all, philosophical problems. But even if such dissolution should occur, it should not be described as a discovery that philosophers have misused language, but rather as a discovery that philosophers' premises are either (a) dubious or plainly false (when the expressions they contain are construed in ordinary ways), or (b) implicit proposals for the reform of language.

It may seem that alternative (b) offers the traditional philosopher a way to escape the unsettling conclusion that his pet problems have been dissolved. For, he may say, I have as good a right to use jargon as any other specialist, and my "disguised proposals" are simply attempts to get a real problem properly into focus — something which ordinary language will not permit. But this, of course, will not do. A specialist may have a right to use jargon when he begins to *answer* questions, but not in the formulation of those primordial questions which originally impelled him to inquire. A philosopher who takes this line will therefore have to swallow the conclusion that philosophical problems are made, not found. If he does so, he will have to explain why he constructs such problems, and justify his no-longer-disguised proposals on the basis of a claim that we *need* these problems. He will have to say that if ordinary beliefs do not raise them, then so much the worse for ordinary beliefs. A few philosophers have consciously taken this road — notably Heidegger, in his discussion of *Seinsvergessenheit*, its cause and cure. But one who takes it is committed to the view that philosophy is not a subject in which agreement may be reached by argument. Clearly, there is no point in arguing with such a philosopher about whether his is the correct view of philosophy, nor is there any need to do so. The linguistic turn in philosophy is a reaction against the notion of philosophy as a discipline which attempts the solution of certain traditional problems — problems (apparently) generated by certain commonsense beliefs. If philosophy in the future becomes Heideggerian meditation, or, more generally, becomes the activity of constructing new language-games for the sheer joy of it (as in Hesse's *Magister Ludi*) — if, in short, philosophers drop their traditional conception of the nature of their discipline — then linguistic philosophers will have nothing left to criticize. The critical thrust of the linguistic movement in contemporary philosophy is against philosophy as a pseudo-science; it has no animus against the creation of a new art form within which, consciously rejecting the goal of "solving problems," we may carry on in the open an activity previously conducted behind a façade of pseudo-scientific argumentation.

Let me now return to Maxwell's and Feigl's criticisms of Ordinary Language Philosophy, and contrast my own approach to the issues they raise with another which might be taken. One might argue that given the development of suitable linguistic theories and techniques, we can in fact do what Maxwell and Feigl think we cannot — that is, construct a grammar and a dictionary for a natural language such as English and discover, by consulting them, that philosophers misuse English, in a perfectly straightforward sense of "misuse." Recent developments in empirical linguistics have suggested ways in which a much more comprehensive grammar, and a much more rationally constructed dictionary, might be composed.[42] These developments have resulted in a cooperative

effort by philosophers and linguists to clarify our ordinary notions of "grammaticalness" and "meaning." On the philosophers' part, this effort has been in large part motivated by a feeling that Austin was on the right track, but that his sensitive ear for usage needs to be supplemented by less subjective tests.[43]

If one answers Maxwell and Feigl in this way, however, one must justify the exclusion of philosophers' utterances from the data which we include in our inductive base — that for which we feel compelled to account. To take a concrete case, when Ziff says that "philosophers who speak of 'the rules of language' (or of 'moral rules'), are, I believe, misusing the word 'rule'," [44] he could presumably defend his belief by saying that we shall fail to find a relatively neat and simple account of the meaning of "rule" which will include most uses of the term plus these philosophers' locutions, whereas by leaving out these locutions (and perhaps some others), we can get such an account. This may well be true. If we want a dictionary whose entries are something more than very long disjunctions of (equally respectable) alternative senses, we shall have to say that some occurrences of a term are, in Ziff's words, "minor, derivative, or deviant." [45] The important point, however, is that although "deviance" is sometimes intuitively detectable, at other times we say that an utterance is deviant simply because an account of the meaning of a word contained in it would otherwise be unbearably complicated. (Ziff's claim about "rule" is certainly one of the latter cases.) But now we are faced with a choice between making life difficult for linguists and making life impossible for tradition-minded philosophers. If the force of the charge that a philosopher is misusing language is merely that his use of a word is hard for the linguist to handle, then it

---

[42] See Fodor and Katz [3], and also Ziff [2].

[43] Thus we find Ziff using *"Miracula sine doctrina nihil valent"* as the epigraph for *Semantic Analysis.*

[44] Ziff [2], p. 35.

[45] Ziff [2], p. 247.

seems best simply to distinguish between senses, or meanings, of the word, and drop the notion of "misuse" altogether. If, as we suggested above, such a distinction will do all that the original charge of "misuse" could do (viz., alert us to the possibility of a "fallacy of ambiguity" in a philosopher's arguments), then nothing except an antecedent prejudice against traditional philosophy would justify our continuing to make the latter charge.

This does not mean that improvements in linguistics are irrelevant to philosophy. An improved science of linguistics and an improved philosophy of language may provide a philosophically neutral, straightforwardly empirical way of sorting out "separate and distinct meanings" (or senses) in ordinary language, and thus allay Maxwell's and Feigl's suspicion that we make, rather than find, such distinctions. To do this would be a great accomplishment, if only because it would put a stop to endless, inconclusive quibbling among Ordinary Language Philosophers about whether, or how, a given word is ambiguous. But such advances would not bring us closer to showing that ordinary, non-philosophical English is Ideal in Bergmann's sense, because it would bring us no closer to showing that a philosopher's use of a term is actually illicit. If a philosopher simply says, for example, "From here on I shall use 'voluntary action' as synonymous with 'action not done under compulsion' " (or if we realize that he is *consistently* treating these two expressions as synonymous), we may then object on aesthetic or practical grounds to his having pointlessly given a new sense to a familiar term, but we cannot use this objection to dissolve the problem which he proceeds to construct. To show that his use was illicit would require a demonstration that his arguments embody the fallacy of ambiguity, through playing back and forth between, for example, the new and the old sense of "voluntary." But that is something we already know how to do, and which philosophers have been doing ever since Aristotle.

4. CRITERIA OF SUCCESS IN ANALYTIC PHILOSOPHY

The results of the preceding section may be summarized as follows: (1) Even if no adequate tests are available for determining whether a given language is Ideal, the sketches of possible new languages drawn by Ideal Language philosophers may nevertheless lead us to abandon the attempt to solve certain traditional philosophical problems. (2) In the absence of such tests, however, no knock-down argument can be given for the claim that these problems are unreal, "merely verbal," meaningless, or "pseudo–." (3) Noting that the senses given to certain ordinary words by philosophers differ from the senses they bear in non-philosophical discourse may enable us to dissolve certain formulations of traditional philosophical problems by noting that the apparently commonsensical primary premises used to construct such problems are actually in need of justification, since a new sense of a crucial word is being employed in them. Although there *may* be a way of formulating the problem which does *not* involve using words in unusual ways, we may legitimately refuse to be bothered by the problem until a new formulation is actually produced. (4) The activity of dissolving problems by detecting such unusual uses of words cannot, however, be described as detection of a philosopher's "misuse" of language, except in a trivial and misleading sense of "misuse" — one which identifies it with "philosophical use."

With these results in mind, we can now take up the question we previously deferred: do linguistic philosophers actually have criteria for philosophical success which are clear enough to permit rational agreement? It is obvious (and uninteresting) that they do, when the subject upon which agreement is required is sufficiently specialized. For example, it has long been a desideratum of Ideal Language Philosophy to produce an inductive logic which would be "extensional" in that its canons could be stated in a language employing only "descriptive" predicates and (roughly) the logical equipment available in *Principia Mathematica* (thus avoiding the use of a primitive notion of "causal connection"). This attempt has thus far failed, but the criteria for success are quite clear. However, when we ask whether there are criteria for success in achieving the primary task of linguistic philosophy — dissolving philosophical problems — things are not so clear. The primary reason that philosophers yearn for an extensional inductive logic is their conviction that once we had one, we would have dissolved the problem of "the nature of causality." But it is by no means clear why a philosopher who could succeed in giving criteria for distinguishing "accidental conjunctions" from "causal connections" without having to appeal to a primitive notion of "causal efficacy" or "nomologicality" would thereby have put to rest the traditional puzzles about causality. For it is not clear what these puzzles are. If, for example, a traditional metaphysician rejoins that inductive logic can only tell us which connections are causal, but not what causality *is*, there is little that the Ideal Language Philosopher can say, except that he now knows as much about causality as he wants to and that he does not understand what further problems arise. If we rejoin that in an Ideal Language we could simply talk, with Goodman, about projectable and unprojectable, ill-confirmed and well-confirmed, hypotheses, and never talk about "causes" and "effects" at all, then we would still have to show that such a language is "adequate" for all non-philosophical purposes. But it is not clear what could show this.

When we turn to Ordinary Language approaches, we find once again that rational agreement is possible on delimited and specialized questions. If a philosopher says "We would not say 'this caused that' unless ———," and is presented with a counter-example — a situation in which ——— is *not* the case and we certainly *would* say "this caused that" — then he is simply wrong. As Austin's work showed, there is sufficient agreement about "what we would say if . . ." to permit us to settle such questions on empirical grounds. (And if there is not sufficient agreement among philosophers, we still can fall back on questionnaires, interviews with men in the street, and the like.) The difficulties arise when we go from such agreement to statements of the form "It is part of our concept of *A* that all *A*'s must be *B*'s" or "It is a conceptual (logical, grammatical) truth about *A*'s that all *A*'s must be *B*'s" and the like. Here all the difficulties about analyticity mentioned by Maxwell and Feigl raise their heads; it becomes embarrassing that there is no agreed-upon theory about when a word's meaning has been *extended* and when it has been *changed*, or about the difference between distinct *senses* and distinct *meanings*. The lack of such a theory is embarrassing because a philosopher who is toying with the idea of non-*B*ish *A*'s can usually dream up a science-fiction-like situation in which most of the usual criteria for *A*hood, but few or none of the usual criteria for *B*hood, are met. He can then insist that we should continue to use "A" to describe the situation in question, and who can prove him wrong? His more conservative colleagues may wish to insist that, given this use, the meaning of "A" (and thus our concept of an *A*) would have changed (or that "A" would now have been given a new sense), but who can prove them right? And what philosophical problem would be clarified, solved, or dissolved by a correct prediction about how people would adjust their linguistic behavior to cope with a changed environment?

These considerations suggest that the extent of agreement among linguistic philosophers about criteria for philosophical success is inversely proportional to the relevance of their results to traditional philosophical problems. Oxford philosophers (like Strawson) noted that Ideal Language philosophers had begun to play the game of building an extensional elementaristic language for its own sake, and had lost touch with the problems which arose from the use of ordinary language. In reaction to this, Oxford philosophers tried to find a logic of ordinary language. But when it became apparent that they could disagree just as heartily and inconclusively about this logic as traditional metaphysicians had differed about the ultimate structure of reality, the need for criteria for "conceptual (as opposed to empirical) truth," for "sameness of meaning (or of sense)," and related notions became painfully evident. Furthermore, it began to seem that Oxford philosophers were playing the game of discovering "what we would say if . . ." for its own sake. Concern about the shaky metaphilosophical foundations of Oxford philosophy has recently expressed itself in an upsurge of interest in the philosophy of language. The philosophical journals are now filled with articles analyzing the notion of "meaning," "(linguistic) use," "rule of language," "speech-act," "illocutionary force of an utterance," and the like. It is too soon to make any firm predictions about the results of these efforts. Although the development of a philosophy of language which is "the philosophy of linguistics, a discipline analogous in every respect to the philosophy of physics, the philosophy of mathematics . . . and the like" [46] will rid us of the off-the-cuff, amateurish dicta about language which have been taken as points of departure by the various schools of linguistic philosophy, it is not clear that this development will help linguistic philosophers obtain the sort of "conceptual truths" they seek. Ziff, for example, at the conclusion of a systematic, thorough, and subtle attempt to construct criteria for answering the question "What does the word '. . .' mean," offers the following hypothesis about what "good" means: answering to certain interests. In the course of his argument, he notes that utterances "which have traditionally been of interest to philosophers" — for example, "It is good to be charitable" and "A

charitable deed is something that is intrinsically good" — must be treated as "deviant." [47] One reason why they must be so treated is they do not fit the hypothesis that "good" means "answering to certain interests," while this hypothesis does cover the great majority of utterances containing the word "good." We may well accept Ziff's hypothesis, but we must then recognize that such an account of the meaning of "good" leaves moral philosophers with nothing to get their teeth into. The traditional problems have, after all, been constructed with the aid of deviant utterances. Practically any ethics, or meta-ethics, is compatible with the fact that the vast majority of relevant linguistic phenomena is accounted for by Ziff's hypothesis. [48] It

[46] Fodor and Katz [2], p. 18.

[47] Ziff [2], pp. 238–39. (For the formal statement of what "good" means, see pp. 247 ff.)

[48] It might be said that the evidence for Ziff's theory about the meaning of "good" is evidence for the truth of a naturalist meta-ethics, and against the truth of an intuitionist or an emotivist meta-ethics. If one conceives Moore (in *Principia Ethica*) and Stevenson (in *Ethics and Language*) as concerned with answering the question "What does 'good' mean?" this would seem to be so. Since both Moore and Stevenson do conceive of themselves, in part at least, as answering this question, it would seem off-hand that if Ziff is right, they are wrong. But things are not that simple. Moore and Stevenson (as well as such naturalists as Dewey and Perry) were concerned with developing a theory about what counts as proper justification of a moral choice, about the possibility of resolving moral disputes, and about the similarities and differences between our knowledge of what is good and our knowledge of other matters. Such a theory is inseparable from a general epistemological theory. Theories of such generality are not knocked down by facts about the meanings of particular words, and it is hard to imagine Moore or Stevenson being greatly bothered by Ziff's result. It is much easier to imagine them saying that most of the questions in which they were interested may be restated in terms of criteria for deciding what interests one should have.

On the other hand, it should be conceded that, faced with such techniques and results as Ziff's, linguistic philosophers will probably cease phrasing their problems as questions about the meanings of words. Their habit of phrasing problems in this way in the past may stand revealed as little more than a handy heuristic device which suggested, misleadingly, that they had clear and straightforward criteria for the truth of their thus seems that all Ziff's account offers to philosophy is the familiar conclusion that philosophers' questions are rather peculiar. In general, we might expect that the interests of empirical linguistics will best be served by treating as deviant, among others, precisely those utterances which have engendered philosophical perplexity, and by providing accounts of the meanings of terms which are too banal to permit the derivation of philosophically interesting "conceptual truths." To the extent to which philosophers transform themselves into empirical linguists, a consensus among inquirers will once again have been bought at the cost of relevance to traditional philosophical problems (not simply relevance to their solution, but relevance to their dissolution, unless "deviance" is taken to be a sufficient condition for dissolubility).

These rather pessimistic conclusions may be reinforced and clarified if we approach the question of agreement among linguistic philosophers from a different angle. Consider the notion of "giving an analysis." "Linguistic philosophy" and "analytic philosophy" are often used interchangeably, and one might expect that the linguistic philosophers' criteria for philo-

sophical success would boil down to criteria for "giving a correct analysis." A full account of the checkered career of this notion is beyond our present scope.[49] Therefore, for the sake of simplicity, let us restrict consideration to cases where both the analysandum and the analysans are statements, rather than propositions, sentences, concepts, or words.[50] Now, one might suggest that S' is a correct analysis of S if some or all of the following conditions are fulfilled:

(1) S' and S are materially equivalent (that is, have the same truth-conditions).
(2) S' and S are materially equivalent by virtue of the structure of English (that is, the fact that they have the same truth-conditions can be determined by linguistics alone, rather than by linguistics plus further empirical research).
(3) A language which contained S' plus the rest of English, but did not contain S, would be as adequate as ordinary English.
(4) A language which contained S' plus the rest of English, but did not contain S, would be less misleading than ordinary English.
(5) S' would normally be accepted (without hesitation, rather than after philosophical debate) by speakers of English as an accurate paraphrase of S, in any non-

---

theories. But if this should happen, it would not be a sign that developments in linguistics had enabled us to answer philosophical questions, but rather a sign that these developments had made us dubious about the questions themselves. Just as the development of an empirical science of psychology caused philosophers to stop phrasing their questions as questions about how the mind works, and the development of modern formal logic made them stop writing works on epistemology (such as Bradley's *Principles of Logic*) in the guise of treatises on reasoning, so the development of empirical linguistics may force them to find new descriptions of what they want to do. (For a contrary view of the relevance of developments in linguistics to philosophy, see Fodor and Katz [3] and the paper by Katz at pp. 340–55 below. I should argue that these writers neglect the possibility that such developments will cause philosophers to have doubts about the thesis that "philosophical questions are questions of language," and force them to find a sense of "question of language" in which certain questions of language are outside the purview both of empirical linguistics and of the philosophy of language.)

[49] See the articles by Black and Stebbing on the nature of philosophical analysis listed in the bibliography, as well as the references listed under the entry for Langford [3]. See also Körner [2] and [5], and the essay by Urmson at pp. 294–301 below.

[50] In making this restriction we are (*pace* Moore) taking methodological nominalism for granted — i.e., assuming that talk about concepts and propositions may be dismissed in favor of talk about linguistic expressions. We are also assuming that since the analysis of the use of a word will usually draw upon analyses of statements in which the word is employed, problems about the criteria for correct analyses of the meanings of words will require solutions to problems about criteria for the correct analyses of statements.

On the issue between Moore and Malcolm, about whether analysis of concepts and propositions can be reduced to explication of linguistic usage, see Malcolm [5] (reprinted at pp. 111–24 below), Langford [3], Moore [3], Carney [2], and Chappell [1].

philosophical conversation in which S occurred.

The last of these conditions might be accepted by a philosopher who insisted on fidelity to ordinary language.[51] But reflection makes clear that (5) is so strong as to forbid any philosophically interesting analyses. A normally accepted paraphrase will usually be felt by philosophers to be as much in need of analysis as the analysandum itself.[52]

When we turn to (3) and (4) we are back with the familiar problem of the vagueness of "adequate" and "misleading." To help eliminate this vagueness it is natural to turn to (1) and (2). If we take "as adequate as" to mean "as well able to permit a differential linguistic response to every given situation as," then the satisfaction of (1) would seem to entail the satisfaction of (3).[53] But for any case in which a cause C invariably produces the effects E and E', and in which nothing else ever produces E and E', the

truth-conditions of "This is E" and "This is E' " will be the same — namely, the occurrence of C. Since, however, E and E' may be, respectively, a certain state of the nervous system and a certain sensation, and since no one wants to say that a statement about the former is an analysis of a statement about the latter, (1) is too weak. We are forced to recognize that "a given situation" may be described in many ways, and that for one language to be as adequate as another entails that the former be able to describe what is, in one sense, "the same situation" in as many ways as the latter. To eliminate such cases as E and E', we must move on to the stronger condition (2), and thus into problems about the nature and the limits of empirical linguistics.

Among these problems are the three difficulties suggested above:

(a) it seems clear that many statements are such that no necessary and sufficient conditions for their truth can be found by inspection of linguistic behavior.[54]

(b) where an S' which expresses necessary and sufficient conditions for the truth of S can be found by the methods of linguistics, it will often tend (for reasons discussed above) to be what we have referred to as a "normally acceptable paraphrase" — a banality which does not meet condition (4) in that it is no less, if no more, "misleading" (in any familiar philosophical sense) than the analysans itself.

(c) analyses produced by inspecting present linguistic behavior of speakers of English leave open the possibility that this behavior will change in such a way that S' will no longer be a necessary or sufficient condition for the truth of S. This would happen if "S, but not S'," ceased to be a deviant utterance, although no new sense, or meaning, of any component of S (nor of S') had been introduced. In such a case, it would seem counter-intuitive to claim that S' remained a correct analysis of S.

---

[51] Indeed such a condition seems to be suggested by Urmson's criticism of Ryle's claim that "to believe something is to manifest a disposition" on the ground that "when we say 'I believe that . . .' we do not say that we are thereby manifesting any profound dispositions" (p. 307 below).

[52] This is true of Ordinary Language philosophers as well as Ideal Language philosophers. Consider as an analysandum a statement used as an example in a debate between Austin and Strawson about truth: "What the policeman said was true." (This debate is included in *Truth*, ed. George Pitcher [Englewood Cliffs, 1964]; see also Strawson's "Truth: A Reconsideration of Austin's Views," *The Philosophical Quarterly*, XV [1965], 289–301.) Normally acceptable paraphrases would be statements like "The policeman was right" or "What the policeman said corresponds to the facts." The latter paraphrase is pounced on by Austin as a take-off point for a defense of the correspondence theory of truth. Strawson, in contesting this defense, never contests that this paraphrase *would*, indeed, normally be accepted. Instead, he argues that it does not, as Austin thinks, provide us with a useful clue to a philosophically interesting account of what it is for a statement to be true.

[53] Construing "given situation" in a way which permits this entailment results from the adoption of what Urmson calls the "*unum nomen, unum nominatum* view of the function of words" (see Urmson [3], pp. 188 ff.).

[54] See Ziff [2], pp. 184–85, the discussion of "cluster concepts" in Putnam [1], and Wittgenstein [1], Part I, Sections 67–107.

How serious these difficulties are, from the point of view of agreement among linguistic philosophers, is hard to say. The first two would be obviated if, in practice, it turned out that the statements which philosophers want analyzed do have non-banal truth conditions which could be discovered by the methods of linguistics. The third might be surmounted by arguing that analyses of how we now use words and statements suffice for philosophical purposes, and that the possibility of linguistic change is no more fruitful a subject for philosophical speculation than the possibility of a change in "the ultimate structure of reality."

There is no point in speculating about whether actual success in practice will surmount the first two difficulties. We just have to wait and see. But something needs to be said about the proposed strategy for getting around the third difficulty. In presenting the difficulty, I suggested that it would be counter-intuitive to say both that

(1) S' is now a satisfactory analysis of S
and
(2) Without any word used in S having changed its meaning, or being used in a new sense, S' might cease to be a satisfactory analysis of S.

It would be counter-intuitive because philosophers think of analysis as having something to do with *meaning*, and they tend to assume that correct analyses cannot lose their correctness while meaning remains unchanged. This cluster of intuitions and assumptions comprises the view that the truth conditions for statements, and the meanings of the words used in statements, are internally related to one another. This view — now usually labeled "Verificationism," and derided as an unfortunate remnant of Logical Positivism — is usually attacked by *reductio ad absurdum* arguments. Such arguments show that if we infer from any change in the truth conditions of the statement of the form "This is an X" to the conclusion that "X" has changed its meaning, or is being used in a

new sense, or now stands for a different concept, then we are forced to say, for example, that the general acceptance of a new experimental method for determining the presence of X's (even in cases in which previous criteria for Xhood are unsatisfied) automatically brings about a change of sense, meaning or concept.[55] If it is agreed that this consequence is absurd, we face the problem of finding a sense of "giving an analysis" of S which either loosens the original connection with "meaning," loosens the original connection with truth conditions, or both. Since, however, it is hard to imagine a sense of "analysis" which does not involve the satisfaction of (1) and (2), only the first of these projects seems promising.

In order to loosen the connection with "meaning," we might say, in accordance with the strategy suggested above, that we are interested not in what an expression means, but in how it is used at present. Granting that S might someday be used quite differently, while all its components retained their present meaning, it does seem reasonable to suggest that if we could get an account of its present use, we would have whatever it is that philosophers want when they ask for "analyses." It further seems reasonable to suggest that "an account of its present use" would be given if non-banal necessary and sufficient conditions for the truth of S were agreed upon by most speakers of English. However, it must be noted that if we settle for this, we are deprived of inferences from statements like

(A) The correct analysis of "This is an X" is "This is Y and Z"

to statements like

(B) It is a necessary truth about X's that they are Y.

Statements such as (B) might well be inferred from statements like (A), as long as we retain the assumption that the correct analysis of "This is an X" could not change unless the meaning of "X"

---

[55] For examples of such arguments, see Putnam [1] and [3], and Chihara and Fodor [1].

changed. But once this assumption is dropped, we are no longer in a position to derive quasi-metaphysical statements such as (B) from statements like (A), for the latter will only concern the way in which X's are talked about at a given time, rather than the "essence" of Xhood. Even if, in accordance with methodological nominalism, we grant that to know the meaning of "X" is to know the essence of X's, no statement about "X" short of a complete account of its meaning could give us such knowledge. We may conclude that the suggested strategy for getting around the difficulty posed by the possibility of linguistic change leads us to a further difficulty: we must now say that the philosophical purposes which lead us to search for analyses of statements will be served even if we are no longer able to make such statements as (B).

Our discussion of possible senses of "giving an analysis" tends to confirm our original pessimism about the ability of linguistic philosophers to come to rational agreement about the solution or dissolution of philosophical problems. But more needs to be said, for two assumptions which have played an important part in our discussion may well be questioned. One hears less and less in the current literature about "dissolving problems" or about "giving analyses." Instead, one finds claims to have discovered necessary truths about various sorts of entities (intentions, actions, sensations, thoughts, etc.), without any suggestion that these truths are deduced from analyses of statements about such entities, and with only cursory reference to the traditional philosophical problems about them. It would seem, then, that neither the assumption that the primary task of linguistic philosophy is to dissolve traditional problems, nor the assumption that its primary method is to produce analyses, corresponds to present practice. Indeed, much current philosophical practice seems to differ from the practice of traditional philosophers *only* in the adoption of what I have called "methodological nominalism."

It is clear that one can defend a statement like (B) above (a "necessary truth" about a kind of entity) and yet not attempt to give necessary and sufficient truth conditions for any statement, or to give a complete account of the meaning of any word. Consider the following thesis.

(T) A person who understands the meaning of the words "I am in pain" cannot utter these words with the intention of making a true assertion unless he *is* in pain (or unless his utterance is a slip of the tongue — a complication that can here be ignored).[56]

We find this common doctrine about pain-reports backed up by arguments stating that unless a sense can be found for the notion of "pain-hallucination," or some similar notion, we cannot imagine a situation which would be a counter-example to the doctrine. Opponents of (T), however, proceed to construct a sense for "pain-hallucination" by describing a hypothetical technique for determining whether a person is in pain other than his own report — for example, by detecting a brain-state constantly conjoined with such reports.[57] Faced with a case in which a person (whose knowledge of the words "I am in pain" has never previously been questioned) sincerely reports that he is in pain, but the appropriate brain-state is absent, would we not find it reasonable to describe him as having a pain-hallucination? In rebuttal, defenders of (T) can say either that "pain" would in this case no longer have its original meaning (or sense), or that *however* we might describe this weird case, it *could* not be in terms of the notion of "pain-hallucination," since this notion is just senseless. But the second alternative is clearly ques-

---

[56] Sidney Shoemaker, *Self-Knowledge and Self-Identity* (Ithaca, 1963), p. 168. Shoemaker says that he "takes this to be a necessary truth."
[57] See Putnam, "Minds and Machines," in *Dimensions of Mind*, ed. S. Hook (New York, 1960), pp. 138–64, esp. pp. 153 ff.; and also Rorty, "Mind-Body Identity, Privacy and Categories," *The Review of Metaphysics*, (1965), 24–54, especially pp. 41 ff.

tion-begging, and the first embodies just that Verificationism which post-positivistic linguistic philosophers unite in rejecting. Defenders of (T) are thus driven to say that it is pointless to introduce such hypothetical science-fiction situations. But this means that instead of talking about "necessary truths" we must rest content with remarks like the following.

(T') Given our present linguistic practices, no objection can be raised to an inference from "Jones, who knows the meaning of the words he uses, sincerely asserts that he is in pain and has not made a slip of the tongue" to "Jones is in pain."

One may, in fact, be willing to stop talking about "necessary truths" if one believes, as most linguistic philosophers do, that many traditional philosophical problems have arisen because philosophers were not sufficiently careful about noting that certain questions are simply silly (where "silly" means something like "such that our present linguistic practice does not provide an agreed-upon way of answering them"). The example of Wittgenstein suggests how extraordinarily effective the detection of such silliness can be. But if we make such a tactical retreat, then our description of our general strategy will have to be changed. We will have to drop the claim to be continuing the great philosophical tradition of finding out the essence of X's, and fall back on the notion of philosophy which was held by the positivists — philosophy as an essentially *critical* activity, an activity whose success is measured by its ability to dissolve such problems. Suppose that one's philosophical claims are restricted to claims about what, as our language now works, it is silly to ask, and that one's criterion of silliness is that no procedure of answering these questions suggests itself naturally to users of the language. The fact that somebody can come up with an imaginative suggestion about how such a procedure might come into existence can then be shrugged off.

For one will have done one's job once one has noted that as things stand, questions like "How do I know that I am in pain?" are silly questions, and that a philosophical theory which insists on answering such questions needs to justify asking them. But if one's aim is to continue the task of traditional philosophy — discovering the nature of, for example, sensations or feelings — then this fact cannot be shrugged off.

These considerations show that the difficulties which beset attempts to offer analyses of statements apply in equal measure to attempts to offer necessary truths ("partial analyses," as they are sometimes called). They also show that the attempt to disassociate linguistic philosophy from its commitment to the positivistic effort to dissolve philosophical problems, and to reunite it to the Great Tradition, is likely to fail. The current practice of linguistic philosophers makes good sense if it is seen as an attempt to dissolve traditional problems by noting, for example, fallacies of ambiguity in arguments which purport to show that philosophical problems exist, or the fact that certain questions which philosophers think need answering are in fact silly, since the language as now used presents no procedures for answering them. It does not make good sense when seen as an attempt, in Austin's words, to use "a sharpened awareness of words to sharpen our perception of, though not as the final arbiter of, the phenomena." [58] This celebrated and cryptic phrase would be intelligible if we had independent criteria for knowing what the phenomena are like, independent of our knowledge of how words are used, and could thus assess the adequacy or accuracy of our language. But the point of methodological nominalism is precisely that no such check is possible. Without it, the claim that we find out something about non-linguistic phenomena by knowing more about linguistic phenomena is either an idle conciliatory gesture or a misleadingly formulated re-

[58] Austin [1], p. 130.

minder of the innocuous fact that statements about "X" can often be paraphrased as statements about X's, and conversely. Our tendency to insist that philosophy is something quite different from lexicography can be assuaged without such gestures. It can be assuaged by seeing philosophy as lexicography with a purpose — the purpose which the positivists originally formulated. Discoveries about how we use words now (without any reference to "meaning," or to "conceptual analysis") do, in practice, help us to dissolve philosophical problems. The extra-linguistic reality which contemporary philosophers help us to understand can thus be taken simply as the history of philosophy (and the temptations to philosophize which threaten to prolong this history). If one finds this view of the work of the linguistic philosopher too restrictive, one must either (a) surmount the difficulties concerning the gap between "our present use of 'X' " and "the meaning of 'X'," or (b) find some way of going from facts about "our present use of 'X' " to statements about "our concept of *X*hood" or "the essence of X's" which does not go through the notion of "meaning," or (c) repudiate methodological nominalism by finding some way of judging the accuracy or adequacy of our present use of language by reference to antecedently-established facts about concepts or essences.

I suspect (but cannot show) that none of these three alternatives is viable. I conclude, therefore, that the question "Do linguistic philosophers have criteria for philosophical success which are clear enough to permit rational agreement?" should be construed as I have thus far: "Do they have criteria for success in dissolving philosophical problems?" If, for the reasons indicated, we cannot have satisfactory criteria for "correct analyses" or for "necessary truths," whereas we can have satisfactory criteria for descriptions of how linguistic expressions are currently used, then the crucial question becomes: "Do linguistic philosophers have agreed-

upon principles in accordance with which they can infer from facts about current linguistic practice to the dissolution of a given philosophical problem?" The answer to this question must be negative, if one means by "the dissolution of a philosophical problem" a demonstration that there is, *tout court*, "no problem" about, for example, perception, free will, or the external world. (To show *that* would require agreement about the correct analyses of all relevant concepts, or on all necessary truths about the relevant entities.) The answer is affirmative if one means instead a demonstration that a *particular formulation* of a given problem involves a use of a linguistic expression which is sufficiently unusual to justify our asking the philosopher who offers the formulation to re-state his problem in other terms.[59] This phrasing may seem rather wishy-washy, but I do not think that any stronger construction can be given to the notion of "dissolution of a philosophical problem" if we are to give an affirmative answer. Nor is it really as wishy-washy as it seems. Granted that "deviance" is not, in itself, a criticism of a philosopher's use of language, and granted that a *prima facie* silly question (like "How do we know that we are in pain?" or "Is pleasurable activity desirable?") might be reinterpreted in an interesting and fruitful way, the insistence that deviance or *prima facie* silliness be recognized for what it is is of the greatest importance. Granting, with Wittgenstein, that any expression has a sense if we *give* it a sense (and, more generally, that any use of any expression can be made non-deviant and non-silly by, so to speak, creating a language-game within which it will be at home), we still ought to ask the philosopher who departs from ordinary linguistic practice to actually *do* the job of explaining why he uses ordinary words in

---

[59] For a reinterpretation of the positivists' original project, which suggests such an interpretation of "dissolution," see Bar-Hillel [4], reprinted below at pp. 356–59.

unfamiliar ways, or of stating the rules of the new language-game which he wants us to play. (In doing this job, of course, he will have to use ordinary uses of language, and antecedently familiar language-games.) If he can do this, well and good. It will then be up to us to decide whether, now that we understand what he is up to, we assent to the premises which generate his problems, and see some point in playing his game. Experience has shown that he often cannot do this job, and that even if he can, his original problem-generating premises, when reinterpreted, seem dubious or false, and his new game pointless.

Adopting this limited notion of the function of linguistic philosophy helps us to see why (despite a growing recognition that all the talk about "logical form," "analysis of concepts," and "necessary truths" has raised more problems than it has solved) philosophers who have taken the linguistic turn remain convinced of the value of doing so. For, despite their dubious metaphilosophical programs, writers like Russell, Carnap, Wittgenstein, Ryle, Austin, and a host of others have succeeded in forcing those who wish to propound the traditional problems to admit that they can no longer be put forward in the traditional formulations. These writers have not, to be sure, done what they hoped to do. They have not provided knock-down, once-and-for-all demonstrations of meaninglessness, conceptual confusion, or misuse of language on the part of philosophers they criticized.[60] But this does not matter. In the light of the considerations about presuppositionlessness advanced in Sections 1 and 2 above, it would be astonishing if they *had* done any of these things. Philosophical discussion, by the nature of the subject, is such that the best one can hope for is to put the burden of proof on one's opponent.[61] Linguistic philosophy, over the last thirty years, has succeeded in putting the entire philosophical tradition, from Parmenides through Descartes and Hume to Bradley and Whitehead, on the defensive. It has done so by a careful and thorough scrutiny of the ways in which traditional philosophers have used language in the formulation of their problems. This achievement is sufficient to place this period among the great ages of the history of philosophy.

5. PROSPECTS FOR THE FUTURE: DISCOVERY VERSUS PROPOSAL

I have now done all that I can, within the restricted compass of an introduction to an anthology, to answer the two questions posed at the beginning of Section 2. In doing so, I have implicitly raised certain other questions which I have not tried to answer. I cannot do so now, but I shall try to point out where some of the unanswered questions lie by taking up, once again, the very general question raised at the outset: Is the linguistic turn doomed to suffer the same fate as previous "revolutions in philosophy"? The relatively pessimistic conclusions reached in the preceding sections entail that linguistic philosophers' attempts to turn philosophy into a "strict science" must fail. How far does this pessimism carry? If linguistic philosophy cannot be a strict science, if it has a merely critical, essentially dialectical, function, then what of the future? Suppose that all the traditional problems are, in the fullness of time, dissolved — in the sense that no one is able to think of any formulations of these questions which are immune to the sort of criticisms made by linguistic philosophers. Does that mean that philosophy will have come to an end — that philosophers will

---

[60] Arguments that linguistic philosophers are no better able to present knock-down "proofs" than traditional philosophers are offered in Waismann [2] and Ayer [13], especially pp. 26–27. For a criticism of Waismann's arguments see Levison [1] and Passmore [3], esp. pp. 33–37.

[61] For arguments for this general dictum about the nature of philosophy, see Johnstone [8]. I find Johnstone's assimilation of philosophical arguments to *argumenta ad hominem* somewhat misleading, but I think that the arguments he advances for this assimilation effectively support the view I set forth here.

have worked themselves out of a job? Is a "post-philosophical" culture really conceivable?

The only sensible thing to say about most of these questions is that it is too soon to answer them. But it may be useful to list some of the alternative standpoints from which they might be answered. One can envisage at least six possibilities for the future of philosophy, after the dissolution of the traditional problems.

(1) Since the single substantive philosophical thesis that unites the various branches of linguistic philosophy is methodological nominalism, a repudiation of this thesis would open new horizons. If there were a way of agreeing upon answers to the traditional philosophical questions which would not involve the reduction of questions about the nature of things either to empirical questions (to be turned over to the sciences) or to questions about language, then the linguistic turn would probably be treated as having led to a dead end. Many contemporary philosophers think that phenomenology offers such a way.

(2) A second possibility is that *both* methodological nominalism *and* the demand for clear-cut criteria for agreement would be dropped. Philosophy would then cease to be an argumentative discipline, and grow closer to poetry. Heidegger's later essays can be seen as an attempt to do philosophy in an entirely new way — one which rejects the *traditional* problems as spurious, yet insists that there *are* problems to be solved which are not simply problems about how it would be best to talk. The fact that these problems are all but unstatable, and consequently are such that no agreement about criteria for their solution is available, would be cheerfully accepted. This would be taken as signifying the difficulty of the subject matter, rather than (as Heidegger's critics take it) the perversity of the methods employed.

(3) Another possibility is that methodological nominalism would be retained, but that the demand for clear-cut criteria

of agreement about the truth of philosophical theses would be dropped. Philosophers could then turn toward creating Ideal Languages, but the criterion for being "Ideal" would no longer be the dissolution of philosophical problems, but rather the creation of new, interesting and fruitful ways of thinking about things in general. This would amount to a return to the great tradition of philosophy as system-building — the only difference being that the systems built would no longer be considered *descriptions* of the nature of things or of human consciousness, but rather *proposals* about how to talk. By such a move, the "creative" and "constructive" function of philosophy could be retained. Philosophers would be, as they have traditionally been supposed to be, men who gave one a *Weltanschauung* — in Sellars' phrase, a way of "understanding how things in the broadest possible sense of the term hang together in the broadest possible sense of the term." [62]

(4) It might be that we would end by answering the question "Has philosophy come to an end?" with a resounding "Yes," and that we would come to look upon a post-philosophical culture as just as possible, and just as desirable, as a post-religious culture. We might come to see philosophy as a cultural disease which has been cured, just as many contemporary writers (notably Freudians) see religion as a cultural disease of which men are gradually being cured. The wisecrack that philosophers had worked themselves out of a job would then seem as silly a sneer as a similar charge leveled at doctors who, through a breakthrough in preventive medicine, had made therapy obsolete. Our desire for a *Weltanschauung* would now be satisfied by the arts, the sciences, or both.[63]

[62] Sellars [6], p. 1.
[63] Goethe said that if you had science and art you thereby had religion, but that if you had neither, you had better go out and get religion (*"Wer Wissenschaft und Kunst besitzt/ Hat auch Religion/ Wer jene beiden nicht besitzt/*

(5) It might be that empirical linguistics can in fact provide us with non-banal formulations of the necessary and sufficient conditions for the truth of statements, and non-banal accounts of the meaning of words. Granted that these formulations and accounts would apply only to our present linguistic practices, it might be that the discovery of such formulations and accounts would satisfy at least some of the instincts which originally led men to philosophize. Linguistic philosophy, instead of being lexicography pursued for an extrinsic purpose, would become lexicography pursued for its own sake. Such a vision of the future of philosophy is put forward, though with many qualifications and reservations, by Urmson's description of the Austinian "fourth method of analysis" at pp. 299–301 below. Though such a project would be related to the tradition neither through sympathy (as in [3]), nor through repudiation (as in [4]), it might nevertheless reasonably be called "philosophy" simply because its pursuit filled part (although obviously not all) of the gap left in the cultural fabric by the disappearance of traditional philosophy.

(6) It might be that linguistic philosophy could transcend its merely critical function by turning itself into an activity which, instead of inferring from facts about linguistic behavior to the dissolution of traditional problems, discovers necessary conditions for the possibility of language itself (in a fashion analogous to the way in which Kant purportedly discovered necessary conditions for the possibility of experience). Such a development is envisaged by Strawson (pp. 318–20 below), when he says that the goal of "descriptive metaphysics" is to show "how the fundamental categories of our thought hang together, and how they relate, in turn, to those formal notions (such as existence, identity, and unity) which

range through all categories." A discipline of this sort would perhaps emerge with very general conclusions, such as "It is a necessity in the use of language that we should refer to persisting objects, employing some criteria of identity through change." [64]

Positions (1) through (6) may be associated respectively with six names: Husserl, Heidegger, Waismann, Wittgenstein, Austin, and Strawson. This is not to say that any of these men would embrace one of these alternatives without many qualifications and restrictions, but rather that those who opt for one of these alternatives often cite one of these six philosophers as a good example of the sort of philosophical attitude and program which they have in mind. For our present purposes, it would be impracticable to take up (1) and (2), the Husserlian and Heideggerian alternatives. Whether orthodox Husserlian phenomenology is in fact a presuppositionless method offering criteria for the accuracy of phenomenological descriptions is too large a question to be discussed. All that can be said is that linguistic philosophers are perennially puzzled by the question of whether Husserlian methods differ, other than verbally, from the methods practiced by linguistic philosophy — whether, in other words, a phenomenological description of the structure of X is more than an Austinian account of our use of "X," phrased in a different idiom. [65] When we turn to "existential phenomenologists" — heretical disciples of Husserl, among them Sartre and the Heidegger of Sein und Zeit — we find that linguistic philosophers are tempted to assimilate such efforts to the sort of proposals for an Ideal Language mentioned in (3). This temptation extends even to the work of the later Heidegger.

---

[64] Hampshire [14], p. 66. See p. 37 below for a more complete quotation from this passage.
[65] See Downes [1], and the articles by Chappell, Turnbull, and Gendlin in the same issue of The Monist (XLIX, No. 1). See also Schmitt [1], Taylor [2], and Ayer [10].

Der habe Religion," Zahme Xenien, Neuntes Buch). Substituting "philosophy" for "religion," I suggest that this expresses the view of many followers of Wittgenstein.

A Waismann-like view of philosophy as "the piercing of that dead crust of tradition and convention, the breaking of those fetters which bind us to inherited preconceptions, so as to attain a new and broader way of looking at things" [66] is able to welcome even such quasi-poetic efforts as Heidegger's "Bauen Wohnen Denken." Once philosophy is viewed as proposal rather than discovery, a methodological nominalist can interpret both the philosophical tradition, and contemporary attempts to break free of this tradition, in equally sympathetic ways.

If we restrict ourselves to alternatives (3) through (6), which all adhere to methodological nominalism, we can see that (3) and (4) share a common ground not shared by (5) and (6). Both (3) and (4) repudiate the notion that there are philosophical truths to be discovered and demonstrated by argument. Waismann says that "To seek, in philosophy, for rigorous proofs is to seek for the shadow of one's voice," [67] and Wittgenstein that "If one tried to advance *theses* in philosophy, it would never be possible to debate them, because everyone would agree with them." [68] What difference there is between these two positions lies in Wittgenstein's apparent feeling that philosophers' attempts to "break the fetters" by inventing new, specifically philosophical, language-games are bound to result only in exchanging new fetters for old. Whereas Waismann thought that philosophical system-building had, and could again, crystallize a "vision," the mystical strain in Wittgenstein led him to strive for an "unmediated vision" — a state in which things could be seen as they are, without the mediation of a new way of thinking about them. Such a difference is not an appropriate topic for argument. It must suffice to say that Waismann and Wittgenstein share the view that philosophy, apart

from its critical and dialectical function, can be *at most* proposal, never discovery.

The view that philosophy should aim at proposing better ways of talking rather than at discovering specifically philosophical truths is, of course, the direct heir of the Ideal Language tradition in linguistic philosophy. There is not a great difference between the metaphilosophical pragmatism of an article like Carnap's "Empiricism, Semantics and Ontology" and Waismann's vision of philosophy-as-vision. In contrast to this attitude, which contemplates with equanimity the lack of a strict decision-procedure for judging between alternative proposals, the Oxford tradition of Ordinary Language analysis has tended to hold out for the view that there are specifically philosophical truths to be discovered. Hampshire says of Austin that

Since it was a constant point of difference between us, he often, and over many years, had occasion to tell me that he had never found any good reason to believe that philosophical inquiries are essentially, and of their very nature, inconclusive. On the contrary he believed that this was a remediable fault of philosophers, due to premature system-building and impatient ambition, which left them neither the inclination nor the time to assemble the facts, impartially and cooperatively, and then to build their unifying theories, cautiously and slowly, on a comprehensive, and therefore secure, base. [69]

Such a view, which serves as the point of departure for much contemporary work, suggests that lexicography, pursued for its own sake and apart from its critical function, will in the end give us something rather like a traditional philosophical system. The body of truths about how we speak, ordered by a complex but precise taxonomic theory, will present itself as a *Weltanschauung*. The claim that this is the *right* world view will be based simply on the fact that it is the one built in our

[66] Waismann [2], p. 483.
[67] Waismann [2], p. 482.
[68] Wittgenstein [1], Part I, Section 128.

[69] Hampshire [6], p. vii (Reprinted at p. 243 below.)

language, and is therefore more likely to be correct than (to quote a phrase which Austin used in another context) "any that you or I are likely to think up in our armchairs of an afternoon." [70] Insofar as Austin had in mind a model for such a system, the model was Aristotle. Like Aristotle's, such a hypothetical system would not consist of answers to all the questions posed by philosophers of the past, but would instead dismiss many (if not all) of these questions as ill-formed, and would proceed to make distinctions which, once explicitly recognized, would free us from the temptation to answer these questions. It would thus accomplish the critical aims which were, for Wittgenstein, the sole justification of continued philosophical inquiry, as a by-product of a search for truths. *Pace* Wittgenstein, it *would* be "possible to question" these truths, but such questions could be answered. They could be answered in the same way as a theorist in any other empirical science answers questions about the truth of his theory — by pointing to its superior ability to account for the facts.

At the present time, this Austinian alternative — (5) above — is (in English-speaking lands) the most widespread conception of what the philosophy of the future will be like. Its strongest rival is neither (3) nor (4), but (6) — the Strawsonian view that we need not restrict ourselves to a theory which accounts for our linguistic behavior, but that we can get a theory about language as such — about any possible language, rather than simply about the assemblage of languages presently spoken. Such a project, which suggests that the study of language can lead us to certain necessary truths as well as to an Austinian empirical theory, holds out the hope that linguistic philosophy may yet satisfy our Platonic, as well as our Aristotelian, instincts — the instincts which impelled Wittgenstein to write the

Tractatus It is far from clear how exponents of this project hope to avoid the usual difficulties arising from the gap between contingent truths about linguistic behavior and necessary truths about language as such, but the general strategy may be glimpsed in the following quotation from Hampshire.

The argument of this chapter has been that it is a necessity in the use of language that we should refer to persisting objects, employing some criteria of identity through change: it is a necessity that the speaker should have the means of indicating his own point of view or standpoint, since he is himself one object among others; that every object must exhibit different appearances from different points of view: and that every object, including persons who are language-users, agents and observers, has a history of changing relations to other things in its environment. These truisms entail consequences in the theory of perception, the theory of mind, the theory of action . . . *We cannot claim an absolute and unconditional finality for these truisms, since the deduction of them is always a deduction within language as we know it. But the deduction only shows that we are not in a position to describe any alternative forms of communication between intentional agents which do not exemplify these truisms.* [71]

Hampshire seems to suggest that a language which we cannot imagine being used is not a language, and that the sort of language we can imagine being used is determined by the language we ourselves use. Consequently, we can fairly infer from features of our own language to features of anything that we shall ever describe as a "language." To put it crudely, if the Martians speak a language which does not exemplify the truisms cited, we shall never know that they do; therefore the suggestion that they do is not one which we can really understand. If we put aside the question of whether Hampshire's "truisms" are in fact true, there remains one obvious difficulty: philoso-

---

[70] *Philosophical Papers*, p. 130.

[71] Hampshire [14], pp. 66–67. [Italics added].

phers are constantly doing something which they describe as "sketching a possible language" — a language which does not exemplify some or all of these truisms.[72] Unless some criteria are developed to test the suggestion that such languages could not be used by someone who did not already know a language which embodied the truisms in question (that such languages are, in Strawson's phrase, "parasitic" upon ordinary language),[73] the strategy will not work. Granted that the limits of the language a man can speak are, in some sense, the limits of his thought and his imagination, it seems nevertheless that our language is so rich that we can pull our imagination up by its own bootstraps. Thus, the difficulty presented to traditional Ordinary Language philosophy by science-fiction-like examples of exotic linguistic behavior remains a difficulty for a project such as (6). It is, however, far too soon to pass judgment on this project. It is presently exemplified by only a few documents — notably Strawson's *Individuals* and Hampshire's *Thought and Action* — and can hardly be said to have had a fair run.[74]

This brief sketch of some possible futures must suffice. The only moral that may be drawn, I think, is that the metaphilosophical struggles of the future will center on the issue of reform versus description, of philosophy-as-proposal versus philosophy-as-discovery — the issue between the least common denominator of (2), (3), and (4) on the one hand, and the least common denominator of (1), (5), and (6) on the other. We have seen, in the course of the preceding sections, a certain oscillation between these two metaphilosophical alternatives. Once the linguistic turn had been taken, and once methodological nominalism had taken hold, it was natural for philosophers to suggest that the function of their discipline is to *change* our consciousness (by reforming our language) rather than to describe it, for language — unlike the intrinsic nature of reality, or the transcendental unity of apperception — is something which, it would seem, *can* be changed. But it was equally natural for philosophers to resist abandoning the hope that their discipline could be a science, an activity in which the principal criterion of success is simply accurate description of the facts. Ever since Plato invented the subject, philosophy has been in a state of tension produced by the pull of the arts on one side and the pull of the sciences on the other. The linguistic turn has not lessened this tension, although it has enabled us to be considerably more self-conscious about it. The chief value of the metaphilosophical discussions included in this volume is that they serve to heighten this self-consciousness.

A final cautionary word: an important (although, I believe, inevitable) defect of this anthology, and of this introduction, is that they do not adequately exhibit the

---

[72] As an example of such a language, consider the "canonical notation," characterized by an absence of singular terms, which Quine develops in *Word and Object*. Another example to be considered is the language which Sellars suggests might come into existence if people stopped thinking of themselves as *persons*, and began thinking only about, say, molecules and their behavior. (See Sellars [6], especially pp. 32–40.) Sellars has Hampshire-like reservations about the possibility of such a language (see pp. 39–40), but the basis for these reservations is not clear.

[73] For this notion of "parasitism," see Strawson's "Singular Terms,, Ontology and Identity," *Mind*, LXV (1956), 433–54. See also Quine's dismissal of Strawson's point as irrelevant in *Word and Object*, p. 158 n., and Manley Thompson's "On the Elimination of Singular Terms," *Mind*, LXVIII (1959), 361–76. For another example of the use of the notion of one language's being "parasitic" on another, see Wilfrid Sellars, "Time and the World-Order," *Minnesota Studies in the Philosophy of Science*, III, especially Sections 1 and 9.

[74] For criticisms of (6), see Black [4] (reprinted at pp. 331–39 below); Julius Moravscik,

"Strawson and Ontological Priority," in *Analytical Philosophy, Second Series*, ed. R. J. Butler (Oxford, 1965), pp. 109–19; Burtt [1]; and Mei [1] and [3] and Price [1] (on whether Ordinary Language philosophers need study Chinese).

interplay between the adoption of a meta-philosophical outlook and the adoption of substantive philosophical theses. This interplay is exceedingly complex, and often subliminal, and the relations involved more often causal than logical. I have discussed the degree to which linguistic philosophy is "presuppositionless," but I have not tried to discuss the more difficult topic of how changes in the vocabulary used in formulating substantive theses produce changes in the vocabulary of metaphilosophy. Nor do I know how to do this. I should wish to argue that the most important thing that has happened in philosophy during the last thirty years is not the linguistic turn itself, but rather the beginning of a thoroughgoing rethinking of certain epistemological difficulties which have troubled philosophers since Plato and Aristotle.[75] I would argue that if it were not for the epistemological difficulties created by this account, the traditional problems of metaphysics (problems, for example, about universals, substantial form, and the relation between the mind and the body) would never have been conceived. If the traditional "spectatorial" account of knowledge is overthrown, the account of knowledge which replaces it will lead to reformulations everywhere else in philosophy, partic-

ularly in metaphilosophy. Specifically, the contrast between "science" and "philosophy" — presupposed by *all* the positions (1) through (6) which I have described — may come to seem artificial and pointless. If this happens, most of the essays in this volume will be obsolete, because the vocabulary in which they are written will be obsolete. This pattern of creeping obsolescence is illustrated by the fate of the notions of "meaninglessness" and "logical form" (and by my prediction that their successors, the notions of "misuse of language" and "conceptual analysis," will soon wither away). The notions which the metaphilosophers of the future will use in the struggle between philosophy-as-discovery and philosophy-as-proposal almost certainly will not be the notions used in the debates included in the present volume. But I do not know what they will be. The limits of metaphilosophical inquiry are well expressed in the following quotation from Hampshire.

The rejection of metaphysical deduction, and the study of the details of linguistic usage, are sometimes supported by the suggestion that all earlier philosophers have been mistaken about what philosophy is, about its necessary and permanent nature. This is an inconsistency. If we have no final insight into the essence of man and of the mind, we have no final insight into the essence of philosophy, which is one of men's recognisable activities: recognisable, both through the continuity of its own development, each phase beginning as a partial contradiction of its predecessor, and also by some continuity in its gradually changing relation to other inquiries, each with their own internal development.[76]

[76] Hampshire [14], p. 243.

---

[75] These difficulties exist only if one holds that the acquisition of knowledge presupposes the presentation of something "immediately given" to the mind, where the mind is conceived of as a sort of "immaterial eye," and where "immediately" means, at a minimum, "without the mediation of language." This "spectatorial" account of knowledge is the common target of philosophers as different as Dewey, Hampshire, Sartre, Heidegger, and Wittgenstein.

PART I

Classic Statements of the Thesis That Philosophical Questions Are Questions of Language

· 1 ·

MORITZ SCHLICK

The Future of Philosophy

The study of the history of philosophy is perhaps the most fascinating pursuit for anyone who is eager to understand the civilization and culture of the human race, for all of the different elements of human nature that help to build up the culture of a certain epoch or a nation mirror themselves in one way or another in the philosophy of that epoch or of that nation.

The history of philosophy can be studied from two distinct points of view. The first point of view is that of the historian; the second one is that of the philosopher. They will each approach the study of the history of philosophy with different feelings. The historian will be excited to the greatest enthusiasm by the great works of the thinkers of all times, by the spectacle of the immense mental energy and imagination, zeal and unselfishness which they have devoted to their creations, and the historian will derive the highest enjoyment from all of these achievements. The philosopher, of course, when he studies the history of philosophy will also be delighted, and he cannot help being inspired by the wonderful display of genius throughout all the ages. But he will not be able to rejoice at the sight that philosophy presents to him with exactly

the same feelings as the historian. He will not be able to enjoy the thoughts of ancient and modern times without being disturbed by feelings of an entirely different nature.

The philosopher cannot be satisfied to ask, as the historian would ask of all the systems of thought — are they beautiful, are they brilliant, are they historically important? and so on. The only question which will interest him is the question, "What truth is there in these systems?" And the moment he asks it he will be discouraged when he looks at the history of philosophy because, as you all know, there is so much contradiction between the various systems — so much quarreling and strife between the different opinions that have been advanced in different periods by different philosophers belonging to different nations — that it seems at first quite impossible to believe that there is anything like a steady advance in the history of philosophy as there seems to be in other pursuits of the human mind, for example, science or technique.

The question which we are going to ask tonight is "Will this chaos that has existed so far continue to exist in the future?" Will philosophers go on contradicting each other, ridiculing each other's opinions, or will there finally be some kind of universal agreement, a unity of philosophical belief in the world?

All of the great philosophers believed that with their own systems a new epoch

Reprinted from *College of the Pacific Publications in Philosophy*, I (1932), 45–62, by permission of Paul A. Schilpp, editor of *The Pacific Philosophy Forum* (successor journal). (Copyright 1932 by P. A. Schilpp.)

of thinking had begun, that they, at least, had discovered the final truth. If they had not believed this they could hardly have accomplished anything. This was true of Descartes, for instance, when he introduced the method which made him "the father of modern philosophy," as he is usually called; of Spinoza when he tried to introduce the mathematical method into philosophy; or even of Kant when he said in the preface to his greatest work that from now on philosophy might begin to work as securely as only science had worked thus far. They all believed that they had been able to bring the chaos to an end and start something entirely new which would at last bring about a rise in the worth of philosophical opinions. But the historian cannot usually share such a belief; it may even seem ridiculous to him.

We want to ask the question, "What will be the future of philosophy?" entirely from the point of view of the philosopher. However, to answer the question we shall have to use the method of the historian because we shall not be able to say what the future of philosophy will be except in so far as our conclusions are derived from our knowledge of its past and its present.

The first effect of a historical consideration of philosophical opinions is that we feel sure we cannot have any confidence in any one system. If this is so — if we cannot be Cartesians, Spinozists, Kantians, and so forth — it seems that the only alternative is that we become skeptics, and we become inclined to believe that there can be no true system of philosophy because if there were any such system it seems that at least it must have been suspected and would have shown itself in some way. However, when we examine the history of philosophy honestly, it seems as if there were no traces of any discovery that might lead to unanimous philosophical opinion.

This skeptical inference, in fact, has been drawn by a good many historians, and even some philosophers have come to the conclusion that there is no such

thing as philosophical advancement, and that philosophy itself is nothing but the history of philosophy. This view was advocated by more than one philosopher in the beginning of the century and it has been called "historicism." That philosophy consists only of its own history is a strange view to take, but it has been advocated and defended with apparently striking arguments. However, we shall not find ourselves compelled to take such a skeptical view.

We have thus far considered two possible alternatives that one may believe in. First, that the ultimate truth is really presented in some one system of philosophy and secondly, that there is no philosophy at all, but only a history of thought. I do not tonight propose to choose either of these two alternatives; but I should like to propose a third view which is neither skeptical nor based on the belief that there can be any system of philosophy as a system of ultimate truths. I intend to take an entirely different view of philosophy and it is, of course, my opinion that this view of philosophy will some time in the future be adopted by everybody. In fact, it would seem strange to me if philosophy, that noblest of intellectual pursuits, the tremendous human achievement that has so often been called the "queen of all sciences" were nothing at all but one great deception. Therefore it seems likely that a third view can be found by careful analysis and I believe that the view which I am going to advance here will do full justice to all the skeptical arguments against the possibility of a philosophical system and yet will not deprive philosophy of any of its nobility and grandeur.

Of course, the mere fact that thus far the great systems of philosophy have not been successful and have not been able to gain general acknowledgment is no sufficient reason why there should not be some philosophical system discovered in the future that would universally be regarded as the ultimate solution of the great problems. This might indeed be expected to happen if philosophy were a "science." For in science we continually find that unexpected satisfactory solutions for great problems are found, and when it is not possible to see clearly in any particular point on a scientific question we do not despair. We believe that future scientists will be more fortunate and discover what we have failed to discover. In this respect, however, the great difference between science and philosophy reveals itself. Science shows a gradual development. There is not the slightest doubt that science has advanced and continues to advance, although some people speak skeptically about science. It cannot be seriously doubted for an instant that we know very much more about nature, for example, than people living in former centuries knew. There is unquestionably some kind of advance shown in science, but if we are perfectly honest, a similar kind of advance cannot be discovered in philosophy.

The same great issues are discussed nowadays that were discussed in the time of Plato. When for a time it seemed as though a certain question were definitely settled, soon the same question comes up again and has to be discussed and reconsidered. It was characteristic of the work of the philosopher that he always had to begin at the beginning again. He never takes anything for granted. He feels that every solution to any philosophical problem is not certain or sure enough, and he feels that he must begin all over again in settling the problem. There is, then, this difference between science and philosophy which makes us very skeptical about any future advance of philosophy. Still we might believe that times may change, and that we might possibly find the true philosophical system. But this hope is in vain, for we can find reasons why philosophy has failed, and must fail, to produce lasting scientific results as science has done. If these reasons are good then we shall be justified in not trusting in any system of philosophy, and in believing that no such system will come forward in the future.

Let me say at once that these reasons do not lie in the difficulty of the problems with which philosophy deals; neither are they to be found in the weakness and incapacity of human understanding. If they lay there, it could easily be conceived that human understanding and reason might develop, that if we are not intelligent enough now our successors might be intelligent enough to develop a system. No, the real reason is to be found in a curious misunderstanding and misinterpretation of the nature of philosophy; it lies in the failure to distinguish between the scientific attitude and the philosophical attitude. It lies in the idea that the nature of philosophy and science are more or less the same, that they both consist of systems of true propositions about the world. In reality philosophy is never a system of propositions and therefore quite different from science. The proper understanding of the relationship between philosophy on one side and of the sciences on the other side is, I think, the best way of gaining insight into the nature of philosophy. We will therefore start with an investigation of this relationship and its historical development. This will furnish us the necessary facts in order to predict the future of philosophy. The future, of course, is always a matter of historical conjecture, because it can be calculated only from past and present experiences. So we ask now: what has the nature of philosophy been conceived to be in comparison with that of the sciences? and how has it developed in the course of history?

In its beginnings, as you perhaps know, philosophy was considered to be simply another name for the "search for truth" — it was identical with science. Men who pursued the truth for its own sake were called philosophers, and there was no distinction made between men of science and philosophers.

A little change was brought about in this situation by Socrates. Socrates, one might say, despised science. He did not believe in all the speculations about astronomy and about the structure of the universe in which the early philosophers indulged. He believed one could never gain any certain knowledge about these matters and he restricted his investigations to the nature of human character. He was not a man of science, he had no faith in it, and yet we all acknowledge him to be one of the greatest philosophers who ever lived. It is not Socrates, however, who created the antagonism that we find to exist later on between science and philosophy. In fact, his successors combined very well the study of human nature with the science of the stars and of the universe.

Philosophy remained united with the various sciences until gradually the latter branched off from philosophy. In this way, perhaps, mathematics, astronomy, mechanics and medicine became independent one after the other and a difference between philosophy and science was created. Nevertheless some kind of unity or identity of the two persisted, we might say, almost to modern times, i. e. until the nineteenth century. I believe we can say truthfully that there are certain sciences — I am thinking particularly of physics — which were not completely separated from philosophy until the nineteenth century. Even now some university chairs for theoretical physics are officially labeled chairs of "natural philosophy."

It was in the nineteenth century also that the real antagonism began, with a certain feeling of unfriendliness developing on the part of the philosopher toward the scientist and the scientist toward the philosopher. This feeling arose when philosophy claimed to possess a nobler and better method of discovering truth than the scientific method of observation and experiment. In Germany at the beginning of the nineteenth century Schelling, Fichte, and Hegel believed that there was some kind of royal path leading to truth which was reserved for the philosopher, whereas the scientist walked the pathway of the vulgar

and very tedious experimental method, which required so much merely mechanical technique. They thought that they could attain the same truth that the scientist was trying to find but could discover it in a much easier way by taking a short cut that was reserved for the very highest minds, only for the philosophical genius. About this, however, I will not speak because it may be regarded, I think, as having been superseded.

There is another view, however, which tried to distinguish between science and philosophy by saying that philosophy dealt with the most general truths that could be known about the world and that science dealt with the more particular truths. It is this last view of the nature of philosophy that I must discuss shortly tonight as it will help us to understand what will follow.

This opinion that philosophy is the science that deals with those most general truths which do not belong to the field of any special science is the most common view that you find in nearly all of the text books; it has been adopted by the majority of philosophical writers in our present day. It is generally believed that as, for example, chemistry concerns itself with the true propositions about the different chemical compounds and physics with the truth about physical behavior, so philosophy deals with the most general questions concerning the nature of matter. Similarly, as history investigates the various chains of single happenings which determine the fate of the human race, so philosophy (as "philosophy of history") is supposed to discover the general principles which govern all those happenings.

In this way, philosophy, conceived as the science dealing with the most general truths, is believed to give us what might be called a universal picture of the world, a general world view in which all the different truths of the special sciences find their places and are unified into one great picture — a goal which the special sciences themselves are thought incapable of reaching as they are not general enough and are concerned only with particular features and parts of the great whole.

This so-called "synoptic view" of philosophy, holding as it does that philosophy is also a science, only one of a more general character than the special sciences, has, it seems to me, led to terrible confusion. On the one hand it has given to the philosopher the character of the scientist. He sits in his library, he consults innumerable books, he works at his desk and studies various opinions of many philosophers as a historian would compare his different sources, or as a scientist would do while engaged in some particular pursuit in any special domain of knowledge; he has all the bearing of a scientist and really believes that he is using in some way the scientific method, only doing so on a more general scale. He regards philosophy as a more distinguished and much nobler science than the others, but not as essentially different from them.

On the other hand, with this picture of the philosopher in mind we find a very great contrast when we look at the results that have been really achieved by philosophical work carried on in this manner. There is all the outward appearance of the scientist in the philosopher's mode of work but there is no similarity of results. Scientific results go on developing, combining themselves with other achievements, and receiving general acknowledgment, but there is no such thing to be discovered in the work of the philosopher.

What are we to think of the situation? It has led to very curious and rather ridiculous results. When we open a text book on philosophy or when we view one of the large works of a present day philosopher we often find an immense amount of energy devoted to the task of finding out what philosophy is. We do not find this in any of the other sciences. Physicists or historians do not have to spend pages to find out what physics or history are. Even those who agree that philosophy in some way is the system of the most general truths explain this generality in rather different ways. I will not go into detail with respect to these varying definitions. Let me just mention that some say that philosophy is the "science of values" because they believe that the most general issues to which all questions finally lead have to do with value in some way or another. Others say that it is epistemology, i. e. the theory of knowledge, because the theory of knowledge is supposed to deal with the most general principles on which all particular truths rest. One of the consequences usually drawn by the adherents of the view we are discussing is that philosophy is either partly or entirely metaphysics. And metaphysics is supposed to be some kind of a structure built over and partly resting on the structure of science but towering into lofty heights which are far beyond the reach of all the sciences and of experience.

We see from all this that even those who adopt the definition of philosophy as the most general science cannot agree about its essential nature. This is certainly a little ridiculous and some future historian a few hundred or a thousand years from now will think it very curious that discussion about the nature of philosophy was taken so seriously in our days. There must be something wrong when a discussion leads to such confusion. There are also very definite positive reasons why "generality" cannot be used as the characteristic that distinguishes philosophy from the "special" sciences, but I will not dwell upon them, but try to reach a positive conclusion in some shorter way.

When I spoke of Socrates a little while ago I pointed out that his thoughts were, in a certain sense, opposed to the natural sciences; his philosophy, therefore, was certainly not identical with the sciences, and it was not the "most general" one of them. It was rather a sort of Wisdom of Life. But the important feature which we should observe in Socrates, in order to understand his particular attitude as well as the nature of philosophy, is that this wisdom that dealt with human nature and human behavior consists essentially of a special *method*, different from the method of science and, therefore, not leading to any "scientific" results.

All of you have probably read some of Plato's Dialogues, wherein he pictures Socrates as giving and receiving questions and answers. If you observe what was really done — or what Socrates tried to do — you discover that he did usually not arrive at certain definite truths which would appear at the end of the dialogue but the whole investigation was carried on for the primary purpose of making clear what was meant when certain questions were asked or when certain words were used. In one of the Platonic Dialogues, for instance, Socrates asks "What is Justice?"; he receives various answers to his question, and in turn he asks what was meant by these answers, why a particular word was used in this way or that way, and it usually turns out that his disciple or opponent is not at all clear about his own opinion. In short, Socrates' philosophy consists of what we may call "The Pursuit of Meaning." He tried to clarify thought by analyzing the meaning of our expressions and the real sense of our propositions.

Here then we find a definite contrast between this philosophic method, which has for its object the discovery of *meaning*, and the method of the sciences, which have for their object the discovery of *truth*. In fact, before I go any farther, let me state shortly and clearly that I believe Science should be defined as the "*pursuit of truth*" and Philosophy as the "*pursuit of meaning*." Socrates has set the example of the true philosophic method for all times. But I shall have to explain this method from the modern point of view.

When we make a statement about anything we do this by pronouncing a sentence and the sentence stands for the proposition. This proposition is either true or false, but before we can know or decide whether it is true or false we must know

what this proposition says. We must know the meaning of the proposition first. After we know its sense we may be able to find out whether it is true or not. These two things, of course, are inseparably connected. I cannot find out the truth without knowing the meaning, and if I know the meaning of the proposition I shall at least know the beginning of some path that will lead to the discovery of the truth or falsity of the proposition even if I am unable to find it at present. It is my opinion that the future of philosophy hinges on this distinction between the discovery of sense and the discovery of truth.

How do we decide what the sense of a proposition is, or what we mean by a sentence which is spoken, written, or printed? We try to present to ourselves the significance of the different words that we have learned to use, and then endeavor to find sense in the proposition. Sometimes we can do so and sometimes we cannot; the latter case happens, unfortunately, most frequently with propositions which are supposed to be "philosophical." But how can we be quite sure that we really know and understand what we mean when we make an assertion? What is the ultimate criterion of its sense? The answer is this: We know the meaning of a proposition when we are able to indicate exactly the circumstances under which it would be true (or, what amounts to the same, the circumstances which would make it false). The description of these circumstances is absolutely the only way in which the meaning of a sentence can be made clear. After it has been made clear we can proceed to look for the actual circumstances in the world and decide whether they make our proposition true or false. There is no vital difference between the ways we decide about truth and falsity in science and in every-day life. Science develops in the same ways in which does knowledge in daily life. The method of verification is essentially the same; only the facts by which scientific statements are verified are usually more difficult to observe.

It seems evident that a scientist or a philosopher when he propounds a proposition must of necessity know what he is talking about before he proceeds to find out its truth. But it is very remarkable that oftentimes it has happened in the history of human thought that thinkers have tried to find out whether a certain proposition was true or false before being clear about the meaning of it, before really knowing what it was they were desirous of finding out. This has been the case sometimes even in scientific investigations, instances of which I will quote shortly. And it has, I am almost tempted to say, nearly always been the case in traditional philosophy. As I have stated, the scientist has two tasks. He must find out the truth of a proposition and he must also find out the meaning of it, or it must be found out for him, but usually he is able to find it for himself. In so far as the scientist does find out the hidden meaning of the propositions which he uses in his science he is a philosopher. All of the great scientists have given wonderful examples of this philosophical method. They have discovered the real significance of words which were used quite commonly in the beginning of science but of which nobody had ever given a perfectly clear and definite account. When Newton discovered the concept of *"mass"* he was at that time really a philosopher. The greatest example of this type of discovery in modern times is Einstein's analysis of the meaning of the word "simultaneity" as it is used in physics. Continually, something is happening "at the same time" in New York and San Francisco, and although people always thought they knew perfectly well what was meant by such a statement Einstein was the first one who made it really clear and did away with certain unjustified assumptions concerning time that had been made without anyone being aware of it. This was a real philosophical achievement — the discovery of meaning by a logical clarification of a proposition. I could give more instances, but perhaps these two will

be sufficient. We see that meaning and truth are linked together by the process of verification; but the first is found by mere reflection about possible circumstances in the world, while the second is decided by really discovering the existence or non-existence of those circumstances. The reflection in the first case is the philosophic method of which Socrates' dialectical proceeding has afforded us the simplest example.

From what I have said so far it might seem that philosophy would simply have to be defined as the science of meaning, as, for example, astronomy is the science of the heavenly bodies, or zoology the science of animals, and that philosophy would be a science just as other sciences, only its subject would be different, namely, "Meaning." This is the point of view taken in a very excellent book, "The Practice of Philosophy," by Susanne K. Langer. The author has seen quite clearly that philosophy has to do with the pursuit of meaning, but she believes the pursuit of meaning can lead to a science, to "a set of true propositions" — for that is the correct interpretation of the term, science. Physics is nothing but a system of truths about physical bodies. Astronomy is a set of true propositions about the heavenly bodies, etc.

But philosophy is not a science in this case. There can be no science of meaning, because there cannot be any set of true propositions about meaning. The reason for this is that in order to arrive at the meaning of a sentence or of a proposition we must go beyond propositions. For we cannot hope to explain the meaning of a proposition merely by presenting another proposition. When I ask somebody, "What is the meaning of this or that?" he must answer by a sentence that would try to describe the meaning. But he cannot ultimately succeed in this, for his answering sentence would be but another proposition and I would be perfectly justified in asking "What do you mean by *this*?" We would perhaps go on defining what he meant by using different words, and repeat his thought over and over again by using new sentences. I could always go on asking "But what does this new proposition mean?" You see, there would never be any end to this kind of inquiry, the meaning could never be clarified, if there were no other way of arriving at it than by a series of propositions.

An example will make the above clear, and I believe you will all understand it immediately. Whenever you come across a difficult word for which you desire to find the meaning you look it up in the Encyclopedia Britannica. The definition of the word is given in various terms. If you don't happen to know them you look up these terms. However, this procedure can't go on indefinitely. Finally you will arrive at very simple terms for which you will not find any explanation in the encyclopedia. What are these terms? They are the terms which cannot be defined any more. You will admit that there are such terms. If I say, e. g., that the lamp shade is yellow, you might ask me to describe what I mean by yellow — and I could not do it. I should have to show you some color and say that this is yellow, but I should be perfectly unable to explain it to you by means of any sentences or words. If you had never seen yellow and I were not in a position to show you any yellow color it would be absolutely impossible for me to make clear what I meant when I uttered the word. And the blind man, of course, will never be able to understand what the word stands for.

All of our definitions must end by some demonstration, by some activity. There may be certain words at the meaning of which one may arrive by certain mental activities just as I can arrive at the signification of a word which denotes color by showing the color itself. It is impossible to define a color — it has to be shown. Reflection of some kind is necessary so that we may understand the use of certain words. We have to reflect, perhaps, about the way in which we learn these words,

and there are also many ways of reflection which make it clear to us what we mean by various propositions. Think, for example, of the term "simultaneity" of events occurring in different places. To find what is really meant by the term we have to go into an analysis of the proposition and discover how the simultaneity of events occurring in different places is really determined, as was done by Einstein; we have to point to certain actual experiments and observations. This should lead to the realization that philosophical activities can never be replaced and expressed by a set of propositions. The discovery of the meaning of any proposition must ultimately be achieved by some act, some immediate procedure, for instance, as the showing of yellow; it cannot be given in a proposition. Philosophy, the "pursuit of meaning," therefore cannot possibly consist of propositions; it cannot be a science. The pursuit of meaning consequently is nothing but a sort of mental activity.

Our conclusion is that philosophy was misunderstood when it was thought that philosophical results could be expressed in propositions, and that there could be a system of philosophy consisting of a system of propositions which would represent the answers to "philosophical" questions. There are no specific "philosophical" truths which would contain the solution of specific "philosophical" problems, but philosophy has the task of finding the meaning of *all* problems and their solutions. It must be defined as *the activity of finding meaning*.

Philosophy is an activity, not a science, but this activity, of course, is at work in every single science continually, because before the sciences can discover the truth or falsity of a proposition they have to get at the meaning first. And sometimes in the course of their work they are surprised to find, by the contradictory results at which they arrive, that they have been using words without a perfectly clear meaning, and then they will have to turn to the philosophical activity of clarification, and they cannot go on with the pursuit of truth before the pursuit of meaning has been successful. In this way philosophy is an extremely important factor within science and it very well deserves to bear the name of "The Queen of Sciences."

The Queen of Sciences is not itself a science. It is an activity which is needed by all scientists and pervades all their other activities. But all real problems are scientific questions, there are no others.

And what was the matter with those great questions that have been looked upon — or rather looked up to — as specific "philosophical problems" for so many centuries? Here we must distinguish two cases. In the first place, there are a great many questions which look like questions because they are formed according to a certain grammatical order but which nevertheless are not real questions, since it can easily be shown that the words, as they are put together, do not make logical sense.

If I should ask, for instance: "Is blue more identical than music?" you would see immediately that there is no meaning in this sentence, although it does not violate the rules of English grammar. The sentence is not a question at all, but just a series of words. Now, a careful analysis shows that this is the case with most so-called philosophical problems. They look like questions and it is very difficult to recognize them as nonsensical but logical analysis proves them none the less to be merely some kind of confusion of words. After this has been found out the question itself disappears and we are perfectly peaceful in our philosophical minds, we know that there can be no answers because there were no questions, the problems do not exist any longer.

In the second place, there are some "philosophical" problems which prove to be real questions. But of these it can always be shown by proper analysis that they are capable of being solved by the methods of science although we may not be able to apply these methods at present for merely technical reasons. We can at least say what would have to be done in order to answer the question even if we cannot actually do it with the means at our disposal. In other words: problems of this kind have no special "philosophical" character, but are simply scientific questions. They are always answerable in principle, if not in practice, and the answer can be given only by scientific investigation.

Thus the fate of all "philosophical problems" is this: Some of them will disappear by being shown to be mistakes and misunderstandings of our language and the others will be found to be ordinary scientific questions in disguise. These remarks, I think, determine the whole future of philosophy.

Several great philosophers have recognized the essence of philosophical thinking with comparative clarity, although they have given no elaborate expression to it. Kant, e. g. used to say in his lectures that philosophy cannot be taught. However, if it were a science such as geology or astronomy, why then should it not be taught? It would then, in fact, be quite possible to teach it. Kant therefore had some kind of a suspicion that it was not a science when he stated "The only thing I can teach is philosophizing." By using the verb and rejecting the noun in this connection Kant indicated clearly, though almost involuntarily, the peculiar character of philosophy as an activity, thereby to a certain extent contradicting his books, in which he tries to build up philosophy after the manner of a scientific system.

A similar instance of the same insight is afforded by Leibniz. When he founded the Prussian Academy of Science in Berlin and sketched out the plans for its constitution, he assigned a place in it to all the sciences but Philosophy was not one of them. Leibniz found no place for philosophy in the system of the sciences because he was evidently aware that it is not a pursuit of a particular kind of truth, but an activity that must pervade *every* search for truth.

The view which I am advocating has at the present time been most clearly expressed by Ludwig Wittgenstein; he states his point in these sentences: "The object of philosophy is the logical clarification of thoughts. Philosophy is not a theory but an activity. The result of philosophy is not a number of 'philosophical propositions', but to make propositions clear." This is exactly the view which I have been trying to explain here.

We can now understand historically why philosophy could be regarded as a very general science: it was misunderstood in this way because the "meaning" of propositions might seem to be something very "general," since in some way it forms the foundation of all discourse. We can also understand historically why in ancient times philosophy was identical with science: this was because at that time all the concepts which were used in the description of the world were extremely vague. The task of science was determined by the fact that there were no clear concepts. They had to be clarified by slow development, the chief endeavor of scientific investigation had to be directed towards this clarification, i. e. it had to be philosophical, no distinction could be made between science and philosophy.

At the present time we also find facts which prove the truth of our statements. In our days certain specific fields of study such as ethics and esthetics are called "philosophical" and are supposed to form part of philosophy. However, philosophy, being an activity, is a unit which cannot be divided into parts or independent disciplines. Why, then, are these pursuits called philosophy? Because they are only at the beginnings of the scientific stage; and I think this is true to a certain extent also of psychology. Ethics and esthetics certainly do not yet possess sufficiently clear concepts, most of their work is still devoted to clarifying them, and therefore it may justly be called philosophical. But in the future they will, of course, become part of the great system of the sciences.

It is my hope that the philosophers of the future will see that it is impossible for them to adopt, even in outward appearance, the methods of the scientists. Most books on philosophy seem to be, I must confess, ridiculous when judged from the most elevated point of view. They have all the appearance of being extremely scientific books because they seem to use the scientific language. However, the finding of meaning cannot be done in the same way as the finding of truth. This difference will come out much more clearly in the future. There is a good deal of truth in the way in which Schopenhauer (although his own thinking seems to me to be very imperfect indeed) describes the contrast between the real philosopher and the academic scholar who regards philosophy as a subject of scientific pursuit. Schopenhauer had a clear instinct when he spoke disparagingly of the "professorial philosophy of the professors of philosophy." His opinion was that one should not try to teach philosophy at all but only the history of philosophy and logic; and a good deal may be said in favor of this view.

I hope I have not been misunderstood as though I were advocating an actual separation of scientific and philosophical work. On the contrary, in most cases future philosophers will have to be scientists because it will be necessary for them to have a certain subject matter on which to work — and they will find cases of confused or vague meaning particularly in the foundations of the sciences. But, of course, clarification of meaning will be needed very badly also in a great many questions with which we are concerned in our ordinary human life. Some thinkers, and perhaps some of the strongest minds among them, may be especially gifted in this practical field. In such instances, the philosopher may not have to be a scientist — but in all cases he will have to be a man of deep understanding. In short he will have to be a *wise* man.

I am convinced that our view of the nature of philosophy will be generally adopted in the future; and the consequence will be that it will no longer be attempted to teach philosophy as a system. We shall teach the special sciences and their history in the true philosophical spirit of searching for clarity and, by doing this, we shall develop the philosophical mind of future generations. This is all we can do, but it will be a great step in the mental progress of our race.

Editor's note: For discussions of the conception of philosophy as the activity of finding meanings, which Schlick presents here, see Ambrose [3] (reprinted below at pp. 147–55); Black [1], [3], [11]; Copi [1], [2]; Hampshire [1] (reprinted below at pp. 284–93); Russell [4]; Stebbing [5], [6], [9]; and Wisdom [2].

· 2 ·

RUDOLF CARNAP

ON THE CHARACTER OF PHILOSOPHIC PROBLEMS[1]

PHILOSOPHY IS THE LOGIC OF SCIENCE

Philosophers have ever declared that their problems lie at a different level from the problems of the empirical sciences. Perhaps one may agree with this assertion; the question is, however, where should one seek this level. The metaphysicians wish to seek their object *behind* the objects of empirical science; they wish to enquire after the essence, the ultimate cause of things. But the logical analysis of the pretended propositions of metaphysics has shown that they are not propositions at all, but empty word arrays, which on account of notional and emotional connections arouse the false appearance of being propositions. This conception that the "propositions" of metaphysics, including those of ethics, have no theoretical content, is to be sure still disputed. We shall not, however, enter here on its demonstration, but, under its guidance, will limit ourselves to non-metaphysical and non-ethical (non-evaluating) philosophical problems.

In order to discover the correct standpoint of the philosopher, which differs from that of the empirical investigator, we must not penetrate *behind* the objects of empirical science into presumably some kind of transcendent level; on the con-

trary we must take a *step back* and *take science itself as the object*. Philosophy is *the theory of science* (wherein here and in the following "science" is always meant in the comprehensive sense of the collective system of the knowledge of any kind of entity; physical and psychic, natural and social entities). This must be appraised more closely. One may consider science from various viewpoints; e.g. whether one can institute a psychological investigation considering the activities of observation, deduction, formulation of theories, etc., or sociological investigations concerning the economical and cultural conditions of the pursuit of science. These provinces — although most important — are not meant here. Psychology and sociology are empirical sciences; they do not belong to philosophy even though they are often pursued by the same person, and have torn loose from philosophy as independent branches of science only in our own times. Philosophy deals with science only from the *logical* viewpoint. *Philosophy is the logic of science*, i.e., the logical analysis of the concepts,

Reprinted from *Philosophy of Science*, I (1934), 5–19, by permission of the author and the publisher, The Williams and Wilkins Company, Baltimore.

[1] Translated by W. M. Malisoff. Attention is called to the following choices taken by the translator: — *Auffassung* has been rendered variously as interpretation, conception, position; *Folgerung* as deduction, conclusion, inference, but in conformance with the discussion, most often as entailment. *Gehalt* which may mean value, has been rendered only as *content; Inhalt* as meaning; but *inhaltlich* as *connotative*, rather than *strict* or *meaningful* or *intensional*, which may convey as much.

propositions, proofs, theories of science, as well as of those which we select in available science as common to the possible methods of constructing concepts, proofs, hypotheses, theories. [What one used to call epistemology or theory of knowledge is a mixture of applied logic and psychology (and at times even metaphysics); insofar as this theory is logic it is included in what we call logic of science; insofar, however, as it is psychology, it does not belong to philosophy, but to empirical science.]

The interpretation that philosophy is the logic of science is not to be justified here. It has been represented previously and is represented now by various philosophic groups, amongst others also by our Vienna circle. With this thesis the question as to the character of philosophic problems is not by any means already solved. Very much comes into question right at this point. We should consequently ask here: what character, what logical nature, do the questions and answers of the logic of science have? For those who are with us in the conception that philosophy is the logic of science the question of the character of philosophic problems will be answered thereby as well.

ARE THE PROPOSITIONS OF THE LOGIC OF SCIENCE MEANINGLESS?

Our antimetaphysical position has been formulated by Hume in the classical manner:—

"It seems to me, that the only objects of the abstract sciences or of demonstration are quantity and number, and that all attempts to extend this more perfect species of knowledge beyond these bounds are mere sophistry and illusion. As the component parts of quantity and number are entirely similar, their relations become intricate and involved; and nothing can be more curious, as well as useful, than to trace, by a variety of mediums their equality or inequality, through their different appearances. But as all other ideas are clearly distinct and different from each other, we can never advance farther, by our utmost scrutiny, than to observe this diversity, and, by an obvious reflection, pronounce one thing not to be another. Or if there be any difficulty in these decisions, it proceeds entirely from the undeterminate meaning of words, which is corrected by juster definitions. . . . All other enquiries of men regard only matter of fact and existence; and these are evidently incapable of demonstration. . . . When we run over libraries, persuaded by these principles, what havoc must we make? If we take in our hand any volume; of divinity or school metaphysics, for instance; let us ask, *Does it contain any abstract reasoning concerning quantity or number?* No. *Does it contain any experimental reasoning concerning matter of fact and existence?* No. Commit it then to the flames: for it can contain nothing but sophistry and illusion." Hume, An Enquiry Concerning Human Understanding, XII, 3.

Against this the following objection, which on first appearance seems indeed destructive, has been repeatedly raised:— "If every proposition which does not belong either to mathematics or to the empirical investigation of facts, is meaningless, how does it fare then with your own propositions? You positivists and antimetaphysicians yourselves cut off the branch on which you sit." This objection indeed touches upon a decisive point. It should be of interest to every philosopher as well as metaphysician to comprehend the character of the propositions of the logic of science; but to the antimetaphysician, who identifies philosophy and the logic of science, this is the *deciding question*, upon the satisfactory answer of which the security of his standpoint depends.

Wittgenstein has represented with especial emphasis the thesis of the meaninglessness of metaphysical propositions and of the identity of philosophy and the logic of science; especially through him has the Vienna circle been developed on this point. How now does Wittgenstein dispose of the objection that his own propositions are also meaningless? He doesn't at all; he agrees with it! He is of the opinion that the non-metaphysical *philosophy* also has no propositions; it operates with words, *the meaninglessness of which in the end it itself must recognize:—*

"Philosophy is not a theory but an activity. A philosophical work consists essentially of elucidations. The result of philosophy is not a number of "philosophical propositions," but to make propositions clear." (Tractatus Logico-philosophicus, 4. 112).

"My propositions are elucidatory in this way: he who understands me finally recognizes them as senseless, when he has climbed out through them, on them, over them. (He must so to speak throw away the ladder, after he has climbed up on it.) He must surmount these propositions; then he sees the world rightly. Whereof one cannot speak, thereof one must be silent." (*ibid.*, 6.54-7).

We shall try in the following to give in place of this radically negative answer a *positive answer* to the question of the character of the propositions of the logic of science and thereby of philosophy.

CONNOTATIVE AND FORMAL CONSIDERATION (INHALTLICHE UND FORMALE BETRACHTUNG)

To construct science means to construct a system of propositions which stand in certain fundamental coherence with one another. The logic of science is thus the logical analysis of this system, of its elements and of the methods of tying these elements. In such an analysis we can start from but two different viewpoints; we shall call them connotative (inhaltlich) and formal.

It is usual in the logic of science to put something like the following and similar questions: What is the meaning of this or that concept? In what relation does the meaning of this concept stand with respect to that? Is the meaning of this concept more fundamental than of that? What meaning (Inhalt, Gehalt) does this proposition have? (Or: What does this proposition say?) Is the meaning of this proposition contained in the meaning of that? Does this proposition say more than that? Is what this proposition asserts, necessary or contingent or impossible? Is what these two propositions say compatible?

All these questions refer to the *meaning* of concepts and propositions. We call them therefore questions of meaning or of *connotation* (inhaltliche). In contrast to this we understand by *formal* questions and propositions such as relate only to the formal structure of the propositions, i.e. to the arrangement and kind of symbols (e.g. words) out of which a proposition is constructed, *without reference to the meaning* of the symbols and propositions. Formal (in the sense here defined) are e.g. (most of) the rules of grammar.

According to prevalent conceptions the connotative questions of the logic of science are much richer and fruitful than the formal; though the formal do belong to the logic of science, they are at most a small, insignificant section. But this opinion is wrong. The logic of science can progress without exception according to the formal method without thereby restricting the wealth of questioning. It is possible in the case of purely formal procedures, that is from a viewpoint in which one does not reckon with the meaning, finally to arrive at the answering of all those questions which are formulated as connotative questions. This possibility is to be shown illustratively in the following. Therewith the question of the character of *philosophy as logic of science* is answered: it is *the formal structure theory of the language of science,* — we shall call it: The logical syntax of the language of science.

LOGICAL SYNTAX OF LANGUAGE

By the "logical syntax" (or also briefly "syntax") of a language we shall understand the *system* of the *formal* (i.e. not referring to meaning) *rules* of that language, as well as to the consequences of these rules. Therein we deal first with the *formative rules* (Formregeln) which decree how from the symbols (e.g. words) of the language propositions can be built up, secondly with the *transformation rules* (Unformungsregeln), which decree how from given propositions new ones can be derived. If the rules are set up strictly formally they furnish mechanical operations with the symbols of the language. The formation and transformation of propositions resembles chess: like chess figures words are here combined and manipulated according to definite rules. But thereby we do not say that language is nothing but a game of figures; it is not denied that the words and propositions have a meaning; one merely abstracts methodically from meaning. One may express it also thus: *language* is treated as a *calculus*.

That the formal, calculus-like representation of the formative rules is possible is evident. What linguists call rules of syntax are indeed such formal (or at least formally expressible) rules for the formation of propositions. We can see, however, that the transformation rules, which one usually calls logical rules of deduction, clearly have the same formal, that is, syntactical character. (And that is the reason why we call the combined system of rules syntax, in widening the terminology of linguists.) Since Aristotle the efforts of logicians (more or less consciously) were directed toward formulating the deductive rules as formally as possible, i.e. possibly so that with their help the conclusion could be "calculated" mechanically from the premisses. This was attained first in a strict manner only in modern symbolic logic; the traditional logic was too much hindered by the defect of the language of words.

For a certain part of the language of science we already know a strictly formal theory, namely *Hilbert's* metamathematics. It considers the symbols and formulas of mathematics without reference to meaning, in order to investigate relations of deducibility, sufficiency, consistency, etc. This metamathematics is hence (in our manner of expression) the logical syntax of mathematical language. The logical syntax of the language of science

meant here is an analogous extension with reference to the language of all of science.

One of the most important concepts of logic and thereby of the logic of science is that of (logical) inference (Folgerungentailment). Can this concept be formulated purely formally? It is often stated that the relation of entailment depends on the meaning of the propositions. In a certain sense we can agree with that; for when the meaning of two propositions is known, it is thereby determined whether one is the entailment of the other or not. The decisive point, however, is: is it also possible to formulate the concept "entailment" purely formally? If the transformation rules of language are set up purely formally, we call a proposition an inference (entailment) of other propositions if it can be constructed from those propositions by the application of the transformation rules. The question, whether a certain proposition is an inference (entailment) of certain other propositions or not, is therefore completely analogous to the question whether a certain position in chess can be played from another or not. This question is answered by chess theory, i.e. a combinatorial or mathematical investigation which is based on the chess rules; that question is thus a formal one, it is answered by a *Combinatorial Calculus or Mathematics of Language*, which rests on the transformation rules of language, that is what we have called the *syntax* of language. Briefly: "entailment" is defined as deducibility according to the transformation rules; since these rules are formal, "entailment" is also a formal, syntactical concept.

The concept "entailment" is, as *Lewis* has correctly seen, quite different from the concept of "(material) *implication*." (Russell, Principles of Mathematics). Implication does not depend on the sense of the propositions, but only on their *truth-value*; but entailment on the contrary is not quite determined by the truth values. From this, however, one may not conclude that in the determination of entailment reference to the *meaning* is necessary; it suffices to refer to the formal structure of the propositions.

The Content of a Proposition

On the basis of the concept of "entailment" one can define the following classification of propositions which is fundamental to the logic of science. A proposition is called *analytic* (or tautological) if it is an entailment of every proposition (more exactly: if it is deducible without premisses, or is the entailment of the empty class of propositions). A proposition is called *contradictory* if any proposition at all is its entailment. A proposition is called *synthetic* if it is neither analytical nor contradictory. Example: "It is raining here" is synthetic; "It is raining or it is not raining" is analytic; "It is raining and it is not raining" is contradictory. An analytic proposition is true in every possible case and therefore does not state which case is on hand. A contradictory proposition on the contrary says too much, it is not true in any possible case. A synthetic proposition is true only in certain cases, and states therefore that one of these cases is being considered — all (true or false) statements of fact are synthetic. The concepts "analytic," "contradictory," "synthetic" can be defined in analogous manner also for classes of propositions; several propositions are said to be *incompatible* (unverträglich) with one another, if their conjunction is a self-contradiction.

And now we come to the principal concept of the logic of science, the concept of the (Inhalt) content of a proposition. Can this central concept of the connotative (inhaltliche) method of consideration be formulated purely formally also? We can be easily convinced that that is possible. For what, to be sure, do we want to know when we ask concerning the content or meaning of a proposition S? We wish to know what S conveys to us; what we experience through S; what we can take out of S. In other words: we ask

what we can deduce from S; more accurately: what propositions are entailments of S which are not already entailments of any proposition at all, and therefore declare nothing. We define therefore: by the *content* (Gehalt) of a proposition S we understand the class of entailments from S which are not analytic. Thereby the concept "Gehalt" is connected to the syntactical concepts defined earlier; it is then also a syntactic, a purely formal concept. From this definition it is apparent that the content of an analytic proposition is empty, since no non-analytic proposition is an entailment of it. Further, that the content of S_2 is contained in that of S_1 when and only when S_2 is an entailment of S_1; that two propositions are of equal content when and only when each is the entailment of the other. Thus the defined concept "Content" corresponds completely to what we mean when we (in a vague manner) are accustomed to speak of the "meaning" (Inhalt) of a proposition; at any rate, insofar as by "meaning" something logical is meant. Often in the investigation of the "meaning" or "sense" of a proposition one also means: What does one think of or imagine in this proposition? This, however, is a psychological question with which we have nothing to do in a logical investigation.

Connotative and Formal Modes of Expression (Inhaltliche und Formale Redeweise)*

We have set out from the fact that a language can be considered in two different ways: in a connotative and in a formal manner. Now, however, we have established that with the aid of the formal method the questions of the connotative approach can also be answered finally. Fundamentally there is really no difference between the two approaches, but only a

* Editor's note: In most English translations of Carnap's writings of this period, "inhaltliche Redeweise" is translated as "material mode of speech."

difference between two modes of expression: In the investigation of a language, its concepts and propositions and the relations between them, one can employ either the connotative or the formal mode of expression. The connotative mode of expression is more customary and obvious; but one must use it with great care; it frequently begets muddles and pseudo-problems. We shall consider several examples of propositions in connotative form and their translation into formal mode of speech; in the case of several of these examples (6a–10a) only on translation do we see that we are dealing with assertions concerning the language.

Connotative Mode of Speech	*Formal Mode of Speech*
1a. The propositions of arithmetical language give the properties of numbers and relations between them.	1b. The propositions of arithmetical language are constructed in such and such a manner from predicates of one or more values and number expressions as arguments.
2a. The expression '5' and '3+2' mean the same number.	2b. 3b. The expressions '5' and '3+2' are synonymous in the arithmetical language (i.e. always interchangeable with one another).
3a. '5' and '3+2' do not mean the same number but two equal numbers.	

On the basis of the connotative formulation *1a* there arise easily a number of metaphysical pseudo-problems concerning the nature of numbers, whether the numbers are real or ideal, whether they are extra- or intramental and the like. The danger of these pseudo-problems disappears when we use the formal mode of expression, where we speak of "number expressions" instead of "numbers." Also the philosophic conflict between *2a* and *3a* disappears in the formal mode of expression: both theses have the same translation.

4a. The word "luna" of the Latin language signifies the moon.	4b. On the basis of the syntactical translation rules between the Latin and the English languages the word "moon" is coördinated with the word "luna."
5a. The concept "red" signifies an ultimate quality; the concept "man" has a more ultimate meaning than the concept "grandson."	5b. The word "red" is an undefined fundamental symbol of language; the word "man" stands on a lower level that the word "grandson" in the definition family-tree of concepts.
6a. The moon is a thing; the sum of 3 and 2 is not a thing but a number.	6b. "Moon" is the designation of a thing; "3+2" is not a designation of a thing but a designation of a number.
7a. A property is not a thing.	7b. A property-word is not a thing-word.
8a. This particular (fact, event, condition) is logically necessary: . . . . logically impossible; . . . . logically possible.	8b. This proposition is analytic; . . . . contradictory; . . . . not contradictory.
9a. This particular (fact, event, condition) is physically necessary; . . . . physically impossible; . . . . physically possible.	9b. This proposition is deducible from the class of physical laws; . . . . is incompatible with . . . .; . . . . is compatible. . . . .
10a. Reality consists of facts, not of things.	10b. Science is a system of propositions, not of names.

Philosophy Is the Syntax of the Language of Science

We had started with the presupposition: Philosophy of Science is the logic of science, the logical analysis of concepts, propositions, structures of propositions of science. Since now the data of every logical analysis can be translated in the formal mode of expression, all the questions and theorems of philosophy consequently find their place in the formal structure theory of language, that is, in the realm which we have called the Syntax of the language of Science. Here it must, however, be noted that a philosophic theorem, formulated as a proposition of syntax, can be meant in different ways:

A. As *Assertion*; e.g.
1. In the language of science available today (or a part of it: of physics, biology, . . .) such and such holds.

2. In every language (or: in every language of such and such a nature) such and such holds.
3. There is a language for which such and such holds.

B. As *Proposal*; e.g.
1. I propose to build up the language of science (or of mathematics, of psychology, . . .) so that it acquires such and such properties.
2. I wish (along with other things) to investigate a language which possesses such and such properties.

The common confusion in philosophic discussions, not only among metaphysicians but also in the philosophy of science, is principally called forth by lack of a clear conception that the object of discussion is the language of science; and further because one does not clearly state (and mostly does not know oneself) whether a thesis is meant as an assertion or as a proposal. Let us consider, for example, in the discussion of the logical foundations of mathematics a point of conflict between the logisticists (Frege, Russell) and the axiomatists (Peano, Hilbert); let the theses be formulated by 12a, 13a. Then we translate the theses in order to formulate them more exactly into the formal mode of expression: 12b, 13b.

12a. The *numbers* are classes of classes of things.
13a. The numbers are unique ultimate entities.

12b. The number-symbols are class symbols of second rank.
13b. The number-symbols are individual-symbols (i.e. symbols of null rank, which appear only as arguments).

If now we interpret 12b and 13b in the manner A3, the conflict disappears: one can say that a language of arithmetic is constructible which has the property 12b; but also one as well which has the property 13b. But perhaps the theses 12b, 13b are meant as proposals in the sense B_1. In that case one is not dealing with a discussion about true or false, but with a discussion as to whether this or that mode of expression is simpler or more pertinent (for certain purposes of a scientific methodical nature). In any case the discussion is oblique and fruitless as long as the discussers do not agree as to which of the interpretations A or B is meant. The situation is similar with regard to the philosophical combat concerning the theses 14a, 15a:

14a. To the ultimate given belong relations.

15a. Relations are never given ultimately but depend always on the nature of the members of the relation.

14b. To the undefined fundamental signs belong two- (or more-) valued predicates.
15b. All two- or more-valued predicates are defined on the basis of one-valued predicates.

The discussion becomes clear only when 14b and 15b are considered as proposals; the problem then consists of putting up languages of this or that form and comparing them with one another.

In the following example we deal with the conflict of two theses 16a, 17a, which correspond more or less to positivism and to realism.

16a. *A thing* is a complex of sensations.

17a. A thing is a complex of atoms.

16b. Every proposition in which a thing-name occurs, is of equal content with a class of propositions in which no thing-names but sensation-names occur.

17b. Every proposition in which a thing-name occurs is of equal content with a proposition in which no thing-names but space-time coödinates and physical functions occur.

16b, 17b can be interpreted here in the sense A₁, namely as assertions concerning the syntactical structure of our language of science. In spite of that they do not contradict one another, since a proposition concerning a thing can be transformed in more than one way with equal content. We see: in using the formal mode of expression the pseudo-problem "What is a thing?" disappears, and therewith the opposition between the positivist and the realist answer disappears.

In taking the position that all philosophical problems are questions of the syntax of the language of science, we do not mean it to be a proposal or even a prescription for limiting inquiry to a definite, seemingly very narrow field of questions. Much more is meant: as soon as one exactly formulates some question of philosophy as logic of science, one notes that it is a question of the logical analysis of the language of science; and further investigation then teaches that each such question allows itself to be formulated as a formal question, to wit a question of the syntax of the language of science. All theorems of philosophy take on an exact, discussable form only when we formulate them as assertions or proposals of the syntax of the language of science.

THE PROBLEM OF THE FOUNDATIONS OF THE SCIENCES

In order to make clearer our position concerning the character of philosophic problems, we shall cast a brief glance on the problems which one customarily designates as the philosophic foundation problems of the individual sciences.

The philosophic *problems of the foundations of mathematics* are the questions of the syntax of mathematical language, not, to be sure, as an isolated language, but as a part of the language of science. This addendum is important. The logistic trend (Frege, Russell) is right in the demand that the foundation-laying of mathematics must not only construct the mathematical calculus but also must make clear the meaning of mathematical concepts, since the application of mathematics to reality rests on this meaning. We restate it in the formal mode of speech: mathematical concepts attain their meaning by the fact that the rules of their application in empirical science are given. If we investigate not only the syntactical rules of mathematical language merely, but also the rules which relate to the appearance of mathematical symbols in synthetic propositions, we formulate thereby the meaning of mathematical concepts (e.g. the meaning of the symbol "2" is formulated by establishing how this symbol can appear in synthetic propositions, and according to what rules such propositions can be derived from propositions without number expressions. If a rule is set up with the aid of which one can derive from the proposition "In this room there are Peter and Paul and otherwise no person" the proposition "In this room there are 2 people," the meaning of "2" is established by that rule).

The *problems of the foundations of physics* are questions of the syntax of physical language: the problem of the verification of physical laws is the question concerning the syntactic deductive coherence between the physical laws (i.e. general propositions of a certain form) and the protocol propositions (singular propositions of a certain form); the problem of induction is the question whether and which transformation rules lead from protocol propositions to laws; the problem of the finitude or infinity and other structure properties of time and space is the question concerning the syntactical transformation rules with reference to number expressions which appear in the physical propositions as time and space coordinates; the problem of causality is the question concerning the syntactical structure of the physical laws (whether unique or probability functions) and concerning a certain property of completeness of the system of these laws (determinism-indeterminism).

The philosophical *problems of the foundation of biology* refer above all to the relation between biology and physics. Here the following two problems are to be distinguished:

1. Can the concepts of biology be defined on the basis of the concepts of physics? (If yes, the language of biology is a part-language of physical language.)

2. Can the laws of biology be derived from the laws of the physics of the inorganic? The second question forms the kernel of the vitalism-problem, if we purge this problem of the usual metaphysical admixtures.

Among the *problems of the foundations of psychology* there are, analogously to the above-mentioned: 1. Can the concepts of psychology be defined on the basis of the concepts of physics? 2. Can the laws of psychology be derived from those of physics? The so-called psycho-physical problem is usually formulated as a problem of the relation of two object-realms: the realm of psychic events and the realm of physical events. But this formulation leads to a maze of pseudo-problems. In using the formal mode of expression it becomes clear that one is dealing only with the relation of both part-languages, that

of psychology and that of physics, or to be more accurate still, with the manner of the syntactical derivation relations (translation rules) between the propositions of both these languages. With the formulation of the psycho-physical problem in the formal mode of expression the problem surely is not yet solved; it may still be quite difficult to find the solution. But at least the necessary condition is satisfied whereby a solution may be sought: the question at least is put clearly.

A point of principle must now be noted so that our position will be understood correctly. When we say that philosophical questions are questions of the syntax of the language of science which permit expression in a formal mode of speech, we do not thereby say that the answers to these questions can be found by merely calculating with logical formulas, without recourse to experience. A proposal for the syntactical formulation of the language of science is, when seen as a principle, a proposal for a freely chooseable convention; but what induces us to prefer certain forms of language to others is the recourse to the empirical material which scientific investigation furnishes. (It is e.g. a question of convention whether one takes as the fundamental laws of physics deterministic or statistical laws; but only by attention to the empirical material, syntactically put — to the protocol propositions — can we decide with which of these two forms we can arrive at a well correlated, relatively simple construction of a system.) From this it follows that the task of the philosophy of science can be pursued only in a close cooperation between logicians and empirical investigators.

Editor's note: The metaphilosophical views which Carnap puts forward in this article are substantially the same as those advanced in Carnap [4]. For criticism of these views see Bar-Hillel [5], Black [7], and Goodman [4]. For Carnap's more recent metaphilosophical views, see Carnap [2] (reprinted below at pp. 72–84) and [7].

GUSTAV BERGMANN

LOGICAL POSITIVISM, LANGUAGE, AND THE

RECONSTRUCTION OF METAPHYSICS

1. *Introduction.* A philosophical movement is a group of philosophers, active over at least one or two generations, who more or less share a style, or an intellectual origin, and who have learned more from each other than they have from others, though they may, and often do, quite vigorously disagree among themselves. Logical positivism is the current name of what is no doubt a movement. The common source is the writings and teachings of G. E. Moore, Russell, and Wittgenstein during the first quarter of the century. However, two of these founding fathers, Moore and Russell, do not themselves belong to the movement. The logical positivists have also greatly influenced each other; they still do, albeit less so as the disagreements among them become more pronounced. There is indeed vigorous disagreement, even on such fundamentals as the nature of the philosophical enterprise itself. The very name, logical positivist, is by now unwelcome to some, though it is still and quite reasonably applied to all, particularly from the outside. Reasonably, because they unmistakably share a philosophical style. They all accept the linguistic turn Wittgenstein

initiated in the *Tractatus*. To be sure, they interpret and develop it in their several ways, hence the disagreements; yet they are all under its spell, hence the common style. Thus, if names in themselves were important, it might be better to choose linguistic philosophy or philosophy of language. In fact, these tags are now coming into use. But they, too, like most labels, are misleading. For one, the concern with language is nothing new in first philosophy or, if you please, epistemology and metaphysics. Certainly all "minute philosophers" have shared it. For another, there is strictly speaking no such thing as the philosophy of language. Language may be studied by philologists, aestheticians, and scientists such as psychologists or sociologists. To bring these studies thoughtfully together is well worth while. Customarily, such synoptic efforts are called philosophy. There is no harm in this provided they are not mistaken for what they are not, namely, technical philosophy. Rather than being philosophers of language, the positivists, who are all technical philosophers, are therefore philosophers through language; they philosophize by means of it. But then, everybody who speaks uses language as a means or tool. The point is that the positivists, newly conscious of it, use it in a new way.

The novelty is, I believe, radical. Even the greatest innovators never do more, can

Reprinted (in a truncated form) from *Rivista Critica di Storia della Filosophia*, VIII (1953), 453–81, by permission of the author and the publisher, La Nuova Italia Editrice, Florence.

do no more, than add one or two features to the tradition, perhaps submerge one or two others. The tradition as a whole persists. Features is a vague word. I had better speak of new questions and methods; for they, not the answers we give, matter. The logical positivists neither added nor submerged a single major question. Their characteristic contribution is a method. This may mean radical novelty; it does, I believe, in their case. There is a sense, though, in which the linguistic turn has not even produced startlingly new answers. The answers the positivists give to the old questions, or those which most of them give to most, are in some respects very similar to what has been said before within the empiricist stream of the great tradition. On the other hand, both questions and answers are so reinterpreted that they have changed almost beyond recognition. At least, alas, beyond the recognition of many. Many of the logical positivists themselves, like other innovators before, even thought that they had disposed of the tradition. Some still believe it. I think there is merely a new method, though one that is radically new, of approaching the old questions.

This is not a historical paper. I wish to speak as a philosopher. Thus, while I am aware of how much I owe to others, I can only speak for myself. Nor is my intent primarily critical. Yet, such is the dialectical nature of philosophy that we cannot either in thinking or in writing do without that foil the ideas of others provide. This makes us all critics as well as, in a structural sense, historians. Thus, while it is my main purpose, or very nearly so, to explain one kind of logical positivism, I shall, almost of necessity, discuss all others. They fall into two main divisions. The one is made up by the ideal linguists, the other by the analysts of usage, more fully, of correct or ordinary usage. The ideal linguists are either *formalists* or *reconstructionists*. The outstanding formalist is Carnap. What the reconstructionists hope to reconstruct in the new style is the old metaphysics. Clearly, from what has been said, I am a reconstructionist. There is, third, the *pragmatist* variety. These writers, we shall presently see, are best counted with the ideal linguists. Usage analysis flourishes above all at Oxford and Cambridge. These philosophers are also known as, fourth, the therapeutic positivists or *casuists*. One variant of this view deserves to be distinguished. For want of a better term I shall, with a new meaning, resuscitate an old one, calling this view, fifth, *conventionalist*. This wing is led by Ryle.

The expositor's position determines, as always, his strategy. The argument will center around reconstructionism. But since I believe the method to be neutral in that it may be used by all and any, I shall set it off as clearly as I can from the specific conclusions to which it has led me. Not surprisingly, these conclusions, or answers to the old questions, lie within the empiricist tradition, if it is conceived broadly enough to include the act philosophies of Moore and Brentano. The debt to Hume and the phenomenalists in general is, naturally, tremendous. One clever Englishman recently proposed the equation: Logical Positivism is Hume plus mathematical logic. He has a point, though by far not the whole story. But whatever these specific conclusions may be, I can hardly do more than hint at a few of them. This must be kept in mind throughout. I have, of course, discussed them elsewhere. Here, however, they serve mainly as illustrations, *pour fixer les idées*, for even in philosophy abstractness cannot without disadvantage be pushed beyond certain limits.

2. *The linguistic turn.* What precisely the linguistic turn is or, to stay with the metaphor, how to execute it properly is controversial. That it must be executed, somehow or other, is common doctrine, flowing from the shared belief that the relation between language and philosophy is closer than, as well as essentially different from, that between language and any

other discipline, What are the grounds of this belief and how did it arise?

First. There is no experiment on whose outcome the predictions of two physicists would differ solely because the one is a phenomenalist, the other a realist. Generally, no philosophical question worthy of the name is ever settled by experimental or, for that matter, experiential evidence. Things are what they are. In some sense philosophy is, therefore, verbal or linguistic. But this is not necessarily a bad sense. One must not hastily conclude that all philosophers always deal with pseudo-problems. Those who thus stretch a point which is telling enough as far as it goes, are overly impressed with the naïve "empiricism" of the laboratory. Most of them are formalists. Scientism and formalism, we shall see, tend to go together. *Second.* Philosophers maintain in all seriousness such propositions as that time is not real or that there are no physical objects. But they also assure us that we do not in the ordinary sense err when, using language as we ordinarily do, we say, for instance, that some event preceded some other in time or that we are perceiving physical objects such as stones and trees. Outside their studies, philosophers themselves say such things. Thus they use language in two ways, in its ordinary sense and in one that is puzzling to say the least. To decide whether what they say as philosophers is true one must, therefore, first discover what they say, that is, precisely what that peculiar sense is. The inquiry is linguistic. It starts from common sense, for what else is there to start from? These points were pressed by G. E. Moore. His emphasis on ordinary usage and common sense reappears, of course, in the British branches of the movement. The commonsense doctrine also influenced the reconstructionists. It is worth noticing, though, that in the form in which all these positivists have adopted it, the doctrine is not itself a philosophical proposition. Rather, it helps to set their style, assigning to philosophy the task of elucidating common sense, not

of either proving or disproving it. In this form the commonsense doctrine also represents at least part of what could be meant by saying, as both Husserl and Wittgenstein do, that philosophy is descriptive. *Third.* This point stands to the second in a relation similar to that between morphology and physiology or, perhaps, pathology. We have seen that philosophers, using language in their peculiar sort of discourse, arrive at such propositions as that there are no physical objects. Taken in their ordinary sense, these propositions are absurd. The man on the street, however, who uses the same language never ends up with this kind of absurdity. We also know that the conclusions one draws depend on the grammatical form of the statements that express the premises. We notice, finally, that sometimes two statements, such as 'Peter is not tall' and 'Cerberus is not real,' exemplify the same grammatical form though they say really quite different things. We conclude that philosophers come to grief because they rely on grammatical form. What they should trust instead is the logical form of statements such as, in our illustration, 'Peter is not tall' and 'There is no dog that is three-headed, etc.'. Consistently pursued, the notion of logical form leads to that of an ideal language in which logical and grammatical form coincide completely. Both notions took shape when Russell answered several philosophical questions, some about arithmetic, some about just such entities as Cerberus, by means of a symbolism. There is one more suggestion in all this, namely, that in an ideal language the philosopher's propositions could no longer be stated so that he would find himself left without anything to say at all. 'Peter exists,' for instance has no equivalent in Russell's symbolism, Peter's existence showing itself, as it were, by the occurrence of a proper name for him. Ontology is, perhaps, but an illusion spawned by language. So one may again be led to think that all philosophy is verbal in a bad sense. The suggestion seduced the formalists as well as those who later became usage analysts. It even seduced Wittgenstein. The reconstructionists reject it. According to them, philosophical discourse is peculiar only in that it is ordinary or, if you please, commonsensical discourse about an ideal language.

Ordinary discourse about an ideal language is, indeed, the reconstructionist version of the linguistic turn. But a statement so succinct needs unpacking. Precisely what is an ideal language? I cannot answer without first explaining what syntax is.

3. *Syntax*. Signs or symbols may be artificial, that is, expressly devised, or they may have grown naturally. In either case they do not say anything by themselves. We speak by means of them; we "interpret" them; having been interpreted, they "refer." Syntax deals only with some properties of the signs themselves and of the patterns in which they are arranged. This, and nothing else, is what is meant by calling syntax formal and schemata syntactically constructed formal languages. It would be safer to avoid any term that suggests interpretation, such as 'language', 'sign', or 'symbol'. I shall simply speak of syntactical schemata and their elements. Or one could use a prefix to guard against confusion, calling the elements f-signs, for instance, 'f' standing for 'formal'. In this section, where I discuss only f-notions, I shall suppress the prefix. Later on I shall occasionally take this precaution. In themselves, signs are physical objects or events. Written signs, and we need not for our purpose consider others, are instances of geometrical shapes. Syntax is thus quite commonsensical business. It is, so to speak, a study of geometrical design. But philosophers are not geometricians. They do not invent and investigate these schemata for their own sake, as mathematical logicians often do, but with an eye upon their suitability for serving, upon interpretation, as the ideal language. Making this claim for any one schema, the geometrician turns philosopher, committing himself to a philosophical position. This is why I insisted that the method as such is neutral. Yet, to introduce neutrally the syntactical notions or categories (f-categories!) which I shall need would be tediously abstract and is, at any rate, quite unnecessary for my purpose. So I shall, instead, introduce them by describing that particular schema which I judge to be, with one later addition, that of the ideal language. Broadly speaking, it is the schema of Russell's *Principia Mathematica*. Very broadly indeed; and I shall have to speak broadly throughout the rest of this section, simplifying so sweepingly that it amounts almost to distortion, though not, of course, as I judge it, to essential distortion.

The construction of the schema proceeds in three steps. First one selects certain shapes and kinds of such as its elements or signs. Then certain sequences of shapes are selected or, if you please, defined as its sentences. Order, as the term sequence implies, enters the definition. Finally a certain subclass of sentences, called analytic, is selected. Turning to some detail, relatively speaking, I shall, in order to fix the ideas, add in parentheses some prospective interpretations from our natural language. *First*. The elements are divided into categories. Though based on shape and nothing else, the divisions are not nominal in that the definitions of sentence and analyticity are stated in their terms. Signs are either logical or descriptive. Descriptive signs are either proper names ('Peter'), or predicates and relations of the first order ('green', 'louder than'), or predicates and relations of higher orders ('color'). Logical signs are of two main kinds. Either they are individually specified signs, connectives ('not', 'and', 'if then') and quantifiers ('all', 'there is something such that'). Or they are variables. To each descriptive category corresponds one of variables, though not necessarily conversely; to proper names so-called individual variables (such phrases as 'a certain particular'), to predicates predicate variables (such phrases as 'a certain property'), and so on. *Second.* Sentences are either atomic or complex. Atomic sentences are sequences of descriptive signs of appropriate categories ('Peter (is) green', 'John (is) taller than James'). Complex sentences contain logical signs ('John (is) tall *and* James (is) short', *'There is something such that* it (is) green'). *Third.* In defining analyticity arithmetical technics are used; in the sense in which one may be said to use such technics who, having assigned numbers to people on the basis of their shapes, called a company unlucky (f-unlucky!) if the sum of the numbers of its members is divisible by 13. A sentence is said to follow deductively from another if and only if a third, compounded of the two in a certain manner, is analytic. ('*p*' implies '*q*' if and only if 'if *p* then *q*' is analytic.) The definition of analyticity is so designed that when a descriptive sign occurs in an analytic sentence, the sentence obtained by replacing it with another descriptive sign of the same category is also analytic. (In 'Either John is tall or John is not tall', the terms 'John' and 'tall' occur vacuously.) Two such sentences are said to be of the same "logical form"; analyticity itself is said to depend on "form" only, which is but another way of saying that it can be characterized by means of sentences which contain none but logical signs. This feature is important. Because of it, among others, f-analyticity can, as we shall see, be used to explicate or reconstruct the philosophical notion of analyticity which, unfortunately, also goes by the name of formal truth. Unfortunately, because the f-notion of logical form which I just defined needs no explication. The philosophical notion, like all philosophical ones, does. To identify the two inadvertently, as I believe Wittgenstein did, leads therefore to disaster. But of this later.

The shapes originally selected are called the undefined signs of the schema. The reason for setting them apart is that many schemata, including the one I am considering, provide machinery for adding new signs. To each sign added corresponds one special sentence, called its definition, the whole construction being so arranged that this sentence is analytic. This has two consequences. For one, the definitions of the language which, in some sense, the schema becomes upon interpretation, are all nominal. For another, interpretation of the undefined signs automatically interprets all others. Defined signs whose definitions contain undefined descriptive signs are themselves classified as descriptive.

4. *Ideal language and reconstruction.* To interpret a syntactical schema is to pair its undefined signs one by one with words or expressions of our natural language, making them "name" the same things or, if you please, "refer" equally. An interpreted schema is in principle a language. In principle only, because we could not speak it instead of a natural language; it is neither rich nor flexible enough. Its lack of flexibility is obvious; it lacks richness in that we need not specify it beyond, say, stipulating that it contains color predicates, without bothering which or how many. Thus, even an interpreted schema is merely, to use the term in a different sense, the "schema" of a language, an architect's drawing rather than a builder's blueprint. The ideal language is an interpreted syntactical schema. But not every such schema is an ideal language. To qualify it must fulfill two conditions. *First,* it must be complete, that is, it must, no matter how schematically, account for all areas of our experience. For instance, it is not enough that it contain schematically the way in which scientific behaviorists, quite adequately for their purpose, speak about mental contents. It must also reflect the different way in which one speaks about his own experience and, because of it, of that of others; and it must show how these two ways jibe. *Second,* it must permit, by means of ordinary discourse about it, the solution of all philosophical problems. This discourse, the heart of the philosophical

enterprise, is the reconstruction of metaphysics. So I must next explain how to state, or restate, the classical questions in this manner and, if they can be so stated, why I insist that this discourse is, nevertheless, quite ordinary or commonsensical though, admittedly, not about the sort of thing the man on the street talks about. Making the range of his interests the criterion of "common sense" is, for my taste, a bit too John Bullish.

Consider the thesis of classical nominalism that there are no universals. Given the linguistic turn it becomes the assertion that the ideal language contains no undefined descriptive signs except proper names. Again, take classical sensationism. Transformed it asserts that the ideal language contains no undefined descriptive predicates except nonrelational ones of the first order, referring to characters exemplified by sense data which are, some ultrapositivists to the contrary notwithstanding, quite commonsensical things. I reject both nominalism and sensationism. But this is not the point. The point is that the two corresponding assertions, though surely false, are yet not absurd, as so many of the classical theses are, as it is for instance absurd to say, as the sensationists must, that a physical object is a bundle of sense data. Obvious as they are, these two illustrations provide a basis for some comments about the reconstruction in general.

First. I did not, either affirmatively or negatively, state either of the two classical propositions. I merely mentioned them in order to explicate them, that is, to suggest what they could plausibly be taken to assert in terms of the ideal language. For the tact and imagination such explication sometimes requires the method provides no guarantee. No method does. But there is no doubt that this kind of explication, considering as it does languages, is quite ordinary discourse. Yet it does not, by this token alone, lose anything of what it explicates. To say that a picture, to be a picture, must have certain features is, clearly, to say something about what it is

a picture of. I know no other way to speak of the world's categorial features without falling into the snares the linguistic turn avoids. These features are as elusive as they are pervasive. Yet they are our only concern; that is why the ideal language need be no more than a "schema." I just used the picture metaphor, quite commonsensically I think, yet deliberately. For it has itself become a snare into which some positivists fell, not surprisingly, since it is after all a metaphor. Of this later. *Second.* A critic may say: "Your vaunted new method either is circular or produces an infinite regress. Did you not yourself, in what you insist is ordinary discourse, use such words as 'naming' and 'referring'? Surely you know that they are eminently philosophical?" I have guarded against the objection by putting quotation marks around these words when I first used them. The point is that I did use them commonsensically, that is, in a way and on an occasion where they do not give trouble. So I can without circularity clarify those uses that do give rise to philosophical problems, either by locating them in the ideal language, or when I encounter them in a philosophical proposition which I merely mention in order to explicate it, or both, as the case may be. But the critic continues: "You admit then, at least, that you do not, to use one of your favorite words, explicate common sense?" I admit nothing of the sort. The explication of common sense is circular only as it is circular to ask, as Moore might put it, how we know what in fact we do know, knowing also that we know it. *Third.* The critic presses on: "Granting that you can without circularity explicate the various philosophical positions, say, realism and phenomenalism, I still fail to see how this reconstruction, as you probably call it, helps you to choose among them." I discover with considerable relief that I need no longer make such choices. With relief, because each of the classical answers to each of the classical questions has a commonsense core. The realist, for instance, grasped some fundamental features of experience or, as he would probably prefer to say, of the world. The phenomenalist grasped some others. Each, anxious not to lose hold of his, was driven to deny or distort the others. From this squirrel cage the linguistic turn happily frees us. Stated in the new manner, the several "cores" are no longer incompatible. This is that surprising turn within the turn which I had in mind when I observed that the old questions, though preserved in one sense, are yet in another changed almost beyond recognition. To insist on this transformation is one thing. To dismiss the classical questions out of hand, as some positivists unfortunately do, is quite another thing. *Fourth.* The method realizes the old ideal of a philosophy without presuppositions. Part of this ideal is an illusion, for we cannot step outside of ourselves or of the world. The part that makes sense is realized by constructing the schema formally, without any reference to its prospective use, strict syntacticism at this stage forcing attention upon what may otherwise go unnoticed. But the critic persists: "Even though you start formally, when you choose a schema as the ideal language you do impose its "categories" upon the world, thus prejudging the world's form. Are you then not at this point yourself trading on the ambiguity of 'form', as you just said others sometimes do?" One does not, in any intelligible sense, choose the ideal language. One finds or discovers, empirically if you please, within the ordinary limits of human error and dullness, that a schema can be so used. Should there be more than one ideal language, then this fact itself will probably be needed somewhere in the reconstruction; equally likely and equally enlightening, some traits of each would then be as "incidental" as are some of Finnish grammar. More important, all this goes to show that the reconstructionist's philosophy is, as I believe all good philosophy must be, descriptive. But it is time to relieve the abstractness by showing, however sketchily, the method at work.

5. *Three issues.* The commonsense core of *phenomenalism* is wholly recovered by what is known as the principle of acquaintance. (Later on I shall restore the balance by reconstructing what I think is the deepest root of realism. Realism, to be sure, has others, such as the indispensability of the quantifiers, which permit us to speak of what is not in front of our noses. But these roots run closer to the surface.) The word principle is unfortunate; for description knows no favorites. The feature in question is indeed a principle only in that quite a few other explications are found to depend on it. What it asserts is that all undefined descriptive signs of the ideal language refer to entities with which we are directly or, as one also says, phenomenally acquainted. Notice the difference from sensationism. Relational and higher-order undefined predicates are not excluded. The indispensability of at least one of these two categories is beyond reasonable doubt. Nor does the principle exclude undefined descriptive signs that refer to ingredients of moral and aesthetic experience. If ethical naturalism is explicated as the rejection of such terms, then one sees that a reconstructionist need not be an ethical naturalist. I, for one, am not.

The ideal language contains proper names, the sort of thing to which they refer being exemplified by sense data; 'tree' and 'stone' and 'physical object' itself are, broadly speaking, defined predicates, closer analysis revealing that the "subjects" of these predicates do not refer to individual trees and stones. That this amounts to a partial explication of the substantialist thesis, accepting a small part of it and rejecting the rest, is fairly obvious. Another aspect of the matter raises two questions. Definitions are linguistic constructions, more precisely, constructions within a language. How detailed need they be? What are the criteria for their success? To begin with the second question, consider the generality 'No physical object is at the same time at two different places'. Call it S and the sentence that corresponds to it in the ideal language S'. Since 'time' and 'place' in S refer to physical time and place, the descriptive signs in S' are all defined. Their construction is successful if and only if S' and a few other such truths, equally crucial for the solution of philosophical problems, follow deductively from the definitions proposed for them in conjunction with some other generalities containing only undefined descriptive signs, which we also know to be true, such as, for instance, the sentence of the ideal language expressing the transitivity of being phenomenally later. The construction is thus merely schematic, in the sense in which the ideal language itself is merely a schema. The building stones from which it starts in order to recover the sense in phenomenalism are so minute that anything else is patently beyond our strength. Nor, fortunately, is it needed to solve the philosophical problems. To strive for more is either scientism or psychologism, scientism if one insists on definitions as "complete" as in the axiomatization of a scientific discipline, psychologism if one expects them to reflect all the subtlety and ambiguity of introspective analysis. Formalists tend to scientism; usage analysts to psychologism.

Analyticity is not a commonsense notion. However, the differences that led philosophers to distinguish between analytic and synthetic propositions are clearly felt upon a little reflection. There is, first, a difference in certainty, one of kind as one says, not merely of degree. Or, as it is also put, analytic truth is necessary, synthetic truth contingent. Certainty is a clear notion only if applied to beliefs. Besides, what is sought is a structural or objective difference between two kinds of contents of belief. There is only this connection that, once discovered, such a structural difference will be useful in explicating the philosophical idea of certainty. Second, analytic (tautological) truths

are empty in that they say nothing about the world, as 'John is either tall or not tall' says nothing. Third, there is even in natural languages the difference, often though not always clear-cut, between descriptive (not f-descriptive!) words such as 'green' and logical (not f-logical!) ones such as 'or'. Analyticity depends only on the logical words and on grammatical "form." Fourth, descriptive words seem to refer to "content," to name the world's furniture, in a sense in which logical words do not. These, I believe, are the four felt differences which philosophers, including many positivists, express by calling analytical truths necessary, or formal, or syntactical, or linguistic. Without explication the formula courts disaster; its explication has four parts, all equally important. First, our knowledge that all "content" variations of analytic "form" ('George is either tall or not tall', 'James is either blond or not blond', etc.) are true is, in the ordinary sense, very certain. But no claim of a philosophical kind for the certainty of this knowledge can be the basis of our explication; it can only be one of its results. Second, the notions of analyticity and of logical and descriptive words correspond to perfectly clear-cut f-notions of the ideal language. Third, the specific arithmetical definition of f-analyticity in the ideal language (that is, in the simplest cases, the well-known truth tables) shows in what reasonable sense analytical truth is combinatorial, compositional, or linguistic. Fourth, arithmetic, the key to this definition, is itself analytic upon it. Taken together these four features amply justify the philosophers' distinction between what is either factual or possible (synthetic) and what is necessary (analytic), between the world's "form" and its "content." But if they are taken absolutely, that is, independently of this explication, then the phrases remain dangerously obscure. Greatest perhaps is the danger of an absolute notion of form as a verbal bridge to an absolute notion of certainty. Nothing is simpler, for instance, than to set aside syntactically a special class of first-order predicates, subsequently to be interpreted by color adjectives, and so to define f-analyticity that 'Nothing is (at the same time all over) both green and red' becomes analytic. Only, this kind of f-analyticity would no longer explicate the philosophical notion. Ours does. But that it does this is not itself a formal or linguistic truth.

Ontology has long been a favorite target of the positivistic attack. So I shall, for the sake of contrast, reconstruct the philosophical query for what there is. The early attacks were not without grounds. There is, for one, the absurdity of the classical formulations and, for another, the insight, usually associated with the name of Kant, that existence is not a property. In Russell's thought, this seed bore double fruit. On the one hand, when 'Peter' is taken to refer to a particular, 'Peter exists' cannot even be stated in the ideal language; his "existence" merely shows itself by the occurrence of a proper name in the schema. On the other hand, such statements as 'There are no centaurs (centaurs do not exist)' or 'There are coffeehouses in Venice' can be expressed in the ideal language, in a way that does not lead to absurdity, by means of quantifiers, which are logical signs, and of defined predicates, whose definitions do not involve the "existence" of the kinds defined. This is as it should be. Ontological statements are not ordinary statements to be located within the ideal language; they are philosophical propositions to be explicated by our method. Logical signs, we remember, are felt not to refer as descriptive ones do. This reconstructs the classical distinction between existence and subsistence. Ontology proper asks what exists rather than subsists. So the answer to which we are led by our method seems to be a catalogue of all descriptive signs. Literally, there can be no such catalogue; but one would settle for a list of categories, that is, of the kinds of entities to which we refer or might have occasion to refer. But then, every serious philosopher claims that he can in his fashion talk about everything. So one could not hope to reconstruct the various ontological theses by means of a list of all descriptive signs. The equivalent of the classical problem is, rather, the search for the undefined descriptive signs of the ideal language.[1] I used this idea implicitly when I explicated nominalism and phenomenalism. To show that it is reasonable, also historically, consider two more examples. Take first materialism or, as it now styles itself, physicalism or philosophical behaviorism. Interpreted fairly, even this silliest of all philosophies asserts no more than that all mental terms can be defined in a schema whose undefined descriptive predicates refer to characters exemplified by physical objects. Quite so. I, too, am a scientific behaviorist. Only, the materialist's schema is, rather obviously, incomplete and therefore not, as he would have to assert, the ideal language. Russell, on the other hand, when he denied the existence of classes, meant, not at all either obviously or sillily, no more than that class names are defined signs of the ideal language.

[1] One could argue that this conception of ontology is anticipated in the *Tractatus* (2.01, 2.02, 2.027). But I was not aware of that when I first proposed it.

Editor's note: Bergmann's views about the nature of philosophy have changed in various ways in recent years. For his later views, see Bergmann [3]. For his criticisms of ordinary language philosophy, see especially Bergmann [1], [8], [10], and [13].

· 4 ·

RUDOLF CARNAP

EMPIRICISM, SEMANTICS, AND ONTOLOGY*

1. THE PROBLEM OF ABSTRACT ENTITIES

Empiricists are in general rather suspicious with respect to any kind of abstract entities like properties, classes, relations, numbers, propositions, etc. They usually feel much more in sympathy with nominalists than with realists (in the medieval sense). As far as possible they try to avoid any reference to abstract entities and to restrict themselves to what is sometimes called a nominalistic language, i.e., one not containing such references. However, within certain scientific contexts it seems hardly possible to avoid them. In the case of mathematics, some empiricists try to find a way out by treating the whole of mathematics as a mere calculus, a formal system for which no interpretation is given or can be given. Accordingly, the mathematician is said to speak not about numbers, functions, and infinite classes, but merely about meaningless symbols and formulas manipulated according to given formal rules. In physics it is more difficult to shun the suspected entities, because the language of physics serves for the communication of reports and predictions and hence cannot be taken as a mere calculus. A physicist who is suspicious of abstract entities may perhaps try to declare a certain part of the language of physics as uninterpreted and uninterpretable, that part which refers to real numbers as space-time coordinates or as values of physical magnitudes, to functions, limits, etc. More probably he will just speak about all these things like anybody else but with an uneasy conscience, like a man who in his everyday life does with qualms many things which are not in accord with the high moral principles he professes on Sundays. Recently the problem of abstract entities has arisen again in connection with semantics, the theory of meaning and truth. Some semanticists say that certain expressions designate certain entities, and among these designated entities they include not only concrete material things but also abstract entities, e.g., properties as designated by predicates and propositions as designated by sentences.[1] Others object strongly to this procedure as violating the basic principles of empiricism and leading back to a metaphysical ontology of the Platonic kind.

It is the purpose of this article to clarify this controversial issue. The nature and implications of the acceptance of a lan-

Reprinted from *Revue Internationale de Philosophie*, IV (1950), 20–40, by permission of the author and the editor.

*I have made here some minor changes in the formulations to the effect that the term "framework" is now used only for the system of linguistic expressions, and not for the system of the entities in question. [Note added by Carnap.]

Editor's note: These changes were made in the original version when the essay was republished in Carnap's *Meaning and Necessity* (Second Edition, Chicago: University of Chicago Press, 1956).

[1] The terms "sentence" and "statement" are here used synonymously for declarative (indicative, propositional) sentences.

guage referring to abstract entities will first be discussed in general; it will be shown that using such a language does not imply embracing a Platonic ontology but is perfectly compatible with empiricism and strictly scientific thinking. Then the special question of the role of abstract entities in semantics will be discussed. It is hoped that the clarification of the issue will be useful to those who would like to accept abstract entities in their work in mathematics, physics, semantics, or any other field; it may help them to overcome nominalistic scruples.

2. Linguistic Frameworks

Are there properties, classes, numbers, propositions? In order to understand more clearly the nature of these and related problems, it is above all necessary to recognize a fundamental distinction between two kinds of questions concerning the existence or reality of entities. If someone wishes to speak in his language about a new kind of entities, he has to introduce a system of new ways of speaking, subject to new rules; we shall call this procedure the construction of a linguistic *framework* for the new entities in question. And now we must distinguish two kinds of questions of existence: first, questions of the existence of certain entities of the new kind *within the framework*; we call them *internal questions*; and second, questions concerning the existence or reality *of the system of entities as a whole*, called *external questions*. Internal questions and possible answers to them are formulated with the help of the new forms of expressions. The answers may be found either by purely logical methods or by empirical methods, depending upon whether the framework is a logical or a factual one. An external question is of a problematic character which is in need of closer examination.

The world of things. Let us consider as an example the simplest kind of entities dealt with in the everyday language: the spatio-temporally ordered system of observable things and events. Once we have accepted the thing language with its framework for things, we can raise and answer internal questions, e.g., "Is there a white piece of paper on my desk?," "Did King Arthur actually live?," "Are unicorns and centaurs real or merely imaginary?," and the like. These questions are to be answered by empirical investigations. Results of observations are evaluated according to certain rules as confirming or disconfirming evidence for possible answers. (This evaluation is usually carried out, of course, as a matter of habit rather than a deliberate, rational procedure. But it is possible, in a rational reconstruction, to lay down explicit rules for the evaluation. This is one of the main tasks of a pure, as distinguished from a psychological epistemology.) The concept of reality occurring in these internal questions is an empirical, scientific, non-metaphysical concept. To recognize something as a real thing or event means to succeed in incorporating it into the system of things at a particular space-time position so that it fits together with the other things recognized as real, according to the rules of the framework.

From these questions we must distinguish the external question of the reality of the thing world itself. In contrast to the former questions, this question is raised neither by the man in the street nor by scientists, but only by philosophers. Realists give an affirmative answer, subjective idealists a negative one, and the controversy goes on for centuries without ever being solved. And it cannot be solved because it is framed in a wrong way. To be real in the scientific sense means to be an element of the system; hence this concept cannot be meaningfully applied to the system itself. Those who raise the question of the reality of the thing world itself have perhaps in mind not a theoretical question as their formulation seems to suggest, but rather a practical question, a matter of a practical decision concerning the structure of our language. We have to make the choice whether or not to accept and use the forms of expression in the framework in question.

In the case of this particular example, there is usually no deliberate choice because we all have accepted the thing language early in our lives as a matter of course. Nevertheless, we may regard it as a matter of decision in this sense: we are free to choose to continue using the thing language or not; in the latter case we could restrict ourselves to a language of sense-data and other "phenomenal" entities, or construct an alternative to the customary thing language with another structure, or, finally, we could refrain from speaking. If someone decides to accept the thing language, there is no objection against saying that he has accepted the world of things. But this must not be interpreted as if it meant his acceptance of a *belief* in the reality of the thing world; there is no such belief or assertion or assumption, because it is not a theoretical question. To accept the thing world means nothing more than to accept a certain form of language, in other words, to accept rules for forming statements and for testing, accepting, or rejecting them. The acceptance of the thing language leads, on the basis of observations made, also to the acceptance, belief, and assertion of certain statements. But the thesis of the reality of the thing world cannot be among these statements, because it cannot be formulated in the thing language or, it seems, in any other theoretical language.

The decision of accepting the thing language, although itself not of a cognitive nature, will nevertheless usually be influenced by theoretical knowledge, just like any other deliberate decision concerning the acceptance of linguistic or other rules. The purposes for which the language is intended to be used, for instance, the purpose of communicating factual knowledge, will determine which factors are relevant for the decision. The efficiency, fruitfulness, and simplicity of the use of the thing language may be among the decisive factors. And the questions concerning these qualities are indeed of a theoretical nature. But these questions cannot be identified with the question of realism. They are not yes-no questions but questions of degree. The thing language in the customary form works indeed with a high degree of efficiency for most purposes of everyday life. This is a matter of fact, based upon the content of our experiences. However, it would be wrong to describe this situation by saying: "The fact of the efficiency of the thing language is confirming evidence for the reality of the thing world"; we should rather say instead: "This fact makes it advisable to accept the thing language."

The system of numbers. As an example of a system which is of a logical rather than a factual nature let us take the system of natural numbers. The framework for this system is constructed by introducing into the language new expressions with suitable rules: (1) numerals like "five" and sentence forms like "there are five books on the table"; (2) the general term "number" for new entities, and sentence forms like "five is a number"; (3) expressions for properties of numbers (e.g., "odd," "prime"), relations (e.g. "greater than"), and functions (e.g., "plus"), and sentence forms like "two plus three is five"; (4) numerical variables ("m," "n," etc.) and quantifiers for universal sentences ("for every n, . . .") and existential sentences ("there is an n such that . . .") with the customary deductive rules.

Here again there are internal questions, e.g., "Is there a prime number greater than a hundred?" Here, however, the answers are found, not by empirical investigation based on observations, but by logical analysis based on the rules for the new expressions. Therefore the answers are here analytic, i.e., logically true.

What is now the nature of the philosophical question concerning the existence or reality of numbers? To begin with, there is the internal question which, together with the affirmative answer, can be formulated in the new terms, say, by "There are numbers" or, more explicitly, "There is an n such that n is a number." This statement follows from the analytic statement "five is a number" and is therefore itself analytic. Moreover, it is rather trivial (in contradistinction to a statement like "There is a prime number greater than a million," which is likewise analytic but far from trivial), because it does not say more than that the new system is not empty; but this is immediately seen from the rule which states that words like "five" are substitutable for the new variables. Therefore nobody who meant the question "Are there numbers?" in the internal sense would either assert or even seriously consider a negative answer. This makes it plausible to assume that those philosophers who treat the question of the existence of numbers as a serious philosophical problem and offer lengthy arguments on either side, do not have in mind the internal question. And, indeed, if we were to ask them: "Do you mean the question as to whether the framework of numbers, *if* we were to accept it, would be found to be empty or not?" they would probably reply: "Not at all; we mean a question *prior* to the acceptance of the new framework." They might try to explain what they mean by saying that it is a question of the ontological status of numbers; the question whether or not numbers have a certain metaphysical characteristic called reality (but a kind of ideal reality, different from the material reality of the thing world) or subsistence or status of "independent entities." Unfortunately, these philosophers have so far not given a formulation of their question in terms of the common scientific language. Therefore our judgment must be that they have not succeeded in giving to the external question and to the possible answers any cognitive content. Unless and until they supply a clear cognitive interpretation, we are justified in our suspicion that their question is a pseudo-question, that is, one disguised in the form of a theoretical question while in fact it is non-theoretical; in the present case it is the practical problem whether or not to incorporate into the language the new linguistic forms which constitute the framework of numbers.

The system of propositions. New variables, "p," "q," etc., are introduced with a rule to the effect that any (declarative) sentence may be substituted for a variable of this kind; this includes, in addition to the sentences of the original thing language, also all general sentences with variables of any kind which may have been introduced into the language. Further, the general term "proposition" is introduced. "p is a proposition" may be defined by "p or not p" (or by any other sentence form yielding only analytic sentences). Therefore, every sentence of the form ". . . is a proposition" (where any sentence may stand in the place of the dots) is analytic. This holds, for example, for the sentence:

(a) "Chicago is large is a proposition."

(We disregard here the fact that the rules of English grammar require not a sentence but a that-clause as the subject of another sentence; accordingly, instead of (a) we should have to say "That Chicago is large is a proposition.") Predicates may be admitted whose argument expressions are sentences; these predicates may be either extensional (e.g., the customary truth-functional connectives) or not (e.g., modal predicates like "possible," "necessary," etc.). With the help of the new variables, general sentences may be formed, e.g.,

(b) "For every p, either p or not-p."

(c) "There is a p such that p is not necessary and not-p is not necessary."

(d) "There is a p such that p is a proposition."

(c) and (d) are internal assertions of existence. The statement "There are propositions" may be meant in the sense of (d); in this case it is analytic (since it follows from (a)) and even trivial. If, however, the statement is meant in an external sense, then it is non-cognitive.

It is important to notice that the system of rules for the linguistic expressions of the propositional framework (of which only a few rules have here been briefly indicated) is sufficient for the introduction of the framework. Any further explanations as to the nature of the propositions (i.e., the elements of the system indicated, the values of the variables "*p*," "*q*," etc.) are theoretically unnecessary because, if correct, they follow from the rules. For example, are propositions mental events (as in Russell's theory)? A look at the rules shows us that they are not, because otherwise existential statements would be of the form: "If the mental state of the person in question fulfils such and such conditions, then there is a *p* such that . . . " The fact that no references to mental conditions occur in existential statements (like *(c)*, *(d)*, etc.) show that propositions are not mental entities. Further, a statement of the existence of linguistic entities (e.g., expressions, classes of expressions, etc.) must contain a reference to a language. The fact that no such reference occurs in the existential statements here, shows that propositions are not linguistic entities. The fact that in these statements no reference to a subject (an observer or knower) occurs (nothing like: "There is a *p* which is necessary for Mr. *X*"), shows that the propositions (and their properties, like necessity, etc.) are not subjective. Although characterizations of these or similar kinds are, strictly speaking, unnecessary, they may nevertheless be practically useful. If they are given, they should be understood, not as ingredient parts of the system, but merely as marginal notes with the purpose of supplying to the reader helpful hints or convenient pictorial associations which may make his learning of the use of the expressions easier than the bare system of the rules would do. Such a characterization is analogous to an extra-systematic explanation which a physicist sometimes gives to the beginner. He might, for example, tell him to imagine the atoms of a

gas as small balls rushing around with great speed, or the electromagnetic field and its oscillations as quasi-elastic tensions and vibrations in an ether. In fact, however, all that can accurately be said about atoms or the field is implicitly contained in the physical laws of the theories in question.[2]

The system of thing properties. The thing language contains words like "red," "hard," "stone," "house," etc., which are used for describing what things are like. Now we may introduce new variables, say "*f*," "*g*," etc., for which those words are substitutable and furthermore the general term "property." New rules are laid down which admit sentences like "Red is a prop-

[2] In my book *Meaning and Necessity* (Chicago, 1947) I have developed a semantical method which takes propositions as entities designated by sentences (more specifically, as intensions of sentences). In order to facilitate the understanding of the systematic development, I added some informal, extra-systematic explanations concerning the nature of propositions. I said that the term "proposition" "is used neither for a linguistic expression nor for a subjective, mental occurrence, but rather for something objective that may or may not be exemplified in nature. . . . We apply the term 'proposition' to any entities of a certain logical type, namely, those that may be expressed by (declarative) sentences in a language" (p. 27). After some more detailed discussions concerning the relation between propositions and facts, and the nature of false propositions, I added: "It has been the purpose of the preceding remarks to facilitate the understanding of our conception of propositions. If, however, a reader should find these explanations more puzzling than clarifying, or even unacceptable, he may disregard them" (p. 31) (that is, disregard these extra-systematic explanations, not the whole theory of the propositions as intensions of sentences, as one reviewer understood). In spite of this warning, it seems that some of those readers who were puzzled by the explanations, did not disregard them but thought that by raising objections against them they could refute the theory. This is analogous to the procedure of some laymen who by (correctly) criticizing the ether picture or other visualizations of physical theories, thought they had refuted those theories. Perhaps the discussions in the present paper will help in clarifying the role of the system of linguistic rules for the introduction of a framework for entities on the one hand, and that of extra-systematic explanations concerning the nature of the entities on the other.

eity," "Red is a color," "These two pieces of paper have at least one color in common" (i.e., "There is an f such that f is a color, and . . ."). The last sentence is an internal assertion. It is of an empirical, factual nature. However, the external statement, the philosophical statement of the reality of properties — a special case of the thesis of the reality of universals — is devoid of cognitive content.

The systems of integers and rational numbers. Into a language containing the framework of natural numbers we may introduce first the (positive and negative) integers as relations among natural numbers and then the rational numbers as relations among integers. This involves introducing new types of variables, expressions substitutable for them, and the general terms "integer" and "rational number."

The system of real numbers. On the basis of the rational numbers, the real numbers may be introduced as classes of a special kind (segments) of rational numbers (according to the method developed by Dedekind and Frege). Here again a new type of variables is introduced, expressions substitutable for them (e.g., "$\sqrt{2}$"), and the general term "real number."

The spatio-temporal coordinate system for physics. The new entities are the space-time points. Each is an ordered quadruple of four real numbers, called its coordinates, consisting of three spatial and one temporal coordinate. The physical state of a spatio-temporal point or region is described either with the help of qualitative predicates (e.g., "hot") or by ascribing numbers as values of a physical magnitude (e.g., mass, temperature, and the like). The step from the system of things (which does not contain space-time points but only extended objects with spatial and temporal relations between them) to the physical coordinate system is again a matter of decision. Our choice of certain features, although itself not theoretical,

is suggested by theoretical knowledge, either logical or factual. For example, the choice of real numbers rather than rational numbers or integers as coordinates is not much influenced by the facts of experience but mainly due to considerations of mathematical simplicity. The restriction to rational coordinates would not be in conflict with any experimental knowledge we have, because the result of any measurement is a rational number. However, it would prevent the use of ordinary geometry (which says, e.g., that the diagonal of a square with the side 1 has the irrational value $\sqrt{2}$) and thus lead to great complications. On the other hand, the decision to use three rather than two or four spatial coordinates is strongly suggested, but still not forced upon us, by the result of common observations. If certain events allegedly observed in spiritualistic séances, e.g., a ball moving out of a sealed box, were confirmed beyond any reasonable doubt, it might seem advisable to use four spatial coordinates. Internal questions are here, in general, empirical questions to be answered by empirical investigations. On the other hand, the external questions of the reality of physical space and physical time are pseudo-questions. A question like "Are there (really) space-time points?" is ambiguous. It may be meant as an internal question; then the affirmative answer is, of course, analytic and trivial. Or it may be meant in the external sense: "Shall we introduce such and such forms into our language?"; in this case it is not a theoretical but a practical question, a matter of decision rather than assertion, and hence the proposed formulation would be misleading. Or finally, it may be meant in the following sense: "Are our experiences such that the use of the linguistic forms in question will be expedient and fruitful?" This is a theoretical question of a factual, empirical nature. But it concerns a matter of degree; therefore a formulation in the form "real or not?" would be inadequate.

3. What Does Acceptance of a Kind of Entities Mean?

Let us now summarize the essential characteristics of situations involving the introduction of a new kind of entities, characteristics which are common to the various examples outlined above.

The acceptance of a new kind of entities is represented in the language by the introduction of a framework of new forms of expressions to be used according to a new set of rules. There may be new names for particular entities of the kind in question; but some such names may already occur in the language before the introduction of the new framework. (Thus, for example, the thing language contains certainly words of the type of "blue" and "house" before the framework of properties is introduced; and it may contain words like "ten" in sentences of the form "I have ten fingers" before the framework of numbers is introduced.) The latter fact shows that the occurrence of constants of the type in question — regarded as names of entities of the new kind after the new framework is introduced — is not a sure sign of the acceptance of the new kind of entities. Therefore the introduction of such constants is not to be regarded as an essential step in the introduction of the framework. The two essential steps are rather the following. First, the introduction of a general term, a predicate of higher level, for the new kind of entities, permitting us to say of any particular entity that it belongs to this kind (e.g., "Red is a *property*," "Five is a *number*"). Second, the introduction of variables of the new type. The new entities are values of these variables; the constants (and the closed compound expressions, if any) are substitutable for the variables.[3] With the help of the variables, general sentences concerning the new entities can be formulated.

After the new forms are introduced into the language, it is possible to formulate with their help internal questions and possible answers to them. A question of this kind may be either empirical or logical; accordingly a true answer is either factually true or analytic.

From the internal questions we must clearly distinguish external questions, i.e., philosophical questions concerning the existence or reality of the total system of the new entities. Many philosophers regard a question of this kind as an ontological question which must be raised and answered *before* the introduction of the new language forms. The latter introduction, they believe, is legitimate only if it can be justified by an ontological insight supplying an affirmative answer to the question of reality. In contrast to this view, we take the position that the introduction of the new ways of speaking does not need any theoretical justification because it does not imply any assertion of reality. We may still speak (and have done so) of "the acceptance of the new entities" since this form of speech is customary; but one must keep in mind that this phrase does not mean for us anything more than acceptance of the new framework, i.e., of the new linguistic forms. Above all, it must not be interpreted as referring to an assumption, belief, or assertion of "the reality of the entities." There is no such assertion. An alleged statement of the reality of the system of entities is a pseudo-statement without cognitive content. To be sure, we have to face at this point an important question; but it is a practical, not a theoretical question; it is the question of whether or not to accept the new linguistic forms. The acceptance cannot be judged as being either true or false be-

---

[3] W. V. Quine was the first to recognize the importance of the introduction of variables as indicating the acceptance of entities. "The ontology to which one's use of language commits him comprises simply the objects that he treats as falling . . . within the range of values of his variables." "Notes on Existence and Necessity," *Journal of Philosophy*, XL (1943), 118. Compare Quine, "Designation and Existence," *Journal of Philosophy*, XXXVI (1939), 701–09, and "On Universals," *Journal of Symbolic Logic*, XII (1947), 74–84.

cause it is not an assertion. It can only be judged as being more or less expedient, fruitful, conducive to the aim for which the language is intended. Judgments of this kind supply the motivation for the decision of accepting or rejecting the kind of entities.[4]

Thus it is clear that the acceptance of a linguistic framework must not be regarded as implying a metaphysical doctrine concerning the reality of the entities in question. It seems to me due to a neglect of this important distinction that some contemporary nominalists label the admission of variables of abstract types as "Platonism."[5] This is, to say the least, an extremely misleading terminology. It leads to the absurd consequence, that the position of everybody who accepts the language of physics with its real number variables (as a language of communication, not merely as a calculus) would be

called Platonistic, even if he is a strict empiricist who rejects Platonic metaphysics.

A brief historical remark may here be inserted. The non-cognitive character of the questions which we have called here external questions was recognized and emphasized already by the Vienna Circle under the leadership of Moritz Schlick, the group from which the movement of logical empiricism originated. Influenced by ideas of Ludwig Wittgenstein, the Circle rejected both the thesis of the reality of the external world and the thesis of its irreality as pseudo-statements;[6] the same was the case for both the thesis of the reality of universals (abstract entities, in our present terminology) and the nominalistic thesis that they are not real and that their alleged names are not names of anything but merely *flatus vocis*. (It is obvious that the apparent negation of a pseudo-statement must also be a pseudo-statement.) It is therefore not correct to classify the members of the Vienna Circle as nominalists, as is sometimes done. However, if we look at the basic anti-metaphysical and pro-scientific attitude of most nominalists (and the same holds for many materialists and realists in the modern sense), disregarding their occasional pseudo-theoretical formulations, then it is, of course, true to say that the Vienna Circle was much closer to those philosophers than to their opponents.

---

[4] For a closely related point of view on these questions see the detailed discussions in Herbert Feigl, "Existential Hypotheses," *Philosophy of Science*, 17 (1950), 35–62.

[5] Paul Bernays, "Sur le platonisme dans les mathématiques" (*L'Enseignement mathématique*, 34 (1935), 52–69). W. V. Quine, see previous footnote and "On What There Is," *Review of Metaphysics*, II (1948), 21–38. Quine does not acknowledge the distinction which I emphasize above, because according to his general conception there are no sharp boundary lines between logical and factual truth, between questions of meaning and questions of fact, between the acceptance of a language structure and the acceptance of an assertion formulated in the language. This conception, which seems to deviate considerably from customary ways of thinking, is explained in his "Semantics and Abstract Objects," *Proceedings of the American Academy of Arts and Sciences*, LXXX (1951), 90–96. When Quine in "On What There Is" classifies my logicistic conception of mathematics (derived from Frege and Russell) as "platonic realism" [p. 33], this is meant (according to a personal communication from him) not as ascribing to me agreement with Plato's metaphysical doctrine of universals, but merely as referring to the fact that I accept a language of mathematics containing variables of higher levels. With respect to the basic attitude to take in choosing a language form (an "ontology" in Quine's terminology, which seems to me misleading), there appears now to be agreement between us: "the obvious counsel is tolerance and an experimental spirit" (*ibid.*, p. 38).

4. ABSTRACT ENTITIES IN SEMANTICS

The problem of the legitimacy and the status of abstract entities has recently again led to controversial discussions in connection with semantics. In a semantical meaning analysis certain expressions in a language are often said to designate (or name or denote or signify or refer to)

---

[6] See Carnap, *Scheinprobleme in der Philosophie; das Fremdpsychische und der Realismusstreit* (Berlin: 1928). Moritz Schlick, *Positivismus und Realismus*, reprinted in *Gesammelte Aufsätze* (Vienna, 1938).

certain extra-linguistic entities.[7] As long as physical things or events (e.g., Chicago or Caesar's death) are taken as designata (entities designated), no serious doubts arise. But strong objections have been raised, especially by some empiricists, against abstract entities as designata, e.g., against semantical statements of the following kind:

(1) "The word 'red' designates a property of things";

(2) "The word 'color' designates a property of properties of things";

(3) "The word 'five' designates a number";

(4) "The word 'odd' designates a property of numbers";

(5) "The sentence 'Chicago is large' designates a proposition."

Those who criticize these statements do not, of course, reject the use of the expressions in question, like "red" or "five"; nor would they deny that these expressions are meaningful. But to be meaningful, they would say, is not the same as having a meaning in the sense of an entity designated. They reject the belief, which they regard as implicitly presupposed by those semantical statements, that to each expression of the types in question (adjectives like "red," numerals like "five," etc.) there is a particular real entity to which the expression stands in the relation of designation. This belief is rejected as incompatible with the basic principles of empiricism or of scientific thinking. Derogatory labels like "Platonic realism," "hypostatization," or " 'Fido'-Fido principle" are attached to it. The latter is the name given by Gilbert Ryle (in his review of my *Meaning and Necessity* [*Philosophy*,

XXIV (1949), 69–76]) to the criticized belief, which, in his view, arises by a naïve inference of analogy: just as there is an entity well known to me, viz. my dog Fido, which is designated by the name "Fido," thus there must be for every meaningful expression a particular entity to which it stands in the relation of designation or naming, i.e., the relation exemplified by "Fido"-Fido. The belief criticized is thus a case of hypostatization, i.e., of treating as names expressions which are not names. While "Fido" is a name, expressions like "red," "five," etc., are said not to be names, not to designate anything.

Our previous discussion concerning the acceptance of frameworks enables us now to clarify the situation with respect to abstract entities as designata. Let us take as an example the statement:

(a) " 'Five' designates a number."

The formulation of this statement presupposes that our language L contains the forms of expressions which we have called the framework of numbers, in particular, numerical variables and the general term "number." If L contains these forms, the following is an analytic statement in L:

(b) "Five is a number."

Further, to make the statement (a) possible, L must contain an expression like "designates" or "is a name of" for the semantical relation of designation. If suitable rules for this term are laid down, the following is likewise analytic:

(c) " 'Five' designates five."

(Generally speaking, any expression of the form " '. . .' designates . . ." is an analytic statement provided the term ". . ." is a constant in an accepted framework. If the latter condition is not fulfilled, the expression is not a statement.) Since (a) follows from (c) and (b), (a) is likewise analytic.

Thus it is clear that *if* someone accepts the framework of numbers, then he must acknowledge (c) and (b) and hence (a) as true statements. Generally speaking, if someone accepts a framework for a cer-

---

[7] See *Meaning and Necessity* (Chicago, 1947). The distinction I have drawn in the latter book between the method of the name-relation and the method of intension and extension is not essential for our present discussion. The term "designation" is used in the present article in a neutral way; it may be understood as referring to the name-relation or to the intension-relation or to the extension-relation or to any similar relations used in other semantical methods.

tain kind of entities, then he is bound to admit the entities as possible designata. Thus the question of the admissibility of entities of a certain type or of abstract entities in general as designata is reduced to the question of the acceptability of the linguistic framework for those entities. Both the nominalistic critics, who refuse the status of designators or names to expressions like "red," "five," etc., because they deny the existence of abstract entities, and the skeptics, who express doubts concerning the existence and demand evidence for it, treat the question of existence as a theoretical question. They do, of course, not mean the internal question; the affirmative answer to *this* question is analytic and trivial and too obvious for doubt or denial, as we have seen. Their doubts refer rather to the system of entities itself; hence they mean the external question. They believe that only after making sure that there really is a system of entities of the kind in question are we justified in accepting the framework by incorporating the linguistic forms into our language. However, we have seen that the external question is not a theoretical question but rather the practical question whether or not to accept those linguistic forms. This acceptance is not in need of a theoretical justification (except with respect to expediency and fruitfulness), because it does not imply a belief or assertion. Ryle says that the "Fido"-Fido principle is "a grotesque theory." Grotesque or not, Ryle is wrong in calling it a theory. It is rather the practical decision to accept certain frameworks. Maybe Ryle is historically right with respect to those whom he mentions as previous representatives of the principle, viz. John Stuart Mill, Frege, and Russell. If these philosophers regarded the acceptance of a system of entities as a theory, an assertion, they were victims of the same old, metaphysical confusion. But it is certainly wrong to regard *my* semantical method as involving a belief in the reality of abstract entities, since I reject a thesis of this kind as a metaphysical pseudo-statement.

The critics of the use of abstract entities in semantics overlook the fundamental difference between the acceptance of a system of entities and an internal assertion, e.g., an assertion that there are elephants or electrons or prime numbers greater than a million. Whoever makes an internal assertion is certainly obliged to justify it by providing evidence, empirical evidence in the case of electrons, logical proof in the case of the prime numbers. The demand for a theoretical justification, correct in the case of internal assertions, is sometimes wrongly applied to the acceptance of a system of entities. Thus, for example, Ernest Nagel (in his review of my *Meaning and Necessity* [*Journal of Philosophy*, XLV (1948), 467–72]) asks for "evidence relevant for affirming with warrant that there are such entities as infinitesimals or propositions." He characterizes the evidence required in these cases — in distinction to the empirical evidence in the case of electrons — as "in the broad sense logical and dialectical." Beyond this no hint is given as to what might be regarded as relevant evidence. Some nominalists regard the acceptance of abstract entities as a kind of superstition or myth, populating the world with fictitious or at least dubious entities, analogous to the belief in centaurs or demons. This shows again the confusion mentioned, because a superstition or myth is a false (or dubious) internal statement.

Let us take as example the natural numbers as cardinal numbers, i.e., in contexts like "Here are three books." The linguistic forms of the framework of numbers, including variables and the general term "number," are generally used in our common language of communication; and it is easy to formulate explicit rules for their use. Thus the logical characteristics of this framework are sufficiently clear (while many internal questions, i.e., arithmetical questions, are, of course, still open). In spite of this, the controversy concerning the external question of the ontological reality of the system of numbers continues. Suppose that one philosopher says: "I believe that there are numbers as real entities. This gives me the right to use the linguistic forms of the numerical framework and to make semantical statements about numbers as designata of numerals." His nominalistic opponent replies: "You are wrong; there are no numbers. The numerals may still be used as meaningful expressions. But they are not names, there are no entities designated by them. Therefore the word "number" and numerical variables must not be used (unless a way were found to introduce them as merely abbreviating devices, a way of translating them into the nominalistic thing language)." I cannot think of any possible evidence that would be regarded as relevant by both philosophers, and therefore, if actually found, would decide the controversy or at least make one of the opposite theses more probable than the other. (To construe the numbers as classes or properties of the second level, according to the Frege-Russell method, does, of course, not solve the controversy, because the first philosopher would affirm and the second deny the existence of the system of classes or properties of the second level.) Therefore I feel compelled to regard the external question as a pseudo-question, until both parties to the controversy offer a common interpretation of the question as a cognitive question; this would involve an indication of possible evidence regarded as relevant by both sides.

There is a particular kind of misinterpretation of the acceptance of abstract entities in various fields of science and in semantics, that needs to be cleared up. Certain early British empiricists (e.g., Berkeley and Hume) denied the existence of abstract entities on the ground that immediate experience presents us only with particulars, not with universals, e.g., with this red patch, but not with Redness or Color-in-General; with this scalene triangle, but not with Scalene Triangularity or Triangularity-in-General. Only entities belonging to a type of which examples were to be found within immediate experience could be accepted as ultimate constituents of reality. Thus, according to this way of thinking, the existence of abstract entities could be asserted only if one could show either that some abstract entities fall within the given, or that abstract entities can be defined in terms of the types of entity which are given. Since these empiricists found no abstract entities within the realm of sense-data, they either denied their existence, or else made a futile attempt to define universals in terms of particulars. Some contemporary philosophers, especially English philosophers following Bertrand Russell, think in basically similar terms. They emphasize a distinction between the data (that which is immediately given in consciousness, e.g., sense-data, immediately past experiences, etc.) and the constructs based on the data. Existence or reality is ascribed only to the data; the constructs are not real entities; the corresponding linguistic expressions are merely ways of speech not actually designating anything (reminiscent of the nominalists' *flatus vocis*). We shall not criticize here this general conception. (As far as it is a principle of accepting certain entities and not accepting others, leaving aside any ontological, phenomenalistic and nominalistic pseudo-statements, there cannot be any theoretical objection to it.) But if this conception leads to the view that other philosophers or scientists who accept abstract entities thereby assert or imply their occurrence as immediate data, then such a view must be rejected as a misinterpretation. References to space-time points, the electromagnetic field, or electrons in physics, to real or complex numbers and their functions in mathematics, to the excitatory potential or unconscious complexes in psychology, to an inflationary trend in economics, and the like, do not imply the assertion that entities of these kinds occur as immediate data. And the same holds for references to abstract entities as designata in semantics. Some of the criticisms by English philosophers against such references give the impression that, probably due to the misinterpretation just indicated, they accuse the semanticist not so much of bad metaphysics (as some nominalists would do) but of bad psychology. The fact that they regard a semantical method involving abstract entities not merely as doubtful and perhaps wrong, but as manifestly absurd, preposterous and grotesque, and that they show a deep horror and indignation against this method, is perhaps to be explained by a misinterpretation of the kind described. In fact, of course, the semanticist does not in the least assert or imply that the abstract entities to which he refers can be experienced as immediately given either by sensation or by a kind of rational intuition. An assertion of this kind would indeed be very dubious psychology. The psychological question as to which kinds of entities do and which do not occur as immediate data is entirely irrelevant for semantics, just as it is for physics, mathematics, economics, etc., with respect to the examples mentioned above.[8]

5. Conclusion

For those who want to develop or use semantical methods, the decisive question is not the alleged ontological question of the existence of abstract entities but rather the question whether the use of abstract linguistic forms or, in technical terms, the use of variables beyond those for things (or phenomenal data), is expedient and fruitful for the purposes for which semantical analyses are made, viz. the analysis, interpretation, clarification, or construction of languages of communication, especially languages of science. This question

is here neither decided nor even discussed. It is not a question simply of yes or no, but a matter of degree. Among those philosophers who have carried out semantical analyses and thought about suitable tools for this work, beginning with Plato and Aristotle and, in a more technical way on the basis of modern logic, with C. S. Peirce and Frege, a great majority accepted abstract entities. This does not, of course, prove the case. After all, semantics in the technical sense is still in the initial phases of its development, and we must be prepared for possible fundamental changes in methods. Let us therefore admit that the nominalistic critics may possibly be right. But if so, they will have to offer better arguments than they have so far. Appeal to ontological insight will not carry much weight. The critics will have to show that it is possible to construct a semantical method which avoids all references to abstract entities and achieves by simpler means essentially the same results as the other methods.

The acceptance or rejection of abstract linguistic forms, just as the acceptance or rejection of any other linguistic forms in any branch of science, will finally be decided by their efficiency as instruments, the ratio of the results achieved to the amount and complexity of the efforts required. To decree dogmatic prohibitions of certain linguistic forms instead of testing them by their success or failure in practical use, is worse than futile; it is positively harmful because it may obstruct scientific progress. The history of science shows examples of such prohibitions based on prejudices deriving from religious, mythological, metaphysical, or other irrational sources, which slowed up the developments for shorter or longer periods of time. Let us learn from the lessons of history. Let us grant to those who work in any special field of investigation the freedom to use any form of expression which seems useful to them; the work in the field will sooner or later lead to the elimination of those forms which have no

---

[8] Wilfrid Sellars ("Acquaintance and Description Again," in *Journal of Philosophy*, XLVI (1949), 496–504; see pp. 502 f.) analyzes clearly the roots of the mistake "of taking the designation relation of semantic theory to be a reconstruction of *being present to an experience.*"

useful function. *Let us be cautious in making assertions and critical in examining them, but tolerant in permitting linguistic forms.*

Editor's note: This essay was published almost simultaneously with Quine's "Two Dogmas of Empiricism" (Quine [7]). These two essays, which had in common a leaning towards pragmatism and a repudiation of distinctions which were basic to positivistic metaphilosophy, had a profound effect on linguistic philosophy in America. The best general treatments of the implications of these essays are Alan Pasch, *Experience and the Analytic* (Chicago: University of Chicago Press, 1958) and Morton White [8]. For comments on the metaphilosophical position which Carnap takes in this essay, see p. 160–67 (Cornman) and 168–71 (Quine) below; see also Cornman [2] and the articles by Bar-Hillel, Cohen, Frank, Morris, and Sellars (with Carnap's replies) in *The Philosophy of Rudolf Carnap*, ed. P. A. Schilpp (La Salle, Illinois: Open Court Publishing Co., 1963).

5

GILBERT RYLE

Systematically Misleading Expressions

Philosophical arguments have always largely, if not entirely, consisted in attempts to thrash out "what it means to say so and so." It is observed that men in their ordinary discourse, the discourse, that is, that they employ when they are not philosophizing, use certain expressions, and philosophers fasten on to certain more or less radical types or classes of such expressions and raise their question about all expressions of a certain type and ask what they really mean.

Sometimes philosophers say that they are analysing or clarifying the "concepts" which are embodied in the "judgments" of the plain man or of the scientist, historian, artist or who-not. But this seems to be only a gaseous way of saying that they are trying to discover what is meant by the general terms contained in the sentences which they pronounce or write. For, as we shall see, "x is a concept" and "y is a judgment" are themselves systematically misleading expressions.

But the whole procedure is very odd. For, if the expressions under consideration are intelligently used, their employers must always know what they mean and do not need the aid or admonition of philosophers before they can understand what they are saying. And if their hearers understand what they are being told, they too are in no such perplexity that they

Reprinted from *Proceedings of the Aristotelian Society*, XXXII (1931–32), 139–70, by permission of the author and the editor.

need to have this meaning philosophically "analysed" or "clarified" for them. And, at least, the philosopher himself must know what the expressions mean, since otherwise he could not know what it was that he was analysing.

Certainly it is often the case that expressions are not being intelligently used and to that extent their authors are just gabbling parrot-wise. But then it is obviously fruitless to ask what the expressions really mean. For there is no reason to suppose that they mean anything. It would not be mere gabbling if there was any such reason. And if the philosopher cares to ask what these expressions *would* mean *if* a rational man were using them, the only answer would be that they would mean what they would then mean. Understanding them would be enough, and that could be done by any reasonable listener. Philosophizing could not help him, and, in fact, the philosopher himself would not be able to begin unless he simply understood them in the ordinary way.

It seems, then, that if an expression can be understood, then it is already known in that understanding what the expression means. So there is no darkness present and no illumination required or possible.

And if it is suggested that the non-philosophical author of an expression (be he plain man, scientist, preacher or artist) does know but only knows dimly or foggily or confusedly what his expression means, but that the philosopher at the end of his exploration knows clearly, distinctly and definitely what it means, a twofold answer seems inevitable. First, that if a speaker only knows confusedly what his expression means, then he is in that respect and to that extent just gabbling. And it is not the rôle — nor the achievement — of the philosopher to provide a medicine against that form of flux. And next, the philosopher is not *ex officio* concerned with ravings and ramblings: he studies expressions for what they mean when intelligently and intelligibly employed, and not as noises emitted by this idiot or that parrot.

Certainly expressions do occur for which better substitutes could be found and should be or should have been employed. (1) An expression may be a breach of, *e.g.*, English or Latin grammar. (2) A word may be a foreign word, or a rare word or a technical or trade term for which there exists a familiar synonym. (3) A phrase or sentence may be clumsy or unfamiliar in its structure. (4) A word or phrase may be equivocal and so be an instrument of possible puns. (5) A word or phrase may be ill-chosen as being general where it should be specific, or allusive where the allusion is not known or not obvious. (6) Or a word may be a malapropism or a misnomer. But the search for paraphrases which shall be more swiftly intelligible to a given audience or more idiomatic or stylish or more grammatically or etymologically correct is merely applied lexicography or philology — it is not philosophy.

We ought then to face the question: Is there such a thing as analyzing or clarifying the meaning of the expressions which people use, except in the sense of substituting philologically better expressions for philologically worse ones? (We might have put the problem in the more misleading terminology of "concepts" and asked: How can philosophizing so operate by analysis and clarification, upon the concepts used by the plain man, the scientist

or the artist, that after this operation the concepts are illumined where before they were dark? The same difficulties arise. For there can be no such thing as a confused concept, since either a man is conceiving, *i.e.*, knowing the nature of his subject-matter, or he is failing to do so. If he is succeeding, no clarification is required or possible; and if he is failing, he must find out more or think more about the subject-matter, the apprehension of the nature of which we call his "concept." But this will not be philosophizing about the concept, but exploring further the nature of the thing, and so will be economics, perhaps, or astronomy or history. But as I think that it can be shown that it is not true in any natural sense that "there are concepts," I shall adhere to the other method of stating the problem.)

The object of this paper is not to show what philosophy in general is investigating, but to show that there remains an important sense in which philosophers can and must discover and state what is really meant by expressions of this or that radical type, and none the less that these discoveries do not in the least imply that the naïve users of such expressions are in any doubt or confusion about what their expressions mean or in any way need the results of the philosophical analysis for them to continue to use intelligently their ordinary modes of expression or to use them so that they are intelligible to others.

The gist of what I want to establish is this. There are many expressions [1] which

---

[1] I use "expression" to cover single words, phrases and sentences. By "statement" I mean a sentence in the indicative. When a statement is true, I say it "records" a fact or state of affairs. False statements do not record. To know that a statement is true is to know that something is the case and that the statement records it. When I barely understand a statement I do not know that it records a fact, nor need I know the fact that it records, if it records one. But I know what state of affairs *would* obtain, if the statement recorded a state of affairs.

Every significant statement is a quasi-record, for it has both the requisite structure and constituents to be a record. But knowing these, we don't yet know that it is a record of a fact. False occur in non-philosophical discourse which, though they are perfectly clearly understood by those who use them and those who hear or read them, are nevertheless couched in grammatical or syntactical forms which are in a demonstrable way *improper* to the states of affairs which they record (or the alleged states of affairs which they profess to record). Such expressions can be reformulated and for philosophy but *not* for non-philosophical discourse must be reformulated into expressions of which the syntactical form is proper to the facts recorded (or the alleged facts alleged to be recorded).

When an expression is of such a syntactical form that it is improper to the fact recorded, it is systematically misleading in that it naturally suggests to some people — though not to "ordinary" people — that the state of affairs recorded is quite a different sort of state of affairs from that which it in fact is.

I shall try to show what I am driving at by examples. I shall begin by considering a whole class of expressions of one type which occur and occur perfectly satisfactorily in ordinary discourse, but which are, I argue, *systematically misleading*, that is to say, that they are couched in a syntactical form improper to the facts recorded and proper to facts of quite another logical form than the facts recorded. (For simplicity's sake, I shall speak as if all the statements adduced as examples are true. For false statements are not formally different from true ones. Otherwise grammarians could become omniscient. And when I call a statement "systematically misleading" I shall not mean that it is false, and certainly not that it is senseless.

statements are pseudo-records and are no more records than pseudo-antiquities are antiquities. So the question, What do false statements state? is meaningless if "state" means "record." If it means, What *would* they record if they recorded something being the case? the question contains its own answer.

By "systematically" I mean that all expressions of that grammatical form would be misleading in the same way and for the same reason.)

I. QUASI-ONTOLOGICAL STATEMENTS

Since Kant, we have, most of us, paid lip service to the doctrine that "existence is not a quality" and so we have rejected the pseudo-implication of the ontological argument; "God is perfect, being perfect entails being existent, ∴. God exists." For if existence is not a quality, it is not the sort of thing that can be entailed by a quality.

But until fairly recently it was not noticed that if in "God exists" "exists" is not a predicate (save in grammar), then in the same statement "God" cannot be (save in grammar) the subject of predication. The realization of this came from examining negative existential propositions like "Satan does not exist" or "unicorns are non-existent." If there is no Satan, then the statement "Satan does not exist" cannot be about Satan in the way in which "I am sleepy" is about me. Despite appearances the word "Satan" cannot be signifying a subject of attributes.

Philosophers have toyed with theories which would enable them to continue to say that "Satan does not exist" is none the less still somehow about Satan, and that "exists" still signifies some sort of attribute or character, although not a quality.

So some argued that the statement was about something described as "the idea of Satan," others that it was about a subsistent but non-actual entity called "Satan." Both theories in effect try to show that something may *be* (whether as being "merely mental" or as being in "the realm of subsistents"), but not be in existence. But as we can say "round squares do not exist," and "real nonentities do not exist," this sort of interpretation of negative existentials is bound to fill either the realm of subsistents or the realm of ideas with walking self-contradictions. So the theories had to be dropped and a new analysis of existential propositions had to begin.

Suppose I assert of (apparently) the general subject "carnivorous cows" that they "do not exist," and my assertion is true, I cannot really be talking about carnivorous cows, for there are none. So it follows that the expression "carnivorous cows" is not really being used, though the grammatical appearances are to the contrary, to denote the thing or things of which the predicate is being asserted. And in the same way as the verb "exists" is not signifying the character asserted, although grammatically it looks as if it was, the real predicate must be looked for elsewhere.

So the clue of the grammar has to be rejected and the analysis has been suggested that "carnivorous cows do not exist" means what is meant by "no cows are carnivorous" or "no carnivorous beasts are cows." But a further improvement seems to be required.

"Unicorns do not exist" seems to mean what is meant by "nothing is *both* a quadruped *and* herbivorous *and* the wearer of one horn" (or whatever the marks of being an unicorn are). And this does not seem to imply that there are some quadrupeds or herbivorous animals.

So "carnivorous cows do not exist" ought to be rendered "nothing is both a cow and carnivorous," which does not as it stands imply that anything is either.

Take now an apparently singular subject as in 'God exists" or "Satan does not exist." If the former analysis was right, then here too' "God" and "Satan" are in fact, despite grammatical appearance, predicative expressions. That is to say, they are that element in the assertion that something has or lacks a specified character or set of characters, which signifies the character or set of characters by which the subject is being asserted to be characterized. "God exists" must mean what is meant by "Something, and one thing only, is omniscient, omnipotent and infinitely good" (or whatever else are the characters summed in the compound character of being a god and the only god). And "Satan does not exist" must mean what is meant by "nothing is both devilish and alone in being devilish," or perhaps "nothing is both devilish and called 'Satan'," or even " 'Satan' is not the proper name of anything." To put it roughly, "x exists" and "x does not exist" do not assert or deny that a given subject of attributes x has the attribute of existing, but assert or deny the attribute of being x-ish or being an x of something not named in the statement.

Now I can show my hand. I say that expressions such as "carnivorous cows do not exist" are systematically misleading and that the expressions by which we paraphrased them are not or are not in the same way or to the same extent systematically misleading. But they are not false, nor are they senseless. They are true, and they really do mean what their less systematically misleading paraphrases mean. Nor (save in a special class of cases) is the non-philosophical author of such expressions ignorant or doubtful of the nature of the state of affairs which his expression records. He is not a whit misled. There is a trap, however, in the form of his expression, but a trap which only threatens the man who has begun to generalize about sorts or types of states of affairs and assumes that every statement gives in its syntax a clue to the logical form of the fact that it records. I refer here not merely nor even primarily to the philosopher, but to any man who embarks on abstraction.

But before developing this theme I want to generalize the results of our examination of what we must now describe as "so-called existential statements." It is the more necessary that, while most philosophers are now forewarned by Kant against the systematic misleadingness of "God exists," few of them have observed that the same taint infects a whole host of other expressions.

If "God exists" means what we have

said it means, then patently "God is an existent," "God is an entity," "God has being," or "existence" require the same analysis. So ". . . is an existent," ". . . is an entity," are only bogus predicates, and that of which (in grammar) they are asserted are only bogus subjects.

And the same will be true of all the items in the following pair of lists.

Mr. Baldwin —
is a being.
is real, or a reality.
is a genuine entity.
is a substance.
is an actual object or entity.
is objective.
is a concrete reality.
is an object.
is.

Mr. Pickwick —
is a nonentity.
is unreal or an unreality, or an appearance.
is a bogus or sham entity.
is not a substance.
is an unreal object or entity.
is not objective or is subjective.
is a fiction or figment.
is an imaginary object.
is not.
is a mere idea.
is an abstraction.
is a logical construction.

None of these statements is really about Mr. Pickwick. For if they are true, there is no such person for them to be about. Nor is any of them about Mr. Baldwin. For if they were false, there would be no one for them to be about. Nor in any of them is the grammatical predicate that element in the statement which signifies the character that is being asserted to be characterizing or not to be characterizing something.

I formulate the conclusion in this rather clumsy way. There is a class of statements of which the grammatical predicate *appears* to signify not the having of a specified character but the having (or not having) of a specified *status*. But in all such statements the appearance is a purely grammatical one, and what the statements really record can be stated in statements embodying no such quasi-ontological predicates.

And, again, in all such quasi-ontological statements the grammatical subject-word or phrase *appears* to denote or refer to something as that of which the quasi-ontological predicate is being predicated; but in fact the apparent subject term is a concealed predicative expression, and what is really recorded in such statements can be re-stated in statements no part of which even appears to refer to any such subject.

In a word, all quasi-ontological statements are systematically misleading. (If I am right in this, then the conclusion follows, which I accept, that those metaphysical philosophers are the greatest sinners, who, as if they were saying something of importance, make "Reality" or "Being" the subject of their propositions, or "real" the predicate. For at best what they say is systematically misleading, which is the one thing which a philosopher's propositions have no right to be: and at worst it is meaningless.)

I must give warning again that the naïve employer of such quasi-ontological expressions is not necessarily and not even probably misled. He has said what he wanted to say, and anyone who knew English would understand what he was saying. Moreover, I would add, in the cases that I have listed, the statements are not merely significant but true. Each of them records a real state of affairs. Nor *need* they mislead the philosopher. We, for instance, I hope are not misled. But the point is that anyone, the philosopher included, who abstracts and generalizes and so tries to consider what different facts of the same type (*i.e.*, facts of the same type about different things) have in common, is compelled to use the common grammatical form of the statements of those facts as handles with which to grasp the common logical form of the facts themselves. For (what we shall see later) as the way in which a fact *ought* to be recorded in expressions *would* be a clue to the form of that fact, we jump to the assumption that the way in which a fact *is* recorded *is* such a clue. And very often the clue is misleading and suggests that the fact is of a different form from what really is its form. "Satan is not a reality" from its grammatical form looks as if it recorded the same sort of fact as "Capone is not a philosopher," and so was just as much denying a character of a somebody called "Satan" as the latter does deny a character of a somebody called "Capone." But it turns out that the suggestion is a fraud; for the fact recorded would have been properly or less improperly recorded in the statement " 'Satan' is not a proper name" or "No one is called 'Satan' " or "No one is both called 'Satan' and is infinitely malevolent, etc.," or perhaps "Some people believe that someone is both called 'Satan' and infinitely malevolent, but their belief is false." And none of these statements even pretend to be "about Satan." Instead, they are and are patently about the noise "Satan" or else about people who misuse it.

In the same way, while it is significant, true and directly intelligible to say "Mr. Pickwick is a fiction," it is a systematically misleading expression (*i.e.*, an expression misleading in virtue of a formal property which it does or might share with other expressions); for it does not really record, as it appears to record, a fact of the same sort as is recorded in "Mr. Baldwin is a statesman." The world does not contain fictions in the way in which it contains statesmen. There is no subject of attributes of which we can say "*there* is a fiction." What we can do is to say of Dickens "*there* is a story-teller," or of Pickwick Papers "*there* is a pack of lies"; or of a sentence in that novel, which contains the pseudo-name "Mr. Pickwick" "*there* is a fable." And when we say things of this sort we are recording just what we recorded when we said "Mr. Pickwick is a

fiction," only our new expressions do not suggest what our old one did that some subject of attributes has the two attributes of being called "Mr. Pickwick" and of being a fiction, but instead that some subject of attributes has the attributes of being called Dickens and being a coiner of false propositions and pseudo-proper names, or, on the other analysis, of being a book or a sentence which could only be true or false *if* someone was called "Mr. Pickwick." The proposition "Mr. Pickwick is a fiction" is really, despite its *prima facies*, about Dickens or else about Pickwick Papers. But the fact that it is so is concealed and not exhibited by the form of the expression in which it is said.

It must be noted that the sense in which such quasi-ontological statements are misleading is not that they are false and not even that any word in them is equivocal or vague, but only that they are formally improper to the facts of the logical form which they are employed to record and proper to facts of quite another logical form. What the implications are of these notions of formal propriety or formal impropriety we shall see later on.

II. Statements Seemingly About Universals, or Quasi-Platonic Statements

We often and with great convenience use expressions such as "Unpunctuality is reprehensible" and "Virtue is its own reward." And at first sight these seem to be on all fours with "Jones merits reproof" and "Smith has given himself the prize." So philosophers, taking it that what is meant by such statements as the former is precisely analogous to what is meant by such statements as the latter, have accepted the consequence that the world contains at least two sorts of objects, namely, particulars like Jones and Smith, and "universals" like Unpunctuality and Virtue.

But absurdities soon crop up. It is obviously silly to speak of an universal meriting reproof. You can no more praise or blame an "universal" than you can make holes in the Equator.

Nor when we say "unpunctuality is reprehensible" do we really suppose that unpunctuality ought to be ashamed of itself.

What we do mean is what is also meant but better expressed by "Whoever is unpunctual deserves that other people should reprove him for being unpunctual." For it is unpunctual men and not unpunctuality who can and should be blamed, since they are, what it is not, moral agents. Now in the new expression "whoever is unpunctual merits reproof" the word "unpunctuality" has vanished in favour of the predicative expression ". . . is unpunctual." So that while in the original expression "unpunctuality" seemed to denote the subject of which an attribute was being asserted, it now turns out to signify the having of an attribute. And we are really saying that anyone who has that attribute, has the other.

Again, it is not literally true that Virtue is a recipient of rewards. What is true is that anyone who is virtuous is benefited thereby. Whoever is good, gains something by being good. So the original statement was not "about Virtue" but about good men, and the grammatical subject-word "Virtue" meant what is meant by ". . . is virtuous" and so was, what it pretended not to be, a predicative expression.

I need not amplify this much. It is not literally true that "honesty compels me to state so and so," for "honesty" is not the name of a coercive agency. What is true is more properly put "because I am honest, or wish to be honest, I am bound to state so and so." "Colour involves extension" means what is meant by "Whatever is coloured is extended"; "hope deferred maketh the heart sick" means what is meant by "whoever for a long time hopes for something without getting it becomes sick at heart."

It is my own view that all statements which seem to be "about universals" are analysable in the same way, and consequently that general terms are never really the names of subjects of attributes. So "universals" are not objects in the way in which Mt. Everest is one, and therefore the age-old question what *sort* of objects they are is a bogus question. For general nouns, adjectives, etc., are not proper names, so we cannot speak of "the objects called 'equality', 'justice', and 'progress'."

Platonic and anti-Platonic assertions, such as that "equality is, or is not, a real entity," are, accordingly, alike misleading, and misleading in two ways at once; for they are both quasi-ontological statements and quasi-Platonic ones.

However, I do not wish to defend this general position here, but only to show that in *some* cases statements which from their grammatical form seem to be saying that "honesty does so and so" or "equality is such and such," are really saying in a formally improper way (though one which is readily understandable and idiomatically correct) "anything which is equal to *x* is such and such" or "whoever is honest, is so and so." These statements state overtly what the others stated covertly that something's having one attribute necessitates its having the other.

Of course, the plain man who uses such quasi-Platonic expressions is not making a philosophical mistake. He is not philosophizing at all. He is not misled by and does not even notice the fraudulent pretence contained in such propositions that they are "about Honesty" or "about Progress." He knows what he means and will, very likely, accept our more formally proper restatement of what he means as a fair paraphrase, but he will not have any motive for desiring the more proper form of expression, nor even any grounds for holding that it is more proper. For he is not attending to the form of the fact in abstraction from the special subject matter that the fact is about. So for him the best way of expressing something is the way which is the most brief, the most elegant, or the most emphatic, whereas those who, like philosophers, must generalize about the *sorts* of statements that have to be made of *sorts* of facts about *sorts* of topics, cannot help treating as clues to the logical structures for which they are looking the grammatical forms of the common types of expressions in which these structures are recorded. And these clues are often misleading.

III. Descriptive Expressions and Quasi-descriptions

We all constantly use expressions of the form "the so and so" as "the Vice-Chancellor of Oxford University." Very often we refer by means of such expressions to some one uniquely described individual. The phrases "the present Vice-Chancellor of Oxford University" and "the highest mountain in the world" have such a reference in such propositions as "the present Vice-Chancellor of Oxford University is a tall man" and "I have not seen the highest mountain in the world."

There is nothing intrinsically misleading in the use of "the"-phrases as unique descriptions, though there is a sense in which they are highly condensed or abbreviated. And philosophers can and do make mistakes in the accounts they give of what such descriptive phrases mean. What are misleading are, as we shall see, "the"-phrases which behave grammatically as if they were unique descriptions referring to individuals, when in fact they are not referential phrases at all. But this class of systematically misleading expressions cannot be examined until we have considered how genuine unique descriptions do refer.

A descriptive phrase is not a proper name, and the way in which the subject of attributes which it denotes is denoted by it is not in that subject's being *called* "the so and so," but in its possessing and being *ipso facto* the sole possessor of the idiosyncratic attribute which is what the descriptive phrase signifies. If Tommy is the eldest son of Jones, then "the eldest

son of Jones" denotes Tommy, not because someone or other *calls* him "the eldest son of Jones," but because he is and no one else can be both a son of Jones and older than all the other sons of Jones. The descriptive phrase, that is, is not a proper name but a predicative expression signifying the joint characters of being a son of Jones and older than the other sons of Jones. And it refers to Tommy only in the sense that Tommy and Tommy alone has those characters.

The phrase does not in any sense *mean* Tommy. Such a view would be, as we shall see, nonsensical. It means what is meant by the predicative expression, ". . . is both a son of Jones and older than his other sons," and so it is itself only a predicative expression. By a "predicative expression" I mean that fragment of a statement in virtue of which the having of a certain character or characters is expressed. And the having of a certain character is not a subject of attributes but, so to speak, the tail end of the facts that some subject of attributes has it and some others lack it. By itself it neither names the subject which has the characters nor records the fact that any subject has it. It cannot indeed occur by itself, but only as an element, namely, a predicative element in a full statement.

So the full statement "the eldest son of Jones was married to-day" means what is meant by "someone (namely, Tommy) (1) is a son of Jones, (2) is older than the other sons of Jones [this could be unpacked further] and (3) was married to-day."

The whole statement could not be true unless the three or more component statements were true. But *that* there is someone of whom both (1) and (2) are true is not guaranteed by their being stated. (No statement can guarantee its own truth.) Consequently the characterizing expression ". . . is the eldest son of Jones" does not *mean* Tommy either in the sense of being his proper name or in the sense of being an expression the understanding of which involves the knowledge that Tommy has this idiosyncratic character. It only *refers* to Tommy in the sense that well-informed listeners will know already, that Tommy and Tommy only has in fact this idiosyncratic character. But this knowledge is not part of what must be known in order to understand the statement, "Jones' eldest son was married to-day." For we could know what it meant without knowing that Tommy was that eldest son or was married to-day. All we must know is that someone or other must be so characterized for the whole statement to be true.

For understanding a statement or apprehending what a statement means is not knowing that this statement records this fact, but knowing what *would* be the case if the statement *were* a record of fact.

There is no understanding or apprehending the meaning of an isolated proper name or of an isolated unique description. For *either* we know that someone in particular is called by that name by certain persons or else has the idiosyncratic characters signified by the descriptive phrase, which require that we are acquainted both with the name or description and with the person named or described. *Or* we do not know these things, in which case we don't know that the quasi-name is a name at all or that the quasi-unique description describes anyone. But we can understand statements in which quasi-names or quasi-unique descriptions occur; for we can know what would be the case if someone were so called or so describable, and also had the other characters predicated in the predicates of the statements.

We see then that descriptive phrases are condensed predicative expressions and so that their function is to be that element or (more often) one of those elements in statements (which as a whole record that something has a certain character or characters) in which the having of this or that character is expressed.

And this can easily be seen by another approach.

Take any "the"-phrase which is naturally used referentially as the grammatical subject of a sentence, as "The Vice-Chancellor of Oxford University" in "The Vice-Chancellor of Oxford University is busy." We can now take the descriptive phrase, lock, stock and barrel, and use it non-referentially as the grammatical predicate in a series of statements and expressions. "Who is the present Vice-Chancellor of Oxford University?" "Mr. So-and-So is the present Vice-Chancellor of Oxford University," Georges Carpentier is not the present Vice-Chancellor of Oxford University," "Mr. Such-and-Such is either the Vice-Chancellor of Oxford University or Senior Proctor," "Whoever is Vice-Chancellor of Oxford University is overworked," etc. It is clear anyhow in the cases of the negative, hypothetical and disjunctive statements containing this common predicative expression that it is not implied or even suggested that anyone does hold the office of Vice-Chancellor. So the "the"-phrase is here quite non-referential, and does not even pretend to denote someone. It signifies an idiosyncratic character, but does not involve that anyone has it. This leads us back to our original conclusion that a descriptive phrase does not in any sense *mean* this person or that thing; or, to put it in another way, that we can understand a statement containing a descriptive phrase and still not know of this subject of attributes or of that one that the description fits it. (Indeed, we hardly need to argue the position. For no one with a respect for sense would dream of pointing to someone or something and saying "that is the meaning of such and such an expression" or "the meaning of yonder phrase is suffering from influenza." "Socrates is a meaning" is a nonsensical sentence. The whole pother about denoting seems to arise from the supposition that we could significantly describe an object as "the meaning of the expression '*x*'" or "what the expression 'x' means." Certainly a descriptive phrase can be said to *refer* to or *fit* this man or that mountain, and this man or that mountain can be described as that to which the expression "*x*" refers. But this is only to say that this man or that mountain has and is alone in having the characters the having of which is expressed in the predicative sentence-fragment ". . . is the so-and-so.")

All this is only leading up to another class of systematically misleading expressions. But the "the"-phrases which we have been studying, whether occurring as grammatical subjects or as predicates in statements, were not formally fraudulent. There was nothing in the grammatical form of the sentences adduced to suggest that the facts recorded were of a different logical form from that which they really had.

The previous argument was intended to be critical of certain actual or possible philosophical errors, but they were errors about descriptive expressions and not errors *due* to a trickiness in descriptive expressions as such. Roughly, the errors that I have been trying to dispel are the views (1) that descriptive phrases are proper names and (2) that the thing which a description describes is what the description means. I want now to come to my long-delayed muttons and discuss a further class of systematically misleading expressions.

Systematically Misleading Quasi-referential "the"-phrases

1. There frequently occur in ordinary discourse expressions which, though "the"-phrases, are not unique descriptions at all, although from their grammatical form they look as if they are. The man who does not go in for abstraction and generalization uses them without peril or perplexity and knows quite well what he means by the sentences containing them. But the philosopher has to re-state them in a different and formally more proper arrangement of words if he is not to be trapped.

When a descriptive phrase is used as the grammatical subject of a sentence in a formally non-misleading way, as in "the King went shooting to-day," we know that if the statement as a whole is true (or even false) then there must be in the world someone in particular to whom the description "the King" refers or applies. And we could significantly ask "Who is the King?" and "Are the father of the Prince of Wales and the King one and the same person?"

But we shall see that there are in common use quasi-descriptive phrases of the form "the so-and-so," in the cases of which there is in the world no one and nothing that could be described as that to which the phrase refers or applies, and thus that there is nothing and nobody about which or whom we could even ask "Is it the so-and-so?" or "Are he and the so-and-so one and the same person?"

It can happen in several ways. Take first the statement, which is true and clearly intelligible, "Poincaré is not the King of France." This at first sight looks formally analogous to "Tommy Jones is not (*i.e.*, is not identical with) the King of England." But the difference soon shows itself. For whereas if the latter is true then its converse "the King of England is not Tommy Jones" is true, it is neither true nor false to say "The King of France is not Poincaré." For there is no King of France and the phrase "the King of France" does not fit anybody — nor did the plain man who said "Poincaré is not the King of France" suppose the contrary. So "the King of France" in this statement is not analogous to "the King of England" in the others. It is not really being used referentially or as a unique description of somebody at all.

We can now redraft the contrasted propositions in forms of words which shall advertize the difference which the original propositions concealed between the forms of the facts recorded.

"Tommy Jones is not the same person as the King of England" means what is meant by (1) "Somebody and — of an unspecified circle — one person only is called Tommy Jones; (2) Somebody, and one person only has royal power in England; and (3) No one both is called Tommy Jones and is King of England." The original statement could not be true unless (1) and (2) were true.

Take now "Poincaré is not the King of France." This means what is meant by (1) Someone is called "Poincaré" and (2) Poincaré has not got the rank, being King of France. And this does not imply that anyone has that rank.

Sometimes this twofold use, namely the referential and the non-referential use of "the"-phrases troubles us in the mere practice of ordinary discourse. "Smith is not the only man who has ever climbed Mont Blanc" might easily be taken by some people to mean what is meant by "One man and one man only has climbed Mont Blanc, but Smith is not he," and by others, "Smith has climbed Mont Blanc but at least one other man has done so too." But I am not interested in the occasional ambiguity of such expressions, but in the fact that an expression of this sort which is really being used in the non-referential way is apt to be construed as if it *must* be referentially used, or as if any "the"-phrase was referentially used. Philosophers and others who have to abstract and generalize tend to be misled by the verbal similarity of "the"-phrases of the one sort with "the"-phrases of the other into "coining entities" in order to be able to show to what a given "the"-phrase refers.

Let us first consider the phrase "the top of that tree" or "the centre of that bush" as they occur in such statements as "an owl is perched on the top of that tree," "my arrow flew through the centre of the bush." These statements are quite unambiguous and convey clearly and correctly what they are intended to convey.

But as they are in syntax analogous to "a man is sitting next to the Vice-Chancellor" and "my arrow flew through the curtain," and as further an indefinite list could be drawn up of different statements having in common the "the-phrases" "the top of that tree" and "the centre of that bush," it is hard for people who generalize to escape the temptation of supposing or even believing that these "the"-phrases refer to objects in the way in which "the Vice-Chancellor" and "the curtain" refer to objects. And this is to suppose or believe that the top of that tree is a genuine subject of attributes in just the same way as the Vice-Chancellor is.

But (save in the case where the expression is being misused for the expression "the topmost branch" or "the topmost leaf of the tree") "the top of the tree" at once turns out not to be referring to any object. There is nothing in the world of which it is true (or even false) to say "that is the top of such and such a tree." It does not, for instance, refer to a bit of the tree, or it could be cut down and burned or put in a vase. "The top of the tree" does not refer to anything, but it signifies an attribute, namely, the having of a relative position, when it occurs in statements of the form "x is at or near or above or below the top of the tree." To put it crudely, it does not refer to a thing but signifies a thing's being in a certain place, or else signifies not a thing but the site or locus of a thing such as of the bough or leaf which is higher than any of the other boughs or leaves on the tree. Accordingly it makes sense to say that now one bough and now another is at the top of the tree. But "at the top of the tree" means no more than what is meant by "higher than any other part of the tree," which latter phrase no one could take for a referential phrase like "the present Vice-Chancellor."

The place of a thing, or the whereabouts of a thing is not a thing but the tail end of the fact that something is there. "Where the bee sucks, there suck I," but it is the clover flower that is there which holds the honey and not the whereabouts of the flower. All that this amounts to is that though we can use quasi-descriptive phrases to enable us to state where something is, that the thing is there is a relational character of the thing and not itself a subject of characters.

I suspect that a lot of Cartesian and perhaps Newtonian blunders about Space and Time originate from the systematically misleading character of the "the"-phrases which we use to date and locate things, such as "the region occupied by x," "the path followed by y," "the moment or date at which z happened." It was not seen that these are but hamstrung predicative expressions and are not and are not even ordinarily taken to be referentially used descriptive expressions, any more than "the King of France" in "Poincaré is not the King of France" is ordinarily treated as if it was a referentially used "the"-phrase.

Take another case. "Jones hates the thought of going to hospital," "the idea of having a holiday has just occurred to me." These quasi-descriptive phrases suggest that there is one object in the world which is what is referred to by the phrase "the thought of going to hospital" and another which is what is referred to by "the idea of having a holiday." And anyhow partly through accepting the grammatical *prima facies* of such expressions, philosophers have believed as devoutly in the existence of "ideas," "conceptions" and "thoughts" or "judgments" as their predecessors did (from similar causes) in that of substantial forms or as children do (from similar causes) in that of the Equator, the sky and the North Pole.

But if we re-state them, the expressions turn out to be no evidence whatsoever in favour of the Lockean demonology. For "Jones hates the thought of going to hospital" only means what is meant by "Jones feels distressed when he thinks of what he will undergo if he goes to hospital." The phrase "the thought of . . ." is transmuted into "whenever he thinks of . . .,"

which does not even seem to contain a reference to any other entity than Jones and, perhaps, the hospital. For it to be true, the world must contain a Jones who is sometimes thinking and sometimes, say, sleeping; but it need no more contain both Jones and "the thought or idea of so and so" than it need contain both someone called "Jones" and something called "Sleep."

Similarly, the statement "the idea of taking a holiday has just occurred to me" seems grammatically to be analogous to "that dog has just bitten me." And as, if the latter is true, the world must contain both me and the dog, so it would seem, if the former is true, the world must contain both me and the idea of taking a holiday. But the appearance is a delusion. For while I could not re-state my complaint against the dog in any sentence not containing a descriptive phrase referring to it, I can easily do so with the statement about "the idea of taking a holiday," *e.g.*, in the statement "I have just been thinking that I might take a holiday."

A host of errors of the same sort has been generated in logic itself and epistemology by the omission to analyse the quasi-descriptive phrase "the meaning of the expression 'x'." I suspect that all the mistaken doctrines of concepts, ideas, terms, judgments, objective propositions, contents, objectives and the like derive from the same fallacy, namely, that there must be *something* referred to by such expressions as "the meaning of the word (phrase or sentence) 'x'," on all fours with the policeman who really is referred to by the descriptive phrase in "our village policeman is fond of football." And the way out of the confusion is to see that some "the"-phrases are only similar in grammar and not similar in function to referentially-used descriptive phrases, *e.g.*, in the case in point, "the meaning of 'x'" is like "the King of France" in "Poincaré is not the King of France," a predicative expression used non-referentially.

And, of course, the ordinary man does

not pretend to himself or anyone else that when he makes statements containing such expressions as "the meaning of 'x'," he is referring to a queer new object: it does not cross his mind that his phrase might be misconstrued as a referentially used descriptive phrase. So he is not guilty of philosophical error or clumsiness. None the less his form of words is systematically misleading. For an important difference of logical form is disguised by the complete similarity of grammatical form between "the village policeman is reliable" and "the meaning of 'x' is doubtful" or again between "I have just met the village policeman" and "I have just grasped the meaning of 'x'."

(Consequently, as there is no object describable as that which is referred to by the expression "the meaning of 'x'," questions about the status of such objects are meaningless. It is as pointless to discuss whether word-meanings (*i.e.*, "concepts" or "universals") are subjective or objective, or whether sentence-meanings (*i.e.*, "judgments" or "objectives") are subjective or objective, as it would be to discuss whether the Equator or the sky is subjective or objective. For the questions themselves are not about anything.)

All this does not of course in the least prevent us from using intelligently and intelligibly sentences containing the expression "the meaning of 'x' " where this can be re-drafted as "what 'x' means." For here the "the"-phrase is being predicatively used and not as an unique description. "The meaning of 'x' is the same as the meaning of 'y' " is equivalent to " 'x' means what 'y' means," and that can be understood without any temptation to multiply entities.

But this argument is, after all, only about a very special case of the systematic misleadingness of quasi-descriptions.

2. There is another class of uses of "the"-phrases which is also liable to engender philosophical misconstructions, though I am not sure that I can recall any good instances of actual mistakes which have occurred from this source.

Suppose, I say, "the defeat of the Labour Party has surprised me," what I say could be correctly paraphrased by "the fact that the Labour Party was defeated, was a surprise to me" or "the Labour Party has been defeated and I am surprised that it has been defeated." Here the "the"-phrase does not refer to a thing but is a condensed record of something's being the case. And this is a common and handy idiom. We can always say instead of "because A is B, therefore C is D" "the D-ness of C is due to the B-ness of A." "The severity of the winter is responsible for the high price of cabbages" means what is meant by "Cabbages are expensive because the winter was severe."

But if I say "the defeat of the Labour Party occurred in 1931," my "the"-phrase is referentially used to describe an event and not as a condensed record of a fact. For events have dates, but facts do not. So the facts recorded in the grammatically similar statements "the defeat of the Labour Party has surprised me" and "the defeat of the Labour Party occurred in 1931" are in logical form quite different. And both sorts of facts are formally quite different from this third fact which is recorded in "the victory of the Labour Party would have surprised me." For this neither refers to an event, nor records the fact that the Labour Party was victorious, but says "if the Labour Party had won, I should have been surprised." So here the "the"-phrase is a protasis. And, once more, all these three uses of "the"-phrases are different in their sort of significance from "the defeat of the Conservative Party at the next election is probable," or "possible," or "impossible." For these mean "the available relevant data are in favour of" or "not incompatible with" or "incompatible with the Conservative Party being defeated at the next election."

So there are at least these four different types of facts which can be and, in ordinary discourse, are conveniently and intelligibly recorded in statements containing grammatically indistinguishable "the"-phrases. But they can be restated in forms of words which do exhibit in virtue of their special grammatical forms the several logical structures of the different sorts of facts recorded.

3. Lastly, I must just mention one further class of systematically misleading "the"-phrases. "The whale is not a fish but a mammal" and "the true Englishman detests foul play" record facts, we may take it. But they are not about this whale or that Englishman, and they might be true even if there were no whales or no true Englishmen. These are, probably, disguised hypothetical statements. But all I wish to point out is that they are obviously disguised.

I have chosen these three main types of systematically misleading expressions because all alike are misleading in a certain direction. They all suggest the existence of new sorts of objects or, to put it in another way, they are all temptations to us to "multiply entities." In each of them, the quasi-ontological, the quasi-Platonic and the quasi-descriptive expressions, an expression is misconstrued as a denoting expression which in fact does not denote, but only looks grammatically like expressions which are used to denote. Occam's prescription was, therefore, in my view, "do not treat all expressions which are grammatically like proper names or referentially used "the"-phrases, as if they were therefore proper names or referentially used "the"-phrases."

But there are other types of systematically misleading expressions, of which I shall just mention a few that occur to me.

"Jones is an alleged murderer," or "a suspected murderer," "Smith is a possible or probable Lord Mayor," "Robinson is an ostensible, or seeming or mock or sham or bogus hero," "Brown is a future or a past Member of Parliament," etc. These suggest what they do not mean, that the subjects named are of a special kind of murderer, or Lord Mayor, or hero, or Member of Parliament. But being an alleged murderer does not entail being a murderer, nor does being a likely Lord Mayor entail being a Lord Mayor.

"Jones is popular" suggests that being popular is like being wise, a quality; but in fact it is a relational character, and one which does not directly characterize Jones, but the people who are fond of Jones, and so "Jones is popular" means what is meant by "Many people like Jones, and many more like him than either dislike him or are indifferent to him," or something of the sort.

But I have, I think, given enough instances to show in what sense expressions may seem to mean something quite different from what they are in fact used to mean; and therefore I have shown in what sense some expressions are systematically misleading.

So I am taking it as established (1) that what is expressed in one expression can often be expressed in expressions of quite different grammatical forms, and (2) that of two expressions, each meaning what the other means, which are of different grammatical forms, one is often more systematically misleading than the other.

And this means that while a fact or state of affairs *can* be recorded in an indefinite number of statements of widely differing grammatical forms, it is stated better in some than in others. The ideal, which may never be realized, is that it should be stated in a completely nonmisleading form of words.

Now, when we call one form of expression better than another, we do not mean that it is more elegant or brief or familiar or more swiftly intelligible to the ordinary listener, but that in virtue of its grammatical form it exhibits, in a way in which the others fail to exhibit, the logical form of the state of affairs or fact that is being recorded. But this interest in the best way of exhibiting the logical form of facts is not for every man, but only for the philosopher.

I wish now to raise, but not to solve, some consequential problems which arise.

1. Given that an expression of a certain grammatical form is proper (or anyhow approximates to being proper) to facts of a certain logical form and to those facts only, is this relation of propriety of grammatical to logical form *natural* or *conventional*?

I cannot myself credit what seems to be the doctrine of Wittgenstein and the school of logical grammarians who owe allegiance to him, that what makes an expression formally proper to a fact is some real and non-conventional one-one picturing relation between the composition of the expression and that of the fact. For I do not see how, save in a small class of specially-chosen cases, a fact or state of affairs can be deemed like or even unlike in structure a sentence, gesture or diagram. For a fact is not a collection — even an arranged collection — of bits in the way in which a sentence is an arranged collection of noises or a map an arranged collection of scratches. A fact is not a thing and so is not even an arranged thing. Certainly a map may be like a country or a railway system, and in a more general, or looser, sense a sentence, as an ordered series of noises might be a similar sort of series to a series of vehicles in a stream of traffic or the series of days in the week.

But in Socrates being angry or in the fact that either Socrates was wise or Plato was dishonest I can see no concatenation of bits such that a concatenation of parts of speech could be held to be of the same general architectural plan as it. But this difficulty may be just denseness on my part.

On the other hand, it is not easy to accept what seems to be the alternative that it is just by convention that a given grammatical form is specially dedicated to facts of a given logical form. For, in fact, customary usage is perfectly tolerant of systematically misleading expressions. And,

moreover, it is hard to explain how in the genesis of languages our presumably non-philosophical forbears could have decided on or happened on the dedication of a given grammatical form to facts of a given logical form. For presumably the study of abstract logical form is later than the entry into common use of syntactical idioms.

It is, however, my present view that the propriety of grammatical to logical forms is more nearly conventional than natural: though I do not suppose it to be the effect of whim or of deliberate plan.

2. The next question is: How are we to discover in particular cases whether an expression is systematically misleading or not? I suspect that the answer to this will be of this sort. We meet with and understand and even believe a certain expression such as "Mr. Pickwick is a fictitious person" and "the Equator encircles the globe." And we know that if these expressions are saying what they seem to be saying, certain other propositions will follow. But it turns out that the naturally consequential propositions "Mr. Pickwick was born in such and such a year" and "the Equator is of such and such a thickness" are not merely false but, on analysis, in contradiction with something in that from which they seemed to be logical consequences. The only solution is to see that being a fictitious person is not to be a person of a certain sort, and that the sense in which the Equator girdles the earth is not that of being any sort of a ring or ribbon enveloping the earth. And this is to see that the original propositions were not saying what they seemed on first analysis to be saying. Paralogisms and antinomies are the evidence that an expression is systematically misleading.

None the less, the systematically misleading expressions as intended and as understood contain no contradictions. People do not really talk philosophical nonsense — unless they are philosophizing or, what is quite a different thing, unless they are being sententious. What they do is to use expressions which, from whatever cause — generally the desire for brevity and simplicity of discourse — disguise instead of exhibit the forms of the facts recorded. And it is to reveal these forms that we abstract and generalize. These processes of abstraction and generalization occur before philosophical analysis begins. It seems indeed that their results are the subject matter of philosophy. Pre-philosophical abstract thinking is always misled by systematically misleading expressions, and even philosophical abstract thinking, the proper function of which is to cure this disease, is actually one of its worst victims.

3. I do not know any way of classifying or giving an exhaustive list of the possible types of systematically misleading expressions. I fancy that the number is in principle unlimited, but that the number of prevalent and obsessing types is fairly small.

4. I do not know any way of proving that an expression contains no systematic misleadingness at all. The fact that antinomies have not yet been shown to arise is no proof that they never will arise. We can know that of two expressions "x" and "y" which record the same fact, "x" is less misleading than "y"; but not that "x" cannot itself be improved upon.

5. Philosophy must then involve the exercise of systematic restatement. But this does not mean that it is a department of philology or literary criticism.

Its restatement is not the substitution of one noun for another or one verb for another. That is what lexicographers and translators excel in. Its restatements are transmutations of syntax, and transmutations of syntax controlled not by desire for elegance or stylistic correctness but by desire to exhibit the forms of the facts into which philosophy is the enquiry.

I conclude, then, that there is, after all, a sense in which we can properly enquire and even say "what it really means to say so and so." For we can ask what is the real form of the fact recorded when this is concealed or disguised and not duly exhibited by the expression in question. And we can often succeed in stating this fact in a new form of words which does exhibit what the other failed to exhibit. And I am for the present inclined to believe that this is what philosophical analysis is, and that this is the sole and whole function of philosophy. But I do not want to argue this point now.

But, as confession is good for the soul, I must admit that I do not very much relish the conclusions towards which these conclusions point. I would rather allot to philosophy a sublimer task than the detection of the sources in linguistic idioms of recurrent misconstructions and absurd theories. But that it is at least this I cannot feel any serious doubt.

[In this paper I have deliberately refrained from describing expressions as "incomplete symbols" or quasi-things as "logical constructions." Partly I have abstained because I am fairly ignorant of the doctrines in which these are technical terms, though in so far as I do understand them, I think that I could re-state them in words which I like better without modifying the doctrines. But partly, also, I think that the terms themselves are rather ill-chosen and are apt to cause unnecessary perplexities. But I do think that I have been talking about what is talked about by those who use these terms, when they use them.]

Editor's note: For Ryle's present view of this essay, see p. 305 below. For critical discussion of Ryle's views in this essay, see the cross-references given under Ryle [11] in the bibliography, especially Shapere [1] (reprinted at pp. 271–83 below).

6

JOHN WISDOM

PHILOSOPHICAL PERPLEXITY

1. *Philosophical statements are really verbal.* I have inquired elsewhere the real nature of philosophical requests such as 'Can we know what is going on in someone else's mind?' 'Can we really know the causes of our sensations?' 'What is a chair?' and of philosophical answers such as 'We can never really know the causes of our sensations', 'A chair is nothing but our sensations', or 'A chair is something over and above our sensations', 'The goodness of a man, of a picture, of an argument is something over and above our feelings of approval and over and above those features of the man, the picture or the argument, which "determine" its goodness'. There is no time to repeat the inquiry here and I have to say dogmatically:

A philosophical answer is really a verbal recommendation in response to a request which is really a request with regard to a sentence which lacks a conventional use whether there occur situations which could conventionally be described by it. The description, for example 'I know directly what is going on in Smith's mind', is not a jumble like 'Cat how is up', nor is it in conflict with conventional usage like 'There are two white pieces and three black so there are six pieces on the board'. It just lacks a conventional usage. To call both 'Can 2 + 3 = 6?' and 'Can I know what is going on in the minds of others?'

nonsensical questions serves to bring out the likeness between them. But if one were to deny that there is a difference between them it would be an instance of that disrespect for other people which we may platitudinously say, so often damages philosophical work. A disrespect which blinds one to the puzzles they raise — in this instance the puzzle of the philosophical *can* which somehow seems between 'Can 2 + 3 = 6?' and 'Can terriers catch hares?' Compare 'Can persons be in two places at once?' 'Do we have unconscious wishes?' 'Can you play chess without the queen?' (W).[1]

Even to say that 'I know directly what is going on in Smith's mind' is *meaningless*, is dangerous, especially if you have just said that 'There are two white pieces and three black so there are six' is meaningless.

It is not even safe to say that 'I know directly what is going on in Smith's mind' lacks a use or meaning and leave it at that. For though it has no meaning it tends to have a meaning, like 'All whiffley was the tulgey wood', though of course it is

[1] Wittgenstein has not read this over-compressed paper and I warn people against supposing it a closer imitation of Wittgenstein than it is. On the other hand I can hardly exaggerate the debt I owe to him and how much of the good in this work is his — not only in the treatment of this philosophical difficulty and that but in the matter of how to do philosophy. As far as possible I have put a W against examples I owe to him. It must not be assumed that they are used in a way he would approve.

Reprinted from *Proceedings of the Aristotelian Society*, XXXVII (1936–37), 71–88, by permission of the author and the editor.

unlike this last example in the important respect that it does not lack a meaning because its constituent words are unknown. Nor does it lack meaning because its syntax is unknown. This makes it puzzling and makes it resemble the logical case. It is clear that for these reasons it would be even more illuminating and more misleading to say that 'God exists' and 'Men are immortal' are meaningless — especially just after saying $2 + 3 = 6$ is meaningless.

2. *Philosophical statements are not verbal.* I have said that philosophers' questions and theories are really verbal. But if you like we will not say this or we will say also the contradictory.[2] For of course (*a*) philosophic statements usually have not a verbal air. On the contrary they have a non-verbal air like 'A fox's brush is really a tail'. (W). And their non-verbal air is not an unimportant feature of them because on it very much depends their puzzlingness.

And (*b*) though really verbal a philosopher's statements have not a merely verbal point. Unlike many statements the primary point of uttering them is not to convey the information they convey but to do something else. Consequently all attempts to explain their peculiar status by explaining the peculiar nature of their subject-matter, fail. For their subject-matter is not peculiar; their truth or falsity, in so far as these are appropriate to them at all, is fixed by facts about words, e.g. Goodness is not approval by the majority, because 'The majority sometimes approves what is bad' is not self-contradictory. But the point of philosophical statements is peculiar. It is the illumination of the ultimate structure of facts, i.e. the relations between different categories of being or (we must be in the mode) the relations between different sub-languages within a language.

The puzzles of philosophical proposi-

tions, of fictional propositions, general propositions, negative propositions, propositions about the future, propositions about the past, even the puzzle about psychological propositions, are not removed by explaining the peculiar nature of the subject-matter of the sentences in which they are expressed but by reflecting upon the peculiar manner in which those sentences work. Mnemonic slogan: It's not the stuff, it's the style that stupefies.

3. *The divergence of point from content.* The divergence of point from content which is found in necessary and near necessary propositions can be explained here only briefly.

Suppose a decoder, though still utterly ignorant of the meaning of both of two expressions 'monarchy' and 'set of persons ruled by the same king', has after prolonged investigation come to the conclusion that they mean the same in a certain code. He will say to his fellow-decoder ' "Monarchy" means the same as "set of persons ruled by the same king" '. The translator, and the philosopher also, may say the same. They all use the same form of words because what they say is the same. But the point of what they say is very different. The decoder's point can be got by anyone who knows the meaning of 'means the same as'; the translator does what he wants with the sentence only if his hearer knows the meaning either of 'monarchy' or of 'set of persons ruled by the same king'; the philosopher does what he wants with the sentence only if his hearer already uses, i.e. understands, i.e. knows the meaning of, *both* 'monarchy' and 'set of persons ruled by the same king'. This condition makes the case of the philosopher curious; for it states that he can do what he wants with the sentence only if his hearer already knows what he is telling him. But this is true in the required sense. The philosopher draws attention to what is already known with a view to giving insight into the structure of what 'monarchy', say, means, i.e. bringing into connection the sphere in which the one ex-

---

[2] I do not wish to suggest that Wittgenstein would approve of *this* sort of talk nor that he would disapprove of it.

pression is used with that in which the other is. Compare the man who says 'I should have the change from a pound after spending five shillings on a book, one and sevenpence-halfpenny on stamps and two and twopence-halfpenny at the grocer's, so I should have eleven shillings and twopence'. This is Moore's example and I beg attention for it. It is tremendously illuminating in the *necessary synthetic* group of puzzles and in a far, far wider field than this, because it illuminates the use of 'means the same' — a phrase which stops so many. When on first going to France I learn the exchange rate for francs, do I know the meaning of 'worth 100 francs' or do I come to know this after staying three weeks?

The philosopher is apt to say 'A monarchy is a set of people under a king' rather than ' "Monarchy" means the same as "a set of people under a king" '. By using the former sentence he intimates his point. Now shall we say 'A monarchy is a set of people under a king' means the same as ' "Monarchy" means "a set of people under a king" ' or not? My answer is 'Say which you like. But if you say "Yes" be careful, etc., and if you say "No" be careful, etc.'

If we decide to describe the difference between the two as a difference of meaning we must not say that the difference in meaning is a difference of subjective intension, nor that it is a difference of emotional significance merely. For these are not adequate accounts of the difference between the two — and not an adequate account of the difference between the use of '3 plus 5 plus 8' and the use of '16'.

4. *Philosophy, truth, misleadingness and illumination.* Now that we have seen that the philosopher's intention is to bring out relations between categories of being, between spheres of language, we shall be more prepared to allow that false statements about the usage of words may be philosophically very useful and even adequate provided their falsity is realized and

there is no confusion about what they are being used for.

The nature of the philosopher's intention explains how it is that one may call a philosophical theory such as *A proposition is a sentence*, certainly false, and yet feel that to leave one's criticism at that is to attend to the letter and not the spirit of the theory criticized.

The nature of the philosopher's intention explains also how it is that one cannot say of a philosopher's theory that it is false when he introduces it in his own terminology, while yet one often feels that such theories are somehow philosophically bad. Thus (W) suppose the word 'sense-datum' has never been used before and that someone says 'When Jones sees a rabbit, has an illusion of a rabbit, has an hallucination of a rabbit, dreams of a rabbit, he has a sense-datum of a rabbit'. One cannot protest that this is false, since no statement has been made, only a recommendation. But the recommendation purports to be enlightening and one may well protest if it is, on the contrary, misleading. This particular recommendation is liable to suggest that sense-data are a special sort of thing, *extremely* thin coloured pictures, and thus liable to raise puzzles, such as 'How are sense-data related to material things?' We can abuse a philosopher as much as we like if we use the right adjectives. *Good is an ultimate predicate* is useless, *A proposition is a subsistent entity* is useless and pretentious,[3] *We can never know the real cause of our sensations* is misleading. And we can praise him although he speaks falsely or even nonsensically. People have considered whether it is true that 'an event is a pattern of complete, particular, specific facts and a complete, particular, specific fact is an infinitely thin slice out of an event'.[4]

You may say 'How absurd of them since the statement is nonsense'. Certainly

[3] Neither of these theories is entirely useless. They are for one thing good antitheses to the naturalistic error.

[4] *Problems of Mind and Matter*, p. 32.

the statement is nonsense and so, if you like, it was absurd of them. But it was better than saying it was nonsense and ignoring it. Suppose I say 'The thoroughbred is a neurotic woman on four legs'. This is nonsense, but it is not negligible.[5]

5. *Provocation and Pacification.* So far, however, little or nothing has been said to explain what sort of things makes a philosophical statement misleading and what makes it illuminating. Only a short answer is possible here.

In the first place there is the misleading feature which nearly all philosophical statements have — a non-verbal air. The philosopher *laments* that we can never really know what is going on in someone else's mind, that we can never really know the causes of our sensations, that inductive conclusions are never really justified. He laments these things as if he can dream of another world where we can see our friends and tables face to face, where scientists can justify their conclusions and terriers can catch hares. This enormous source of confusion we cannot study now.

Secondly philosophical statements mislead when by the use of like expressions for different cases, they suggest likenesses which do not exist, and by the use of different expressions for like cases, they conceal likenesses which do exist.

Philosophical theories are illuminating in a corresponding way, namely when they suggest or draw attention to a terminology which reveals likenesses and differences concealed by ordinary language.

I want to stress the philosophical usefulness of metaphysical surprises such as 'We can never really know the causes of our sensations', 'We can never know the real causes of our sensations', 'Inductive conclusions are never really justified', 'The laws of mathematics are really rules of

grammar'. I believe that too much fun has been made of philosophers who say this kind of thing. Remember what Moore said about 1924 — words to this effect: When a philosopher says that really something is so we are warned that what he says is really so is not so really. With horrible ingenuity Moore can rapidly reduce any metaphysical theory to a ridiculous story. For he is right, they are false — only there *is* good in them, poor things. This shall be explained.

Wittgenstein allows importance to these theories. They are for him expressions of deep-seated puzzlement. It is an important part of the treatment of a puzzle to develop it to the full.

But this is not enough. Wittgenstein allows that the theories are philosophically important not merely as specimens of the whoppers philosophers can tell. But he too much represents them as merely symptoms of linguistic confusion. I wish to represent them as also symptoms of linguistic penetration.

Wittgenstein gives the impression that philosophical remarks either express puzzlement or if not are remarks such as Wittgenstein himself makes with a view to curing puzzlement.

This naturally gives rise to the question 'If the proper business of philosophy is the removal of puzzlement, would it not be best done by giving a drug to the patient which made him entirely forget the statements puzzling him or at least lose his uneasy feelings?'

This of course will never do. And what we say about the philosopher's purposes must be changed so that it shall no longer seem to lead to such an absurd idea.

The philosopher's purpose is to gain a grasp of the relations between different categories of being, between expressions used in *different manners*.[6] He is confused about what he wants and he is confused by

---

[5] The matter can be put in terms of truth and falsehood. A philosophical theory involves an explicit claim, an equation, and an implicit claim that the equation is not misleading and is illuminating. The explicit claim may be false and the implicit true on one or both counts, or vice versa.

[6] See 'different level' in *Proceedings of the Aristotelian Society*, Supplementary Volume XIII, p. 66.

the relations between the expressions, so he is very often puzzled. But only such treatment of the puzzles as increases a grasp of the relations between different categories of being is philosophical. And not all the philosopher's statements are either complaints of puzzlement or pacificatory. Philosophers who say 'We never know the real causes of our sensations', 'Only my sensations are real', often bring out these 'theories' with an air of triumph (with a misleading air of empirical discovery indeed). True the things they say are symptoms of confusion even if they are not of puzzlement. But they are also symptoms of penetration, of noticing what is not usually noticed. Philosophical progress has two aspects, provocation and pacification.

6. *Example of the pointless doubts: (a) how misleading they are.* Let us consider this with examples. Take first the philosopher who says to the plain man: 'We do not really know that there is cheese on the table; for might not all the sense evidence suggest this and yet there be no cheese — remember what happened at Madame Tussaud's'.

Our assertion with confidence that there is cheese on the table or our assertion that we know that there is cheese on the table raises as last these three puzzles: (1) *the category puzzle*, which finds expression in 'We ought not to speak of a cheese (of the soul) but of bundles of sense-data'; (2) *the knowledge puzzle*, which finds expression in 'We ought not to say "I know there is cheese on the table" but "Very, very probably there is cheese on the table" '; (3) *the justification puzzle*, which finds expression in 'Empirical conclusions are not really justified'.

We cannot here speak of all these. We are considering (2) the *knowledge* or *pointless doubt* puzzle. There are a group of pointless doubt puzzles including the following: 'We don't really know that there is cheese on the table'; 'We ought to say only "It is probable that there is cheese on the table" '; 'It is improper to say "I know that there is cheese on the table" '; 'It would be well if we prefixed every remark about material things with "probably" '.

All these suggestions are misleading — they all suggest that it has been discovered that we have been over-confident about material things. They should have slightly different treatment but I have only just *realized* this multiplicity. Let us take the puzzle in the crude form 'Couldn't there be no cheese here although all the sense-evidence suggests there is?'

Wittgenstein explains that this sentence though of the verbal form we associate with doubt and though it may be uttered with the intonation, expression and gestures we associate with doubt is not *used* as a sentence expressing doubt. To utter it is to raise a pseudo-doubt. People say 'We ought not to say "There *is* cheese on the table" but "Probably there is cheese on the table" or "The sense-evidence suggests ever so strongly that there is cheese on the table." For whatever we do we never observe a cheese, we have to rely upon our senses. And we may be suffering from a joint hallucination of all the senses or a consistent dream. Remember how people are deceived at Madame Tussaud's. And we may see and touch cheesy patches, smell cheesy smells, obtain cheesy pictures from cameras and cheesy reactions from mice and yet the stuff to-morrow be soap in our mouth. And then to-morrow we shall say "Yesterday we were mistaken." So our "knowledge" to-day that there is cheese here is not real knowledge. Every one ought really to whisper "Possibly hallucinatory" after *every* sentence about material things however much he has made sure that he is right'.

What those who recommend this should notice is how not merely unusual but pointless a use of words they recommend. As language is at present used, I raise my hungry friends' hopes if I say 'There is cheese on the table', and I damp them if I add 'unless it is hallucinatory'. But this additional clause has its effect only because I do *not always* use it. If a parent adds 'be very careful' to everything he says to a child he will soon find his warnings ineffective. If I prefix every statement about material things with 'probably' this doubt-raiser will soon cease to frighten hungry friends, that is cease to function as it now does. Consequently in order to mark those differences which I now mark by saying in one case 'Probably that is cheese on the table' and in another case 'I know that is cheese on the table', I shall have to introduce a new notation, one to do the work the old did. 'To do the work the old did!' that is, to claim what I formerly claimed with 'know'!

It may now be said 'In the ordinary use of "know" we may know that that is cheese on the table, but this knowledge is not real knowledge'.

This gives the misleading idea that the philosopher has envisaged some kind of knowing which our failing faculties prevent us from attaining. Terriers cannot catch hares, men cannot really know the causes of their sensations. Nothing of the kind, however. For when we say to the philosopher 'Go on, describe this real knowledge, tell us what stamp of man you want and we will see if we can buy or breed one' then he can never tell us.

It may now be said, 'No, no, the point is this: There is some inclination to use[7] "know" strictly so that we do not know that insulin cures diabetes, that the sun will rise to-morrow, because these propositions are only probable inferences from what we have observed. There is some inclination to use "know" only when what is known is observed or is entailed by something known for certain. Now you do not know in this sense that you will not have to correct yourself to-morrow and say "I was mistaken yesterday, that was not cheese," since nothing you know for certain to-day is incompatible with this. And if you do not know but what you may

have to correct yourself to-morrow you do not know that you are right to-day'.

But what is meant by 'certain'? I should claim to know for certain that that is cheese on the table now. And as the objector rightly points out this entails that I shall not have to correct myself to-morrow. I therefore know in the strict sense that I shall not have to correct myself to-morrow.

It will be said that it is not *absolutely* certain that that is cheese on the table. But I should reply that it is.

It will be said that it is not *senseless to doubt* that that is cheese on the table, not even after the most exhaustive tests. I should reply that it is.

But, of course, by now I see what the sceptic is driving at. It is not senseless to doubt that that is cheese on the table, in the sense in which it is senseless to doubt 'I am in pain', 'I hear a buzzing' — not even after the most exhaustive tests — indeed the exhaustive tests make no difference to this. For, in this sense, it is not senseless to doubt that that is cheese on the table provided only that 'He says that that is cheese but perhaps he is mistaken' has a use in English. You see, 'He says he is in pain, but perhaps he is mistaken' has no use in English. Hence we may be 'absolutely certain' that he is not mistaken[8] about his pain, in the very special sense that 'He is mistaken' makes no sense in this connection.

Thus the sceptic's pretended doubts amount to pointing out that, unlike statements descriptive of sensations, statements about material things make sense with 'perhaps he is mistaken'. And the sceptic proposes to mark this by an extraordinary use of 'know' and 'probably'. He proposes that we should not say that we know that that is cheese on the table unless it is entailed by statements with regard to which a doubt is not merely out of the question but unintelligible, i.e. such that where S is P is one of them, then 'S is P unless I

---

[7] Another form would be: 'It is proper' as opposed to 'usual' to use 'know' so that, etc.

[8] Of course he may be *lying*.

am mistaken' raises a titter like 'I am in pain unless I am mistaken'. 'That is cheese on the table' is not such a statement and so of course it does not follow from such statements — otherwise a doubt with regard to it would be unintelligible, i.e. it would be absolutely certain in the strict, philosophic sense.

The sceptic's doubts become then a recommendation to use 'know' only with statements about sense-experience and mathematics and to prefix all other statements with 'probably'.[9]

This is very different talk and much less misleading. But still it is misleading unless accompanied by the explanation given above of the astounding certainty of statements about sense-experience. Even with the explanation the suggestion is highly dangerous, involving as it does a new and *manner*—indicating' use of the familiar words 'know' and 'probable'. Without the explanation it suggests that there is a difference in degree of certainty between statements about material things and statements about sense-data, a difference in certainty dependent upon their subject-matter, in a sense analogous to that in which we say 'I am certain about what happened in Hyde Park — I was there — but I am not certain about what happened in Spain — I was not an eye-witness'. This suggests that I know what it would be like to be an eye-witness of cheese, but am in fact unfortunately obliged to *rely upon the testimony of* my senses.

Now the difference between statements about sense-experiences and statements about material things is not at all like this. The difference is not one of subject-matter (stuff) but of a different manner of use (style). And statements about sense-experiences are certain only because it makes no sense to say that they may be

wrong.[10] Notice the connection between 'He says he is in pain but I think he is mistaken' and 'He cries "Ow!" but I think he is mistaken'. The difference between sense-statements and thing-statements cannot be adequately explained here. And consequently the full misleadingness of such a use of 'probably' as is recommended in what we may call the last form of the pseudo-doubt, cannot be adequately explained here.

But I hope I have said enough to bring out in good measure the misleadingness of saying such things as 'O dear, we can never know the causes of our sensations', and even 'It would be philosophically excellent to put "probably" before all statements about material things'.

7. *Example of the pointless doubts: (b) how importantly illuminating they are.* But though the recommended use of 'probably' would be pointless as a cautionary clause and would thus be extremely misleading, the recommendation to use it so is not pointless, is not prompted wholly by confusion, but partly by penetration. The philosopher says to the plain man 'You do not really know that that is a cheese on the table'. We have pacified those who are opposed to this statement by bringing out the sources of their reluctance to agree with it. But the philosopher must pacify everyone and we must now pacify those philosophers who are pleased with it, and complete the pacification of those who are puzzled by it, being tempted to deny it and at the same time tempted to assert it. What *is* the point behind the misleading statement 'We can never know statements about material things'? The answer has been given already by the method of forcing reformulations. But we may now approach the answer by a different route. Under what circumstances are such things usually said?

It is when after considering hallucinations, illusions, etc., one wishes to empha-

[9] Compare the tendency to use 'what ought to be done' irrevocably. People who do this lament thus: 'What one ought to do is always for the best, but unfortunately we never know what we really ought to do.' Others lament thus: 'We can know what we ought to do but unfortunately this does not always turn out for the best'.

[10] This, I realize, stands very much in need of pacifying explanation.

size (1) the likeness between such cases and cases in which there was 'something really there', and to emphasize the continuity between (a) cases in which one says 'I think that is cheese on the table', 'I believe that is a real dagger', 'Probably that is a snake, not a branch' and (b) cases in which one says 'That *is* cheese on the table', 'I found that it *was* a snake'; and to emphasize (2) the unlikeness between even so well assured a statement as 'This is my thumb' and such a statement as 'I see a pinkish patch', 'I feel a softish patch', 'I am in pain'.

It is not at all easy at first to see how in being revocable and correctable by others the most assured statement about a thing is more like the most precarious statement about another thing than it is to a statement descriptive of one's sensations. Ordinary language conceals these things because in ordinary language we speak both of some favourable material-thing-statements and of statements about our sensations, as certain, while we speak of other statements about material things as merely probable. This leads to pseudo-laments about the haunting uncertainty of even the best material-thing-statements and pseudo-congratulations upon the astounding certainty of statements about our sensations.

We are all, when our attention is drawn to those cases so often described in which it looks for all the world as if our friend is standing in the room although he is dying two thousand miles away, or in which we think we see a banana and it turns out to be a reflection in a greengrocer's mirror, we are all, in such cases, inclined to say 'Strictly we ought always to add "unless it is a queer looking stick and not a banana, or a reflection or an hallucination or an illusion" '.[11] We do not stop to consider what would happen if we did always add this. Horrified at the deceptions our senses have practised upon us

[11] Then every statement would be tautologous but *absolutely* certain!

we feel we must abuse them somehow and so we say that they never *prove* anything, that we never *know* what is based on them.

The continuity and the difference which are concealed by ordinary language would be no longer concealed but marked if we used 'probably' in the way recommended. But what an unfortunate way of obtaining this result! And in what a misleading way was the recommendation made! I do not really know that this is a thumb. The huntsman's coat is not really pink. A fox's brush is really a tail. (W).

8. *Other Examples.* Now many other examples should be given. 'What is a mathematical proposition?' 'Do inductive arguments give any probability to their conclusions?' These other puzzles should be re-created; the temptations to give the answers which have been given should be re-created. But this cannot be done in this paper. Without bringing up the puzzles and temptations the following accounts are half dead, but I offer them for what they are worth.

Take 'The laws of mathematics and logic are really rules of grammar'. With this instructive incantation people puzzle themselves to death. Is it or isn't it true? And if false what amendment will give us the truth? If not rules then what? The answer is 'They are what they are, etc. Is a donkey a sort of horse but with *very* long ears?' People are puzzled because of course it isn't true that the laws of mathematics are rules of grammar (more obvious still that they are not commands). And yet they cannot bring themselves to lose the advantages of this falsehood. For this falsehood draws attention to (1) an unlikeness and (2) a likeness concealed by ordinary language; (1) an unlikeness to the laws of hydraulics and an unlikeness in this unlikeness to the unlikeness between the laws of hydraulics and those of aeronautics; for it is an unlikeness not of subject-matter but of manner of functioning — and (2) a likeness but not an exact likeness to the functioning of rules.

Again 'Inductive arguments do not

really give any probability to their conclusions' gives the misleading idea that the scientists have been found out at last, that our confidence in our most careful research workers is entirely misplaced, their arguments being no better than those of the savage. Nothing of the kind of course. What is at the back of this lament is this: In ordinary language we speak of 'Dr. So and so's experiment with a group of 100 children whose teeth improved after six months extra calcium' as having very much increased the probability of the proposition that bad teeth are due to calcium deficiency. We also say that my having drawn 90 white balls from a bag which we know to contain 100 balls, each either white or black, has very much increased the probability of the proposition that all the balls in that bag are white. We even speak numerically in connection with empirical probability — we not only argue *a priori* and say 'There were six runners, there are now only five, we still know nothing of any of them, so it is now 4–1 against the dog from trap 1' but we also argue empirically and say 'It was 5–1 against the dog from trap 1; but I hear a rumour that each of the others has been provided with a cup of tea, and I think we may now take 4–1 against him'.

The similarity in the way we speak of these cases leads us when asked how empirical arguments give probability to their conclusions to try to assimilate them to the formal cases, balls in bags, dice, etc. But when this attempt is made it begins to appear that the investigation of nature is much less like the investigation of balls in a bag than one is at first apt to think.

At the same time is revealed the shocking continuity between the scientist's arguments by the method of difference and the savage's *post hoc ergo propter hoc*,[12] between the method of agreement and the reflexes of rats, and struck by the difference and the continuity and how they are concealed by ordinary language,

[12] See Keynes, *A Treatise on Probability*.

we provoke attention to them with 'Even the best established scientific results are nothing but specially successful superstitions'. We say this although we have made no shocking discovery of scientists faking figures, although the scientist's reasons for his belief in insulin still differ from my landlady's reasons for belief in Cure-all, in exactly the way which, in the ordinary use of language, makes us call the one belief scientifically grounded and the other a superstition. Similarly we may say, having seen a butterfly die or been told the age of an oak 'The strongest of us have really only a short time to live'. We say this although we have made no discovery of impending disaster, or we may say 'Man is nothing but a complicated parasite' when we watch the arrival of the 9.5 at the Metropolis.

CONCLUSION

The plain man has come to expect of philosophers paradoxical, provoking statements such as 'We can never really know the causes of our sensations', 'Causation is really nothing more than regular sequence', 'Inductive conclusions are really nothing but lucky superstitions', 'The laws of logic are ultimately rules of grammar'. Philosophers know that the statements are provocative; this is why they so often put in some apologetic word such as 'really' or 'ultimately'.

These untruths persist. This is not merely because they are symptoms of an intractable disorder but because they are philosophically useful. The curious thing is that their philosophical usefulness depends upon their paradoxicalness and thus upon their falsehood. They are false because they are needed where ordinary language fails, though it must not be supposed that they are or should be in some perfect language. They are in a language not free from the same sort of defects as those from the effects of which they are designed to free us.

To invent a special word to describe the

status of, for example, mathematical propositions would do no good. There is a phrase already, 'necessary yet synthetic'. It is, of course, perfectly true that mathematical propositions are 'necessary synthetics' — it should be true since the expression was made to measure. True but no good. We are as much inclined to ask 'What are necessary synthetic propositions?' as we were to ask 'What are mathematical propositions?' 'What is an instinct?' An innate disposition certainly. But philosophically that answer is useless. No — what is wanted is some device for bringing out the relations between the manner in which mathematical (or dispositional) sentences are used and the manners in which others are used — so as to give their place on the language map. This cannot be done with a plain answer, a single statement. We may try opposite falsehoods or we may say, 'Be careful that this expression "mathematical proposition" does not suggest certain analogies at the expense of others. Do not let it make you think that the difference between mathematical propositions and others is like that between the propositions of hydraulics and those of aeronautics. Do notice how like to rules, etc., and yet, etc'.

If you will excuse a suspicion of smartness: Philosophers should be continually trying to say what cannot be said.

Editor's note: For Wisdom's later views on the nature and method of philosophy, see the various items listed in the bibliography, especially the essays included in Wisdom [8].

7

NORMAN MALCOLM

MOORE AND ORDINARY LANGUAGE

I

In this paper I am going to talk about an important feature of Professor Moore's philosophical method, namely, his way of refuting a certain type of philosophical proposition.

I shall begin by giving a list of propositions all of which have been maintained or are now maintained by various philosophers. Every one of these statements would, I am sure, be rejected by Moore as false. Furthermore, if with regard to each of these statements, he were asked to give a *reason* for rejecting that statement, or were asked to *prove* it to be false, he would give a *reason* or *proof* which would be strikingly similar in the case of each statement. I want to examine the general character of this common method of proof in order to show the point and the justification of it. I think that showing the point and the justification of Moore's method of attacking this type of philosophical statement will throw great light on the nature of philosophy, and also explain Moore's importance in the history of philosophy.

Reprinted from *The Philosophy of G. E. Moore*, Volume IV of *The Library of Living Philosophers*, ed. Paul A. Schilpp (Evanston and Chicago: Northwestern University, 1942), pp. 345–68, by permission of the author and the editor. (Copyright 1942 by *The Library of Living Philosophers*.)

The following is my list of philosophical statements:

(1) There are no material things.

(2) Time is unreal.

(3) Space is unreal.

(4) No one ever perceives a material thing.

(5) No material thing exists unperceived.

(6) All that one ever sees when he looks at a thing is part of his own brain.

(7) There are no other minds — my sensations are the only sensations that exist.

(8) We do not know for *certain* that there are any other minds.

(9) We do not know for *certain* that the world was not created five minutes ago.

(10) We do not know for *certain* the truth of any statement about material things.

(11) All empirical statements are hypotheses.

(12) *A priori* statements are rules of grammar.

Let us now consider Moore's way of attacking these statements. With regard to each of them I am going to state the sort of argument against it which I think Moore would give, or at least which he would approve.

(1) Philosopher: "There are no material things."

Moore: "You are certainly wrong, for

here's one hand and here's another; and so there are at least two material things." [1]

(2) Philosopher: "Time is unreal."

Moore: "If you mean that no event ever follows or precedes another event, you are certainly wrong; for *after* lunch I went for a walk, and after that I took a bath, and after that I had tea." [2]

(3) Philosopher: "Space is unreal."

Moore: "If you mean that nothing is ever to the right of, or to the left of, or behind, or above anything else, then you are certainly wrong; for this inkwell is to the left of this pen, and my head is above them both."

(4) Philosopher: "No one ever perceives a material thing." [3]

Moore: "If by 'perceive' you mean 'hear', 'see', 'feel', etc., then nothing could be more false; for I now both see and feel this piece of chalk."

(5) Philosopher: "No material thing exists unperceived."

Moore: "What you say is absurd, for no one perceived my bedroom while I was asleep last night and yet it certainly did not cease to exist."

(6) Philosopher: "All that one ever sees when one looks at a thing is part of one's own brain." [4]

Moore: "This desk which both of us now see is most certainly not part of my brain, and, in fact, I have never seen a part of my own brain."

(7) Philosopher: "How would you prove that the statement that your own sensations, feelings, experiences are the only ones that exist, is false?"

Moore: "In this way: I know that *you*

now see me and hear me, and furthermore I know that my wife has a toothache, and therefore it follows that sensations, feelings, experiences other than my own exist."

(8) Philosopher: "You do not know for *certain* that there are any feelings or experiences other than your own."

Moore: "On the contrary, I know it to be *absolutely* certain that you now see me and hear what I say, and it is absolutely certain that my wife has a toothache. Therefore, I do know it to be absolutely certain that there exist feelings and experiences other than my own."

(9) Philosopher: "We do not know for certain that the world was not created five minutes ago, complete with fossils." [5]

Moore: "I know for certain that I and many other people have lived for many years, and that many other people lived many years before us; and it would be absurd to deny it."

(10) Philosopher: "We do not know for certain the truth of any statement about material things."

Moore: "Both of us know for *certain* that there are several chairs in this room, and how absurd it would be to suggest that we do not know it, but only believe it, and that perhaps it is not the case!"

(11) Philosopher: "All empirical statements are really hypotheses."

Moore: "The statement that I had breakfast an hour ago is certainly an empirical statement, and it would be ridiculous to call it an hypothesis."

(12) Philosopher: "*A priori* statements are really rules of grammar."

Moore: "That 6 times 9 equals 54 is an *a priori* statement, but it is most certainly wrong to call it a rule of grammar."

It is important to notice that a feature which is common to all of the philosophical statements in our list is that they are *paradoxical*. That is, they are one and all statements which a philosophically un-

---

[1] See Moore's "Proof of an External World," *Proceedings of the British Academy*, XXV (1939).

[2] See Moore's "The Conception of Reality," *Philosophical Studies*, 209–211.

[3] This is the philosopher who says that all we really perceive are sense-data, and that sense-data are not material things, nor parts of material things.

[4] "I should say that what the physiologist sees when he looks at a brain is part of his own brain, not part of the brain he is examining." Bertrand Russell, *The Analysis of Matter* (1927), 383.

[5] Cf. B. Russell, *Philosophy* (1927), 7. This is a way of expressing the view that no statements about the *past* are known with certainty.

sophisticated person would find shocking. They go against "common sense." This fact plays an important part in the explanation of the nature of Moore's attacks upon these statements.

Let us examine the general nature of Moore's refutations. There is an inclination to say that they one and all *beg the question*. When the philosopher said that *a priori* statements are rules of grammar he meant to include the statement that 6 times 9 equals 54, among *a priori* statements. He meant to say of *it*, as well as of every other *a priori* statement, that it really is a rule of grammar. When Moore simply denies that it is a rule of grammar, he seems to beg the question. At least his reply does not seem to be a fruitful one; it does not seem to be one which ought to convince the philosopher that what he said was false.

When the philosopher says that there are no material things, is it not the case that part of what he means is that there are no hands; or, if he would allow that there are hands, part of what he means is that hands are, not material things? So that Moore's refutation, which asserts of two things that they are hands, and asserts that hands are material things, in one way or another begs the question.

And when the philosopher says that one does not know for certain that there are any sensations, feelings, experiences other than one's own, part of what he means to say is that one never knows for certain that one's wife has a toothache; and when Moore insists that he does know for certain that his wife has a toothache, he begs the question. At least it seems a poor sort of refutation; not one which ought to convince any philosopher that what he said was wrong.

I hold that what Moore says in reply to the philosophical statements in our list is in each case perfectly true; and furthermore, I wish to maintain that what he says is in each case a *good* refutation, a refutation that shows the falsity of the statement in question. To explain this is the main purpose of my paper.

The essence of Moore's technique of refuting philosophical statements consists in pointing out that these statements *go against ordinary language*. We need to consider, first, in what way these statements do go against ordinary language; and, second, how does it refute a philosophical statement to show that it goes against ordinary language?

When Russell said that what the physiologist sees when he looks at a brain is part of his own brain, not part of the brain he is examining, he was of course not referring to any particular physiologist, but to all physiologists, and not only to all physiologists, but to every person whomsoever. What he meant to imply was that whenever in the past a person has said that he sees a tree or a rock or a piece of cheese on the table, what he has said was really false; and that whenever in the future any person will say that he sees a house or a car or a rabbit, what he will say really will be false. All that will ever really be true *in any case whatever* in which a person says that he sees something, will be that he sees a part of his own brain.

Russell's statement is a most startling one. Nothing could be more paradoxical! And what sort of a statement is it? Did Russell mean to imply that whenever in the past any physiologist has thought that he was seeing someone else's brain he has been *deceived*? Suppose that, unknown to the physiologist, a section of his cranium had been removed and furthermore there was, also unknown to him, an ingenious arrangement of mirrors, such that when he tried to look at a brain in front of him, what he actually saw was a part of his own brain in his own skull. Did Russell mean to say that this is the sort of thing which has always happened in the past when a physiologist has tried to examine a brain, and which will always happen in the future? If he were making this straightforward empirical statement, then it is clear that he would have no evidence whatever for it. It is not the sort of empirical statement that an intelligent man would make.

No, Russell was not making an empirical statement. In the normal sort of circumstances in which a person would ordinarily say that he sees the postman, Russell would agree with him as to what the particular circumstances of the situation were. Russell would not disagree with him about any question of empirical fact; yet Russell would still say that what he really saw was not the postman, but part of his own brain. It appears then that they disagree, not about any empirical facts, but about what *language* shall be used to describe those facts. Russell was saying that it is really *a more correct way of speaking* to say that you see a part of your brain, than to say that you see the postman.

The philosophical statement, "All that one ever sees when one looks at a thing is part of one's brain" may be interpreted as meaning, "Whenever one looks at a thing it is really more correct language to say that one sees a part of one's brain, than to say that one sees the thing in question." And Moore's reply, "This desk which both of us see is not a part of my brain," may be interpreted as meaning, "It is correct language to say that what we are doing now is seeing a desk, and it is not correct language to say that what we are doing now is seeing parts of our brains." [6]

When the dispute is seen in this light, then it is perfectly clear that Moore is right. We can see that the philosophical statement which he is attacking is false, no matter what arguments may be advanced in favor of it. [7] The "proofs" of it may be ever

so tempting, but we are right in rejecting them as false statements without even examining them. For it is obvious to us upon the slightest reflection, that a person may wish to see the Empire State building; and that a way in which we might describe in ordinary language, what happened when he fulfilled his wish, would be by saying the words "He is now seeing the Empire State building for the first time"; and that we would never accept as a correct description of what happened, the words "He is now seeing a part of his brain." What Moore's reply reminds us of is that situations constantly occur which ordinary language allows us to describe by uttering sentences of the sort "I see my pen," "I see a cat," etc. and which it would be outrageously incorrect to describe by saying "I see a part of my brain." It is in this way that Moore's reply constitutes a refutation of the philosophical statement.

Let us consider the philosophical statement "We do not know for *certain* the truth of any statement about material things," and Moore's typical sort of reply, "Both of us know for *certain* that there are several chairs in this room, and how absurd it would be to suggest that we do not know it, but only believe it, and that perhaps it is not the case — how absurd it would be to say that it is highly probable, but not certain!" The view that we do not know for certain the truth of any statement about material things, and the wider view that we do not know for certain the truth of *any* empirical statement, are very popular views among philosophers. [8] Let us notice

---

[6] It must not be assumed that Professor Moore would agree with my interpretation of the nature of the philosophical paradoxes, nor with my interpretation of the nature of his refutations of those paradoxes. That Moore does employ such refutations anyone knows, who is familiar with his language and discussions. But this paper's analysis of the philosophical paradoxes and of Moore's refutations is not one that Moore has ever suggested.

[7] What led Russell to make the statement was

his being led to the view (1) that what we really see are "percepts"; and (2) that each person's "percepts" are located in that person's brain. Neither of these statements expresses an empirical proposition.

[8] E.g., ". . . all empirical knowledge is probable only." C. I. Lewis, *Mind and the World-Order* (1929), 309.

"We have . . . found reason to doubt external perception, in the full-blooded sense in which common-sense accepts it." Bertrand Russell, *Philosophy* (1927), 10.

". . . we can never be completely certain that any given proposition is true. . . ." Russell, *An Inquiry into Meaning and Truth* (1940), 166.

how sweeping and how paradoxical is the philosopher's statement that we never know for certain any statement about material things is true.

In ordinary life everyone of us has known of particular cases in which a person has said that he knew for certain that some material-thing statement was true, but that it has turned out that he was mistaken. Someone may have said, for example, that he knew for certain by the smell that it was carrots that were cooking on the stove. But you had just previously lifted the cover and seen that it was turnips, not carrots. You are able to say, *on empirical grounds*, that *in this particular case* when the person said that he knew for certain that a material-thing statement was true, he was mistaken. Or you might have known that it was wrong of him to say that he knew for certain it was carrots, not because you had lifted the cover and seen the turnips, but because you knew from past experience that cooking carrots smell like cooking turnips, and so knew that he was not entitled to conclude from the smell alone that it was *certain* that it was carrots. It is an empirical fact that *sometimes* when people use statements of the form: "I know for certain that p," where p is a material-thing statement, what they say is false.

But when the philosopher asserts that we never know for certain *any* material-thing statements, he is not asserting this empirical fact. He is asserting that *always* in the past when a person has said "I know for certain that p," where p is a material-thing statement, he has said something false. And he is asserting that *always* in the future when any person says a thing of that sort his statement will be false. The philosopher says that this is the case no matter what material-thing statement is referred to, no matter what the particular circumstances of the case, no matter what

evidence the person has in his possession! If the philosopher's statement were an empirical statement, we can see how absurdly unreasonable it would be of him to make it — far more unreasonable than it would be of a man, who knew nothing about elephants, to say that an elephant never drinks more than a gallon of water a day.

The philosopher does not commit *that* sort of absurdity, because his statement is not an empirical one. The reason he can be so cocksure, and not on empirical grounds, that it never has been and never will be right for any person to say "I know for certain that p," where p is a material-thing statement, is that he regards that *form of speech* as *improper*. He regards it as improper in just the same way that the sentence "I see something which is totally invisible," is improper. He regards it as improper in the sense in which every self-contradictory expression is improper. Just as it would never be proper for you to describe *any* experience of yours by saying "I see something which is totally invisible," so the philosopher thinks that it would never be proper for you to describe any state of affairs by saying "I know for certain that p," where p is a material-thing statement.

Among the philosophers who maintain that no material-thing statement can be certain, Mr. Ayer is one who realizes that when he makes this statement he is not making an empirical judgment, but is condemning a certain form of expression as improper. He says,

We do indeed verify many such propositions [i.e., propositions which imply the existence of material things] to an extent that makes it highly probable that they are true; but since the series of relevant tests, being infinite, can never be exhausted, this probability can never amount to logical certainty. . . .

It must be admitted then that there is a sense in which it is true to say that we can never be sure, with regard to any proposition implying the existence of a material thing, that we are not somehow being deceived; but at the same time one may object to this statement on the ground that it is misleading. It

---

". . . no genuine synthetic proposition . . . can be absolutely certain." A. J. Ayer, *Language, Truth, and Logic* (1936), 127.

". . . statements about material things are not conclusively verifiable." Ayer, *The Foundations of Empirical Knowledge* (1940), 239.

is misleading because it suggests that the state of 'being sure' is one the attainment of which is conceivable, but unfortunately not within our power. *But, in fact, the conception of such a state is self-contradictory.* For in order to be sure, in this sense, that we were not being deceived, we should have to have completed an infinite series of verifications; and it is an analytic proposition that one cannot run through all the members of an infinite series. . . . Accordingly, what we should say, if we wish to avoid misunderstanding, is not that we can never be certain that any of the propositions in which we express our perceptual judgments are true, but rather that *the notion of certainty does not apply to propositions of this kind.* It applies to the *a priori* propositions of logic and mathematics, and the fact that it does apply to them is an essential mark of distinction between them and empirical propositions.[9]

The reason, then, that Ayer is so confident that it never has been and never will be right for anyone to say of a material-thing statement that he knows it for certain, is that he thinks it is self-contradictory to say that a material-thing statement is known for certain. He thinks that the phrase "known for certain" is properly applied only to *a priori* statements, and not to empirical statements. The philosophical statement "We do not know for certain the truth of any material-thing statement," is a misleading way of expressing the proposition. "The phrase 'known for certain' is not properly applied to material-thing statements." Now Moore's reply, "Both of us know for certain that there are several chairs in this room, and how absurd it would be to suggest that we do not know it, but only believe it, or that it is highly probable but not really certain!" is a misleading way of saying "It is a proper way of speaking to say that we know for certain that there are several chairs in this room, and it would be an improper way of speaking to say that we only believe it, or that it is only highly probable!" Both the philo-

[9] A. J. Ayer, *The Foundations of Empirical Knowledge*, 44–45. My italics.

sophical statement and Moore's reply to it are disguised linguistic statements.

In this as in all the other cases Moore is right. What his reply does is to give us a *paradigm* of absolute certainty, just as in the case previously discussed his reply gave us a paradigm of seeing something not a part of one's brain. What his reply does is to appeal to our language-sense; to make us feel how queer and wrong it would be to say, when we sat in a room seeing and touching chairs, that we *believed* there were chairs but did not know it for certain, or that it was only highly probable that there were chairs. Just as in the previous case his reply made us feel how perfectly proper it is in certain cases to say that one sees a desk or a pen, and how grossly improper it would be in such cases to say that one sees a part of one's brain. Moore's reply reminds us of the fact that if a child who was learning the language were to say, in a situation where we were sitting in a room with chairs about, that it was "highly probable" that there were chairs there, we should smile, *and correct his language.* It reminds us of such facts as this: that if we were driving at a rapid speed past some plants in a cultivated field, it might be proper to say "It's highly probable that they are tomato plants, although we can't tell for certain"; but if we had ourselves planted the seeds, hoed and watered them, and watched them grow, and finally gathered the ripe tomatoes off them, then to say the same thing would, to use John Wisdom's phrase, "raise a titter." By reminding us of how we ordinarily use the expressions "know for certain" and "highly probable," Moore's reply constitutes a refutation of the philosophical statement that we can never have certain knowledge of material-thing statements. It reminds us that there *is* an ordinary use of the phrase "know for certain" in which it is applied to empirical statements; and so shows us that Ayer is wrong when he says that "The notion of certainty does not apply to propositions of this kind."

Indeed the notion of *logical* certainty

does not apply to empirical statements. The mark of a logically certain proposition, i.e., an *a priori* proposition, is that the negative of it is self-contradictory. Any proposition which has this character we do not *call* an empirical statement. One of the main sources of the philosophical statement, "We can't ever know for certain the truth of any empirical statement," has been the desire to point out that empirical statements do not have logical certainty. But this truism has been expressed in a false way. The truth is, not that the phrase "I know for certain" has no proper application to empirical statements, but that the sense which it has in its application to empirical statements is *different* from the sense which it has in its application to *a priori* statements. Moore's refutation consists simply in pointing out that it has *an* application to empirical statements.

II

It may be objected: "Ordinary men are ignorant, misinformed, and therefore frequently mistaken. Ordinary language is the language of ordinary men. You talk as if the fact that a certain phrase is used in ordinary language implies that, when people use that phrase, what they say is *true*. You talk as if the fact that people *say* 'I know for certain that p', where p is a material-thing statement, implies that they *do* know for certain. But this is ridiculous! At one time everyone said that the earth was flat, when it was actually round. Everyone was mistaken; and there is no reason why in these philosophical cases the philosophers should not be right and everyone else wrong."

In order to answer this objection, we need to consider that there are two ways in which a person may be wrong when he makes an empirical statement. First, he may be making a mistake as to what the empirical facts are. Second, he may know all right what the empirical facts are, but may use the wrong language to describe those facts. We might call the first "being

mistaken about the facts," and the second "using incorrect language" or "using improper language" or "using wrong language."

It is true that at one time everyone said that the earth was flat, and what everyone said was wrong. Everyone believed that if you got into a ship and sailed west you would finally come to the edge and fall off. They did not believe that if you kept on sailing west you would come back to where you started from. When they said that the earth was flat, they were wrong. The way in which their statement was wrong was that they were making a mistake about the facts, not that they were using incorrect language; they were using perfectly correct language to describe what they thought to be the case. In the sense in which they said what was wrong, it is perfectly possible for *everyone* to say what is wrong.

Now suppose a case where two people agree as to what the empirical facts are, and yet disagree in their statements. For example, two people are looking at an animal; they have a clear, close-up view of it. Their descriptions of the animal are in perfect agreement. Yet one of them says it is a fox, the other says it is a wolf. Their disagreement could be called linguistic. There is, of course, a right and a wrong with respect to linguistic disagreements. One or the other, or both of them, is using incorrect language.

Now suppose that there were a case like the one preceding with this exception: that the one who says it is a wolf, not only agrees with the other man as to what the characteristics of the animal are, but furthermore *agrees that that sort of animal is ordinarily called a fox*. If he were to continue to insist that it is a wolf, we can see how absurd would be his position. He would be saying that, although the other man was using an expression to describe a certain situation which was the expression ordinarily employed to describe that sort of situation, nevertheless the other man was using incorrect language. What makes his statement absurd is that ordinary language *is* correct language.

The authors of the philosophical paradoxes commit this very absurdity, though in a subtle and disguised way. When the philosopher says that we never really perceive material things, since all that we really perceive are sense-data and sense-data are not material things nor parts of material things, he does not disagree with the ordinary man about any question of empirical fact. Compare his case with the case of two men who are proceeding along a road. One of them says that he sees trees in the distance; the other says that it is not true that he sees trees — that it is really a mirage he sees. Now this is a genuine dispute as to what the facts are, and this dispute could be settled by their going further along the road, to the place where the trees are thought to be.

But the philosopher who says that the ordinary person is mistaken when he says that he sees the cat in a tree, does not mean that he sees a squirrel rather than a cat; does not mean that it is a mirage; does not mean that it is an hallucination. He will agree that the facts of the situation are what we should ordinarily describe by the expression "seeing a cat in a tree." Nevertheless, he says that the man does not *really* see a cat; he sees only some sense-data of a cat. Now if it gives the philosopher pleasure always to substitute the expression "I see some sense-data of my wife," for the expression "I see my wife," etc., then he is at liberty thus to express himself, *providing* he warns people beforehand so that they will understand him. But when he says that the man does not *really* see a cat, he commits a great absurdity; for he implies that a person can use an expression to describe a certain state of affairs, which is the expression ordinarily used to describe just such a state of affairs, and yet be using incorrect language.

One thing which has led philosophers to attack ordinary language, has been their supposing that certain expressions of ordinary language are self-contradictory.[10] Some philosophers have thought that any assertion of the existence of a material thing, e.g., "There's a chair in the corner," is self-contradictory. Some have thought that any assertion of the perception of a material thing, e.g., "I see a fly on the ceiling," is self-contradictory. Some have thought that any assertion of the existence of an unperceived material thing, e.g., "The house burned down, when no one was around," is self-contradictory. Some have seemed to think that statements describing spatial relations, e.g., "The stove is to the left of the icebox," are self-contradictory.

Some have seemed to think that statements describing temporal relations, e.g., "Charles came later than the others, but before the doors were closed," are self-contradictory. Some philosophers think that it is self-contradictory to assert that an empirical statement is known for certain, e.g., "I know for certain that the tank is half-full."

The assumption underlying all of these theories is that an ordinary expression *can* be self-contradictory. This assumption seems to me to be false. By an "ordinary expression" I mean an expression which has an ordinary use, i.e., which is ordinarily used to describe a certain sort of situation. By this I do not mean that the expression need be one which is frequently used. It need only be an expression which *would* be used to describe situations of a certain sort, if situations of that sort were to exist, or were believed to exist. To be an ordinary expression it must have a commonly accepted *use*; it need not be the case that it is ever *used*. All of the above statements, which various philosophers have thought were self-contradictory, are ordinary expressions in this sense.

---

[10] I think that this is really behind *all* attacks upon ordinary language. For how could a philosopher hold, on non-empirical grounds, that the using of a certain expression will *always* produce a false statement, unless he held that the expression is self-contradictory?

The reason that no ordinary expression is self-contradictory, is that a self-contradictory expression is an expression which would *never* be used to describe *any* sort of situation. It does not have a descriptive usage. An ordinary expression is an expression which would be used to describe a certain sort of situation; and since it would be used to describe a certain sort of situation, it *does* describe that sort of situation. A self-contradictory expression, on the contrary, describes nothing. It is possible, of course, to *construct* out of ordinary expressions an expression which is self-contradictory. But the expression so constructed is not itself an ordinary expression — i.e., not an expression which has a descriptive use.

The proposition that no ordinary expression is self-contradictory is a tautology, but perhaps an illuminating one. We do not *call* an expression which has a descriptive use a self-contradictory expression. For example, the expression "It is and it isn't" looks like a self-contradictory expression. But it has a descriptive use. If, for example, a very light mist is falling — so light that it would not be quite correct to say that it was *raining*, yet heavy enough to make it not quite correct to say that it was *not* raining — and someone, asking for information, asked whether it was raining, we might reply "Well, it is and it isn't." We should not say that the phrase, used in this connection, is self-contradictory.

The point is that, even if an expression has the appearance of being self-contradictory, we do not *call* it self-contradictory, providing it has a use. Nor do we say of *any* expression which is used to describe or refer to a certain state of affairs that *in that use* it is self-contradictory. It follows that no ordinary expression is, in any ordinary use of that expression, self-contradictory. Whenever a philosopher claims that an ordinary expression is self-contradictory, he has misinterpreted the meaning of that ordinary expression.

A philosophical paradox asserts that, whenever a person uses a certain expression, what he says is false. This could be either because the sort of situation described by the expression never does, *in fact*, occur; or because the expression is self-contradictory. Now the point of replying to the philosophical statement, by showing that the expression in question does have a descriptive use in ordinary language, is to prove, first, that the expression is not self-contradictory; and, second, that therefore the only ground for maintaining that when people use the expression what they say is always false, will have to be the claim, that *on the basis of empirical evidence* it is known that the sort of situation described by the expression never has occurred and never will occur. But it is abundantly clear that the philosopher offers no empirical evidence for his paradox.

The objection set down at the beginning of this section contains the claim that it does not follow from the fact that a certain expression is used in ordinary language that, on any occasion when people use that expression, what they say is true. It does not follow for example, from the fact that the expression "to the left of" is an ordinary expression, that anything ever *is* to the left of another thing. It does not follow from the fact that the expression "it is certain that" is an ordinary expression applied to empirical statements, that any empirical statements ever *are* certain. Let us, next, consider this question.

The expression "There's a ghost" has a descriptive use. It is, in my sense of the phrase, an ordinary expression; and it does not follow from the fact that it is an ordinary expression that there ever have been any ghosts. But it is important to note that people can learn the meaning of the word "ghost" without actually seeing any ghosts. That is, the meaning of the word "ghost" can be explained to them in terms of the meanings of words which they already know. It seems to me that there is an enormous difference in this respect between the learning of the word "ghost" and the learning of expressions like "earlier," "later," "to the left of," "behind," "above," "material things," "it is possible that," "it is certain that." The difference is that, whereas you can teach a person the meaning of the word "ghost" without showing him an instance of the true application of that word, you cannot teach a person the meaning of these other expressions without showing him instances of the true application of those expressions. People could not have learned the meaning of the expressions "to the left of," or "above," unless they had actually been shown instances of one thing being to the left of another, and one thing being above another. In short, they could not have learned the meanings of expressions which describe spatial relations without having been acquainted with some instances of spatial relations. Likewise, people could not have learned the use of expressions describing temporal relations, like "earlier" and "later," unless they had been shown examples of things standing in these temporal relations. Nor could people have learned the difference between "seeing a material thing," and "seeing an after-image" or "having an hallucination," unless they had actually been acquainted with cases of seeing a material thing. And people could not have learned the meaning of "it is probable that," as applied to empirical statements, and of "it is certain that," as applied to empirical statements, unless they had been shown cases of empirical probability and cases of empirical certainty, and had seen the difference or differences between them.

In the case of all expressions the meanings of which must be *shown* and cannot be explained, as can the meaning of "ghost," it follows, from the fact that they are ordinary expressions in the language, that there have been *many* situations of the kind which they describe; otherwise so many people could not have learned the correct use of those expressions. Whenever a philosophical paradox asserts, therefore, with regard to such an expression,

that always when that expression is used the use of it produces a false statement, then to prove that the expression is an *ordinary* expression is completely to refute the paradox.

III

An empirical statement can be paradoxical and not be false. A philosophical statement cannot be paradoxical and not be false. This is because they are paradoxical in totally different ways. If an empirical statement is paradoxical, that is because it asserts the existence of empirical facts which everyone or almost everyone believed to be incompatible with the existence of other well-established empirical facts. But if a philosophical statement is paradoxical, that is because it asserts the impropriety of an ordinary form of speech. It is possible for everyone to be mistaken about certain matters of empirical fact. That is why an empirical statement can be paradoxical and yet true. But it is not possible for an ordinary form of speech to be improper. That is to say, ordinary language is correct language.

When a philosopher says, for example, that all empirical statements are hypotheses,[11] or that *a priori* statements are really rules of grammar,[12] Moore at once attacks. He attacks because he is sensitive to the violations of ordinary language which are implicit in such statements. " '49 minus 22 equals 27' *a rule of grammar*? 'Napoleon was defeated at Waterloo' an *hypothesis*? What an absurd way of talking!" Moore's attacks bring home to us that our ordinary use of the expressions "rule of grammar" and "hypothesis" is very different from that suggested by the philosophical statements. If a child learning the language were to call "49 minus 22 equals 27" a *rule of grammar*, or "Napoleon was defeated at

[11] "Empirical statements are one and all hypotheses. . . ." Ayer, *Language, Truth and Logic*, 132.
[12] I do not know that *exactly* this statement has ever been made in print, but it has been made in discussions in Cambridge, England.

Waterloo" an *hypothesis*, we should *correct* him. We should say that such language is not a proper way of speaking.

The reason that the philosopher makes his paradoxical statement that all empirical propositions are hypotheses, is that he is impressed by and wishes to emphasize a certain similarity between the empirical statements which we should ordinarily call hypotheses and the empirical statements which we should ordinarily call, not hypotheses but absolutely certain truths. The similarity between the empirical proposition the truth of which we say is not perfectly established, but which we will assume in order to use it as a working hypothesis, and the empirical proposition the truth of which we say is absolutely certain, is that neither of them possesses *logical* certainty. That is, neither of them has a self-contradictory negative. The falsehood of the absolutely certain empirical proposition, as well as of the hypothesis, is a logical possibility. The philosopher, wishing to emphasize this similarity, does so by saying that all empirical statements are really hypotheses. Likewise, one of the main sources of the paradoxical statement that no empirical statements ever have absolute certainty but at most high probability, lies, as we have said, in the desire to stress this same similarity. This linguistic device of speaking paradoxically, which the philosopher adopts in order to stress a similarity, does of course ignore the *dis*-similarities. It ignores the dissimilarities, which *justify* the distinction made in ordinary language, between absolutely certain empirical propositions and empirical propositions which are only hypotheses or have only high probability.

Let us consider another example of the philosophical procedure of employing a paradox in order to emphasize a similarity or a difference. Philosophers have sometimes made the statement "All words are vague." It is the desire to emphasize a similarity between words with vague meanings and words with clear meanings which has tempted the philosophers to utter this paradox. The meaning of a word is vague, if it is the case that in a large number of situations where the question is raised as to whether the word applies or not, people who know the use of the word and who know all the facts of the situations are undecided as to whether the word does apply or not, or disagree among themselves without being able to come to any consensus of opinion. Let us call such situations "undecidable cases." A word is vague, then, if with regard to the question of its application there is a *large* number of undecidable cases. But even with respect to the words which we should ordinarily say have clear meanings, it is possible to produce undecidable cases. The only difference between the clear words and the vague ones is that with respect to the former the number of undecidable cases is relatively smaller. But then, says the philosopher, the difference between a large number of undecidable cases and a small number is only a difference of *degree*! He is, therefore, tempted to say that *all* words are really vague. But, we might ask, why should not the use of the words "vague" and "clear," in ordinary language, simply serve to call attention to those differences of degree?

Similarly, a philosophizing biologist, finding it impossible to draw a sharp line separating the characteristics of inanimate things from the characteristics of animate things, may be tempted to proclaim that all matter is really animate. What he says is philosophical, paradoxical, and false. For it constitutes an offense against ordinary language, in the learning of which we learn to call things like fish and fowl animate, and things like rocks and tables inanimate.

Certain words of our language operate in pairs, e.g., "large" and "small," "animate" and "inanimate," "vague" and "clear," "certain" and "probable." In their use in ordinary language a member of a pair *requires* its opposite — for animate is *contrasted* with inanimate, probability with certainty, vagueness with clearness.

Now there are certain features about the criteria for the use of the words in these pairs which tempt philosophers to wish to remove from use one member of the pair. When the philosopher says that all words are really vague, he is proposing that we never apply the word "clear" anymore, i.e., proposing that we abolish its use.

But suppose that we did *change* our language in such a way that we made the philosophical statements true — that is, made it true that it was no longer correct to call any material thing inanimate, no longer correct to call any empirical statement certain, no longer correct to say of any word that its meaning is clear. Would this be an improvement?

It is important to see that by such a move we should have gained nothing whatever. The word in our revised language would have to do double duty. The word "vague" would have to perform the function previously performed by two words, "vague" and "clear." But it could not perform this function. For it was essential to the meaning of the word "vague," in its previous use, that vagueness was *contrasted* with clearness. In the revised language vagueness could be contrasted with nothing. The word "vague" would simply be dropped as a useless word. And we should be compelled to adopt into the revised language a new pair of words with which to express the same distinctions formerly expressed by the words "clear" and "vague." The revision of our language would have accomplished nothing.

The paradoxical statements of the philosophers are produced, we have suggested, by their desire to emphasize similarities or differences between the criteria for the use of certain words. For example, the statement that no empirical propositions are certain arises from the desire to stress the similarity between the criteria for applying the phrases "absolutely certain" and "highly probable" to empirical propositions; and also from the desire to stress the difference between the criteria for applying "certain" to empirical statements, and for applying it to *a priori* statements. The desire to stress various similarities and differences tempts the philosophers to make their paradoxes.

The reason I have talked so much about the nature of paradoxical philosophical statements and the temptations which produce them, is to throw light on Moore's rôle as a philosopher. A striking thing about Moore is that he never succumbs to such temptations. On the contrary, he takes his stand upon ordinary language and defends it against every attack, against every paradox. The philosophizing of most of the more important philosophers has consisted in their more or less subtly repudiating ordinary language. Moore's philosophizing has consisted mostly in his refuting the repudiators of ordinary language.

The rôle which Moore, the Great Refuter, has played in the history of philosophy has been mainly a destructive one. (His most important constructive theory, the theory that good is a simple indefinable quality like yellow, was itself a natural outcome of his own destructive treatment of innumerable attempts to define "good.") To realize how much of philosophy consists of attacks on ordinary language, on common sense, and to see that ordinary language must be right, is to see the importance and the justification of Moore's destructive function in philosophy.

It might be asked: "You say that the philosopher's paradox arises from his desire to stress a similarity or a difference in the criteria for the use of certain expressions. But if the similarity or the difference does really exist, and if all that his philosophical statement does is to call attention to it, why not let him have his paradox? What harm is there in it?" The answer is that if that were the whole of the matter, then there would be no harm in it. But what invariably happens is that the philosopher is misled by the form of his philosophical statement into imagining that it is an empirical statement. "There is no certainty about empirical matters" is so very much like "there is no certainty about the future of the present generation." "What one really sees when one looks at a thing is a part of one's brain" is so very like "What really happens when one sees a thing is that light rays from it strike the retina." Misled by the similarity in appearance of these two sorts of statements, and knowing that the paradoxicalness of empirical statements is no objection to their being true, the philosopher imagines that his paradox is really true — that common sense is really wrong in supposing that empirical matters are ever certain, that any words ever have clear meanings, that anything other than a part of one's brain is ever seen, that anything ever does happen later or earlier than something else, and so on.

When the philosopher supposes that his paradox is literally true, it is salutary to refute him. The fact that the authors of the paradoxes nearly always fancy themselves to be right and common sense to be wrong, and that they then need to have it proved to them that their statements are false, explains Moore's great importance in philosophy. No one can rival Moore as a refuter because no one has so keen a nose for paradoxes. Moore's extraordinarily powerful language-sense enables him to detect the most subtle violations of ordinary language.

Two things may be said against Moore's method of refutation.[13] In the first place, it often fails to convince the author of the paradox that he is wrong. If, for example, the paradox is, that no one ever knows for certain that any other person is having sensations, feelings, experiences; and Moore replies "On the contrary, I know

[13] This must be taken as qualifying my previous statement that Moore's refutations are *good* ones.

that you now see and hear me," it is likely that the man who made the paradox will not feel refuted. This is largely because Moore's reply fails to bring out the linguistic, non-empirical nature of the paradox. It sounds as if he were opposing one empirical proposition with another, contradictory, empirical proposition. His reply does not make it clear that what the paradox does is to attack an ordinary form of speech as an incorrect form of speech, *without disagreeing as to what the empirical facts are,* on *any* occasion on which that ordinary form of speech is used.

In the second place, Moore's style of refutation does not get at the sources of the philosophical troubles which produce the paradoxes. Even if it shows the philosopher that his paradox is false, it only leaves him dissatisfied. It does not explain to him what it was that made him want to attack ordinary language. And it does not remove the temptation to attack ordinary language by showing how fruitless that attack is. In short, even if Moore does succeed in making the philosopher feel refuted, he does not succeed in curing the philosophical puzzlement which caused the philosopher to make the paradox which needs to be refuted.

Although Moore's philosophical method is an incomplete method, it is the essential first step in a complete method. The way to treat a philosophical paradox is first of all to resist it, to prove it false. Because, if the philosopher is pleased with his paradox, fancies it to be true, then you can do nothing with him. It is only when he is dissatisfied with his paradox, feels refuted, that it is possible to clear up for him the philosophical problem of which his paradox is a manifestation.

However, to say that Moore's technique of refutation is the essential first step in the complete philosophical method does not adequately describe the importance of the part he has played in the history of philosophy. Moore's great historical rôle

consists in the fact that he has been perhaps the first philosopher to sense that any
philosophical statement which violates
ordinary language is false, and consistently to defend ordinary language against its
philosophical violators.[14]

[14] My present belief (1963) is that my article
gives an accurate description of Moore's reaction
to typical philosophical assertions, and also that
in most fundamental points the article is sound.
I do not like its youthfully overconfident tone,
my remarks about "paradoxical" philosophical
statements are unnecessarily paradoxical, what I
say about *certainty* is certainly unsatisfactory,
and I no longer think that Moore is to be under-

stood as presenting paradigms of perception,
knowledge, and so on. For a somewhat different
interpretation of Moore's defense of ordinary
language the reader is referred to the lecture
"George Edward Moore" in my book *Knowledge
and Certainty* (Englewood Cliffs, N.J.: Prentice-
Hall, Inc., 1963). [Note added by Professor
Malcolm in 1963.]

Editor's note: For criticisms of the views expressed in this essay (and for replies by Malcolm), see the cross-references under Malcolm
[5] in the bibliography, especially Chisholm [3]
(reprinted below at pp. 175–82), and Malcolm's
reply to Chisholm (Malcolm [7]). See also the
literature on the "argument of the paradigm
case," listed under Watkins [3], especially the
chapter from Passmore [3], reprinted below at
pp. 182–92.

PART II

Metaphilosophical Problems of Ideal-Language Philosophy

IRVING M. COPI

LANGUAGE ANALYSIS AND METAPHYSICAL INQUIRY

The traditional attitude of philosophers towards the analysis of language is that it may have some corrective value, but can make no positive contribution to philosophy. The world must be investigated in itself: an analysis of the language in which we describe it will perhaps give us greater insight into the description, but not into what is described. Many philosophers have been suspicious of language, considering it a hindrance rather than an aid in philosophical investigation. This tradition has a long history, some of whose high points we can mention briefly.

Like so many others, this view has its source in Plato, who remarked in the *Cratylus* that: ". . . . the knowledge of things is not to be derived from names. No; they must be studied and investigated in themselves."[1] This view was shared by the founder of modern philosophy. In his second Meditation, Descartes complained: ". . . words often impede me and I am almost deceived by the terms of ordinary language."[2] Empiricists as well as rationalists have held this view. In his *Essay*

Locke referred to ". . . those fallacies which we are apt to put upon ourselves by taking words for things."[3] And Berkeley, in the Introduction to his *Principles of Human Knowledge*, stated that: ". . . most parts of knowledge have been so strangely perplexed and darkened by the abuse of words, and general ways of speech wherein they are delivered, that it may almost be made a question whether language has contributed more to the hindrance or advancement of the sciences."[4]

In view of this heavy weight of tradition, it is very interesting that one of the most eminent of living philosophers should hold the contrary opinion, and maintain it almost constantly for over forty years. Bertrand Russell has departed from this tradition by asserting that a careful study of language may lead to positive philosophical conclusions. In 1903, in his *Principles of Mathematics*, he wrote that: "The study of grammar, in my opinion, is capable of throwing far more light on philosophical questions that is commonly supposed by philosophers."[5] In 1940, in his *Inquiry into Meaning and Truth*, Russell asserted that: "For my part, I believe that,

Reprinted from *Philosophy of Science*, XVI (1949), 65–70, by permission of the author and the publisher. (Copyright 1949 by The Williams and Wilkins Company, Baltimore.)
Paper read at the Meeting of the Western Division of the American Philosophical Association, at Knox College in May, 1948.
[1] *The Dialogues of Plato*, Jowett translation. Random House edition, 1937. "Cratylus," p. 439.
[2] *Descartes Selections*, edited by R. M. Eaton. Charles Scribner's Sons, 1927. "Meditations on First Philosophy," p. 104.

[3] *Essay on Human Understanding*. John Locke. Book II, Chapter XIII, §18.
[4] *Berkeley: Essay, Principles, Dialogues, etc.*, edited by M. W. Calkins. Charles Scribner's Sons. 1929. "A Treatise Concerning The Principles of Human Knowledge." p. 120 f.
[5] *Principles of Mathematics*, Bertrand Russell. Cambridge University Press, 1903. 2nd ed. Norton & Company, 1938. p. 42.

partly by means of the study of syntax, we can arrive at considerable knowledge concerning the structure of the world." [6]

This faith was not constant; it wavered from time to time. In 1923 he wrote that he did *not* think that the study of the principles of symbolism would yield any positive results in metaphysics.[7] But a study of Russell's literary biography reveals that such waverings were only occasional and temporary. His faith in language analysis as a key to metaphysical knowledge has remained with Russell during the greater part of his philosophical career.

To the question, how language analysis can yield philosophical knowledge, a definite answer is given. The path by which a study of language is supposed to yield knowledge about the rest of the universe is charted by what Russell regarded as "perhaps the most fundamental thesis" of Wittgenstein's *Tractatus Logico-Philosophicus*. Wittgenstein had written that in order that a certain sentence should assert a certain fact there must, however the language may be constructed, be something in common between the structure of the sentence and the structure of the fact.[8]

The linguistic program for metaphysical inquiry may be described in these terms. Each of the facts of which the world is composed has a certain ontological structure. In order for a given sentence to assert a particular fact, the sentence must have a *logical* structure which has something in common with the *ontological* structure of the fact. Hence, on the not unreasonable presumption that sentences are easier to investigate than the facts they assert, the royal road to metaphysical knowledge consists of investigating the structures of sentences. For a study of grammar will yield us knowledge of that part of the ontological structure of the world which is common to facts, on the one hand, and sentences asserting those facts, on the other.

Russell was as aware as anyone else of the pitfalls that beset this pathway. He had even suggested a name for the mistake of too naïve an application of this principle, calling it the ". . . fallacy of verbalism . . . the fallacy that consists in mistaking the properties of words for the properties of things."[9] It is clear that not all properties of sentences are also properties of the facts asserted by the sentences. Language has many 'accidental' features: the same fact may be asserted by several sentences with widely different structures.

Recognizing the sometimes pernicious influence of language, and at the same time persuaded that language analysis can be a valuable tool in philosophical inquiry, Russell concluded that ". . . common language is not sufficiently logical. . . . We must first construct an artificial logical language before we can properly investigate our problem." [10] Wittgenstein too was concerned with this problem. He wrote that: "In order to avoid these errors of philosophy, we must employ a symbolism which excludes them, . . . A symbolism, that is to say, which obeys the rules of grammar . . . of logical syntax." [11] We have Russell's word that Wittgenstein was here: ". . . concerned with the conditions which would have to be fulfilled by a logically perfect language." [12]

In order, then, to gain metaphysical knowledge through investigating language, one must *first* construct an 'ideal' or 'logically perfect' language to investigate.

The nature of such an 'ideal' language has never been completely specified. Perhaps it could only be explained completely by giving an actual example, that is, by actually constructing such a 'logically

---

[6] *An Inquiry into Meaning and Truth*, Bertrand Russell. Norton & Company, 1940. p. 438.

[7] "Vagueness," Bertrand Russell, *Australasian Journal of Psychology and Philosophy*, I(1923), 84.

[8] *Tractatus Logico-Philosophicus*, Ludwig Wittgenstein. Introduction by Bertrand Russell. Harcourt, Brace and Company, 1922, p. 8.

[9] "Vagueness," Russell, p. 85.

[10] *Inquiry into Meaning and Truth*, Russell, p. 415.

[11] *Tractatus*, 3.325.

[12] *Tractatus*, Introduction, p. 7.

perfect' language. However, the following requirements have, from time to time, been laid down. An 'ideal' language must be neither vague nor ambiguous. Perhaps even more important is the requirement of being 'logical'. On this Russell wrote that: "A logically perfect language has rules of syntax which prevent nonsense . . ."[13] Wittgenstein pointed to the ideal of ". . . language itself preventing every logical mistake."[14] It seems to me that the notion of such an 'ideal' or 'logically perfect' language is perfectly intelligible, although it has been found otherwise by some writers.[15]

The notion of a 'logically perfect' language may be explained partially by some examples of steps in its direction. I shall describe two such steps, both designed to eliminate certain defects of 'natural' language, and both of which have been incorporated into symbolic logic.

The first of these has to do with *existence*. Perhaps the most famous example of a philosophical mistake attributable to imperfect language is the ontological argument. Of such subtlety that it took the genius of Kant to refute and explain it, that argument must, nevertheless, be attributed to defective language. The very form of the refutation reveals that fact; the crux of Kant's argument is his phrase: "*Being* is evidently not a real predicate . . ."[16]

There is certainly linguistic excuse for this mistake: certain grammatical forms of natural language treat *existence* in the same way as a predicate. For example, "Men think" and "Men exist" are sentences of the same grammatical form. The fact that they have grammatically the same appearance may lead one to assume

that they have the same logical structure. Yet making this assumption leads to the ontological paralogism, which is best refuted by denying the assumption. Thus treating *existence* in the same grammatical way as genuine or ordinary predicates is seen to be a flaw in ordinary language, which would have to be eliminated in a 'logically perfect' language. The language of logistic, while not perfect, is an improvement over ordinary language in that it has the required distinction embedded right in the symbolism itself. If we abbreviate "*x* is a man" by "m*x*" and "*x* thinks" by "t*x*," then "men think" is written

$$(x) : \mathrm{m}x \supset \mathrm{t}x$$

while "men exist" is written

$$(\mathrm{E}x) : \mathrm{m}x.$$

Here we note immediately that there is no misleading resemblance in grammatical form between the notion of *existence*, on the one hand, and ordinary properties, on the other. In logistic they are governed by different syntactical rules, and the temptation to confuse them has disappeared. In this sense, and to this extent, the language of logistic is a step in the direction of a 'logically perfect' language.

The other example has to do with the confusion in natural language of the notions of *class membership* and *class inclusion*. In the last chapter of his *Inquiry*, Russell posed this question: "Consider first a group of sentences which all contain a certain name (or synonym for it). These sentences all have something in common. Can we say that their verifiers also have something in common?"[17] Earlier "verifier" had been defined as "That occurrence in virtue of which my assertion is true (or false)."[18] More generally, the question is whether we can validly infer the structures of facts from the structures of sentences asserting those facts. In particular, given two true sentences of grammatically the same structure,

---

[13] *Ibid.*, p. 8.

[14] *Tractatus*, 5.4731.

[15] See, for example "Russell's Philosophy of Language," by Max Black, *The Philosophy of Bertrand Russell*, ed. P. A. Schilpp. Library of Living Philosophers, 1944. [Reprinted (in part) below at pp. 136–46.]

[16] *Critique of Pure Reason*, Kant. Müller translation. Macmillan Company, 1927. p. 483.

[17] *Inquiry into Meaning and Truth*, Russell, p. 431.

[18] *Ibid.*, p. 291.

can we infer that the facts which they assert have the same structure? The basic tenet of the Russell-Wittgenstein conception of language is that this question is to be answered in the affirmative — but *only* if the syntax of the language is logical. In ordinary English, the two sentences "men are rational" and "men are numerous" have exactly the same form or structure. Yet any inference from this to similarity of structure of the two facts would be invalid. Failure to recognize this permits the well-known fallacies of composition and division. The reason for this is that the English language is improperly structured here. It is not the structures of the facts, but a faulty syntax that leads to their being asserted by sentences of the same form. In English, using obvious abbreviations, we have "M is R" and "M is N." These have the same structure, and this is misleading. In the symbolism of logistic the facts are asserted by "$M \subset R$" and "$M \ \varepsilon \ N$," and *these* sentences have clearly different structures. In this sense, and to this further extent, the language of logistic is closer than English to 'logical perfection'.

The relevance of an 'ideal' language to the program for investigating metaphysics by means of investigating language is clear. If we have a 'logically perfect' language, then its structure will have something in common with the structure of the world, and by examining the one we shall come to understand the other. Thus an 'ideal' language is a sufficient tool for this technique of philosophical inquiry. But it is also a *necessary* tool, in that an imperfect language will have a misleading structure which will render unsound any inferences drawn from *its* structure to the structure of the world.

Some of the specifications for an 'ideal' or 'logically perfect' language seem to me to be objectionable. For example, ordinary languages have the relational property of *vagueness*. When this property is fully described, it may be found to involve reference to the apparent *continuity* of forms in the world (that is, the absence of 'fixed species'), and also to certain limitations of our human powers of discrimination. If such an analysis of vagueness is correct, then no language which is perfect in the sense of not being vague could be used by us in this world. It could only be used in this world by beings with perfect (superhuman) powers of discrimination; and it could only be used by us if we were transported to a world in which all species were fixed, and no border-line cases could occur.

Again, the requirement that an 'ideal' language be unambiguous is perhaps improper. This would seem to follow from the fact that *indexical symbols* (in the sense of Peirce) are essentially ambiguous, although in a systematic way, and that indexical symbols cannot be eliminated from any language that is to be adequate for expressing singular propositions.

Finally, the requirement that an 'ideal' or 'logically perfect' language must itself prevent every logical mistake seems to require that an 'ideal' language must have a *complete* and *consistent* logic embedded into its symbolism. But any effort to achieve this must necessary run afoul of the general decision problem, whose unsolvability has been demonstrated by Gödel and others.

I do not wish to develop any of these criticisms of the notion of an ideal language, but desire instead to criticize the project that seems to require it.

Even if a 'logically perfect' language could be devised, the proposed program for investigating the ontological structure of the world by means of investigating the logical structure of an 'ideal' language is impossible of fulfilment. For the project must have the following sequence: *first*, an 'ideal' language must be set up, and *then*, through it, the metaphysical structure of the world is to be discovered. On this view, the construction of a 'logically perfect' language is not an end in itself, but a *means* to the end of more general philosophical inquiry. I submit that this program cannot possibly be realized. A 'logically perfect' language cannot be utilized as a *means* to philosophical inquiry, because no language could possibly be known to be 'ideal', in the present sense, until after the completion of such a philosophical investigation. Surely no device can seriously be proposed as a *means* to an end if the end must already have been attained before the device can be acquired and recognized to be what is required. No proposal could be more circular, in the most vicious sense.

That the setting up of an 'ideal' language *does* presuppose the completion of a metaphysical inquiry of the kind indicated is shown by the following considerations.

Historically, the few steps that logicians have taken in the direction of an 'ideal' language have been achieved only on the basis of previous philosophical insight. The difference between *existence* and properties of things was not discovered by means of investigating logistic. No, logistic took its present form because Kant had already pointed out that important difference. Frege and Peano did not distinguish between class membership and class inclusion by examining a language in which both " ⊂ " and " ε " were present. No, such a language was set up because they had already perceived the distinction in question. That this sequence was necessary rather than accidental is readily shown.

The point is that an 'ideal' language is characterized only incompletely by reference to vagueness, ambiguity, and the like. The essence of an 'ideal' language, as conceived by the proponents of the program under discussion, is that its logical structure 'corresponds with' or 'mirrors' in some sense the ontological structure of fact. Hence a language can be known to be 'ideal' only by comparing its logical structure with the ontological structure of the world, which must be known independently if the comparison is to be significant.

An analogy with geometry may clarify the point. There are many geometries, Euclidean and non-Euclidean. Mathematically, one is as good as another. But physically they are of different value. If their undefined terms, such as point and line and so on are interpreted the same way, then at most one is true and the rest all false as descriptions of the real space in which we move. But this difference cannot be discovered mathematically, but only by empirical investigation of the physical world. Similarly, we may conceivably achieve alternative languages, candidates for the title of the 'ideal' language. They may — conceivably — each be completely precise (that is, not vague), and unambiguous, and consistent and complete (in the senses of these words that are important to logicians). But the question which is 'ideal' in the important sense here intended can only be answered by comparing their structures with the ontological structure of the world. It is clear that this can only be done if this metaphysical structure has already been investigated, *independently*, without using any of the candidate languages with whose logical structures it is to be compared.

I conclude, then, that Russell's program for investigating the metaphysical structure of the world by means of examining the logical structure of an 'ideal' language, must be rejected because of the circularity inherent in the program proposed. It must be concluded that the general program of inferring the structure of the world from the structure of language must be rejected, because if the language is 'ideal', there is a vicious circle involved, while if the language is *not* 'ideal', it will have misleading 'accidental' features.

· 8b ·

GUSTAV BERGMANN

TWO CRITERIA FOR AN IDEAL LANGUAGE

The lucidity of Mr. Copi's argument makes the task of the reviewer very pleasant, even if he disagrees as completely as I do with the conclusion, which is the main thesis Mr. Copi attempts to prove. Only at one minor point does his exposition not quite suit my taste. He chose to preface his argument with a string of quotations supposedly supporting the position he wishes to defend. It seems to me that with the proper historical precautions these passages allow for a very different interpretation. Yet I shall not pursue this matter, partly because I believe that Mr. Copi merely followed a literary stereotype, but mainly because the issue ought to be discussed on its merits rather than through the clouds of witnesses one could adduce on either side.

The thesis itself, as I understand it, asserts that by and large language analysis is of no philosophical significance. However, Mr. Copi shows his judiciousness by not defending his thesis, or attacking its contradictory, in this vague preliminary form. Instead, he attacks a position that may be stated as follows: *The proper way of exhibiting the structure of our world is to*

Reprinted from *Philosophy of Science*, XVI (1949), 71–74, by permission of the author and the publisher. (Copyright 1949 by The Williams and Wilkins Company, Baltimore.)

Paper read, in reply to the preceding one, at the Meeting of the Western Division of the American Philosophical Association, at Knox College in May, 1948.

construct an ideal language in which to talk about it; for the structure of such a language is, in some sense, a picture of the structure of the world. Before I retrace the strategy of Mr. Copi's attack on this position — we shall see that it proceeds along two different lines — I wish to forestall, without attributing it to him, one very crude and obvious misunderstanding. No one in his right mind will deny that as long as one studies symbolic systems as such, all one can learn from them about the world belongs to the physics of pencils and papers and to the psychology of those who play these fascinating and intricate games. But from this it does not follow that the products of the formalists are not invaluable and, perhaps, even indispensable tools of the philosopher, though his concern, as far as he is a philosopher, is admittedly not with symbols as such. The situation is, I believe, closely analogous to a very familiar one in physics. For, are there not many among us who would agree, irrespective of other differences in opinion, that the gap between pure mathematics on the one hand and theoretical physics on the other is, in one sense, unbridgeable? Yet no one denies that mathematics is an invaluable and even an indispensable tool of physics. But now for the two prongs of the attack.

The main thrust, or what I believe Mr. Copi considers to be the main thrust, is as massive as it is simple; I daresay, a little too massive and a little too simple. Its point is that the capacity of reflecting accurately the relevant features of the world is part of the definition of an ideal language. Thus, in order to know whether any given language is ideal, one must first know what these features are. To be sure, if a criterion were set up this way, those who propose it would be caught in a circularity as obvious as it is inescapable. I submit, therefore, that irrespective of what some "linguistic philosophers" may have said, the criterion of adequacy they actually use is not what Mr. Copi believes it to be. In my opinion, a language that can be spoken about the world has to fulfill two criteria to be ideal in the sense of the thesis I wish to defend. One of these criteria — the one relevant here — demands that in such a language the so-called philosophical puzzles disappear, or, as some put it, that they cannot even be stated in it. The accuracy of this particular formulation of the criterion is not the point in jeopardy. The point is that *I do know what those puzzles are* and that *I can know it before I know what the ontological structure of the world is*. In other words, the critical phrase is not 'ideal language' but, rather, 'ontological structure of the world'. What I, for one, mean by a metaphysical or ontological feature is what corresponds to certain structural features of the ideal language. Consider, for instance, that according to some the ideal language is a subject-predicate pattern. I have no doubt that this grammatical feature — which, as such, is best clarified and put into relief by the formalistic study of symbolisms that do not possess it — corresponds to that structural or, if you please, ontological feature of the world to which "nonlinguistic philosophers" refer as exemplification. But some critics feel that while language analysis *may* thus be used to guide us to a counterpart of ontology, there is no reason to believe that if we want to be safe, we *must* always talk about the reflection (e.g., the subject-predicate form) instead of talking about the thing itself (e.g., exemplification). Yet the "linguistic philosophers" make much

of this latter point. It should at least be mentioned that this claim raises a further question which, as far as I can see, has not been raised by Mr. Copi and which I shall, therefore, not discuss. I turn to another question or, rather, objection which he does raise. The answer to it, though not difficult, is very enlightening.

So far I have spoken of *the* ideal language. But just as there are several ways of axiomatizing Euclidean geometry, there could be (provided that there is any) two or more ideal languages. If two of these were to differ in structure, how are we to know which reflects the structure of the world? To clear up this apparent difficulty, I shall, like Mr. Copi, use a mathematical analogy, which, like his, is really more than a mere analogy. Whenever two formalisms stand in the relation, mediated by something each of them is about, of being both representations of this something, then there are also certain purely formal features — the sort of thing mathematicians call invariants — that characterize the two formalisms *qua* formalisms. And it is only such invariant traits of an ideal language that can be called ontological features in a strict sense; for only about them could there be nonverbal disagreement. So we see that this particular objection does not embarrass the linguistic philosopher; it merely gives him an opportunity to explain what is, mathematically speaking, a truism, though admittedly an important one.

I turn now to the second prong of the attack. This time we are not told that one of our criteria is circular but, rather, that certain other criteria an ideal language is supposed to satisfy are impossible of fulfillment. Faced with this attack, the defense will have to change its tactics. Accordingly, I shall argue, *first*, that it would be foolish indeed to expect the ideal language to satisfy the criteria that Mr. Copi thinks we, the linguistic philosophers, expect it to satisfy. *Second*, I shall myself state a certain condition of completeness, in a specific sense of the term, which is, in my opinion, the second criterion an ideal language must satisfy and which it may very well satisfy without satisfying those other criteria that are ideal only in the spurious sense of being impossible of fulfillment. Mr. Copi mentions three such criteria; I shall discuss the two which I understand. First, he observes that according to a celebrated mathematical theorem a symbolism as complex as the ideal language must be expected to be cannot have a certain mathematical property technically known as completeness. Why, of course not! But then, what has this sort of completeness to do with "logical perfection," a very curious and, to me, quite unintelligible notion Mr. Copi introduces on this occasion? And, again, whatever the term signifies to him, why should the ideal language be logically perfect? All I can see here is, not an argument, but a verbal bridge designed to lead us, by two unpermissible substitutions, from 'complete' over 'perfect' to 'ideal'. Next we are told that because of the vagueness of many descriptive characters in our world no language could be completely precise. Thus, or so the argument goes, no language can be ideal. All that needs to be said in reply is that this time the bridge leads from 'precise' to 'ideal'.

Let me now try to explain briefly the peculiar sense in which I believe the ideal language must be complete or exhaustive. First I shall say what I do not mean and, as we so often must in philosophy, I shall say it through an analogy. Physical science is becoming ever more complete and exhaustive; in this sense it approaches a goal or ideal. But does that mean that our physicists know, or, for that matter, care to know which leaves the next storm will shake from the tree in front of my window? Such futile exhaustiveness is not an ideal in any sense; so I see no reason why the ideal language should be expected to realize it, the less so since, unlike the language of science, it is not one actually to be

spoken for the sake of greater efficiency, precision, exhaustiveness, or what not. Who wants to use it for such purposes acts like the man who tried to live, not in a house, but in the blueprint of one. But then, a blueprint or schema may or may not, according to its function, be complete and this, in either case, without showing all the details in the granulation of the wall paint. The ideal language, as I conceive it, is not a language actually to be spoken but a blue print or schema, complete only in the sense that *it must show, in principle, the structure and systematic arrangement of all the major areas of our experience.* The following three examples will help to explicate this meaning of completeness. First, it is not sufficient for our schema to show, in principle, how behavioristic psychology reconstructs the other fellow's mind; it must also provide, and relate to the first, an account of awareness as given. Second, it must contain, not only the logic of the sociology of value judgments, but also what some call their phenomenology. Third, it must have a place, not only for such statements as 'this is green', but also for the kind exemplified by 'I know (see, remember, etc.) that this is green'.

The interplay between my two criteria is, I trust, obvious. Only if the second is satisfied can we be sure — or, at least, as sure as we may be of anything — that some of the puzzles mentioned in the first have not been ignored rather than dissolved. Thus there is only one more thing I should like to say. I do believe that the two criteria are both intelligible and defensible, yet I would be the first to admit the grave shortcomings of many of the ideal languages or schemata so far proposed by linguistic philosophers. The less sophicated positivists, in particular, have violated the second criterion by their proneness to mistake the language of science for the ideal language.

IRVING M. COPI

REPLY TO PROFESSOR BERGMANN

I appreciate the force of Professor Bergmann's genial criticisms, even though I am unsure of their direction. They indicate the need, however, to clarify some aspects of my paper. To this I shall proceed.

1. I do not mean to argue that language analysis is not important for philosophy. It is of the greatest importance for logic, aesthetics, ethics, and perhaps epistemology. But it cannot have the importance for metaphysics that Russell and Wittgenstein have claimed, because their program does involve a vicious circle.

2. The criteria for an ideal language that I mention are just those to which Russell and Wittgenstein attach greatest importance. My remarks on completeness, precision, etc., were not "verbal bridges" to lead by "unpermissable substitutions" to the notion of an ideal language. These are the properties in terms of which the authors I was criticizing characterize or define their conception of an ideal language. An examination of their texts will show this to be the case.

3. Professor Bergmann's ideal for language is clearly different from the Russell-

Wittgenstein conception. *Chacun à son goût*. In defending his own notion, he is not defending theirs; and it was theirs, not his, that I was criticizing.

4. I shall allow myself the luxury of one criticism of Professor Bergmann's criteria. They depend, in part, upon "the so-called philosophical puzzles" which must "disappear" in an ideal language. I admit that there are some philosophical puzzles, but I insist that there are also some real philosophical problems. I am willing for the first to disappear, but I must insist that the problems be solved rather than exorcised. But puzzles and problems cannot be distinguished except on the basis of a given metaphysics. For example, Zeno's paradox of the arrow becomes a platitude within the framework of Russell's cinematographic metaphysics. But in a metaphysics of substance, the matter is otherwise. The inference is simple, but not "too simple." Distinguishing philosophical problems from puzzles is necessary for the establishment of an ideal language. Since they can only be distinguished within the framework of a particular metaphysics, a metaphysics must be chosen or constructed prior to the construction of an ideal language. These remarks serve to point further my thesis that metaphysical questions are prior to linguistic ones, and cannot be decided by means of the latter.

Reprinted from *Philosophy of Science*, XVI (1949), 74, by permission of the author and the publisher. (Copyright 1949 by The Williams and Wilkins Company, Baltimore.)

MAX BLACK

Russell's Philosophy of Language

The influence of language on philosophy has, I believe, been profound and almost unrecognized. Russell

1. Introduction

Russell's Influence. For the purpose of preliminary definition we might adapt a remark of William James and identify philosophy of language as "what a philosopher gets if he thinks long enough and hard enough about language." This characterization may serve as a reminder of the persistence and intensity of Russell's preoccupation with language, displayed in much of his philosophical writing during the past twenty-five years.[1] The flourishing condition of present-day "semiotic" is a

Reprinted from *The Philosophy of Bertrand Russell*, Volume V of *The Library of Living Philosophers*, ed. Paul A. Schilpp. (Evanston and Chicago: Northwestern University, 1944), pp. 229–32, 244–55, by permission of the author and the editor. (Copyright 1944 by *The Library of Living Philosophers*.)

[1] The quotation at the head of this essay is taken from the article "Logical Atomism," in *Contemporary British Philosophy* (1924), vol. 1, which is, for all its brevity, the best statement of Russell's early program for philosophical inquiries into language. It is a matter for regret that the earlier lectures, published under the title of "The Philosophy of Logical Atomism" in *The Monist* (XXVIII [1918], 495–527; XXIX [1919], 32–63, 190–222, 345–380), have never been reprinted. [Editor's Note: These lectures have now been reprinted in *Logic and Language*, ed. R. C. March (London: George Allen and Unwin, 1956).] Language is a topic of central importance also in "On Propositions: What They

sufficient testimony to the fertility of Russell's ideas; today, some twenty years after the epigraph of this essay was composed, it would be more accurate to say: "the influence of language on philosophy is profound and almost universally recognized."[2] If it is true that "language has, so to speak, become the *Brennpunkt* of present-day philosophical discussion,"[3] hardly another philosopher bears a greater share of the responsibility.

Are and How They Mean" (*Aristotelian Society Proceedings*, Supplementary Volume II [1919], 1–43), in *The Analysis of Mind* (London, 1921), especially Chapter 10: "Words and Meaning," and in *Philosophy* (New York, 1927), Chapter 4: "Language." *An Inquiry into Meaning and Truth* (New York, 1940) is, of course, almost entirely devoted to the same topic.

[2] Contemporary concern with philosophy of language is most apparent in the members and sympathizers of the philosophical movement known as "Logical Positivism" or "Scientific Empiricism." In this instance the transmission of ideas can be traced with rare accuracy. It is known that the Vienna Circle was much influenced, in the postwar years, both by Russell's own work and that of his pupil Wittgenstein. Although the *Tractatus* owes much to Russell, there can be no question that the influence here was reciprocal, as Russell has frequently and generously acknowledged. The *Monist* articles are introduced with the words: "The following articles are . . . very largely concerned with explaining certain ideas which I learnt from my friend and former pupil, Ludwig Wittgenstein" (*The Monist*, XXVIII [1918], 495). A more detailed discussion of sources would call for some reference to the work of G. E. Moore. Cf. *The Philosophy of G. E. Moore* (Evanston, 1942), pp. 14 ff.

[3] W. M. Urban, *Language and Reality* (London, 1939), p. 35.

Philosophical study of language, conceived by Russell as the construction of "philosophical grammar,"[4] may have been regarded by him, at an early period, as a mere "preliminary" to metaphysics; it soon became much more than this. Philosophical linguistics may be expected to provide nothing less than a pathway to the nature of that reality which is the metaphysician's goal. To this very day the hope persists that "with sufficient caution, *the properties of language may help us to understand the structure of the world.*"[5] So ambitiously conceived, as a study potentially revealing ontological structure, philosophy of language cannot be restricted to the examination of uninterpreted formal systems, still less, as with earlier philosophers, to the rhetorical art of avoiding unintentional ambiguity. Its successful pursuit requires the use of data drawn from logic, psychology, and empirical linguistics and the formulation of reasoned decisions concerning the scope of metaphysics and the proper methods of philosophical research. Such questions as these arise constantly in Russell's discussions, even on occasions when he is most earnestly avowing the "neutrality" of his devotion to scientific method.

Since the full-bodied suggestiveness of Russell's work on language is a function of his refusal to adopt the self-imposed limitations of the mathematical logician, it would be ungrateful to regret the complex interweaving of themes which results. But any selection of topics, considered in abstraction from the context of Russell's general philosophical doctrines, is bound to be somewhat misleading. It must be hoped that the aspects of Russell's earlier procedures here chosen for brief critical examination so typically manifest his style of philosophic thought at this period that an understanding of their merits and defects will serve as a guide to the evaluation of the more extensive doctrines of which they are a part.

The Scope of This Essay. The main topics discussed in the remainder of this essay are:

(i) *The consequences of applying the theory of types to "ordinary language."*[*] A new paradox will be presented whose resolution requires extensive reformulation of Russell's theory, and a critical judgment will be made of the value of the renovated theory.

(ii) *The search for "ultimate constituents" of the world.* The procedure here, so far as it is relevant to the criticism of language, will be shown to be, in part, susceptible of a neutral interpretation, and, for the rest, to be based upon an unproved epistemological principle (reducibility to acquaintance), which will, after examination, be rejected.

(iii) *The notion of the "ideal language."* This branch of the investigation concerns the goal of the entire method. The construction of an "ideal language" will be condemned, for due reason presented, as the undesirable pursuit of an ideal incapable of realization.

These headings cover most of Russell's *positive* contributions to philosophy of language.[6] There will be no space for discussion of the genesis of the whole inquiry in the destructive criticism of "ordinary language."[7] The bare reminder must suffice that the English language, as now used by philosophers, offends by provoking erroneous metaphysical beliefs. Syntax induces misleading opinions concerning the

---

[4] "I have dwelt hitherto upon what may be called *philosophical grammar.* . . . I think the importance of philosophical grammar is very much greater than it is generally thought to be . . . philosophical grammar with which we have been concerned in these lectures" (*The Monist*, XXIX [1919], 364).

[5] *An Inquiry into Meaning and Truth*, p. 429 (italics supplied).

[*] Editor's note: The section of this essay which covers this topic has been omitted for reasons of space.

[6] The only serious omission is reference to Russell's behavioristic analysis of meaning (cf. especially the last four works cited in footnote 1 above).

[7] *Contemporary British Philosophy*, 1 (1924), 368.

structure of the world (notably in the attribution of ontological significance to the subject-predicate form), while vocabulary, by promoting the hypostatization of pseudo-entities, encourages false beliefs concerning the *contents* of the world. In either case we are "giving metaphysical importance to the accidents of our own speech." [8] It is in trying to remedy these defects of ordinary language by searching for what is *essential* in language that we arrive finally at the "ideal language" and its valid metaphysical implications.

[Section 2 omitted]

3. THE SEARCH FOR ULTIMATE CONSTITUENTS OF THE WORLD

The Genesis of the Theory of Descriptions. For all their drastic character, the segregatory techniques of the theory of types prove insufficient to cure *all* the philosophical confusions which can be attributed to excessive confidence in grammatical structure as a guide to logical form. A notable instance of such confusion arises in connection with the syntactical properties of phrases of the form "the so-and-so."

If the phrase, "The present king of France," be compared, in respect of identity or diversity of type, with a personal name, say that of Stalin, it will be found that the noun clause may be substituted for the name without producing nonsense. [9] More generally, it is a fact that some descriptive phrases and some nouns can replace each other in some or all contexts without producing nonsense. If the theory

of types were to be relied upon to provide a sufficient criticism of ordinary language, it would be necessary to conclude that "Stalin" and "The present king of France" are syntactically similar. [10] This conclusion is maintained in a more colloquial form by anybody who claims that "The present king of France" names or denotes a person.

Upon such a foundation of identification of the syntactical properties of the descriptive phrase and the name, curious arguments have sometimes been erected. Since "The present king of France" refers to a person who does not exist, it must be conceded that there are *nonexistent persons* who can appear as subjects of true propositions. Though nonexistent, they must accordingly be capable of sustaining predicates. Thus it is certain, by the law of excluded middle, that one of the two propositions, "The present king of France is a parent" and "The present king of France is childless," is true. And there must be countless other properties by which the nonexistent present king of France is characterized (among them the property of being under discussion in this essay). It can scarcely be doubted that whatever is characterized by properties is not a mere nonentity, that in order to be a subject of which characters are genuinely predicable it is required to have some kind of objective "being," not to be confused with the vacuity of sheer nothingness on the one hand or the full actuality of "existence" on the other.

The argument culminates, then, in the assertion that the present king of France has some shadowy mode of participation in the world — some tenuous sort of "reality" compatible with nonexistence. And, if so much prove acceptable, the stage is set for similar argument in defense of the right to a recognized objective status of fictions, self-contradictory entities, and even nonentity itself. Hamlet and the Snark, the

---

[8] *The Analysis of Mind*, p. 182.

[9] This statement would need some qualifications for complete accuracy. It is not easy to provide an account of the theory of descriptions that will succeed in being tolerably brief. The best short version known to me is that of Professor L. S. Stebbing in her *A Modern Introduction to Logic*, 2d ed., pp. 144–158 ("The Analysis of Descriptions") and pp. 502–505 ("Logical Constructions"). Cf. also G. E. Moore's article (in *The Philosophy of Bertrand Russell* (Evanston, 1944)) on "Russell's 'Theory of Descriptions'."

[10] Or that Stalin and the present King of France belong to the same type.

philosopher's stone and the round square, being all characterized by predicates, must all, in some versions of this position, have their being in a multiplicity of distinct limbos, realms of *Sosein, Aussersein,* and *Quasisein* in which to enjoy their ambiguous status of partial or quasi existence.[11] The exploration and portrayal in "a terminology devised expressly for the purpose" of such *Lebensräume* of Being, will, of course, provide philosophers of this persuasion with endless material for mystification and dialectical ingenuity.

That arguments so remarkable should have appealed to some philosophers is a matter of historical record; and many another argument in good standing today might be shown to involve patterns of thought essentially similar. The suppression of such invalid trains of inference, against which the theory of types provides no protection, is the main object of Russell's theory of descriptions.

This part of Russell's program may still be plausibly interpreted as a contribution to the reform of common syntax; improvement of the vocabulary of ordinary language (which will be remembered as the second plank of the platform) is provided rather by the doctrine of logical constructions. Although this is intimately connected both in origin and content with the theory of descriptions, it requires the use of certain epistemological considerations which need not be invoked in the case of the latter.

The Theory of Descriptions as a Metaphysically Neutral Technique of Translation. That the theory of descriptions can be construed as a method of logical translation, capable of justification independently of adherence to any disputable epistemology, is a point that is commonly overlooked by critics. The reader may be reminded that Russell's contribution to the interpretation of descriptive phrases consists in the circumstantial demonstration that every sentence containing a descriptive phrase can be translated into another sentence having the same meaning but a different, and normally more complex, grammatical form. Thus, to take the familiar illustration once again,

(5) The present king of France is married

becomes

(6) Exactly one thing at present reigns over France, and nothing that reigns over France is not married.[12]

The feature upon which the usefulness of this procedure depends is the absence in the expanded form (6) of any ostensible reference to an alleged constituent (a "nonexistent person") designated by the original phrase "The present king of France." Not only has the descriptive phrase disappeared in the course of translation, but no part of the expansion of (5) can be identified as capable of abbreviation by the original descriptive phrase. Thus the procedure is not one of definition, in the dictionary sense, of the phrase "The present king of France," but rather a method for recasting every sentence in which the original phrase occurs.[13]

Mastery of the character of the translations appropriate to the different kinds of contexts in which descriptive phrases may occur having once been achieved, a permanent protection is provided against the blandishments of grammatical analogy which lend the doctrine of Realms of Being its spurious plausibility. Reference to the expanded form (6) above shows that the original sentence (5) differs quite radically in form from such a sentence as "Stalin is married." It becomes obvious that adherence to the principle of excluded middle

---

[11] The classical source of this agrument is A. R. v. Meinong's *Untersuchungen zur Gegenstandstheorie* (Leipzig, 1904). For a sympathetic exposition cf. J. N. Findlay's *Meinong's Theory of Objects* (London, 1933), especially Chapter 2.

[12] Here again some accuracy has been deliberately sacrificed. Cf. Stebbing, *op. cit.,* foot of p. 157, for a better statement.

[13] There is no reason, however, why the notion of definition should not be extended so as to cover the kind of reduction involved in the example cited.

is consistent with the assertion that *every* ascription of a predicate to the present king of France results in a false statement; more generally, a valuable instrument is thereby provided for the expulsion of illegitimate inferences and the clarification of ideas, as the successful application of methods essentially similar to a variety of other philosophical problems amply demonstrates.[14]

It is important to recognize that the enjoyment of such welcome benefits exacts no prior commitment to any epistemological theses. The gist of the method is the proof of the equivalence in meaning of given sentences. Only if appeal to some philosophical principle is involved in verifying the truth of any such proposed translation will it be necessary to deny that the method is epistemologically neutral.

Now the manner in which the equivalence of two *English* sentences is established does not differ in principle from that involved in proving the correctness of a translation from one European language into another. In both cases there is more or less explicit and direct appeal to congruence of behavior and linguistic utterance in cognate situations. The criteria are of a sociological order and may, for that very reason, provide a basis for agreement between philosophers elsewhere advocating very diverse epistemological or metaphysical doctrines. Since an idealist and a materialist can agree upon the correct translation of a passage from Homer, there seems to be no reason why they should have much more difficulty in coming to an understanding about the soundness of a proposed translation within their native tongue; they might both therefore make equal and equally good use of the methods provided by the theory of descriptions. It is not extravagantly optimistic to hope that, once the theory has been separated from the more specifically metaphysical

components with which it is associated in Russell's presentation, it may ultimately achieve a measure of common agreement (without prejudice to eventual differences of opinion concerning the interpretation and value of the method) such as may be found in the elementary propositional calculus or the other well-established branches of symbolic logic.

The Doctrine of Logical Constructions and Its Reliance upon the Principle of Reducibility to Acquaintance. It is to be noted that the foregoing noncontroversial portion of Russell's theory is concerned with the logical expansion of *logical symbols.* When sentence (5) was equated with sentence (6), such words as "present," "king," "France," etc., occurred *vacuously* (to use a convenient term of Quine's);[15] they were present merely as illustrative variables indicating how "The X of Y is Z" might, *in general*, be translated. Thus the translations offered by the theory of descriptions provide further insight into the manner in which the logical words "the," "and," "of" are used in ordinary language; but no information is yielded concerning the syntactical relationships of nonlogical material words.

The shift from the consideration of logical to that of nonlogical or material words corresponds exactly to the line drawn in this brief exposition between the theory of descriptions and the doctrine of logical constructions; it will now be shown that when this boundary is crossed the validity of an epistemological principle concerning the reducibility of knowledge to acquaintance becomes relevant to the criticism of Russell's method.

Anybody who maintains, with Russell, that tables are logical constructions, or that the self is a logical construction, is claiming *at least* that sentences containing the material words "table" or "I" submit to the same type of reductive translation as was demonstrated in connection with de-

---

[14] A good example is G. E. Moore's article, "Is Existence a Predicate?" (*Aristotelian Society Proceedings,* Supplementary Volume XV [1936], 175–188).

[15] W. V. Quine, *Mathematical Logic* (New York, 1940), p. 2.

scriptive phrases.[16] If tables are logical constructions it is necessary that every sentence containing the word "table" shall be capable of transformation into another sentence from which that word is absent and no part of which could be abbreviated by the word. It is quite certain that *some* material words, such as "average," satisfy such a condition; and it would seem initially plausible that some elements of vocabulary do and others do not admit of such reduction. If this were the case the claim in respect of any specific X that it was a logical construction would seem to require a specific demonstration. On Russell's principles, however, it can be known in advance of specific investigation that the entities referred to by the vast majority, if not indeed the totality, of the words of ordinary language *must be* logical constructions.

For very much more than mere translation of the kind specified is implied by Russell's contention that tables are logical constructions: the procedure must, on his view, have a *direction*, determined by progressive approach toward a *final translation*. A sentence is a final translation only if it consists entirely of "logically proper names" (demonstrative symbols) for "ultimate constituents"; it may then conveniently be referred to as a *pictorial sentence*.[17] To say that X is a logical construction is to claim that sentences containing "X" may be *finally* translated, in this drastic sense, into pictorial sentences.

What are these "ultimate constituents"?[18] They are, on Russell's view, pre-cisely those entities "with which we can be acquainted"; more specifically, sense-data (particulars) now presented to us and universals characterizing sense-data with which we are or have been acquainted. The assurance that every sentence can be finally translated into a pictorial sentence is provided by the principle that "every proposition which we can understand must be composed wholly of constituents with which we are acquainted."[19]

The reasons should now be obvious for distinguishing between the theory of descriptions and the theory of logical constructions. The latter predicts that sentences containing "table" will prove to admit of translation into pictorial sentences in which each element refers to an object with which we are acquainted. But ordinary language contains no logically proper names and can therefore provide no pictorial sentences.[20] The verification of the thesis here requires the invention of a new vocabulary departing drastically in character from that which it is to replace.

The case for the validity of the doctrine of logical constructions accordingly is quite different from that which supports the theory of descriptions. The latter is established by empirical grounds manifested in achieved success in translation; the former is, in the absence of the successful provision of the new vocabulary desiderated, rather the expression of a stubborn aspiration, whose plausibility rests entirely upon the supposed truth of the principle of reducibility to acquaintance.

No mention has hitherto been made of the metaphysical consequences of the doctrine of logical constructions. The reader will hardly need to be reminded that Rus-

---

[16] Russell, of course, did not use so linguistic a version. Cf. the statement in the text with the following typical utterance: "The real man, too, I believe, however the police may swear to his identity, is really a series of momentary men, each different one from the other, and bound together, not by a numerical identity, but by continuity and certain intrinsic causal laws" (*Mysticism and Logic* [New York, 1918], p. 129).

[17] The term is due to Stebbing.

[18] "Neither the word [a proper name] nor what it names is one of *the ultimate indivisible constituents of the world*" (*Analysis of Mind*, p. 193; italics supplied).

[19] *The Problems of Philosophy* (London, 1912), p. 91.

[20] "We cannot so use sentences [i.e., pictorially] both because our language is not adapted to picturing and because we usually do not know what precisely are the constituents of the facts to which we refer" (Stebbing, *op. cit.*, p. 157). "No word that we can understand would occur in a grammatically correct account of the universe" (Russell, *Philosophy*, p. 257).

sell has drawn such consequences freely, characteristically maintaining that matter, the self, and other minds (to cite some striking instances of alleged logical constructions) are "symbolic fictions" or even "myths." [21] But for these supposed consequences it is unlikely that Russell's theory of constructions would have received the critical attention which has been lavished upon it. If, as the next section will try to show, the principle of reduction to acquaintance has no evidential support, discussion of these alleged consequences becomes redundant. [22]

Criticism of the Principle of Reducibility to Acquaintance. Since the various formulations of the principle which Russell has

given [23] hardly vary except in unimportant details of phraseology, the version of 1905 might be taken as standard: "in every proposition that we can apprehend (i.e., not only in those whose truth or falsehood we can judge of, but in all that we can think about) all the constituents are really entities with which we have immediate acquaintance." [24]

The confidence with which this principle is presented for acceptance contrasts strikingly with the baldness of the grounds offered in its defense. "The chief reason," says Russell, "for supposing the principle true is that it seems scarcely possible to believe that we can make a judgment or entertain a supposition without knowing what it is that we are judging or supposing about." [25] And in another place, after this statement is repeated almost verbatim, there is added merely the comment: "We must attach *some* meaning to the words we use, if we are to speak significantly and not utter mere noise, *and the meaning we attach to our words must be something with which we are acquainted.*" [26]

Whatever persuasiveness attaches to this defense of the principle can be shown to arise from equivocation upon the crucial words "know," "mean," and "acquaintance." It may be just permissible so to use the term "acquaintance" that the sentence, "I know the meaning of '*X*'," is synonymous with "I am acquainted with *X*," where the word "meaning" is used in the sense it has in *ordinary language*. This is hardly a sense of "acquaintance" which can be relied upon not to engender confusion, but a philosopher may nevertheless find its introduction expedient. In this

---

[21] The following are typical statements: "The persistent particles of mathematical physics I regard as logical constructions, symbolic fictions . . ." (*Mysticism and Logic*, p. 128); ". . . matter, which is a logical fiction. . . ." (*Analysis of Mind*, p. 306); ". . . [desire] merely a convenient fiction, like force in mechanics . . ." (*op. cit.*, p. 205).

[22] The standard argument against Russell's attribution of a fictitious status to logical constructions (viz., the proof that "X is a logical construction" does not entail "X does not exist"), though accurate, does less than justice to Russell's point, however misleadingly expressed. The critics of Russell's language of "fictions" would not allow that the average man is a "fiction" or "unreal"; but they would be prepared to admit that the average *unicorn* is "unreal" (though no doubt stigmatizing the choice of terms as perverse). Now there is a sense in which the plain man would want to claim that both the average man *and* the average unicorn are fictions, because the phrases referring to them can be dispensed with in a complete account of the world. And more generally, if "X" is a dispensable symbol it is natural to say something like: " 'X' is a mere symbolic expedient, corresponding to nothing ultimate and irreducible in the world." It is this kind of statement that Russell wishes to make. Now, if all nonpictorial sentences were finally translatable, it would be natural to say that the world consists only of particular sense-data and the universals by which they are characterized, and to attribute the apparent presence of *other* entities to unwarranted inferences drawn from the nature of the symbols used in abbreviating pictorial sentences. It would, in short, be natural to say that facts about tables are *nothing but* facts about objects of acquaintance. This is the gist of Russell's position.

[23] "On Denoting," *Mind*, XIV (1905), 492; *Mysticism and Logic*, pp. 219, 221; *The Problems of Philosophy*, p. 91. Cf. J. W. Reeves, "The Origin and Consequences of the Theory of Descriptions," *Aristotelian Society Proceedings*, XXXIV (1934), 211–230.

[24] *Mind*, XIV (1905), 492.

[25] *Mysticism and Logic*, p. 219.

[26] *The Problems of Philosophy*, p. 91 (italics supplied). I am not aware of any other defense of the principle by Russell.

sense of the word, however, the assertion that "the meaning we attach to our words must be something with which we are acquainted" is merely the tautology that "the meaning of our words must be the meaning of our words." This can hardly be Russell's intention in the passages cited. Since we understand the word "Attila" we may be said either to "know the meaning of the word" or, alternatively and synonymously, to "be acquainted with Attila." Now Attila is neither a sense-datum nor a universal capable of characterizing sense-data; it is impossible, then, for anybody to be acquainted with Attila in the narrow technical sense of acquaintance which makes Russell's principle, whether true or false, something more than a mere tautology. If his assertion is to have any content, he must be interpreted as meaning "It seems scarcely possible to believe that we can make a judgment without knowing *by acquaintance* what it is that we are judging about" and "It is impossible that our words should have meaning unless they refer to entities *with which we are acquainted.*"

The alleged defense of the favored principle ("the chief reason for supposing the principle true") is now seen to be a mere repetition of that which was to be demonstrated. One of two things must be the case. Either Russell is using the term "meaning" in one of its customary senses; in that case the argument adduced in favor of the principle is refuted quite simply by pointing out that "Attila" *means* a certain person with whom we are *not* acquainted in Russell's sense. Or, alternatively, a new sense of meaning is implicitly *introduced* in which only objects with which we are acquainted can be meant by words: in that case the argument is a *petitio principii.* In either case the principle remains unproved.

Grounds for Rejecting the Principle of Reducibility to Acquaintance. It is likely that the reasons why the principle, in default of persuasive argument in its defense, should have seemed to so many philosophers self-evident are connected with the supposed necessity of "directness" in relations of meaning and knowing. Underlying Russell's position throughout is the conviction that in all genuine knowledge or meaning there must be some such ultimate fusion of intimacy between the knower and what is known as is provided by the notion of "acquaintance."

Let the validity of such an approach be tested in some less controversial area. Suppose it were argued that "every proposition about the *possession* of material objects must be reducible to a proposition about *contact* with objects" on the ground that "it seems hardly possible to believe that we can hold an object without really being in contact with it." Would it not be clear in such a case that there was being introduced a restricted and misleading sense of "holding" or "possession," in virtue of which it becomes logically impossible to hold anything except the surface with which one is in contact? And would it not be quite as clear that the mere introduction of a stipulation concerning the meaning of a term could succeed in demonstrating precisely nothing?

It may be objected that the analogy is unsound; and it is true that there might be *independent* grounds for supposing the relationship of *meaning,* unlike that of physical possession, to be necessarily direct. But although this may be allowed as an abstract possibility, neither Russell nor anybody else has yet provided good grounds for believing it to be anything more. And there are good opposing reasons for rejecting the principle.

Whenever sentences containing a symbol (such as "the present king of France" or "the average man") can be translated in such a manner that the symbol neither appears explicitly nor can be identified with any portion of the translation, it will be convenient to speak of the symbol as being *dispensable.* Now there is good reason to believe that "table" and "I" are not dispensable symbols, i.e., that there are truths concerning tables and the self which are not capable of being expressed without the use of these or synonymous symbols. It can be demonstrated, in connection with quite elementary examples of deductive theories, that "auxiliary" or "secondary" symbols can be introduced in such a way that they are not capable of *explicit* definition in terms of the basic experiential terms of the theory.[27] This does not render them undefined, in a wide sense of that term, since the mode of introduction of the auxiliary symbols into the system provides both for their syntactical relations with associated symbols and for inferential relations between the sentences in which they occur and the "primary" observational sentences of the system. This seems to be precisely the situation in respect of such scientific terms as "energy," "entropy," and "field," none of which are "dispensable."[28] There appears to be no *a priori* reason why this should not be the case also in respect of the names of material objects and other terms of ordinary language.

Indeed a careful scrutiny of the attempts made (especially by phenomenalists) to prove that words denoting material objects are dispensable will render this last suggestion something more than plausible. For these attempts invariably terminate in sceptical conclusions. When Russell, in a later book, undertakes to provide a phenomenalistic analysis of "You are hot,"[29] he arrives at a proposition which in order to be known to be true requires the speaker to know *inter alia* that the hearer is aware of a multitude of events in the same sense of "aware" in which he himself is aware of events and, further, that whole classes of events which *could* be perceived exist in the absence of such perception. Now neither of these truths could be known by acquaintance; the conclusion drawn is that the original prop-

osition analyzed is not *strictly* known to be true. At best we can "assume" its truth, "in the absence of evidence to the contrary."[30] But to assume or postulate the truth of a proposition is only to *hope* that it may be true. There are circumstances in which the truth of the assertion "You are hot" is *certain*; nothing could be more absurd than to doubt that this remark, when addressed to a philosopher in the warmest chamber of a Turkish bath, may sometimes be both true and known to be true. Now if the truth of the principle of acquaintance requires the rejection of even a single certain truth, there would seem to be sufficient reason to abandon it.

4. THE NOTION OF THE "IDEAL LANGUAGE"

The Character of the "Ideal Language." An examination of the character of that "ideal language" which Russell recommends as the goal of the philosophy of language provides a very precise test of the value of his early doctrines. For the "ideal language" is, by definition, the symbolism which would be entirely free from the philosophical defects which Russell claims to find in ordinary language. If language "had been invented by scientifically trained observers for purposes of philosophy and logic,"[31] just this symbolism would have resulted. And it would be "logically perfect"[32] in the sense of conforming to "what logic requires of a language which is to avoid contradiction."[33] The character of the ideal language is calculated, then, to reveal in a vivid fashion the benefits to be expected from a successful outcome of Russell's program of reform.

The discussion of the preceding sections should have made clear the features which would be manifested by such a paradigm of philosophical symbolism. Every symbol will be a "logically proper name" de-

[27] Cf. Ramsey's discussion of the place of explicit definitions in a theory (*Foundations of Mathematics*, p. 229).
[28] Further detail would be needed to prove this statement.
[29] *An Inquiry into Meaning and Truth*, pp. 280–282, 284–291.

[30] *Ibid.*, p. 292.
[31] *The Analysis of Mind*, p. 193.
[32] *The Monist*, XXVIII (1918), 520.
[33] *Contemporary British Philosophy*, 1, p. 377.

noting objects of acquaintance: "There will be one word and no more for every simple object and everything that is not simple will be expressed by a combination of words."[34] How closely will these logically proper names for ultimate constituents resemble the words at present in use? By definition, they must be unintelligible in the absence of the entities they denote. Thus no proper names, in the familiar *grammatical* sense, can qualify for inclusion in the ideal language, just because, in virtue of referring to complex series of causally related appearances, they function as logical descriptions. The descriptive character of such a name as "Napoleon" is recognized by the circumstance that the name is intelligible to persons who never met the Corsican.[35]

Similar considerations would seem to disqualify all other types of words in the ordinary language. The names of universals characterizing sense-data (e.g., the name of a specific shade of color) might seem to be exceptions; but it would be hard to deny that even these have meaning in the absence of instances of the universals they denote. Now if universals are among the ultimate constituents, as Russell claims, they must be represented in the ideal language by arbitrary noises of such a character that it is logically impossible that they should be uttered in the absence of instances of the universals concerned.

The attempt might be made to construct illustrative instances of sentences of the ideal language composed entirely of demonstratives, by inventing such words as "thet" and "thot" to supplement the present meager stock of "this" and "that."[36] But even "This thet thot"[37] would still convey to a hearer some such meaning as "Something with which the speaker is ac-

quainted has some relation, with which the speaker is acquainted, to some other thing with which he is acquainted."[38] The proposition understood by the hearer would not then be the proposition intended by the speaker; the "perfect sentence," having meaning only to the speaker and to him only at the time of utterance, would be perfectly unintelligible. If this criticism is based upon a misinterpretation of Russell's intention, and if it were permissible for the names of such ultimate constituents as are universals to be intelligible at a variety of times and to more than a single person, it would still be necessary that the names of particulars should be private; and communication would be possible only by the grace of some kind of pre-established speaker-hearer ambiguity in virtue of which what was a logically proper name for the one functioned as a description for the other.

What becomes under such conditions of the intention that the ideal language shall be "completely analytic and . . . show at a glance the logical structure of the facts asserted or denied"?[39] Such a system, containing "no words that we can [at present] understand"[40] would be so remote from our present means of expression and so unsuited to perform the functions of unambiguous and logically accurate communication which may be desired of an efficient language, that to urge its capacity to provide "a grammatically correct account of the universe"[41] is to be extravagantly implausible. The "ideal language" in practice would resemble a series of involuntary squeaks and grunts more closely than anything it is at present customary to recognize as a language.

It is by no means certain that Russell ever seriously supposed that the ideal language could be realized; and some of his remarks suggest that he regarded it on

[34] *The Monist*, XXVIII (1918), 520.
[35] *The Analysis of Mind*, pp. 192–193.
[36] As suggested by John Wisdom (*Mind*, XL [1931], 204).
[37] Somewhat more drastic than Wisdom's "This son that, and that brother thet, and thet mother thot, and thot boy, and this kissed Sylvia" (*ibid.*).

[38] Cf. Wisdom's discussion of this point, *op. cit.*, p. 203.
[39] *The Monist*, XXVIII (1918), 520.
[40] *Philosophy*, p. 257.
[41] *Ibid.*

occasion as a mere device of exposition.[42] If, as has been argued above, the ideal language is not capable of realization, it becomes impossible seriously to defend indefinite progression toward such an "ideal" as a desirable procedure for the philosophical criticism of language.

It is not difficult to see, in retrospect, why Russell should have been led into this untenable position of defending as the aim of the philosophy of language the construction of a language which could never work. For the "ideal language" would satisfy perfectly the intention to make the relation of "picturing" the sole essential basis of symbolism. Whatever else Russell is prepared to regard as "accidental" in language, he is unwilling to abandon the notion that language must "correspond" to the "facts," through one-one correlation of elements and identity of logical structure. But there is no good reason why we should expect language to correspond to, or "resemble," the "world" any more closely than a telescope does the planet which it brings to the astronomer's attention.

Consequences of Abandoning the Pursuit of an "Ideal Language." To abandon the image of language as a "picture" of the world, which has, on the whole, wrought so much mischief in the philosophy of language, is to be in a position to make the most intelligent use of the products of Russell's analytical ingenuity.

[42] Cf. *The Monist*, XXVIII (1918), 520.

For it would be both unfair and ungrateful to end without acknowledging the pragmatic value of the techniques invented by Russell. Rejection of the possibility or desirability of an "ideal language" is compatible with a judicious recourse to the methods of translation and analysis which have been criticized in this paper. It is a matter of common experience that philosophical confusion and mistaken doctrine are sometimes connected with failure to make type distinctions or to reveal, by the technique of translation, the correct deductive relations between sentences of similar grammatical, though differing logical, forms. And where such confusion is manifested it is helpful to follow Russell's new way of "philosophical grammar." It will be well, however, to be unashamedly opportunistic, making the remedy fit the disease and seeking only to remove such hindrances to philosophical enlightenment as are demonstrably occasioned by excessive attachment to the accidents of grammar and vocabulary. In this way there is some hope of avoiding the temptation to impose, by way of cure, a predetermined linguistic structure — of seeking to eliminate the philosophical ills of the language at present in use by proposing an "ideal language" which never could be used. Nor need such a program be aimless. For the object will be to remove just those linguistic confusions which are actually found to be relevant to doctrines of philosophical importance.

· 10a ·

ALICE AMBROSE

Linguistic Approaches to Philosophical Problems[1]

Views about the nature of philosophical theories answer to one of two rough descriptions, one orthodox and seemingly having the best claim to truth, the other heterodox and seemingly false. In this paper I shall set out the considerations both for and against accepting various forms of the heterodox position; but I shall argue without reservation against the orthodox position. The latter commonly describes philosophy as a pursuit of truth, where "pursuit of truth" is interpreted in conformity with common usage as the attempt to acquire knowledge about our world. The contrasting position comprises a series of views held by philosophers whose primary concern appears to be the language in which purported truths are expressed. This concern reflects a conception of philosophy, a conception often not explicit and sometimes even disclaimed, namely, that a philosophical theory has its sources in linguistic facts rather than in facts about our world, and that despite appearances it gives us information only about language. A theory about causation, for example, tells us something about the word "cause" rather than about causation as a feature of our world.

This rough description of the position of

linguistic philosophers makes it appear to ignore a distinction we all know, between the use and mention of a word. It is clear, for example, that philosophical views about causation do not translate into any statements about the word "cause." But of course this fact is already known to philosophers whose approach is linguistic. To maintain their thesis it is therefore incumbent upon them to specify in what way philosophical theories yield only verbal information and, first of all, to show that such theories are not what they seem. This latter thesis I want now to defend.

Descartes remarked that "Philosophy teaches us to speak with an appearance of truth on all things, and causes us to be admired by the less learned." [2] But this appearance of truth is much more an appearance than he ever supposed. Philosophical views quite clearly have an empirical air, i.e., they appear to state matters of fact. To take some sample illustrations: a physical object is a bundle of properties, perception of physical objects involves an inference to something beyond one's experience, man's mind is necessarily given to antinomies, one cannot know one

Reprinted (with revisions by Professor Ambrose) from *The Journal of Philosophy*, XLIX (1952), 289–301, by permission of the author and the editor.

[1] Read at a Symposium on Linguistic Conceptions of Philosophy, Smith College, May 20, 1951.
[2] Descartes, *Discourse on the Method of Rightly Conducting the Reason and Seeking for Truth in the Sciences*, Part I.

is not dreaming, it is impossible to know other people exist, motion is impossible, etc.

I want to hold that despite appearances these are *not* factual statements about physical objects, perception, the human mind, one's knowledge; first, because investigations which come to these conclusions are clearly not empirical. I do not propose here to discuss in a positive way the kind of evidence the philosopher adduces for a theory; here I can only say the evidence is not empirical. And I back this claim by pointing out that he has no laboratory, no experiments figure in his demonstrations or refutations, he cannot claim to closer observation of phenomena than other folk. Empirical conclusions cannot be expected to derive from non-empirical evidence. Second, they are not empirical because philosophic disputants come to opposite conclusions although the same facts are available to them and no possible further fact can decide betwixt them; i.e., their dispute cannot, even theoretically, be settled by recourse to any sort of matter of fact. Examples of such disputes are: the long-standing controversy over whether universals exist (consider Russell's, Carnap's, and Quine's changing positions), Locke and Berkeley's dispute over the existence of abstract ideas, disputes over the existence of sense data and over the extent of our knowledge. Third, some (possibly all) philosophical theories cannot be empirical because they imply the logical impossibility of what is patently and undeniably possible. For example, it appears to be a consequence of some of Bradley's views that it is self-contradictory (not merely false) that we should all be here now, or somewhere else before, or that we should have walked here, or that I should be sitting next to B.

There are two points to be made about views which have this sort of consequence, (1) that a philosopher need make no appeal to fact to show the incorrectness of such views, and (2) that whatever implies that something is logically impossible cannot

itself be empirical. (1) It is an adequate objection to such a philosophical view that it has as a consequence the impossibility of what is clearly possible. (I am taking the position that if we know anything at all we know, for example, that sitting next to B is entirely possible. This is a minimum claim of knowledge. It requires only the understanding of the sentence asserting it.) Citing the relevant *possibility* constitutes a sufficient objection to such a view; if a philosopher cites a fact he has merely cited something logically stronger than is necessary. It is the mere possibility, not the fact, that he requires. The possibility of there being a right act the total consequences of which do not contain as great a balance of pleasure over pain as any act the agent could do is enough to refute the theory that every right act must have consequences containing such a balance. That the possibility is remote or fantastic does not prevent it from being a test case. In other words, the theory is tested by a mere logical possibility. And what is merely possible cannot serve to refute a statement of fact. This is support for my claim that philosophical investigation of a theory is not empirical and hence that the theory itself is not empirical. (2) An additional reason for asserting the theory to be non-empirical is that whatever implies that something is logically impossible cannot itself be factual. No factual statement has as a consequence a logical impossibility.

The three considerations cited against holding philosophical views to be empirical are obviously different in character. The first two call attention to matters of fact about philosophical investigations and philosophical disputes, while the last one rests on the logical points (1) that only a non-empirical statement can be tested by citing a possibility, and (2) that whatever implies that something is logically impossible cannot itself be factual. All entail the consequence that a philosophical investigation does not consist in the attempt to ascertain the truth-value of a theory.

Without pretending to have met various

reasons that might be advanced for the thesis that a philosophical theory does assert something factual, I am now going to proceed as though enough had been said to dispose of this thesis, in order to take up another view, which at least in appearance contests the claim that philosophical theories inform us only about the use of words. Philosophers holding this view do make a careful examination of the language used to express a theory, but they consider this linguistic task merely as a preliminary necessity for ascertaining truth. This view is the most plausible alternative both to the view that philosophical theories are factual truths or falsities and to the view that their function is to convey facts about words. It is the most plausible, first, because it is consistent with the fact that philosophical investigations are not empirical and that philosophical disputes are not settled by appeal to fact, and second, because it has the support of the undeniable fact that philosophical theories are expressed in what may be called the ontological as opposed to the linguistic idiom.[3] According to this alternative view philosophical statements are analyses of puzzling concepts; and philosophical reasoning, at least a good deal of it, is directed to defending or attacking the correctness of an analysis. Philosophical questions and answers, and philosophical disputes, all have on this view a non-linguistic description. A philosophical question is a request for the analysis of a concept, i.e., for a statement of what concepts constitute (are logically entailed by) the given concept. The analysis will be correct if the statement of it is a logically necessary truth. Vagueness of concepts is the explanation of philosophical disputes.

Now the history of philosophy is full of what appear to be attempts to arrive at necessary truths. The following are illustrations: (1) Body is extended. This was set out by Descartes as an indubitable

truth, indubitable because ascertainable by reason alone. Being a physical body necessarily implies being extended in space. (2) Socrates' attempts in the *Republic* and other dialogues to find the "essence" of justice, courage, virtue, etc. are also good illustrations of attempted analyses, as is evidenced by his procedure of dismissing any feature not characterizing all possible instances of the concept in question. (3) Zeno's argument that motion is impossible was directed to showing the concept of motion to have contradictory consequences. At least this is the natural description of his argument that the hypothesis that a body moves from A to B is self-contradictory. (4) Bradley's argument for the impossibility of relations, namely, that in order for two things to be related there would have to be an infinity of relations between them, also clearly derives from an investigation of the notion of a relation. (5) Hume's claim that a cause is nothing more than an invariable sequence appears likewise to be an analytic account of causation.

Now the activity illustrated in these examples is according to some philosophers not to be described as in any way requiring the examination of language, except as language is a crutch to our apprehension of concepts. Some go so far as to lodge a general complaint against language, not only because it is so often abused but because it is a barrier rather than a window to our ideas. Berkeley, for example, enjoins each of us to "use his utmost endeavors to obtain a clear view of the ideas he would consider, separating from them all that dress and incumbrance of words which so much contribute to blind the judgment and divide the attention. . . . We need only draw the curtain of words to behold the fairest tree of knowledge, whose fruit is excellent and within the reach of our hand."[4] For himself, since ideas so little profit from their quite fortuitous associa-

---

[3] I have taken the phrase "ontological idiom" from M. Lazerowitz.

[4] Berkeley, *The Principles of Human Knowledge*, Introduction, Section 24.

tion with words, he says that "whatever ideas I consider, I shall endeavor to take them bare and naked into my view, keeping out of my thoughts, so far as I am able, those names which long and constant use hath so strictly united with them. . . . So long as I confine my thoughts to my own ideas, divested of words, I do not see how I can easily be mistaken. The objects I consider, I clearly and adequately know. . . . To discern the agreements and disagreements there are between my ideas, to see what ideas are included in my compound idea and what not, there is nothing more requisite than an attentive perception of what passes in my own understanding."[5] This evidently is what C. H. Langford in our time calls considering a statement, "not verbally, but in terms of genuine ideas."[6]

If any philosopher takes the position that a concern with ideas is positively hampered by attention to words, and that ideas are the philosopher's proper concern, he clearly will be far from admitting that philosophical views are in any way about words or that examination of language is anything more than an unfortunate necessity. It is my contention that complaints which philosophers have made against language are pseudo-complaints — pseudo because they express dissatisfaction with the fact that language does not come up to a standard which it is self-contradictory that it should come up to. But I have argued this point elsewhere[7] and so shall not discuss it here. If it is correct, then philosophers are robbed of an important reason for holding that analysis should be of concepts but not of language, and that attention to language is a second-best to inspection of ideas. I suspect it is nonsense to speak, as Berkeley did, of taking ideas

"bare and naked" into one's view, divested of their linguistic encumbrances. But disregarding this point, what I want to propose (though with some reservation) is that an analyst, even though he claims linguistic study is merely a tool in the analysis of concepts, is in fact engaging in *one* linguistic approach to philosophical problems.

I define a linguistic approach to philosophy as one arising from the view that what a philosopher does when he produces or tries to refute a philosophical theory is to inform one about language. Whether or not the so-called analytic approach in philosophy can be classified as a linguistic approach I admit is uncertain. But we may take it as evidence that it can be, if the analysis of a concept which a philosophical theory is claimed to state turns out to be a linguistic analysis. This evidence is provided by G. E. Moore's statement in Cambridge lectures that the analysis of a notion is identical with the definition of a word, in a strictly limited sense. Roughly, "analytic definition" covers what that sense is. An analytic definition is intended to clarify a concept by making explicit those concepts implicitly contained in it. This it will succeed in doing only if the words occurring in the expression of the analysans stand for, "such ideas as common use has annexed them to," to quote Locke. That is, if the analysans is expressed by means of words not having a usage in the language or by means of old words used in a new way, the analysis will not clarify a concept. A successful analysis then will secure the same end as a correct definition: state how a word or phrase is conventionally used. However, from his Cambridge lectures there is reason to suppose that Moore, who would I think agree that some philosophical theories state analyses, would deny that they state something about the correct or established use of language, and for reasons over and above the fact that they are not *about* words.

Whether or not Moore would deny this thesis about what analysis does I am not

[5] *Ibid.*, Sections 21 and 22.
[6] C. I. Lewis and C. H. Langford, *Symbolic Logic*, p. 475.
[7] Alice Ambrose, "The Problem of Linguistic Inadequacy," *Philosophical Analysis, A Collection of Essays*, ed. Max Black (Ithaca, New York: Cornell University Press, 1950), pp. 15–37.

concerned here to decide. I am concerned to evaluate it since it is an emphatically linguistic view in which the increasing attention to language naturally eventuates. According to this view the appearance which a philosophical theory has of being about empirical fact, or of being about the implications of concepts, merely conceals an attempt to express correct usage. Philosophical theories are to be examined neither for their necessary truth nor for their correspondence with those non-linguistic facts which make up our spatio-temporal world, but for their linguistic correctness — that is, for their correspondence with the linguistic fact that words are customarily used in such-and-such a way. I am not sure that anyone has ever held this view about philosophical theories. However, though one might not explicitly hold it, one might do philosophy as though one did. Moore and Norman Malcolm have often proceeded in such a way as to suggest this, for example, when they criticize a theory for misuse of words. Recall Moore's criticisms of views, say on the nature of material objects, for going counter to ordinary English, and Malcolm's recent criticisms of Moore's use of "know" in the claim "I know material objects exist" and of Russell's use of "perception" in his claim that perception involves an inference. This type of criticism at least suggests that a philosopher was interpreted as attempting, but failing, to give a proper account of conventional usage.

The attempt to answer one or other of the questions, "Does this analysis state a necessary truth?" "Does this account of the use of the word correctly describe its established, conventional use?," characterizes the tasks, respectively, of the two positions I have thus far called linguistic. Either position differs markedly from one further linguistic approach to philosophical problems, stated explicitly by Morris Lazerowitz, and by John Wisdom in some of his papers, according to which philosophers are neither analyzing concepts nor stating correct usage in giving a view, but

are doing something else equally linguistic, namely, revising language. This approach stems from the view that philosophical theories are not, as they appear to be, answers to questions, but are proposals to alter language: that they do not in fact attempt to clarify a concept or to explain a current usage, but instead, in a concealed way, propose that a word's use shall be modified for philosophical purposes. Practitioners of this persuasion conduct what might be called meta-philosophical investigations — that is, they do not aim at establishing or refuting a theory, i.e., at answering a philosophical question, but instead show what linguistic features a philosopher is emphasizing in order to persuade other philosophers of the need of a linguistic change. They try to show what a philosophical theory comes to; and they arrive in the end at the Wittgenstein position that once one sees what a question comes to the craving for an answer disappears.

We have now three views about the nature of philosophical theories, one that they state analyses of concepts, another that they state what is the established usage of words, and another that they conceal a proposal for linguistic change. In order to make clear the differences between the first two and the last I shall try to set out what, ideally, their proponents would say about Berkeley's defense of his theory about physical objects. Berkeley grants that the expression "What we eat, drink, and are clothed with are ideas" departs from the familiar use of language. But he asserts he is not disputing "about the propriety, but the truth of the expression." "If . . . you agree with me that we eat and drink and are clad with the immediate objects of sense, which cannot exist unperceived . . . I shall readily grant it is more proper or conformable to custom that they should be called *things* rather than *ideas*." [8] In other words, he seems to say that "We are

[8] Berkeley, *The Principles of Human Knowledge*, Part First, Section 38.

clothed with material things" is proper enough language, that is, that what we are clothed with *is* the sort of thing to which "material things" is applied, but that it fails to express what is true; while "We are clothed with ideas" offends against linguistic properties but does say what is true. He recommends our compromising between these two facts by employing "those inaccurate modes of speech which use has made inevitable," [9] but with full awareness of their inaccuracy. For purposes of philosophizing "We are clothed with fine raiment" will be understood to mean "We are clothed with raiment-ideas." Thus we shall "think with the learned, and speak with the vulgar." In this way he insists that "the common use of language will receive no manner of alteration . . . from the admission of our tenets," that "in the tenets we have laid down there is nothing inconsistent with the right use and significancy of language, and that discourse, so far as it is intelligible, remains undisturbed." [10]

About these claims there are two things to say: (1) Quite clearly, as English is at present, "We are clothed with ideas" is not a proper interpretation of "We are clothed with material things." There is no rule of synonymy which makes it correct to replace "material thing" by "class of ideas." (2) Berkeley preserves the *status quo* of ordinary English at the cost of constructing a philosophical language to which his arbitrary rule of translation, "material thing" = "class of ideas," provides no bridge. For "We are clothed with ideas," which he says is true, cannot translate into "We are clothed with material things," because that is, according to Berkeley, false, or, by turns, nonsense.

About these facts proponents of the three linguistic theories about philosophy would take, respectively, the following positions: the first two that Berkeley is misusing language; the third that he is

[9] *Ibid.*, Section 51.
[10] *Ibid.*, Section 83.

suggesting an alteration, for academic purposes, of philosophic discourse, and that it is a misinterpretation of his intention to suppose he is stating the accepted meaning of the phrase "material thing." Only in philosophical usage is his meaning to obtain, which is to say that the phrase "material thing" will come to have no function in philosophical discourse since "class of ideas" will displace it.

The sharp difference between these positions shows up when each is considered with reference to the question "Why is it so often asserted that Berkeley's position on material objects, though not substantiated, is unrefuted?" Accepting the view that Berkeley is either analyzing the nature of material objects or defining the phrase "material object," the charge that he is misusing language would imply that his analysis, or definition, is *in*correct. But as the quotations make clear, Berkeley was perfectly aware, even admits, that his account uses "ideas" in a way not in accord with ordinary linguistic proprieties. Yet he insists on his account nevertheless. If the aim of a philosophical theory is to give a correct analysis or a correct account of established usage, then the theory should be refuted so soon as it is shown that it fails to do this. And it would then be inexplicable why his theory is thought to remain unrefuted.

The third linguistic view, on the other hand, is constructed to explain just this phenomenon. If Berkeley's theory is an attempt to alter language for purposes of *philosophic* (as against ordinary) discourse, then it is understandable why pointing out a linguistic impropriety in no way persuades him to relinquish his view. Berkeley's reasoning for this view also has its explanation: if his view conceals an attempt to persuade one to accept a modification of language — conceals because of its being expressed in the indicative and its using but not mentioning words — then his reasoning will be construed not as showing its correctness but as urging the virtue of a proposed re-definition and the demerits of present usage. The first two linguistic approaches would thus take Berkeley's theory as an attempt to give a correct answer to one or other of the questions, "What is the analysis of the concept 'physical object'?," "What is the proper use of the words 'physical object'?"; the last takes it as not attempting a true answer to any question whatever. It therefore directs its efforts, not to refuting Berkeley but to showing what his view comes to, i.e., what linguistic features he emphasizes in order to persuade one of the need for a linguistic alteration.

Although a number of philosophers have, in working with a particular philosophical theory, done the kind of metaphilosophical analysis I have just described, i.e., shown what specific linguistic modification is being recommended, they have not always proceeded in this fashion and consequently have not subscribed to the above general account of the nature of philosophical theories. Norman Malcolm, for example, describes the sceptic as recommending the discontinuance of the application of the word "certain" to empirical statements, but in some of his writings he seems not to take this kind of view. Max Black describes the critics of induction as proposing a change of terminology, viz., of "practically know" for "know for certain," holding that their criticism arises because they prefer to construe "know" in a limiting sense, that is, as meaning "deductively certain." [11] Nevertheless, Black denies he is analyzing the dispute between defenders and critics of induction as being about how inductive inference ought to be described. Similarly, Moore denies, in his comment on a paper of mine, that the sceptic is proposing how the word "know" ought to be used, and in a comment on a paper by Morris Lazerowitz, that he is proposing anything about the use of the word "unreal." [12]

I should like now to canvass briefly the objections to the view that a philosophical theory proposes a linguistic change. In *Language and Philosophy* Max Black, in referring to Moore, cites the fact that "the man who might be supposed to know best whether he is making a recommendation strenuously resists the suggestion." [13] This it seems to me is not a convincing reason. Normally it would be, but when one considers the scandalous fact that after more than 2000 years philosophers are still so unclear about what philosophy is as not to be puzzled by the fact that no single theory remains undisputed, I think we can grant Moore nothing further than that he certainly *thinks* he is not making linguistic recommendations. What one thinks one is doing and what one is in fact doing may be quite different things. Hume certainly thought he was urging us to establish empirically, by introspection, that there could not be a simple idea without a correspondent impression; and yet he had already stated that "by *ideas* I mean the faint images of [impressions]." [14] It should be pointed out that to hold that traditional philosophers are making linguistic proposals is not the same as to say they are making *conscious* linguistic proposals. Any person holding the proposal theory would certainly say that philosophers are unaware of the fact that they are revising language, and that what they do with language deludes them as well as others. Freud's wellknown study on the psychopathology of everyday life is sufficient evidence for the possibility of this being the case.

But there is one much more crucial criticism, directed against every linguistic theory about the nature of philosophy, which must be weighed. This criticism rests on the obvious fact that philosophical views are not ostensibly about the use of

---

[11] Max Black, *Language and Philosophy* (Ithaca, New York: Cornell University Press, 1949), pp. 75–78.

[12] *The Philosophy of G. E. Moore*, Volume IV of *The Library of Living Philosophers*, pp. 673–75.

[13] Max Black, *Language and Philosophy*, p. 79.

[14] Hume, *A Treatise of Human Nature*, Book I, Part I, Section I.

words at all. Philosophical statements use but do not mention words. They are expressed as though they were about matters of fact, or, alternatively, about relations between concepts. Some philosophers appear to claim they are about both, for example, rationalists who hold the task of metaphysics to be discovery of the necessary features of *reality*. I should like to hold that just as the form of expression of philosophical theories misleads some philosophers into saying they are about our world, so the form misleads critics of linguistic approaches into supposing they do not convey merely verbal information.

What then about the view that they state the relation between concepts, and further, that their function is in no way to convey any fact about words? It seems to me that the likeness of an analysis, that is, a necessary proposition, to an empirical one, and its unlikeness to such a proposition as "The word 'triangle' means three-sided figure," deceive one about the linguistic information it provides, information about the application of a word. It would be too great a task here for me to show in detail that necessary propositions yield only verbal information, but I shall try to sketch some reasons for holding this. However, it must be admitted to begin with that it is simply incorrect to say that a necessary proposition is directly about words. "Material bodies are extended" will not translate into any statement mentioning the phrase "material bodies." Nevertheless it is a fact that in understanding a sentence for a necessary proposition and knowing that what it expresses is necessarily true, what one knows is a *verbal* fact. In understanding the sentence "Material bodies are extended" and knowing that it expresses a necessary truth one knows the phrase "unextended material body" has no application.

Nevertheless, you might say, in understanding the sentence "There are no white crows" and knowing that it expresses something true, one likewise knows that "white crows" has no application. This is correct, but putting the matter in this way obscures an important difference, which it is essential to be clear about: viz., that, in knowing that the one sentence expresses something contingently true, one knows the verbal fact that "white crows" has in our language a descriptive use and the non-verbal fact that it applies to nothing; while, in knowing that the other expresses something necessarily true, one knows that "unextended material bodies" has no descriptive use and one need know no non-verbal fact to know that what the sentence expresses is true. Knowing the verbal fact is sufficient for knowing a truth-value; there is no further fact to know. And this I take as grounds for holding that what a necessary proposition conveys is merely verbal information. One can understand the expression for a contingent proposition but lack knowledge as to whether what is described exists or not. But in knowing that "unextended material bodies" describes nothing conceivable, no such knowledge can be lacking. For nothing is described; if it were, then "Material bodies are extended" could theoretically be false — when what is described by "unextended material bodies" exists. The sentence "It is impossible for unextended material bodies to exist," into which "Material bodies are extended" translates, suggests that an imaginable state of affairs, namely, a state of affairs expressed by "Unextended material bodies exist," is impossible. But when we understand the sentence "It is impossible . . ." we know the linguistic fact that "unextended material bodies" has no descriptive use, not that it describes what is counter to natural law. Thus, although our necessary proposition does not assert any linguistic fact it does indirectly give us information about usage. And further, it gives us no more than this, since when we understand an expression not to have a use we cannot go on to say we either know or can come to know a non-linguistic fact. For we cannot know that what is described by a phrase which does not describe either could or could not, or does or does not, exist.

This linguistic aspect of necessary propositions is what justifies the linguist in philosophy in maintaining the relevance of attending to the verbal information concealed by the form of expression. Both the philosopher who interprets a theory as attempting either a correct analysis or a correct account of usage and the philosopher who interprets it as proposing a revision of language are attending to just this concealed information. The latter arrives at his position via the thesis that a philosophical theory is being proposed for acceptance, in philosophical discourse, as a logical necessity, for example, that "Physical objects are classes of ideas" shall be understood by philosophers to express a necessary truth. And thus what is proposed on the verbal level is that "unperceived physical object" shall not have a use. On all of these views about philosophical theories then, the focus is on the verbal fact which the theories conceal.

Something should be said about one remaining view which is usually construed as linguistic, namely, the positivistic view that metaphysical statements are nonsense. This view is arrived at by the use of a criterion for determining the meaningfulness of indicative sentences, the so-called principle of verifiability in sense experience. This criterion has a number of different formulations, but each of them seems open to conclusive objections. One formulation is as follows: a declarative sentence which does not express an *a priori* proposition is meaningful if and only if the proposition it expresses can be confirmed or refuted in sense experience. So formulated the criterion implies a contradiction, for it implies that a sentence open to testing by the criterion expresses a proposition and at the same time might fail to express one, since the criterion may show the sentence to be literally meaningless. For there must be a proposition in order for the criterion to have a non-vacuous application, and if the proposition fails to meet the test the criterion implies that no proposition was expressed.[15] This objection can be avoided by saying that a declarative sentence which does not express an *a priori* proposition is meaningful if and only if it expresses a proposition verifiable (or refutable) in sense experience. But this formulation avoids the contradiction only by begging the question: it is artificially tailored to exclude as meaningless any sentence failing to express a proposition open to *sense* testing. Metaphysical sentences are eliminated from intelligible discourse by linguistic fiat — by an arbitrary decision to apply "senseless" to them.[16] Despite these difficulties, it must in fairness be said that the positivist critique of philosophical language has the merit of making perspicuous the unique position occupied by the sentences of metaphysics. It has underlined the need for a correct understanding of the differences between these and common-sense, scientific, and mathematical statements.

[15] For an attempt to meet this criticism, which was made in M. Lazerowitz' "The Principle of Verifiability," *Mind*, XLVI (1937), 372–78, see A. J. Ayer's Introduction to the revised edition of *Language, Truth and Logic* (1948).

[16] This criticism, together with others, are elaborated in M. Lazerowitz' *The Structure of Metaphysics*, pp. 49–57.

Editor's note: For another statement, parallel to Miss Ambrose's, of the "proposal" theory of philosophy, see Nowell-Smith [2]. Compare also Waismann [2], Wisdom [8], and the various articles and books by M. Lazerowitz listed in the bibliography. For a concrete application of this theory, see Ayer, *The Foundations of Empirical Knowledge* (London: Macmillan and Co., 1940), Chapter I, Section 5; for criticisms of Ayer's invocation of the theory, see Austin [3], pp. 55–61, and Sellars [1], Section 5.

· 10b ·

RODERICK M. CHISHOLM

Comments on the "Proposal Theory"
of Philosophy[1]

Miss Ambrose discusses a number of "linguistic approaches" to philosophical problems and seems inclined to accept what might be called the "proposal theory" of philosophy. According to this theory, philosophical statements "are not, as they appear to be, answers to questions, but are proposals to alter language"; "in a concealed way," they "propose that a word's use shall be modified for philosophical purposes."[2] She points out, however, that

to hold that traditional philosophers are making linguistic proposals is not the same as to say that they are making *conscious* linguistic proposals. Any person holding the proposal theory would certainly say that philosophers are unaware of the fact that they are revising language, and that what they do with language deludes them as well as others. Freud's well-known study of the psychopathology of everyday life is sufficient evidence for the possibility of this being the case.

According to the suggestion, then, the philosopher, in expressing what may seem to be a "factual" statement, is merely making subconscious (or unconscious) linguistic proposals — or, better perhaps, he is making such proposals subconsciously. The philosopher who says, "Matter is unreal," for example, may be proposing subconsciously that the word "matter" be used in some different way. Any theory about the psychopathology of philosophers is, of course, a psychological or psychiatric theory and, as such, falls within the sphere of psychology or medicine rather than of philosophy. (It may be significant to note, however, that the kind of evidence offered in behalf of this theory is not the sort of evidence to which the psychiatrist usually appeals.) But the question whether philosophical statements are *mere* proposals and thus not "factual" is not a question of psychology or medicine. Miss Ambrose, accordingly, appeals to evidence other than that of psychopathology to show that philosophical statements are not "empirical." In what follows, I shall comment upon these points.[3]

1. Miss Ambrose's first reason for saying that philosophical statements are not empirical is that they are not based upon empirical evidence; the philosopher "has no laboratory, no experiments figure in his demonstrations or refutations, he cannot claim to closer observation of phenomena than other folk." Yet philosophers very often *do* appeal to evidence. In books

Reprinted from *The Journal of Philosophy*, XLIX (1952), 301–306, by permission of the author and the editor.
[1] Read at a Symposium on Linguistic Conceptions of Philosophy, Smith College, May 20, 1951.
[2] Unless otherwise indicated, references are to Alice Ambrose, "Linguistic Approaches to Philosophical Problems."

[3] I have discussed other aspects of this question in "Philosophers and Ordinary Language," *The Philosophical Review*, LX (1951), 317–328. [Editor's note: Reprinted below at pp. 175–82.]

on ethics, for example, we find reference to anthropological facts, e.g., the similarities and differences of ethical preferences and customs among different peoples; or to psychological facts, e.g., facts about motivation; or to autobiographical facts concerning the preferences of the authors. In books on epistemology, we are reminded that light takes time to travel, that stars sometimes cease to exist, that straight sticks often appear bent, that people sometimes have hallucinations and make mistakes, that things look yellowish to people who have jaundice. In books on metaphysics, we may read about molecules, or about evolution, or about the functioning of the brain and nervous system. It may be agreed that such facts as these are not the *discoveries* of philosophers; the philosopher may become aware of them by studying psychology or physics or some other branch of knowledge. Or, as Peirce emphasized, the philosopher may appeal to "those observations which every person can make in every hour of his waking life"; G. E. Moore, for example, appealed to this sort of observation when he showed his audience that he had a hand.[4] "The observational part of philosophy," Peirce said, "is a simple business, compared, for example, with that of anatomy or biography, or any other special science." [5] Miss Ambrose's point may be that the facts to which the philosopher appeals for his evidence are generally accessible; but this itself is hardly ground for saying that his conclusions are not factual.

2. I feel certain that Miss Ambrose would have the discussion turn, at this point, upon the second of her three reasons for supposing that philosophy is not empirical or factual. The second reason is that "philosophic disputants come to opposite conclusions although the same facts are available to them and no further fact can decide betwixt them; i.e., their dis-

pute cannot, even theoretically, be settled by recourse to any sort of matter of fact." An example is the dispute over the proposition, "Universals exist." Miss Ambrose formulates the point in a way which may seem question-begging, for the philosopher may reply, "The matter of fact which would decide our dispute is the fact that universals exist, or the fact that they don't exist." But I think Miss Ambrose would hold that facts pertaining to the existence or non-existence of universals are not the sort of facts which she has in mind when she speaks of certain facts as being "available." Although she does not discuss her use of the term "available," I think we may safely re-express her point by using the term "experience." Thus we might say that the philosophical dispute "cannot, even theoretically, be settled by recourse to any experience," or better, that the conflicting philosophical statements are statements whose truth or falsity "cannot, even theoretically, be determined by recourse to any experience." And this can be expressed more briefly simply by saying that the philosophical statements are statements which are not *verifiable*. Let us interpret Miss Ambrose's second argument, then, as involving two points: (a) philosophical statements, unlike scientific statements, are not verifiable; and (b) if a statement is not verifiable it cannot be factual.

(a) How are we to show that philosophical statements, unlike those of science, are not verifiable? The critics of early logical positivism, it will be recalled, had pointed out that the term "verifiable" is used in a number of different ways and that it is difficult to formulate a criterion of *verifiability* which will enable us to make the desired distinction between philosophical and scientific statements. Thus it may be easy to formulate a criterion of verifiability which allows us to say that the statements of science and common sense *are* verifiable. And it is easy enough to formulate a criterion of verifiability which allows us to say that the statements of philosophy or metaphysics are *not* verifi-

---

[4] C. S. Peirce, *Collected Papers*, 1.126. G. E. Moore, "Proof of an External World" (British Academy Annual Philosophical Lecture, 1939).
[5] *Op. cit.*, 1.133.

able. But I think it is safe to say that no one has yet succeeded in formulating a criterion of verifiability which will allow us to say *both* that the statements of science and common sense *are* verifiable and that those of philosophy or metaphysics are *not* verifiable.[6] If this is so, then Miss Ambrose's second reason for saying that philosophical statements are not factual is, at least at present, problematic, for it seems to presuppose that such a criterion is already at hand.

(b) But suppose we *should* be able to show that philosophical statements are unverifiable, in the desired sense. Would it follow that they are not *factual*? What if, as is likely, the philosopher continues to hold that they *are* factual and we find ourselves in disagreement over the question, "Are unverifiable statements factual?" I think that this disagreement, into which we would be led by Miss Ambrose's contention, may be exactly the sort of dispute she has in mind. It concerns the kind of question that Cardinal Mercier called *criteriological*.[7] Let us recall, briefly, the peculiarities of this kind of question.

Suppose, to use an example from another field, two psychologists cannot agree that a certain man is intelligent. If they have a common criterion of intelligence, probably they can resolve their dispute by examining him. And if they disagree concerning the criterion of intelligence, perhaps they can resolve their dispute by noting the characteristics shared by people whom both agreed to count as intelligent. But if they do not agree either as to who is intelligent or as to the criterion of intelligence there is little likelihood of settling their dispute. Their predicament would be similar to that of many philosophers who disagree about ethics: they can't agree which things are good because they use different criteria of goodness and they can't work out a common criterion of goodness because they can't even reach a preliminary agreement about which things are good. Philosophers who disagree about what things are to be counted as "ultimately real," or who disagree about what statements are to be counted as "meaningless" or "making no sense," sometimes reach a similar stalemate. One philosopher may contend, for example, that the statements "Time is unreal" and "A necessary being exists" are meaningless (or nonsense, or make no sense); another may deny it. They find that they employ different criteria of nonsense and then seek to work out a common criterion, possibly by generalizing from two groups of cases which each will agree to count as meaningful and meaningless respectively.[8] But then they learn that they can't even agree on these. One wants to count "Animals have vital entelechies," "There are contingent beings," and other such statements, among the meaningful cases; otherwise, he argues, the criterion will be too narrow. But the other wants to leave them out or count them as meaningless; otherwise, he argues, the criterion will be too broad. It is reasonable to suppose that, in such a situation, there is little hope of coming to terms. Similarly, if philosophers find themselves in disagreement over Miss Ambrose's contention that unverifiable statements are not *factual*, their dispute will, in all probability, lead to a similar impasse. I have said it may have

---

[6] Compare C. G. Hempel, "The Empiricist Criterion of Meaning," *Revue Internationale de Philosophie*, Quatrième Année, N° 11 (1950), 41–63; A. J. Ayer, *Language, Truth, and Logic*, Second Edition, pp. 11–16; Alonzo Church, review of same, *Journal of Symbolic Logic*, XIV (1949), 52–53; R. M. Blake, "Can Speculative Philosophy be Defended?" *Philosophical Review*, LII (1943), 127–134; Karl Popper, *Logik der Forschung*, pp. 21 ff. My remarks above, concerning what kinds of statements may be said to be "verifiable," could, of course, be re-expressed by substituting for the technical term "verifiable" some longer expression, such as "capable of being settled by recourse to empirical matters of fact."

[7] Compare Cardinal Mercier, *Critériologie génerále*. Compare also A. E. Murphy, "Can Speculative Philosophy be Defended?" *Philosophical Review*, LII (1943), 135–143.

[8] This is the method which Hempel describes, *loc. cit.*, p. 60.

been just this sort of dispute which led Miss Ambrose to say that philosophical disputes "cannot, even theoretically, be settled by recourse to any sort of matter of fact." But there are, of course, many non-philosophical disputes which are of this sort; compare our example involving the two psychologists. And there are many philosophical disputes which are *not* of this sort; for example, those which concern such questions as "Is there a necessary being?"

3. Miss Ambrose's third reason for holding that philosophical theories are not factual or empirical is the following: "Certain philosophical theories cannot be empirical because they imply the logical impossibility of what is patently and undeniably possible." For example, one of Bradley's views entails that the sentence, "We walked to the library," is self-contradictory. Concerning this view, Miss Ambrose makes two rather different points. (a) The view is obviously false; the sentence is not self-contradictory. (b) It is a fact that "whatever implies that something is logically impossible cannot itself be factual." Of these two points, the first is not relevant to our discussion. The second depends upon the doctrine that necessary propositions convey "merely verbal information." What reason is there for accepting this doctrine?

Miss Ambrose admits that "it is simply incorrect to say a necessary proposition is directly about words." The sentence, "Material bodies are extended," does not *mention* any words. But she holds that, in knowing and understanding this sentence, one knows a *verbal fact* — viz., that the phrase "unextended material bodies" has no descriptive use. She also admits that, in knowing and understanding the contingent sentence, "There are no white crows," one could similarly be said to know and understand a *verbal* fact, viz., that the phrase "white crow" has no application. And, by similar reasoning, I suppose, one could show that *any* sentence conveys a verbal fact. The sentence, "There are tigers in India," conveys that the word "tiger" has an application and that some of the things it applies to live in a place designated by the word "India"; the sentence, "The roof needs repair," conveys that what is designated by the word "roof" needs the operation designated by the word "repair"; and so on.[9] But Miss Ambrose offers a reason for saying that a necessary sentence, unlike a contingent one, conveys *merely* verbal information. She states this as follows, using the examples "There are no white crows" and "There are no unextended material bodies":

. . . in knowing that the one sentence expresses something contingently true, one knows that "white crows" has in our language a descriptive use and the non-verbal fact that it applies to nothing; while, in knowing that the other expresses something necessarily true, one knows that "unextended material bodies" has no descriptive use and one need know no non-verbal fact to know that what the sentence expresses is true. Knowing the verbal fact is sufficient for knowing a truth-value; there is no further fact to know. And this I take as grounds for holding that what a necessary proposition conveys is merely verbal information.

The cogency of this argument depends, therefore, upon the manner in which Miss Ambrose's technical terms "descriptive use" and "application" are to be distinguished. If, for example, the term "descriptive use" were defined by making use of the concepts of *necessity* or *contingency* (e.g., "A phrase may be said to have a descriptive use if and only if there *could* be something to which it would apply"), Miss Ambrose's argument would hardly be conclusive. But she has provided us with no definition or explication of this important term. I think it is fair to conclude, therefore, that until she tells us what she means by "descriptive use" she cannot be said to have shown that "what a necessary proposition conveys is merely verbal information."

[9] Compare C. J. Ducasse, *Philosophy as a Science*, pp. 95–103.

· 11 ·

JAMES W. CORNMAN

LANGUAGE AND ONTOLOGY

Generally, ontology has been thought to be the theory or study of the nature of being — or, to use more modern terminology, the study of what kinds of entities are basic. Traditionally, it has been thought that ontology is the job of the metaphysician who sits pondering about reality. In some quarters, however, the current conception of ontology is quite different; although it is still thought to be concerned with the question of what there is, as conceived by some it is the work of the scientists rather than the philosophers which has ontological implications. Indeed, the correct scientific theory states what essentially there is, e.g., elementary particles such as electrons, protons, and photons. On this view, each scientific theory, whether correct or not, is committed to some position about what is ontologically basic. The philosopher deals only with the logical analysis of language, i.e., with the analysis of relations among certain expressions of languages, which has little or no significance for ontology. Others, however, have still another view of ontology. They claim that although logical analysis is the sole domain of the philosopher, it is still he who engages in ontology, because given a theory, scientific

or otherwise, then merely by getting the logical relationships among the expressions of the theory correctly characterized, we can arrive at the ontological position to which the theory is committed. Thus, on this view not only the scientist but also the man on the street is ontologically committed to some position, although he requires the help of the linguistic analyst to discover what his position is.

It is my view that both of these "contemporary" views of ontology are misguided, because no ontological position follows from the work of either the scientist or the analytic philosopher. I shall attempt to show that what ontologically commits the holder of a particular theory, or the user of a certain form of discourse, is the theory of linguistic reference that he maintains, i.e., his theory about which expressions refer and to what they refer. Furthermore, since philosophers, rather than scientists and other non-philosophers, are concerned with theories of reference, only philosophers engage in ontology. And since a theory of reference is not a subject matter of logic (either formal or informal), philosophers who do logical analysis are not doing ontology.

In order to show that the two "contemporary" views of ontology are wrong I wish to establish two points. First, I wish to show that there are senses of 'refer' for which it is true to say that an expression is a referring expression but that we are not entitled to infer from this that anything

An abridged and revised version of a paper first published in *The Australasian Journal of Philosophy*, XLI (1963), 291–305, used by permission of the author and the editor.

Editor's note: I am most grateful to Professor Cornman for having consented to shorten his article in order to make it possible for me to include it in this volume.

exists in any sense of 'exist'. This is a vital point for if there were no such sense of 'refer', then, as will be shown, we would be ontologically committed merely by our language and apparently committed to some very queer things. As a consequence ontology would be merely a linguistic concern, one of the views I am trying to refute. To develop this point I shall first distinguish several senses of 'refer' and then use Quine's development of a similar point in "On What There Is"[1] to show that although certain expressions can be substituends for the variable x in " 'x' refers to q" it does not follow from this that anything exists.

Second, I wish to show that even for that sense of 'refer' for which we can infer from " 'p' refers to q" that something exists, we are ontologically committed to whatever it is that 'p' refers to, but not to any particular ontological view about what it is that 'p' refers to. To find what that is, what ontological position we are committed to, requires in addition a theory of reference. Here I shall be attacking some things said by Quine.

This second point is also essential to my purposes because unless this point is correct not only is at least one of the two "contemporary" views of ontology correct, but also certain ontological positions are self-defeating. To see this, consider the following ontological theory concerning the mind-body problem. This theory as held by J. J. C. Smart states that what sensation-expressions really refer to are certain brain-processes rather than sensations, although no sensation-expressions mean the same as any brain-process-expression.[2] Furthermore, the theory does not deny that either "There are sensations" or "There are brain-processes" is true. But if it is

legitimate to infer from the truth of these sentences that we are ontologically committed to both brain-processes and sensations, as it would be on both "contemporary" views of ontology, then this theory is indeed ontologically committed to sensations, i.e., committed to the view that sensations are ontologically basic. But this is just what the theory denies, because it is the view that even though sensation-expressions denote, we are ontologically committed to brain-processes but not to sensations. Thus this theory, if the above move is legitimate, is surely in a paradoxical situation because it would be ontologically committed to sensations while at the same time denying that anyone is so committed.

In order to establish the first point, I must first distinguish among certain senses of 'refer' so that we can work with just the sense or senses relevant to ontological commitment and the problems we are trying to solve. To do so let us consider the words 'Alaska', 'Pegasus', and 'loud'. For each of these words the following sentences seem, at least before undergoing philosophical scrutiny, to be true: "The word 'Alaska' refers to the largest state of the United States," "The word 'Pegasus' refers to the winged horse captured by Bellerophon," and "The word 'loud' refers to a property of things." Thus each of these words seems to be a substituend for x in " 'x' refers to y." Yet there also seem to be differences relevant to reference among these words. 'Alaska' and 'Pegasus' seem to be substituends for x in "What 'x' refers to exists." However, 'loud' is not such a substituend because such substituends are nouns and 'loud' is not a noun. Furthermore, when 'Alaska' is substituted for x the resulting sentence is true, but when 'Pegasus' is substituted the sentence is false, for at least one sense of 'exist'.

To distinguish these three differences let us say that a linguistic expression refers₁ if and only if it is a substituend for x in " 'x'

[1] W. V. Quine, *From a Logical Point of View* (Cambridge, Massachusetts: 1961), pp. 1–19.
[2] See J. J. Smart, "Sensations and Brain Processes," *The Philosophical Review*, LXVIII (1959); and my paper "The Identity of Mind and Body," *The Journal of Philosophy*, LIX (1962).

refers to y"; a linguistic expression refers $_2$ if and only if it is a substituend for x in "What 'x' refers to exists"; and a linguistic expression refers $_3$ if and only if when it is a substituend for x in "What 'x' refers to exists" the resulting sentence is true. Expressions that refer $_2$ are commonly called denoting expressions and those that refer $_3$ are denoting expressions that denote something.

It is obvious, I think, that the only sense of 'refer' which is relevant to ontological commitment is 'refer $_3$' because it would seem that we should be ontologically committed to something only if a sentence of the form "What 'p' refers to exists" is true. That is, it seems that only in the case in which an expression denotes do we have any right to infer that something exists. It would seem, then, that there are senses of 'refer' for which we are not entitled to infer from the truth of sentences of the form " 'x' refers to y" that something exists. However, this may not be true. Someone might argue in a Meinongian way that because a certain expression refers in at least one sense, it is legitimate to infer that what it refers to exists in at least some sense. We must prove that there are no grounds for such a view because if we cannot then there will be a very good sense in which it will be true to say that a language ontologically commits its users. This would be true because for certain senses of 'refer' expressions of the form " 'x' refers to x" are surely true. Thus, for example, the expression " 'Pegasus' refers $_1$ to Pegasus" and the expression " 'the number two' refers $_1$ to the number two" both seem to be true. If we are entitled to infer from the truth of these statements that what 'Pegasus' refers to and what 'the number two' refers to exist, we will be ontologically committed to the existence of certain things just on the basis of the truth of referring $_1$ statements. In this way we could prove that all sorts of strange things exist. What this view in its most extreme form amounts to is a claim that any expression which refers in some sense also denotes or names

something. What I must do here is to show that there is no reason to think that we are ontologically committed to anything by any sense of referring except referring $_3$, i.e., denoting. Then I shall show that even for referring $_3$ we are not ontologically committed to any view of what it is that is denoted by any expression.

The argument I wish to refute, which is, I believe, the only argument put forth to substantiate the view that if an expression refers in any sense, what it refers to exists, goes as follows: Although for one sense of 'exist' the sentence "What 'Pegasus' refers to exists" is false there must be some other sense of 'exist' for which that sentence is true. For, even if "What 'Pegasus' refers to exists" is false (for one sense of 'exist'), what 'Pegasus' refers to must exist (in some other sense of 'exist') because even when we deny that what 'Pegasus' refers to exists we are talking about or referring to what 'Pegasus' refers to and there must be something we are talking about or referring to. Thus what 'Pegasus' refers to must exist (for some sense of 'exist'). To show that this argument has no force I shall, as Quine does, employ the method developed by Russell in "On Denoting." [3]

Using Russell's technique we can translate "What 'Pegasus' refers to exists" as follows: "At least one thing that exists is referred to by 'Pegasus' and there exists no more than one thing referred to by 'Pegasus'." On this translation the sentence is false. Should we still infer that what 'Pegasus' refers to exists (in some sense)? I think not on the basis of the reason given above and I can find no other. On this translation the sentence is false because the first conjunct is false. But if that is false then "Each thing that exists is not referred to by 'Pegasus'" is true. But we cannot infer from the truth of this sentence that what 'Pegasus' refers to exists for the above reason, because this sentence does not use the ex-

[3] See B. Russell, "On Denoting," in *Readings in Philosophical Analysis* (New York, 1949), pp. 103–115.

procoion "what 'Pegasus' refers to" and therefore there is no reason to suppose that in uttering the sentence we are talking about or referring to what 'Pegasus' refers to. Rather we would seem to be referring to each thing that exists and denying that 'Pegasus' refers to any of these things.

It seems, then, that there is no reason to suppose that an expression, 'p', denotes anything unless that sentence "What 'p' refers to exists" is true for all senses of 'exist', or, better, for the usual sense of 'exist' since the other "odd" senses seem to be needed if and only if the argument we have destroyed is sound. Thus there is no reason to conclude that what 'Pegasus' refers to exists merely because the sentence "What 'Pegasus' refers to exists" is meaningful. Thus we have established the first point. I shall now proceed to the second.

What I wish to show now is that even for that sense of 'refer' for which we can infer from " 'p' refers to q" that something exists, i.e., 'refer₃', we are only ontologically committed to what 'p' refers to, whatever it is, but not to any particular view of what that is. No matter what the language is, the users of that language are not committed to any particular ontological positions merely because an expression of that language denotes. What is necessary, in addition, is some theory about what the expression denotes. However, some philosophers have denied this. Quine, for example, sometimes says things which imply that no such theory is necessary, such as:

We find philosophers allowing themselves not only abstract terms but even pretty unmistakable quantifications over abstract objects ("There are concepts with which . . . ," ". . . some of which propositions . . . ," ". . . there is something that he doubts or believes"), and still blandly disavowing within the paragraph, any claim that there are such objects.[4]

The philosophers who assert sentences containing the phrases mentioned in the

[4] W. V. Quine, *Word and Object* (New York, 1960), p. 241.

above quotation surely, as Quine says, use abstract terms, and what is more, at least imply that they are substituends for variables. But the inference from a premise concerning commitments to the use of certain terms as substituends for variables to the conclusion that we are ontologically committed to certain entities as the values of those variables is surely not legitimate without an additional premise concerning the reference of the substituends.

In order to show that this additional premise is necessary and, at the same time, to establish the second of the two points I am trying to make, I wish to examine the criteria for ontological commitment implicit in the two views about ontology that I wish to refute. One of these criteria is as follows:

A theory, T, is ontologically committed to an entity, E, if and only if "E exists" or some statement which implies "E" exists" (e.g., "What 'E' refers to exists") is used to make one of the affirmations of T.

If this is the correct criterion then it follows that if an expression 'E' refers₃, we are ontologically committed to E. Thus a scientific theory, or any other kind of theory, is ontologically committed to E merely because one of its assertions is or implies "E exists." This is the first of the two positions I wish to refute. Furthermore such a criterion would justify Quine's claim that those who assert sentences such as "There are concepts with which . . ." are ontologically committed to concepts and thereby to abstract entities.

But is this criterion correct? Let us examine it. To find the mistake in this criterion we need only remember the method of avoiding an ontological commitment to Pegasus considered earlier in the paper. There I utilized Russell's theory of descriptions to show that an assertion containing a term which seemingly denotes Pegasus could be paraphrased in such a way that there is no reason to think that there was any such reference to Pegasus. We can generalize this point, as does

Quine, by saying that in any case where we can paraphrase a statement such as "E exists" so that there is no reason to think that there is any reference to E, we are not ontologically committed to E. There is, then, at least one way to avoid the charge that we are ontologically committed to an entity, E, even when we assert "E exists" or some statement which implies "E exists." For example, if I assert "The average American family has 1.2 cars," then on the above criterion I am ontologically committed to an entity, the average American family, because the assertion implies "There is something which is the average American family." However, we can paraphrase this sentence as "The number of family-run cars in the United States divided by the number of American families equals 1.2," in which the phrase 'the average American family' does not occur. Thus there is no reason to think I am referring to the average American family when I assert the sentence and, as a result, no reason to think I am ontologically committed to the average American family.

Thus this first criterion will not do. It would ontologically commit us to more entities than there is any reason to think we should be committed to. It follows from this that the view about ontology which states that a theory, scientific or otherwise, is ontologically committed to an entity merely because one of its assertions is or implies a sentence such as "E exists" is mistaken. However, Quine's claim, which is correct if this criterion is acceptable, does not fail because this criterion fails. He stresses the importance of paraphrasing. We must stress it also if we are to find some way to avoid the problems of the above criterion. We are ontologically committed to entities not in all cases in which we do assert or imply a sentence of the form "x exists" but perhaps only in those cases in which we must assert, i.e., cannot avoid asserting, a sentence which is of that form or which implies one of that form in order to say what we wish to say.

Let us now examine a criterion which

accounts for this point. It would be expressed as follows:

A theory, T, is ontologically committed to an entity, E, if and only if "E exists" or some statement which implies "E exists" must be used to make one of the assertions of T.[5]

If this criterion is correct then the ontological commitments of a theory don't follow merely from the assertions of the theory, but from those assertions which contain referring expressions the logical analyst cannot paraphrase away. Thus this is the criterion implicit in the second of the two contemporary views about ontology which I wish to refute. It is also a criterion which justifies Quine's claim concerning 'concepts' and abstract entities.

Let us now examine the criterion. If we work with the English language one problem becomes immediately apparent. Consider the following assertion: "Hesperus exists." It seems that any theory which makes that assertion would be ontologically committed to at least one astronomical body. But this is not so if we adopt the presently discussed criterion. Since both 'Venus' and 'Phosphorus' refer to the same entity as 'Hesperus,' it is false that "Hesperus exists" or any statement which implies "Hesperus exists" must be used to make any affirmation of any theory.[6] Either "Phosphorus exists" or "Venus exists" would do equally as well. Therefore in this case, as in any other in which there is in a language more than one non-synonymous term to refer to the same entity, no theory would have any ontological commitments. This surely is mistaken. Unlike the previously examined criterion, this one would not ontologically commit us to as

[5] See W. Alston, "Ontological Commitments," *Philosophical Studies*, IX (1958), for a criterion of this kind.

[6] I assume here that the implication is logical. For this my objections hold. If the implication is extensional then my objection will not hold. However, in that case, to establish such an implication requires some consideration of the reference of the relevant expressions, which is one of the points I am trying to make.

many entities as it seems we should be committed to.

Is there any way to correct this second criterion to avoid the above problem? I believe that any correction that will work must at least add to the disjunction on the right side of the criterion a disjunct such as "or some expression which refers to the same entity as 'E'." More than this addition is needed to avoid all the problems such a criterion faces, but it is, I believe, necessary to avoid the above problem. And if it is a necessary addition then one of my claims is established, i.e., a premise concerning linguistic reference is essential to make the inference from what is asserted to a conclusion about ontological commitments. But more of this later. What is important to emphasize here is that at least for a language such as English neither of the two criteria discussed above is correct.

However, the above conclusion may bother no one who accepts either of the two criteria we have discussed. He might well say that the problems arise not because there is something wrong with the criteria but because there is something wrong with the English language as ordinarily used. If a language were such that there was in that language one and only one expression to denote each entity, then the users of that language would be committed to use one particular expression to denote each thing they wish to talk about. Thus for this language no additional premise about linguistic reference would be needed to infer validly from assertions to ontological commitments. We could in such a language read off a theory's ontological commitments directly from its assertions. For such an "ideal" language, then, both of the above criteria would work.[7] But should we infer from this that in this case a theory of reference is un-

necessary for the criteria which apply? Let us see.

Suppose that someone constructed or discovered a language, S, which he claimed was "ideal." Suppose further that this language contained both sensation-expressions and brain-process-expressions. Should we conclude that, at least for S, Smart's identity thesis is wrong and that we are ontologically committed to both brain-processes and sensations, or should we conclude that S is not "ideal"? Or suppose that S contained brain-process-expressions but not sensation-expressions. Should we conclude that sensation-expressions are unnecessary for an "ideal" language, or would we conclude that S is not "ideal"? In neither case would we know what to conclude unless the "inventor" or "discoverer" established his claim about S. But how could he do this?

First, he would have to show that what I shall call, modifying one of Ryle's phrases, the 'Fido' — Fido theory of reference applies to all the denoting expressions of S. That is, he could only establish that S is the kind of ideal language he claims it is by showing that for any denoting expressions of S, e.g., 'q', the sentence " 'q' denotes q" is true but for any other denoting expression not synonymous with 'q', e.g., 'p', the sentence " 'p' denotes q" is false. If this 'Fido' — Fido theory of reference were true of S, then if an expression 'p' denotes something, it could denote only one thing, p, and thus we would be ontologically committed to p if we asserted "p exists." Secondly, he would have to show that those denoting expressions of other languages which denote but which are not in S, denote some entity which is denoted by some denoting expressions which are in S.

It is then necessary, in order to justify a claim that a language is "ideal," to show that one particular theory of reference applies to the language, i.e., the 'Fido' — Fido theory of reference. From this we can conclude that for the purposes of ontology there is no essential difference between an

[7] See B. Russell in his introduction to *Tractatus Logico-Philosophicus* by L. Wittgenstein (London, 1958), p. 9, for a discussion of such an "ideal" language.

"ideal" language such as S, and a "non-ideal" language such as ordinary English. In both cases some premise about the reference of expressions of the language is needed in order to draw conclusions about ontological commitments. The only difference is that whereas in the latter case the premise concerning linguistic reference is needed to justify the inference from assertions to ontological commitments, in the former case it is needed to justify the claim that the language in which the assertions are made is "ideal." Thus somewhere or other such a premise is necessary for any inference from language to ontological commitments.

The consequences of the above conclusion for the matters with which we are presently concerned are twofold. First, neither of the two "contemporary" criteria of ontological commitment are by themselves correct. Both at least require in addition some theory of reference. Secondly, Quine cannot justify his claim that those who assert "There are concepts with which . . ." are ontologically committed to abstract entities unless he justifies the 'Fido' — Fido theory of reference, because only if at least one of the two "contemporary" criteria is by itself sufficient, is his inference valid without an additional premise about linguistic reference. But we have just seen that neither criterion is sufficient. Thus Quine's claim is no better substantiated than the claim of his "Meinongian" opponent, because both require what neither has substantiated: the 'Fido' — Fido theory of reference, a theory which is no more obviously correct for one language than for any other. In fact, for English as ordinarily used, it is surely incorrect, as we can see if we remember that 'Hesperus', 'Phosphorus', and 'Venus' all denote the same entity. Thus, whether it is true of any particular language is at least debatable.

We are now, I think, ready to draw some final conclusions. As we have seen, the possibility of inconsistency in certain ontological positions arises because these positions condone assertions such as "E exists," yet deny any ontological commitment to E. One such position, previously mentioned, is Smart's version of the Identity Theory, which agrees that assertions such as "There are sensations" are true, yet claims that because sensation-expressions really refer to brain-processes, we are not ontologically committed to sensations; that is, sensations are ontologically derivative. We have also seen that this position is indeed inconsistent if either of the two "contemporary" criteria for ontological commitment is correct. But since we have found that inferences from such assertions to ontological commitments are valid only if some premise regarding linguistic reference is included, we can conclude that theories such as Smart's can be consistently held if we are careful about which theory of reference we adopt.

The second conclusion is that no ontological position follows from the work of the scientist or the work of the logical analyst. That this is true of the scientist can be seen from the fact that the only scientific claims relevant to ontology are assertions such as "E exists." But since no ontological commitments follow from such assertions, ontology does not follow from the work of the scientist. That no ontological position follows from the work of the logical analyst can be seen from the fact that whereas the logical analyst is solely concerned with the relationships among various linguistic expressions (e.g., he is concerned with paraphrasing sentences or showing how the functions of certain expressions are different from or similar to the functions of other expressions), what is necessary for ontology are the relationships between linguistic expressions and entities. Thus, we can conclude that ontology is the job of neither the scientist nor the analytic philosopher. Whether or not we should also conclude from this that ontology is a misguided pursuit will not be discussed here. I shall only say, briefly and dogmatically, that the usual attempts to show that such a pursuit is illegitimate because it invokes utterances which are neither scientifically verifiable nor analytic, can be justified only by employing some particular theory of reference. But because employing such a theory is in itself an ontological pursuit, these attempts are self-defeating.

WILLARD v. O. QUINE

SEMANTIC ASCENT

This chapter has been centrally occupied with the question what objects to recognize. Yet it has treated of words as much as its predecessors. Part of our concern here has been with the question what a theory's commitments to objects consist in (§ 49)*, and of course this second-order question is about words. But what is noteworthy is that we have talked more of words than of objects even when most concerned to decide what there really is: what objects to admit on our own account.

This would not have happened if and insofar as we had lingered over the question whether in particular there are wombats, or whether there are unicorns. Discourse about non-linguistic objects would have been an excellent medium in which to debate those issues. But when the debate shifts to whether there are points, miles, numbers, attributes, propositions, facts, or classes, it takes on an in some sense philosophical cast, and straightway we find ourselves talking of words almost to the exclusion of the non-linguistic objects under debate.

Carnap has long held that the questions of philosophy, when real at all, are questions of language; and the present observation would seem to illustrate his point. He holds that the philosophical questions of what there is are questions of how we may most conveniently fashion our "linguistic framework," and not, as in the case of the wombat or unicorn, questions about extra-linguistic reality.[1] He holds that those philosophical questions are only apparently about sorts of objects, and are really pragmatic questions of language policy.

But why should this be true of the philosophical questions and not of theoretical questions generally? Such a distinction of status is of a piece with the notion of analyticity (§ 14), and as little to be trusted. After all, theoretical sentences in general are defensible only pragmatically; we can but assess the structural merits of the theory which embraces them along with sentences directly conditioned to multifarious stimulations. How then can Carnap draw a line across this theoretical part and hold that the sentences this side of the line enjoy non-verbal content or meaning in a way that those beyond the line do not? His own appeal to convenience of linguistic framework allows pragmatic connections across the line. What other sort of connection can be asked anywhere, short of direct conditioning to nonverbal stimulations?

Reprinted from *Word and Object* (Cambridge, Massachusetts: The Massachusetts Institute of Technology Press, 1960), pp. 270–76, by permission of the author and the publisher. (Copyright 1960 by the Massachusetts Institute of Technology Press.)

*Editor's note: The section numbers refer to previous portions of *Word and Object*.

[1] Carnap, "Empiricism, semantics, and ontology. [Editor's note: Reprinted above at pp. 72–84.]

Yet we do recognize a shift from talk of objects to talk of words as debate progresses from existence of wombats and unicorns to existence of points, miles, classes, and the rest. How can we account for this? Amply, I think, by proper account of a useful and much used manoeuvre which I shall call *semantic ascent*.

It is the shift from talk of miles to talk of 'mile'. It is what leads from the material (*inhaltlich*) mode into the formal mode, to invoke an old terminology of Carnap's. It is the shift from talking in certain terms to talking about them. It is precisely the shift that Carnap thinks of as divesting philosophical questions of a deceptive guise and setting them forth in their true colors. But this tenet of Carnap's is the part that I do not accept. Semantic ascent, as I speak of it, applies anywhere.[2] 'There are wombats in Tasmania' might be paraphrased as "Wombat' is true of some creatures in Tasmania', if there were any point in it. But it does happen that semantic ascent is more useful in philosophical connections than in most, and I think I can explain why.

Consider what it would be like to debate over the existence of miles without ascending to talk of 'mile'. "Of course there are miles. Wherever you have 1760 yards you have a mile." "But there are no yards either. Only bodies of various lengths." "Are the earth and moon separated by bodies of various lengths?" The continuation is lost in a jumble of invective and question-begging. When on the other hand we ascend to 'mile' and ask which of its contexts are useful and for what purposes, we can get on; we are no longer caught in the toils of our opposed uses.

The strategy of semantic ascent is that it carries the discussion into a domain where both parties are better agreed on the objects (viz., words) and on the main terms concerning them. Words, or their inscriptions, unlike points, miles, classes, and the rest, are tangible objects of the size so popular in the marketplace, where men of unlike conceptual schemes communicate at their best. The strategy is one of ascending to a common part of two fundamentally disparate conceptual schemes, the better to discuss the disparate foundations. No wonder it helps in philosophy.

But it also figures in the natural sciences. Einstein's theory of relativity was accepted in consequence not just of reflections on time, light, headlong bodies, and the perturbations of Mercury, but of reflections also on the theory itself, as discourse, and its simplicity in comparison with alternative theories. Its departure from classical conceptions of absolute time and length is too radical to be efficiently debated at the level of object talk unaided by semantic ascent. The case was similar, if in lesser degrees, for the disruptions of traditional outlook occasioned by the doctrines of molecules and electrons. These particles come after wombats and unicorns, and before points and miles, in a significant gradation.

The device of semantic ascent has been used much and carefully in axiomatic studies in mathematics, for the avoidance, again, of question-begging. In axiomatizing some already familiar theory, geometry say, one used to be in danger of imagining that he had deduced some familiar truth of the theory purely from his axioms when actually he had made inadvertent use of further geometrical knowledge. As a precaution against this danger, a device other than semantic ascent was at first resorted to: the device of disinterpretation. One feigned to understand only the logical vocabulary and not the distinctive terms of the axiom system concerned. This was an effective way of barring information extraneous to the axioms and thus limiting one's inferences to what the axioms logically implied. The device of

---

[2] In a word, I reject Carnap's doctrine of "quasi-syntactic" or "pseudo-object" sentences, but accept his distinction between the material and the formal mode. See his *Logical Syntax*, §§ 63–64. (It was indeed I, if I may reminisce, who in 1934 proposed 'material mode' to him as translation of his German.)

disinterpretation had impressive side effects, some good, such as the rise of abstract algebra, and some bad, such as the notion that in pure mathematics "we never know what we are talking about, nor whether what we are saying is true."[3] At any rate, with Frege's achievement of a full formalization of logic, an alternative and more refined precaution against question-begging became available to axiomatic studies; and it is a case, precisely, of what I am calling semantic ascent. Given the deductive apparatus of logic in the form of specified operations on notational forms, the question whether a given formula follows logically from given axioms reduces to the question whether the specified operations on notational forms are capable of leading to that formula from the axioms. An affirmative answer to such a question can be established without disinterpretation, yet without fear of circularity, indeed without using the terms of the theory at all except to talk about them and the operations upon them.

We must also notice a further reason for semantic ascent in philosophy. This further reason holds also, and more strikingly, for logic; so let us look there first. Most truths of elementary logic contain extralogical terms; thus 'If all Greeks are men and all men are mortal . . .'. The main truths of physics, in contrast, contain terms of physics only. Thus whereas we can expound physics in its full generality without semantic ascent, we can expound logic in a general way only by talking of forms of sentences. The generality wanted in physics can be got by quantifying over nonlinguistic objects, while the dimension of generality wanted for logic runs crosswise to what can be got by such quantification. It is a difference in shape of field and not in content; the above syllogism about the

Greeks need owe its truth no more peculiarly to language than other sentences do.

There are characteristic efforts in philosophy, those coping e.g. with perplexities of lion-hunting or believing (§§ 30–32), that resemble logic in their need of semantic ascent as a means of generalizing beyond examples.[4] Not that I would for a moment deny that when the perplexities about lion-hunting or believing and its analogues are cleared up they are cleared up by an improved structuring of discourse; but the same is true of an advance in physics. The same is true even though the latter restructuring be led up to (as often happens) within discourse of objects, and not by semantic ascent.

For it is not as though considerations of systematic efficacy, broadly pragmatic considerations, were operative only when we make a semantic ascent and talk of theory, and factual considerations of the behavior of objects in the world were operative only when we avoid semantic ascent and talk within the theory. Considerations of systematic efficacy are equally essential in both cases; it is just that in the one case we voice them and in the other we are tacitly guided by them. And considerations of the behavior of objects in the world, even behavior affecting our sensory surfaces by contact or radiation, are likewise essential in both cases.

There are two reasons why observation is felt to have no such bearing on logic and philosophy as it has on theoretical physics. One is traceable to misapprehensions about semantic ascent. The other is traceable to curriculum classifications. This latter factor tends likewise to make one feel that observation has no such bearing on mathematics as it has on theoretical physics. Theoretical assertions in physics, being terminologically physics, are generally conceded to owe a certain empirical content to the physical observations which, however indirectly, they help to systema-

---

[3] Russell, *Mysticism and Logic and Other Essays*, p. 75. The essay in question dates from 1901, and happily the aphorism expressed no enduring attitude on Russell's part. But the attitude expressed has been widespread.

[4] Wittgenstein's characteristic style, in his later period, consisted in avoiding semantic ascent by sticking to the examples.

tize, whereas laws of so-called logic and mathematics, however useful in systematizing physical observations, are not considered to pick up any empirical substance thereby. A more reasonable attitude is that there are merely variations in degree of centrality to the theoretical structure, and in degree of relevance to one or another set of observations.

In § 49 I spoke of dodges whereby philosophers have thought to enjoy the systematic benefits of abstract objects without suffering the objects. There is one more such dodge in what I have been inveighing against in these last pages: the suggestion that the acceptance of such objects is a linguistic convention distinct somehow from serious views about reality.

The question what there is is a shared concern of philosophy and most other nonfiction genres. The descriptive answer has been given only in part, but at some length. A representative assortment of land masses, seas, planets, and stars have been individually described in the geography and astronomy books, and an occasional biped or other middle-sized object in the biographies and art books. Description has been stepped up by mass production in zoology, botany, and mineralogy, where things are grouped by similarities and described collectively. Physics, by more ruthless abstraction from differences in detail, carries mass description farther still. And even pure mathematics belongs to the descriptive answer to the question what there is; for the things about which the question asks do not exclude the numbers, classes, functions, etc., if such there be, whereof pure mathematics treats.

What distinguishes between the ontological philosopher's concern and all this is only breadth of categories. Given phys-

ical objects in general, the natural scientist is the man to decide about wombats and unicorns. Given classes, or whatever other broad realm of objects the mathematician needs, it is for the mathematician to say whether in particular there are any even prime numbers or any cubic numbers that are sums of pairs of cubic numbers. On the other hand it is scrutiny of this uncritical acceptance of the realm of physical objects itself, or of classes, etc., that devolves upon ontology. Here is the task of making explicit what had been tacit, and precise what had been vague; of exposing and resolving paradoxes, smoothing kinks, lopping off vestigial growths, clearing ontological slums.

The philosopher's task differs from the others', then, in detail; but in no such drastic way as those suppose who imagine for the philosopher a vantage point outside the conceptual scheme that he takes in charge. There is no such cosmic exile. He cannot study and revise the fundamental conceptual scheme of science and common sense without having some conceptual scheme, whether the same or another no less in need of philosophical scrutiny, in which to work. He can scrutinize and improve the system from within, appealing to coherence and simplicity; but this is the theoretician's method generally. He has recourse to semantic ascent, but so has the scientist. And if the theoretical scientist in his remote way is bound to save the eventual connections with non-verbal stimulation, the philosopher in his remoter way is bound to save them too. True, no experiment may be expected to settle an ontological issue; but this is only because such issues are connected with surface irritations in such multifarious ways, through such a maze of intervening theory.

PART III

Metaphilosophical Problems of Ordinary-Language Philosophy

· 13 ·

RODERICK CHISHOLM

PHILOSOPHERS AND ORDINARY LANGUAGE

The point of a philosophical symposium on ordinary language, I take it, is to discuss certain contemporary views about the relation between ordinary language and philosophy. Among these are: (1) that many apparently important philosophical statements "violate" ordinary language in that they use it incorrectly; (2) that such statements are misleading and often seem comparatively unimportant when formulated correctly; and (3) that "any philosophical statement which violates ordinary language is false." The first two of these theses seem to me to be true, but the third seems to be false; accordingly, I shall restrict this paper to an examination of the third.[1]

The clearest defense of this thesis is to be found in Norman Malcolm's important paper, "Moore and Ordinary Language," in Volume IV of the "Library of Living Philosophers." Malcolm describes and defends what he takes to be G. E. Moore's method of defending ordinary language "against its philosophical violators."[2] "The philosophizing of most of the more important philosophers," according to Malcolm, "has consisted in their more or less subtly repudiating ordinary language";[3] but Moore, sensing that "any philosophical statement which violates ordinary language is false,"[4] has devised a method of refuting such statements. "The essence of Moore's technique of refuting philosophi-

cal statements consists in pointing out that these statements *go against ordinary language.*"[5] Whether this is in fact Moore's technique need not concern us.

Most philosophical views, it seems to me, *cannot* be refuted so easily. My hope, in criticizing this paper, which Malcolm wrote a number of years ago, is to elicit clarification of what is surely one of the most significant movements in contemporary philosophy. I shall first discuss the concept of correctness and then I shall examine two linguistic theories upon which Malcolm bases the thesis.

I

Let us begin by asking how we would show that a philosopher is using language *incorrectly.* Suppose we have found an epistemologist who holds that *certainty* is very difficult to attain: he tells us that, although people may *believe* that there is furniture in the room or that the earth has existed for hundreds of years past, no one can be *certain* that such beliefs are true. We might point out to him that people *do*

[1] Read at the annual meeting of the American Philosophical Association, University of Toronto, December 27–29, 1950.
[2] Norman Malcolm, "Moore and Ordinary Language," *The Philosophy of G. E. Moore,* Volume IV of *The Library of Living Philosophers.* ed. P. A. Schilpp. (Evanston and Chicago: Northwestern University, 1942), p. 124. [Editor's note: Reprinted above at pp. 111–24. References are to the pagination in this volume.]
[3] Ibid., p. 122.
[4] Ibid., p. 124.
[5] Ibid., p. 113.

Reprinted from *The Philosophical Review,* LX (1951), 317–28, by permission of the author and the editor.

call such beliefs "certain"; we might go on to note that, ordinarily, one would apply the word "uncertain" only to beliefs of a much more problematic sort, for instance to conjectures about the weather; we might add that, if anyone were to teach a child the meaning of the words "certain" and "uncertain," he would never cite as an *uncertain* belief the one about the furniture; and so on. This sort of technique, which is frequently used, would show that the epistemologist disagrees with most people about the denotation of the word "certain," since he does not apply that word to the beliefs to which it is ordinarily applied. But would it show that he is using the word incorrectly? To see that it would not, let us consider a different case. A fifteenth-century geographer might have pointed out to Columbus that ordinarily people apply the word "flat" and not the word "round" to the earth; that they apply the word "round" to entities of quite a different sort, possibly to peaches and olives; that if a man wanted to teach his children the meaning of the word "round" he would never cite the earth as an example; and so on. But, Malcolm holds, this would not show that Columbus was using language incorrectly, since in this case ordinary people were making a *mistake* and Columbus was not.[6]

If we are thus to distinguish between *mistaken* usage and *incorrect* usage, we need, apparently, some such concept as that of *connotation* or *intension* for describing incorrectness. In the Columbus case, where *mistaken* usage was involved, we may assume that the word "round," as well as the word "flat," had the same intension for each of the persons concerned. Thus it is possible to say that the disagreement was unlike those which often arise because someone uses language incorrectly. For example, people sometimes argue over the question "Is a whale a fish?" and yet seem to be in agreement about the properties of whales; usually, in such cases, the word "fish" does *not* have the same intension for each of the persons concerned. In the whale case, unlike the Columbus case, at least one person is using language incorrectly. It is possible, therefore, that our epistemologist is using the word "certain" correctly, even though he disagrees with most people concerning its denotation. For it may be that, although his language is correct, he is mistaken about the facts. Or, as he might insist, it may be that his language is correct and that, as in the Columbus case, ordinary people are mistaken about the facts.[7]

To say that someone uses a word correctly, then, is to say, in part at least, that it has for him the same intension it has for most people.[8] Language as it is ordinarily used cannot be incorrect since "correct language" is synonymous with "ordinary language"; "ordinary language *is* correct language."[9] Thus the principal way to find out whether someone is using a word incorrectly would be to find out what intension the word has for him and

---

[6] "There are two ways in which a person may be wrong when he makes an empirical statement. First he may be making a mistake as to what the empirical facts are. Second, he may know all right what the empirical facts are, but may use the wrong language to describe those facts. We might call the first 'being mistaken about the facts', and the second 'using incorrect language' or 'using improper language' or 'using wrong language' . . . [When people] said that the earth was flat, they were wrong. The way in which their statement was wrong was that they were making a mistake about the facts, not that they were using incorrect language; they were using perfectly correct language to describe what they thought to be the case. In the sense in which they said what was wrong, it is perfectly possible for *everyone* to say what is wrong" (*ibid.*, p. 117).

[7] Compare C. A. Campbell, "Common-Sense Propositions and Philosophical Paradoxes," *Aristotelian Society Proceedings*, XLV (1944–1945); also Morris Weitz, "Philosophy and the Abuse of Language," *Journal of Philosophy*, XLIV (1947), 533–546.

[8] The *intension* of a word, say "horse," for some person, might be said to comprise those characteristics which it is necessary for him to believe an object to have before he will refer to it as a "horse" (or apply the word "horse" to it). Compare C. I. Lewis, *An Analysis of Knowledge and Valuation*, p. 43.

[9] Malcolm, "Moore and Ordinary Language," p. 118.

what it has ordinarily, and then to compare intensions.[10] It is not enough, then, to provide a technique which merely shows that the philosopher disagrees with most people concerning the *denotation* of a word.

But when, finally, we *have* learned that a philosopher is using words incorrectly, what follows? Suppose the epistemologist does use the word "certain" incorrectly; he uses it, not as it is ordinarily used, but, say, to refer to a type of cognition which it would be logically impossible for any man to attain. Clearly, when we have pointed this out, we have not *refuted* him. To be sure, now that we *understand* him, we are no longer shocked by his statement that "certain," in his sense, does not apply to beliefs about the furniture. In all probability his statement which formerly seemed paradoxical now seems trivial and uninteresting. But we have not refuted him, since we have not shown that what he is saying is *false*. Indeed we now see, what we had not seen before, that what he is saying is *true*, since, presumably, our beliefs about the furniture *do not* have what he calls "certainty."[11]

Malcolm believes, however, that "a philosophical statement cannot be paradoxical and not be false."[12] We must look further, then, if we are to find a technique of refutation. This brings us to the first of the two theories mentioned above.

II

According to the first theory, "if a philosophical statement is paradoxical, that is because it asserts the impropriety of an ordinary form of speech."[13] The philosopher who says "Nothing is certain" may *seem* to be concerned, not with language, but with knowledge and belief; according to the theory, however, his statements are *really* "disguised linguistic statements."[14] He may not even realize that they are disguised; what the philosopher does may be "concealed from himself as well as from others."[15] And similarly for the other paradoxical philosophers: e.g., those who deny the reality of space and time; those who hold that no material thing exists unperceived; those who hold that we cannot be certain there are other minds; those who hold, as Russell does, that we see, not external objects, but only parts of our brains; and so on. It is important to realize, moreover, that this theory is intended to apply not merely to those philosophers who are out to "entertain, dazzle, and bewilder the customers"; according to Mal-

[10] Malcolm and others have suggested that correctness can sometimes be determined without elaborate lexicographical investigation. For example, if we can show that the epistemologist so uses "certain" that the ordinary statement "I am certain it's raining" is contradictory, his use is probably incorrect, since, if Malcolm is right, people do not ordinarily make statements which are contradictory. A similar short cut is available in connection with words which "operate in pairs, e.g., 'large' and 'small', 'animate' and 'inanimate', 'vague' and 'clear', 'certain' and 'probable'. In their use in ordinary language a member of a pair requires its opposite — for animate is *contrasted* with inanimate, . . ." etc. ("Moore and Ordinary Language," p. 121. Compare Alice Ambrose, "Moore's Proof of an External World," also in *The Philosophy of G. E. Moore*.) However, it would be hazardous to suppose, whenever we find such a pair, that each member denotes something. Compare such pairs as "real" and "unreal," "possible" and "impossible," "actual" and "fictitious," "angels" and "devils," "elect" and "damned." "Creation" and "Creator," "mortals" and "immortals," and so on. Some have held that the principal business of philosophy is the difficult task of finding out and making articulate the ordinary intensions of words such as "certain" and the like. Compare C. J. Ducasse, *Philosophy as a Science*.

[11] Compare J. L. Cobitz, "The Appeal to Ordinary Language," *Analysis*, XI (1950), 9–11; also Norman Malcolm, "Certainty and Empirical Statements," *Mind*, LI (1942), 18–46, esp. p. 25. When we show that the epistemologist's statement is trivial, we may not refute him, but possibly we will *silence* him. One of the more important contributions of Malcolm and others concerned with correctness has been to show that many philosophical statements may be trivialized in this way.

[12] "Moore and Ordinary Language," p. 120.

[13] *Ibid.*

[14] *Ibid.*, p. 116.

[15] Morris Lazerowitz, "The Existence of Universals," *Mind*, LV (1946), 1–24; the quotation appears on p. 23.

colm, "the philosophizing of *most* of the more important philosophers has consisted in their more or less subtly repudiating ordinary language."[16] Thus, wherever we find a philosophy which is really a disguised attack upon ordinary language, we have only to remove the disguise and refute the philosophy (if it is false) by purely linguistic considerations.

This technique evidently involves three steps, each of them very doubtful, it seems to me. (1) First we show that the philosophical statement is not an "empirical statement," that it does not concern the "empirical facts." (2) From this it will follow, according to the theory, that the philosopher is really trying to tell us something about language. (3) Then, with the philosopher's disguise thus removed, an easy refutation is at hand.

(1) What does it mean to say, of a statement, that it does not concern the "empirical facts"? No meaning is provided for the technical term "empirical" (or "empirical facts"), and it seems to be used in a number of different ways.

When Malcolm says that a philosopher's statement is not *empirical*, he usually means that, in the (incorrect) sense in which the philosopher interprets his statement, its denial is contradictory. In other words, in the (incorrect) language the philosopher uses, his paradoxical statements are *necessary*. And Malcolm has shown with considerable care and ingenuity that many philosophical statements *are* nonempirical in this sense; among these are many statements which have been made about certainty.[17] But it is very difficult to see the justifica-

tion for saving, as our theory would require, that *all* of the paradoxical statements of philosophy are statements which in the language of the philosophers are necessary. After all, for every paradoxical philosophical statement which is necessary, in a philosopher's language, we can find a variant of it, equally paradoxical, which is not necessary in that language. Suppose, for example, our philosopher uses "know" (incorrectly) to describe a type of cognition which one can have only of one's own experience. Then he may say, for example, "No one can know the content of anyone else's experience," and this paradoxical statement, let us assume, will turn out to be *necessary*, in his language. But suppose " Jones is other than his grocer" is *not* necessary in that language. Then the paradoxical statement "Jones can never know the content of his grocer's mind" will not be necessary; hence we will have a paradoxical philosophical statement which is yet *empirical*, on the present account.

The other possible meanings of "empirical" do not fare much better. We might, for example, interpret it to mean the same as "capable of being supported by evidence."[18] But in *this* sense probably *all* of the paradoxical statements cited are empirical, since each is supported by *some* evidence, however inadequate; the epistemologist reminds us that people *do* make mistakes, even when they feel certain; Russell reminds us of the speed of light, its effect in the brain, and so on.[19] And, if we take the term "empirical" even more narrowly to mean, say, "translatable into a

---

[16] Moore and Ordinary Language," p. 122 (my italics). Malcolm holds, consistently, that the *denials* of the paradoxical philosophies — Moore's defence of common sense, for example — are also disguised linguistic statements. But these assert the "propriety" rather than the "impropriety" of ordinary language.

[17] See Malcolm's "Certainty and Empirical Statements"; also his "The Verification Argument," *Philosophical Analysis*, ed. Max Black (Ithaca, New York: Cornell University Press, 1950).

[18] In "Certainty and Empirical Statements" Malcolm seems to interpret "empirical" this way; cf. p. 20. In that paper he seems also to use "empirical statements" synonymously with "statement which makes sense"; cf. p. 33. The expression "making sense," of course, involves the same difficulties as does "empirical."

[19] Whether the evidence is *good*, is another point. Malcolm has pointed out, in fact, that it is *not* very good. See "Certainty and Empirical Statements," p. 42. On this point, compare Ralph M. Blake, "Can Speculative Philosophy be Defended?" *Philosophical Review*, LII (1943), 127–134.

phenomenalistic language," perhaps we can show that none of the statements cited is empirical; but now the problem is to show that the ordinary statements of science and common sense *are* empirical, in this narrow sense. In short, the success of the program we are discussing will depend upon showing that there is a sense of the term "empirical" attributable to the statements of common sense and the sciences and not to those of the paradoxical philosophers. The difficulty of the program is not lessened, of course, if for the technical term "empirical" we substitute some other, say "factual" or "informational," or some combination, such as "conveying information about empirical matters of fact."

(2) The second general problem is that of showing that the disputes, instigated by paradoxical philosophers, are really linguistic. If we *do* find that a philosophical dispute does not concern the "empirical facts" (in some significant sense), may we conclude that the disputants therefore disagree about "what language shall be used to describe those facts?" It seems clear to me that we cannot. Even in the whale case, the most we have a right to conclude is that people *use* language differently and *mistakenly believe* that they are in disagreement about the facts. From the fact that they *use* words differently, it does not at all follow that they have different *beliefs* concerning which use is more nearly correct. Possibly, like people who use different regional accents, they have *no* beliefs about the correctness or other virtues of their different uses. Nor does it even follow that they have what Stevenson calls a disagreement in *attitude* concerning their respective uses; they might be people who are tolerant linguistically. Of course it may be, as is often intimated, that the linguistic difference is symptomatic of some significant subconscious disagreement. And some philosophers (though not Malcolm, so far as I know) are interested in speculating about the motives *other* philosophers may have for using one locution

rather than another.[20] But the most a psychiatrist could tell us about our problem is that a philosopher might *say* one thing, while wishing, subconsciously or otherwise, for something else, possibly wishing that he were *saying* something else. But it would be incorrect to describe this fact by saying that the philosopher is "really asserting" the something else. From the fact that people use language differently, then, it does not follow that they disagree about language.

(3) The third problem is that of providing a refutation. Suppose (to discount all of the foregoing) we agree that the paradoxical philosophers really *are* trying to convey something about the "propriety" of ordinary language; the epistemologist is saying that it is "incorrect" or "improper" to ascribe certainty to beliefs about material things; or Russell is stating "that it is really a more correct way of speaking to say that you see a part of your brain than to say that you see the postman,"[21] and so on. Do we now have a technique of refutation?

Unfortunately there is still room for doubt concerning what it is, according to the theory we are examining, that the paradoxical philosophers are supposed to be trying to say. We may choose between two quite different types of interpretation. According to the first, the epistemologist is saying that ordinarily people never *do* use the word "certain" to refer to beliefs about material things; Russell is saying that people ordinarily talk the way *he* likes to talk in his philosophical writings, that when

[20] Compare B. A. Farrell's critical discussion, "An Appraisal of Therapeutic Positivism," *Mind*, LV (1946), 25–48, 133–150. In addition to the works cited there, see Morris Lazerowitz, "Strong and Weak Verification, II," *Mind*, LIX (1950), 345–57; "Are Self-Contradictory Expressions Meaningless?" *Philosophical Review*, LVIII (1949), 563–84. See also various papers by John Wisdom, particularly *Aristotelian Society Proceedings*, XXXXVII (1936–37); also J. Findlay, "Some Reactions to Recent Cambridge Philosophy," *Australasian Journal of Psychology and Philosophy*, XVIII (1940), 193–211.

[21] Malcolm, "Moore and Ordinary Language," p. 114.

they look at the mailman or the sun they say "I see a part of my brain" and that they never say "I see the sun" or "I see the mailman." The other shocking philosophical views would be interpreted similarly; when philosophers seem to deny the existence of time, or of space, or of matter, and such like, what they are really trying to tell us is that people ordinarily talk in these paradoxical ways. This interpretation of Malcolm's thesis, however, implausible it may seem, is suggested by the fact that the term "correct language," as we have seen, is to be taken to mean language as it is ordinarily used; thus if someone says that a certain way of speaking is the *correct* way, he means it is the *ordinary* way. The paradoxical philosophers, then, would really be trying to tell us how people ordinarily use words. If *this* is the true interpretation of what the paradoxical philosophers are saying, then, clearly, we *can* refute their views by appealing to the facts of ordinary language, for it is obvious that people *do not* talk in these strange ways. But it is also obvious, it seems to me, that the philosophers are not trying to *say* that they do. The epistemologist is not contending, even subconsciously, that ordinarily people do not use the word "certain." And surely what Russell is fond of telling us is *not* that the ordinary man never *says* that he sees the sun, but that he *does* say it and that when he does he is mistaken. Moreover, I can not believe that *this* is the sort of view which is being attributed to Russell and the others. It is more plausible to suppose that the alternative interpretation is intended: these philosophers are not trying to *describe* ordinary language; they are *proposing* that we change it. This is the way Lazerowitz would interpret them: according to him, paradoxical philosophical statements should be in the "language of proposal" rather than in the "language of assertion." [22] The epistemologist is pro-

posing that we change the meaning of "certain" and Russell is proposing that we use the word "see" in a different way: "Henceforth let us say that we see our brains and not that we see the mailman." This is the alternative to saying that the paradoxical philosophers are really trying to *describe* ordinary language. But if we decide that they are merely making *proposals*, then, once again, we are without a method of refutation, since, as Lazerowitz puts it, proposals "have no refutation." [23] A proposal may be ill-advised, but *being* a proposal it is neither true nor false and hence cannot be refuted.

Thus we haven't yet found a general technique for showing that the paradoxical statements of philosophy are false.

III

Malcolm's second linguistic theory, if true, does provide us with a method of refutation. This theory, which is of quite a different sort from the one we have been discussing, concerns the psychology of language. There are words in ordinary language, Malcolm believes, whose *use* implies that they have a denotation. That is to say, from the fact that they are used in ordinary language, we may infer that there is something to which they truly apply. Of course, this is not true of all words; from the fact that the word "God" and the word "ghost" have an ordinary use, we may not infer that there is a God or that there are ghosts. But, Malcolm believes, from the fact that "expressions like 'earlier,' 'later,' 'to the left of,' 'behind,' 'above,' 'material things,' 'it is pos-

---

[22] Morris Lazerowitz, "Moore's Paradox," *The Philosophy of G. E. Moore*, p. 391. Lazerowitz also applies this interpretation to those who, like

Moore, deny the paradoxical views. Moore comments: "Mr. Lazerowitz concludes that when, for instance, I tried to show that time is not unreal, all that I was doing was to recommend that we should not use certain expressions in a different way from that in which we do! If this is all I was doing, I was certainly making a huge mistake, for I certainly did not think it was all. And I do not think so now." ("A Reply to My Critics," *The Philosophy of G. E. Moore*, p. 675).

[23] "Moore's Paradox," p. 376.

sible that,' 'it is certain that',"[24] have a use, we *may* infer that there is something to which they truly apply. And thus if we know that such words *are* used in ordinary language, we may say of any philosopher who says there are *no* cases of certainty or *no* material things, etc. that he is mistaken. These philosophical words, according to Malcolm, are expressions the meanings of which must be shown; they cannot be explained to people "in terms of the meanings of words which they already know."[25]

In the case of all expressions the meanings of which must be *shown* and cannot be explained, as can the meaning of "ghost," it follows, from the fact that they are ordinary expressions in the language, that there have been *many* situations of the kind which they describe; otherwise so many people could not have learned the correct use of those expressions. Whenever a philosophical paradox asserts, therefore, with regard to such an expression, that always when that expression is used the use of it produces a false statement, then to prove that the expression is an ordinary expression is completely to refute the paradox.[26]

Let us assume for the moment that this theory is true. What philosophers can we refute with it? Not an epistemologist who says we cannot be certain of beliefs about material things; he can deny the certainty of all such beliefs and still be immune, provided only that he allows us an occasional instance of certainty, say, for example, in the case of sense-data or elementary arithmetic. For the technique applies only to those philosophers who hold there are *no* instances to which the philosophical words in question apply. And if we *could* find a philosopher who said, "Nothing is certain," or who said, "The word 'certain' interpreted in its ordinary sense, has no denotation," we could not refute *him* by

this method, unless we knew he was using these words correctly. If our epistemologist, for example, were to say, "Nothing is certain," the technique would not apply, since we happen to know that *he* uses the word "certain" incorrectly and *not* as it is understood in ordinary language. This technique, then, would seem to apply normally to cases in which these special words are being used *correctly*, not to cases in which they are used incorrectly.[27] Thus we have yet to find how a proof of linguistic incorrectness can provide us with a method of refutation. The technique applies most obviously to those philosophers who, using ordinary language correctly make false statements about it — or, rather, make statements which *would* be false if this theory were true.

What reason is there for believing then, that these philosophically interesting words, such as "certain," "material thing," and the others listed above, can be explained only ostensively, that is to say, by exhibiting instances of their application? It is difficult to imagine how this type of explanation could be achieved, for example, in the case "it is possible that," which Malcolm cites. It is even more difficult to imagine how we could produce instances of the true application of "fictitious," "imaginary," "nothing," "nonexistent," and "impossible," which he does not cite. The philosopher whom we are refuting by this method may tell us that ordinary people learn the meaning of "certain," "material thing," and so on, by whatever method they learn the meaning of such words as "impossible" and "nothing." He may tell us, for instance, that people have recourse to some "method of contrast"; we learn the meaning of "impossible" by having it contrasted with "possible." Similarly, he might say we learn the meaning of "certain" by having it con-

---

[24] "Moore and Ordinary Language," p. 120.
[25] *Ibid.*, p. 119.
[26] *Ibid.*, p. 120. Compare Max Black, *Language and Philosophy* (Ithaca, New York: Cornell University Press, 1949), pp. 16–17.

[27] Of course, one could provide an *incorrect* formulation for the view that some of these words, as ordinarily used, have no denotation. And if we could find a philosopher who held such a view and formulated it incorrectly, the technique *would* apply to him.

trasted with "doubtful." And there may be other methods of conveying the meaning of words. There might be a "method of limits"; one might convey the meaning of "perfect circle" by exhibiting a sequence of shapes which seem to approach circularity as a limit.[28] Similarly, if there are no cases of certainty, one might convey the meaning of "certain" by arranging conjectures or opinions in such a series. And there could even be a "method of illusion." Suppose, for example, we teach a child the meaning of the word "courage" by showing him someone calming accepting situations which we mistakenly believe he regards as dangerous. If the child also has this mistaken belief, he may be able to abstract the quality of courage in the manner required; but, since the belief is mistaken, the ostensive explanation has been accomplished without exhibiting an instance of the true application of the word. It might well be that some of the philosophically interesting words have been learned in this fashion. The skeptic might tell us that we have learned the meaning of "certain" by observing situations (i.e., beliefs) which we mistakenly took to have characteristics they did not have in fact. McTaggart probably would

have said that this is the way we learn the meaning of the expression "material thing." And doubtless a study of the psychology of language would reveal still other ways of explaining the meanings of words. Such suggestions as these are not likely to seem unacceptable to one who can accept a paradoxical philosophy.

Our philosopher, therefore, should not have great difficulty in countering this type of refutation. And probably it is just as well: most philosophers are ready enough, as it is, to infer entities answering to the expressions which occur in ordinary language.

Thus we have failed to find sufficient reason for believing that "any philosophical statement which violates ordinary language is false."

Many philosophical statements *do* violate ordinary language; as a result, they are misleading, they may seem more important than they are, and philosophers may become entangled in verbal confusions. One of Mr. Malcolm's valuable contributions has been to show us how readily all of this does occur. But for the rest, so far as I can see, ordinary language does not have the philosophical significance which he and others attribute to it.

[28] Compare C. D. Broad, *Five Types of Ethical Theory*, pp. 57–59.

Editor's Note: For Malcolm's reply to this essay, see Malcolm [7].

JOHN PASSMORE

ARGUMENTS TO MEANINGLESSNESS:

EXCLUDED OPPOSITES AND PARADIGM CASES

At the beginning of the *Monadology*, Leibniz argues as follows: 'There must be simple substances, since there are compounds; for a compound is nothing but a collection or aggregate of simple things'. As it stands, Leibniz' argument has an arbitrary air. On the face of it, every compound could be a compound of complex things; thus there could be compounds even if there were not simples.

Suppose, however, Leibniz' argument were recast in a 'formal' or 'linguistic' mode. It might run as follows: 'Our language contains the adjective "complex"; "complex" can act as an adjective — i.e. can distinguish one thing from another — only if what is complex can be contrasted with what is not-complex, the simple. Thus, from the fact that the word "complex" plays a certain role in our language, it follows that there are simples'.

Pretty obviously, this would be a bad argument, for the reasons advanced by Wittgenstein in his *Philosophical Investigations* (§47). Our ordinary way of using the words 'simple' and 'complex' is such that we contrast a simple problem with a complex problem; a simple character with a complex character; a simple design with a complex design — and so have

plenty of occasions for contrasting the 'simple' and the 'complex'. But the problem, the character, the design, is neither 'simple' nor 'complex' in some metaphysically absolute sense of the word. Indeed, 'simple' and 'complex' are not contradictory descriptions; a plastic tumbler can be simple in design and yet complex in molecular structure. Metaphysicians have wanted to say that there are some entities —the 'objects' of Wittgenstein's *Tractatus*, the 'simple natures' of Descartes' *Regulae*, the 'elements' of Plato's *Theaetetus* — which are simple, in a sense which prevents them from also being complex. "But what," Wittgenstein asks, "are the simple constituent parts of a chair? — The bits of wood of which it is made? Or the molecules, or the atoms? — 'Simple' means: not composite. And here the point is: in what sense 'composite'? It makes no sense at all to speak absolutely of 'the simple parts of a chair'." And again: "Asking 'Is this object composite?' *outside* a particular language-game is like what a boy once did, who had to say whether the verbs in certain sentences were in the active or passive voice, and who racked his brains over the question whether the verb 'to sleep' meant something active or passive."

Wittgenstein will not allow, I take it, that metaphysics is itself a 'language-game.' It would be as improper, on his account of the matter, for the metaphysi-

Reprinted from *Philosophical Reasoning* (New York: Basic Books, Inc.; London: Gerald Duckworth & Co. Ltd., 1961), pp. 100–18 by permission of the author and the publishers. (© by John Passmore.)

cian to assert that 'everything is complex' as for him to assert that 'some entities are simple'. Yet on the face of it, the metaphysician can produce *arguments* against the view that 'some entities are simple', e.g. the sort of argument which Plato brings forward in the *Sophist* and the *Parmenides*, and we can, at least, understand what these arguments are about. 'Simple' and 'complex' play a part in the metaphysician's 'language-game' which is rather different from the part they play in our everyday talk about designs, or characters, or problems — or chairs and tables — but it does not follow that the metaphysician's remarks are senseless. Yet one can see why Wittgenstein should think that they are. Take the metaphysician who says: 'Everything is complex'. 'Complex' cannot be, in this sentence, a distinguishing adjective — as it is in 'a complex design'. The metaphysician is, indeed, ruling out the possibility of using 'complex' to distinguish one sort of thing from another thing. Yet this is precisely how we ordinarily do use adjectives in general, and 'complex' in particular. In telling us not to use 'complex' in a distinguishing way the metaphysician, it might be suggested, is telling us to do what cannot be done — 'cannot' because it cuts across 'the grammar of 'complex' '.

Aristotle was aware of this particular problem. In his *Topics*, discussing the ways in which a definition can be criticized, he writes: 'Next, for destructive purposes, see whether he has rendered in the property any such term as is a universal attribute. For one which does not distinguish the subject from other things is useless, and it is the business of the language of "properties," as also of the language of definitions, to distinguish' (Bk. V, §2, 130b). Yet even in this passage Aristotle still refers to 'universal attributes', as if not every attribute had to distinguish.

Frege, on the other hand, raises a formal objection to the conception of 'universal attributes'. "It is only in virtue of the possibility of something not being wise," he writes in *The Foundations of Arithmetic*, "that it makes sense to say 'Solon is wise'. The content of a concept diminishes as its extension increases; if its extension becomes all-embracing, its content must vanish altogether. It is not easy to imagine how language could have come to invent a word for a property which could not be the slightest use for modifying the description of any object at all" (trans. J. L. Austin, p. 40e).

A good deal depends on what Frege means in this passage by 'the possibility of something not being wise'. Two interpretations suggest themselves. On the first, there must *actually* be something that is not wise, if the description of Solon as 'wise' is to make sense; on the second, all that is necessary is that something's not being wise should be *conceivable*. If, as seems most likely, the first is the correct interpretation — that 'not-wise' must have an actual extension if 'wise' is to be intelligible — an obvious difficulty at once arises. What of such predicates as 'possessing an extension which is not all-embracing'? Are we to say that assertions such as 'this concept has not an all-embracing extension' have no sense, since nothing has an all-embracing extension? If so, Frege's own argument would be unintelligible.

Admittedly, this predicate consists of a complex phrase, not a word. But that seems to be an accident. Aristotle, supposing that some predicates have, and others have not, an all-embracing extension, might well have invented words to refer to the two distinct cases, or his translator might have done so. Let us suppose that the translator used the word 'properties' to mean 'predicates which have not an all-embracing extension' and the word 'transcendentals' to mean 'predicates which have an all-embracing extension'. Then a Frege arises, who wishes to deny that there are any predicates which have an all-embracing extension. It will be natural for him to say: 'All predicates are properties', or 'There are no transcendentals'. But then, it would seem, it immediately follows that what he is saying must be unintelligible, since if he is right there is nothing to which the predicate 'being a transcendental predicate' applies, and so the description 'being a predicate-property' has no use. But it would clearly be an extraordinary doctrine that once some philosopher had divided things in a certain kind of way, it was impossible for anybody else — on pain of unintelligibility — to reject the view that they could be divided in that way.

Let us look then at the second alternative: suppose Frege is arguing that it must be 'conceivable', as distinct from being actually the case, that something should not have a certain predicate, if the use of that predicate is to be significant. Here, of course, the word 'conceivable' is by no means clear. But it is reasonable to presume, at least, that whatever anyone has ever conceived is conceivable; so that if philosophers have maintained, and have got others to believe, that there are simple entities, then it is conceivable that there are 'simple entities'; if they have suggested, and won agreement to the view, that some concepts have an all-embracing extension, then it is conceivable that some concepts have an all-embracing extension. Then to demand only that a predicate should have a 'conceivable' opposite will not rule out metaphysical assertions and counter-assertions about the complexity of all things as 'senseless' — as Wittgenstein wanted to do.

Wittgenstein, all the same, was drawing attention to an important fact: the metaphysician is not using the word 'simple' as we use it in our non-metaphysical thinking. By itself, that settles nothing, but at least it emphasizes the peculiarity of the metaphysical use, which might otherwise escape our notice. It drives us to consider how the metaphysician does use 'simple' and 'complex', which involves, of course, a close consideration of the actual arguments by which metaphysicians have sought to establish, or to overthrow, the supposition that there are simple entities. Such an examination soon makes it ap-

parent that when metaphysicians have described ideas, natures or forms as simple, they have taken the consequence to follow that we cannot be mistaken about those ideas, natures or forms. This is not surprising, for in the everyday use of the word 'simple', a 'simple' design is one we can easily describe, a 'simple' character is one we can easily understand, a 'simple' problem is one we can easily solve — in each case, then, the reference is to something about which we are unlikely to make mistakes. But the *metaphysically* simple is that about which it is logically impossible, as distinct from merely unusual, to be mistaken. Why should this be? Because in knowing the metaphysically simple entity at all, we know it completely; and this in turn is because all true descriptions of it are synonymous, i.e. we cannot, as we can in the case of complexes, know that it is of a certain description while overlooking the fact that it is also of some other description.

It turns out, then, that 'simple' is a predicate of a distinctly peculiar kind; to say that 'this entity is simple' is not to say that it possesses the descriptive property of being simple. If there were such a property, it would at once follow that no entity could possess it, since any entity which did would be describable as being 'simple' as well as being the sort of entity it is — say, a red sense-datum — and so would not be simple; it could be described in either of two non-synonymous ways, as 'red' or as 'simple'. To call an entity 'simple' — in the metaphysical sense — is not to describe it but to make a logical point about it, the point that only one empirical description can be offered of it.

If we wish to say, against the doctrine of 'simples', that 'every entity is complex', then too, we are not, in the ordinary fashion, offering a description of things: we are making the logical point that every entity can be described in a variety of ways. Asked to list the properties of animals, we should not include in our list 'they are complex' (any more than we should include 'they have properties');

asked to define an animal, we could not use 'complex' as our genus. If 'complex' appeared in a definition, it would serve, like 'thing', as a linguistic filler — 'an organism is a complex which . . .' — not as the descriptive part of the definition. Aristotle was right, then, to point out that 'it is the business of the language of properties, as also of the language of definitions, to distinguish'; but he was also right not to conclude that there are no 'universal attributes'.

For, we are suggesting, there is a wide class of propositions — metaphysical propositions — where the use of a predicate does not presuppose that there is something to which the predicate does not apply. 'Everything is describable' does not imply that there are indescribables; this proposition is not senseless, either; and there is a point in uttering it, in so far as there are metaphysicians who have taken the view that some entities are indescribable. 'Everything that happens is natural' does not imply that there are things which are not natural — or things which have the property of not-happening — but rather that any happening is describable in terms of physical laws and spatio-temporal occurrences. But the predicates, in these cases, turn out to be of an unusual, formal, kind. Their 'content' is that propositions of a certain form are true, not that some thing is distinguishable from some other thing in virtue of possessing a special property — a characteristic which could be used in classifying or defining it.

But are such metaphysical propositions the only ones in which there are universal predicates? To say that such predicates as 'possessing a mass' or 'being in motion' are also universal predicates would at once arouse protests; for it is very commonly supposed that there are entities such as 'thoughts' and that to those entities the predicates of physics have no application. But let us suppose that they did have a universal application. Would it then be senseless to apply them at all? It would seem not. For in distinguishing between

the mass and the velocity of objects we do not in any way rely upon the fact (if it is a fact) that there are some objects which lack mass or velocity. In this case, too, the predicate "possessing a mass' would be of no use to us in classifications and definitions — or more generally, in those processes of discrimination and identification which are normally our major concern; but it need not even be pointless to remark 'that thing has a mass' — for somebody might wrongly have supposed that it was an exception — and certainly it could be a scientifically interesting statement that everything has a mass. The doctrine that a predicate cannot be both useful and have an all-embracing extension seems to rest, indeed, upon the supposition that predicates can only be used to discriminate and to identify classes of objects.

With these general considerations in the back of our mind, let us look at certain recent attempts to use the 'excluded opposites' argument as a rapid way of ruling out, as senseless, a diversity of philosophical positions.[1] Thus, writing about 'The Objectivity of History' in *Mind* (1955) Christopher Blake maintains that it is logically impossible to take the view that no historical writings are objective, since it would make no sense to talk about 'non-objective' history unless there is 'objective' history. Blake is going a lot further than Frege. Frege said only that *something* must be not wise if the assertion 'Solon is wise' is to have sense; Blake is arguing that *some historical writings* must be objective if the phrase 'non-objective history' is to have any sense.

What Blake could properly have said, and this is sufficiently obvious, is that if all history is non-objective, then 'non-objective' cannot serve as a differentiating predicate within history. Phrases like 'Macaulay's non-objective *History of England*' will then be of no use in discriminating between Macaulay's historical writings

[1] See also C. K. Grant: 'Polar Concepts and Metaphysical Arguments'. Proceedings of the Aristotelian Society, LVII (1956–57).

and the historical writings of, say, Ranke. But it could still be useful to describe all historical writings as 'non-objective', in order to distinguish them from the writings of physicists. There may be some point, even, in using the phrase 'Macaulay's non-objective *History of England*', although it will not be a classifying or defining point.

Suppose, for example, it is true that 'All men are fallible' or that 'All accountants love accuracy'. The consequences will follow that 'fallible' is of no use for distinguishing between men, or 'accuracy-loving' for distinguishing between accountants. But the statement 'We fallible men ought always to check quotations' or 'Accuracy-loving accountants naturally dislike vague financial estimates' are in no way logically-improper. 'Fallible' and 'accuracy-loving' have in these statements a reminding function, not a discriminating function; but it is perfectly proper to use predicates as a way of reminding.

If, then, when Ryle writes in *Dilemmas* (p. 95) that 'ice could not be thin if ice could not be thick' he means that it would be senseless, or logically-improper, to describe ice as 'being thin' unless some ice is thick, he is clearly mistaken. (Compare 'Ice could not be cold, if ice could not be hot'.) Quinine is always bitter; silk is always soft; men are always mortal — yet one can say 'He drank down the bitter quinine as if it were lemonade'; 'the soft silk was soothing to the touch'; 'we mortal men do act absurdly, in that we care for the future'. If all ice were thin, then certainly we should not put up a notice: 'The ice is thin', but we should still have to remind children or imprudent adults: 'Beware, ice is thin!'

In a certain range of cases, however — including some philosophically important cases — the existence of an opposite seems to be 'written into' the sense of a predicate. The most obvious instances are predicates like 'counterfeit', 'imitation', 'copied'. Thus, to take Ryle's example, there cannot be counterfeit money unless there is legal money. 'All Icelandic coins are coun-

terfeit' cannot be true because it would be equivalent to 'All Icelandic coins are imitations of Icelandic coins'. Even then, it is worth noting, if 'All Icelandic coins are counterfeit' simply means that 'All the Icelandic coins circulating *at the moment* are counterfeit', this could be true. Suppose the coinage is entirely silver-metallic; in principle, a gang of forgers could completely replace it by a nickel-metallic coinage, melting down the silver. But they must have something to copy, i.e. there must at some time have been genuine Icelandic coinage. Similarly, even although the original manuscript of Shakespeare's plays does not survive, it makes sense to speak of what we do in fact have as 'copies' only on the presumption that there was such an original. The argument in this instance, however, is not from the general logical principle that every predicate must have an 'opposite' but from the special characteristics of a particular class of predicates.

An unusually explicit presentation of 'the argument from excluded opposites' or 'the principle of non-vacuous contrasts' is to be found in Malcolm's essay on 'Moore and Ordinary Language'.[2] The argument, as he presents it, refers only to certain kinds of predicate. "Certain words of our language," he says, "operate in pairs, e.g. 'large' and 'small', 'animate' and 'inanimate', 'vague' and 'clear', 'certain' and 'probable'. In their use in ordinary language, a member of a pair *requires* its opposite — for animate is *contrasted* with inanimate, probability with certainty, vagueness with clearness" (p. 121). Suppose, then, a philosopher tries to persuade us that 'all statements are vague'; he is really proposing, according to Malcolm, that we give up our ordinary use of the predicate 'vague' — for that is, precisely, to *distinguish* within the class of statements between those which are vague and those which are not. There would be nothing to gain from accepting the philoso-

[2] *The Philosophy of G. E. Moore*, ed. P. A. Schilpp, pp. 345–68.
Editor's note: Reprinted above at pp. 111–24. References are to the pagination in this volume.

pher's proposal, he objects, for if we did we should have to invent another pair of distinguishing words to take the place of 'clear' and 'vague' — so as to be able still to distinguish, say, between statements like 'Shakespeare was born at Stratford-on-Avon' and statements like 'Shakespeare's genius lies outside space and time'.

Malcolm's is, on the face of it, a quite moderate and reasonable objection to what is certainly, if he is right, a very strange philosophical procedure. If it be true, as Malcolm urges, that 'when the philosopher says that words are really vague, he is proposing that we never apply the word "clear" any more, i.e. proposing that we abolish its use', we might well complain that we cannot easily get along without it. But, in fact, of course, one does not find that a philosopher who says that 'all statements are vague' no longer praises certain utterances for their clarity or condemns the vagueness of others. Similarly, even if a philosopher denies that any empirical proposition can be certain, this does not prevent him from saying, for example: 'One thing's certain: Jones won't get a scholarship'. Is this merely because not even the philosopher himself can take his linguistic innovations seriously?

A contrast, and a comparison, with the practice of scientists now suggests itself. Scientists quite often drop *both* of a pair of contrasting opposites, replacing them — for scientific purposes — by a reference to a difference of degree on a sliding scale. Thus they replace 'hot' and 'cold' by 'degrees of temperature', 'loud' and 'soft' by 'number of decibels', 'fast' and 'slow' by 'feet per second' and so on. But, of course, the scientist does not give up using the contrast-words in all circumstances. If he is talking informally about his work he might well say: 'the lab get pretty hot with all that stuff cooking, and noisy, too; I'm out of it fast enough when five o'clock comes, I can tell you'. Nor does the scientist commit himself to such utterances as 'everything is really hot', 'everything is really fast', 'everything is really loud' when

he discovers that the familiar contrast-predicates of everyday life are unsatisfactory in serious scientific descriptions. Nor is a motorist, even if he gives up talking about 'steep hills' and 'slight hills' as distinct from 'hills of such-and-such a gradient', tempted into the assertion that 'Really, all hills are steep'. Simply, the ordinary distinction does not discriminate enough for the motorist's purposes and is too indecisive in its application to a range of cases. Everybody would agree that a hill with a grade of one in five is 'steep', but when it comes to a grade of one in twelve, a cyclist, a pedestrian, a lorry-driver, the owner of a small car, a racing driver are likely to describe it in very different terms.

A similar situation can arise in regard to the pairs of opposites in which philosophers are interested. Thus in *The Brown Book* (p. 87) Wittgenstein writes: "Looking at it as we did just now, the distinction between automatic and non-automatic appears no longer so clear and final as it did at first. We don't mean that the distinction loses its practical value in particular cases, e.g. if asked under particular circumstances: 'Did you take this bolt from the shelf automatically, or did you think about it?' we may be justified in saying that we did not act automatically and give as an explanation that we had looked at the material carefully, had tried to recall the memory-image of the pattern and had uttered to ourselves doubts and decisions. This may *in the particular case* be taken to distinguish automatic from non-automatic." So a distinction which we might at first have supposed to be one we could readily make in regard to any action at all turns out, if Wittgenstein is right, to be applicable only in a certain range of cases. But how absurd it would be to conclude that all action is really automatic — or, for the matter of that, really non-automatic — when the truth of the matter, only, is that the distinction between automatic and non-automatic is not in every case a useful one.

Something, we begin to feel, has gone wrong. Philosophers cannot be as foolish as they are now being made to appear; it cannot really be the case that they are exhorting the ordinary man to drop such words as 'clear' from his vocabulary, or trying to persuade him no longer to distinguish between cases where he picks up a book automatically and cases where he picks it up because it looks interesting. Such assertions as 'all statements are vague' *cannot* mean what, as ordinary men and women, we should naturally suppose them to mean; the counter-examples are so obvious, and so often and so explicitly drawn to our attention, that it is impossible to suppose that even the loftiest of transcendentalists could overlook them.

In fact, of course, we have been forgetting that philosophers are addressing themselves to the community of their fellow-philosophers, not to humanity at large. It is as if an economist were to be rebuked for overlooking the fact that a person can 'demand' something which he has no means of paying for. If 'all statements are vague' is in some respects queer, this is because it is a response to a — less apparent — queerness, or to a very special definition of clarity.

When Ramsey said that although we can make many things clearer, we cannot make anything clear, he was, considered from the standpoint of ordinary language, very obviously mistaken. There are a great many occasions on which we could rightly claim that we have made something clear to somebody; yet in the context of philosophical controversy, Ramsey's remark was called-for, sensible and true. We cannot 'make anything clear' if that means formulating it in such a way that it is logically impossible for anybody to misunderstand us, and that is the sort of 'clarity' Ramsey's philosophical contemporaries were looking for. 'All statements are vague' is a perfectly natural response to the attempt to construct statements which are 'clear' in this very special, philosophical, sense of the word. One could no doubt

formulate the same point on a somewhat different way, by saying something like this: 'On the criterion of "clarity" you suggest, no statement could ever truly be described as "clear"'. But to dismiss 'all statements are vague' as senseless, by an appeal to the principle of excluded opposites, would be quite to ignore the contribution of that statement to philosophical controversy.

In a similar way, the statement 'No bodies are solid' is, considering the history of the idea of solidity, a quite natural way of making the point that there are no bodies which are wholly impenetrable. 'No empirical propositions are certain', similarly, is an emphatic way of asserting that it is always logically possible for an empirical statement to be false. Only by considering how such statements are actually used in philosophical controversy can we possibly hope to understand them; we need to know the history behind them. But they are none the worse for that. The crucial point is that they are not attempts to purge the language of everyday life — to rid it of words like 'solid' and 'certain' and 'clear'; rather, they are emphatic ways of pointing out that particular philosophical criteria of solidity, certainty, clarity are never in fact satisfied. Nor do they make that point in an outrageous, wilfully paradoxical way; on the contrary, they make it in the most natural manner, if the historical context of controversy is taken into account.

To sum up: there is no general argument from a predicate's having no opposite to its being 'senseless', or even useless. If a predicate has no opposite, then it will, indeed, be useless *for certain purposes* — as a mode of distinguishing between or of identifying particular kinds of thing. That fact is worth pointing out; but it does not follow that such a predicate is useless for all purposes. Predicates may be used to remind, or to make a formal point, or to reject a *conceivable* classification, as well as to distinguish and identify. Philosophers have their special concerns, and in devoting themselves to these concerns they, in particular, may need to use non-distinguishing predicates or to deny that a predicate, if used in a certain way, will in fact distinguish. But in this latter case, they are not denying that the predicate can also be used in a differentiating way, although their mode of expression may easily lead, if the controversial context is ignored, to the supposition that they are doing so.

Very similar considerations apply to the 'paradigm case' argument. This argument, too, is stated in a particularly clear way by Malcolm in "Moore and Ordinary Language." He distinguishes between two classes of expression: those which could be learnt through descriptions and those which must be learnt by reference to cases. 'It is probable that' and 'It is certain that' belong, he argues, to this second class; we can learn how to use these expressions only by being shown cases where they apply and cases where they do not apply and seeing the difference between them. So it is then senseless for a philosopher suddenly to assert 'No empirical statements are certain'. We know when to use 'certain' of empirical statements; we have learnt to do so from being shown cases. There cannot possibly be no such cases; for then we could never have learnt how to use the word 'certain'.

Then are we to conclude that there must be 'ghosts' since, again, people know how to use that word correctly? The correct use of 'ghosts', Malcolm would reply, could be learnt by description; we could simply be told 'if you were to see a being with such-and-such characteristics, you would be seeing a ghost'. A person can intelligibly deny that it is possible to see a ghost; he can argue that those who profess to have done so are really suffering from an illusion. In contrast, a philosopher cannot sensibly deny, as some have tried to do, that it is possible to see a cat; he cannot sensibly suppose that everybody who has ever thought he has seen a cat was the victim of a strange sort of hallucination. "When he says that a man does not *really*

see a cat," writes Malcolm, "he commits a great absurdity; for he implies that a person can use an expression to describe a certain state of affairs, which is the expression ordinarily used to describe just such a state of affairs, and yet be using incorrect language" (p. 118).

Malcolm has presumed, however, that there is a sharp distinction between what is learnt ostensively and what is learnt descriptively. In fact, the two sorts of learning ordinarily go hand in hand. Consider the situation of a child brought up in a society in which it is firmly believed that miracles are of daily occurrence. Then he will certainly learn how to apply the word 'miracles' by reference to cases: someone has a narrow escape from an accident, or recovers unexpectedly from an illness, or a house is saved, by a sudden shift of wind, from being burnt to the ground, and the child will be told 'that's a miracle'. But at the same time he will learn that miracles involve supernatural invention.

Similarly, a person could learn the use of the phrase 'possessed by the devil' in a purely ostensive fashion. When he sees somebody behaving in a strange fashion he is told: 'that man is possessed by the devil'. Hippocrates, presumably, learnt how to use the phrase 'the sacred disease', by watching epileptics. So when Hippocrates wanted to say 'there is no sacred disease', the paradigm-case exponents of his day would certainly reply: 'When a man says that there are no sacred diseases, he is committing a very great absurdity, for he implies that a person can use an expression to describe a certain state of affairs, which is the expression ordinarily used to describe such a state of affairs and yet be using incorrect language'.

But, Malcolm might reply, even if Hippocrates did in fact learn to use the phrase 'the sacred disease' ostensively, he *could* have learnt it descriptively. The fundamental question, then, is whether there are in fact any expressions which could only be learnt ostensively, so that we could never have learnt them unless there are cases to which they apply. That question, in its full extent, we need not discuss; it will be sufficient to suggest that the philosophically-interesting phrases to which Malcolm explicitly refers are certainly not so ostensively tied. The phrases 'material things', 'it is possible that', 'it is certain that' could certainly be learnt descriptively. 'Material things', indeed, plays no part in ordinary language. It is a philosopher's phrase; Berkeley was so far right when he argues that in denying material things he was not denying anything which the ordinary man believes. Our parents say to us: 'Bring me a chair', 'Bring me my book', but never 'Bring me a material thing'. Unless they are philosophers, we shall never hear the phrase from their lips, except, perhaps, in referring to the tastes of the philistine — 'He cares only for material things' — and that phrase, certainly, could be explained to us descriptively. When we first hear of 'material things', in any other sense, it is as things which, for example, are 'solid and extended', i.e. we meet the phrase as a philosophical description.

As for 'it is certain that' and 'it is probable that', these phrases are learnt both in cases and through descriptions. If we misuse them, we are corrected in either of two ways. Suppose we say: 'It is certain that Jones will write a great poem', then we might be told, simply, that this is not the sort of thing anybody can be certain about. Or the rebuke may be generalized. 'It is wrong to say that anything is certain if there is the slightest possibility that it will not happen', i.e. there is an appeal to an explicit criterion.

In that way a clash may arise between cases and criteria. The same thing happens with miracles, or sacred diseases, or diabolic possessions. On the one side, no one would wish to deny that men are sometimes, quite unexpectedly, not killed in accidents, nor that houses which look as if they cannot possibly escape a fire may none the less do so; nor again that people sometimes suffer from epilepsy; nor that they become insane. No one wishes to deny, that is, that there are circumstances which it is, or was, conventional to describe by the expressions 'miracle', 'sacred disease', 'diabolic possession', and that we might have been taught to use these expressions precisely by reference to such cases. What we may well wish to deny, however, is that these cases satisfy a certain criterion: that the house or the man was saved by divine intervention, that the disease is a gift from the gods, that there is a demon inside the person who is 'possessed by a devil'. We know the circumstances in which it is conventional to use the expressions; we are not denying that there are such circumstances. But we wish to deny that in these circumstances a particular supernatural agency is at work. Or on the practical side, we may wish to deny that prayer, reverence and exorcism are the best ways — as they were the conventionally appropriate ways — of dealing with difficult situations, epileptics and madmen. Yet the criteria and the methods of handling have been taught along with the circumstances of correct employment. So it is perfectly natural for us to say: 'There are no miracles, no disease is sacred, nobody is ever possessed by a devil' rather than that 'miracles do not involve divine intervention, sufferers from the sacred diseases are not stricken by the gods, people possessed by the devil have not a supernatural being inside them'.

Similarly, a philosopher may on reflection decide that the criterion of certainty he has been taught when he was told 'It is wrong to say that anything is certain if there is the slightest possibility it will not happen' has in fact no application. Or that whereas he has commonly supposed that 'seeing a cat' involved some sort of direct confrontation with the cat's qualities, no such direct confrontation ever occurs. Then it is not merely arbitrary for him to express his conclusions — whether they are correct is not our present concern — in the form 'No empirical propositions are certain'; 'No one ever really sees a cat'.

It is true that the philosopher has a

choice. He *could* say, instead, 'Some of the ordinary criteria for certainty, or the ordinary criteria for seeing, will have to be abandoned' — he could, that is, go on using the expressions 'empirically certain', 'seeing a cat' but without accepting what are ordinarily regarded as implications of 'I am certain that . . .' or 'I see a cat'. To some extent, that has happened with 'miraculous' and 'possessed'; we say of a narrow escape that it is 'miraculous', or of a man who works with ferocious energy that he is 'a man possessed' — just as we allow that a man can be 'inspired' without supposing that there are Muses. As I said in discussing 'providential', no philosophical argument can lead to the conclusion that an expression must be banished from the language. But neither can it issue in the conclusion that an expression *must* be retained. Newton was able to assert that no bodies are free from gravitational influences, even if the distinction between gravitational and levitational had been taught ostensively — as the difference between the falling apple and the balloon. Philosophers are equally free to assert that 'we never really see a cat'. Take an unsophisticated person through the physicist's and the physiologist's story about perception, and 'then we don't really see *things*' is the form in which he will naturally express his bewilderment; it isn't just a philosopher's paradox. Similar considerations apply to 'things aren't really coloured'; 'I can't really be sure of anything'; 'I don't really have free will'.

This last instance has achieved a certain notoriety, thanks to Flew's treatment of it in his essay on 'Philosophy and Language'.[3] Flew draws attention to the fact that we have all learnt the use of the expression 'of his own free will', to cover

[3] *Philosophical Quarterly*, 1955; reprinted in *Essays in Conceptual Analysis*, 1956, ed. A. G. N. Flew.

such cases as that in which a bridegroom marries 'of his own free will'. So far so good. There are certainly circumstances in which we are accustomed to employ this expression. But we have also learnt criteria: we have been told that a person acts of his own free will only when his action proceeds from an act of will and when that act of will has the metaphysical peculiarity of being uncaused. If we wish to deny, as we well might, that this criterion is ever satisfied, then a natural way of expressing our conclusion is that 'there is no such thing as free will'. In a philosophical context we shall be quite well understood; nor will it follow that we shall no longer make such statements as that 'Hamlet returned to Denmark of his own free will but did not leave for England of his own free will'. But we shall have given notice, as it were, that this in no way commits us to accepting the conclusion that before he returned to Denmark he went through an uncaused act of will.

The paradigm case argument, then, does nothing to show that certain philosophical positions are 'absurd' or 'senseless'. At best, it serves to remind us — as, I suggested, the 'excluded opposite' argument may also remind us — that a philosopher's statements are not to be interpreted quite as a wholly unsophisticated person might interpret them. When Hippocrates denied that any disease was sacred, perhaps some innocent reader thought he was denying that anybody has ever suffered from epilepsy. Certainly if the bare statement 'there are no sacred diseases' were made out of its context, it could easily be ridiculed. 'Do you *really* mean that nobody ever suffers from fits, or rolls on the ground in a frenzy?' But our motto ought to be: 'Don't ask what a philosopher *could* mean; look and find out what he *did* mean'. If that is our motto we shall not find much use for paradigm case or excluded opposite arguments.

GROVER MAXWELL AND HERBERT FEIGL

WHY ORDINARY LANGUAGE NEEDS REFORMING[1]

Most philosophers, including many "ordinary-language"[2] philosophers, would agree that it is often permissible, even desirable, to "reform" ordinary language for scientific and for some philosophical purposes. But many of them would also maintain that most or, at least, a large portion of philosophical problems arise in ordinary language and, hence [sic!], must be solved in ordinary language — to attempt to solve them by "rational reconstructions," etc., would be to do something "utterly irrelevant."[3] We shall devote a large portion of this study to an examination of both

Reprinted from *The Journal of Philosophy*, LVIII (1961), 488–98, by permission of the authors and the editor.
[1] Contribution to the Symposium "Must Philosophers Reform Ordinary Language," meeting of the American Philosophical Association (Western Division), Chicago, May, 1960.
[2] See especially: J. L. Austin, "A Plea for Excuses," *Proceedings of the Aristotelian Society*, LVIII (1956–57), 11–12, 29; P. F. Strawson, "Construction and Analysis," in A. J. Ayer, *et al., The Revolution in Philosophy* (London: Macmillan, 1956), pp. 109–110, and *Introduction to Logical Theory* (New York: John Wiley & Sons, 1952), p. 230; and John Wisdom, "Philosophical Perplexity," *Proceedings of the Aristotelian Society*, XVI (1936).
Editor's note: Wisdom's article is reprinted above at pp. 101–10.
[3] See, for example, P. F. Strawson, "Carnap's Views on Constructed Systems *vs.* Natural Languages in Analytic Philosophy," in *The Philosophy of Rudolf Carnap*, ed. P. A. Schilpp (La Salle, Illinois: Open Court, 1963), pp. 503–18.
Editor's note: This essay overlaps Strawson's "Analysis, Science, & Metaphysics," reprinted below at pp. 312–20. See note, p. 312.

the premise and the conclusion of this argument.

To begin with, we wonder whether the ordinary-language philosopher can remain true to his own dictum. The terms of ordinary language are notoriously ambiguous and vague. We shall quickly be told that it is just this feature which renders it such a rich and effective instrument and that in many cases the ambiguity and vagueness do not cause any difficulty. We agree. But will it not also be agreed, even insisted, that some philosophical problems do arise from failure to distinguish among the various meanings or uses of a term and that one of the tasks of the philosopher is to "sort out" the various relevant meanings? But in what sense, if any, are these various *separate and distinct* meanings *already there* in ordinary language, waiting for the philosopher to unearth them? Surely the ordinary man (including ourselves) is not always conscious of their being there — otherwise, the "philosophical problems" that rendered the "sorting out" desirable would never have arisen. It might be retorted that by calling attention to the various uses of relevant terms we can often elicit agreement from the ordinary man (including ourselves) and in so doing remove his philosophical puzzlement. But how are we to decide whether this is the correct description of such a situation or whether we should say that we have persuaded the ordinary man to accept "tightened-up," perhaps modified — in short, *re-*

formed — meanings? Perhaps some cases are more aptly described in the former and others in the latter manner; but we know of no decision procedure for classifying each particular case, and we strongly suspect that many cases of putative ordinary-usage analysis are, in fact, disguised reformations. Perhaps such activity differs only in degree from that of the avowed reconstructionist or system builder. (This is, of course, *not* to say that the difference in degree may not be important.) For example, Professor Stephen Toulmin, in his recent book, *The Uses of Argument*,[4] takes William Kneale to task for supposing that it is appropriate in certain circumstances to say, "Improbable but true." But, surely, if we tell someone of having witnessed a friend make twenty consecutive "passes" with the dice, he might well exclaim, "How improbable!" And we might well reply, "Yes, improbable but true." In fact, we *have* heard such an expression so used on various occasions — by no means always only by philosophers, either. Professor Toulmin is, of course, engaged in adumbrating his own theory of probability, and he has every right, according to our view, to tighten up — to *reform* — the concept of probability in this manner, provided he produces reasonable grounds for so doing. But Professor Toulmin stoutly maintains that the *only legitimate* grounds for a theory of probability (and, we suppose, any philosophical theory) must be adduced from ordinary usage. Had Professor Toulmin permitted himself a bit of additional *reformation* and utilized the distinction, emphasized by Carnap (who also gets his wrist slapped by Professor Toulmin) and others, between individual events and kinds of events, he could have made a good case for maintaining that the expression at which he is so outraged *is* improper *unless* it is an ellipsis for something like, 'The event in question (which did occur) is a member of such-and-such a class of events. The occurrence of members of this

class of events is improbable. However, *this* event *did* occur'.

Consider a closely related point. Strawson[5] has pointed out that "in the effort to describe our experiences we are constantly putting words to new uses, connected with, but not identical with, their familiar uses; applying them to states of affairs which are both like and unlike those to which the words are most familiarly applied." Surely, something like this accounts, in large measure, for the evolution of "natural" languages; ordinary language is constantly *being* reformed. (Cf. Jespersen's point that an enormous number of the words in ordinary language are "dead metaphors."[6]) And quite often we find it necessary to help this evolution along a bit simply because ordinary language provides no univocal guide as to what should properly be said when novel situations arise, whether these arise in actuality or in thought experiments. Consider William James's example of the dog running round a tree on the trunk of which is a squirrel that encircles the trunk so that he always faces the dog. Does the dog go around the squirrel? Or consider the old conundrum: When a tree falls out of earshot of any sentient being, is there or is there not any sound? In what sense are the relevant *distinct* uses of 'go around' and 'sound' already lurking in ordinary language, waiting to be unearthed? Even in these extremely simple, perhaps puerile, "philosophical problems," a modest degree of reformation seems to be required.

A large proportion of philosophical problems arise from consideration of unusual cases. Many of the problems concerning perception, the reality of the external world, etc., arise quite naturally from consideration of abnormal cases such as illusions, hallucinations, and so on.

[4] Cambridge: University Press, 1958, p. 54.

[5] *Loc. cit.*
[6] *Language: Its Origins, Nature and Development* (London, 1925), p. 432; cited by D. J. O'Connor, "Philosophy and Ordinary Language," *Journal of Philosophy*, XLVII (1951), 797–808.

We do not condone all of the nonsense these problems have elicited (nor do we condemn it wholesale, either; any difficult and fascinating problem will produce some nonsense). But we see absolutely no reason to believe that examination of ordinary use in the "paradigm," normal cases can provide us with definitive rules for "proper" use in the unusual and novel cases. The "paradigm" cases can provide us with a starting point — a jumping-off place; ordinary language *is* (often) the first word — but, quite often, this is all that it can do.

Furthermore — and this is of crucial importance — consideration of atypical cases often points up possible inadequacies and may suggest improvements in our conceptualization of the "normal" cases. Carnap, in a penetrating examination of some of the claims of ordinary-language philosophers,[7] considers the following example:

"Does it follow from the fact that the same object can feel warm to one man and cold to another, that the object really is neither cold nor warm nor cool nor has any such property?" In order to solve this puzzle, we have first to distinguish between the following two concepts: (1) "the thing x feels warm to the persons y" and (2) "the thing x is warm," and then to clarify the relation between them. The method and terminology used for this clarification depends upon the specific purpose we may have in mind. First, it is indeed possible to clarify the distinction in a simple way in ordinary language. But if we require a more thorough clarification, we must search for explications of the two concepts. The explication of concept (1) may be given in an improved [reformed] version of the ordinary language concerning perceptions and the like. If a still more exact explication is desired, we may go to the scientific language of psychology. The explication of concept (2) must use an objective language, which may be a carefully selected, qualitative part of the ordinary language. If we wish the explicatum to be more precise, then we use the quantitative term "temperature" either as a term of the developed ordinary language, or as a scientific term of the language of physics.

Perhaps the prescientific gestation of the concept of temperature proceeded in a manner something like this, perhaps not; at any rate, it easily could have.

As an example of a philosophical problem which arises in ordinary language but which need not — perhaps cannot — be solved in ordinary language, Carnap cites the paradoxes of Zeno. He says:[8]

For their solution, certain parts of mathematics are needed which go far beyond elementary arithmetic, such as the theory of real numbers, the concept of the limit of a series, and finally the proof that certain infinite series are convergent, i.e., that every member of the series is greater than zero and nevertheless the sum of the whole series is finite. In this case, the perplexities were formulated in the natural language. But the diagnosis consists in the demonstration that certain apparently valid forms of inference involving the infinite are fallacious and lead to contradictions. The therapy consists in the use of a new language, with terms suitable for the formulation of the problem and with rules of deduction preventing the old contradictions.

We are aware of a number of attempts to resolve these paradoxes within the rubric of ordinary language. We do not think that any of these has been successful, and, indeed, some of them seem to commit the "fallacy of irrelevant conclusion."[9] Be that as it may, it is sufficient for our purposes that, although the paradoxes arise in ordinary language, they *can* be solved in nonordinary language.[10] And we suggest that, even if it could be shown that some of the ordinary-language attempts succeed, the

---

[7] "P. F. Strawson on Linguistic Naturalism," in *The Philosophy of Rudolf Carnap*, p. 934.

[8] *Ibid.*, p. 939.

[9] See, especially, G. Ryle, *Dilemmas* (Cambridge: University Press, 1954), pp. 36–53, critically commented upon by A. Ambrose, *Journal of Philosophy*, LII (1955), 157–58.

[10] See, for example, A. Grünbaum, "Modern Science and Refutation of the Paradoxes of Zeno," *The Scientific Monthly*, LXXXI (1955), 234–39.

non-ordinary resolution is more thorough, more complete, more elegant, and actually simpler.

By far the greater number of important and interesting traditional philosophical problems, it seems to us, have arisen out of those non-paradigmatic cases which are either *the results of scientific discoveries* or of *speculation along scientific lines*. The problems of primary and secondary qualities, as well as many of the questions concerning substance, had their origins in considerations of Renaissance science and speculation that many of the observable properties of physical objects would some day be explained by microstructure. The "nature" of space and time; the free-will problems and their relation to causality, determinism, and indeterminism; the mind-body problem (particularly in connection with its neurophysiological aspects); the problems of teleology; etc., etc., provide other examples.

What can we say, briefly, about the actual role reformation plays in these and in other philosophical problems? As a beginning let us consider what might seem to be a digression. Ordinary-language philosophers often contend that reformation, systematization, etc., tend to neglect and to destroy the immense richness and complexity of ordinary language and to replace it with "neat simplicities." But surely this is only one edge of the sword, and perhaps the other edge is sharper: the "richness" of ordinary language often turns out to be an *embarras de richesse*. It is a commonplace that science proceeds, in large measure, by simplifying, by abstracting, by neglecting factors that are irrelevant and, even in some cases, by neglecting factors that have a measure of relevance in order to arrive at viable approximations. It seems to us that philosophy, too, should often proceed in a similar manner. The Oxbridge analysts remind us that each statement has its own logic; they should also point out, further, that each statement may have several logics, for they *do* point out, quite correctly, that a single

tokening of a sentence may simultaneously play several roles, e.g., cognitive, emotive, performatory, etc. An epistemologist, for example, who is interested in an analysis of the validation of knowledge claims will need to extract from this tangle, and concentrate on, the *cognitive* aspects. He will want to determine certain general cognitive features which a large variety of sentences have in common. He will want to eliminate or minimize the much vaunted "context dependence" as much as is feasible, partly by abstracting context-invariant features and partly by formulating *general* principles which themselves specify the relevant contextual conditions. In short, he will need to systematize to some extent. For this purpose he may even find it necessary to introduce new terms. Some of these may be merely notational conveniences, introduced by *explicit* definition; but others may be introduced in a manner similar to the introduction of certain theoretical terms in science — it may *not* be possible, even in principle, to define them explicitly. They will be *implicitly* defined by some of the principles of the theory of knowledge that employs them. The dichotomy, *term of ordinary language* vs. *technical term*, if by 'technical term' is meant a term for which explicit definition or neat "criteria" are given, is chimerical both in theoretical science and in philosophy. This should not be surprising. Even in teaching the meanings of many terms of *ordinary language*, it is often impossible to give helpful explicit definitions *or* to give the meanings of such terms "ostensively." Here, as in science and philosophy, we have to proceed by giving *some* of the rules for the use of such a term and by exhibiting its use on *some* occasions. We have to show how it is located in a network of other concepts — or we may say that we call attention to the *meaning postulates* that implicitly define the term by relating it to other terms. It is neither possible nor necessary nor desirable that every term, expression, or sentence of science or philosophy be *trans-*

latable into ordinary language, the observation language, or the like.

This discussion, incidentally, shows how technical philosophy of science may have important implications for the analysis of ordinary language; i.e., the analysis of scientific theories results in a model useful in explaining how many of the terms of our ordinary language "get their meaning"; they are, in a sense, implicitly defined by the meaning postulates of the (somewhat primitive) theories presupposed by ordinary language. Another case in point, closely related to the one above, is the analytic-synthetic distinction. Surely this distinction is crucial for analytic philosophy; for the central concern of the analyst is the set of moves made according to the rules of the relevant language game. The move from 'Joe is a bachelor' to 'Joe is male' is sanctioned wholly by such rules; but a move from 'Joe is a bachelor' to 'Joe is neurotic', even if justified, cannot be certified by the analyst, for it depends upon the factual premise, 'All (or most, or many) bachelors are neurotic' rather than, as in the case with the former, upon an analytic premise such as 'All bachelors are male'. Unfortunately, most moves, and virtually all of these which are philosophically interesting, are not so easily classified as the simple examples cited above. Search ordinary usage of a particular linguistic move as much as we may, the most we are usually able to come up with is the fact that sometimes it seems to be made on the basis of an analytic premise, at others on the basis of a factual premise; in most cases, ordinary use does not provide any definitive basis for placing it in either category. The ordinary-language analyst will, thus, in most cases, not be able to decide whether the move is within his province of certification or not. When he professes to do so, we contend, *he is actually indulging in tacit reformation and issuing a stipulation* as to what the terms in question *are to* mean. The parallel (actually the identical) problem in philosophy of science is concerned with the distinc-

tion between those lawlike statements which are true solely by virtue of the meanings of the terms involved (the meaning postulates which implicitly — or explicitly — define the relevant terms) and those which express contingent truths. Here, again, a statement such as '$f = ma$' seems sometimes to be used merely as a definition of 'force', at others as an empirical law ('force' being defined perhaps by Hooke's law), and, in many cases, its use provides no definitive basis for classifying it as either. (In some, though not all, of the cases of the last type, 'force' seems to function as a theoretical term that is not explicitly definable at all.) The terms are what one of us has called "systematically ambiguous." [11]

But we do not share the views of Quine *et al.*, who hold that there is no analytic-synthetic distinction or that it is of no importance. It seems to us that, in any responsible, reflective use of language, the meanings of words should be determined entirely by the intent of the language user concerning their use. So, when we wish to speak of meaning at all, our proposal is that we yield gracefully (to borrow a phrase from an unpublished manuscript by Professor Roger Buck) to the temptation to issue stipulations — to reform.[12] An analysis of a theory — a set of lawlike statements — will almost always reveal that it is possible to distribute analyticity and contingency in a number of different ways so that each member of the resulting *family* of reformations will be consistent with the actual use of the theory in a

[11] H. Feigl, "Some Major Issues and Developments in the Philosophy of Science of Logical Empiricism," in *Minnesota Studies in the Philosophy of Science*, ed. H. Feigl and M. Scriven (Minneapolis: University of Minnesota Press, 1956).

[12] In connection with this problem, the terms 'reform' and 'reformation' had already been used as "technical terms" by one of us before this symposium topic was assigned; see G. Maxwell, "Meaning Postulates in Scientific Theories," in *Current Issues in the Philosophy of Science*, ed. H. Feigl and G. Maxwell (New York: Holt, Rinehart and Winston, 1961).

given situation or context. The value of such reformation stands out most sharply when it becomes desirable to enrich or otherwise modify the theory, usually in view of new discovery or new speculation. In such cases, that reformation should be selected which results in the greatest simplicity, elegance, heuristic fertility, etc., of the modified theory. Thus a meaning postulate cannot be false, nor can a belief in it be mistaken; it is necessarily true and (therefore) factually empty simply because it is merely a "surrogate"[13] for a linguistic rule. *But* such rules often indirectly "reflect" facts or beliefs via considerations of simplicity, theoretical fertility, etc.; and if we stubbornly cling to all of the "old" rules in the face of new discoveries, we must be prepared to pay the price of having some of our concepts become vacuous and of having our conceptual system become more and more cumbersome — perhaps practically unmanageable.[14]

We contend that this segment of the philosophy of science, at the very least, provides a helpful model for analogous problems in ordinary language. We believe, of course, that it is more than a model and that it provides the most plausible theory which explains how our everyday concepts grew and evolved as a result of the facts and beliefs deemed most important throughout the history of mankind. And it shows why the language of science is continuous with ordinary language and why scientific discoveries are potentially relevant to *any* philosophical problem.

The need for reform, then, is at least threefold. First, there is the need, for certain philosophical purposes, to abstract and systematize, eliminating irrelevancies. Second, in many cases, we must reform in

order to analyze at all, because mere examination of ordinary use will not reveal the sought-for rule and because the more interesting terms of ordinary language are also systematically ambiguous. Third, the implicit rules that *are* present in the ordinary language game may *indirectly* reflect beliefs which are false.

But now let us offer an olive branch. Ordinary language is indeed (usually) the *first* word. The *groundwork* for almost any philosophical investigation should consist of a careful and detailed study of the actual use to which terms designating the relevant concepts are put (a task which Oxbridge analysts often perform so admirably). And this is not all: for the purpose of effective communication, among other things, let the *meanings* we give to the pertinent terms in our reformations be such that the resulting *use* corresponds as closely with their *ordinary use* as is consistent with other desiderata such as simplicity, heuristic fertility, etc. (provided, of course, that we can discover what the ordinary use actually is). Finally, when our reformations do depart from ordinary use, let us explicitly note this fact and point out, insofar as is possible, both the nature of the differences and the grounds for the departure. A philosopher who violates these maxims, in order to get started, must pull himself up by his bootstraps; and even if he succeeds in this, he will in all probability be seriously misunderstood, not only by others, but, quite possibly, even by himself. Even the system-builder who, having proposed wholesale a new terminology and notation, makes his use of his conceptual apparatus in principle clear (although he is exercising a prerogative we would not deny him) must be prepared to find himself, perhaps justifiably, ignored. The kind of systematization that *we* advocate is similar to that of science. It should be a cooperative venture and should, in the main, proceed slowly, aided by criticisms and suggestions exchanged among coworkers.

We must admit that most philosophers

[13] See Max Black, "Necessary Statements and Rules," *Philosophical Review*, LXVII (1958), 313–41.

[14] For a more detailed treatment of these points, see Maxwell, *loc. cit.* Also, Feigl, "Confirmability and Confirmation," in *Readings in Philosophy of Science*, ed. P. P. Wiener (New York: Scribner's, 1953).

have failed to observe the maxims listed above, and we are astounded to note among them those who, of all people, should know better. For example, Professor Gilbert Ryle[15] adduces a kind of ontological proof[16] or transcendental deduction of the nonexistence of private mental states or events such as pain, anger, elation, etc. He purports to do this by exhibiting our actual use of such terms and comes to the remarkable conclusion that they *mean* or refer to nothing but actual and/or possible behavior. Professor Ryle's failure has at least three facets. First, such ontological proofs are highly suspect on elementary logical grounds — unless it could be shown, e.g., that the concept of immediate experience is inconsitent; we do not think that Professor Ryle demonstrates *this*. Second, it would be hard to imagine a more radical departure from common sense and ordinary usage than that which Professor Ryle proposes. We are more sure of the fact that when we token 'Jones is in pain', we do not *mean* or intend to refer to his actual or possible behavior than we are of any philosophical thesis. (It is true, of course, that we use his behavior as probabilistic indicators of his pain.) Third, Professor Ryle does not and cannot justify his flagrant violation of ordinary usage because he deliberately ignores the relevant scientific considerations (particulary those of neurophysiology). Professor Norman Malcolm goes even further and suggests that sentences such as 'I am in pain' are perhaps not reports at all but are to be classified with such acts as limping, crying, holding one's leg, etc.[17] It is one of those delightful ironies of philosophy that Professor Malcolm, for whom *any* departure from ordi-

nary language was, at least at one time, anathema and who emphatically maintained that ordinary use is *correct use*[18] should propose the most radical departure from ordinary language of which we have ever heard. Professor Malcolm arrives at his position, of course, by following the footsteps of the master. He finds it nonsensical to say, "I have a pain and Jones has something similar to or qualitatively identical with it," because *I* have no "criteria" for saying that *Jones's* immediate experience is similar to mine. If by a 'criterion', following the early logical postivists, one means something like a *logically* necessary or sufficient condition, then of course: no criteria, no meaning. But this argument has for us no force at all and simply reflects a narrow verificationism, or an anti-theoretical bias on the part of Ryle and the later Wittgenstein. Do we not lack criteria, in exactly the same way, for asserting that a past event was (qualitatively) similar to a present one? Or for saying that a hydrocarbon molecule has roughly the *same* shape as a certain tinker-toy model? The justification of such "transcendent" assertions is indirect, and depends on the acceptance of an entire conceptual frame. This is in some (though not in all) respects similar to the justification of scientific theories. The adoption of a conceptual frame can be pragmatically justified, and while this includes quite prominently empirical considerations, these alone are not sufficient — simply because they function as "evidence" only within such a frame. To ask for absolute or *a priori* demonstrations, here as elsewhere, is to chase a will-o'-the-wisp — reflecting a quixotic "quest for certainty."

If space permitted, we should like to "view with alarm" other fashionable but highly questionable recent tendencies among some of the ordinary-language phi-

---

[15] *The Concept of Mind* (London: Hutchinson's University Library, 1949).

[16] We are indebted to Professor P. K. Feyerabend for this point.

[17] "Knowledge of Other Minds," *Journal of Philosophy*, LV (1958), 969–78. Cf. also the counterarguments by H. Feigl in "Other Minds and the Egocentric Predicament," *ibid.*, pp. 978–87.

[18] N. Malcolm, "Moore and Ordinary Language," in *The Philosophy of G. E. Moore*, ed. P. A. Schilpp (New York: Tudor, 1946), pp. 345–68.

Editor's note: Reprinted above at pp. 111–24.

losophers. For example, religion (if not also theology) is again the subject of very peculiar defenses. If literal interpretations of the scripture are excluded, i.e., if "demythologization" is attempted, one must ask whether the remaining core of significance in religious expressions can consist in anything more than edification, exhortation (including, of course, self-exhortation), and consolation. There is no doubt that these functions of language play important roles in our lives. But "faith," "creed," or "belief" in this religious sense does not involve any knowledge claims, and is exclusively a matter of attitude and ritual and reduces to the expression-appeal (plus perhaps some "performatory") functions of language. If so, should not the self-professed linguistic therapists and clarifiers make it perfectly explicit that "belief" ("faith," "creed," etc.) in that sense is not to be confused with "belief" in the well-known and entirely different sense in which we use it in connection, eg., with predictions or conjectures — be it in common life or in science? We think that the basic distinction between cognitive and noncognitive significance is indispensable and that its neglect can lead us only back to obscurity, or worse still, to obscurantism. The clarity of thought aspired to by Wittgenstein himself can be attained only if, while granting the *fusions* of the various functions of language, we remain on our guard against their *confusions*. This in fact seems to us to be the first step in all cases of philosophical analysis and, hence, a prerequisite for any subsequent reformation.

Editor's note: At the same symposium in which Thompson presented his reply to this essay by Maxwell and Feigl, another reply was presented by O. K. Bouwsma. This reply is entitled "The Terms of Ordinary Language Are . . ." and is included in Bouwsma [1].

MANLEY THOMPSON

When Is Ordinary Language Reformed?[1]

According to Professors Maxwell and Feigl, "it does not seem that we ordinarily speak of reforming ordinary language." But what shall we say about the rather frequent proposals to simplify spelling, verb formation, plural endings, and the like? These proposals for the most part are not concerned primarily, if indeed at all, with reforms in specialized languages like those of law, medicine, physics, chess, or business. They are concerned primarily with reforms in the language all of us speak in our everyday living, and surely we would ordinarily speak of these reforms as reforms of ordinary language. I suspect the point is that Professors Maxwell and Feigl are not at all concerned with reforming ordinary language in the way that these proposals are concerned with reforming it. We do not ordinarily speak of reforming language in the way that Professors Maxwell and Feigl think that philosophers must reform it. In this paper I shall take the liberty of referring to the latter as "the extraordinary way of reforming ordinary language." We shall see presently that there is some point in keeping this contrast in mind when we discuss the question of whether philosophers must reform ordinary language.

The contrast, unfortunately, is not

Reprinted from *The Journal of Philosophy*, LVIII (1961), 498–504, by permission of the author and the editor.
[1] Read at the meeting of the Western Division of the American Philosophical Association at Chicago, May, 1960.

brought out very well by Maxwell and Feigl's initial characterization of how they are going to use the phrase "reforming ordinary language." They say that their use of this phrase will be the same as that of the phrase "changing the ordinary use of terms or introducing new terms by specifying what use they are to have." The trouble is that the latter phrase can be readily applied to many of the reforms that seem to be ordinary. It is apparent from what is said later in the Maxwell-Feigl paper that its authors do not mean in their initial characterization of reforming ordinary language just any change in the ordinary use of a term, nor do they mean the introduction of a new term to serve just any of the uses that a new word may serve. On the contrary, their main concern is with the cognitive functions of language, and they are concerned with the various noncognitive functions only to the extent of isolating the latter and keeping them from being confused with the cognitive functions. The extraordinary way of reforming ordinary language is thus a cognitive reform — a reform which aims to improve the capacity of language to perform its cognitive functions.

I shall not have time to discuss separately each of the three needs for cognitive reform listed by Professors Maxwell and Feigl. I want instead to raise the general question: Have they given us a satisfactory account of what philosophers should do (or try to do) with ordinary language? I want to suggest another way, which I believe is more fruitful, of regarding the relation between philosophy and ordinary language. The central point I shall try to urge is that when we speak of instituting any of the Maxwell-Feigl reforms of language we have in mind something that applies to what we are inclined to call "specialized" rather than "ordinary" language.

Consider the case of a head waiter who refers to all the medium-sized tables in his restaurant as "six-foot tables." The other waiters know his use of this phrase and understand his orders when he says, "Do thus and so with the six-foot tables." But one day a workman comes to the restaurant and is told by the head waiter to revarnish the tops of all the six-foot tables. The head waiter discovers later that the workman has departed after revarnishing the tops of only three of the tables. He recalls the workman and asks why the job was not finished. Producing a ruler, the workman demonstrates that only the three tables with revarnished tops measure approximately six feet. The others are barely five feet. The head waiter admits the fault is his and announces to the other waiters and workmen that henceforth in his instructions the phrase "six-foot table" will not be used. The new phrase "medium table" will be used instead. Has the head waiter reformed ordinary language? Clearly not, but he has reformed what we might call the specialized language he uses for giving orders in the restaurant.

I do not wish to press this rather crude example too far, but I think it illustrates the principal factors that are present when we speak of cognitive reforms of language. In an obvious sense the head waiter used ordinary language in giving his instructions, but in an important sense he did not. The later point is brought out by the fact that the workman misunderstood the instructions, although we hardly want to say he misunderstood ordinary language. There is nothing in ordinary language which tells us exactly how close to six feet a table must measure in order to be cor-

rectly referred to as a "six-foot table." Presumably Professors Maxwell and Feigl would say that here we must stipulate a meaning postulate, and this in effect is what the workman did. He stipulated that when the measurement is short by at least a foot the table is not a six-foot table. But this stipulation is a tacit reform of the specialized language of the head waiter's instructions and not of ordinary language.

In his *Introduction to Mathematical Philosophy*, when speaking of the logical distinction between the *is* of identity and the *is* of predication, Lord Russell comments: "It is a disgrace to the human race that it has chosen to employ the word 'is' for these two entirely different ideas — a disgrace which a symbolic logical language of course remedies" (p. 172). Here, I suppose, is as clear-cut a case as we can find of a philosopher claiming to reform ordinary language in a manner that is philosophically necessary. But is the reform philosophically necessary? To be sure, two sentences like "Chicago is the largest city on the Great Lakes" and "Chicago is larger than any other city on the Great Lakes" both have the surface grammar of a subject and predicate connected by "is." But that "is" functions differently in the two cases at a deeper level of grammar is shown clearly by differences in linguistic context. It is unnecessary to go to differences in context afforded by the nonspeech environment. In the first sentence, "is" functions predicatively with reference to a phrase beginning with the definite article; in the second, with reference to a phrase beginning with an adjective in comparative form. The relevant grammatical rule applicable in the linguistic context provided by the first sentence is that "is" has the force of "is identical with." The addition of the phrase "identical with" immediately after the "is" in the first sentence always makes grammatical sense, although the need for such an addition (usually as a matter of emphasis) arises only when "is" is taken in a wider context than that afforded by the sentence itself. On the other hand, "Chicago is identical with larger than any other city on the Great Lakes" is grammatical nonsense. A different rule governing the use of "is" is obviously at work here.

Russell's only quarrel with ordinary language on this score is thus that all occurrences of the word "is" are not governed by exactly the same set of rules, not even by the same set of typically ambiguous rules. But why is this a disgrace to the human race? For one thing, Russell takes note of the fact that in ordinary English the sign of identity is never "is" alone but "is" in conjunction with certain specifiable types of words (such articles and nouns), and that the sign of predication is likewise never "is" alone but "is" in conjunction with certain specifiable types of words (such as verbs and adjectives). Russell notes only that confusion is bound to arise if one takes "is" by itself, regardless of its linguistic context, as a connective sign. But this is simply a misunderstanding of ordinary language, and the only reform called for is a correction of the misunderstanding. However, if a logician tried to operate with a logical calculus that symbolized identity and predication in exactly the same way, the result would not only be disgrace, it would be disaster.

The point is that Russell's need for reform arises only when ordinary language is regarded as a logical calculus. I suspect Russell was led to this view by the fact that in many presentations of Aristotelian logic "is" seems to occur indifferently as the symbol of identity and predication. But then the reform called for is a reform of the specialized language of these logicians. The fact that in their specialized language they borrow the word "is" from ordinary language does not make their language ordinary any more than the language of the head waiter's instructions is made ordinary because he uses only words from ordinary language. We develop specialized languages for many purposes, including that of serving as an intellectual tool in logical analysis; and we add new words, stipulate further meaning postulates, and otherwise reform a specialized language whenever the occasion arises. In instituting these reforms, as well as in the actual development of a specialized language, we also make use of ordinary language. But we neither develop nor reform ordinary language in the way that we do a specialized language. Ordinary language in this respect stands at rock bottom — it is not a tool which we develop while using another language as we develop a specialized language while using it. We speak of reforming ordinary language in what I called the "ordinary way," simplifications in spelling, verb formations, plural endings, and the like, because words as subject to changes of this sort are already tools which we can make easier to use. But when we construct a specialized language we may give ordinary words special uses and thus make them tools in a way that they were not tools before, as the phrase "six-foot table" became a tool in the language of the head waiter's instructions or the word "is" in the language of classical logicians. My suggestion, then, is that many extraordinary reforms of ordinary language are in fact reforms of these tools in specialized rather than in ordinary language.

I said *many* extraordinary reforms. What of the rest? Suppose that at some time ordinary language reflected the belief mentioned in Aristotle that thunder is a quenching of fire in the clouds. An analyst of ordinary language at this time might conclude that the move from "That is thunder" to "That is fire being quenched in the clouds" was analytic in ordinary language. Do we want to say that in this case ordinary language needs reform because one of its discernible rules reflects a false belief? Surely what is needed here is reform in belief and not in language. Once the mistaken belief about thunder is abandoned, the linguistic reform takes care of itself; people will no longer say the things they used to say about thunder — the word "thunder" will behave according to new rules. But as long as the old belief is retained, it is utterly misleading to describe the situation as one calling for linguistic reform. I suggest, then, that when extraordinary reforms of ordinary language are not in fact reforms of specialized language, they are reforms in belief misconstrued as linguistic reforms.

There may of course be a cultural lag. People may continue to talk in the old way even after their beliefs have been changed, and a man may find himself saying things in an ordinary conversation which are incompatible with things he would say in a specialized language of inquiry. In this situation one may speak of reforming ordinary language by bringing it up to date. But is this anything more than proposing that we consciously accelerate and direct the natural evolution of language? People are hardly going to continue indefinitely talking in a manner contrary to what they believe. As new beliefs gradually become ordinary beliefs, adjustments in ordinary language are bound to occur. While the adjustments that come about naturally without conscious planning may often be less satisfactory than those which fit in with particular plans, it is hardly the peculiar job of the philosopher to draw up such plans and urge their adoption. This forms no part of philosophical inquiry. It seems to me that these planned adjustments belong with the ordinary reforms of ordinary language. Those who propose planned reforms in spelling, verb formations, and the like are certainly proposing to accelerate and direct the natural evolution of language, and this is also true of planned reforms designed to make usage correspond with new beliefs.

But does ordinary language, then, have any special relation to philosophy? Ordinary language is the pre-theoretical language in which we first express our beliefs, our doubts, our wonders, our puzzles, and our problems. Ordinary language thus has the first word, and it remains *the* word until inquiry changes our beliefs. When

philosophical inquiries, despite extensive use of specialized language, end in confusion and disagreement, philosophers may turn (or return) to ordinary language because they suspect that the source of trouble lies in the initial statement of the problem. Of course, the initial statement may have been in a specialized language, say the language of physics; and in this case philosophers may be led to re-examine what they have assumed about physics and what they have borrowed from it. Yet as philosophers, their primary job is neither to add to physics nor to make it intelligible to the non-specialist. The peculiarly philosophic task concerns the relation of physics to something else, and sometimes what this something else is is stated in ordinary language simply because there is no other language at hand. Does physics say what this table in front of me really is? We might have a special metaphysical language in which we gave a meaning to the phrase "really is," but when our metaphysics ends in confusion and dispute we still have ordinary language. "What is it really?" may occur in ordinary language as an expression of doubt, wonder, or puzzlement, and philosophers in despair of metaphysical language may seek the word of ordinary language on this point. But here the concern is to understand, not to reform, ordinary language.

When philosophers turn in this way to ordinary language, specialized philosophical language about ordinary language inevitably results, and there is thus the problem, rightly emphasized by Maxwell and Feigl, of deciding when philosophers have got the word of ordinary language and when they have read their own philosophical prejudices into ordinary language. There is, I believe, no easy solution to this problem — no single set of criteria we can appeal to. But we only make matters worse when we regard ordinary language as if it were just another specialized language subject to cognitive reforms in the way that all such languages are. In using ordinary language one is always faced with the question, "Does this sentence say what I mean?" If the answer is "no," one has no alternative but to find another sentence of ordinary language which does say what one means. Communication fails unless the search is successful. This is the situation even when one introduces for the first time expressions of specialized language, since one has to make clear in ordinary language what these primitive expressions of specialized language mean. But in using an already developed specialized language one always has the alternative of introducing new expressions into the specialized language, using ordinary language to relate these new primitive expressions to the already existing expressions of the specialized language. It is just because of this rock-bottom character of ordinary language that it makes sense to speak of *the* word of ordinary language. That it makes sense, in other words, to distinguish between what ordinary language says and what philosophers may say that it says. Yet it is also just this rock-bottom character of ordinary language that we lose when we speak of reforming it as Russell did, and, it seems to me, as Professors Maxwell and Feigl have, too.

· 16a ·

R. M. HARE

Philosophical Discoveries[1]

I

There are two groups of philosophers in the world at present who often get across one another. I will call them respectively 'analysts' and 'metaphysicians', though this is strictly speaking inaccurate — for the analysts are in fact often studying the same old problems of metaphysics in their own way and with sharper tools, and the metaphysicians of an older style have no exclusive or proprietary right to the inheritance of Plato and Aristotle who started the business. Now metaphysicians often complain of analysts that, instead of doing *ontology*, studying *being qua being* (or for that matter *qua* anything else), they study only *words*. My purpose in this paper is to diagnose one (though only one) of the uneasinesses which lie at the back of this common complaint (a complaint which

Reprinted from *Mind*, LXIX (1960), 145–62, by permission of the author and the publisher. (Copyright 1960 by Thomas Nelson and Sons Ltd.)

Sections 2–5 and 7 were first published in *The Journal of Philosophy*, LIV (1957), 741–50, and are reprinted by permission of the editor.

[1] Sections 2–5 and 7 of this paper appeared in the *Journal of Philosophy*, in a symposium with Professors Paul Henle and S. Körner entitled 'The Nature of Analysis'. The whole paper could not be printed there for reasons of space, and I am grateful to the editors of the *Journal* for permission to include in this revised version of the complete paper the extract already printed.

Editor's note: References to Henle and to Körner in this essay are to Henle [1], reprinted below at pp. 218–23, and Körner [5] (which was, like Henle's paper, written in reply to the original version of Hare's essay).

analysts of all kinds, and not only those of the 'ordinary-language' variety, have to answer). The source of the uneasiness seems to be this: there are some things in philosophy of which we want to say that we *know* that they are so — or even that we can *discover* or *come to know* that they are so — as contrasted with merely deciding arbitrarily that they are to be so; and yet we do not seem to know that these things are so by any observation of empirical fact. I refer to such things as that an object cannot both have and not have the same quality. These things used to be described as metaphysical truths; now it is more customary, at any rate among analysts, to express them metalinguistically, for example by saying that propositions of the form '*p* and not *p*' are analytically false. An analyst who says this is bound to go on to say what he means by such expressions as 'analytically false'; and the account which he gives will usually be of the following general sort: to say that a proposition is analytically false is to say that it is false in virtue of the meaning or use which we give to the words used to express it, and of nothing else. But this way of speaking is not likely to mollify the metaphysician; indeed, he might be pardoned if he said that it made matters worse. For if philosophical statements are statements about how words are *actually* used by a certain set of people, then their truth will be contingent — whereas what philosophers seem to be after are necessary truths: but if they are expressions of a certain philosopher's *decision* to use words in a certain way, then it seems inappropriate to speak of our *knowing* that they are true. The first of these alternatives would seem to make the findings of philosophy contingent upon linguistic practices which might be other than they are; the second would seem to turn philosophy into the making of fiats or conventions about how a particular writer or group of writers is going to use terms — and this does not sound as if it would provide answers to the kind of questions that people used to be interested in, like 'Can an object both have and not have the same quality, and if not why not?' This is why to speak about 'decisions' (Henle, *op. cit.* pp. 753 ff.) or about 'rules' which are 'neither true nor false' (Körner, *op. cit.* pp. 760 ff.) will hardly assuage the metaphysician's legitimate anxiety, although both of these terms are likely to figure in any successful elucidation of the problem.

It is worth pointing out that this dilemma which faces the analyst derives, historically, from what used to be a principal tenet of the analytical movement in its early days — the view that all meaningful statements are either analytic (in the sense of analytically true or false) or else empirical. From this view it seems to follow that the statements of the philosopher must be either empirical or analytic; otherwise we can only call them meaningless, or else not really statements at all but some other kind of talk. Many analysts failed to see the difficulty of their position because of a confusion which it is easy to make. It is easy to suppose that the proposition that such and such another proposition is analytically true, or false (the proposition of the analyst) is itself analytic, and therefore fits readily into one of the approved categories of meaningful discourse. But, though it may *perhaps* be true, it is not *obviously* true that to say 'Propositions of the form "*p* and not *p*" are analytically false' is to make an analytically true statement; for is not this a statement about how the words 'and not' are

used? And is it analytically true that they are used in this way? There are conflicting temptations to call the statement analytic, and empirical, and neither. The early analysts therefore ought to have felt more misgivings than most of them did feel about the status of their own activities; and this might have made them more sympathetic towards the metaphysicians, whose activities are of just the same dubious character (neither clearly empirical nor clearly analytic).

This is not to say that the matter has not been widely discussed since that time; and indeed there are certain well-known simple remedies for the perplexity. But I am not convinced that the disease is yet fully understood; and until it is, metaphysicians and analysts will remain at cross purposes. It is a pity that the early analysts, in general, tended to follow the lead, not of Wittgenstein, but of Carnap. Wittgenstein was moved by doubts on this point among others to describe his own propositions as 'nonsensical' (*Tractatus*, 6:54); but Carnap wrote, '[Wittgenstein] seems to me to be inconsistent in what he does. He tells us that one cannot state philosophical propositions and that whereof one cannot speak, thereof one must be silent; and then instead of keeping silent, he writes a whole philosophical book' (*Philosophy and Logical Syntax*, p. 37), thus indicating that he did not take Wittgenstein's misgivings as seriously as he should have. At any rate, the time has surely come when metaphysicians ought to co-operate in attacking this problem, which touches them both so nearly.

Once it is realised that the propositions of the analyst are not obviously analytic, a great many other possibilities suggest themselves. Are they, for example, empirical, as Professor Braithwaite has recently affirmed?[2] Or are some of them analytic and some empirical? Or are they sometimes ambiguous, so that the writer has no clear idea which of these two things

[2] An Empiricist's View of the Nature of Religious Belief, p. 11.

(if either) they are? Or are they, not statements at all, but resolves, stipulations or rules? Or, lastly, are they (to use an old label which has little if any explanatory force) synthetic *a priori*? These possibilities all require to be investigated.

This paper is intended to serve only as a prolegomenon to such an investigation. It takes the form of an analogy. If we could find a type of situation in which the same sort of difficulty arises, but in a much clearer and simpler form, we might shed some light on the main problem. In choosing a much simpler model, we run the risk of over-simplification; but this is a risk which has to be taken if we are to make any progress at all. If we are careful to notice the differences, as well as the similarities, between the model and that of which it is a model, we shall be in less danger of misleading ourselves.

The suggestion which I am going tentatively to put forward might be described as a demythologised version of Plato's doctrine of *anamnesis*. Plato says that finding out the definition of a concept is like remembering or recalling. If this is correct, some of the difficulties of describing the process are accounted for. To remember (whether a fact, or how to do something) is not (or at any rate not obviously) to make an empirical discovery; yet it is not to make a decision either. So there may be here a way of escaping from the analyst's dilemma.

II

Suppose that we are sitting at dinner and discussing how a certain dance is danced. Let us suppose that the dance in question is one requiring the participation of a number of people — say one of the Scottish reels. And let us suppose that we have a dispute about what happens at a particular point in the dance; and that, in order to settle it, we decide to dance the dance after dinner and find out. We have to imagine that there is among us a sufficiency of people who know, or say they know, how to dance the dance — in

the sense of 'know' in which one may know how to do something without being able to *say* how it is done.

When the dance reaches the disputed point everybody may dance as he thinks the dance should go; or they may all agree to dance according to the way that one party to the dispute says it should go. Whichever of these two courses they adopt, there are several things which may, in theory, happen. The first is, chaos — people bumping into one another so that it becomes impossible, as we should say, for the dance to proceed. The second is that there is no chaos, but a dance is danced which, though unchaotic, is not the dance which they were trying to dance — not, for example, the dance called 'the eightsome reel'. The third possibility is that the dance proceeds correctly. The difficulty is to say how we tell these three eventualities from one another, and whether the difference is empirical. It may be thought that, whether empirical or not, the difference is obvious; but I do not find it so.

It might be denied that there is any empirical difference between the first eventuality (chaos) and the second (wrong dance). For it might be said, we could have a dance which consisted in people bumping into one another. In Michael Tippett's opera *The Midsummer Marriage* the character called the He-Ancient is asked reproachfully by a modern why his dancers never dance a new dance: in reply, he says 'I will show you a new dance' and immediately trips one of the dancers up, so that he falls on the ground and bruises himself. The implication of this manoeuvre is the Platonic one that innovations always lead to chaos — that there is only one right way of dancing (the one that we have learnt from our elders and betters) and that all deviations from this are just wrong. But whether or not we accept this implication, the example perhaps shows that we *could* call *any* series of movements a dance. If, however, we started to call it a dance, we should have to stop calling it chaos. The terms 'dance' and 'chaos' mutually exclude one another; but although we cannot call any series of movements *both* chaos *and* dance, we can call any series of movements *either* chaos *or* dance; so the problem of distinguishing dance from chaos remains.

The first and the second eventualities (chaos and wrong dance) are alike in this, that, whether or not we can say that *any* series of movements is *a* dance, we cannot say that *any* series of movements is *the* dance (*viz.* the eightsome reel) about the correct way of dancing which we were arguing. It might therefore be claimed that, although it may be difficult to say what counts as *a* dance, and thus distinguish between the first and second eventualities, we can at least distinguish easily between either of them and the third (right dance). And so we can, *in theory*; for obviously both the wrong dance, and chaos or no dance at all, are distinct from the right dance. That is to say, the terms of my classification of things that might happen make it analytic to say that these three things that might happen are different things. But all distinctions are not impirical distinction (for example evaluative distinctions are not); and the question is rather, How, empirically (if it is done empirically) do we tell, of these three logically distinct happenings, which has happened? And how, in particular, do we tell whether the third thing has happened (whether the dance has been danced correctly)?

III

Let us first consider one thing that might be said. It might be said: 'The dance has been danced correctly if what has been danced is the dance *called* the eightsome reel'. On this suggestion, all we have to know is how the expression 'eightsome reel' is used; then we shall be able to recognize whether what has been danced *is* an eightsome reel. This seems to me to be true; but it will be obvious why I cannot rest content with this answer to the problem. For I am using the dance analogy in an attempt to elucidate the nature of the discovery called 'discovering the use of words'; and therefore I obviously cannot, in solving the problems raised within the analogy, appeal to our knowledge of the use of the expression 'eightsome reel'. For this would not be in the least illuminating; the trouble is that we do not know whether knowing how the expression 'eightsome reel' is used is knowing something empirical. We shall therefore have to go a longer way round.

It may help if we ask, What does one have to assume if one is to be sure that we have danced the right dance? Let us first introduce some restrictions into our analogy in order to make the dance-situation more like the language-situation which it is intended to illustrate. Let us suppose that the dance is a traditional one which those of the company who can dance it have all learnt in their early years; let us suppose that they cannot remember the circumstances in which they learnt the dance; nothing of their early dancing-lessons remains in their memory except: how to dance the dance. And let us further suppose that there are no books that we can consult to see if they have correctly danced the dance — or, if there are books, that they are not authoritative.

What, then, in such a situation, do we have to rely on in order to be sure that we have really established correctly what is the right way to dance the eightsome reel? Suppose that someone is detailed to put down precisely what happens in the dance that the dancers actually dance — what movements they make when. We then look at his description of the dance and, under certain conditions, say, 'Well then, *that* is how the eightsome reel is danced'. But what are these conditions?

We have to rely first of all upon the accuracy of the observer. We have to be sure that he has correctly put down what actually happened in the dance. And to put down correctly what one actually sees happening is, it must be admitted, empirical observation and description. But what else do we have to rely on? There are, it seems to me, at least two other requirements. As Henle correctly observes (I do not know why he thinks I would disagree) we cannot 'discover the rules of a ballroom dance simply by doing it' (*op. cit.* p. 753). The first requirement is that the dance which is being danced is indeed the eightsome reel; the second is that it is being danced right. These are not the same; for one may dance the eightsome reel but dance it wrong. Though the distinction between dancing a dance and dancing it right is not essential to my argument, it is in many contexts a crucial one (and with games, even more crucial than with dances; it must, *e.g.* be possible to play poker but, while playing it, cheat). Even Körner, who on page 759 of his paper objects to the distinction, uses it himself on page 762, where he says, 'If it [*sc.* a performance of a dance] is relevant but uncharacteristic, it is incorrect'. For both these requirements, we have to rely on the *memory* of the dancers; and, as I have said, to remember something is not (or at any rate not obviously) to make an empirical discovery.

IV

The sort of situation which I have been describing is different from the situation in which an anthropologist observes and describes the dances of a primitive tribe. This, it might be said, *is* an empirical enquiry. The anthropologist observes the behaviour of the members of the tribe, and *he* selects for study certain parts of this behaviour, namely those parts which, by reason of certain similarities, *he* classifies as dances. And within the class of dances, *he* selects certain particular patterns of behaviour and names them by names of particular dances — names which *he* (it may be arbitrarily or for purely mnemonic reasons) chooses. Here we have nothing which is not included in the characteristic activities of the empirical scientist; we have the observation of similarities

in the pattern of events, and the choosing of words to mark these similarities.

In the situation which I have been discussing, however, there are elements which there could not be in a purely anthropological enquiry. If a party of anthropologists sat down to dinner before starting their study of a particular dance, they could not fall into the sort of argument that I have imagined. Nor could they fall into it *after* starting the study of the dance. This sort of argument can arise only between people who, first of all, know how to dance the dance in question or to recognise a performance of it, but secondly are unable to say how it is danced. In the case of the anthropologists the first condition is not fulfilled. This difference between the two cases brings certain consequences with it. The anthropologists could not, as the people in my example know, know *what* dance it is that they are disputing about. In my example, the disputants know that what they are disputing about is how *the eightsome reel* is danced. They are able to say this, because they have learnt to dance a certain dance, and can still dance it, and know that if they dance it it will be distinctively different from a great many other dances which, perhaps, they can also dance. The anthropologists, on the other hand, have not learnt to dance the dance which they are going to see danced after dinner; and therefore, even if they have decided to *call* the dance that they are to see danced 'dance no. 23', this name is for them as yet unattached to any disposition of theirs to recognise the dance when it is danced. The anthropologists will not be able to say, when a particular point in the dance is reached, 'Yes, *that's* how it goes'. They will just put down what happens and add it to their records. But the people in my example, when they say 'eightsome reel', are not using an arbitrary symbol for *whatever* they are going to observe; the name 'eightsome reel' has for them already a determinate meaning, though they cannot as yet say what this meaning is. It is in this same way that a logician knows, before he sets out to investigate the logical properties of the concept of negation, *what* concept he is going to investigate.

The second consequence is that, when my dancers have put down in words the way a dance is danced, the words that they put down will have a peculiar character. It will not be a correct inscription of their remarks to say that they have just put down how a particular set of dancers danced on a particular occasion; for what has been put down is not: how a particular set of dancers *did* dance on a particular occasion, but: how *the* eightsome reel *is* danced. It is implied that if *any* dancers dance like *this* they are dancing an eightsome reel correctly. Thus what has been put down has the character of universality — one of the two positive marks of the *a priori* noted by Kant (we have already seen that what has been put down has the negative characteristic which Kant mentioned, that of not being empirical). What about the other positive mark? Is what we have put down (if we are the dancers) *necessarily* true? Is it necessarily true that the eightsome reel is danced in the way that we have put down?

What we have put down is 'The eightsome reel is danced in the following manner, *viz.* . . .' followed by a complete description of the steps and successive positions of the dancers. We may feel inclined to say that this statement is necessarily true. For, when we have danced the dance, and recognised it as an eightsome reel correctly danced, we may feel inclined to say that, if it had been danced differently, we *could* not have called it, correctly, an eightsome reel (or at any rate not a correct performance of one); and that, on the other hand, danced as it was, we could not have denied that it was an eightsome reel. The statement which we have put down seems as necessary as the statement 'A square is a rectangle with equal sides'. I do not wish my meaning to be mistaken at this point. I am not maintaining that there is any temptation to say that the statement 'The dance which we have just danced is an

eightsome reel' is a necessary statement; for there is no more reason to call this necessary than there is in the case of any other singular statement of fact. The statement which I am saying is necessary is 'The eightsome reel is danced as follows, *viz.* . . .' followed by a complete description.

We may, then, feel inclined to say that this statement, since it has all the qualifications, is an *a priori* statement. But there is also a temptation to say that it is synthetic. For consider again for a moment the situation as it was before we began to dance. Then we already knew how to dance the eightsome reel, and so for us the term 'eightsome reel' had already a determinate meaning; and it would be plausible to say that, since we knew the meaning of 'eightsome reel' already before we started dancing, anything that we subsequently discovered could not be something attributable to the meaning of the term 'eightsome reel'; and therefore that it could not be something analytic; and therefore that it must be something synthetic. Have we not, after all, *discovered* something about how the eightsome reel is danced?

There is thus a very strong temptation to say that the statement 'The eightsome reel is danced in the following way, *viz.* . . .' followed by a complete description, is, when made by people in the situation which I have described, a synthetic *a priori* statement. Perhaps this temptation ought to be resisted, for it bears a very strong resemblance to the reasons which made Kant say that 'Seven plus five equals twelve' is a synthetic *a priori* statement. Yet the existence of the temptation should be noted. Certainly to call this statement 'synthetic *a priori*' would be odd; for similar grounds could be given for considering all statements about how words are used as synthetic *a priori* statements. If, which I have seen no reason to believe, there is a class of synthetic *a priori* statements, it can hardly be as large as this. Probably what has to be done with the term 'synthetic *a priori*' is to recognise that it has been used to cover a good many different kinds of statements, and that the reasons for applying it to them differ in the different cases. It is, in fact, an ambiguous label which does not even accurately distinguish a class of statements, let alone explain their character. What would explain this would be to understand the natures of the situations (as I said, not all of the same kind) in which we feel inclined to use the term; and this is what I am now trying, in one particular case, to do.

V

The peculiar characteristics of the situation which I have been discussing, like the analogous characteristics of the language-situation which I am trying to illuminate, all arise from the fact (on which Professor Ryle has laid so much stress) that we can know something (*e.g.* how to dance the eightsome reel or use a word) without being able yet to say what we know. Professor Henle has objected to the extension of Ryle's distinction to the language-situation. 'This distinction is no longer clear', he says, 'when one comes to language, and it is by no means apparent that one can always know how to use a word without being able to say how it is used' (*op. cit.* p. 750). But, although I do not claim that the distinction is entirely clear in any field, in language it is perhaps clearer than elsewhere. To say how a term is used we have, normally, to *mention* the term inside quotation marks, and to *use*, in speaking of the quoted sentence or statement in which it occurs, some such logician's term as 'means the same as' or 'is analytic'. In saying how a term is used, we do not have to use it; and therefore we may know fully how to use it in all contexts without being able to say how it is used. For example, a child may have learnt the use of 'father', and use it correctly, but not be able to say how it is used because he has not learnt the use of 'mean' or any equivalent expression. Henle seems to confuse being able to 'decide on logical grounds' that a statement is true with being able to say 'the statement is logically true'.

A person who did not know the use of the expression 'logically true' could do the former but not the latter.

Besides noticing that the dance-situation has the characteristics which I have described, we should also be alive to certain dangers. There is first the danger of thinking that it could not have been the case that the eightsome reel was danced in some quite different way. It is, of course, a contingent fact, arising out of historical causes with which I at any rate am unacquainted, that the dance called 'the eightsome reel' has the form it has and not some other form. If it had some different form, what my dancers would have learnt in their childhood would have been different, and what they would have learnt to call 'the eightsome reel' would have been different too; yet the statement 'the eightsome reel is danced in the following manner, etc.' would have had just the same characteristics as I have mentioned (though the 'etc.' would stand for some different description of steps and movements).

Next, there is the danger of thinking that if *anthropologists* were observing the dance, and had been told that the dance which they were to observe was called 'the eightsome reel', *they*, in reporting their observations, would be making the same kind of statement — namely a non-empirical, universally necessary statement which at the same time we are tempted to call synthetic. They would not be making this sort of statement at all, but an ordinary empirical statement to the effect that the Scots have a dance which they dance in a certain manner and call 'the eightsome reel'.

VI

There is also a third thing which we must notice. If a completely explicit definition were once given of the term 'eightsome reel', it would have to consist of a specification of what constitutes a correct performance of this dance. To give such a definition is to give what is often called a 'rule' for the performance of the dance.

Now if we already have such a definition, then statements like 'The eightsome reel is danced in the following way, *viz*. . . .' , followed by a specification of the steps, will be seen to be analytic, provided only that we understand 'is danced' in the sense of 'is correctly danced'. It might therefore be said that, once the definition is given, there remains no problem — no proposition whose status defies classification. Similarly, if we were to *invent* a dance and give it explicit rules of performance, there would be no problem. But in this latter case there would be no *discovery* either. It is because, in my problem-case, we do not *start off* by having a definition, yet do start off by having a determinate meaning for the term 'eightsome reel', that the puzzle arises. It is in the *passage* to the definition that the mystery creeps in — in the passage (to use Aristotle's terms) from the ἡμῖν γνώριμον to the ἀπλῶς γνώριμον.[3] What we have to start with is not a definition, but the mere ability to recognise instances of correct performances of the dance; what we have at the end is the codification in a definition of what we know. So what we have at the end is different from what we have at the beginning, and it sounds sensible to speak of our *discovering* the definition — just as those who first defined the circle as the locus of a point equidistant. etc., thought that they had discovered something about the circle, namely what later came to be called its essence. We see here how definitions came to be treated as synthetic statements; and, since the real or essential definition (the prototype of all synthetic *a priori* statements) is one of the most characteristic constituents of metaphysical thinking, this explains a great deal about the origins of metaphysics.

Briefly, there are two statements whose status is unproblematical, both expressed in the same words. There is first the anthropologist's statement that the eightsome reel (meaning 'a certain dance to which the Scots give that name') is (as a matter of observed fact) danced in a certain manner.

This is a plain empirical statement. Secondly, there is the statement such as might be found in a book of dancing instructions — the statement that the eightsome reel is danced (meaning 'is correctly danced') in a certain manner. This statement is analytic, since by 'eightsome reel' the writer *means* 'the dance which is (correctly) danced in the manner described'. Should we then say that the appearance of there being a third, mysterious, metaphysical, synthetic *a priori* statement about the dance, somehow intermediate between these two, is the result merely of a confusion between them, a confusion arising easily from the fact that they are expressed in the same words? This, it seems to me, would be a mistake. For how do we *get* to the second, analytic statement? Only *via* the definition or rule; but if the definition is not a mere empirical description, then there is, on this view, nothing left for it to be but a stipulative definition, the result of a decision. So there will be again no such thing as discovering how the eightsome reel is danced. There will only be something which might be described as 'inventing the eightsome reel'. It is preferable, therefore, to say that there is a third kind of statement, intermediate between the first and the second, which forms, as it were, the transition to the second — we settle down in the comfortable analyticity of the second only after we have discovered that this definition of the term 'eightsome reel', and no other, is the one that accords with our pre-existing but unformulated idea of how the dance should be danced. And this discovery seems to be neither a mere decision, nor a mere piece of observation. But, since I am still very perplexed by this problem, I do not rule out the possibility that, were I to become clearer about it, I should see that there is no third alternative.

Before I conclude this section of my paper, and go on to describe more complicated kinds of dances which resemble talking even more closely, I have two remarks to make. The first is that, unless *some* people knew how to dance dances, anthropologists could not observe empiri-

[3] Eth. Nic. 1095 b 2; An. Post. 71 b 33.

cally how dances are danced; and that therefore there could not be empirical statements about dances unless there were at least the possibility of the kind of non-empirical statement that I have been characterising. The situation is like that with regard to moral judgments; unless *some* people make genuine evaluative moral judgments, there is no possibility of other people making what have been called 'inverted commas' moral judgments, *i.e.* explicit or implicit descriptions of the moral judgments that the first set of people make.[4] So, if philosophical analysis resembles the description of dances in the respects to which I have drawn attention, empirical statements about the use of words cannot be made unless there is at least the possibility of these other, non-empirical statements about the use of words. This perhaps explains the odd fact that analytical enquiries seem often to start by collecting empirical data about word-uses, but to end with apparently *a priori* conclusions.[5]

The second remark is that I have nothing to say in this paper which sheds any direct light on the question (often confused with the one which I am discussing) — the question of the distinction between logic and philology. The features which I am trying to pick out are features as well of philological as of logical discoveries, and this makes them more, not less, perplexing.

VII

I will now draw attention to some differences between the comparatively simple dance-situation which I have been discussing so far and the language-situation which is the subject of this paper. Talking is an infinitely more complex activity than dancing. It is as if there were innumerable different kinds of steps in dancing, and a dancer could choose at any moment (as is to a limited extent the case in ballroom dancing) to make any of these steps. Talking is in this respect more like ballroom dancing than like reels — there is a variety of different things one can do, and if one's partner knows how to dance, she reacts appropriately; but to do *some* things results in treading on one's partner's toes, or bumping into other couples and such further obstacles as there may be, however well she knows how to dance. Nevertheless there are a great many things which one can do; and not all of them are laid down as permissible in rules which have been accepted before we do them. There can be innovations in dancing and in speech — and some of the innovations are understood even though they are innovations.

Both dancing and talking can become forms of creative art. There are kinds of dancing and of talking in which the performer is bound by no rules except those which he cares to make up as he goes along. Some poetry is like this; and so is 'creative tap-dancing' (the title of a book which once came into my hands). The most creative artists, however, are constrained to talk or dance *solo*. It is not about these highest flights of talking and dancing that I wish to speak, but about these more humdrum activities which require the co-operation of more than one person, and in which, therefore, the other people involved have to know a good deal about what sort of thing to expect one to do, and what they are expected to do in answer. It is in this sense that I am speaking of 'knowing how to dance' and 'knowing how to talk'.

What makes co-operation possible in both these activities is that the speaker or dancer should not do things which make the other people say 'We don't know what to make of this'. That is to say, he must not do things which cannot be easily related to the unformulated rules of speaking or dancing which everybody knows who has learnt to perform these activities.

[4] See my *Language of Morals*, pp. 124 f.
[5] See the remarks of Professor Ayer on Mr. Wollheim's valuable paper 'La Philosophie Analytique et les Attitudes Politiques' in *La Philosophie Analytique* (Cahiers de Royaumont; Paris: Editions de Minuit, 1962), and compare also Aristotle, *An. Post.* 100 a 7 and *Eth. Nic.* 1143 b 4.

The fact that these rules are unformulated means that to learn to formulate them is to make some sort of discovery — a discovery which, as I have said, cannot be described without qualification as an empirical one. If a person in speaking or dancing does something of which we say 'We don't know what to make of this', there are only two ways of re-establishing that *rapport* between us which makes these co-operative activities possible; either he must explain to us what we *are* to make of what he has done; or else he must stop doing it and do something more orthodox. He must either teach us his new way of dancing or talking, or go on dancing or talking in our old way. I should like to emphasise that I am not against what Körner calls 'replacement-analysis'; the last chapter of my *Language of Morals* is evidence of this. But we need to be very sure that we understand the functioning of the term that is being replaced before we claim that a new gadget will do the old job better.

It might be said, dancing is not like talking, because dancing is a gratuitous activity, and talking a purposeful one; therefore there are things which can go wrong in talking that cannot go wrong in dancing — things which prevent the purposes of talking being realised. This I do not wish to deny; though the existence of this difference does not mean that there are not also the similarities to which I have been drawing attention. And the difference is in any case not absolute. Some talking is gratuitous; and some dancing is purposeful. When dancing in a crowded ballroom, we have at least the purpose of avoiding obstacles, human and inanimate. If we imagine these obstacles multiplied, so that our dance-floor becomes more like its analogue, the elusive entity which we call 'the world', dancing becomes very like talking. And all dance-floors have at least a floor and boundaries of some kind; so no kind of dancing is *completely* gratuitous; all dancers have the purpose of not impinging painfully against whatever it is that limits

their dance-floor (unless there are penitential dances which consist in bruising oneself against the walls — but this too, would be a purpose). And there are some markedly purposeful activities which, though not called dances, are like dances in the features to which I have drawn attention — for example, the pulling up of anchors (old style).

This analogy points to a way of thinking about our use of language which is a valuable corrective to the more orthodox representational view, in which 'facts', 'qualities', and other dubious entities flit like untrustworthy diplomats between language and the world. We do not need these intermediaries; there are just people in given situations trying to understand one another. Logic, in one of the many senses of that word, is learning to formulate the rules that enable us to make something of what people say. Its method is to identify and describe the various sorts of things that people say (the various dances and their steps) such as predication, conjunction, disjunction, negation, counting, adding, promising, commanding, commending — need I ever stop? In doing this it has to rely on our knowledge, as yet unformulated, of how to do these things — things of which we may not even know the names, and which indeed may not *have* names till the logician invents them; but which are, nevertheless, distinct and waiting to be given names. Since this knowledge is knowledge of something that we have learnt, it has, as I have said, many of the characteristics of memory — though it would be incorrect, strictly speaking, to say that we *remember* how to use a certain word; Plato's term 'recall' (ἀναμιμνήσκεσθαι)', is, perhaps more apt. As in the case of memory however, we know, without being, in many cases, able to give further evidence, that we have got it right. And often the only test we can perform is: trying it out again. In most cases there comes a point at which we are satisfied that we have got the thing right (in the case of speaking, that we have formulated correctly what we know). Of course, the fact that we are satisfied does not show that we are not wrong; but if once satisfied, we remain satisfied until we discover, or are shown, some cause for dissatisfaction.

VIII

Meno, in the Platonic dialogue named after him, is asked by Socrates what goodness is (a question much more closely akin than is commonly allowed to the question, How and for what purposes is the word 'good' used?). Being a young man of a sophistical turn of mind, Meno says 'But Socrates, how are you going to look for something, when you don't in the least know what it is? . . . Or even if you do hit upon it, how are you going to know that this is *it*, without having previous knowledge of what *it* is?'[6] In more modern terms, if we do not already know the use of the word 'good' (or, in slightly less fashionable language, its analysis), how, when some account of its use (some analysis) is suggested, shall we know whether it is the correct account? Yet (as Socrates goes on to point out) if we knew already, we should not have asked the question in the first place. So philosophy either cannot begin, or cannot reach a conclusion.

It will be noticed that my dancers could be put in the same paradoxical position. If they know already how the dance is danced, what can they be arguing about? But if they do not know already, how will they know, when they have danced the dance, whether they have danced it correctly? The solution to the paradox lies in distinguishing between knowing how to dance a dance and being able to say how it is danced. Before the enquiry begins, they are able to do the former, but not the latter; after the enquiry is over they can do the latter, and they know that they are right because all along they could do the former. And it is the same with the analysis of concepts. We know how to use a certain expression, but are unable to say how it

is used (λογὸν διδόναι, give an analysis or definition, formulate in words the use of the expression). Then we try to do the latter; and we know we have succeeded when we have found an analysis which is in accordance with our hitherto unformulated knowledge of how to use the word. And finding out whether it *is* in accordance involves talking (dialectic), just as finding out whether the account of the dance is right involves dancing.

Dialectic, like dancing, is typically a co-operative activity. It consists in trying out the proposed account of the use of a word by using the word in accordance with it, and seeing what happens. It is an experiment with words, though not, as we have seen, an altogether empirical experiment. In the same way, we might dance the dance according to someone's account of how it is danced, and see if we can say afterwards whether what we have danced is the dance that we were arguing about (*e.g.* the eightsome reel) or at least *a* dance, or whether it is no dance at all. There is no space here to give many examples of dialectic; but I will give the most famous one of all.[7] It is a destructive use of the technique, resulting in the *rejection* of a suggested analysis. An account of the use of the word 'right' is being tried out which says that 'right' means the same as 'consisting in speaking the truth and giving back anything that one has received from anyone'. The analysis is tried out by 'dancing' a certain statement, *viz.* 'It is always right to give a madman back his weapons which he entrusted to us when sane'. But the dance has clearly gone wrong; for this statement is certainly not (as the proposed definition would make it) analytic, since to deny it, as most people would, is not to contradict oneself. So the analysis has to be rejected.

Plato was right in implying that in recognising that such a proposition is not analytic we are relying on our memories. It is an example of the perceptive genius of that great logician, that in spite of being

---

[6] *Meno*, 80 d.

[7] Adapted from *Republic*, 331 c.

altogether at sea concerning the *source* of our philosophical knowledge; and in spite of the fact that his use of the material mode of speech misled him as to the *status* of the analyses he was looking for — that in spite of all this he spotted the very close logical analogies between philosophical discoveries and remembering. He was wrong in supposing that we are remembering something that we learnt in a former life — just as more recent mythologists have been wrong in thinking that we are discerning the structure of some entities called 'facts'. What we are actually remembering is what we learnt on our mothers' knees, and cannot remember learning.

Provisionally, then, we might agree with the metaphysicians that philosophy has to contain statements which are neither empirical statements about the way words are actually used, nor yet expressions of decisions about how they are to be used; but we should refuse to infer from this that these statements are about some non-empirical order of being. The philosopher elucidates (not by mere observation) the nature of something which exists before the elucidation begins (for example, there is such an operation as negation before the philosopher investigates it; the philosopher no more invents negation than Aristotle made man rational). He neither creates the objects of his enquiry, nor receives them as mere data of experience; yet for all that, to say that there is such an operation as negation is no more mysterious than to say that there is such a dance as the eightsome reel. But even that is quite mysterious enough.

Editor's note: For comment on this article, see (in addition to Henle [1] and Körner [3], previously mentioned) Compton [1], and compare Hare [2]. For discussion of the issues raised, see the references given in footnote 41 of the Introduction.

· 16b ·

PAUL HENLE

Do We Discover Our Uses of Words?

Mr. Hare builds his paper on analogy between physical skills and the uses of language. People with physical skills may be able to perform certain activities without being able to say what they do or what rule they follow. The contrast between what one does and how one describes what one does is perfectly clear and no one, to take Mr. Hare's example, would confuse dancing the eightsome reel with describing the dance. This distinction is no longer clear, however, when one comes to language and it is by no means apparent that one can always know how to use a word without being able to say how it is used. To take a simple example, a person would hardly be said to know how to use the term "father" unless he could decide on logical grounds the truth of the sentence, "A father is a parent," "A father is a male," and "All male parents are fathers." Yet one way of giving at least a rough formulation of the rules for using the term "father" would be to say "Use 'father' synonymously with 'male parent'." Thus knowing how to use the term involves knowing some of the rules of use and knowing them not merely in the sense of being able to follow them, but in the sense of being able to formulate them. More generally terms have, among other uses, uses in statements

Reprinted from *The Journal of Philosophy*, LIV (1957), 750–58, by permission of Mrs. Jeanne Henle and the editor.
Editor's note: This essay is a reply to Hare's (16a).

which are logically true, and among these are analyses and definitions.

It may be the case, therefore, that one cannot know how to use a term without also knowing how to analyze it. Certainly one cannot know all the uses of a term without knowing its analysis, but "knowing how to use a term" is a loose expression and probably does not require knowing all the uses. I would not want to insist that what has been said about "father" applies equally to every other term, and while I would think that one could not know how to use the term "father" without knowing its definitions, there would be other terms such as "space" and "substance" where one could. At most a partial set of rules would be required and perhaps not even that. My point, however, is not that knowing the use of a term always requires knowing its analysis, but rather that the distinction between knowing how to act and saying what rules one follows is not clear in language. Language, in fact, is the one place where it is not clear, and this means that analogies to other activities have their least value here. Insofar as they suggest that the clear distinction can be made within language, they are definitely misleading.

In spite of this difficulty, the analogy seems attractive and perhaps it could be revived by a clearer specification of what it is to use a term. Uses of language are multifarious and perhaps some division among them may enable us to distinguish the uses which are like doing or acting from those which are like speaking about actions. If this is the case, speaking, or at least some sorts of speaking, may be put on all fours with dancing; and a discussion such as Mr. Hare's would once more become illuminating.

One easy suggestion as a start is to equate using a term to applying it. We use a word when we point to or otherwise indicate something and say that the word applies. "This is a chair," "That is red" became paradigms of use. No one could doubt that this is a use of language and an important one, one which children learn perhaps as the first. It has the advantage, moreover, of being easily separable from anything like the analysis of the term. It would be almost impossible to apply a term correctly without following the rules for its use, but at the same time, one need not be able to formulate the rules in order to follow them. Thus, we may say along the lines Mr. Hare at least suggests, to analyze a term is to formulate the rules we follow in applying it.

As far as it goes, this suggestion is not bad, but a difficulty becomes apparent at once: Not all terms can be applied in the sense of our paradigms. In general, adjectives and common nouns can be used as indicated, but verbs, prepositions, and adverbs cannot. One cannot point and say "This is between" in the sense in which one can say "This is a chair." A number of possibilities are open. A well-known one is to invent an object to be pointed at or indicated, in this case perhaps the ordered triad of objects, one of which is between the other two. We may then say that "between" is applied to this triad in the sense in which "chair" is applied to the chair. Some such procedure will work in a number of cases and of course is enshrined in Russell's logic. It is by no means clear that all terms can be handled in this manner, and adverbs would particularly be troublesome. To say of an action that it was done slowly would involve the further artificiality of treating "slowly" as an adjective applying to the ordered pair involved.

If this procedure is considered too artificial, there is an alternative. We may relax the narrow requirement of being able to apply a term in the sense of pointing to what the term is predicated of and we may then say that, given a situation and a term, we can use the term of that situation if we know how to decide what sentences containing the term are true of the situation. This is not intended as a final statement but merely as an indication of the sort of statement which is required. One would, for example, not be expected to know how to decide the truth of all sentences but only of relatively short sentences — say those which can be uttered at a normal speed in five minutes or less. Again, the requirement of knowing how to decide may appear to be too strong, since one knows the truth of some scientific statements without knowing how their truth is decided. Again, perhaps the whole discussion should be restated in terms of probability rather than truth — this raises another host of questions. Whatever the emendations, however, a formula along the lines of the one given will serve merely to indicate what it is to know how to use a term of a situation. To know how to use a term in general would have to be explained as knowing how to use it in many, or most, or common situations.

It may be thought that I am leaving this account in entirely too vague a state and, certainly, much more discussion would be necessary before it became explicit; but my purpose at the moment is not to work a sense of "using a term" which will exclude knowing the analysis of the term, but rather to indicate some of the complexity of the problem. I have barely indicated two ways of solving it, one by restricting use of denotation and inventing denotata as needed. Alternatively, one may speak in terms of situations in which the term may be used. I am sure there are other possibilities, though I very much doubt that they would be simpler than those mentioned. The question I wish to raise is this: When we explicate "use of a term" by means of denotata or situations or in some other way, how much help are analogies to dancing, pulling up anchors, and the like? It would seem that if we are to avoid being misled, "knowing how to use a term" must be hedged with so many and such complete restrictions that the parallel to knowing how to dance is unimportant. The discussion must be carried on in terms of logic and logic alone. I am forced, therefore, to reject Mr. Hare's analogy as being misleading at its face value and useless when the complexity of the problem is seen.

We have noticed some general reasons for suspecting analogies between the use of language and any other activity. There is, however, a more particular objection to the form in which Mr. Hare develops the analogy, a difficulty which he himself half recognizes. His first analogy to speaking is doing the eightsome reel, a dance with which I am unacquainted but which, I gather, prescribes a rigidly fixed routine. In such a case, if one knows the dance, one can formulate its rules simply by noticing what one does as he dances it. Such a dance might form an analogue to reciting, but it does not reflect the variety of possibilities allowable in carrying on a conversation. Mr. Hare, of course, realizes this and so shifts his analogy to ball-room dancing which, like conversation, allows a number of alternatives at various junctures. What he does not recognize, however, or at least does not recognize explicitly, is that one cannot discover the rules of a ball-room dance simply by doing it. At most one can find one way of doing the dance and admittedly there are a number of others. The only way in which one could comprehend all of these possibilities would be to consider all of the alternatives at every step of the dance. This might be possible, but it is no longer the case that simply performing a physical action enables us to formulate rules; rather, the whole investigation moves into the mental sphere and it is by considering possibilities that we arrive at our rules. I do not doubt, of course, that a consideration of possible cases is an im-

portant aspect of the working out of rules, but this is a far less startling claim than what I, at least, understood Mr. Hare to be implying — that we could do philosophical analysis simply by listening to ourselves talk.

With all these objections to Mr. Hare's analogy, there still remains the central problem to which he addresses himself. We use words in a variety of ways on a variety of occasions. This, of course, is an empirical truth. Other people use words in the same way or very nearly the same way as we do. This, again, is an empirical truth, and it is also an empirical truth that just these people rather than others use words in this way. We cannot always or even in general formulate complete rules for our use of terms. This, once more, is an empirical truth. Philosophers engage in formulating these rules. Again, an empirical truth. What they do in formulating these rules, however, according to Mr. Hare is not to discover one more empirical truth, but rather to make a discovery which one might well call a synthetic *a priori* truth if it were not for the ambiguities of the term "synthetic *a priori*."

In opposition to Mr. Hare, I shall contend that what is involved is primarily a matter of reaching a decision. There may be discovery incidental to the decision, but if so it is discovery of the ordinary empirical sort. The decision is not, of course, arbitrary — it is made for good and often self-conscious reasons; but it is none the less to be thought of as a decision to act rather than a discovery of truth.

We may begin by considering a situation like that of Mr. Hare's anthropologist watching a dance, a situation in which I am interested in another person's use of language. It may be his use of a term or of a sentence or of a type of grammatical construction, it does not matter; for the sake of the illustration let it be a term. Boswell-like, I would listen to his conversation and keep a record of his usage. To get more material I might introduce topics of conversation which would involve the term. I might even ask hypothetical questions as to how he would use the term under conditions which did not in fact obtain. Probably I would attach less weight to these latter than to the actual employment of the term but still they would be taken into account. After obtaining a large sample of this sort I would attempt to codify the usage, to formulate rules to which his use of language conformed. There are two aspects of the conclusions which might be reached which are worth pointing out.

First, strictly speaking, I would have found rules according to which he had used the term during a given time-interval. The record would probably not even be complete, but certainly it would be no more than a record of use during a certain span. Since "How X uses a term" presumably means something different from "How X used the term between times t_1 and t_2," I have not found how X uses the term but must merely make a more or less probable inference from the rules he followed during the observation period. The probability would, as usual, depend on the completeness of the record, the frequency with which the term was used, the length of the time-span, and the occurrence of any unusual incidents which would upset the tenor of X's life.

Second, I have not found the only set of rules compatible with X's utterances. Presumably there would be others, perhaps more complicated, which, had he been following them, would have led X to use the term in the same way. New situations would help discriminate between alternative sets of rules, but no finite experience could give rise to a unique set of rules. Thus, if one were investigating someone's use of the term "mammal" before the discovery of the platypus, it would have been equally compatible with the rule "Apply 'mammal' to all haematothermal viviparous lactiferous quadrupeds" and "Apply 'mammal' to all haematothermal lactiferous quadrupeds." Even today one cannot tell from other people's use of the term

whether the requirement of being lactiferous is necessary; and even if asked whether they would call a warm-blooded quadruped which didn't give milk a mammal, most people would not know. The set of rules derived from such observations is clearly not unique.

There is no doubt, then, that the set of rules arrived at as constituting another person's use of a term is at best an inductive generalization. The set of rules formulating observations are only one formulation among many, and the transition from past use so formulated to use in general represents a typical inductive inference. These conclusions are hardly controversial and are interesting not for themselves, but for comparison in the case in which I am trying to formulate rules of my own usage.

In this case, as well as the other, I may remember or invoke other evidence of instances of my use of the term. I may as before and in a quite impersonal way formulate rules which codify my past uses of the term. As before, these rules will not be unique, but there is an advantage in one's own case. Given some pair of rules, both of which conform with one's actual past usage, but which differ in their prescription for some case which has not arisen, I can at once ask myself what I would do in that case. It is not sure that I would get any important information. I may be unable to make up my mind. I may favor one rule over the other and I may tell myself that I would decide so as to confirm that rule — which would hardly be evidence in the ordinary sense. Still I may come up with something useful and so might be able to eliminate some alternatives. This could not be expected, however, to go so far as to give one a unique set of rules. There would be too many situations in which one would just not be sure how he would use the word. Here there is no difference in principle between formulating rules for one's own use and those of other people.

When it comes to the step of going from one's past use to his use in general, however, the situation is more complex. As before, one could distinguish between "my use of a term" and "how I have used a term," and I take it that the difference would be of the following sort: If I have used a term in a certain way, but no longer intend to use it in that way, the way does not constitute my use of the term. Neither does the way in which I intend to use it. That way becomes my use only after I have used it for a little while at least. Thus having used a term in a certain way is a necessary, but not sufficient, condition of using it in that way. I do not insist on this way of speaking, though it seems quite natural to me; and my point can be made equally well so long as having used a term in a certain way is not a sufficient condition of that being my use of it.

Granted this last claim we are, as in the case of another person, confronted with the transition between "I have used a term according to a certain rule" to "I shall continue to use it according to that rule." If this were a simple induction as in the case of another person, one could agree that analysis represents a discovery, though, of course, it would be an empirical discovery. One does not, however, predict his own conduct in the same way that he predicts that of another person, and the reasons for this are simple and well-known.

Every prediction, as distinguished from a mere guess, is based on certain evidence and assumes that certain factors will be decisive in the occurrence or non-occurrence of the event predicted. If some new factor enters the situation, the result of the prediction is rendered uncertain; and if one knows that a new factor will enter, he must have less confidence in his prediction. Suppose I predict a friend's conduct, basing my predictions on my knowledge of his habits, his interests, and the situation in which he will find himself. Suppose I also tell him what I have predicted about him. The fact that I have told him, along with any desires he may have to vindicate my judgment or else perhaps to show that he is an inscrutable person, will certainly in-

fluence his conduct and render my prediction doubtful. Of course, if I know him well enough I may try to predict how he will react to this information and so predict his conduct on the basis of his knowing the first prediction. But if I tell him of this second prediction it will be vitiated in the same manner as the first.

The point of this discussion is that if I am predicting my own behavior I cannot conceal the prediction from myself and there is the same sort of interference as when one tells another what has been predicted concerning him. Any prediction I make about myself is vitiated by the fact that I make it. This is not to say that one cannot predict one's own future. One can, insofar as the future does not depend upon oneself but upon external circumstances. One can also predict some events of his own action if these are minor or far distant so that the prediction is likely to be forgotten and does not interfere. This is recognized in daily life. While I may predict the weather or coming political events or your conduct, I do not predict at what time I shall have lunch or go to bed. These are questions which I simply decide.

It is the same, I believe, with the formulation of rules governing how I use terms. If I am interested in making the rules explicit (not everyone is, of course), when I notice that alternative sets of rules would account for my usage, I either decide between them or else I decide not to decide. I may even, for various reasons, decide to follow somewhat different rules than previously, as a reader of Russell's logic might decide to use the definite article in a somewhat different manner than he had before. Thus, it seems we do not formulate our own use of terms inductively as we formulate another person's, nor do we invoke any synthetic *a priori* principles to get at rules of use. We simply decide them. Mr. Hare is right that there is something new involved, but this is not a synthetic statement but merely a decision.

To say that an analysis represents a decision is not of course to claim that it is an arbitrary decision. Philosophers have reasons for these decisions as well as any others, and it may be well to examine the chief sorts.

(1) Philosophers like other people wish to be understood. They do not, therefore, depart far from their own and established usage. This is to say that an excellent reason for deciding to follow a certain rule for the use of a term is the fact that one has spoken in accordance with the rule and that other people do so as well. Where usage is not fixed and where there are doubts, there is greater freedom to set up an arbitrary rule.

(2) Philosophers find certain ideas clearer than others. It is not always evident why that is the case and there seem to be fashions in the matter. Idealists of the nineteenth century seem to have found mental terms clearer than physical and tried to analyze physical terms by means of them. Today the opposite tendency seems stronger. I do not know of any way of deciding who is right or, for that matter, how one can escape his own findings; perhaps one must start with whatever he finds clear. Mr. Hare, for example, has indicated his mistrust for any analysis in terms of "facts." He seems willing, however, in constructing a surrogate for "ought," to use such notions as "please" and "part of a sentence common to indicative and imperative moods." I cannot see that there is a marked advantage. My purpose is not,

however, to dispute Mr. Hare's choice of terms to use in analysis, but rather to point out that one does make such a choice and the analysis is considered valuable only if it explains by means of terms already considered clear. Many logicians, for example, would rejoice in an analysis of contrary-to-fact conditionals in terms of a truth-value logic, but not if intensional concepts were brought in.

Another way of making the same point is to say that analysis is essentially reductionistic and what it reduces to is something antecedently clear. I do not mean to disparage it by calling it reductionistic, but merely to point out that it provides a means of eliminating a term and replacing it with clearer terms.

I do not claim that these are the only considerations which lead to an adoption of a certain rule of use but they are enough to show that the decision is not arbitrary. What we have, then, is no discovery involving a new kind of knowledge, but merely making up one's mind to follow a certain rule. Though this, I believe, is what the philosopher does, this is not always the way in which he presents his conclusions. More often he will offer them as proposals, as recommendations of rules to be followed. Sometimes. even, crediting the reader with intentions of conformity to usage and desire for clarity, he will say that the analysis represents what the reader really means.

17

P. T. GEACH

ASCRIPTIVISM

The statement that an act x was voluntary, or intentional, or done with intent, or the like, on the part of an agent A has often been analyzed as a causal statement that x was initiated by some act of A's mind that was an act of bare will — a volition, or an act of A's setting himself to do x, or an act of intending to do x, or the like. Latterly there has been a reaction against this type of analysis; it has been held (in my opinion, quite rightly) that the attempt to identify and characterize these supposed acts of bare will always runs into insuperable difficulties. To avoid such difficulties, some Oxford philosophers, whom I shall call Ascriptivists, have resorted to denying that to call an act voluntary, intentional, and so forth, is any sort of causal statement, or indeed any statement at all. In this note I shall try to expound and to refute Ascriptivism.

Ascriptivists hold that to say an action x was voluntary on the part of an agent A is not to describe the act x as caused in a certain way, but to ascribe it to A, to hold A responsible for it. Now holding a man responsible is a moral or quasi-moral attitude; and so, Ascriptivists argue, there is no question here of truth or falsehood, any more than there is for moral judgments. If B agrees or disagrees with C's ascription of an act to A, B is himself taking up a quasi-moral attitude toward A. Facts may support or go against such

a quasi-moral attitude, but can never *force* us to adopt it. Further, the Ascriptivists would say, there is no risk of an antinomy, because ascription of an act to an agent can never conflict with a scientific account of how the act came about; for the scientific account is *de*scriptive, and *de*scriptive language is in quite a different logical realm from *a*scriptive language. Though it has not had the world-wide popularity of the distinction between *de*scriptive and *pre*scriptive language, the Ascriptivist theory has had quite a vogue, as is very natural in the present climate of opinion.

Now as regards hundreds of our voluntary or intentional acts, it would in fact be absurdly solemn, not to say melodramatic, to talk of imputation and exoneration and excuse, or for that matter of praise and reward. Ascribing an action to an agent just does not *in general* mean taking up a quasi-legal or quasi-moral attitude, and only a bad choice of examples could make one think otherwise. (As Wittgenstein said, when put on an unbalanced diet of examples philosophy suffers from deficiency diseases.)

Again, even when imputation and blame are in question, they can yet be distinguished from the judgment that so-and-so was a voluntary act. There are savage communities where even involuntary homicide carries the death penalty. In one such community, the story goes, a man fell off a coconut palm and broke a bystander's neck; the dead man's brother demanded blood for blood. With Solomonic wisdom

Reprinted from *The Philosophical Review*, LXIX (1960), 221–25, by permission of the author and the editor.

the chief ordered the culprit to stand under the palm-tree and said to the avenger of blood, "Now you climb up and fall off and break his neck!" This suggestion proved unwelcome and the culprit went free. Though the vengeful brother may still have thought the culprit ought to have been punished, his reaction to the suggested method of execution showed that he knew as well as we do the difference between falling-off-a-tree-on-someone-and-breaking-his-neck *voluntarily* or *intentionally* and just having it happen to you. To be sure, on his moral code the difference did not matter — his brother's death was still imputable to the man who fell on him — but this does not show that he had no notion of voluntariness, or even a different one from ours.

I said that Ascriptivism naturally thrives in the present climate of opinion; it is in fact constructed on a pattern common to a number of modern philosophical theories. Thus there is a theory that to say "what the policeman said is true" is not to describe or characterize what the policeman said but to corroborate it; and a theory that to say "it is bad to get drunk" is not to describe or characterize drunkenness but to condemn it. It is really quite easy to devise theories on this pattern; here is a new one that has occurred to me. "To call a man happy is not to characterize or describe his condition; macarizing a man" (that is, calling him happy: the words "macarize" and "macarism" are in the O.E.D.) "is a special non-descriptive use of language." If we consider such typical examples of macarism as the Beatitudes or again such proverbial expressions as 'happy is the bride that the sun shines on; happy are the dead that the rain rains on', we can surely see that these sentences are not used to convey propositions. How disconcerting and inappropriate was the reply, 'Yes, that's true', that a friend of mine got who cited 'happy are the dead that the rain rains on' at a funeral on a rainy day! The great error of the Utilitarians was to suppose that 'the greatest happiness of the greatest number'

was a descriptive characterization of a state of affairs that one could aim at; but in fact the term 'happiness' is not a descriptive term: to speak of people's happiness is to macarize them, not to describe their state. Of course 'happy' has a secondary descriptive force; in a society where the rich were generally macarized, 'happy' would come to connote wealth; and then someone whose own standards of macarism were different from those current in his society might use 'happy', in scare-quotes so to say, to mean 'what most people count happy, that is rich' . . ." There you are; I make a free gift of the idea to anybody who likes it.

There is a radical flaw in this whole pattern of philosophizing. What is being attempted in each case is to account for the use of a term "P" concerning a thing as being a performance of some other nature than describing the thing. But what is regularly ignored is the distinction between calling a thing "P" and predicating "P" of a thing. A term "P" may be predicated of a thing in an *if* or *then* clause, or in a clause of a disjunctive proposition, without the thing's being thereby called "P." To say, "If the policeman's statement is true, the motorist touched 60 mph" is not to *call* the policeman's statement true; to say "If gambling is bad, inviting people to gamble is bad" is not to *call* either gambling or invitations to gamble "bad." Now the theories of non-descriptive performances regularly take into account only the use of a term "P" to *call* something "P"; the corroboration theory of truth, for example, considers only the use of "true" to *call* a statement true, and the condemnation theory of the term "bad" considers only the way it is used to *call* something bad; predications of "true" and "bad" in *if* or *then* clauses, or in clauses of a disjunction, are just ignored. One could not write off such uses of the terms, as calling for a different explanation from their use to *call* things true or bad; for that would mean that arguments of the pattern "if *x* is true (if *w* is bad), then *p*; but *x is* true (*w is* bad); *ergo p*" contained a fallacy of equivocation, whereas they are in fact clearly valid.

This whole subject is obscured by a centuries-old confusion over predication embodied in such phrases as "a predicate is *asserted of* a subject." Frege demonstrated the need to make an absolute distinction between predication and assertion; here as elsewhere people have not learned from his work as much as they should. In order that the use of a sentence in which "P" is predicated of a thing may count as an act of *calling* the thing "P," the sentence must be used assertively; and this is something quite distinct from the predication, for, as we have remarked, "P" may still be predicated of the thing even in a sentence used nonassertively as a clause within another sentence. Hence, calling a thing "P" has to be explained in terms of predicating "P" of the thing, not the other way round. For example, condemning a thing by calling it "bad" has to be explained through the more general notion of predicating "bad" of a thing, and such predicating may be done without any condemnation; for example, even if I utter with full conviction the sentence, "If gambling is bad, inviting people to gamble is bad," I do not thereby condemn either gambling or invitations to gamble, though I do predicate "bad" of these kinds of act. It is therefore hopeless to try to explain the use of the term "bad" in terms of nondescriptive acts of condemnation; and, I maintain, by parity of reasoning it is hopeless to try to explain the use of the terms "done on purpose," "intentional," or the like, in terms of non-descriptive acts of ascription or imputation.

With this I shall dismiss Ascriptivism; I adopt instead the natural view that to ascribe an act to an agent is a causal description of the act. Such statements are indeed paradigm cases of causal statements: cf. the connection in Greek between αἰτία ("cause") and αἴτιος ("responsible"). Let us recollect the definition of will given by Hume: "the internal impression we feel and are conscious of when we knowingly give rise to any new motion of our body or new perception of our mind." Having offered this definition of will, Hume concentrates on the supposed "internal impression" and deals with the causal relation between this and the "new motion" or "new perception" on the same lines as other causal relations between successive events. Like a conjurer, Hume diverts our attention; he makes us forget the words "knowingly give rise to," which are indispensable if his definition is to have the least plausibility. If Hume had begun by saying, "There is a peculiar, characteristic, internal impression which we are sometimes aware *arises in us* before a new perception or new bodily motion; we call this volition or will," then his account would have had a fishy look from the outset. To say we *knowingly give rise to* a motion of mind and body is already to introduce the whole notion of the voluntary; an "internal impression" need not be brought into the account, and is anyhow, I believe, a myth. But without the "internal impression" Hume's account of causality cannot be fitted to voluntary causality; without it we no longer have *two* sorts of event occurring in succession but only, on each occasion, *one* event to which "we knowingly give rise" — words that express a non-Humian sort of causality.

For an adequate account of voluntary causality, however, we should need an adequate account of causality in general; and I am far from thinking that I can supply one. To develop one properly would require a synoptic view of the methods and results of the strict scientific disciplines — a labor of Hercules that far exceeds my powers; and it would take a better man than I am to see far through the dust that Hume has raised. All I have tried to do here is to make it seem worthwhile to investigate non-Humian ideas of causality in analyzing the voluntary, instead of desperately denying, as Ascriptivists do, that voluntariness is a causal concept.

18

JAMES W. CORNMAN

USES OF LANGUAGE AND PHILOSOPHICAL PROBLEMS

But how many kinds of sentences are there? Say assertion, question, and command? — There are countless kinds: countless different kinds of use of what we call "symbols," "words," "sentences." L. Wittgenstein, *Philosophical Investigations*, p. 23.

One looks at the above quotation and cannot help but agree with it. It surely seems true, almost trivial, something it would not take a philosopher to figure out. Why then do so many philosophers find the idea expressed in the quotation so important for their work? What have uses of language to do with philosophers and the problems they consider? It is this latter question I wish to consider.

Many philosophers of late have contended that other philosophers have been misled by language into making some strange claims. Such philosophers also claim that many so-called enduring philosophical problems can be solved and in many cases dissolved by properly classifying the uses of the language in which the problems are expressed. This approach to philosophical problems, which stems in a large part from the later Wittgenstein, involves pointing out logical similarities or differences or both between the linguistic expressions in which the problem

being considered is expressed and other linguistic expressions the use of which is clear. Two well-known attempts to handle specific philosophical problems by employing this approach are the attempt by H. L. A. Hart to dissolve the problem of human agency by properly understanding the use of sentences such as 'He did it' and 'He raised his arm', and the attempt by P. H. Nowell-Smith to dissolve the problem concerning the nature of ethical properties by showing the correct use of sentences of the form 'x is right', and 'x is good'.

What I shall try to do in this paper is show that although both men, and others who approach philosophical problems in the same way, are justified in their philosophical conclusions *if* they can establish their claims about the correct uses of certain sentences, what none of these men have done is establish those claims.[1] Do-

Reprinted from *Philosophical Studies*, XV (1964), 11–16, by permission of the author and the editor.

This paper was presented at the sixty-first annual meeting of the American Philosophical Association, Western Division, May 3, 1963.

[1] Some others whom it seems reasonable to interpret as using or implying this approach are the following: J. L. Austin in "Other Minds," *Proceedings of the Aristotelian Society*, Supplementary Volume XX (1946), where he tries to show that because 'I know' is logically like 'I promise' in certain respects, it is a performatory utterance and thus not used to refer to some kind of mental event; R. M. Hare in *The Language of Morals* (New York: Oxford University Press, 1952), where in Chapters 6 and 7 he compares and contrasts the logical features of 'good' and 'red' to show that 'good' is not the name of a property, either simple or complex; Gilbert Ryle in *The Concept of Mind* (New York: Barnes and Noble, 1949) where he claims that sentences such as 'John is vain' are in important ways law-

ing this, as I hope to indicate, would involve these followers of the Wittgenstein of the *Investigations* in the problems which motivated the Wittgenstein of the *Tractatus*.

HART: DESCRIPTION AND ASCRIPTION

The problem Hart is interested in, the problem of human action, can be put in terms of the following question: "What is the difference between someone raising his arm and his arm going up?" If there is a difference as the question presupposes, it would seem that there must be some difference between the kinds of events or states which cause the arm to go up in each case. Traditionally there have generally been three kinds of answers concerning the unique feature of the cause which results in someone raising his arm rather than it merely going up. It has been thought that in the former case the cause of the arm going up is either some unique physical event, e.g., some unique brain process, or some unique mental event, e.g., an act of will or volition, or the person himself in some nondeterministic way. However, no one of these three kinds of solutions seems to be satisfactory. The first leads us into the problems connected with free will and materialism, the second into the problems for dualistic interactionism, and the third leaves us with a mysterious causal force which has been called "the self" but which when we try to explain it usually leads us back to one of the first two kinds of solutions and their problems.

Hart, however, looks at this problem in a different way. It is wrong, he believes, to talk about what certain expressions are supposed to refer to until we have found whether the logical features of the sentences containing those expressions are the correct kind for such a job. For Hart, although sentences such as 'He raised his arm' and 'His arm went up' are indicative sentences, they have quite different uses.

While the second is used descriptively, i.e., used solely to refer to something, in this case to some event, the first sentence is not. It is used to ascribe responsibility to someone for his arm going up, rather than to refer to some event or process which differs in some way from the kind of event or process referred to by 'His arm went up'.[2] Hart reaches this conclusion by comparing the decisions of judges with the sentences relevant to the problem of human agency and finding many similarities between the two. He brings out the similarities by exhibiting the logical peculiarities of judges' decisions and then showing how sentences about human agency have many of the same peculiarities. In light of these similarities he concludes that just as a judge is not referring to a property someone has, i.e., is not describing him, when he gives his legal decisions, neither are we referring to something that goes on in a person when we use sentences such as 'He raised his arm'.

For Hart, then, there is no problem connected with the difference between someone raising his arm and his arm going up because the question which formulated the problem presupposes that sentences such as 'He raised his arm' and 'His arm went up' are both descriptive sentences and therefore are used to describe two quite different goings on. But Hart denies that indicative sentences such as 'He raised his arm' are used descriptively. Thus he denies a presupposition of the problem thereby dissolving rather than solving this problem which had defied solution.

Is Hart's conclusion justified? That is, granted that Hart has established logical similarities between the sentences concerning human agency and judges' decisions, is he then justified in claiming that such sentences are not descriptive? Before considering this question I would first like to turn to Nowell-Smith's claims because his

___

like, and, being like laws, are merely inference tickets and thus do not describe or refer to ghostly goings on.

[2] H. L. A. Hart, "The Ascription of Responsibility and Rights" in *Logic and Language*, first series, ed. A. Flew (Oxford: Blackwell, 1951), pp. 160ff.

quite explicit use of this approach will make clear where its problems lie.

NOWELL-SMITH: DESCRIPTION AND ETHICAL PROPERTIES

Nowell-Smith is concerned with the problem many moral philosophers have tried to solve, that is, the problem of what kind of properties ethical properties are. Nowell-Smith sets out to dissolve the problem by showing that terms such as 'right' and 'good' in their ethical use do not have certain logical features that terms which refer to properties have. As a consequence 'right' and 'good' do not refer to properties, and the problem about what kind of properties they refer to is dissolved. He does this by showing that because there are important logical differences between indicative sentences such as 'x is right' and descriptive sentences such as 'x is blue', the former sentences are not descriptive and as a result their predicates do not refer to properties. In so doing he is primarily attacking intuitionists such as G. E. Moore on whose view, claims Nowell-Smith, sentences such as 'x is good' are, like 'x is blue', descriptive, the primary difference between the two being that 'good' refers to a non-natural rather than a natural property. Such intuitionists, then, seem to presuppose that 'good' and 'right' refer to some kind of property. Nowell-Smith, however, wishes to show that this is where they made their mistake. I should like to state in some detail the two main arguments he uses so that we can later more clearly see the problems facing the approach he uses.

In the first argument Nowell-Smith claims that Moore is guilty of the same fallacy of which Moore had found the naturalists guilty, that is, what Moore called the naturalistic fallacy. Actually, as Nowell-Smith interprets the fallacy it might more appropriately be called the descriptivist fallacy. An example of this fallacy is the situation when from a descriptive premise such as 'x maximizes pleasure' someone infers the normative conclusion 'I ought to do x'. This inference is fallacious because there is nothing logically odd about accepting the premise yet asking, "Why should I do x?" Similarly, claims Nowell-Smith if 'x is right' is descriptive, i.e., is used to refer to a property of x, as it is for the intuitionists, then between it and 'I ought to do x' there should also be a logical gap. That is, it should not be odd to ask "Why should x be done?" while at the same time admitting that x is right. But Nowell-Smith says that the question is logically odd in such a context from which he concludes that 'x is right' unlike 'x maximizes happiness' is not descriptive and therefore 'right' does not refer to any kind of property.[3]

Nowell-Smith in the other argument I wish to consider uses the 'is' and 'seems' distinction to try to show another respect in which 'right' differs logically from descriptive predicates such as empirical predicates. Empirical predicates are used to refer to certain properties something may have or merely seem to have. Thus we can and do say "This is red" and "That seems red." And a color-blind man who realizes that he is color-blind might very well say, "That seems red to me but I realize that it is really brown." According to Nowell-Smith if ethical predicates are used to refer to properties we should, as with color predicates, be able to say, "That seems right to me, but I realize that it is really wrong." But this is surely in some sense logically odd. Thus 'right' differs logically from 'blue', and consequently 'right' unlike 'blue' does not refer to a property.[4] In this argument as in the previous one Nowell-Smith has attempted to dissolve the problem about what kind of properties ethical properties are by showing that ethical predicates do not refer to any kind of properties because they are logically different from predicates which do refer to properties in important respects.

[3] P. H. Nowell-Smith, *Ethics* (London and Baltimore: Penguin Books, 1954), pp. 36–43.
[4] *Ibid.*, pp. 48–60.

HART AND NOWELL-SMITH: THE COMMON ARGUMENT

We are now ready to ask whether the conclusions of Hart and Nowell-Smith that certain indicative sentences have a nondescriptive use are justified on the basis of what they have shown concerning certain logical similarities and differences. Although Hart emphasizes logical similarities with nondescriptive sentences and Nowell-Smith emphasizes logical differences from descriptive sentences, their approach is basically the same. They and others like them move to a conclusion about the use of certain sentences which phrase the problems they are concerned with, from premises about the logical similarities or differences between these sentences and certain other sentences the use of which seems to be clear. They then use this conclusion to either solve or dissolve the relevant problem. The argument made specific by considering Nowell-Smith's use of it would be somewhat as follows: (1) The empirical predicate 'blue' is used descriptively, i.e., refers to a property. (2) The ethical predicate 'right' in indicative sentences such as 'This is right' is logically unlike empirical predicates such as 'blue' in indicative sentences such as 'This is blue' in respects A, B, C . . . Therefore: (3) The ethical predicate 'right' is not used descriptively, i.e., does not refer to a property (either natural or non-natural).

This argument has two premises. Premise (2) is the kind of statement which Nowell-Smith and the others presumably establish by examining the logical features of 'This is right'. We will for our purposes assume that it is true. Therefore if the argument is valid we can assume that the conclusion is justified. However, as it stands the argument is not valid. What seems to be required is a premise that relates certain logical characteristics of predicates to properties. This is achieved if we replace premise (1) with the following: (1') If a predicate is logically unlike empirical predicates such as 'blue' in re-

spects A, B, C . . . then it is not used descriptively, i.e., does not refer to a property.

Nowell-Smith and the others do not seem to consider such a premise perhaps because they think that it is obviously true. Indeed this is the case with Nowell-Smith. He says, "To say that goodness is a property commits us to the very debatable assertion that the logic of 'good' is like that of 'blue', 'loud', and 'round'."[5] This assertion is not only debatable but is false if what Nowell-Smith has shown about the logic of ethical predicates is true. But the reason he thinks that anyone who says that goodness is a property is committed to this debatable assertion seems to be that he accepts the equally debatable assertion that if P is a property then 'P' functions logically like predicates such as 'blue', 'loud', and 'round'. This assertion is roughly equivalent to premise (1'). On what grounds could this claim by Nowell-Smith rest? If not on intuition then only, it would seem, on the claim that certain logical characteristics are the linguistic symptoms of properties.[6] Thus wherever we find these symptoms we can conclude there is a property referred to and wherever we find no such characteristics we can conclude there is no property referred to.

But why should we accept this claim? An ethical intuitionist would see no reason to. He might well agree with Nowell-Smith that 'right' and 'blue' differ logically in many important ways, but he would ex-

---

[5] *Ibid.*, p. 64.

[6] Nowell-Smith briefly indicates another way to justify his claim. He says that because 'property' is a technical term of the logician we must, in order to find out what adjectives refer to properties, examine the adjectives "that most typically fit what the logician has to say about properties; and these are the names of empirical, descriptive properties" (*ibid.*). But aside from the fact that we cannot validly deduce the required conclusion from the premises implicit in Nowell-Smith's claim, this kind of attempt will fail because at least certain nonempirical properties such as mathematical and surely logical properties typically fit what the logician says about properties.

plain the differences in another way entirely. Ethical predicates differ logically from empirical predicates not because they do not refer to properties but because they refer to properties of an entirely different kind. They have certain logical characteristics which are symptoms of non-natural, i.e., nonempirical properties, symptoms, which are, obviously, quite different from the symptoms of empirical properties. Surely this is *prima facie* as likely an explanation as Nowell-Smith's. In a similar manner someone who thought that in using 'He raised his arm' we are referring to some kind of mental going on might wonder why a sentence's being like judges' decisions in certain ways makes the sentence nondescriptive. He might well question why certain logical characteristics are considered to be symptoms of the absence of things referred to rather than symptoms of the presence of mental (nonempirical?) acts. Hart, it seems, like Nowell-Smith has not answered such a question.

CONCLUSION

Men such as Nowell-Smith and Hart, although they have focused attention on important alternatives to the kinds of solutions traditionally offered to certain philosophical problems, have not justified our adopting the alternatives they propose. The obvious question to ask at this point is what they must do to justify their conclusions. I shall not attempt to answer that question here. However, I do wish to indicate what this would seem to involve. They must justify a premise something like one of the form " 'P' is used descriptively if and only if 'P' functions in such a way that it has logical features A, B, C . . ." This brings up two related problems. First, there is the problem of showing why an expression used descriptively must have any special logical features. This, as I have tried to show, involves justifying the claim that there are in the logic of a language symptoms of the kinds of things the expressions of the language refer to, a claim, incidentally, like the one Wittgenstein made in 1916 when he said, "The way in which language signifies is mirrored in its use." [7] Second, if the first problem is solved, there is the problem of showing just what those special features are. Using the language of the Wittgenstein of the *Tractatus*, we can say that these followers of the Wittgenstein of the *Investigations* must show, first, that some logical features of descriptive expressions are essential to their referring; and, second, just which features are essential rather than accidental. [8] Can such claims be justified? About this I can here offer only one clue. They cannot be justified if the early Wittgenstein is correct because to do so would involve us in the relationship between language and reality about which, according to Wittgenstein, we can say nothing.

[7] Wittgenstein, *Notebooks 1914–1916* (New York: Harper, 1961), p. 82e.
[8] See L. Wittgenstein, *Tractatus Logico-Philosophicus* (London, 1958), 3.34.

19

J. O. URMSON

J. L. AUSTIN

Austin, though he admired the methods and objectives of some philosophers more than others, held no views whatever about *the* proper objective or *the* proper method of philosophy. One reason for this is that he thought that the term 'philosophy', without any stretching, covered, and always had covered, a quite heterogeneous set of inquiries which clearly had no single objective and which were unlikely to share a single method. Another reason is that he thought that those inquiries which had continued to be called philosophical and had not hived off under some special name (as have, for example, physics, biology, psychology, and mathematics) were precisely those for the solution of whose problems no standard methods had yet been found. No one knows what a satisfactory solution to such problems as those of free will, truth, and human personality would look like, and it would be baseless dogmatism to lay down in advance any principles for the proper method of solving them.

All philosophers, therefore, are entitled to pursue those problems which most urgently claim their attention and to which their ability and training are best suited; and they are entitled to use any technique that seems hopeful to them, though we cannot expect that every technique will be equally successful. Austin, for his part,

Reprinted from *The Journal of Philosophy*, LXII (1965), 499–508, by permission of the author and the editor. (Copyright 1965 by the Journal of Philosophy, Inc.)

thought that he had developed a technique for tackling certain problems that particularly interested him, problems about the nature of language. He did not imagine that he had first formulated the problems and he did not imagine that he had discovered the only possible method of tackling them; but he thought that he had devised a sort of "laboratory technique" which could be fruitfully used for finding solutions to them very much fuller, more systematic, and more accurate than any hitherto. The justification for the use of the technique was its success in practice; if another technique proved more successful it would be better. In deserting Austin's technique for this we would not be abandoning one theory of the nature of philosophy for another, but doing something more like substituting the camera for the human eye in determining the winners of horse races. This technique, like other research techniques, could not be fully exhibited in action in the conventional book, article, or lecture. Though Austin gave some general indications about it in his writings, particularly in "A Plea for Excuses" and "Ifs and Cans," its details are inevitably less widely known than his more conventional work, though this clearly drew heavily on the results obtained by the use of the technique. Yet Austin himself thought it his most important contribution, and hoped that a systematic use of it might lead to the foundation of a new science of language, transcending and superseding the work of traditional philosophers, grammarians, and linguisticians in that field. So a fairly full account of it by someone (myself) who frequently observed Austin employing it may well be of more value than any critical comments I might make on his published writings. Moreover, I think that a knowledge of it does help in the understanding of the general character of the published writings. In giving my account of this technique of Austin's I shall make use of some notes by Austin, too fragmentary, brief, and disordered for publication, characteristically entitled "Something about one way of possibly doing one part of philosophy."

It will be best to start with as factual as possible an account of the actual employment of the technique, not searching as yet for a philosophically helpful account of what it is being used for. Let it suffice at present to say that the aim is to give as full, clear, and accurate account as possible of the expressions (words, idioms, sentences, grammatical forms) of some language, or variety of language, common to those who are engaged in using the technique. In practice the language will usually be the mother tongue of the investigators, since one can employ the technique only for a language of which one is a master.

We cannot investigate a whole natural language at a sitting, or series of sittings; so we must first choose some area of discourse[1] for investigation — discourse about responsibility, or perception, or memory, or discourse including conditional clauses, to mention first areas traditionally of interest to philosophers; or discourse about artifacts, or discourse in

the present perfect tense, to add less traditional fields of investigation. Austin always recommended that beginners on the technique should choose areas that were not already philosophical stamping grounds. Having chosen our area of discourse, we must then collect as completely as possible all the resources of the language, both idiom and vocabulary, in that area. If we have chosen the field of responsibility, for example, we must not start by offering generalizations about voluntary and involuntary actions, but must collect the whole range of terms and idioms adumbrated in "A Plea for Excuses" — words like 'willingly', 'inadvertently', 'negligently', 'clumsily', and 'accidentally', idioms like 'he negligently did X' and 'he did X negligently'. In the field of artifacts we must collect all such terms as 'tool', 'instrument', 'implement', 'furniture', 'equipment', and 'apparatus'. In this task common sense is needed; a useful collection of terms and idioms require art and judgment; thus it probably would be a mistake to omit the term 'furniture' when examining discourse about artifacts, but it is unlikely to be necessary to include all names for all kinds of furniture — 'table', 'chair', 'stool', etc. Moreover, the notion of a field of discourse is imprecise, and we may initially be unclear whether a given term should or should not be included in it. Austin's precept was that, when in doubt whether a term was necessary or really belonged to the field in question, we should start by including it, since it is easier to strike out later terms that turn out to be intruders than it is to repair omissions. The most obvious devices for getting a fairly complete list are: (*a*) free association, where the investigators add any terms to the initial few that occur to them as being related; (*b*) the reading of relevant documents — not the works of philosophers but, in the field of responsibility, such things as law reports, in the field of artifacts such things as mail-order catalogues; (*c*) use of the dictionary, less ambitiously by looking up terms already noted and adding those

---

[1] I write 'area of discourse'; Austin's notes speak merely of an 'area'. There is little point in searching for a precise definition of an 'area of discourse'; terms are part of a single area of discourse if it is of interest to compare and contrast their employment, and if not, not. Some expressions may usefully be studied as falling into two different areas. There is no certain test of whether a term falls into a given area or not, prior to our investigation.

used in the definitions until the circle is complete, or, more ambitiously, by reading right through the dictionary — Austin, who must have read through the *Little Oxford Dictionary* very many times, frequently insisted that this did not take so long as one would expect.

At the stage of preliminary collection of terms and idioms the work is more quickly and more exhaustively done by a team. Austin always insisted that the technique was at all stages best employed by a team of a dozen or so working together; the members supplemented each other and corrected each other's oversights and errors. Having collected its terms and idioms, the group must then proceed to the second stage in which, by telling circumstantial stories and conducting dialogues, they give as clear and detailed examples as possible of circumstances under which this idiom is to be preferred to that, and that to this, and of where we should (do) use this term and where that. Austin's two stories of the shooting of the donkey to illustrate the circumstances in which we should, when speaking carefully, prefer to say 'accidentally' or 'by mistake' will indicate the sort of thing to be done at this stage ("A Plea for Excuses," *Philosophical Papers*, p. 133). It is also important to tell stories and make dialogues as like as possible to those in which we should employ a certain term or idiom in which it would not be possible, or would strike us as inappropriate, to use that term or idiom. We should also note things which it is not possible to say in any circumstances, though not manifestly ungrammatical or otherwise absurd (Aristotle's observation that one cannot be pleased quickly or slowly is the sort of thing that it meant here). This second stage will occupy several sessions; it is not a matter to be completed in a few minutes.

We have now got our list of terms and idioms (first stage), and a list of circumstantial stories illustrating how these expressions can and cannot occur, according to context. Experience shows that a group, not just a group of Oxford philosophers

but, say, a mixed American and British group, can reach virtual unanimity on these matters. Maybe something that seems perfectly in order to all the rest will sound odd to one member, or vice versa. When this happens it can be noted down and it may be of interest. But getting things right up to this stage is a group activity, and it is easy for a single individual to make mistakes initially that he can be brought to see. The device of a statistical survey of "what people would say" by means of a questionnaire is no substitute for the group, (1) because there cannot be the necessary detail in the questionnaire, (2) because the untrained answerers can so easily make mistakes, (3) because we are raising questions where unanimity is both desirable and obtainable. The group is its own sample, and its members can always ask their friends and relations "What would you say if . . . ?" as required.[2]

Austin always insisted that during the work so far described all theorizing should be rigidly excluded. We must make up detailed stories embodying the felicitous and the infelicitous, but carefully abstain from too early an attempt to explain why. Premature theorizing can blind us to the linguistic facts; premature theorizers bend their idiom to suit the theory, as is shown all too often by the barbarous idiom found in the writings of philosophers who outside of philosophy speak with complete felicity. But eventually the stage must come at which we seek to formulate our results. At this stage we attempt to give general accounts of the various expressions (words, sentences, grammatical forms) under con-

---

[2] An illustration: so shrewd an operator as Noam Chomsky says on page 15 of his admirable *Syntactic Structures* that "Read you a book on modern music" is not a grammatical sentence of English. Consider the dialogue: A. "Please read me a book on modern music." B. "Read you a book on modern music? Not for all the gold in Fort Knox!" Chomsky should have been working in a group. The statistical datum that Urmson allows, Chomsky disallows: this sentence is of no interest. Chomsky has made one of his few errors, as a group of us discovered while reading him.

sideration; they will be correct and adequate if they make it clear why what is said in our various stories is or is not felicitous, is possible or impossible. Thus it is an empirical question whether the accounts given are correct and adequate, for they can be checked against the data collected. Of course, if we have rushed the earlier stages new linguistic facts may be later adduced that invalidate the accounts; this is the universal predicament of empirical accounts. But though the accounts are empirical, the discovery and formulation of adequate ones is a matter requiring great skill and some luck; there is no rule of thumb available.

We may now, if we wish, go on to compare the accounts that we have thus arrived at with what philosophers have commonly said about the expressions in question (or with what grammarians have said). If one does so one may go on to a further project, the examination of traditional philosophical arguments in the light of the results of the technique. This type of project is illustrated by Austin's *Sense and Sensibilia*; here a thumbnail sketch only is given of the use of the technique on various groups of terms: 'illusion', 'delusion', and 'hallucination'; 'looks', 'appears', 'seems', etc.; 'real', 'apparent', 'imaginary', etc.; Austin then tries to show that various traditional arguments depend for their apparent plausibility on the systematic misconstruction and interchange of these and similar key terms. The book illustrates this stage of the inquiry; I do not now ask whether it is a successful illustration.

So much for the actual technique which Austin recommended. Briefly, a group of interested people collects the terms and idioms specially connected with an area of discourse; produces examples in context of the healthy use of these expressions and morbid examples of their misapplication; finally, gives accounts of these expressions which will explain the observed facts about what we do and what we do not say when employing them.

Why did Austin want to do this?

1. He thought that by the use of this technique one could make explicit a surprisingly and excitingly rich and subtle set of distinctions, of sufficient practical importance to have been incorporated into the structure of the language under investigation. In making them explicit one simultaneously gains a richer understanding of a language in which one is interested and of the non-linguistic world the language is used to talk about (in distinguishing mistakes from accidents, etc., one sees more clearly the ways in which actions can be defective). The distinctions made in one language need not be the same as those made in another; one does not discover distinctions that must be made, but ones which can be, and are, made. No doubt for special technical purposes or when we are faced with new situations, the distinctions we can thus find ready-made are inadequate, and we need to invent new ones. But Austin thought that the distinctions which *philosophers* thought up in their studies and employed instead of those in ordinary language were very jejune and poverty-stricken by comparison with those already made in ordinary[3] language. Certainly many of the philosophers who so act do so because they maintain that the distinctions of the natural languages are un-

[3] Here, as commonly among Austin and his associates, 'ordinary' is a technical term, meaning 'nonphilosophical'; thus the terms of modern physics are for present purposes part of ordinary language. The term is unfortunate because it is also true that Austin investigated mainly the resources of ordinary (= 'everyday', 'nontechnical') as opposed to technical language. Austin was not opposed to the coining by scientists and other technical people of useful terms, nor to the investigation of them by philosophers; he himself did not investigate them partly because he thought that he had not the necessary background knowledge, partly because the philosophical problems that most interested him did not arise in such areas. Also Austin was not opposed to philosophers' inventing technical terms for their own use, which he constantly did himself; the point made in the text is that in studying the expressions of a natural language we shall find matter of greater interest than in studying the proposed alternatives of philosophers.

worthy of serious interest and must make way for those of a specially constructed "scientific" language; Austin thought that this could be explained only by the unawareness of these philosophers of the subtlety of ordinary language. Austin did not want to deny that in various places and ways a natural language could embody conceptual muddles; he had no *a priori* certainty that language must always be "perfectly in order as it stands"; he merely thought that a far closer examination of the resources of language than has been traditionally made yields surprisingly rich dividends.

This first aim, as Austin well knew, is no novelty; but he thought that it had been pursued in too piecemeal and too unsystematic a manner, with insufficient effort to collect data, to yield a full reward.

2. Austin hoped that this work might be the beginning of a new science of language, which would incorporate the work of philosophers, grammarians, and linguisticians. A close look at the actual facts of language quickly invalidated, he maintained, most of the prevalent schemata, theories, and generalizations. A new terminology was needed for the accurate study of language, which would emerge in its study; the distinction of locutionary, illocutionary, and perlocutionary acts, made in *How to Do Things with Words*, was intended as a contribution to this new terminology.

3. Austin also believed that the careful examination of the ways in which we talk in a given field would save us from some of the muddles into which philosophers fall in discussing the traditional problems of philosophy. These problems at least arise in ordinary language; so a close examination of this language will be at least a "begin-all" if not an "end-all" in the prudent examination of them. If a philosopher wishes to use words in "special" senses, no doubt he may, and is not necessarily mistaken in principle; but a conceptual revision will prudently be based on a thorough understanding of what is being

revised. Too often philosophers do not use words in new carefully thought-out ways, but rather use ordinary language in a rather deviant manner, while at the same time relying on the entailments and implications of nondeviant use. I have already mentioned Austin's attempt to illustrate this unhappy feature of philosophical practice in *Sense and Sensibilia*.

4. Austin hoped that both the detailed examinations of areas of speech and the new concepts about language therein evolved would be of help to such other disciplines as jurisprudence and economics. I imagine that Hart would not object to my pointing to his work on jurisprudence as a case where this has happened.

Finally, the question may be raised: why do this sort of thing rather than something else? Let me quote quite literally Austin's own note on this point, which is intelligible enough as it stands:

Shan't learn everything, so why not do something else? Well; not whole even of philosophy but firstly always has *been* philosophy, since Socrates. And some slow successes. Advantages of slowness and cooperation. Be your size. Small men. Foolproof × geniusproof. Anyone with patience can do something. Leads to discoveries and agreement. Is amusing. Part of *personal* motive of my colleagues to avoid interminable bickering or boring points of our predecessors: also remember all brought up on classics: no quarrel with maths etc., just ignorant.

This sketch of Austin's techniques is now complete. As is clear, and as he knew, neither his aims nor his methods were wholly new in outline. What is new is the insistence on a technique designed to produce something much more precise and systematic than had hitherto been achieved, and the belief that the technique, patiently and systematically followed, could be the beginning of a new science of language, capable of standing alone with its own procedures and secure results.

But, though the sketch is complete, I should like to add some remarks of my own about Austin's claim that it was possible for a group to attain virtual unanimity about what can and cannot be said in various contexts and on the accounts of the various expressions based on these data. It is on this point that he has been most often criticized and misunderstood.

First let us consider the status of this claim. It is well known to everybody else, and need not be presumed to have escaped Austin's attention, that natural languages are not unchanging and monolithic; in fact they evolve continuously through time, and at any given time dialects and idiolects of geographically and socially separated groups and persons can be distinguished. If Austin had therefore claimed that any group of, say, English speakers, however collected, would give unanimous reports on what they would say in various circumstances, his claim would obviously be false. But though not an unchanging monolith, language is not a Heraclitean river either, certainly not a set of private Heraclitean rivers. Though I do have to guess, divine, speculate, in trying to follow a sports report in an American newspaper, my interpretation of American writings on law, music, history, and the like is no more speculative than that of British writings, though one has to be aware of a few special idioms. What Austin essentially wished to claim was that it was not as a matter of fact difficult to collect a group together in which speech differences were of marginal importance, and that where initially there was disagreement it should not be too readily ascribed to divergent speech habits; nearly always these initial disagreements would disappear after careful discrimination and presentation of cases. The claim is, therefore, the empirical one that groups are readily to be formed the members of which would all make the same linguistic discriminations. It is no doubt true that groups could be contrived of which this would be false, and Austin did not need to deny it.

Secondly, let us consider on what questions unanimity is to be achieved; critics who misunderstand Austin on this point often think that he is obviously wrong and

that nothing better than unrevealing statistics can ever be available. Let us suppose that a vocabulary including the words 'fleshy', 'chubby', 'fat', 'portly', and 'obese' is under consideration and we embark on the difficult task of trying to discriminate among them. Now it is easy to imagine a human figure such that, if asked to choose one of these words to describe it, members of a group would give widely different answers; it is absurd to imagine that Austin intended to deny this. He would rather have claimed that if this happened the group could arrive at unanimity that all the different answers were possible answers. This would be ground for the conclusion that the words in question were not mutually exclusive. But to pose questions where such an array of answers is possible is a clumsy use of the technique. More valuable questions would be such as: "Consider Winston Churchill; would you call him (a) chubby, (b) portly?" Would we not give a virtuously unanimous answer to each of those questions? We could go on to ask such a question as "Can you envisage a figure which we should describe as chubby but not fleshy or as fleshy but not chubby?" Austin thought that unanimity could be obtained on whether such figures could be envisaged, and, if so, which. In sufficiently imprecise situations it will always be possible to say different things; it is essential to ask questions in so sufficiently detailed and precise circumstances that one thing will be seen to be more appropriate to say than another. Austin's claim was that it was easy to gather groups such that there would be agreement on what was most appropriate. In making this claim Austin was certainly not wholly wrong; I have been a member of such a group under Austin's guidance more than once where his claim was abundantly fulfilled I have also joined in groups, with and without Austin, where little headway was made. In these latter cases were we inefficient or was Austin's claim falsified in them? I do not know how to answer that question. Certainly Austin.

more than anybody, has enabled many of us to find a richness in language greater than we had ever expected to find.

But what of those, and there are such, who, when confronted with the data and results of what seems to the group to be a successful exercise of the Austinian technique, reply that the refinements and the subtle distinctions claimed to be discovered in language are the products of the imagination of the group, that they themselves do not find these riches in language? Or what of those who use a quite different language, such as ancient Greek, of which the conceptual framework is importantly different? Some of the former objectors may just have dirty ears; but to neither group need the results, provided that they are clear and definite, be devoid of interest.

For while part of the interest of them is claimed to lie in their illumination of actual language, of our own ways of talking, nonetheless any set of fine discriminations may be of interest. Clarification of, say, the ancient Greek distinction between *arete* ('virtue') and *enkrateia* ('continence') does not cease to be of interest to us because we do not employ it ourselves; similarly, such distinctions as Austin indicates in "A Plea for Excuses" would not cease to be of interest even if we did not recognize them, as I largely do, as giving us a better understanding of our own way of talking.

Editor's note: For discussion of this paper, see the abstracts of the comments read by Stuart Hampshire, Norman Malcolm, and Willard v. O. Quine at the symposium at which this paper was given (*Journal of Philosophy*, LXII (1965), 508–13).

STUART HAMPSHIRE

J. L. AUSTIN

Philosophy is more than any other inquiry burdened with the knowledge of its own past. Like the descendants of an ancient family who still live in a small apartment, equipped with every modern device, in a corner of their ancestral home, philosophers at this time are apt to be at once proud of the great ambitions of their ancestors, and of the monuments that they have left, and at the same time half-ashamed of their heritage, as of something now embarrassingly over-ambitious, from which they must hasten to dissociate themselves. Consequently an anxious and defensive tone has crept into much of the philosophical writing and discussion of the last thirty years, the one of men who are anxious to show that in spite of their conspicuous origins, they are no less productive, unpretentious, unassuming, and modern in outlook, than workers in other fields. They may still live in the great house, but only in a corner of it, in which they lead very ordinary useful lives. As for the rest of the building, they are always available to show the public round with the proper historical explanations. This uncertainty about the relation of the present to the past has produced a certain strain and ambiguity of intention, also an undue sensitiveness to public opinion.

Of all the philosophers whom I have known as contemporaries, or as near-

Reprinted from *Proceedings of the Aristotelian Society*, LX (1959–60), 2–14, by permission of the author and the editor.

contemporaries, Austin was the least embarrassed, and the least uncertain, about philosophy itself and its role. He had made up his mind for himself independently of the current slogans, and he knew exactly what he was doing. As G. E. Moore in an earlier generation, so Austin in his generation had an authority that was immediately recognised by his colleagues, and in both cases the authority was founded, not only on unequalled intellectual powers, but also on a startling directness and sureness of purpose. Austin stood aside from all the indirectness and uncertainties of method, to which philosophers are now liable, for a simple reason: that he was constitutionally unable to refrain from applying the same standards of truthfulness and accuracy to a philosophical argument, sentence by sentence, as he would have applied to any other serious subject-matter. He could not have adopted a special tone of voice, or attitude of mind, for philosophical questions. He was by training a classical scholar and he thought as a classical scholar thinks. Clause by clause, sentence by sentence, a sequence of thought is constructed, until no rough approximations are left. If it is accurate in each one of its parts, it is accurate as a whole. This is the only way in which truthful prose can be written or spoken, and it is the only way in which anything already written can be truthfully interpreted and assessed. He had no need of a theory of philosophical method and therefore no need of a theory of philosophy itself. From the earliest date of which I can speak from personal knowledge, the year 1936, his 'method', which is better described as a style or habit of thought, was unvarying, in spite of at least one conversion in his philosophical interests. Before the war he was already characteristically suspicious of traditional formulations of the traditional problems of metaphysics, and to this extent he agreed with the logical positivists of that time. But he had not yet found his own way with dictionaries and grammars and the exact observation of usage. This was a gradual conversion. But from the beginning he refused to adopt any special and elevated tone for the discussion of philosophy, and he refused to accept from others any peculiar inherited canons of argument. Particularly during the 1930's, when technical pretensions were rife, these refusals had the effect of fair, and devastating, comment on the Emperor's New Clothes. He continued in this vein of patient literalness, through changing fashions, until the end. He could not have brought himself to approach philosophical problems in any other way. Any other way would simply have seemed to him untruthful.

As with Moore, so also with Austin there was a tendency among those who felt his authority to turn his individual style of thought into a general method of solving problems. There is always this desire to make any outstanding individual a type. The distinction and individuality are then comfortably reduced to manageable and imitable proportions. But the results of such a reduction of an individual style to a general method are often trivialities. History may, or may not, show that this has happened again; it is still too early to judge. But we are concerned at this time with Austin's own philosophical conclusions and achievements, as they appeared in discussion and in his publications.

There is a central problem of interpretation. Did he propose a general theory of language, as a structure that, accurately

interpreted, 'is in order as it is' (Wittgenstein's phrase)? Did he believe, and believe for good reasons, that a careful, systematic plotting of the distinctions already marked in standard usage would undermine the foundations of all, or of most, philosophical problems? After recalling his programmatic remarks in the Presidential Address "A Plea for Excuses," the symposium on "Other Minds" and many oral discussions, it seems to me that the evidence is not clear. He distrusted programmatic discussions for two reasons, each in itself a sufficient reason for him: first, that from their nature they must involve vague and sweeping generalisations which cannot be altogether accurate: secondly, that they are a diversion from the detailed inquiries that are needed at the present time. But in the assessment of his own work, particularly on Knowledge ("Other Minds," *Proc. Arist. Soc.*, Symposium, *Supplementary Volume XX*, 1946) and on problems connected with free-will ("Ifs and Cans," British Academy, 1956 and "A Plea for Excuses," *Proc. Arist. Soc.*, 1956/7), the issue cannot now be avoided. Did he try to show, and did he succeed in showing, that the kind of considerations that he here adduced would by themselves lead to adequate solutions, if they were pressed further with equal care and subtlety?

I shall distinguish two slightly different theses that can plausibly be attributed to him: a strong and a weak thesis.

II

The strong thesis may be seen as something like an application of Leibniz's Principle of Sufficient Reason to established forms of speech. For every distinction of word and idiom that we find in common speech, there is a reason to be found, if we look far enough, to explain why this distinction exists. The investigation will always show that the greatest possible number of distinctions have been obtained by the most economical linguistic means. If, as philosophers, we try to introduce an altogether new distinction, we shall find that we are disturbing the economy of the language by blurring elsewhere some useful distinctions that are already recognised. This, as a corollary of the Principle of Sufficient Reason, is a Principle of Continuity in language: every possible position (sense) is occupied (signified). Conversely, there is a presumption that to every verbal difference there corresponds a difference of sense which has its indispensable place. In very detailed lectures on perception, famous in Oxford under the title "Sense and Sensibilia," Austin tried to show that each of the great variety of idioms clustering round the apparently simple verbs 'look' and 'seem' plays a necessary part, and that the clumsy and naïve dichotomy of sense-datum and material object blurs every necessary distinction and is inadequate to the complexity of experience. He delighted to show that this dichotomy, which was in recent times supposed to rest on distinctions already marked on language, in fact rests on pure invention. In general he considered philosophers' inclination towards dramatic dichotomies as essentially primitive, as a mark of the pre-history of the subject, from which we could now at last escape by attention to the complex facts of language. In regular discussions with colleagues at Oxford, he methodically pursued the facts connected with the notion of a rule, examining the rules of many different kinds of games, and of course finding that there are many different kinds of rules. With this range of subtly varying examples in mind, a philosopher will be less confident that the rules of language are like the rules of a game, as if this were a triumphantly clear conclusion: which kind of rules in which kind of game? All that is philosophically interesting will disappear in the vagueness of the comparison at this level of generality. The comparison only comes alive when we descend to the details and set one kind of rule against another. Similarly in the article "A Plea for Excuses," and in seminars and discussions, he explored the variety of significant

ways in which our language allows us to modify the bald statement 'He did so-and-so', strengthening or diminishing its force and its implications. Each of the adverbial qualifications — 'deliberately', 'intentionally', 'on purpose', 'by mistake' and so on — had its own place in a system of graduated differences, and in each case we shall grasp the peculiar point by assembling typical examples. It would be a mistake to neglect any distinction as trivial, because it has played no familiar part in any philosophical problem. Only accuracy and completeness over the whole range of distinctions will locate disputed distinctions in their proper position. Austin had begun this kind of investigation in a class with Professor Hart in 1948, concentrating on legal concepts associated with action and responsibility. He had found a rich vein of 'facts' in the legal cases.

If we methodically investigate the whole spectrum of qualifications of the bald statement 'He did it', we may hope that, by this method of approximation, we shall have finally marked the boundaries of the central concept of action. A frontal assault on the typical philosopher's question 'What is an action?' will lead nowhere, because it is an invitation to smother the facts with an invented formula. 'What is an action?' Compare 'What is real?' and 'What is Truth?' It is the mark of the primitive, of the pre-history of philosophy, to pose questions in this linguistically abstract, and utterly general, form. I recall a lecture to a surprised summer-school audience not long after the war in which he listed some of the many different contrasts that may be implied in the various uses of the phrase '[a] real so-and-so': real [flowers] versus artificial, a real [character in a story] versus an imaginary one, real [courage] versus imperfect, and so on, with more and more subtly varying examples. What then is the use and basis of any generalized contrast between Reality and some supposed antithetical term, e.g., Appearance? The conclusion was that 'real' is an 'adjuster-word' which has to be watched in its role. It is a vulgarity to insist that anything less than a frontal assault on the 'great' problems is a retreat into triviality. If we are to arrive at a clear notion of Truth, we need a detailed review of the various ways in which a statement may go wrong, of the various dimensions of failure in statement-making. And we must not from the beginning assume a simple ungraduated notion of a statement, or of a descriptive utterance, as of something uniform and unmistakable. Here again we shall find, if we will only pause to look at the facts, a continuous spectrum of kinds of utterance, each with its peculiar liabilities to mistake. The most famous of his discoveries in this field was of the element of performativeness that enters into many kinds of utterance ordinarily classified as statements, and particularly into utterances that are claims to knowledge. This was certainly a substantial discovery, which no one can henceforth neglect in giving an account of knowledge ("Other Minds," *Proc. Arist. Soc., Supplementary Volume XX*, 1946).

Behind this policy of looking for graduated differences, and shades of qualification, around the hypnotising central concept (Action, Knowledge, Real, True, Rule), was the conviction that every difference of idiom has its justification in the subtle economy of language as a whole. On occasion, both in discussion and in publications ("Excuses," *Proc. Arist. Soc.*, 1956/57), Austin would suggest that the implied Principle of Sufficient Linguistic Reason is to be justified as Burke justified some other established institutions of England — social and political institutions. These are the distinctions that have stood the test of time and that embody the wisdom of long experience. They must represent a gradual effort of adaptation to 'the human predicament', and they cannot easily be bettered by any projecting reformer (Russell, Quine, Goodman), who sits down in an armchair to determine how we should speak clearly in the light of reason. No workable alternative will be found by *a priori* legislation and by brisk projects of logical reform. The distinctions are organically connected, and the amputation of an offending part will destroy the mutual adjustment, and therefore the life, of the whole.

The weaker thesis is a negative one, and claims no single and exclusive programme for advance in philosophy. It is a fact that we introduce and explain the distinctions that are required for the special purposes of philosophical analysis by reference to some existing distinctions marked in common speech. The philosophical distinctions, and the technical terms in which they are stated, may be refinements of established usage, refinements needed only in answering unusual questions. But they cannot be clear and intelligible, and the philosophical answers cannot be clear and intelligible, unless the distinctions from which they have been refined are themselves accurately recorded. In talking about sense-data, we shall be talking about we-know-not-what, if we have introduced these entities by reference to such phrases as 'the penny looks elliptical', and if we have in fact misreported, and over-simplified, the conditions under which such phrases are used, and the implications that they in fact carry with them. The weaker, or negative, thesis is that we must first have the facts, and all the facts, accurately stated before we erect a theory upon the basis of them. And this is much more difficult, and demands more patient and co-operative labour, than has ever been recognised by philosophers up till the present time. They have been content to seize on a few favourite examples, constantly recurring in the literature, and have then built their theories on this thin and biased foundation. We cannot be sure of the place, and therefore of the representative value, of any particular specimen of the use of an idiom, unless we have once traversed the whole range of its possible uses, and of the uses of other adjacent idioms that belong to the same range. Philosophers are not, unconsciously, to choose the very example from current usage that constitutes plausible evidence for the particular rational reconstruction that they wish to advocate. A rival school of philosophers concentrates attention on another range of well established uses of the philosophically interesting word or phrase, and, on this selected basis, suggests a quite different rational reconstruction of the essential purpose and meaning that lie behind the various uses of the word or phrase. The effect of this casualness and impatience is the notorious and scandalous inconclusiveness of philosophical argument.

It is the most important of all the facts that now need to be recorded about Austin, as a philosopher, that he certainly did himself consider this alleged scandal of inconclusiveness to be a scandal. Since it was a constant point of difference between us, he often, and over many years, had occasion to tell me that he had never found any good reason to believe that philosophical inquiries are essentially, and of their very nature, inconclusive. On the contrary he believed that this was a remediable fault of philosophers, due to premature system-building and impatient ambition, which left them neither the inclination nor the time to assemble the facts, impartially and co-operatively, and then to build their unifying theories, cautiously and slowly, on a comprehensive, and therefore secure, basis. To stop the endless pendulum motion of rival theories, each as plausible and partially founded as the other, is the serious work of philosophy at this time. During a sabbatical year, free from teaching and lecturing, he tried by himself to accumulate a vast range of examples of different types of predication with a view to building, on this unbiased foundation, a general theory of naming and describing. He did not succeed in this enterprise, and he did not believe that he had succeeded. The article "How to Talk" (*Proc. Arist. Soc.*, 1952–3), with which he was altogether dissatisfied, emerged from this work. But he still believed that a group of philosophers, working together for some considerable time, could collect a sufficient range of graded examples to permit, for the first time, some really well-founded generalisations. If this were not done, and if philosophers remained content with their hasty improvisations, we should continue on the old round of rival theories, each resting on its selected examples, and each and all of them exposed by evident counter-examples.

Austin believed at this time that the accepted grammatical-logical classifications of terms, and of types of statement (the classifications of non-formal logic) could be made far more precise and specific. A new set of technical terms was needed for a new philosophical grammar. The grammar books — and he read them carefully — were full of the ghosts of a primitive logic and of a primitive ontology. Here was constructive work that needs to be done, and only philosophers are sufficiently disrespectful of old theories to do it with undeceived attention to the facts. But, clinging to their ancient amateur status, as Platonic gentlemen who do not handle mere facts, they continue to discuss (for example) hypothetical statements in terms of the utmost generality, without distinguishing among the great variety of forms, syntactically or pragmatically different, of 'If . . . then' sentences. Austin had a scholar's feeling for grammar and for the shades of meaning to which a translator attends. Both as a teacher and in discussion among his colleagues, he was an enemy of the easy amateur tradition of linguistic analysis in all its surviving forms. His idea of organised and co-operative work in the philosophical study of language was the belief that amateurs must become artisans. On the one side mathematical logic, which has substituted disciplined work and established results for casual speculation in one large area of philosophy: on the other side, as the other heir of speculative, post-Russell philosophy, a real, in the place of a pretended, study of language. At a time when American foundations were considering means of promoting philosophical research, Austin privately expressed the belief that a large, co-operative, centrally directed project of linguistic analysis might indeed lead to solidly based results, and that uncontrolled private enterprise could accomplish very little. The sceptical arguments of his friends left him quite unmoved.

I may seem to have established no clear difference between Austin's stronger and weaker theses about the existing forms of language. The difference can perhaps be best summarised in a few sentences. The weaker thesis was that an exhaustive and methodical, and, ideally, a co-operative, study of the full facts of common usage in all traditionally disputed areas, is an indispensable *preliminary* to any philosophical advance. The stronger thesis was that the multiplicity of fine distinctions, which such a study would disclose, would by itself answer philosophical questions about freewill, perception, naming and describing, conditional statements. The crude distinctions, which are presupposed in every statement of these questions, will be seen to be intolerably remote from the facts. Thereafter we should move forward from the artificial questions, posed in these inaccurate and intolerably general terms, to the precise and various distinctions that in fact concern us in the conduct of life or in science. Almost all the semi-informed discussions of the linguistic method in philosophy have centered on this second thesis, because it can be much more easily and satisfactorily confused with Wittgenstein's theory of language in *Philosophical Investigations*. Even those who want to overlook significant differences in order to create a man of straw, called 'linguistic philosophy', as a target, cannot plausibly assimilate the weaker thesis to Wittgenstein's later teaching.

Plainly there was no immediate need for Austin to decide between these alternatives. Whatever the ultimate issue, the work immediately to be done, in teaching and in criticism, was the same. For Austin

philosophy as an inquiry, and the teaching of philosophy, were so intimately connected that it often seemed impossible to distinguish the ends that he prescribed for philosophy from those that he prescribed for the teaching of philosophy. He very strongly believed in the educational value of philosophy, rightly taught, and believed in it in a way that is traditionally associated with Greats at Oxford: namely, that it is an irreplaceable training in habits of exact argument, and that it is a prophylactic against intellectual pretentiousness and muddle. In this, and in several other respects, he had been influenced by the example of Prichard, who, as the scourge of pretentiousness and muddle, was the dominant figure among Oxford philosophers when Austin was an undergraduate. Of Prichard it was often said that, a strict and unworldly philosopher, he had in effect, and without explicit intention, trained several generations of civil servants in exact drafting, and that he had only reinforced habits of mind that had first been formed by Latin and Greek proses. This is the effect of the peculiar position of philosophy at Oxford as an accepted educational instrument. It has its continuing effects also on the quality and direction of Oxford philosophy, considered as an independent inquiry. In Austin's generation, the social and political implications of the teaching of philosophy, and of the forming of habits of thought in a ruling class, were certainly not unnoticed, and he was acutely conscious of them. He seriously wanted to 'make people sensible' and clear-headed, and immune to ill-founded and doctrinaire enthusiasms. He believed that philosophy, if it inculcated respect for 'the facts' and for accuracy, was one of the best instruments for this purpose. He had a great respect for practical activities of reform, and, as was shown during the war and within the university, immense and devoted ability in them. It is necessary to mention these facts, because the general tendency of the kind of linguistic analysis with which Austin is associated is constantly misjudged, at least as far as he is concerned. He was always responsibly interested in public affairs. As a young Fellow of All Souls, he began to learn Russian and visited the Soviet Union. At that time he would argue fiercely about politics from an uncommitted, but characteristic, point of view, which was half authoritarian and yet never conservative. So far from being neutral, detached, and therefore conservative, in relating philosophy to wider interests, he sometimes seemed to subordinate philosophy itself to education. He thought that a training in the true, patient method of philosophical analysis was having, and would continue to have, an effect that was the reverse of conservative. He certainly was not surprised by the hostility of the various established orders, whether Christian or secular, and of the merely conventional, *bien pensant* publicists. He was consciously a radical reformer, who had suggested a specific, and largely original, interpretation of that which constitutes clear thinking on abstract topics. He knew that this was an achievement that would rightly be regarded as subversive. He knew that he was (in his own words) 'tampering with the beliefs' of his audience, merely by insinuating unusual standards of verbal accuracy into the dissection of hallowed arguments. The true conservatives, in philosophy as in politics, are those who accept discussion of traditional problems within the traditional terms. However heterodox the conclusions on which the supposed rebels congratulate themselves, no Church or ruling party feels itself seriously threatened by this re-shuffling of the officially approved cards. But there are signs of official fear, and therefore of righteous anger, when the whole game of established argument and counter-argument is held up to ridicule. Austin did, with intention and responsibly, use the weapon of ridicule as a natural side-effect of analysing philosophical pomposity: for example, in examining the arguments for the existence of sense-data and many other traditional arguments. If you considered this style of detailed analysis ill-adapted to the material and ineffective, you would reasonably consider the ridicule to be misplaced also. But it is dishonest to pretend that linguistic analysis of a minute, literal, word-by-word kind is not revolutionary, both in intention and in effect, in philosophy, or to pretend that it confirms the plain man in his uncritical opinions. One of the strongest of the plain man's uncriticised opinions is that philosophical issues are too profound and peculiar to be discussed in any such pedestrian, literal terms. Those of us who, as philosophers, are not convinced of the final effectiveness of linguistic analysis know only too well that we are never without these, and other, embarrassing allies.

If one advances step by step, from one particular truth, accurately stated, to another, and if one never rushes forward to a premature generalisation, until the ground has been fully surveyed, one may indeed find oneself arriving at revolutionary conclusions, at least in philosophy. For no one had ever followed this path before, and it is therefore impossible to tell in advance where it may lead. In at least one case, the theory of knowledge (*Proc. Arist. Soc., Supplementary Volume XX*, 1946, "Other Minds") it did in fact lead to results, which are everywhere acknowledged as relevant, as new, and as of permanent significance.

III

In conclusion there are more scattered, personal and particular features of Austin's philosophical development between the 1930's and 1960 which ought to be recorded. In virtue of his authority and his innovations in the years after the war, the personal history is of some general significance for philosophers.

He arrived at his own distinctive position in philosophy slowly in the five years before the war. As an undergraduate at Balliol, he had been influenced by Prichard, whose lectures and classes he attended and whom he bombarded with questions and objections. I think that his interest in performative utterances was in part traceable to Prichard, who used to ask 'What do we mean when we say "I agree"', and then add 'I am blowed if I know'. Secondly, he read essays to the famous and eccentric Balliol tutor, half Roman historian and half philosopher, Stone, the author of *The Social Contract of the Universe*. Austin was deeply impressed by him as a person and as a tutor. In 1936 he and Professor Berlin held an unconventional and unforgettable class on C. I. Lewis' *Mind and the World Order*. He was already challenging the validity of any technical term for which no clear rule of use could be derived from within ordinary language. But he had not yet made this habit a principle. From 1936 to 1939, Austin attended informal weekly discussions in Berlin's rooms, with Ayer, Woozley, MacNabb, and myself. On these occasions he challenged every technical term in the discussion, as part of a philosophical mythology, unless a plain example, or set of examples, had first been made the focus of the discussion. As the philosophical atmosphere was at that time full of the technical terms of the Vienna Circle, the effect was powerfully negative. In these years we discussed principally sense-data and phenomenalism, hypothetical propositions, and necessary truth. Austin was at that time interested also in Leibniz, and read a rather formal paper to the Philosophical Society, within a Leibnizian framework, which questioned the grounds for believing that every proposition has a contradictory. He was at this time still uncommitted to any general programme in philosophy, but he was strongly influenced by Moore. In common with others of his generation at Oxford, he knew very little of Wittgenstein's later work. Although he shared their hostility to the pretensions of traditional metaphysics, he always attacked both the methods of argument, and the summary conclusions, of the philosophers of the Vienna Circle. Above all, he disliked the rapidity with which they arrived at their conclu-

sions. A philosophical argument with Austin, which was always concentrated on one, or perhaps two, definitely stated examples, commonly lasted for about three hours, until the various plausible interpretations had been exhausted: and he would often return to the topic later in the week, and these arguments would prolong themselves over a term. From 1937 onwards, and increasingly as the war approached, we discussed politics, and he regularly attended the electoral meetings of one of our colleagues, Lord Hailsham, as a heckler. During the war, and during his service as an intelligence officer, there were few opportunities for discussing philosophy. I think that it is certain, from the evidence of a particular conversation, that his natural love of concrete and detailed investigations, and of discoveries that gradually emerge from careful accumulations of fact, had already during the war led to fixed intentions in philosophy. Must philosophy always be unscholarly, vague, inconclusive, tentative? How can we know what would emerge from a planned and patient assault on the facts of the conceptual scheme, as it actually exists? Should there not be a moratorium on all theories until the facts that might form intelligent grammars and dictionaries are reasonably well ordered? Is it not laziness and dishonesty to continue to exchange one hasty theory for another, and to prolong indefinitely that pattern of plausible pretence which we call the history of philosophy? The plausibility of Descartes and, worst of all, of Hume were particular examples that he would quote. He distrusted their literary skill, the smoothness of the surface, and their light attitude towards recalcitrant facts, which made the total scheme brilliant and convincing. Aristotle stood for virtue and on the other side, because his conclusions were not unearned, and because he was more interested in making true statements, however dull, than in being interesting and dramatic. If due allowance is made for the great difference of scale, Austin's strong reaction against the sweeping generalisations about language, which were the legacy of logical positivism, was not unlike Aristotle's patient pruning of the Platonic philosophy. Many, perhaps most, of the great philosophers have survived in memory by the force of their exaggerations. Austin was always suspicious of the dramatic rhetoric of philosophers, and of that further exploitation of personality which has been such a comical, and perhaps harmful, feature of contemporary philosophy. He tried, in lecturing and in teaching and in writing, to reduce the tone of discussion to a plain, underlabourer's style, and to make philosophical argument as unassuming and relaxed as a botanist's argument. He was disgusted by those (and there have been many) who find in philosophy an excuse for re-making the world in their own image, and who realise their fantasies and wishes in an intellectual construction that pretends to be truth. The first virtue, in any inquiry, is respect for existence and for its variety. If this modesty is not taught in universities, and by philosophers, concern for truth will nowhere survive.

I think that there was more to be learnt from him than from any other philosopher of his generation. He had an entirely original and unprejudiced mind, a very strong instrument of natural scholarship, and serious and generous purposes. He was certainly the cleverest man that I have known among teachers of philosophy. He made a contribution, which was entirely his own, to one particular strand in English thought, and the consequences of his work will remain a living issue.

J. O. URMSON AND G. J. WARNOCK

J. L. AUSTIN

Professor Hampshire's account, in the *Proceedings of the Aristotelian Society*, of the late J. L. Austin is felicitous, perceptive, and valuable. However, it seems to us at certain points liable to disseminate just the kind of misunderstanding of Austin's position which Hampshire himself deplores, and it is not, we think, overofficious to say so at once.

Hampshire distinguishes and discusses at length two theses, 'strong' and 'weak', which can, he thinks, "plausibly be attributed" to Austin. The 'strong' thesis states as follows: "For every distinction of word and idiom that we find in common speech, there is a reason to be found, if we look far enough, to explain why this distinction exists. The investigation will always show that the greatest possible number of distinctions have been obtained by the most economical linguistic means. If, as philosophers, we try to introduce an altogether new distinction, we shall find that we are disturbing the economy of the language by blurring elsewhere some useful distinctions that are already recognized."

It is, however, quite certain that Austin did not accept this thesis — or at least that he did not accept all of its several parts. No doubt he believed that there was always a reason why the distinctions of word and idiom in common speech should have

come to be drawn; but he did not take for granted that such reasons must be good and sufficient. No doubt he believed also that linguistic innovation, the introduction of new kinds of terms into a body of existing usage, was more dangerous and difficult than philosophers by habit have been ready to recognize. But in *A Plea for Excuses* (P.A.S. 1956–7) he wrote: "Certainly, then, ordinary language is *not* the last word: in principle it can everywhere be supplemented and improved upon and superseded." In that same article he recognized that systematic investigation of human behaviour might give grounds for modifying, or for supplementing, our existing linguistic resources for commenting upon it. We recollect his saying in conversation that certain areas of 'common speech' — those, namely, in which common speakers for common purposes had no strong interest in, no occasion for, nicety and clarity of distinction — were most unlikely to prove fruitful subjects for investigation. Finally, in his own philosophical practice, particularly in his lectures on 'Words and Deeds', he had no hesitation in marking new distinctions with his own new technical terms, of which 'performative' and 'constative' are only the best-known examples. Such terminological invention he regarded not only as admissible, but as sometimes necessary.

Austin would certainly have regarded the notion of "the greatest possible number of distinctions" as incoherent, but this perhaps is a minor matter.

Reprinted from *Mind*, LXX (1961), 256–57, by permission of the authors and the editor. (Copyright 1961 by Thomas Nelson and Sons Ltd.)

Later Hampshire re-states this 'strong' thesis in words which seem actually to express a rather different thesis, as the proposition that "the multiplicity of fine distinctions which such a study [sc. of common speech] would disclose, would by itself answer philosophical questions about free-will, perception, naming and describing, conditional statements." There is some risk of ambiguity here. Is the expression "philosophical questions" to be understood as prefixed by "some," or by "all"? If the former, then the thesis is scarcely a 'strong' one and scarcely controversial; *some* questions, surely, could be answered by attention to "fine distinctions." But if the thesis is intended to express a claim about *all* philosophical questions, then it is quite certain that Austin did not subscribe to it. In the last sentence of *Ifs and Cans* he wrote that, if some parts of present day philosophy should be taken up into a new and comprehensive 'science of language', there would still be plenty left. In his lectures called 'Sense and Sensibilia' he undertook to deal only with a certain *kind* of philosophical worry. In general, as Hampshire himself quite rightly says, Austin "had no need for a theory of philosophical method and therefore no need of a theory of philosophy itself." His regard for "truthfulness and accuracy" in the use, and in description of the use, of words and phrases stands in no need of a specially philosophical justification; and he regarded it as merely premature to make general claims for the efficacy of this 'method'. What its limitations might be, and what, if it should prove at some point inefficacious, should then be tried instead — these

were questions which only time and hard work could answer.

To Hampshire's 'weak' thesis, that "we must first have the facts, and all the facts, accurately stated before we erect a theory upon the basis of them," Austin might well have agreed — with reservations as to the significance of the phrase '*all* the facts'. But this unambitious statement cannot properly, or even plausibly, be magnified into a guiding *doctrine* for his own, or into a recipe for anyone else's, philosophical practice.

Austin defended his own way of doing philosophy — which he sometimes called "one fashion" of philosophy — as congenial to one who had, as he had, predominantly linguistic interests and training; and he claimed that, when applied to fairly definite and limited problems, it was capable of producing definite results. Large assertions such as those 'strong' theses tentatively attributed to him by Hampshire he would certainly have regarded, besides repudiating them, as worthless. Such theses are not propounded in his writings published or unpublished; and we at least do not recollect, from many years of philosophical discussion with Austin, any hint that he accepted them. The notion that, all the same, they are somehow implied by his philosophical practice could be substantiated only if, as is plainly not the case, that practice could be made intelligible in no other way. But Austin sometimes gave, in much less ambitious terms, his own explanations. Why should these not be taken as meaning just what they say?

· 20c ·

STANLEY CAVELL

Austin At Criticism

Except for the notable translation of Frege's *Foundations of Arithmetic* and whatever reviews there are, *Philosophical Papers* collects all the work Austin published during his lifetime.[1] In addition, this modest volume includes two papers which will have been heard about, but not heard, outside Oxford and Cambridge. The first is one of the two pieces written before the war ("Meaning," 1940) and shows more clearly than the one published a year earlier ("Are There A Priori Concepts?," 1939) that the characteristic philosophical turns for which Austin became famous were deep in preparation.[2] The second previously unpublished paper ("Unfair to Facts," 1954) is Austin's rejoinder to P. F. Strawson's part in their symposium on truth, a debate which, I believe, Austin is widely thought to have lost initially, and to lose finally with this rejoinder. Austin clearly did not concur in this opinion, repeating the brunt of his countercharge at the end of the course of lectures he gave at Berkeley in 1958–1959.[3] The remaining five papers have all become part of

the canon of the philosophy produced in English during the past generation, yielding the purest version of what is called "Oxford philosophy" or "ordinary language philosophy." I will assume that anyone sharing anything like his direction from the English tradition of philosophy, and forced into his impatience with philosophy as it stands (or patience with the subject as it could become), will have found Austin's accomplishment and example inescapable.

As with any inheritance, it is often ambiguous and obscure in its effects. Two of these provide the subjects of my remarks here: the first concerns Austin's methods or purposes in philosophy; the second, related effect concerns the attitudes toward traditional philosophy which he inspires and sanctions.

Reprinted from *The Philosophical Review*, LXXIV (1965), 204–19, by permission of the author and editor, and included in Cavell, *Must We Mean What We Say* (New York: Charles Scribner's Sons, 1969).

[1] J. L. Austin, *Philosophical Papers*, ed. J. O. Urmson and G. J. Warnock (Oxford: 1961).

[2] Curiously, the 1940 paper is the most Wittgensteinian of Austin's writings, in presenting an explicit theory of what causes philosophical disability and in the particular theory it offers (sc., "We are using a working-model which fails to fit the facts that we really wish to talk about").

[3] These lectures, which he gave for many years at Oxford, were published posthumously under their Oxford title, *Sense and Sensibilia*, edited by G. J. Warnock. Austin's original paper on "Truth" (1950) is, of course, reprinted in the book under review. The remaining previously published papers are "Other Minds" (1946), "A Plea for Excuses" (1956), "Ifs and Cans" (1956), "How to Talk — Some Simple Ways" (1953), and "Pretending" (1958). All page references to these papers are cited according to their occurrence in *Philosophical Papers*. The concluding paper — "Performative Utterances" — is the transcript of a talk Austin gave for the B.B.C. in 1956; it is now superseded by the publication of the full set of lectures he used to give on this topic, and gave as the William James Lectures at Harvard in 1955, under the title *How to Do Things with Words*, edited by J. O. Urmson.

I

I wish not so much to try to characterize Austin's procedures as to warn against too hasty or simple a description of them: their characterization is itself, or ought to be, as outstanding a philosophical problem as any to be ventured from within those procedures.

To go on saying that Austin attends to ordinary or everyday language is to go on saying, roughly, nothing — most simply because this fails to distinguish Austin's work from anything with which it could be confused. It does not, in the first place, distinguish his work from ordinary empirical investigations of language, a matter which has come to seem of growing importance since Austin's visits to the United States in 1955 and 1958. I do not say there is *no* relation between Austin's address to natural language and that of the descriptive linguist; he himself seems to have thought there was, or could be, a firmer intimacy than I find between them. The differences which, intuitively, seem to me critical, however, are these. In proceeding from ordinary language, so far as that is philosophically pertinent, one is in a frame of mind in which it seems (1) that one can as appropriately or truly be said to be looking at the world as looking at language; (2) that one is seeking necessary truths "about" the world (or "about" language) and therefore cannot be satisfied with anything I, at least, would recognize as a description of how people in fact talk — one might say one is seeking one kind of explanation of *why* people speak as they do; and even (3) that one is not finally interested *at all* in how "other" people talk, but in determining where and why one wishes, or hesitates, to use a particular expression oneself. What investigations pursued in such frames of mind are supposed to show, I cannot say — perhaps whatever philosophy is supposed to show. My assumption is that there is something special that philosophy is about, and that Austin's procedures, far from avoiding this oldest question of philosophy, plunge us newly into

it. I emphasize therefore that Austin himself was, so far as I know, never anxious to underscore philosophy's uniqueness, in particular not its difference from science; he seemed, indeed, so far as I could tell, to like denying any such difference (except that there is as yet no *established* science — of linguistics or grammar perhaps — to which philosophy may aspire to be assimilated).

The qualification "ordinary language," secondly, does not distinguish this mode of philosophizing from any other of its modes — or, I should like to say, does not distinguish it philosophically. It does tell us enough to distinguish hawks from handsaws — Austin from Carnap, say — but not enough to start a hint about *how* ordinary language is appealed to, how one produces and uses its critical and characteristic forms of example, and why; nor about how and just where and how far this interest conflicts with that of any other temper of philosophy. The phrase "ordinary language" is, of course, of no special interest; the problem is that its use has so often quickly suggested that the answers to the fundamental questions it raises, or ought to raise, are known, whereas they are barely imagined. Austin's only positive suggestion for a title to his methods was, I believe, "linguistic phenomenology" ("Excuses," p. 130), and although he apologizes that "that is rather a mouthful" (what he was shy about, I cannot help feeling, was that it sounds rather pretentious, or anyway philosophical) he does not retract it. This title has never caught on, partly, surely, because Austin himself invests no effort in formulating the significance of the phenomenological impulses and data in his work — data, perhaps, of the sort suggested above in distinguishing his work from the work of linguistic science.

Another characterization of Austin's procedures has impressive authority behind it. Professor Stuart Hampshire, in the memorial written for the *Proceedings of the Aristotelian Society* (1959–1960) on the occasion of Austin's death,* provides various kinds of consideration — personal, social, historical, philosophical — for assessing Austin's achievement in philosophy. The device he adopts in his own assessment is to "distinguish two slightly different theses that can plausibly be attributed to him: a strong and weak thesis" (p. 240). The strong thesis is this: "For every distinction of word and idiom that we find in common speech, there is a reason to be found, if we look far enough, to explain why this distinction exists. The investigation will always show that the greatest possible number of distinctions have been obtained by the most economical linguistic means" (*ibid.*). "The weaker, or negative, thesis is that we must first have the facts, and all the facts, accurately stated before we erect a theory upon the basis of them" (p. 242). The weaker thesis is "negative," presumably, because it counsels study of ordinary language as a preliminary to philosophical advance, whereas the stronger claims "that the multiplicity of fine distinctions, which such a study would disclose, would by itself answer philosophical questions about free-will, perception, naming and describing, conditional statements" (p. 244).

Hampshire's characterizations were quickly repudiated by Austin's literary executors (J. O. Urmson and G. J. Warnock, *Mind* [1961], 256–257),* the weaker thesis on the ground that it is an "unambitious statement which cannot properly, or even plausibly, be magnified into a guiding *doctrine* . . . or recipe," the stronger on various grounds according to its various parts or formulations, but primarily on two: that Austin did sanction at least *some* new distinctions, and that he certainly did not claim that *all* philosophical questions could be answered by attention to fine distinctions. Urmson and Warnock are concerned, it emerges, to repudiate the idea that any such "large assertions" are contained or implied in

*Editor's note: Reprinted above at pp. 239–47. References are to the pagination in this volume.
*Editor's note: Reprinted above at pp. 248–49.

Austin's writings (or conversations). They conclude by saying: "Austin sometimes gave . . . his own explanations. Why should they not be taken as meaning just what they say?"

I want in Section II to take up that challenge explicitly, if briefly. Immediately, it seems clear to me that Urmson and Warnock have trivialized Hampshire's formulations, whatever their several shortcomings. His weak thesis is hardly affected by being called an "unambitious statement" rather than a doctrine or a recipe, partly because it is not unambitious in Austin's practice, and partly because of Austin's conviction, and suggestion, that most philosophers have not merely proceeded in the absence of "all the facts," but in the presence of practically *no facts at all*, or facts so poorly formulated and randomly collected as to defy comprehension. The issue raised is nothing less, I suggest, than the question: what is a philosophical fact? What are the data from which philosophy may, and must, proceed? It would be presumptuous to praise Austin for having pressed such questions to attention, but it is just the plain truth that nothing he says in "his own explanations" begins to answer them.[4]

The strong thesis, in turn, is unaffected by switching its quantification from "all"

[4] If such questions strike a philosopher as fundamental to his subject, or even as relevant, then I do not see how it can be denied that their answer is going to entail "large assertions" for which, moreover, so far as they concern Austin's practice, all the facts are directly at hand, sc., in Austin's practice. To accept Austin's explanations as full and accurate guides to his practice would be not only to confuse advice (which is about all he gave in this line) with philosophical analysis and literary-critical description (which is what is needed), but to confer upon Austin an unrivaled power of self-discernment. It is a mystery to me that what a philosopher says about his methods is so commonly taken at face value. Austin ought to be the last philosopher whose reflexive remarks are treated with this complacency, partly because there are so many of them, and partly because they suffer not merely the usual hazards of self-description but the further deflections of polemical animus. I return to this in the following section.

to "some," for the issue raised is whether attention to fine distinctions can "by itself" answer *any* philosophical question. At the place where Urmson and Warnock confidently assert that *some* questions can be answered in this way — a matter they take as "scarcely controversial" — they omit the qualification "philosophical," and offer no suggestion as to the particular way in which such answers are effected.[5] Finally, were we to let Urmson and Warnock's deflations distract us from philosophical curiosity about Austin's procedures, that could only inflame our psychological curiosity past composure; for the gap between Austin's unruffled advice to philosophical modesty and his obsession, to say the least, with the fineness of ordinary language and his claims to its revelation would then widen to dream-like proportions. His repeated disclaimer that ordinary language is certainly not the last word, "only it *is* the *first* word" (alluded to by Urmson and Warnock), is reassuring only during polemical enthusiasm. For the issue is why the first, or *any*, word can have the kind of power Austin attributes to it. I share his sense that it has, but I cannot see that he has anywhere tried to describe the sources or domain of that power.

My excuse for butting into this controversy is that both sides seem to me to sanction a description of Austin's concerns which is just made to misdirect a further understanding of it and which is the more harmful because of its obvious plausibility, or rather its partial truth. I have in mind simply the suggestion that Austin's fundamental philosophical inter-

est lay in drawing distinctions. Given this description of the method, and asked to justify it, what *can* one answer except: these are all the distinctions there are, or all that are real or important or necessary, and so forth, against which, it cannot be denied, Austin's own words can be leveled. Too obviously, Austin *is* continuously concerned to draw distinctions, and the finer the merrier, just as he often explains and justifies what he is doing by praising the virtues of natural distinctions over home-made ones. What I mean by saying that this interest is not philosophically fundamental is that his drawing of distinctions is always in the service of further purposes, and in particular two. (1) *Part* of the effort of any philosopher will consist in showing up differences, and one of Austin's most furious perceptions is of the slovenliness, the grotesque crudity and fatuousness, of the usual distinctions philosophers have traditionally thrown up. Consequently, one form his investigations take is that of repudiating the distinctions lying around philosophy — dispossessing them, as it were, by drawing better ones. And better not merely because finer, but because more solid, having, so to speak, a greater natural weight; appearing normal, even inevitable, when the others are luridly arbitrary; useful where the others seem twisted; real where the others are academic; fruitful where the others stop cold. This is, if you like, a negative purpose. (2) The positive purpose in Austin's distinctions resembles the art critic's purpose in comparing and distinguishing works of art, namely, that in this cross-light the capacities and salience of an individual object in question are brought to attention and focus. Why comparison and distinction serve such purposes is, doubtless, not easy to say.[6] But it is, I take it,

---

[5] Part of Hampshire's suggestion is that accepted philosophical theses and comparisons are drained, set against Austin's distinctions, of philosophical interest (cf. p. 241). This is a familiar enough fact of contemporary philosophizing, and it suggests to me that one requirement of new philosophical answers is that they elicit a new source of philosophical interest, or elicit this old interest in a new way. Which is, perhaps, only a way of affirming that a change of *style* in philosophy is a profound change, and itself a subject of philosophical investigation.

[6] That it is as much a matter of *comparing* as of distinguishing is clear — and takes its importance — from the way in which examples and, most characteristically, stories set the stage for Austin's distinctions. This is plainly different from their entrance in, say, philosophers like Russell or Broad or even Moore, whose distinc-

amply clear that their unique value is not accidentally joined to a particular task of criticism. They will not do everything, but nothing else evidently so surely defines areas of importance, suggests terms of description, or locates foci of purpose and stresses of composition: other works tell what the given work is about. In Austin's hands, I am suggesting, other words, compared and distinguished, tell what a given word is about. To know why they do, to trace how these procedures function, would be to see something of what it is he wishes words to teach, and hints at an explanation for our feeling, expressed earlier, that what we learn will not be new empirical facts about the world, and yet illuminating facts about the world. It is true that he asks for the difference between doing something by mistake and doing it by accident, but what transpires is a characterization of *what a mistake is* and (as contrasted, or so far as contrasted with this) what an accident is. He asks for the difference between being sure and being certain, but what is uncovered is an initial survey of the complex and mutual

___

tions do not serve to compare and (as it were) to elicit differences but rather, one could say, to provide labels for differences previously, somehow, noticed. One sometimes has the feeling that Austin's differences penetrate the phenomena they record — a feeling from within which the traditional philosopher will be the one who seems to be talking about mere words. The differing role of examples in these philosophical procedures is a topic of inexaggeratable importance, and no amount of words about "ordinary language" or "make all the distinctions" will convey to anyone who does not have the hang of it how to produce or test such examples. Anyone who has tried to teach from such materials and methods will appreciate this lack, which makes it the more surprising that no one, to my knowledge, has tried to compose a useful set of directions or, rather, to investigate exactly the ways one wishes to describe the procedure and notice their varying effectiveness for others, or faithfulness to one's sense of one's own procedures. Perhaps what is wanted really is a matter of conveying "the hang" of something, and that is a very particular dimension of a subject to teach — familiar, for example, in conservatories of music, but also, I should guess, in learning a new game or entering any new territory or technique or apprenticing in a trade.

alignments between mind and world that are necessary to successful knowledge. He asks for the difference between expressing belief and expressing knowledge (or between saying "I believe" and saying "I know") and what comes up is a new sense or human responsibilities, of human knowland assessment of the human limitations, edge; and so on.

As important as any of these topics or results within his investigations is the opportunity his purity of example affords for the investigation of philosophical method generally. Here we have or could have — appearing before our eyes in terms and steps of deliberate, circumstantial obviousness — conclusions arrived at whose generality and convincingness depend, at least intuitively, upon a play of the mind characteristically philosophical, furnished with the usual armchairs and examples and distinctions and wonder. But how can such results have appeared? How can we learn something (about how we — how I — use words) which we cannot have failed to know? How can asking when we would *say* "by mistake" (or what we call "doing something by mistake") tell us what in the world a mistake *is*? How, given such obvious data, have philosophers (apparently) so long ignored it, forgetting that successful knowledge is a human affair, of human complexity, meeting human need and exacting human responsibility, bypassing it in theories of certainty which compare knowledge (unfavorably) with an inhuman ideal; or elaborated moral philosophies so abstracted from life as to leave, for example, no room for so homely, but altogether a central, moral activity as the entering of an excuse? What is philosophy that it can appear periodically so profound and so trivial, sometimes so close and sometimes so laughably remote, so wise and so stone stupid? What is philosophy that it causes those characteristic hatreds, yet mysterious intimacies, among its rivals? What kind of phenomenon is it whose past cannot be absorbed or escaped (as in the case of science) or parts of it freely admired and envied while other parts are despised and banished (as in art), but remains in standing competition, behind every closed argument waiting to haunt its living heirs?

II

One pass to these questions is opened by picking at the particular charges Austin brings against his competitors, past and present. His terms of criticism are often radical and pervasive, but this should not blunt an awareness that they are quite particular, characteristic, and finite. And each of them, as is true of any charge, implies a specific view taken of a situation. This is, indeed, one of Austin's best discoveries, and nothing is of more value in the example of his original investigations than his perfect faithfulness to that perception: it is what his "phenomenology" turns on. That it fails him in criticizing other philosophers will have had various causes, but the productive possibility for us is that he has shown us the value of the procedure and that we are free to apply it for our better judgment.

I must limit myself to just one example of what I have in mind. Take Austin's accusing philosophers of "mistakes." It is worth noticing that the man who could inspire revelation by telling us a pair of donkey stories which lead us to take in the difference between doing something "by mistake" and doing it "by accident" ("Excuses," p. 133, n. 1) uses the term "mistake" in describing what happens when, for example, Moore is discussing the question whether someone could have done something other than what in fact he did ("If and Cans"). Now in the case of shooting your donkey when I meant to shoot mine, the correctness of the term "mistake" is bound to the fact that questions like the following have definite answers. What mistake was made? (I shot your donkey.) What was mistaken for what? (Your donkey was mistaken for mine.) How can the mistake have oc-

curred? (The donkeys look alike.) (How) could it have been prevented? (By walking closer and making sure, which a responsible man might or might not have been expected to do.) But there are no such answers to these questions asked about Moore's discussion — or perhaps we should say that the answers we would have to give would seem forced and more or less empty, a fact that ought to impress a philosopher like Austin.

What has Moore mistaken for what? Should we, for example, say that he mistakes the expression "could have" for "could have if I had chosen"? Then how and why and when can such a mistake have occurred? Was it because Moore has been hasty, thoughtless, sloppy, prejudiced . . . ? But though there are the sorts of answers we are now forced to give (explanations which certainly account for mistakes, and which Austin is free with in accounting for the disasters of other philosophers), they are fantastic in this context; because there is no plausibility to the suggestion, taken seriously, that, whatever Moore has done, he has made a mistake: these charges are thus, so far, left completely in the air. Such charges can equally account for someone's having been involved in an accident or an inadvertence or the like. But, as Austin is fond of saying, each of these requires its own story; and does either of them fit the conduct of Moore's argument any better than the term "mistake"? Then perhaps the mistake lies in Moore's thinking that "could have" *means* "could have if I had chosen." But now this suggests not that Moore *took one thing for another* but that he took a tack he should not or need not have taken. This might be better expressed, as Austin does sometimes express it, by saying that Moore *was mistaken* in this, or perhaps by saying that *it was a mistake for him to*. But to say someone is mistaken requires again its own kind of story, different from the case of doing something by mistake or from making a mistake. In particular it suggests a context in which it is obvious, not that one thing looks like another, but why one would be led to do the mistaken, unhappy thing in question. The clearest case I think of is one of poor strategy: "It is a mistake to castle at this stage." This charge depends upon there being definite answers to questions like the following. Why does it seem to be a good thing to do? Why is it nevertheless not a good thing to do? What would be a better (safer, less costly, more subtle, stronger) thing to do instead? Such questions do fit certain procedures of certain intellectual enterprises, for example, the wisdom of taking a certain term as undefined, the dangers of appealing to the natural rights or the cult emotions of a certain section of the voting population, the difficulties of employing a rhyme scheme of a particular sort. What is Moore trying to do to which such a consideration of plusses and minuses would be relevant?

One may feel: "Of course it is not a matter of better or worse. If Moore (or any philosopher) is wrong he is just wrong. What is absurd about the suggestion that he may have reasons for doing things his way is the idea that he may wish to tally up the advantages of being right over those of being wrong, where being right (that is, arriving at the truth) is the whole point. Cannot to say he has made a mistake — or, rather, to say he is mistaken — just mean that he is just wrong?" But it seems, rather, that "mistaken" requires the idea of a wrong alternative (either taking one thing for another, or taking one tack rather than another). Is such an alternative, perhaps, provided by Austin's account of "could have" (as sometimes indicative rather than subjunctive), and is Moore to be considered mistaken because he did not adopt or see Austin's line? But of course the problem of alternatives is a problem of what alternatives are open to a particular person at a particular moment: and what is "open to" a particular person at a particular moment is a matter of some delicacy to determine — nothing less than determining whether someone

could have done or seen something. However this may be, we still need, if we are to say "mistaken," an account of why he took the "alternative" he did. There seem to be just two main sorts of answers to such a question: either you admit that it is an attractive or plausible or seemingly inevitable one, *and account for such facts*, or you will find nothing of attraction or plausibility or seeming inevitability in it and assign its choice to ignorance, stupidity, incompetence, prejudice, and so forth. When Austin is discussing Moore, his respect pushes him to suggest the former sort of explanation, but he is clearly impatient with the effort to arrive at one and drops it as soon as possible (see, for example, pp. 154, 157).

Calling philosophers prejudiced or thoughtless or childish is a common enough salute among classical philosophers: one thinks of Bacon's or Descartes's or Hume's attitudes to other, especially to past, philosophers. It is time, perhaps, to start wondering why such charges should be characteristic of the way a philosophy responds to a past from which it has grown different or to a position with which it is incommensurable.

Other terms of criticism are implied in Austin's occasional recommendations of his own procedures. For example, one reason for following out the branches of Excuses thoroughly and separately is that "Here at last we should be able to unfreeze, to loosen up and get going on agreeing about discoveries, however small, and on agreeing about how to reach agreement." It is hard to convey to anyone who has not experienced it the rightness and relief words like these can have for students who have gone over the same distinctions, rehearsed the same fallacies, trotted out the same topics seminar after term paper, teaching assistant after lecturer, book after article. And the rightness and relief were completed in his confession that the subject of Excuses "has long afforded me what philosophy is so often thought, and made, barren of — the fun of discovery, the pleasure of cooperation, and the satisfaction of reaching agreements." These are real satisfactions, and I can testify that they were present throughout the hours of his seminar on this topic. It would hardly have occurred to anyone, in the initial grip of such satisfactions, to question whether they are appropriate to philosophy (as they obviously are to logic or physics or historical scholarship) any more than they are, in those ways or proportions, to politics or religion or art; to wonder whether their striking presence in our work now did not suggest that we had changed our subject.

The implied terms of criticism in this recommendation are, of course, that we are frozen, tied up, stopped. Granted a shared sense that this describes our position, one wants to know how we arrived at it. Sometimes Austin attributes this to our distended respect for the great figures of the past (see, for example, "Excuses," p. 131), sometimes to general and apparently congenital weaknesses of philosophy itself: "over-simplification, schematization, and constant obsessive repetition of the same small range of jejune 'examples' are . . . far too common to be dismissed as an occasional weakness of philosophers." And this characteristic weakness — something he refers to as "scholastic," following the call of the major line of British Empiricists — he attributes "first, to an obsession with a few particular words, the uses of which are over-simplified, not really understood or carefully studied or correctly described; and second, to an obsession with a few (and nearly always the same) half-studied 'facts'" (*Sense and Sensibilia*, p. 3). So far the criticisms proceed on familiar Baconian or Cartesian ground; the philosopher of good will and the man of common sense will work together to see through philosophy and prejudice to the world as it is.

At some point Austin strikes into criticisms which go beyond the impatience and doubt which begin modern philosophy, new ones necessary perhaps just because philosophy seems to have survived that impatience and doubt (or emasculated them, in turn, into academic subjects). I find three main lines here. (1) Most notably in *Sense and Sensibilia*, he enters charges against philosophers which make it seem not merely that their weakness is somehow natural to the enterprise, imposed on men of ordinary decency by an ill-governed subject, but that their work is still more deeply corrupt: we hear of philosophers having "glibly trotted out" new uses of phrases (p. 19); of subtle "insinuation" which is "well calculated" to get us "where the sense-datum theorist wants to have us" (p. 25); of bogus dichotomies, grotesque exaggeration, gratuitous ideas (p. 54) — phrases which, at this point, carry the suggestion that they are deliberate or willful exaggerations and the like, and pursued with an absence of obvious motivation matched only by an Iago. (2) On more than one occasion he suggests that philosophical delinquency arises from a tendency to Dionysian abandon: we are warned of the blindness created in the *"ivresse des grandes profondeurs"* (p. 127) and instructed in the size of problems philosophers should aim at — *"In vino*, possibly, *'veritas'*, but in a sober symposium *'verum'* "* ("Truth," p. 85). (3) Finally, and quite generally, he conveys the impression that the philosophers he is attacking are not really serious, that, one may say, they have written inauthentically (cf. *Sense and Sensibilia*, p. 29).

I cannot attempt here to complete the list of Austin's terms of criticism, any more than I can now attempt to trace the particular target each of them has; and I have left open all assessment of their relative seriousness and all delineation of the particular points of view from which they are launched. I hope, however, that the bare suggestion that Austin's work raises, and helps to settle, such topics will have served my purposes here, which, in summary, are these: (1) To argue that, without such tracing and assessment and delineation, we cannot know the extent to which these criticisms are valid and the extent to which they project Austin's own temper. (2) To point out that Austin often gives no reasons whatever for thinking one or other of them true, never making out the application to a philosopher of a term like "mistaken" or "imprecise" or "bogus" or the like according to anything like the standards he imposes in his own constructions. This discrepancy is not, I believe, peculiar to Austin, however clearer in him than in other philosophers; my feeling is that if it could be understood here, one would understand something about the real limitations, or liabilities, of the exercise of philosophy. (3) To register the fact that his characteristic terms of criticism are new terms, new for our time at least, though not in all cases his alone; and that these new modes of criticism are deeply characteristic of modern philosophy. (4) To suggest that if such terms do not seem formidable directions of criticism, and perhaps not philosophical at all (as compared, say, with terms such as "meaningless," "contradiction," "circular," and so forth), that may be because philosophy is only just learning, for all its history of self-criticism and self-consciousness, to become conscious of itself in a new way, at further ranges of its activity. One could say that attention is being shifted from the character of a philosopher's argument to the character of the philosopher arguing. Such a shift can, and perhaps in the Anglo-American tradition of philosophy generally does, serve the purest political or personal motive: such criticism would therefore rightly seem philosophically irrelevant, if sometimes academically charming or wicked. The shift could also, one feels, open a new literary-philosophical criticism, in a tradition which knows how to claim, for example, the best of Kierkegaard and Nietzsche. Whatever the outcome, however, what I am confident of is that the relevance of the shift should itself become a philosophical problem. (5) To urge, therefore, a certain caution

or discrimination in following Austin's procedures, using his attempts to define in new and freer and more accurate terms the various failings — and hence the various powers — of philosophy, without imitating his complacency, and even prejudice, in attaching them where he sees (but has not proven) fit. It suggests itself that a sound procedure would be this: to enter all criticisms which seem right, but to treat them phenomenologically, as temptations or feelings; in a word, as data, not as answers.

These purposes are meant to leave us, or put us, quite in the dark about the sources of philosophical failure, and about the relation between the tradition of philosophy and the new critics of that tradition, and indeed about the relation between any conflicting philosophies. For quite in the dark is where we ought to know we are. If, for example, that failure of Moore's which we discussed earlier is not to be understood as a mistake, then what is it? No doubt it would be pleasanter were we able not to ask such a question — except that philosophy seems unable to proceed far without criticizing its past, any more than art can proceed without imitating it, or science without summarizing it. And anything would be pleasanter than the continuing rehearsals — performable on cue by any graduate student in good standing — of how Descartes was mistaken about dreams, or Locke about truth, or Berkeley about God, or Kant about things-in-themselves or about moral worth, or Hegel about "logic," or Mill about "desirable," and so forth; or about how Berkeley mistook Locke, or Kant Hume, or Mill Kant, or everybody Mill, and so forth. Such "explanations" are no doubt essential, and they may account for everything we need to know, except why any man of intelligence and vision has ever been attracted to the subject of philosophy. Austin's criticisms, where they stand, are perhaps as external and snap as any others, but he has done more than any philosopher (excepting

Wittgenstein) in the Anglo-American tradition to make clear that there is a coherent tradition to be dealt with. If he has held it at arm's length, and falsely assessed it, that is just a fault which must bear its own assessment; it remains true that he has given us hands for assessing it in subtler ways than we had known. The first step would be to grant to philosophers the ordinary rights of language and vision Austin grants all other men: to ask of them, in his spirit, why they should say what they say where and when they say it, and to give the *full story* before claiming satisfaction. That Austin pretends to know the story, to have heard it all before, is no better than his usual antagonist's assumption that there is no story necessary to tell, that everything is fine and unproblematic in the tradition, that philosophers may use words as they please, possessing the right or power — denied to other mortals — of knowing, without investigating, the full source and significance of their words and deeds.

It is characteristic of work like Austin's — and this perhaps carries a certain justice — that criticism of it will often take the form of repudiating it as philosophy altogether. Let me conclude by attempting to make one such line of criticism less attractive than it has seemed to some philosophers to be.

A serviceable instance is provided by a sensational book published a few years ago by Mr. Ernest Gellner (*Words and Things*, London, 1959) in which this author congratulates himself for daring to unmask the sterility and mystique of contemporary English philosophy by exposing it to sociology. First of all, unmasking is a well-turned modern art, perhaps *the* modern intellectual art, and its practitioners must learn not to be misled themselves by masks, and to see their own. I mean both that unmasking is itself a phenomenon whose sociology needs drawing, and also that the philosophy Gellner "criticizes" is itself devoted to unmasking. If, as one supposes, this modern art develops with the weakening or growing irrelevance of given conventions and institutions, then the position of the unmasker is by its nature socially unhinged, and his responsibility for his position becomes progressively rooted in his single existence. This is the occasion for finding a mask or pose of one's own (sage, prophet, saint, and so forth). Austin was an Englishman, an English professor. If I say he *used* this as a mask, I mean to register my feeling that he must, somewhere, have known his criticisms to be as unjustified as they were radical, but felt them to be necessary in order that his work get free, and heard. It would have served him perfectly, because its Englishness made it unnoticeable as a pose, because what he wanted from his audience required patience and cooperation, not depth and upheaval, and because it served as a counterpoise to Wittgenstein's strategies of the sage and the ascetic (which Nietzsche isolated as the traditional mask of the Knower; that is, as the only form in which it could carry authority).

Far from a condemnation, this is said from a sense that in a modern age to speak the truth may require the protection of a pose, and even that the necessity to posture may be an authentic mark of the possession of truth. It may not, too; that goes without saying. And it always is dangerous, and perhaps self-destructive. But to the extent it is necessary, it is not the adoption of pose which is to be condemned, but the age which makes it necessary. (Kierkegaard and Nietzsche, with terrible consciousness, condemned both themselves and the age for their necessities; and both maintained, at great cost, the doubt that their poses were really necessary — which is what it must feel like to know your pose.)

The relation of unmasking to evaluation is always delicate to trace. Gellner vulgarly imagines that his sociological reduction in itself proves the intellectual inconsequence and social irrelevance or political conservatism of English philosophy. (His feeling is common enough; why such psychological or sociological analyses appear to their performers — and to some of their audience — as reductive in this way is itself a promising subject of psychological and sociological investigation.) Grant for the argument that his analysis of this philosophy as a function of the Oxford and Cambridge tutorial system, the conventions of Oxford conversation, the distrust of ideology, the training in classics and its companion ignorance of science, and so forth, is accurate and relevant enough. Such an analysis would at most show the conditions or outline the limitations — one could say it makes explicit the conventions — within which this work was produced or initiated. To touch the question of its value, the value of those conventions themselves, as they enter the texture of the work, would have to be established. This is something that Marx and Nietzsche and Freud, our teachers of unmasking, knew better than their progeny.

Still, it can seem surprising that radical and permanent philosophy can be cast in a mode which merges comfortably in the proprieties of the common room — in the way it can seem surprising that an old man, sick and out of fortune, constructing sayings (in consort with others) polite enough for the game in a lady's drawing room,

and entertaining enough to get him invited back, should have been saying the maxims of La Rochefoucauld.

Seven published papers are not many, and those who care about Austin's work will have felt an unfairness in his early death, a sense that he should have had more time. But I think it would be wrong to say that his work remains incomplete. He once said to me, and doubtless to others: "I had to decide early on whether I was going to write books or to teach people how to do philosophy usefully." Why he found this choice necessary may not be clear. But it is as clear as a clear Berkeley day that he was above all a teacher, as is shown not merely in any such choice, but in everything he wrote and (in my hearing) spoke, with its didactic directions for profitable study, its lists of exercises, its liking for sound preparation and its disapproval of sloppy work and lazy efforts. In example and precept, his work is complete, in a measure hard to imagine matched. I do not see that it is anywhere being followed with the completeness it describes and exemplifies. There must be, if this is so, various reasons for it. And it would be something of an irony if it turned out that Wittgenstein's manner were easier to imitate than Austin's; in its way, something of a triumph for the implacable professor.

21

STUART HAMPSHIRE

THE INTERPRETATION OF LANGUAGE:

WORDS AND CONCEPTS

There are many languages, constantly changing and widely different from each other, not only in vocabulary, but also in structure. It would be a mistake to think of Language, with a capital L, as some Platonic ideal language to which actual languages in different degrees approximate. Different languages have enough in common, as signalling systems, and serve sufficiently similar purposes in social behaviour, to make us call them languages. But we do not in philosophy need to state precisely what are the necessary and sufficient conditions for calling a signalling system a language; for we are not particularly concerned with defining the word 'language'. Nor are we concerned with a systematic classification of the different grammatical forms of language; the interest of contemporary philosophers in forms of speech neither is, nor should be, scientific or systematic. They describe the use of particular idioms in particular languages, and the adaptation of the idioms to particular purposes, only as instances of different functions in speech; and the instances are not selected as evidence in support of some generalization about Language; there is no serious attempt to arrive

by induction at a list of ultimate categories or ultimate functions of language. (Philosophy is not an inductive inquiry; its statements of fact are the citation of examples, not the production of evidence.) This painstaking description of actual, contemporary English or German idioms has so far had a largely negative and destructive purpose: to upset philosophical preconceptions about the necessary forms and functions of language, particularly the preconceptions of Hume and Mill and Russell. No positive conclusions about the necessary forms of language could properly be based on such narrow and haphazard investigations. Perhaps it may sometimes seem that the linguistic analysts are themselves deceived, and that they have some preconceptions of their own about the necessary and universal forms of language. They sometimes write as if there were just so many statable functions which language must fulfil, or (worse) they sometimes write as if all languages must be intertranslatable dialects of the Platonic ideal language. With unacknowledged provincialism, they seem sometimes to be generalizing about a whole range of discourse on the basis of a few contemporary idioms. They sometimes ignore the history of the concepts which they examine, where a 'concept' is a whole family of related idioms taken together. Every concept has a history, and the clearest way of introducing the concept

Reprinted from *British Philosophy in the Mid-Century*, ed. C. A. Mace (London: George Allen & Unwin Ltd.; New York: The Macmillan Co., 1957), pp. 267–79; by permission of the author and the publisher. (Copyright 1957 by George Allen & Unwin Ltd.)

is to trace its history, the changes through which it has passed, as old idioms drop out and new idioms come in. If philosophers were positively and primarily interested in describing and distinguishing the different uses of language, as they sometimes now claim that they are, they would be historians before all else; but they are conspicuously not historians. They are in fact content with a haphazard selection of instances from any one field of discourse, because, whether they acknowledge it or not, they are generally making a negative point — that the discourse of the kind examined does not serve the purposes which previous philosophers had implied that it must serve.

Ambiguity of purpose in linguistic analysis might mislead philosophers seriously; they might step outside the purely negative conclusions, and try to deduce philosophical conclusions from the description of a few English idioms. I will give two examples of how this mistake may be made:

(a) In the characterization of moral judgments;

(b) In the characterization of mental concepts, and in recent discussions of the concept of mind.

In learning a language, which is part of a civilization largely different from one's own, one would expect to be able to pick out a class of utterances which play a part in social behaviour analogous to the part played in our own behaviour by what we call moral judgments; and one would also expect, with rather less confidence, that there would be sentence-forms which occupy, within this unfamiliar language, some place analogous to the place occupied by ought-sentences, or by quasi-imperative or (perhaps) gerundive forms, in English or Latin. If both these expectations were correct and there was this identifiable class of utterances having some distinguishing grammar of its own, it still would not follow that our moral judgments would be translatable, in any ordinary sense of 'translation', into the strangers'

language, or that theirs would be translatable into ours. We might have to say that they had a central concept (e.g. of 'virtue') which we had not got, and that they did not have our corresponding concept of 'virtue', i.e. the concept which would seem to have the nearest corresponding place in our terminology. We might learn to understand their language, in the sense of being able to use it in full communication with them, producing the appropriate expressions in the appropriate situations; we should so far have entered into their manner of thought and into their way of classifying and assessing human behaviour. Partly because we understood their idioms so well, in this ordinary sense of 'understand', we might see that it was impossible to find any equivalents in our own store of moral terms for those expressions which we have singled out as their moral terms; when we lay one language over the other, as a piece of tracing paper, we find that the lines and divisions do not sufficiently coincide at any point. To take a comparatively trivial and easy example: we find this non-correspondence even in Greek discussions of 'virtue', and we find it wherever no distinction of any kind is marked between the moral and natural qualities of persons. A choice is then presented: we may say, if we choose, that the users of this language have a radically different morality from ours, that their moral views and attitudes are altogether different: or we may say that, strictly speaking, they do not make what can properly be called moral judgments at all. It is not incorrect to take the first alternative, provided this kind of difference of moral view is distinguished from the difference of view which is adopted, as a matter of choice and reflection, within a common terminology providing for the expression of other views. And it is not incorrect to take the second, or Kantian alternative, provided that it is made plain that 'moral judgment' is not now being used to single out a speech-function, and is no longer on the same level as 'factual statement', 'command', 'recommendation', etc. It is of little importance for philosophers to decide what makes a moral judgment a moral judgment, that is, to settle the necessary and sufficient conditions for the use of the *expression* 'moral judgment'. But it has been useful, again negatively, to insist that we would in any language single out a class of utterances as moral judgments at least partly on the ground that they are used to prescribe or recommend conduct, where the conduct is not directed towards some given end. This characterization of moral judgments as essentially prescriptive or quasi-imperative is not (or should not be) intended to be precise — indeed the explicatory terms are themselves vague in their application. It is intended solely to counter certain accounts which previous philosophers had given or implied of the use and function of moral judgments. It was a denial of the assumption that they must function in those ways, and in accordance with that logic, which current philosophies recognized; it was negative only, a warning against a false assimilation.

But we are seriously misled if we begin to generalize about the nature of moral judgment on the basis of some examination of the form of our own arguments on moral questions; for then it will seem that there cannot be very different terminologies in which recognizably moral questions (questions of 'What is it, or was it, right to do?'), can be discussed. Here again some study of history is needed in order to engender a decent scepticism. Examination of idioms, and forms of argument, used in current moral discussion, cannot by itself lead to any positive answer to any question posed in moral philosophy; at the most it can lead to an historically interesting description of one conventional morality. It is possible for someone fully to understand, and to be able to use correctly, the idioms of conventional morality, while rejecting this whole terminology as superstitious or as in some other way inadequate. For instance, he may fully understand, in the ordinary sense of 'understand', the familiar

Protestant-Christian notion of personal responsibility, and the distinction now conventionally accepted between the moral and the natural qualities of persons. He may be able always to apply this distinction correctly in particular cases, and he may be able to state in general terms how the line of distinction is ordinarily drawn, that is, to give an analysis of the notion of moral responsibility as it now occurs in ordinary language. But he may at the same time consider that the distinction itself is untenable, when all its implications are traced to the end; he may even intelligibly deny that there is such a thing as personal responsibility, while admitting that he understands the ordinary rules of application of the term. He is then in a position similar to (but not the same as) that of the anthropologist, or the student of comparative religion, who learns to use and to understand a language, or part of a language, while denying that many of the distinctions and classifications involved in the language correspond to any reality.

It is not possible consistently to maintain both of the following two propositions: (1) that to understand an expression is to be able to use the expression correctly, and to recognize the standard occasions of its use: and (2) that existential statements have no place among philosophical conclusions, philosophy being solely concerned to analyse the actual meanings of terms in use. One may deny proposition (1), and give reasons for saying that many expressions which have, or have had, an easily recognizable and statable use in this or that language, are strictly meaningless. This was the paradoxical way of the earlier positivists. Alternatively, one may allow that arguments on philosophical questions, arguments which are in no ordinary sense empirical, may properly terminate in existential statements of the form — 'there are no so-and-so's'. This seems to me the more honest and less misleading way out of the dilemma, and certainly it involves no departure from ordinary usage; for this is the form of statement which has generally been used in repudiating a concept. Entirely unrestricted and unqualified existential statements of the form 'There are no so-and-so's' are perhaps uncommon, but their characteristic use is in expressing quasi-philosophical conclusions: 'There is no God' or 'There are no entirely disinterested actions' or 'There is no such thing as sin'. Many examples could be cited, in which the unrestricted existential form is commonly used to repudiate the use of a concept, or of a distinction, on grounds which are not in any simple sense empirical. The step from these quasi-philosophical existential statements to strictly philosophical conclusions is much smaller than the step from 'meaningless' (ordinary use) to 'meaningless' (philosophical use). A man who understands and can explain what is ordinarily meant by 'sin' cannot properly say that the word is meaningless. But he can properly say that there is no such thing as sin. He is not objecting to the *word*, as having no established place in the vocabulary, and no recognized conditions of use; he is objecting to the concept, that is, to the customary application of the whole set of distinctions which are involved in the use of the word. To reject a concept is to reject a whole system of classification as in one way or another inadequate; and the sufficient grounds for the rejection cannot be given without some comparison between different terminologies and systems of classification, a comparison which involves stepping outside any one terminology, and contrasting its method of application with that of some other. A description of the actual use of any one terminology cannot by itself yield an answer to any problem of moral philosophy, since the problem always lies in the choice, and in the grounds of choice, between different terminologies. Methods of classifying, assessing and prescribing human conduct, with the patterns of argument which support the assessments and prescriptions, come into being and disappear in history one after the other, and they are often mutually exclusive. The lines

drawn cannot always be made to coincide and translations are not always possible; we have to find grounds for thinking and talking in one set of idioms rather than another. A moral philosopher must to this extent moralize himself, or he will be confined to the purely negative work of indicating the difference between moral judgments and judgments of other kinds.

The concept of mind has a long and various history, extending through many languages; it is a history which it would be difficult to write, even if one were confined to Greek, Latin, French, German and English. The outlines of the concept of mind have largely changed in the last fifty years, even more largely since Descartes wrote on the passions of the soul, or since Hume wrote on the sentiments and passions. Mind, motive, passion, sentiment, character, mood, heart, soul, temperament, spirit — these are words for which there have at many times been no translations in other languages, or which have radically changed their meanings in complicated ways. The conception of human beings as having master passions, and constant dispositions, has come into being and passed away more than once. The concept of will, or a concept closely related to it, has existed at some time in some languages, and at other times and in other languages it has not existed at all in any easily recognizable form. There have been times and phases in the history of some languages, when states of mind were conceived as entities easily and definitely identified and labelled, very much as physical things are identified and labelled. Our whole conception of personality, and of the limits of self-knowledge and of knowledge of the minds of others, has changed often, and will certainly change again. Regarded as linguistic analysis, Descartes's and Hume's discussions of the concept of mind are largely out of date; and, regarded as linguistic analysis, Professor Ryle's discussion will soon seem out of date also. But through all the phases of its history, the concept of mind preserves some rough continuity;

there is something common to the various different vocabularies which have been used to talk about human personality and experience. Just as there are largely different moral terminologies, which yet form a single type of discourse, to be called 'moral', so one can speak of different conceptions of human personality as conveyed in different vocabularies. A philosopher may be concerned, not to clarify the conventions of use of any one vocabulary, but rather to take instances to show the conditions of use of any such vocabulary; if so, the proper title of this work is 'The Concept of Mind', and not the word 'mind'. Professor Ryle, like Descartes and Hume before him, takes examples from the contemporary English vocabulary to illustrate the requirements which any such vocabulary must satisfy in its application. His philosophical thesis consists of the statement of these requirements, in direct opposition to the conditions of application which Descartes and Hume insist upon. This is where their philosophical difference lies — that they each have a pattern, a different one, of the conditions under which statements can be confirmed, and expressions applied, with the greatest possible confidence and clarity; and they compare and criticize the actual use of psychological expressions by reference to this standard. From this comparison emerges a general thesis about the proper outlines of the concept of mind. But I must first explain what I mean by the conditions of application of an expression.

To understand an expression in common use involves being able to recognize the standard occasions of its use, and the normal way to explain its meaning is to give specimens of these standard occasions. For every element of the vocabulary of a language which we understand, we could describe some conditions which would be the ideal conditions for the application of the expression in question; we could also describe some contrasting conditions in which its application would have to be qualified as dubious and uncertain. When

we have described the conditions of certainty and uncertainty, we have given the conventions of application for the expression in question. One can draw the outlines of the concept of mind, as it is embodied at any one time in any one language, by giving the conventions of application (the method of verification in this sense) of a whole cluster of expressions in the vocabulary; this would so far be a purely descriptive and historical work (e.g. The Greek concept of the soul — The concept of the passions in the eighteenth century). But a more fundamental inquiry may suggest itself: among all the different types of expression in the present vocabulary — descriptions of states of mind, of sensations, dispositions, processes of thought and many others — there are some that seem, in the conventions of their application, entirely clear and unproblematical; for the conditions of certainty in the application of them are not peculiar and have evident parallels in other familiar and unquestioned kinds of discourse; for this reason they do not provoke doubt or philosophical scepticism. There are other types of expression which seem to have altogether peculiar conditions of certainty, without parallel outside this one kind of discourse; and it is at this point that philosophical scepticism and inquiry begins. 'Can we ever be really certain that anything is a so-and-so? When we claim to know, do we really know?' In any period there is a tendency to take one method of confirmation, appropriate to some one type of expression, as the self-explanatory model to which all other types of expression are to be assimilated. To Hume a direct description of a feeling or sensation seemed the type of expression which, in the standard conditions of its use, provided the model of certain knowledge; the different conditions of certainty appropriate to expressions of other types seemed to him open to challenge; it seemed to him that there could not be any certainty comparable with the certainty attached to the description of a sensation. In some contemporary philosophy the model of certainty has become almost exactly the reverse of Hume's. The conditions of certainty appropriate to descriptions of sensations seem problematical and peculiar, the model being descriptions of the behaviour of bodies; therefore a contrary thesis is developed, which tries to assimilate the conditions of certainty for descriptions of sensations to the conditions of certainty appropriate to descriptions of bodily behaviour. The philosophical thesis in each case consists in the assimilation of the different methods of confirmation in actual use to some single self-explanatory pattern. In the ordinary use of language, and until philosophical doubts arise, every type of description in any language is accepted as having its own appropriate conditions of certainty and its own appropriate method of confirmation. The philosophical doubt takes the form of a more general comparison of the degrees of certainty obtainable in the use of different expressions, a comparison which deliberately cuts across the divisions of type. A philosopher in effect says: 'I know of course that these are the conditions which are ordinarily taken as the standard conditions for the use of expressions of this type: but can we ever be certain about the application of any expression of this type, in the sense in which we can have certainty in the application of expressions of this other type?' In asking this question, he is in effect challenging the accepted rules of application for the family of expressions considered; he is suggesting that the concept is otiose, since, when we reflect, we realize that there is no satisfactory way of determining whether something falls under the concept or not. It is a mistake, in exaggerated respect for established usage, to represent this form of scepticism as a pointless eccentricity of philosophers. Even outside philosophy we do make these comparisons between the certainty which can be obtained in the application of expressions of different types, and we do sometimes become dissatisfied with the vagueness of the conventions of application of a whole range of expressions. The family of expressions then tends to drop out of the language and to be replaced by others, which have clearer and more definite (as it seems) conventions of application; this is the process by which concepts are modified, and which makes their history. One example: I may have learnt to use a vocabulary which permits me to explain human behaviour in terms of a small range of passions, each taken to be definitely identifiable. I might be able to use this vocabulary correctly myself, and be able to distinguish, among statements expressed in these terms, those which are certainly true, given the conventions of the vocabulary, from those which are certainly false. But I might at the same time wish to reject the whole vocabulary, perhaps on the ground that its classifications are 'inadequate to the complexity of the facts'. I know how the passions are conventionally identified, but the identification seems to me too uncertain, when judged by some external standard of certainty which I have taken as a model. I might argue that the conditions under which certainty is conventionally claimed in the application of such expressions do not sufficiently resemble the standard conditions of certainty for expressions of similar type. Even in the more favourable conditions for distinguishing one passion from another, there too often remains a greater possibility of doubt than would be allowed in (for instance) the identification of natural kinds. The proportion of borderline cases to unchallengeable cases is too high, and higher than the form of the statements themselves would suggest. If I am persuaded that, judged by these external standards, no ideally certain case of the identification of a passion exists, or could exist, then I am persuaded that the use of this vocabulary is radically misleading; the concept of simple passions will be discredited. I could correctly express my conviction that the whole terminology is inapplicable by saying that in reality there are no simple passions to be found, and that the facts cannot in general be represented within this framework. Many modern writers, not mainly philosophers, have in fact wished to make exactly this negative existential statement ('There are no simple passions'), and their influence, together with the influence of Freudian psychology, has been enough to make the old classifications of motives almost obsolete over a large range of human conduct: or if not obsolete, at least suspect, so that in conditions in which the identifications would formerly have been made confidently and without qualification, they are now made tentatively and with qualifications and this, if pressed far enough, will amount to a change in the conditions of use of the expressions, and so will amount to a change in their meaning. The concept of the passions will no longer be what it was. Ordinarily sections of the vocabulary become obsolete, and concepts (e.g. the concept of motive) change their outlines, very gradually and without conscious planning or decision; the conventions of application of expressions of different types are not explicitly compared, and the scepticism about a particular range of expressions is felt in practice, rather than worked out in theory. As soon as scepticism is based on a weighted comparison between the conditions of certainty attached to expressions of different types, one has entered the domain of philosophy; this is the form of argument to be found in Professor Ryle's *Concept of Mind*, no less than in all his predecessors. And the argument naturally leads him, for the reasons which I have suggested, to make unqualified existential statements, e.g. in denying the existence of acts of will or of impalpable mental processes, and in asserting the existence of hankerings, cravings and itchings. He has been criticized for expressing any conclusions in an existential form, on the grounds that no existential conclusions can follow from a second-order inquiry into the common uses of words. But the criticism is misplaced, since he is not merely describing the actual uses of words. He

quotes instances of the conventions of application of different expressions, and then tries to represent these conventions of application as fitting into a common pattern. In respect of any expression taken as an example, his first questions always are — 'How do we know when to apply it? What are the standard and most favourable conditions for its use?' He circumscribes the permissible uses of psychological expressions by reference to his own standard of verification. And so he can maintain that there could not be a 'neat sensation' vocabulary, since nothing which he would count as verification, or as certainty in application, would be attached to expressions so used. The conventions of application suggested for a vocabulary of this type diverge too widely from what he takes to be the standard; for he finds this standard of certainty in the conventions governing the use of physical descriptions. He argues his thesis against Hume and Russell by trying to show that, even in apparently recalcitrant cases, the actual conventions of application attached to expressions of different types conform more nearly to his standard than to theirs; and this is the relevance of the instances from ordinary language to the general philosophical thesis. But it remains true that it is a positive thesis, setting up one standard of clear discourse as against another.

In order to define somebody's philosophy, it is enough to discover what existential statements he takes to be unproblematical and in need of no further explanation. And in order to discover what existential statements he takes as unproblematical, it must be enough to discover what kind of discourse provides him with his model of absolute certainty in the use of language — 'this is as certain as anything can be' (e.g. 'as that $2+2=4$', or 'as that I am sitting in this room'). There has always been this connection between the so-called theory of knowledge — i.e. the critical comparison of the conditions of certainty in application attached to expressions of different types — and metaphysics; in fact the two cannot be separated, or even in the end distinguished. Someone who, in exaggerated respect for the common sense of the moment, refuses to make such weighted and critical comparisons, refuses to enter the domain of philosophy. Any vocabulary that we use carries with it its own existential implications; if, applying the actual conventions in use, one distinguishes between true and false statements about acts of will, or about motives, or character, or the soul, it is inevitable that one should sometimes pause to ask whether these conventions provide that kind of certainty in identification which, unreflectingly, we had assumed that they do provide. If, after the comparison, we have lost confidence in our ordinary method of identifying the passions (it was more unlike the standard cases of identification than it seemed), we shall properly say that there are no simple emotions to be identified. This will not imply that there is no difference between what we have counted, by applying the ordinary conventions, as true and as false statements about the passions; it will imply only that the difference between a particular passion existing or not existing was not as sharply marked as we had assumed, for we noticed the enormous possibilities of uncertain and borderline cases and the few possibilities of certain cases. And when we draw attention to this misleadingness, we go beyond the mere plotting of the ordinary uses of words. This plotting is a necessary check within philosophy, but it is not the whole of philosophy.

· PART IV ·

Recapitulations, Reconsiderations, and Future Prospects

22

DUDLEY SHAPERE

PHILOSOPHY AND THE ANALYSIS OF LANGUAGE

Both Wittgenstein, in the *Tractatus Logico-Philosophicus*, and Russell, advancing the philosophy of Logical Atomism, maintained that statements are. or purport to be, records of facts. Wittgenstein held that philosophers, by improperly interpreting language, create for themselves pseudoproblems, and that, to avoid confusion, we should throw statements into a form in which their true function, that of picturing facts, would be revealed more clearly and readily than it is in ordinary language.

Russell agreed that the statements of ordinary language should be translated into another form. But for him the reason for such translation was not just that ordinary language, while it functions perfectly well in ordinary life, misleads philosophers, but also, and more important, that ordinary language really gives an incorrect portrayal of facts. And only by translating the statements of ordinary language into a form which *does* reflect facts accurately can philosophical progress be made. For Russell, such progress was not merely (as it was for Wittgenstein) of the negative sort that consists of the elimination of confusion, but of the positive sort that consists of the discovery of new information about facts.[1]

In this paper, I wish, first, to consider

Reprinted from *Inquiry*, III (1960), 29–48, by permission of the author and the editor. (Copyright 1960 by The Norwegian Research Council for Science and the Humanities.)

these two views, showing some of the reasons why they are open to severe criticisms, not all of which have yet been made fully clear; and second, to show how, by dropping or modifying some of the fundamental theses of these two views, certain positions highly influential in philosophy today have arisen.

I will begin my discussion with a study of one of the most famous and influential articles of what might be called the "Transition Period" of Twentieth Century philosophical analysis — the period, that is,

[1] In sharpening this distinction between the views of the *Tractatus* and Logical Atomism, this essay will be in disagreement with several current interpretations of Wittgenstein's early thought. Warnock, for example, in expounding the view of the *Tractatus*, claims that "This was in fact closely related to Russell's Logical Atomism; it could be called perhaps a more consistent, more thorough, and therefore more extreme working out of some of Russell's principles and ideas." (G. J. Warnock, *English Philosophy Since 1900* (London: Oxford, 1958), p. 64.) Urmson, though he admits that Wittgenstein's early thought was probably different from Russell's (as Wittgenstein himself insisted it was), nevertheless maintains that "it was the sort of interpretation I have given" — of Wittgenstein as a Logical Atomist, — "right or wrong, which was accepted in the period under examination." (J. O. Urmson, *Philosophical Analysis* (Oxford: Clarendon, 1956), pp. ix–x.) It will be an incidental purpose of the present essay to argue that the differences between the views of the *Tractatus* and those of the *Philosophical Investigations* are not as great as the Logical Atomist interpretation of the former would suggest; and to show that the influence of the purely therapeutic character of the *Tractatus* was greater than Urmson says it was.

between the *Tractatus* and Logical Atomism on the one hand, and the later views of Wittgenstein and the present views of Austin and others on the other. This article, which even today holds the place of honor in one of our most-used anthologies, is Ryle's "Systematically Misleading Expressions."[2] My reasons for centering attention on this article are as follows. First, it advances, simultaneously and inconsistently, both of the views outlined above; and in spite of this inconsistency, it advances each of its incompatible theses in a clear and powerful way, making plain the changes which it had to make in the original formulations of them. Second, because of its clearness, it wears its difficulties (and hence those of a whole tradition) on its sleeve, and thus points the way to later developments. Thus, through a close examination of this article, we will be able to survey the whole development of at least one side of Twentieth Century philosophy deriving from the above-mentioned views of Russell and Wittgenstein, and to evaluate some of the strengths and weaknesses of the earlier phases of that tradition.

I

The argument of "Systematically Misleading Expressions" departs from the following thesis:

There are many expressions which occur in non-philosophical discourse which, though they are perfectly clearly understood by those who use them and those who hear or read them, are nevertheless couched in grammatical or syntactical forms which are in a demonstrable way *improper* to the states of affairs which they record (or the alleged states of affairs which they profess to record). (pp. 86–87)

[2] G. Ryle, "Systematically Misleading Expressions," *Proceedings of the Aristotelian Society*, (1931–32); reprinted in A. G. N. Flew, *Logic and Language*, First Series (Oxford: Blackwell, 1952).
Editor's note: Also reprinted above at pp. 85–100. References are to the pagination in this volume.

Although such grammatical forms do not obscure from the ordinary man in his everyday business the true meaning of the expressions, to anyone who tries to analyze them closely they present a vicious trap.

. . . those who, like philosophers, must generalize about the *sorts* of statements that have to be made of *sorts* of facts about *sorts* of topics, cannot help treating as clues to the logical structures for which they are looking the grammatical forms of the common types of expressions in which these structures are recorded. And these clues are often misleading. (p. 92)

Such expressions, Ryle finds, fall into fairly definite groups or classes, each class being misleading in a certain way. Hence they are not simply misleading; they are "systematically misleading," in that they can be classified according to the type of presupposition which, in our attempt to analyze them, they tempt us to make. Thus in speaking of such expressions he says:

. . . all alike are misleading in a certain direction. They all suggest the existence of new sorts of objects, or, to put it in another way, they are all temptations to us to 'multiply entities'. In each of them . . . an expression is misconstrued as a denoting expression which in fact does not denote, but only looks grammatically like expressions which are used to denote. (p. 98)

Ryle lists several types of systematically misleading expressions: quasi-ontological, quasi-platonic, quasi-descriptive, and quasi-referential. Each type is misleading in its own way: what they all have in common is that they mislead philosophers to add entities beyond what the facts really warrant. We might put Ryle's point metaphorically by saying that philosophers are led to add entities "behind" (quasi-ontological), "above" (quasi-platonic), and "along side of" (quasi-descriptive and quasi-referential) entities which are elements of states of affairs. (Ryle incidentally lists two other types of systematically misleading expressions (pp. 32–33), but these do not seem to differ radically from the above, for they too suggest to the analyst a multiplication of entities.)

This trap must and can be avoided; for

what is expressed in one expression can often be expressed in expressions of quite different grammatical forms, and . . . of two expressions, each meaning what the other means, which are of different grammatical forms, one is often more systematically misleading than the other.

And this means that while a fact or state of affairs *can* be recorded in an indefinite number of statements of widely differing grammatical forms, it is stated better in some than in others. (p. 98)

From these considerations Ryle draws a conclusion pertinent to philosophy.

Such expressions can be reformulated and for philosophy but *not* for non-philosophical discourse must be reformulated into expressions of which the syntactical form is proper to the facts recorded (or the alleged facts alleged to be recorded). (p. 87)

II

Underlying Ryle's argument is a theory of the relationship between language and the world which statements are about. This theory is a development, often in the same terminology, of certain views which were for the most part due to Wittgenstein, and which were presented in the *Tractatus* and Russell's papers on Logical Atomism. Ryle, however, often gives detail where Wittgenstein gave only bare sketches; he also tries to avoid some of the objections which had been or could be raised against the views of Russell and the *Tractatus*.

For Ryle, as for Wittgenstein and Russell, every significant statement is, or rather purports to be, a record. What a statement records they called a "fact," a "state of affairs," or "(what is) the case," using these expressions interchangeably. (But *cf.*, below, Note 3.)

Developing this Wittgensteinian theory of the relation of language to reality in detail, Ryle states that in order to qualify as purporting to be a record, a sequence of words must fulfill two conditions: (1) it must have certain constituents, and (2) these constituents must be arranged in a certain order or structure. (p. 87) Presumably corresponding to these two conditions of a significant statement, there are two aspects or components of a state of affairs: (1) a "subject of attributes" or several such subjects, together with their attributes, and (2) the "logical form" or "logical structure" of the fact. Sometimes Ryle also speaks as though expressions in general — single words and phrases as well as whole statements — record facts (though he also speaks of "events" in this connection[3]); but this usage does not seem consonant with his main trend of thought.

Ryle fails to analyze for our benefit the "certain structure" which a significant statement must have in order to be significant; but the constituents of a true statement seem for him to record either the subjects or the attributes, depending on unspecified syntactical factors. To parallel this, we would expect to find him saying that the grammatical form of the statement bears (or ought to bear) some kind of reference to the logical structure of a fact. On this point, however, there is a great deal of obscurity in the article. Certainly Wittgenstein supposed that the logical syntax of language parallels the structure of facts,[4] and held that the structure of facts

---

[3] Whitehead's metaphysics took events rather than facts as the ultimate building-blocks of reality; and perhaps this accounts for Ryle's otherwise unaccountable introduction here of the term "event," and also for his habitual alternation of "facts or states of affairs": possibly he wanted to surmount the whole problem of facts versus events by relying on an expression which would allow for either solution: "state of affairs" could be construed as *either* "fact" *or* "event," depending on the way philosophers finally decided the question. Ryle's attention would certainly have been called to Whitehead's views by Russell's frequent admiring references to them: Whitehead had explained points in terms of events, and Russell was fond of giving this analysis as a second example (in addition to his own theory of descriptions, which Ramsey pronounced a "paradigm of philosophy") of the technique of logical construction.

[4] "That the elements of the picture are combined with one another in a definite way, repre-

would be most clearly reflected by some syntax such as that provided by the system of *Principia Mathematica* (*cf.*, *Tractatus*, 3.325). But much had happened to logic and philosophy in the decade since the publication of the *Tractatus Logico-Philosophicus*. For one thing, Gödel's Theorem had done much to shake the confidence of those who idolized logical systems. Furthermore, difficulties had already been revealed in the supposition that everything in ordinary language can be cast into an extensionalist syntax without gain or loss of meaning; and finally, and most important, the possibility of syntactical systems other than that of *Principia* was beginning to be understood. Why, then, should the grammatical structure provided by *Principia* have any special priority, in that the structure of facts should be represented better or more naturally by it than by any alternative system? Where, indeed, had Russell and Wittgenstein gotten the incredible assumption that the world must conform to the specifications of logic? (No wonder Russell said that "My philosophy is the philosophy of Leibniz"!) Only one step more needed to to be taken to reach an even more fundamental question: Why should it not be that the choice of syntax is simply a matter of convention, rather than of the nature of things?

That Ryle was aware of these difficulties is shown in the "consequential" question he raises toward the end of the article: ". . . is this relation of propriety of grammatical to logical form *natural* or *conventional*?" p. 99) On the one hand, he does "not see how, save in a small class of specially-chosen cases, a fact or state of affairs can be deemed like or even unlike

in structure a sentence, gesture or diagram." (p. 99) For in a fact, he "can see no concatenation of bits such that a concatenation of parts of speech could be held to be of the same general architectural plan as it." (p. 99) Certainly here is a denial of the Wittgensteinian view that "In order to understand the essence of the proposition, consider hieroglyphic writing, which pictures the facts it describes. And from it came the alphabet without the essence of the representation being lost." (*Tractatus*, 4.016) And it makes us wonder about Ryle's own statement, in this very same article, that systematically misleading expressions

must be reformulated into expressions of which the syntactical form is proper to the facts recorded (or the alleged facts alleged to be recorded). (p. 87)

Yet on the other hand, Ryle finds that "it is not easy to accept what seems to be the alternative that it is just by convention that a given grammatical form is specially dedicated to facts of a given logical form." (p. 99) Thus he feels himself unable to reject entirely the idea that there is at least some kind of parallel between grammatical form and the form of facts, though he is unable to describe the exact locus of that parallel.

But not only is the relationship between statements and the facts they record obscure; Ryle's account of "facts" themselves is also unclear — again, no doubt, an effect of the critical analysis to which that notion had been subjected (it is to be noted particularly that Ryle speaks only of "facts," never — as did Russell and Wittgenstein — of "atomic facts"). For we are told that "a fact is not a collection — even an arranged collection — of bits in the way in which a sentence is an arranged collection of noises or a map an arranged collection of scratches. A fact is not a thing and so is not even an arranged thing" (p. 99) Contrast this with the simple (perhaps naïve) view expressed by Wittgenstein in the *Tractatus*: "The configuration

---

sents that the things are so combined with one another. This connection of the elements of the picture is called its structure" (*Tractatus*, 2.15); "The logical picture of the facts is the thought" (*ibid.*, 3); "The thought is the significant proposition" (*ibid.*, 4); "To the configuration of the simple signs in the propositional sign corresponds the configuration of the objects in the state of affairs" (*ibid.*, 3.21).

of the objects forms the atomic fact" (2.0272); "The way in which objects hang together in the atomic fact is the structure of the atomic fact" (2.032). Ryle has told us that we are not to understand the term "fact" as Wittgenstein did; but he has not told us how we are to understand it.

Sometimes, too, he speaks as though there were only one kind of fact — the kind which we should shape statements to meet — and sometimes as though there were *sorts* of facts, so that even systematically misleading expressions indicate or seem to indicate "sorts" of facts. Indeed, according to some passages, such expressions really only record *real* facts and only seem to record unreal ones. (*Cf.* the following quotations: " . . . they are couched in a syntactical form improper to the facts recorded and proper to facts of quite another logical form than the facts recorded" (p. 87); " 'Satan is not a reality' from its grammatical form looks as if it recorded the same sort of fact as 'Capone is not a philosopher' " (p. 90).

III

The difficulties of Ryle's account of the relationship between language and the world, and his failure to define the "form" and "content" of each, leave much to be desired; and these problems were not peculiar to his view, either, but were the common heritage of his tradition. But closer inspection of the article leads us beyond these questions, exposing still deeper ambiguities and more profound problems: problems which are, in fact, among the most profound in Twentieth Century philosophy; for, in essence, they are among the questions over which Wittgenstein, re-evaluating the ideas of the *Tractatus*, brooded for a decade.

These questions which we must now ask in reference to Ryle's views are: Why should he have supposed it necessary, for the theories which he advances, to introduce the notion of facts? Was he correct in assuming that his view of translation — of analysis — requires some such notion? And finally, if his notion of facts is superfluous, what remains of his theory?

It would indeed be a mistake to suppose that, if a criterion for distinguishing between two classes cannot be formulated explicitly and precisely, the distinction is useless or non-existent. But particularly when the distinction is a fundamental one, introduced partly for the technical purpose of refuting opponents, philosophers cannot afford to let it rest on an uncritical and intuitive basis; for it is the very distinction that must be defended in order to justify the criticisms which it makes possible. And Ryle must often have felt that, for his special kind of translation, which consists of going from a "more misleading" to a "less misleading" form of expression, he would have to formulate some criterion of misleadingness, or, conversely, of propriety of grammatical form: some clear procedure or technique by which we can decide, at least in many cases, whether or not a statement is misleading, and, further, by which we can go about remedying this misleadingness.

One possible view would be that extra-linguistic facts serve as the grounds or standards according to which we, as philosophers, strive to model our ways of saying things. In order to serve as such standards, these facts would have to be known clearly, at least to a careful observer — whatever might be meant by "careful." This view naturally assumes the explication of the exact relationship between statements and the facts which they record; only then could we understand what is meant by "modelling" statements after facts.

A great many of Ryle's statements suggest that this is actually his view: ". . . there is, after all, a sense in which we can properly inquire and even say 'what it really means to say so and so'. For we can ask what is the real form of the fact recorded when this is concealed or disguised and not duly exhibited by the expression in question." (p. 100) But if in some moods he did hold this, at other moments he must have been deeply troubled by the difficulties — discussed at such length in this century — of defining explicitly the "given" in experience. For a large number of other statements suggest that Ryle believes, not that facts are clearly known to an observer and can therefore be used as the criteria of the form into which philosophers ought to throw expressions, but the entirely different view that expressions properly formulated can give us a clue to the form of facts otherwise not clearly known.

. . . as the way in which a fact *ought* to be recorded in expressions *would* be a clue to the form of that fact, we jump to the assumption that the way in which a fact *is* recorded *is* such a clue. And very often the clue is misleading and suggests that the fact is of a different form from what really is its form. (p. 90)

. . . those who, like philosophers, must generalize about the *sorts* of statements that have to be made of *sorts* of facts about *sorts* of topics, cannot help treating as clues to the logical structures for which they are looking the grammatical forms of the common types of expressions in which these structures are recorded. And these clues are often misleading. (p. 92)

Philosophy "must then involve the exercise of systematic restatement. . . . Its restatements are transmutations of syntax . . . controlled . . . by desire to exhibit the forms of the facts *into which philosophy is the inquiry.*" (p. 100; italics mine.)

Thus the reader may from some remarks be led to think that Ryle holds that the common man is able to discern the true form of facts, and that only a few overly analytical philosophers are misled by the form in which those facts are expressed — so that with just the proper amount of attention to the facts, the true form of those facts can be made clearly discernible in the grammatical form, and the philosophers' errors avoided; and this

is a view quite reminiscent of the *Tractatus.*[5] But now it appears that Ryle believes, with Russell in his Logical Atomism period, that the true form of facts is to be *discovered*, at least by philosophers, through an analysis of the proper form of expressions; philosophy is again, as it was not for Wittgenstein (*cf., Tractatus,* 4.111), a science.

The philosopher errs, it appears now, not in trying to discover the form of the facts, but in considering the grammatical form of an expression as a clue to the discovery of that form; whereas what would really furnish such a clue (and what should therefore be the object of the philosopher's search) would be the true form of the expression. How, then, are we to find this true form? It is perhaps in line with this new suggestion, that a well-expressed statement would give a clue to the form of facts, that Ryle introduces, at the very end of the article, a new procedure for deciding about the propriety or impropriety of a statement.

How are we to discover in particular cases whether an expression is systematically misleading or not? I suspect that the answer to this will be of this sort. We meet with and understand and even believe a certain expression such as 'Mr. Pickwick is a fictitious person' and 'the Equator encircles the globe.' And we know that if these expressions are saying what they seem to be saying, certain other propositions will follow. But it turns out that the naturally consequential proposi-

[5] The *Tractatus* itself does not employ "facts" (or anything else, for that matter) as criteria for discovering what is the correct formulation of propositions. Wittgenstein is there concerned to show what the logical structure of any possible language must be; and, though he holds that some forms of expression would exhibit the logical form of facts more clearly than others, he does not deal with the question of how we would tell which forms of expression are actually clearest. (Probably he would have held that we simply understand expressions, and need no criterion to tell us what they mean; this is a view also suggested by some passages in Ryle, and I will discuss it presently.) For his successors, however, who wanted to apply his views and eliminate some philosophical confusions, the problem could not fail to arise.

sion such as 'Mr. Pickwick was born in such and such a year' and 'the Equator is of such and such a thickness' are not merely false but, on analysis, in contradiction with something in that from which they seemed to be logical consequences. The only solution is to see that being a fictitious person is not to be a person of a certain sort, and that the sense in which the Equator girdles the earth is not that of being any sort of ring or ribbon enveloping the earth. And this is to see that the original propositions were not saying what they seemed on first analysis to be saying. Paralogisms and antinomies are the evidence that an expression is systematically misleading. (p. 99)

Whether or not a statement is misleading is to be discovered, then, not by an appeal to extralinguistic facts which the statement records more or less properly, but by a direct examination of the statement itself, and the statements which it implies. For example, a statement like, "The wall encircles the city," would, in ordinary contexts, in some sense "imply" the statement, "The wall is of a certain thickness." Now the statement "The equator encircles the globe," might "seem to be saying" something very like what "The wall encircles the city" says — so that the former would imply "The equator is of a certain thickness" in the same way that the latter implies "The wall is of a certain thickness." But in the equator case, such an implication would contradict (in some sense correlative with the sense in which "imply" is used in these contexts) "something" in the original statement. The only way to escape this contradiction, Ryle tells us, is to see that the original statement was not saying what it seemed "on first analysis" to be saying: that statements of this sort "disguise instead of exhibiting the forms of the facts recorded." (p. 100)

Ryle's new procedure for discovering when an expression is misleading, or when an interpretation is incorrect, offers a more modest prize than we might at first have expected; for we find, now, not what the true form of the expression is, but only what it is not (and hence, not what the true form of the fact is, but only what it is not). But can this new criterion show us, "in a demonstrable way" (p. 87), even this?

According to Ryle, the contradiction between "The equator is of a certain thickness" and "The equator encircles the globe" can be removed only if we realize that the latter does not have the "form" the philosopher thinks it has. Yet why is this the only solution? Could an opponent of a Rylean analysis not say, with perfect consistency, that his own analysis of the proposition is the correct one — that the form he attributes to the proposition is the one which truly reveals the form of the facts? Of course he would not take such a line in regard to cases like those Ryle gives as examples. But he might well do so in regard to cases which he claims to be more difficult and important; and in such cases, we might well, on the present view of analysis, have a problem as to which interpretation is the one that really gives a clue to the form of the facts.

Certainly some such answer would be what a Plato or a Meinong or a Russell of *The Problems of Philosophy* would want to give in reply to a Rylean critique. If the philosopher does take such a line, he will be maintaining that he really understands the statement (the form he attributes to it really revealing the facts), while Ryle does not; and Ryle will be maintaining that he really understands the statement, while the philosopher does not. Ryle cannot then prove the philosopher's interpretation to be wrong unless he assumes his own to be right. But simply to assert the denial of the philosopher's contention as a premise, and so "prove" the latter's contention to be wrong, will not serve to prove anything. The philosopher may well be wrong; but Ryle's argument, at least, will not show him to be so.

Ryle is at liberty, of course, to begin by assuming that he understands correctly the expressions under consideration. Only then he must abandon a number of claims he makes in the paper. He must, as we have just seen, abandon his claim to be demonstrating something about the true form of an expression; and this entails abandonment of the claim to be demonstrating something about the form of facts. Further, he must drop the claim that "there is, after all, a sense in which we can properly *inquire* and even say 'what it really means to say so and so' " (p. 100; italics mine), and that the propositions supposedly deducible, under the philosopher's interpretation, from the expression in question prove "*on analysis*, in contradiction with something in that form from which they seemed to be logical consequences" (p. 99; italics mine). For if we understand the expression to begin with — as we must in order to employ the paralogisms and antinomies method — then we need not "inquire" about the meaning, or go through a process of "analysis" to see that it implies or contradicts some other expression which we also understand. And finally, such an approach would make a sham of the paralogisms and antinomies method: for the involved process of finding a contradiction in the philosopher's interpretation of a statement is utterly useless if we know to begin with that that interpretation is incorrect.

Worst of all, still, is the fact that this approach loses the advantage of proving the philosopher in error; and the desire to keep this advantage lies at the heart of the search for a criterion. Some criterion of proper form of an expression seems needed in order to make Ryle's position really an argument. For we would not be able to tell, without first knowing the real intention of a statement, whether or not considering it to have a certain other intention would lead to contradiction; but the real intention is itself what is at issue. Without some criterion, the paralogisms and antinomies procedure amounts either to mere assertion, devoid of any kind of proof or even disproof, or else to an elaborately disguised case of circular reasoning: assuming the denial of a position in order to prove that that position is in error.

The remedies that suggest themselves, however, seem worse than the disease. To reintroduce "facts" as the criteria of misleadingness would again beg the question if the discovery of the facts (or their form) is the goal. And "meanings" or "intentions," even if there were such things, and we could have access to them, and be sure we had not made any error about them, would not settle the present problem; for they would still have to be "correlated" somehow with facts, and this correlation could itself always be questioned consistently by a determined philosopher.[6]

One might hope to salvage the view by a compromise along Logical Atomist lines, by maintaining that we *do* know the structures of *enough* facts to tell us what the structure of language ought to be; and that, once we throw our statements into this form, we will, by inspection of that form, be able to discover new forms of facts (or, perhaps, the forms of new facts).[7] But this line is open to at least two objections: (1) it still hinges on successful analysis of the obscure technical notion of "fact," and its companion notions of "constituents" and "logical form" and their linguistic correlates and the nature of that correlation; and (2) there is no guarantee that all or even any undiscovered facts will necessarily comply with the forms of already known facts.

IV

What lies at the root of the difficulties we have encountered in Ryle's position? Are they peculiar to him — mere products

---

[6] Yet another criterion of misleadingness is suggested by Ryle in this paper, *viz.*, Occam's Razor: a statement is misleading if it tempts us to multiply entities. This criterion is not necessarily connected with the "facts" and "paralogisms" criteria discussed above. I will not deal with it in this paper.

[7] In this paper I will pass over the question whether the Logical Atomists believed that the analysis of language would lead to the discovery of the forms of new facts, or of new forms of facts.

of his own confusion of two distinct theories? Or is there something more fundamentally wrong with the theories themselves — something which encourages or even perhaps forces such confusion? And will the difficulties be removed if some overhauling of the whole approach is made say, for example, the abandonment of the view of language as a record of "facts"?

In order to answer these questions, let us briefly summarize the doctrines we have examined. Beneath the views of the *Tractatus* and Logical Atomism and the traditions they engendered are three fundamental theses, the first two of which were held in common by Russell and Wittgenstein, but the third of which is different for each.

1. *Ordinary language, if it is not flatly self-contradictory, is at least vague, ambiguous, and misleading, and generally fails to permit clear and accurate expression of what we want to say.* This doctrine is fundamental to the *Tractatus*, despite Wittgenstein's remark (5.5563) that "All propositions of our colloquial language are actually, just as they are, logically completely in order": the whole trend of that work, and certainly its influence on others, was along the lines of saying that reconstruction of ordinary language is needed.[8] It is not too much, indeed, to attribute this doctrine to almost the entire philosophical tradition from Thales on; for the program of traditional philosophy has nearly always been conceived, at least tacitly, as the replacement of ordinary ways of looking at the world — and of talking about it — with a new and more precise one.[9]

2. *For a proposition to be expressed clearly and accurately is for the sentence in which it is expressed to "picture" or "record" facts, or, more precisely, for it to "purport to picture or record" facts* (Wittgenstein: to represent a possible combination of "objects"). *This picturing relation between facts and sentences has two aspects:*

i. *A "form" of the sentence which corresponds to or represents the "form" or "structure" of the fact.* The "form" of the sentence (which is the true form of the "proposition") is, of course, not necessarily — not even usually, in ordinary language — the grammatical form; it is rather a "logical" one.

ii. *A "matter" or "content" of the sentence which corresponds to or represents the "constituents" of the fact.* Again, the "content" of a fact or proposition was not necessarily ordinary nouns, pronouns, adjectives, or their factual correlates as ordinarily conceived, but, especially for Wittgenstein, something more fundamental.

This doctrine is a version of the old Correspondence Theory of Truth; and the distinction between "form" and "content" of a proposition did not, either, spring full-grown from the brow of Wittgenstein, but is fundamental to Aristotle's whole philosophy, and reappears clearly in the logical writings of Leibniz; it probably underlies the old distinction between "syncategorematic" and "categorematic" expressions, and certainly underlies the Twentieth Century distinction between "Syntax" and "Semantics." The weighty

---

[8] *Tractatus* 5.5563 must be understood in the light of such passages as 4.014–4.015, and 4.002: ordinary language is (and must be) as much a picture of reality as any other language; but the "law of projection" which projects reality into language (as a "law of projection . . . projects the symphony into the language of the musical score") is an extremely complex one; hence "The silent adjustments to understand colloquial language are enormously complicated." It is to reveal the picturing relation more simply and clearly that philosophical translation is needed: the picturing relation is there, even in ordinary language (otherwise it could not be a language); hence that language is "logically completely in order."

[9] Needless to say, traditional philosophers have looked on this doctrine as a conclusion drawn from a detailed analysis of ordinary ways of looking at things and talking about them — not as an assumption made in advance of their thinking. And the critics of the doctrine — to be discussed below — have not just baldly denied it, but claim that detailed analyses of the particular arguments from which philosophers have drawn this thesis, show these arguments to be in error; and that this fact suggests that perhaps the whole doctrine is in error.

a priori considerations (with which I have not dealt explicitly in this paper) which led Wittgenstein to adopt it and its trailers seem, however, to have been brought into the open first by him.

With regard to the third thesis, Russell and Wittgenstein disagreed. (Whether Russell was fully aware of the disagreement is highly questionable.)

3a. *The function of philosophy is to remove misunderstandings which are the products of linguistic confusions.* (Wittgenstein)

3b. *The function of philosophy is not merely to remove confusions, but, more important, to discover the true form (or forms) of facts.* (Logical Atomism)[10]

These, then, are the fundamental doctrines of Twentieth Century analytic philosophy up to the later thought of Wittgenstein.[11] In this essay we have examined some aspects of these doctrines, and have seen how philosophers of that period struggled to make them precise: how they tried to specify in just what ways ordinary language is vague, ambiguous, and misleading; and to pin down the relations which a perfect language would have to the world — to literalize the picturing metaphor

[10] Some theses of Ryle's own position have been passed over in this essay: (1) that misleadingness is a matter of degree; (2) that perhaps no sentence can ever be freed entirely of misleadingness (*i.e.*, that the ideal language can never be achieved); (3) that misleading statements fall into definite types or classes; and (4) that misleadingness is not relative to the reader or hearer of a sentence, but is an inherent property of it. I have ignored these theses, despite their considerable intrinsic interest, because they are not of such central importance in the overall historical picture with which I am here concerned.

[11] It is sometimes said that the "fundamental assumption" (or "mistake") of these early analytic philosophers lay in the crucial place which they conceived logic to have in the philosophical quest; or, again, that their basic doctrine (and error) was that meaning is naming. But these are merely the trailers of Thesis 2: the crucial importance of logic is asserted by 2i, the doctrine that meaning is naming, by 2ii. All of the theses which I have outlined are central to the positions with which I have been concerned; to maintain that any one of them, or any part of any one of them, is more fundamental than any other, is to falsify the historical picture.

which they believed must indicate the character of that relationship; and to state clearly what the goal of philosophical inquiry is, and to lay down the methods of achieving that goal. We are now in a position to understand the basis of the difficulties which we have encountered.

If one begins — as Wittgenstein began, and as Ryle apparently began — with Thesis 3a, he will be driven to propose some criterion of misleadingness; merely to assume a certain interpretation of an expression will not suffice to refute a contrary interpretation. To these philosophers, with their picture theory of language, the most natural thing to say here seemed to be that a statement is misleading if it does not reflect the facts clearly and accurately: that is, the facts (Thesis 2) provide the starting-point of philosophy, the model according to which the ideal language (Thesis 2) is to be shaped. But the notion of "facts" proved so intractable that ultimately it could achieve nothing; and these philosophers were forced more and more — like Ryle — to fall back on other criteria (which, however, they still thought of as somehow correlated with "facts"): such were "propositions," "(real) meanings," "(real) intentions." And this policy, of course, begs the question; for, stripped bare, it tells us that we can find the real meaning by looking at the real meaning. By this procedure, as we have seen, no *proof* is offered that traditional philosophers were mistaken or misled; the assertions made on the basis of circular reasoning remain just that: mere assertions.

If, on the other hand, one begins with Thesis 3b, supposing to begin with that the logical form of the proposition (the real meaning of the sentence) is known, and uses this to determine what the (forms of the) facts are, he falls into similar difficulties. For how do we tell that *this* is the "proper" form of language, the real meaning of the sentence? Surely not by noting that it conforms to the facts! For that would be saying that we discover the facts by examining sentences which are shaped according to the facts. Yet this is exactly the position in which we found Ryle at one juncture.

In short, it appears that whichever aspect of Thesis 2 we take as primary — whether, in line with Thesis 3a, we take facts as our starting-point and the ideal language as our goal, or, in line with 3b, we take the ideal language as known and the discovery of the facts as the goal — we are driven into circularity: we seem forced to assume *both* that we know the facts, and so can discover the true meaning or real intention or true form of the proposition, *and* that we know the true meaning or real intention or true form of the proposition, and so can discover the facts.[12] It is this tendency, arising necessarily from the weaknesses of the two positions, and not a mere mental lapse, that accounts for the inconsistencies which we have found in Ryle's paper, and which, I believe, close attention will reveal in so many of the basic papers of the early and middle periods of the analytic movement.

V

It is impossible not to ask, at this stage, whether the later developments of analytic philosophy have succeeded in overcoming these weaknesses. To deal with such a question is obviously far beyond the scope of any single essay; but a brief account of the course of development, with regard to the above theses, of later philosophical analysis, can serve as a background for further and more detailed investigations.

Some of the most important developments have emerged from a repudiation of Thesis 1:[13] many philosophers now hold that when we properly understand the roles, the functions, the jobs, the uses (let us avoid the difficult and problem-generating term "meanings") of ordinary expres-

[12] When the next step is taken, and we begin looking for a criterion to tell us *both* what is the true form of the proposition *and* what is the true form of the fact, the differences between the two approaches begin to disappear. This fact has increased the tendency of interpreters to conflate the two fundamentally different initial positions stemming from Theses 3a and 3b.

sions, we will see truly, as Wittgenstein had seen earlier, that "All propositions of our colloquial language are actually, just as they are, logically completely in order."

It must not be supposed, however, that the abandonment of Thesis 1 by many philosophers has resulted in agreement among them as to what the function of philosophy is. But behind the many minor differences as to what that function is, two divergent views can be discerned, one claiming kinship with the later thought of Wittgenstein, the other (agreeing with the first group in abandoning Thesis 1) being led by Professor Austin.

[13] Another very important tradition has refused to relinquish Thesis 1, holding that ordinary language must still be translated into another form. But even for this tradition, this other form is no longer considered to be "correct" in the sense of being a true or accurate representation of the world. Thus Carnap says that "the widely held opinion" that the language recommended by philosophers "must be proved to be 'correct' and to constitute a faithful rendering of 'the true logic'" has led to "pseudo-problems and wearisome controversies." (R. Carnap, *The Logical Syntax of Language* (London: Routledge and Kegan Paul, 1937), pp. xiv–xv.) He maintains rather "that we have in every respect complete liberty with regard to the forms of language; that both the forms of construction for sentences and the rules of transformation . . . may be chosen quite arbitrarily" (*ibid.*, p. xv). The choice of a syntactical system is not to be made on the basis of the "correctness" or "incorrectness" of the system — of whether it corresponds to the "logical form of the facts" — but on the basis of purely pragmatic considerations. And although Carnap in this work explicitly applies his "Principle of Tolerance" only to "syntax," it was not long before the choice of "semantics," too, retreated from the high ground of correctness: the choice, say, between a "sense-datum language" and a "language of appearing" is not to be made on the basis of whether the expressions of one "reach out" to "objects" or "simples" in the world (as Wittgenstein would have had it in the *Tractatus*), but on the basis of "convenience." It was not too long a step from such views to the full-fledged "Logical Pragmatism" of Quine, White, and Goodman; or to the disturbing difficulties concerning "analyticity" and related concepts. But I will not discuss this line of development here; I wish only to point out that it still remains in the tradition of Thesis 1: ordinary language, common sense, is still "vague, cocksure, and self-contradictory," as Russell remarked in *An Outline of Philosophy* (p. 1); and the philosopher's task is still a reconstruction of ordinary language.

(1) This latter group, which really seems to be in the majority at present, will be discussed first, as it is not as much a departure from the views of the early Russell as is sometimes supposed. For, with these philosophers, the "ideal language" of Russell — an artificial construction by philosophers — has been dropped; but in its place, playing a role analogous to that of Russell's ideal language, is ordinary language.

Such a view could, in the light of the criticisms noted in this essay, only be expected to evolve from Logical Atomism; after all,

. . . our common stock of words embodies all the distinctions men have found worth drawing, and the connexions they have found worth marking, in the lifetimes of many generations: these surely are likely to be more numerous, more sound, since they have stood up to the long test of the survival of the fittest, and more subtle, at least in all ordinary and reasonably practical matters, than any that you or I are likely to think up in our armchairs of an afternoon — the most favored alternative method.[14]

Thus, "if a distinction works well for practical purposes in everyday life (no mean feat, for even ordinary life is full of hard cases), then there is sure to be something in it, it will not mark nothing." (Austin, p. 11) It follows that

When we examine what we should say when, what words we should use in what situations, we are looking again not *merely* at words (or "meanings," whatever they may be) but also at the realities we use the words to talk about: we are using a sharpened awareness of words to sharpen our perception of, though not as the final arbiter of, the phenomena. (Austin, p. 8; the qualification, "though not as the final arbiter of," is discussed in Note 15, below.)

The basic error of the Logical Atomists, then, was not in their view that language "marks" something about "realities," but

only in their oversimple view that such "marking" must consist in "picturing." And because the relation between ordinary ways of talking and "the phenomena," "the realities," is not a simple "picturing" one, those early thinkers were led to suppose that ordinary language is imperfect, and so to search for an ideal language. Once we eliminate the naïve mistakes of Thesis 2, therefore, we can deny Thesis 1 and carry out the program of Logical Atomism as expressed in Thesis 3b — remembering, of course, that the word "facts" must not be taken in the way the Logical Atomists took it.[15]

(2) In Part I, Sections 89–107, of the *Philosophical Investigations*, Wittgenstein summarizes and analyzes the development of his own earlier views — the views of the *Tractatus*, and, therefore, of the tradition that developed from those views. He explains why he was led — mistakenly — to think of the task of philosophy as the construction or at least the outlining of

a final analysis of our forms of language, and so a *single* completely resolved form of every expression. That is, as if our usual forms of expression were, essentially, unanalyzed; as if there were something hidden in them that had to be brought to light. . . . It can also be put like this: we eliminate misunderstandings by making our expressions more exact; but now it may look as if we were moving towards a particular state, a state of complete exactness; and as if this were the real goal of our investigation. (*Philosophical Investigations*, I, 91).

The essence of language, he thought then, " 'is hidden from us'; this is the form our problem now assumes. We ask, '*What is language?*' " (I, 92) And this question —

---

[14] J. L. Austin, "A Plea for Excuses," *Proceedings of the Aristotelian Society*, LVII (1956–57), 8.

[15] Austin places two very important qualifications on the use of his technique: (1) we should restrict our application of it to areas of ordinary language which have not been corrupted by philosophical disputes (p. 8); (2) ordinary language must not be considered to be "the final arbiter" of "the phenomena": "ordinary language is *not* the last word: in principle it can everywhere be supplemented and improved upon and superseded. Only remember, it *is* the *first* word." (p. 11)

of what is the essential form of language — he wanted to answer by means of the apparatus of "logical form" and "atomic facts" and their accoutrements. "Thought, language, now appear to us as the unique correlate, picture, of the world." (I, 96) "Its essence, logic, presents an order, in fact the *a priori* order of the world." (I, 97) But

the more narrowly we examine actual language, the sharper becomes the conflict between it and our requirement. (For the crystalline purity of logic was, of course, not a *result of investigation*: it was a requirement.) The conflict becomes intolerable; the requirement is now in danger of becoming empty. . . . Back to the rough ground! (I, 107).

In Sections 108–33, he continues explaining his criticisms of these views, and outlines his new procedures. "It was true to say," as he had said in the *Tractatus*, "that

our considerations could not be scientific ones. . . . We must do away with all *explanation*, and description alone must take its place. And this description gets its power of illumination — i.e. its purpose — from the philosophical problems. These are, of course, not empirical problems; they are solved, rather, by looking into the workings of our language, and that in such a way as to make us recognize those workings: *in despite of* an urge to misunderstand them." (I, 109).

In order to bring out the "workings" of an expression, we point, among other things, to examples of its use in actual contexts, and particularly to uses which the philosopher's employment of the expression fails to cover, or with which his uses conflict; we try to show how his problem arises out of his peculiar use of the expression, his use of it in a peculiar context; to show what makes such a misunderstanding not only possible, but seemingly plausible and even appealing; and to show that, once one sees the workings of the expression, all temptation to misunderstand it — to understand it in the peculiar way the philosopher does — disappears, and with that, the philosopher's problem and his

doctrine disappear. "The results of philosophy are the uncovering of one or another piece of plain nonsense and of bumps that the understanding has got by running its head up against the limits of language" (I, 119); and this will indeed mean "*complete* clarity. But this simply means," not the achievement of perfect formulation, but "that the philosophical problems should *completely* disappear." (I, 133). Not only will the philosopher's problems dissolve, but also his positive doctrines which are either the attempted answers to or the misguided sources of those problems.

Thus, as Austin continues in the tradition of Logical Atomism, so Wittgenstein carried on the therapeutic conception of philosophy which he advanced in his earlier work.[16] To what extent have these approaches been successful? The present essay has provided a context, a basis, in terms of which a thorough critical examination of them can be made.

[16] New reasons are sometimes given in contemporary philosophy for fusing or confusing these two approaches. "What probably happened is this: in the process of dissolving philosophical problems it was gradually seen that certain of these problems arose because of systematic deviations from the ordinary logic of certain concepts. Soon the interest in the logic rather than the deviation became paramount; and philosophy reconstituted itself as a positive, quite autonomous logical activity which is important independently of its ability to clean up traditional mistakes." (M. Weitz, "Oxford Philosophy," *Philosophical Review*, LXII (1953), 188.) In the light of this interpretation, one might ask whether there is any fundamental difference between the Austinian and the Wittgensteinian approaches. But although there is a sense in which it can be said that Wittgenstein's therapeutic measures are supposed to result in something "positive" (namely, an understanding of the logic of our language), he would never have subscribed to Austin's remarks, quoted above, about the results of philosophy. According to Wittgenstein, we explain our ordinary uses by looking at certain "general facts of nature"; extralinguistic facts are no more revealed by the study of ordinary concepts (uses) than by the examination of any other usable set of concepts. The difference between the two approaches is seen in the fact that, for Wittgenstein, the concepts we choose to examine are not (as for Austin) the ones with which philosophers have *not* dealt, but rather those with which philosophers *have* dealt.

23

STUART HAMPSHIRE

ARE ALL PHILOSOPHICAL QUESTIONS QUESTIONS OF LANGUAGE?

1. The typical philosophical question which constitutes the title of this symposium is naturally interpreted as a request for a clear statement, firstly, of the criterion by which we normally distinguish philosophical from non-philosophical questions, and, secondly, of the criterion by which we distinguish questions of language from questions which would not normally be described as questions of language; the question is finally answered when we have decided whether, from agreed statements of the criteria which we apply in the normal use of these two expressions, it follows logically that any philosophical question must be a question of language.

In formulating a criterion for the correct use of an expression, the philosopher, unless he is introducing an entirely new expression or recommending an entirely new use for an old and perhaps discredited expression, must attend to the habits and conventions which actually govern its normal use. He must assume that there are some nuclear contexts in which normal users will agree that the expression is applicable, although there may be peripheral contexts in which its application would be widely disputed. At least one purpose of his formulation of a rule or criterion is to enable disagreements about the pro-

Reprinted from *Proceedings of the Aristotelian Society*, Supplementary Volume XXII (1948), 31–48, by permission of the author and the editor.

priety of the use of the expression in peripheral contexts to be settled.

It seems to me that no very serious disagreements in fact arise now in distinguishing philosophical from non-philosophical questions; at least there is a solid nucleus of questions which almost all philosophers in fact recognise as distinctively philosophical questions. Certainly there are border-line or peripheral cases of questions which some philosophers wish to include among the philosophical and which others wish to exclude; and different criteria or definitions may be proposed in order to widen or narrow the use of the expression in these peripheral contexts. But the expression has a tolerably definite use or meaning, in the sense that the proportion of border-line to nuclear cases is not uncomfortably high. We can draw up a generally agreed list of persons properly called philosophers and a generally agreed list of the questions which they have tried to answer, and this list would be at least as long as the list of border-line cases. There therefore seems to me to be no very urgent need for a precisely formulated criterion of what is and is not a philosophical question.

But the expression "question of language" does seem to me in need of clarification, because, although it is now often used by philosophers, it seems to be used by them in many different senses, that is the proportion of disputed contexts of application to agreed contexts is so high that we cannot say with confidence that it has *any* standard or proper use. So I shall attempt to disentangle some of the different senses in which this expression is used; and then, assuming that we generally agree in recognising a philosophical question when we meet one, I shall ask for a decision whether all admittedly philosophical questions are questions of language in *any* of the senses which I have suggested for this expression. (I cannot show that all philosophical questions *must* be or *cannot* be questions of language, unless I *define* both these expressions, which I do not propose to do.)

2. The expression "question of language" is often loosely used in antithesis to the expression "question of fact." At first sight the implication of this use seems to me that all questions can be classified as either questions of language or questions of fact. But on closer investigation it is not clear in ordinary use whether the alternatives are intended to be complete and exclusive, that is, whether the same question can be described as partly a question of language and partly a question of fact. Some philosophers talk as if a question *must* be described as *either* a question of fact *or* a question of language, and cannnot significantly be described as both or neither; their arguments sometimes suggest that the distinction is *intended* to be exclusive, although they may admit that the principle of distinction has never in fact been so formulated as to exclude border-line cases. But other philosophers and (I think) most non-philosophers generally use the expressions in such a way as to suggest that while there are questions which are *purely* questions of language and also questions which are *purely* questions of fact, they wish to allow a third category which are both or neither; that is, they do not intend the classification to be, even in principle, complete and exclusive.

It is not difficult to suggest a variety of types of questions about which there would in fact be no general agreement in ordinary non-philosophical usage in describing them either as *wholly* questions of fact or as *wholly* questions of language. A few simple specimen cases. (*a*) I am hesitating whether to describe a flower as mauve or purple. Is this hesitation either purely linguistic or purely factual? My decision will be affected both by what other people say about the colour of this and other flowers (facts about their use of the two words), and also by direct comparison of this particular flower with other flowers which I myself unhesitatingly classify as either one or the other. (*b*) I am arguing with someone about whether he really believes the political or religious doctrine which he professes, or whether he is, as we say, self-deceived and only pretends to himself that he believes. Our argument would probably develop partly as an argument about the criterion which we apply in the use of the word 'belief', and partly as a so-called factual dispute about his probable behaviour and states of mind. (*c*) I am asked by the doctor whether my tiredness is mental or physical. Clearly the doctor is not professionally interested in clarifying a question of language, and in some sense his question is certainly a question of fact; but I could not answer him satisfactorily without clarifying what looks like a question of language, namely, without establishing what criterion is to be used in distinguishing the 'mental' from 'physical'.

I do not deny that, of each of these three specimen cases, one might properly decide that the question proposed is *more* a question of language than a question of fact or vice versa; probably one could arrange these and perhaps almost any other suggested questions, in a roughly agreed order as being more or less linguistic, or more or less factual questions. My only contention is that, if we insist on a *complete and exclusive* classification into linguistic and factual, the ratio of doubtful or border-line cases to the cases which are generally agreed as either one or the other will be absurdly high; which amounts to saying that in ordinary usage the two expressions are in fact not used as relatively complete and exclusive antitheses; they are not ordinarily used as polar terms in the same way as, for example, the words 'mental' and 'physical'; the proportion of borderline cases to generally agreed cases is, in the classification of events as either mental or physical, though not negligible, *comparatively* low.

If therefore philosophers decide for their own purposes to introduce a definite criterion by which we can, in the great majority of cases, definitely discriminate a question of fact from a question of language, then they will be introducing a largely new use of these expressions; and the statement "All philosophical questions are questions of language," if established by the application of this new criterion, will be largely uninformative. As so often before, they will be representing an abnormally restricted or expanded use of a familiar expression as a significant discovery. Then the only question which can profitably be asked is — What is the purpose of introducing this new and precisely formulated use of a familiar expression? What problems or pseudo-problems is this new and more exact use intended to solve or dissolve?

I have not in fact been able to find in the writings of those philosophers who might be expected to say 'All philosophical questions are questions of language' any precise criterion for the use of 'question of language'. What one does find instead are precisely formulated criteria for distinguishing between analytic and synthetic statements; and this is the distinction to which most importance seems to be attached when philosophical questions are discriminated from other kinds of questions. But can these two distinctions be interpreted as identical? For the proper answers to many so-called questions of language are certainly not always, or even generally, analytic statements — e.g., what one looks for in grammars and dictionaries are not, in the sense ordinarily prescribed, analytic statements. The usual

answer to this objection is that there are some questions of language which are not empirical questions about actual usage in a particular language, and this subclass of questions of language constitutes the class of properly philosophical questions; they are questions about language with a capital L, and the proper answer to such questions is never a synthetic statement about actual usage in particular languages or even a generalisation from such statements, but always definitions or analytic statements. 'Question of language', in this use, seems to mean what is meant by 'question of definition'.

It now becomes clear how far the expression 'questions of language' is being stretched beyond its ordinary use by philosophers who say 'All philosophical questions are questions of language'; for in ordinary use one would be inclined to say what one means by a question of language is precisely a question which can be answered, and perhaps can *only* be answered, by reference to lexicon, grammar or observation of people's normal linguistic habits; this might even be taken as the definition of 'a question of language' in the ordinary loose sense. The redefinition or expression of the expression by philosophers is achieved by the use of the word Language as an abstraction, so that statements about Language are allowed which are not empirical generalisations about a number of actual languages.

This extension of the use of 'questions of language' to include questions which certainly cannot be answered by the empirical study of the actual use of particular languages has been misleading, as unfamiliar uses of familiar expressions for philosophical purposes must always tend to mislead, unless the unfamiliar use is explicitly acknowledged. But the use of the word 'Language' in this unusual and extended sense in spite of the inevitable but always corrigible misunderstandings involved, may bring out some philosophical point which could not be made in any other way. Philosophers' re-definitions, or calculated disregard of ordinary usage, although they must always to some extent provoke misunderstandings, are held to be useful and justified if they also serve to remove misunderstandings arising out of ordinary usage. So the question at issue is — what philosophical point is made by speaking of philosophical questions as always questions of Language in an extended sense of the word Language — that is, in a sense in which the answer to a question of language is not simply a synthetic statement about the normal use of a particular language?

3. Most philosophers who might be expected to answer the title question affirmatively (e.g., Prof. Ayer in *Language, Truth and Logic* and Prof. Carnap in *Logical Syntax of Language*) have, I think, wanted to assert and emphasise at least the four following theses.

(*a*) All problems, which would ordinarily be described as philosophical problems, disappear, or in fact cease to be regarded as problems, as soon as attention is drawn to some misuse of, or ambiguity in, the words or expressions used in the formulation of the problem.

(*b*) In solving or dissolving problems by this method of drawing attention to misuses or ambiguities of words in their formulation, it is unnecessary, if the problem is genuinely philosophical, to consider any matters of fact, other than (possibly) facts about the normal use of particular words and expressions.

(*c*) All questions normally called philosophical, if they are significant and answerable questions, can be re-expressed, and are more clearly expressed as requests for definite criteria of use, or definitions, of the terms which they contain.

(*d*) In so far as we succeed in formulating agreed rules of use for the expressions of our language, we will not want or need to ask philosophical questions.

Although I think most of the philosophers who would answer the title question affirmatively would probably assent to all four of these theses, they seem to me to be different and logically independent, at least in the sense that it is logically possible to deny any one of them and to accept at least some of the others, and to accept any of them and to deny at least some of the others. In particular there are certainly some philosophers who would accept (*a*) and (*b*) almost without qualification, but who would either firmly deny (*c*) and (*d*), or who would only accept them with substantial qualifications. I think there are good reasons for qualifying and amending all four statements; but (*c*) and (*d*), unlike (*a*) and (*b*), seem to me so misleading as to be properly described as false.

(*a*) and (*b*) seem to be misleading in so far as they may suggest that, as a matter of fact, all or most of the more notorious questions of philosophy have their origin in, or are answered exclusively by reference to, muddles or paradoxes in the use of our ordinary spoken languages. The history of the subject shows that many of the most important philosophical problems have been suggested by, and solved by a clarification of new developments in the methods of the physical sciences and of mathematics. It could even be argued, as a matter of history, that almost all the major philosophical problems have had their origin in the changing methods of the physical sciences and of mathematics. Even philosophical questions about our perception of material objects were originally asked, and still continue to be asked, not only or even primarily because people noticed a not easily clarified ambiguity in the use of the words 'see' and 'touch' and their equivalents in other languages; but also because people have been inclined to believe, or to assume, that the well-attested statements of physical science about the nature of material objects and of our sense-organs are incompatible with our ordinary non-scientific statements about the physical world; and they have therefore come to express doubts about, or dissatisfaction with, ordinary non-scientific statements. But probably most of those who would be inclined to say 'all philosophical questions are questions of language' would retort that even if it is true as a matter of fact that many philosophical questions have been suggested by, and refer to new methods in science and mathematics, and not solely paradoxes or ambiguities of ordinary language, these questions are still usefully and properly described as questions of language; for, whatever may be the historical and psychological facts about their origin, they can all be answered by drawing attention to confusions between the terminology of physical science and of ordinary language, or to confused description in ordinary language of the syntax and vocabulary of the scientific language; these philosophical problems cease to be regarded as problems when the essential differences between the language of common-sense and the language of science have been explained.

This (to me convincing) reply would be a typical example of the philosopher's extended use of the word 'language'. When we talk about the 'language of physical theory', and even more if 'the language of physical theory' is contrasted with 'the language of common-sense', we should in ordinary usage be said to be talking not about two languages, but perhaps about two *kinds of language*; and we would discriminate between these two kinds of language by reference to the different *purposes* for which they are used.

Consider a typical philosophical question — e.g., Can thinking be defined as sub-vocal talking or a set of movements in the brain and larynx? The philosopher will not be considered in any sense to have answered this question if he merely draws attention to standard uses of the word 'thinking' and its equivalents in other languages; the questioner is intentionally going *beyond* our ordinary use of language. Suppose the same questioner goes on to ask 'Can all so-called mental processes, and states of mind, be described in terms of publicly observable physical motions?' Then it would be even more clear that he

was not asking a question about the criterion which governs the use of a particular language but a more general question. There is a sense (the extended sense now established by philosophers) in which he might be said to be asking questions about Language with a capital L, and not asking questions about the standard or proper use of particular expressions in a particular language; that is, he would be asking for a comparison between different kinds of language.

It seems to me undeniable that philosophers always have been, and still are, confronted with questions of this kind, namely, questions which cannot be interpreted as requests for the formulation of the rules of use of particular expressions in particular languages. But I think that some (certainly not all) philosophers who want to say 'all philosophical questions are questions of language' would say that these questions, which are requests for *comparisons* between languages or kinds of languages, are in principle unanswerable; and they would probably go on to say that *therefore* they are not genuine questions, but are pseudo-questions or meaningless questions, though this inference seems to me dubious;[1] or, if they did not say that they are literally unanswerable, they would say that the only possible answer is not the kind of answer which the questioner expects. The answer would consist in setting out the rules of use for a language which might be called a behaviourist language, and then prescribing rules for the translation of those sentences in our ordinary language, which would ordinarily be said to describe states of mind, into sentences of this constructed language; and the answer would end by saying that this logical exercise is the only answer to the

[1] Surely a question cannot properly be described as meaningless unless it can be *shown* to be in principle unanswerable; that is, unless we can formulate the rules for the proper use of the words which are misused in the question. And not all unanswerable questions can in this sense be shown to be unanswerable; and that is generally the point of posing them.

question 'Can all so called mental processes, or states of mind, be described in terms of publicly observable physical motions?' If the questioner is dissatisfied with this answer, he must be told that all philosophical answers — that is, answers which are not empirical or scientific — must be either prescriptions of rules for the use of particular expressions in a particular language, or prescriptions of rules for the translation of sentences of one language into sentences of the other; and this is the thesis expressed in (c) and (d) above, which I wish to dispute.

If the questioner were dissatisfied with this kind of answer, as I think he almost certainly would be, how would he express his dissatisfaction? What more would he be asking? He would be asking for a *comparison* between the *purposes* for which these two languages are used or are useful, and he might express his dissatisfaction with this narrowly logical answer by saying: — 'I agree of course that we can construct a purely physical language, if we choose, and also provide rules for the translation of the psychological statements of ordinary languages with the physical statements of the constructed language'. I agree that it is meaningless to deny that this is logically possible unless we are referring to some further set of linguistic rules which forbid this translation; in that case, by definition, we should not be concerned with two independent languages, but with the rules governing the use of psychological and physical statements within a *single* language. But, although I agree that we can (logically) use whatever language we choose, provided that we use it consistently, I proposed my question in order to discover why, that is, for what purposes, we prefer one language to another; if you like to express it in that way, I was interested not in syntax but in pragmatics. I wanted the philosopher to tell me, not how we may translate psychological statements into a physical language *if* we choose, but why, for some purposes, we in fact choose not to translate. We are inclined to say that something is lost in any such translation; we seem to be unable to communicate in the new language what we wanted to say, and succeeded in saying, in the old. I asked my question because I thought that it was part of the function of philosophy, as the study of language in general as opposed to the study of the grammar of particular languages, to state our intuitive dissatisfaction with such translations more explicitly; that is, the difference between the purposes which the grammar of the language of physical theory is designed to serve, and the purposes which ordinary language is designed to serve. For most of the traditional questions of philosophy can be re-stated as questions about kinds of language in this very general sense of the word. He would be dissatisfied, I suggest, only because he had been refused an answer to his philosophical question as a question of language *in the wider sense* of 'question of language' — that is, the sense in which a question of language is not necessarily a question exclusively about the rules prescribed for, or actually observed in, the use of a particular language.[2]

Questions which are properly called questions of language in this wider sense may certainly be answered in part by drawing attention to the differences in the use of, for example, the word 'emotion' in a behaviourist language and in ordinary language; it may also be useful to try to formulate definitions of the word which may summarise its use in the two kinds of language. But this clarification by definition cannot constitute the whole answer, because it will always make sense to ask whether one definition is better, or more useful for certain purposes, than another;

---

[2] I have not space to try to analyse what arguments we use in showing that one kind of language is useful for one purpose, another for another. I have used the word "purpose" vaguely; perhaps it can be clarified. I am only concerned to assert that such questions are asked and sometimes (I think) answered. What kind of argument can show that such questions *cannot* be answered?

and in defending or attacking a choice of a particular definition or rule for the use of 'emotion', we may use arguments which would not ordinarily be called *wholly* arguments about language, even in the widest of the now established uses of this word. We might appeal to two facts, or sets of facts, which would not naturally be described as *wholly* linguistic facts: (*a*) we might point to the fact that those who have been using (for example) the behaviourist definition of the word 'emotion' have not in fact succeeded in formulating by the use of their definitions simple laws which can be used to predict and control experience; or (*b*) we might point to the fact that the use of the word 'emotion' in the sense suggested has always tended to mislead and confuse people, perhaps because the word has become inseparably associated in their minds with different uses. Whether a particular way of talking and thinking is useful or misleading, whether the adoption of a particular set of definitions or conventions enables us to discover and communicate what we want to communicate, or whether it only suggests unanswerable questions, is in the last resort settled by experience and observation; the test of whether the adoption of a certain rule for the use of a familiar expression is helpful or misleading is an empirical test — does it in fact mislead? Strictly it is not language which is clear or muddled, but we who are clear or muddled. There are many syntactical irregularities and ambiguities in' our languages which do not in fact mislead or perplex people; that some irregularities and ambiguities do mislead, as we learn by experience, could properly be called as much a fact of human psychology as a fact about language; and it is to facts of this kind that philosophers must, and do, attend.

4. But the philosophers who would maintain theses (*c*) and (*d*) would deny that the empirical study of the comparative usefulness for different purposes, either of different kinds of language or

of different rules of use suggested within the same language, is a proper part of philosophy. Questions which can only be answered by reference to psychology or to any other empirical science cannot, given their definition, be described as philosophical questions, since they are partly scientific, and in so far as they are scientific they cannot (logically) be philosophical; they ought therefore to be described as partly philosophical and partly scientific. This argument depends on so defining or using the word 'philosophical' that 'philosophical' and 'empirical' are antithetical terms; it implies that the answer to any *wholly* philosophical question must be an analytic statement or statements.

I do not intend to discuss the empirical question (largely a matter of history) of whether this use of 'philosophical question' to entail 'question answered by purely analytic statements' is or is not in accordance with normal use (even supposing that there is a definite and well-established normal use); even if it is not in accordance with this use, there may be good reasons for adopting a more restricted use; and again it is the *reasons* which have led philosophers to recommend this use, which are important.

But when we ask for these reasons, a dilemma arises; while the sentence 'the answer to any genuinely philosophical question is an analytic statement', may itself be an analytic statement, the adoption of this convention may be recommended by philosophers in statements which are (in part at least) empirical and not analytic; but if it is so recommended, there is a sense in which the conclusion is incompatible with the arguments which are used to support it; for the arguments used to support this *philosophical* conclusion would contain *empirical* statements. If on the other hand the conclusion is supported by arguments consisting *wholly* of analytic statements, that is, if this rule for the use of the word "philosophical" is shown to be the logical consequence of other rules for the use of other expressions, it will still be possible to ask why we should adopt this whole set of rules or definitions. And yet anyone who attempted to answer would thereby forfeit the title of philosopher.

The reasons for classifying questions as philosophical only if empirical statements are not required in answering them are in fact more often implied than directly stated (perhaps in part to avoid this charge of inconsistency). The reasons usually given or implied are partly logical, and partly historical and psychological. The logical doctrine is (roughly) that all significant questions must be answered *either* by appeal to experiment and observation, or by appeal to definitions or axioms (and this thesis is usually presented as an analytic statement showing the proper use of 'significant'); the historical and psychological doctrine usually implied is that *in fact* philosophical arguments have in the past led to interminable misunderstandings largely because philosophers have generally failed to make clear, either to themselves or to others, which of the two kinds of question they were trying to answer; we learn by experience that whenever the two kinds of questions are carefully distinguished, philosophical perplexities tend to disappear and outstanding problems are seen to be soluble; empirical questions are remitted to scientists for solution, and the remainder which can now be clearly classified as genuinely philosophical, are interpreted as requests for definitions or rules of use.

Whether or not philosophical perplexities do in fact tend to disappear and problems to be solved when, and only when, this method is used is surely an empirical question to be decided by experiment and observation of the results. Since the publication of Wittgenstein's *Tractatus Logico–Philosophicus*, the experiment has in fact been made and the results have in fact been generally favourable; many misunderstandings have been clarified and many perplexities removed; and precisely this *fact* is the best *reason* or *justification*

for insisting on a clear distinction between a philosophical question and a scientific or factual question. The justification of the adoption of one method (or, in the wider sense, language) rather than another, in philosophy as in any other enquiry, is a pragmatic one — that, when we use it, we find answers to the questions which we want to answer. Conversely we call methods or terminologies misleading if we find that we are thinking to no purpose when we use them. And it is certainly true that philosophers have in fact been generally misled by failing to distinguish clearly in their manner of expression between empirical and non-empirical questions; it is therefore, in a strict sense of the word, less misleading to distinguish clearly between the two kinds of question; and it is this point which philosophers have wished to stress when so defining or using the word 'philosophical' that 'philosophical' and 'empirical' exclude each other, that a question cannot be both 'philosophical' and 'empirical'.

This neat classification of questions into philosophical and scientific is useful and even necessary, provided that it is not so rigidly applied as to be made the basis of a new scholasticism. Like almost all such classifications of statements or questions into types or compartments, it is useful as a rule which throws into relief the exceptions to the rule. The rule has been used very effectively in the last twenty-five years as an axe to clear away the undergrowth of the tangled cross-purposes of *a priori* psychology called philosophy. But it may be useful now, when the reasons for saying 'no philosophical question is a question of fact' are so widely appreciated, to emphasise the reasons for *not* saying it, to draw attention to the respects in which it may be (and I think already has been) misleading, and so to emphasise the exceptions to the rule. It is for this reason that I have emphasised the difference between proposing definitions, or rules of use, and giving reasons for preferring one set of definitions or rules to another, between showing that a certain use of language is self-contradictory and showing that it is misleading. If any one chooses to accord the title of philosopher only to those who are wholly engaged in the first of each of these activities, he will be adopting an abnormally restricted use of the word; and, if he at the same time declares himself a philosopher, he will be unable consistently to provide any satisfactory reasons for departing so widely from normal use.

5. I think many contemporary philosophers would be inclined to say both (a) 'all philosophical questions are questions of language' and (b) 'no philosophical questions are empirical questions'; given these philosophers' use of 'question of language' to mean 'question of definition', these two theses are logically equivalent. But if one considers (a) alone, as the title of this symposium requires, and disregards the abnormal use of 'question of language' to mean 'question of definition' a relevant historical parallel suggests itself. Philosophy was once conceived as the study of Reality, but was displaced by the application of empirical methods in the physical sciences; it was also conceived (by Locke, Hume, Kant, and so many others) as the *a priori* study of Mind with a capital M, or Knowledge with a capital K, but is being gradually but firmly displaced by the application of empirical methods in psychology; it is now generally conceived as the *a priori* study of Language. Surely it is reasonable to suppose that people will once again become discontented with *a priori* generalisations about an abstraction, and will turn to a methodical study of the facts, to comparative linguistics and semantics, only recently discernible as sciences. It seems historically to be the function of philosophy to initiate genuine science by speculation; in all its phases (outside pure logic) it is pre-science.

But, whether or not this prediction is confirmed, philosophers who claim that all philosophical problems are dissolved when attention is drawn to confusions and ambiguities in the use of words cannot reasonably neglect the comparative study of actual languages; they must ask whether particular metaphysical perplexities *in fact* only suggest themselves in languages in which particular grammatical forms and idioms are used, and whether some philosophical problems are *in fact* not felt to be problems, and perhaps cannot even be formulated, in languages which have very different grammars. Until this evidence is available, it is impossible to decide how many current philosophical questions can be said to be questions of language in the narrower sense, and how many are questions of language only in the wider sense. And if they do ask these questions, they will be asking questions of fact which are also (in the normal sense) questions of language.

6. To summarise:

(a) No criterion has been suggested by philosophers by which we can distinguish a question of language from a question which is not a question of language. In ordinary non-philosophical usage a pure question of language is generally a question which can be answered by observation of actual verbal habits observed in particular languages.

(b) But philosophers, for their own good reasons, have established a wider use of the expression; in this wider but so far unformulated sense, a question of language is not necessarily a question about the proper use of a particular expression in a particular language. It has been found illuminating, although it also has sometimes been misleading, to describe a philosophical question as a question of language in this wider sense.

(c) Some philosophers would probably use the sentence 'all philosophical questions are questions of language' to mean what is meant by 'no philosophical questions are empirical questions'; or 'all philosophical questions are questions of definition'. There were good reasons for suggesting this rule of distinction between philosophical and scientific questions; but if one asks what these reasons are, one is asking a question which would ordinarily be called philosophical and which would (I think) ordinarily be called, at least in part, an empirical question, or which would ordinarily be said to *involve* empirical questions. Therefore the dictum 'all philosophical questions are questions of definition' cannot be accepted. Probably no philosophical questions are *purely* empirical questions, and some philosophical questions are *purely* questions of definition, but certainly some philosophical questions are partly one, and partly the other.

The title-question is certainly a philosophical question, and my answer shows that I at least have interpreted it as *largely* a question of language, even in the narrower sense of the words; and, in some extended but so far unanalysed sense of the words, I might be said to have treated the question as *wholly* a question of language. But I have made some statements which are certainly empirical statements; and I think I can safely defy anyone to answer the question satisfactorily without making at least one empirical statement. Therefore my general conclusion is that, although one may say 'all philosophical questions are questions of language' (in an abnormally extended sense of 'question of language'), a question of language, in this sense and in this context, may also sometimes be, at least in part, an empirical question. 'All philosophical questions are questions of language' is misleading if an identity of meaning is implied between 'questions of language' and 'questions of definition'; but this does seem to be implied in some of the arguments of some philosophers who would wish to maintain that all philosophical questions are questions of language.

Editor's note: For comment on this essay, see Duncan-Jones [1] and Körner [1]. See also Wisdom [9], reprinted above at pp: 101–10.

· 24a ·

J. O. URMSON

THE HISTORY OF PHILOSOPHICAL ANALYSIS

The philosopher, by virtue of his profession, finds ways of thinking and conceptual structures which are normally employed without trouble, and which everyone handles easily and with satisfactory results, problematic and riddled with difficulties. Why, he asks himself, does one ordinarily believe that *this* is a sufficient proof of *that*? For instance, how is it that what is presented to our senses serves as a sufficient proof of the existence of some physical object? What are the concepts of "body," "mind," "causality," and the like, and how can we make use of them without falling into error?

In this situation, the philosopher usually makes a choice between two ways of resolving his problems. There are philosophers who conclude that our usual patterns of thought (and, therefore, ordinary language) are worthless, and that the concepts of every-day life are irredeemable. It is necessary, they believe, to replace them by a way of thinking, a system of concepts, and a use of words which will permit an exact and satisfactory description of reality. This view was, roughly, that of Plato, for whom the every-day vision of the world was mere illusion, and

a lie. It was also the view of the English philosopher F. H. Bradley, who, in his *Appearance and Reality*, found the fundamental features of our thought, including such basic concepts as "time," "relation," and "thing" inadequate and, indeed, self-contradictory. Allowing for over-simplification, we may say that this is the typical view of the metaphysician.

But there are also philosophers who, faced with the same problems, decide that the trouble does not lie with the concepts of common sense, but that they themselves have an insufficient comprehension of these concepts. Accordingly, they try to deepen their understanding of these concepts, and to master all their nuances. Through an exact and thorough analysis of these concepts, and of common-sense ways of thinking, they hope to arrive at a better understanding of common sense itself, and, at the same time, a better understanding of reality. This was the strategy of Aristotle in his *Nichomachean Ethics* (cf. 1145b, 2–7). It is also the point of departure of analytic philosophy.

So interpreted, one can easily see that analysis is a familiar philosophical method. I shall not attempt to offer you a complete historical account of analytic philosophy. Even the minute examination of a particular analytic philosopher, or group of analytic philosophers, would not be of great interest. I propose rather to sketch, in broad strokes, four major forms of philosophical analysis which I think important

A translation of a paper, and the ensuing discussion, presented at the Royaumont Colloquium of 1961, printed in the proceedings of the colloquium (*La philosophie analytique* [Paris: Editions de Minuit, 1962], pp. 11–39). Translated and printed by permission of the author and the publisher. (Copyright 1962 by Les Editions de Minuit.)

to distinguish carefully from one another. I shall call the first of these: classical analysis. It corresponds, roughly, to the traditional method of analysis used by English philosophers, a method which Russell did so much to develop. I shall then examine three other, more recent forms of philosophical analysis: (1) the type of analysis which involves the construction of artificial languages; (2) the type of analysis practiced by Wittgenstein in his later period; (3) the type of analysis which characterizes present-day Oxford Philosophy.

The fundamental notion of classical analysis is that propositions couched in ordinary language are correct, in the sense that they are not objectionable in principle. They are neither logically nor metaphysically absurd. On the other hand, insofar as the form of these propositions of ordinary language hides their true meaning, they are neither metaphysically nor logically satisfactory. The task of the analyst is, therefore, to reformulate them so that this meaning will be clearly and explicitly presented, rather than to reject them. To analyze, is to reformulate, — to translate into a better wording.

But still, what does this involve? We have said that a proposition may be inadequately formulated either logically or metaphysically. One will have recourse to *logical analysis* in the cases in which the verbal form of the proposition obscures its logical import — when, for example, a complex proposition appears to be simple, or a general proposition appears to be singular. Russell's well-known "theory of descriptions" offers us a rule for conducting logical analyses of a category of propositions which combine both of these defects. The proposition which says, for example, "The author of *Waverley* was Scotch" is true, but it appears to be a simple, singular, proposition. In analyzing it, however, we discover that it is complex and general.

One will have recourse to *metaphysical analysis*, on the other hand, when, by virtue of its form, a proposition seems to refer to things, relations, and qualities that, from a metaphysical point of view, are simply complexes of more fundamental entities. In this case, analysis becomes a reformulation, or translation, of the proposition, by means of which the names of these complexes are eliminated in favor of the names of the more fundamental entities — without, however, changing the meaning of the proposition. These complexes are what Russell called "logical constructions." For example, the phenomenalist, if he is an analytic philosopher, will not deny the reality of material objects, but will rather say that these objects are logical constructions — complexes whose elements are the data of sense-perception. In other words, any proposition which contains names of such objects may be translated into a proposition which contains only names for such "givens," without its meaning being thereby changed. In still other terms, we can *reduce* such objects to such sensory data. Everything we can say by talking about such objects can be said better by talking only about what is given to the senses. The names of such objects are (in theory, at least) superfluous.

(It may be necessary to note, however, that an analytic philosopher need not be a phenomenalist. Although, as it happened, most of the practitioners of classical analysis were adherents of traditional empiricism, there is no necessary connection between empiricism and analytic philosophy. Anyone who claims that the only real things are A's and B's — whatever "A" and "B" may stand for — must either say that any proposition of the form "All C's are D's" tells us nothing about the real, or else analyze this proposition in terms of A's and B's, by reducing C's and D's to A's and B's.)

I shall offer three reasons to account for the seductive effect of this program of analysis.

(1) Philosophers who were embarrassed by wanting to refer to entities which seemed to them unknowable sought a metaphysical demonstration of the existence of these entities. Others adopted a paradoxically skeptical attitude, firmly denying that *any* sort of knowledge of these entities was possible. Now if we follow Russell's maxim ("Replace inferred entities by logical constructions") and thus analyze these problematic entities in terms of better-known entities, we easily escape this dilemma.

(2) The point of metaphysics is to discover the fundamental nature of reality, and classical analysis seems to give us a method for doing so: each entity which we can analyze away as a logical construction is no longer a candidate for being ultimately real. Each successful analysis eliminates a certain number of possible candidates. Although, of course, we may never come to the end of such analyses, we shall at least be kept on the straight path.

(3) The analyst is able to state the distinctive nature and goal of metaphysical inquiry, and the difference between metaphysics and the natural sciences, in a particularly simple and elegant way. Natural science, we are told, tells us new facts, of which we were previously ignorant. Metaphysical analysis, on the other hand, gives us a new, and better, understanding of the facts which science has already disclosed.

I think that I have now said enough about classical analysis, which is, in any case, very familiar.

The logical positivism of the Vienna Circle did not modify the methodology of classical analysis. However, because of the anti-metaphysical standpoint which was characteristic of positivism, it could not accept the notion of the goal of analysis as metaphysical discovery. For the positivists of this school, the goal of philosophical analysis is to clarify the language of science, a clarification which would result from, for example, elucidating the relationships between observation and theory, or between scientific concepts at different levels of abstraction. In England at least, as we can see from A. J. Ayer's *Language, Truth and Logic*, positivism led to no important changes in the practice of philosophical analysis. For this reason, it is unnecessary for our present purposes to go over the positivists' theses in detail. We may note, however, that anyone who still calls contemporary English philosophy "positivism" will be seriously mistaken, for it is strikingly different from the Vienna Circle both in the type of analysis which it practices and in its philosophical aims.

As long as twenty-five years ago, the classical conception of analysis already showed signs of losing its grip on analytic philosophers. In saying this, I merely state a fact, and neither rejoice in it nor deplore it. Classical analysis was replaced, not by one, but simultaneously by several quite different conceptions of the nature and function of analytic philosophy. The remainder of this article will be devoted to describing three of these new conceptions.

What seemed to justify abandoning classical analysis, or at least to necessitate reshaping it, was the sterility of this type of analysis outside of logic and mathematics — the areas in which it had obtained its spectacular successes. Although energetic and subtle attempts were made, no satisfactory reformulations of propositions were forthcoming. For instance, it was generally thought that the state was simply a complex of individual people, and thus a logical construction out of these individuals. Thus, it seemed possible to reduce the state to individuals, without modifying the meaning of the word "state" — a project which seemed no more ambitious than that of reducing the notion of "numbers" to that of classes. But in spite of very determined efforts, this reduction was not performed. Propositions about individuals were found which said *more or less* the same thing as propositions about the state, but this was hardly good enough. No one could deny that classical analysis had failed in this area, as well as everywhere else (except in the deductive sciences). But a different interpretation was placed upon this failure by the proponents of each of the new conceptions of analysis.

Some philosophers sought a way out from the dead-end of classical analysis by turning to the construction of artificial languages. Classical analysis was bound to fail outside of the deductive sciences, because beyond these limits our concepts were too vague and our language too imprecise. These latter ways of thinking and talking are neither meaningless nor worthless; to say that they are would be to go over to skepticism or to return to speculative metaphysics. But ordinary propositions are too flexible and ambiguous to permit a truly scientific analysis of their meaning. So the analyst, they argued, must construct his own, ideal, language — or at least fragments of such a language, or a schema of such a language — of which the logical form, and the concepts, will be clear and unambiguous. In this artificial language, the procedures of classical analysis will be applicable, for one will have basic concepts and propositions, on the basis of which everything else can be deduced, and to which everything else can be reduced.

The study of such a language, these philosophers added, is not an end in itself. For if we can succeed in constructing such a language, making it as similar as possible to natural languages save in respect to its greater precision, then the study of such a language will give us all the clarification of our every-day ways of thinking that we can reasonably hope for. This study will make intelligible the conceptual apparatus which is implicit in natural languages, in the way in which an architect's blueprint can clarify an impressionistic sketch.

Here then we have a theory (or, rather, the sketch of a theory) of the nature of philosophical analysis. This was the theory of those philosophers who constructed calculi and formalized languages, not simply as exercises in formal logic, but for spe-cifically philosophical purposes. This theory took very different forms. One finds it first expressed in occasional passages in Russell. Under another form, it is the position of Carnap and of his disciples. Our statement of it approximates the position of Nelson Goodman and of Quine. This theory is still widespread in the United States, but is held by hardly anyone in England.

A second school was inspired (largely, but not entirely) by the thought of Wittgenstein in his later period. Wittgenstein had himself been led to this new point of view in his criticism of his own *Tractatus Logico-Philosophicus* (*Logische-Philoso-phische Abhandlung*), a book which itself espoused implicitly a certain form of classical analysis. According to Wittgenstein, classical analysis rested upon a false conception of language and of thought. No doubt our usual notions are vague and mutable, but it is not for this reason that classical analysis failed. Further, one should not consider this lack of precision as a fault, which can be corrected through the use of an ideal language, but rather as an essential characteristic of any empirical concept. The concepts of an ideal language distort our ordinary concepts, rather than expressing them. (See, for example, Waismann's article on "Verifiability" in *Proceedings of the Aristotelian Society*, Supplementary Volume for 1945, reprinted in *Logic and Language, First Series*, edited by Anthony Flew [Oxford: Blackwell, 1951].)

Wittgenstein and his school made a great point of the heterogeneity of our concepts and of our ordinary linguistic practices. There are, Wittgenstein said, a great number of "language games" (*Sprachspiele*) having widely different rules. There is often no way of telling whether one concept is more complex than another, or of equal complexity, simply because the roles they play are so different. Classical analysis, to be sure, had recognized a similar disparity between empirical concepts and logical concepts, but this dichotomy is entirely insufficient. To talk about our sensations, for example, is to play one language-game. To talk about material objects is to play quite another: To try to reduce the one to the other is like trying to talk about tennis in the vocabulary usually used for talking about soccer. One cannot range the concepts of a language in a hierarchy, as the classical analysts had wished to do, because in principle, and not because of some "defect" in our language, no such hierarchy exists. To put the matter in terms of an image borrowed from Wittgenstein, the words of a language differ among themselves as much as the various tools in a toolbox. To understand a word, or to be familiar with a tool, is to know its function, to know how to use it.

Wittgenstein, and many of the English philosophers who rallied around him, thought that the majority of traditional philosophical problems had arisen from philosophers having failed to grasp the variety of functions which concepts serve, and having therefore drawn erroneous conclusions. Thus, to apply Wittgenstein's method to the solution of a philosophical problem is to correct an erroneous notion of the functions of language rather than to acquire a deeper understanding of language. From this point of view, a philosophical problem is an enigma to be dissolved rather than a question which is susceptible of a straightforward answer.

It follows from this that, for an analyst of this sort, philosophical problems do not result from ignorance of the precise meaning of a concept, but from an entirely false conception of its function. (From this point of view, the more or less imprecise character of empirical concepts is not important.) Such a false conception is what Ryle calls a "category mistake." To resolve a philosophical problem, one should exhibit the generic character of the concepts involved in it, rather than attempting to give a perfect definition or explication of these concepts. This is Ryle's thesis in his *Concept of Mind*: for him, the philosophical pseudo-problems concerning the nature of mind result from the mistaken notion that the mind is a sort of ghost inhabiting a machine (the body). This notion cannot withstand close examination, and should simply be discarded. In the same way, Wittgenstein suggests that the philosopher who seriously asks "What does the act of intending consist in?," and goes on to attempt an introspective examination of what happens inside himself when he wishes to do something, is the victim of a similar mistake. He is, perhaps, attempting to assimilate "intending" to some sort of experience. (See Wittgenstein's *Philosophical Investigations* I, 591 et seq.)

To correct such mistaken notions, one must try to clarify the logical function of the concepts which have been misunderstood, using whatever method proves, in practice, to be efficacious. Perhaps this will lead one to reformulations similar to those produced by classical analysis, or perhaps to a quite different sort of reformulation. Perhaps one will succeed through an application of the verificationist criteria formulated by the positivists. All that matters is the result, and any method that works is a good one. There are no rules for finding such a method. One must rely on philosophical acumen.

To exhibit the results of the adoption of this thesis, I shall offer a brief description of the conception of philosophical problems which it produces. In doing so, I make no pretense of having discovered a uniquely efficacious method.

Analytic philosophers of this persuasion cheerfully admit that ordinary language does not meet all of the philosopher's needs. To express the results of philosophical inquiry, we shall need to modify ordinary language, and fill the gaps which it leaves by introducing new terminology to serve our special philosophical purposes (just as the physicist introduces new terminology to serve *his* purposes). For example, one will invent such technical terms as "language game." But this is not to say that the inadequacy of ordinary language is an important source of philosophical difficulties. Formalized languages, therefore, despite their interest for the logician, are without much interest for the philosopher. For once we have properly understood the logical function of a given concept, it ceases to be problematic, and thus we have no need to resort to an artificial language. We cannot, after all, construct an ideal model of a concept before understanding that concept.

It is often said that philosophers of this stripe have an exaggerated respect for common usage, a superstitious belief in familiar idioms and linguistic conventions. This criticism rests upon a misunderstanding. They study ordinary language carefully only because they believe that ordinary usage offers precious hints about the functions of the concepts used in nontechnical thinking, and because they believe that the principal philosophical problems concern these concepts. There are problems about matter, mind, time, and space; there is a general problem about inference to non-observable entities; but there are no special philosophical problems about protons, mesons, or neutrons.

This conception of philosophical analysis — of analysis as the resolution of conceptual enigmas — has sometimes been condescendingly called "therapeutic positivism." One finds it formulated as early as 1932 in Ryle's "Systematically Misleading Expressions" (*Proceedings of the Aristotelian Society*, 1931–2; reprinted in *Logic and Language, First Series*, edited by Anthony Flew). Ryle presented a new formulation in his *Dilemmas* (Cambridge: Cambridge University Press, 1954). Wittgenstein's version of this conception will be found in his *Philosophical Investigations (Philosophische Untersuchungen)*. Anyone who wishes to understand this conception of analysis should also read the works of John Wisdom and of Friedrich Waismann.

But the sort of analytic philosophy which we have just described is not the same, I believe, as that which is characteristic of Oxford Philosophy, in the form which this movement has taken since the Second World War. Oxford analysis and Wittgensteinian analysis are not incompatible, and may join hands for the achievement of common purposes. But they should not be confused with one another. The fourth method of analysis, which I shall now discuss, is that of Oxford Philosophy. (It goes without saying that few of the philosophers at Oxford would assent without qualification to everything which I am going to say about the characteristic methods of this school.)

The analytic philosophers of the Cambridge School — for example, Russell and Wittgenstein — came to philosophy after considerable work in the sciences and in mathematics. Philosophy of mathematics was the first topic to which Russell applied his classical method of analysis. But the Oxford philosophers came to their subject, almost without exception, after extensive study of classics. Thus they were naturally interested in words, in syntax, and in idioms. They did not wish to use linguistic analysis simply to resolve philosophical problems; they were interested in the study of language for its own sake. Therefore these philosophers are, perhaps, both more given to making linguistic distinctions, and better at finding such distinctions, than most.

For them, natural languages, which philosophers had often stigmatized as awkward and inadequate for exact thought, appeared rather to contain an extraordinary wealth of concepts and of subtle distinctions — concepts which fulfilled a vast variety of functions to which philosophers had usually closed their eyes. Furthermore, since these languages were developed to meet the needs of those who used them, Oxford philosophers thought it likely that only those concepts would have been retained which had proved useful, and that the distinctions which were retained would be adequate — that they would be precise when precision was required, and vague when it was not. All those who speak a natural language have, no doubt, an implicit understanding of its concepts and its nuances. But, Oxford philosophers say, the philosophers who have attempted to describe these concepts and distinctions have either misunderstood them or vastly oversimplified them. In any case, they gave them only superficial study, and thus the true richness of natural languages remained hidden.

This is why Oxford Philosophy is devoted to very detailed and minute studies of ordinary language — studies through which, it is hoped, this richness may be revealed by making explicit the distinctions of which we usually have only a confused knowledge, and by describing the disparate functions of many sorts of linguistic expressions. It is difficult for me to describe the method used in these studies in any general terms. Often, for example, one studies two or three expressions which are at first sight synonymous, and discovers that they cannot, in fact, be used interchangeably. One then scrutinizes the contexts in which each is employed, in order to bring to light the principle which implicitly determines our choice of which expression to use. The best way of seeing how this discipline is practiced is to look to its undoubted master — J. L. Austin — and in particular to two of his articles: (1) his study of the concept of "knowing," in "Other Minds" (*Proceedings of the Aristotelian Society*, Supplementary Volume **XX**, reprinted in *Logic and Language, Second Series*, edited by Anthony Flew [Oxford: Blackwell, 1953]); (2) "A Plea for Excuses" (*Proceedings of the Aristotelian Society*, 1957), in which Austin discusses the closely related terms "mistake," "accident," "inadvertence," etc., and their function in formulating judgments of responsibility.

If one asks these philosophers what such minute description is good for, and why they attempt so close a study of the nuances of ordinary language, they will answer, first of all, that they consider it interesting in itself and useful for discovering the conceptual resources of our language. They will add that one thereby gains a better understanding of the world to which these concepts are applied. To the frequently-posed question "Are these studies really *philosophical?*," they will answer that, if they are useful, it does not matter what one calls them. Neither philosophers nor lexicographers have previously studied language from this point of view. Wittgenstein, of course, regarded his own method as the heir of traditional philosophy. His method of analysis was the true method of philosophy, in that its principal aim was to help us solve the traditional problems. The Oxford school has no such audacious pretensions. They hold that philosophy is large enough to contain many diverse projects. Their modesty does not, however, prevent them from granting that their linguistic studies may have importance for traditional philosophy, for to undertake a philosophical inquiry without having studied the resources of the relevant parts of our language is folly. The shipwreck of most philosophical schemes, they say, is largely due to this folly. Furthermore, after such analysis many problems simply vanish (as Wittgenstein had suggested), and many more are shown to have been badly framed. As Austin said, if such analysis is not the end-all of philosophy, it is at least the begin-all.

There is nothing revolutionary about this view. All the great philosophers (or almost all) have demanded a scrutiny of the words we use, and have recognized that one can be blinded by a misinterpretation of a word. But, according to the Oxford philosophers, only now have we recognized the importance and the necessary complexity of such preliminary inquiries. They devote whole articles, and indeed entire books, to an inquiry which was previously disposed of in a few sentences. (However, one can find good examples of Oxonian analysis in Aristotle — for example, his analysis of "chance" in the *Physics*.)

Wittgensteinian analysis and Oxford analysis, as I have described them, overlap at many points and complement each other elsewhere. Many English philosophers (including many who owe allegiance to Oxford Philosophy) would place themselves at a position between that of Wittgenstein and the view I have just sketched. It may therefore be in point to indicate briefly the principal differences between the two schools:

(1) Wittgensteinian analysis has, for its sole end, the resolution of philosophical enigmas. If there were no such enigmas, there would be no need for analysis. For Oxford, on the other hand, analysis has an intrinsic value.

(2) According to Wittgenstein and his disciples, all that is necessary is to exhibit the *generic* character of the concepts which we analyze. For Oxford, a minute analysis is indispensable.

(3) For Wittgenstein, analysis is the only useful method in philosophy. For Oxford, it is only one among others, and no one claims that it is sufficient, by itself, to resolve all philosophical problems.

Obviously, however, the resemblances between the two schools are important. Both abandon the fundamental thesis of classical analysis, namely, that there is a hierarchy of concepts and of propositions, stretching from the ultimately simple to the highly complex, and that the principal job of analysis is to reformulate complex propositions in order to understand their meaning better, and to reduce the complex to the simple. Both deny that a language can be considered a homogeneous calculus. Both would say that, for philosophical purposes, it is rarely in point to define a co. ·ept in terms of another; it is much mo. ften a matter of distinguishing the function of one concept from the very different function of another.

The type of analysis which involves the construction of artificial languages, on the other hand, differs only slightly from classical analysis — and indeed it is often difficult to distinguish the two. In Wittgenstein's earlier thought, everything is clear. The propositions of ordinary language give a perfect picture of the facts which they describe. The propositions of an ideal language are simply more perspicuous. Often, however, in reading Russell, it is not clear whether the analyses offered are simply more perspicuous reformulations of the analysanda, or whether Russell is trying to say in precise terms what can only be said imperfectly in ordinary language. Nevertheless, classical analysis must be distinguished in principle from ideal-language analysis, even when classical analysis makes use of symbolic logic. For the construction of artificial languages may be seen simply as an auxiliary technique, which leaves the methodological program of classical reductive analysis unchanged. However, if one believes that the construction of an artificial language is in itself a philosophical success, because it is intrinsically a better formulation (rather than a reduction of ordinary formulations), then one goes beyond classical analysis and adopts a disguised form of speculative metaphysics.

We have traced the development of three new methods of philosophical analysis which have replaced classical analysis. We have not attempted a complete picture, but only to sketch outlines. I hope nonetheless that these outlines may aid our approach to analytic philosophy by helping us to avoid mixing up the various forms which analysis has recently taken. It is not sensible to ask for *the* method of making one's fortune (or of ruining oneself); there are many. It is no more sensible to ask "What is the analytical method?" There is not one "analytic philosophy." There are several.

Discussion of Urmson's "The History of Analysis"

(Chaired by L. J. Beck)

Mr. H. B. Acton: I am well aware of the traps and dangers of an attempt of the sort which Mr. Urmson has made. He could hardly be expected to have given us, in the brief sketch of the history of the analytic movement which he presented, details on each of the philosophers connected with that movement. Nevertheless, there is one omission which I regret: he made no mention of Moore. I regret it the more because I think that Mr. Urmson tends to attribute to Wittgenstein certain widely-held views which actually derive from Moore. Without taking up too much time, I should like at least to cite, by way of illustration, Moore's article "The Conception of Reality," which appeared in 1917–18 — a date well before the beginning of the twenty-five years which, as I understand him, Mr. Urmson has taken to cover the recent history of this movement.

I should like to note certain interesting points in this article. In the first place, Moore sets out to discover what lurks behind the various contradictions which he believed himself to have found in certain theses contained in Bradley's *Appearance and Reality*. The first of these is that time is unreal. The second is that time exists. Moore asked himself how Bradley had been able to arrive at these two *prima facie* contradictory views. How does he set about his analysis? He begins by noting that if someone, in the course of an ordinary conversation, remarked that time was unreal, we would take him to mean that

nothing happened before, during, or after anything else. But this is not what Bradley means. The second step of Moore's analysis led him to ask "But how, then, was Bradley able to write both that time was unreal and that time existed — or, more precisely, how could he suppose both that time was unreal and that some things did happen before, during or after certain other things happened?" I shall not now try to enumerate the reasons which Moore offers in order to explicate this apparent contradiction of Bradley's. I wish only to focus attention on the fact that Moore applies to these two Bradleian propositions one of the techniques which is familiar to the analytic philosophers of today. Anticipating Wittgenstein's metaphor, we can say that Moore here "shows the fly the way out of the fly-bottle." *Appearance and Reality* is the fly-bottle, and Bradley is the fly.

Mr. Urmson: I quite agree with Professor Acton that Moore had a very great influence at the beginning of the analytic movement. No doubt I should have mentioned this influence, which was probably as important as that of Wittgenstein. The reason why I thought I might be able to leave Moore out of the story is that Moore devoted little attention (in his writings, at least, if not in his lectures) to theoretical discussions of the analytic method. He practiced analysis, but he did not care to discuss the nature of the analysis which he practiced. This is why I preferred to concentrate on such philosophers as Russell and Wittgenstein, who spent a good deal of time trying to lay down a *theory* of analysis, rather than to talk about someone like Moore, whose influence was of a different sort. Moore approached problems from whatever angle seemed most likely to lead to their solution, and his practice interests us more than the theoretical aspect of his thinking about method, which he never made explicit. So if (doubtless mistakenly) I have omitted reference to him, it is because I see him as a practitioner of the art of analysis, rather than as a theoretician of the analytic method.

Mr. W. v. O. Quine: I have only two short questions to ask Mr. Urmson. The first concerns a phrase which appears towards the end of his paper: "For Wittgenstein, analysis is the only useful method in philosophy. For Oxford, it is only one among others . . ." If, according to Mr. Urmson, there are other useful methods which are practiced by Oxford philosophers, can he tell us what they are?

My second question bears upon the distinction which he draws between "practical" analysis and "metaphysical" speculation. I should simply like to ask if he could give us the name of a single philosopher who practices the sort of analysis he calls "practical" who is not at the same time a speculative philosopher, in the metaphysical sense of the term "speculative."

Mr. Urmson: If I were to speak in the name of all analytic philosophers, Professor Quine, I should find it very difficult to answer your first question. Speaking for myself alone, (if I may, for the sake of argument, count myself among the analysts), I should point to certain moral philosophers, such as John Stuart Mill, who have formulated certain rules of conduct, or certain ways of envisaging the proper approach to moral problems, and who seem to me to have employed a useful method. I have in mind only very general views, such as those which Mill puts forward in his *Utilitarianism*, where he proposes utility as the general criterion of the worth of actions. I do not wish to suggest that I would subscribe without qualifications to Mill's views, but simply to say that he is an example of someone who practices a method which is not analysis (although it often resembles it), and which I should not like to say is useless. I think that it is perfectly legitimate for a philosopher to try to give a general account, in a rational way, of the way in which he proposes to approach the study of the facts of morality.

That is one of the examples I would cite. I think also that nothing prevents a philosopher looking for, and discovering, a new method of envisaging the world. This search seems to me perfectly legitimate. I would simply, as an analyst, reserve the privilege of examining all the other ways of envisaging the world, side-by-side with his.

About the distinction that I drew between philosophy and speculative metaphysics: I shall not try to give the name of an analytical philosopher who has completely succeeded in maintaining this distinction, but I think that they all *try* to do so. To take the example of Moore, whom we were just discussing, I should place him among the practitioners of classical analysis, but I am quite certain that he had no intention whatever of establishing a metaphysical system. I think that Russell, on the other hand, at certain periods in his career quite consciously practiced speculative metaphysics. At other periods, however, for example when he adopted "logical atomism," I think that he was simply trying to express the accumulated experience of science and of every-day life, and that he tried to say nothing which would be incomprehensible to a non-philosopher. (I do not say that he succeeded; that is a separate question.) Moore is probably the best example I can offer of someone who constantly tried to steer clear of all metaphysical speculation, and who came close to succeeding. In this matter, it seems to me that it is the intention which counts, since the intention suggests a deep mistrust of the value of any sort of speculation.

Mr. Bernard Williams: I should like to ask Mr. Urmson for a clarification of the passage in his paper where he alludes to Ryle's notion of "category mistakes." He seems to suggest that one can assimilate the method which Ryle proposes for diagnosing such mistakes to the method practiced by the later Wittgenstein.

Now it seems to me that it is precisely here that we need to make a distinction. I do not wish to pre-empt Professor Ryle's right to his own exegesis of his position on this question, but I think that (or, at least, the method which he actually employs in *The Concept of Mind* suggests to me that) the categories whose existence he presupposes are more than simply a classification of linguistic expressions, and are intended to correspond to true ontological categories, the differences between which are revealed precisely by the examination of the expressions of ordinary usage. (Professor Ryle will tell me if I am wrong on this point.) They are categories such as "tendencies," "events," and the like, and which correspond to certain ways of being-in-the-world.

Such a notion is, I think, in no way implied by the methods which Wittgenstein practiced towards the end of his life, and I think that one can highlight the difference by saying that Ryle's method implies the existence of philosophical truths which permit us to discern which are the true categories, and thus to clear up the philosophical confusions which led us to confuse categories with one another. It seems to me that for Wittgenstein, on the other hand, there is no such thing as a philosophical truth, but that there are perfectly banal truths about matters of fact which we all know, and that we can be cured of our philosophical mistakes simply by reminding ourselves of these truths.

It seems to me that this distinction is related to the method which Mr. Urmson attributes to the post-classical analysts of

the third type — "the method of Oxford" — a method practiced by philosophers who regard the analysis of linguistic facts as an end in itself. (I am not, of course, saying that Mr. Urmson would deny that there are plenty of philosophers at Oxford who are in no way connected with what he has called "Oxford Philosophy." I say this in order to avoid the suggestion that all the philosophers at Oxford devote themselves to studying linguistic facts and pass their time discussing fine points of philology.) But I think that the method of analysis which certain philosophers at Oxford do practice is equivocal on a certain point: these philosophers do not make clear whether they take Professor Ryle's point of view (which was also Aristotle's), the point of view according to which there are ontological categories which can be discovered by looking at linguistic expressions, or whether they take Wittgenstein's view that there are only philosophical problems, which trouble the mind when they are first encountered but which are capable of a simple resolution, by a sort of psychoanalytic method, through bringing these troublesome problems face to face with the solid truths of common sense, and comparing them with plain fact. It seems to me (though I do not dare to lay this down flatly) that the Oxford school, if there is such a thing, still wobbles between these two alternatives.

Mr. Urmson: Very well, let us ask ourselves whether Professor Ryle's method is or is not the same as Wittgenstein's. But you will agree that there is something a little odd about debating this question in Professor Ryle's presence. Turning to him, I would say that he strikes me as having made a certain amount of progress as he has grown older. I think that in the first articles in which he discussed these questions — such as "Systematically Misleading Expressions" — one gathers that there exist "logical forms" which we need to discover and which he takes to correspond to what is fundamentally real. But as his thought developed, this notion seemed to disappear, and if you look at his discussion of the nature of philosophy in his *Dilemmas* (although, even there, his view is different from Wittgenstein's in several important respects), the differences do not seem to me to lead to the firm distinction which Mr. Williams wished to draw.

As for what I called (for the sake of simplicity) "Oxford Philosophy," it is obvious that the description I gave was highly schematic, and I think it corresponds only in a very general way to the tactics of each of the philosophers whom I would place under this heading. I think I have already said, and for the sake of clarity I shall now repeat, that if you read the works of these philosophers, you will find the pervasive influence of Wittgenstein much more easily than you will find any rigorous employment of the method which I described summarily in order to characterize them as a group. If I have stuck to the term "the Oxford method," it is because it seems to me to represent something distinctive which I regard as Oxford's original contribution to the notion of analysis.

Mr. L. J. Beck: It seems to me that we might usefully consult the original sources, and I should like to ask Professor Ryle to offer a gloss on his own text.

Mr. Gilbert Ryle: It is rare that one can witness one's own autopsy. The experience is not without charm. I shall say this to begin with: when I was much younger — I was much younger. This is not a tautology.

It is certain that when I wrote "Systematically Misleading Expressions" I was still under the direct influence of the notion of an "ideal language" — a doctrine according to which there were a certain number of logical forms which one could somehow dig up by scratching away at the earth which covered them. I no longer think, especially not today, that this is a good method. I do not regret having traveled that road, but I am happy to have left it behind me.

As far as the differences and similarities between Ryle and the later Wittgenstein

go, I think that the essential difference is this: I come from a medical background, where I picked up the habit of distinguishing sharply between diseases, which make you sick, and other states of health, which do not. Wittgenstein talks as if philosophical problems were symptoms of a sickness of which the patient must be cured. I think, for myself, that *not* finding these problems troublesome would be a sign of remarkable stupidity. Therefore I use a language which is, so to speak, less clinical than Wittgenstein's, and I am less inclined than he to practice surgery. In part for that reason, and in part for others, I have no compunction about saying that some of the things which philosophers have said are true, and that others are false. The latter, to be sure, are the vast majority.

Wittgenstein did not like using words such as "true" or "false" because he wanted to avoid blurring the line of demarcation between philosophy and science, as had been done in the past. For reasons which seemed to him sufficient, he thought the word "true" belonged, or at least should belong, to the scientist. For myself, I do not see any good reason why the use of the word should be restricted in this way. I think that to say that a philosophical proposition is true, and to say that a scientific proposition is true, does not entail that the two propositions are of the same order. And I see no reason for not using the word "true" — or, more often, the word "false" — in both cases.

For the rest, I agree.

Mr. Leon Apostel: My first question concerns the criteria of adequacy for, or the criteria for correcting, a specimen of linguistic analysis in the "fourth manner" — that is, a pure case of the manner of Oxford Philosophy.

I understand what counts as a good analysis in the classical sense: analysis is a reduction to what is metaphysically basic. I understand what counts as good analysis in the logistic sense: analysis is reconstruction in a more perspicuous language. I also understand what counts as a good analysis in the sense given to "analysis" by therapeutic positivism: the criterion here is the therapeutic efficacy of the analysis. But I have not understood the criterion for a good analysis in the fourth manner — that of the Oxford School.

I ought to explain why this question seems important to me. If I have understood what has been said, then I would wish to put forward the hypothesis that the criterion of a good analysis in this school is simply the same criterion of adequacy which the lexicographer would use. For now one is simply interested in language as it is, and engages in this study for its own sake. One wishes to construct a semantics, and to do so without bothering about philosophical positions. If this is so, then I do not see why the Oxford School persists in using its present method. Why not simply do for semantics what phonology does for sounds? One does not formalize, if one simply constructs a formal model. One does not formalize crystals by developing a science of crystallography. Nor does one formalize the system of sounds by developing phonology. Now the goal of the semantical portion of the science of linguistics seems to me to be the construction of a model — just as in the case of any other respectable science. This will be a formal model of the data, of all relevant material. If my hypothesis is sound, I do not see why one should continue to use a method which prohibits the construction of such a model. Since one in fact does continue to use this method, I suppose that my hypothesis must be false. But if it is false, I need further clarification, since I do not see what alternative hypothesis might be true.

My second question is about the passage in Mr. Urmson's paper which reads as follows: "If one asks these philosophers what such minute description is good for, and why they attempt so close a study of the nuances of ordinary language, they will answer . . ." I am not at the moment interested in what they will answer, but in what they add to their answer. Mr. Urmson tells us that "they will add that one thereby gains a better understanding of the world to which these concepts are applied." Now to pose my question: what is the relation between the structure of language and the structure of the world, and how does one get from the former to the latter? Could you give us some examples?

A final request: could someone give us an example of a *good* analysis, of the "Oxford School" type, and of a *bad* one, so that we can see what the difference is supposed to be?

Mr. Urmson: These are the most difficult questions which I have been asked so far. I confess my embarrassment. Nevertheless, I do not think that one can say that the end which, according to my account, analytical philosophers have had in view is the same as that of lexicographers and semanticists who have used the traditional methods of their disciplines. I willingly grant, however, that anything the lexicographer or the semanticist can offer will be of the greatest interest for the analytic philosopher.

I think that the analysts of the contemporary Oxford School are less interested in giving a general empirical description of how people talk than in discovering (if I dare use this phrase) the *logical* rules which govern the use we make of words and of turns of phrase. Thus, for example, they are not particularly concerned with the history of the language, although they may be led, in the course of their investigations, to certain views in this area.

If I may go on for a moment to your second question before having finished answering your first, I do not think that there is any real agreement among analysts on the problem of knowing to what extent, and in what way, the practice of philosophical analysis can help us in acquiring a deeper understanding of the world. I may perhaps suggest how it *might* help by taking an example. Consider two concepts which are near neighbors, and have generally been confused with one another in the usual course of philosophical discussion. Suppose that by applying our method we discover differences between them which have escaped the attention of those who have carelessly manhandled them — differences, let us say, between the circumstances or the contexts in which we would choose to use one of the two concepts in preference to the other. We will thereby have laid bare a distinction to which we had hitherto been blind, a distinction between two types of circumstances which will be revealed by the discriminations which we have found ourselves making between different linguistic expressions. Our contribution will consist precisely in having revealed a nuance at a point where a confused usage had prevented philosophers from realizing that a distinction existed.

Let us see what actual example of such a procedure I can find. I do not wish to invent one out of my head, but Professor Austin will doubtless excuse me for borrowing one from him. When he undertook to study the concept of "mistake" and that of "accident," he looked over a whole series of expressions in connection with which the two notions arise — "I didn't do it on purpose," "I was mistaken," "It was a mistake," "Wrong number," — and many others. (He also considered other notions, but let us restrict ourselves to these two.) It seems to me that most philosophers have either not tried hard enough to distinguish these two notions, or have not succeeded in doing so. Aristotle is a good example (despite the fact that I greatly admire him). A false distinction, such as that between "*voluntary* mistake" and "*involuntary* mistake," which gives rise to so many confusions, is no great help to us. If, on the other hand, we put forward every employment of these expressions, the circumstances in which we should say that we have done something by mistake, and those in which we would say that we had done it by accident, then we shall have indicated, by looking at what goes on in the world, two

of the things which may occur in the world. We will have helped ourselves to get clear about the difference which separates, in the area of human activity, two notions which philosophy had not previously succeeded in distinguishing.

You have asked me for an example of a *bad* analysis. Very well, I shall take one from Ryle's *Concept of Mind*. When he says that "to believe something, is to manifest a disposition," I think that he has produced a typically defective analysis. He assimilates a proposition about what people believe to a proposition about what they are disposed to do in certain circumstances. In choosing this example, I am deliberately treading on dangerous ground (and Professor Ryle will excuse me), but I would repeat that this seems to me a typical example of a bad analysis, just because when we say "I believe that . . ." we do not say that we are thereby manifesting any profound dispositions. For instance, "I think that it will rain" is an answer to a question about what the weather will be like, not a question which directly concerns *me*. It is not dispositions which are in question here, but simply rain or good weather. This example will show you, perhaps, in what direction we look when we are constrained to lay down criteria for a *good* analysis.[1] We could go on like this for a long time. But I do not wish to try the audience's patience.

Mr. Charles Perelman: Philosophical analysis, as you understand it, differs sharply from lexicographical analysis, for it proposes to exhibit *logical rules* which are implicit in linguistic usage.

We all know that judges, for example, also interpret and analyze language. But they would not, I think, claim to be discerning the logical rules implicit in the use of judicial language. What is it that

---

[1] I fail here utterly to answer Mr. Apostel's first question. The criterion of a satisfactory account of the use of certain expressions can only be the failure of philosophers to find counter-examples.
Editor's Note: Footnote added later (1965) by Mr. Urmson.

characterizes your own activity, and what sense is given to "logical rules" in philosophical analysis? How does this analysis differ from what men normally do when they interpret the terms used in the practice of their respective professions?

Mr. Urmson: I think my reply would be that the difference between the judge who undertakes to discuss the use of the terms he employs when he tries to interpret a law so as to give it a practical application, and the philosophical analyst, is principally a matter of degree. In the first place, the judge will bring in some factors which are irrelevant for the philosophical analyst: for instance, legal precedents (if the context is one in which precedents help to determine what judgment will be rendered). This boils down to saying that his understanding of the circumstances to which the law is to be applied will be determined by what his predecessors have said. It is certainly not the case that the remarks of his predecessors will determine the results reached by the philosophical analyst. In the first place, therefore, the judge relies upon certain criteria which are irrelevant for the analyst.

In the second place, the difference consists in the fact that the analyst will persist in his inquiry, no matter what concept he is trying to analyze, as far as he believes it possible to go. The judge, on the other hand, will limit himself to what is necessary for the study of the particular case which he is called upon to adjudicate.

I should grant that one can glean from the writings of some judges passages which can be incorporated, almost without change, in a work of analytical philosophy. And on this point, I am entirely in agreement with you.

However, you pose a very difficult question when you ask me to specify exactly the field of application of the "implicit logical rules" which we look for in linguistic usage. I shall not try to give a complete answer in a few words, but shall simply suggest where, in my own thinking, I see a line of demarcation between the area of application of philosophical analysis and that of philology. It sometimes happens that the philologist who is interested in semantics will appeal to usage in order to clear up a disputed etymological point, for example, or a stylistic question (such as the classical problem, in English of the use of terms of Latin origin and those of Anglo-Saxon origin). This sort of inquiry seems not directly relevant to the analytic philosopher's concerns. But who can say where the divide comes? I think that no one knows exactly. For this reason, it is very hard to say just what we mean when we use such an expression as "implicit logical rules." I only used this notion for the sake of self-defense in the course of discussion, and I do not find it very clear myself.

Mr. Jean Wahl: I will make two brief remarks: the first, perhaps, in defense, of Aristotle, and the second in defense of Bradley.

I think that if we look in Aristotle, we shall find the possibility of seeing a distinction between "faults" and "accidents" — just as Greek tragedy is, in a general way, a reflection on the distinction which it is necessary to make between these two. Perhaps in Sophocles' *Oedipus* we can find suggestions of such a distinction.

But I especially want to say something in favor of Bradley. Before doing so, I want to mention one of Moore's seminars at Columbia University (at which I was present), where the subject, for two hours, was one which we might well discuss here: the question of whether "It is true that there are two ashtrays on that table" is the same as "There are two ashtrays on that table." For two hours, Moore was a veritable Socrates, and no conclusion was reached. I think that he thought that "It is true that . . ." was useless, and that it sufficed to say "There are . . ." That was the entire content of the discussion.

Coming back to Bradley: for him, time *is* an appearance. Now if one says that it is an appearance, is this to say that it *does not exist*? Remember that we still discuss the question of the relation between the two parts of Parmenides' poem. A similar question arises here, and I do not think that there is any contradiction. Finally when Bradley wrote his book, he must have had some such thought as "This book will be printed." So he knew very well that time existed. Nevertheless, it lay in the domain of appearance.

Mr. Urmson: The last thing I want to do is to launch an attack against Aristotle. All I meant, when I said that he did not distinguish between an accident and a mistake, is that the examples he gives us confuse the two. I am thinking specifically of a passage in which he cites, as examples of the same thing, the case of a man who thinks that a certain bottle, which actually contains poison, contains an innocuous medicine (which, for me, is the archtype of a mistake) and that of a man who, throwing a javelin, misses the target and hits a spectator (which seems to me a clear case of an accident). It was this passage which I had in mind when I alluded to Aristotle. But it is quite likely that he noted the distinction elsewhere.

As to Bradley, I am well aware that he repeated over and over again that what he had to say on this subject was contradictory, absurd, and unthinkable, and yet nevertheless expressed the essence of what we all say all the time, when we are not philosophizing. I still find it mysterious that he could attach so much importance to what was, by his own admission, irredeemably absurd, contradictory, and unthinkable, and still seemed to merit keeping in mind for twenty-three hours out of every twenty-four.

Mr. Jean Brun: What I am going to say may perhaps suggest a historical background for our problem. I was very happy to learn that Aristotle was — so early — an Oxonian. But can one say the same of Aeschylus? You may reply that he was a poet rather than a philosopher. But that is just the issue. Is the analytical philosopher, in studying language as he does, attempting to exhaust the problem of lan-

guage? I may sound like a metaphysician, but still, isn't there a more important dimension of language, one which lies quite outside the sphere of the conceptual inquiry you are conducting? Is not language an attempt to translate a lived experience — one which is not entirely subjective, in the sense that its validity or meaning is not simply limited to *one* subject? When we read Aeschylus, or any other poet, and are interested in what we read, it is not exclusively or even chiefly because his language is a simple autobiographical language, pertaining only to a particular individual who lived at a certain point in time and space. Does the study of language to which you devote yourself simply dismiss this function of language as a translation of lived experience — recognizing it, but putting it off to one side? Does not etymology give us, through studying the history of a word, the chance of seeing different aspects of the vicissitudes of life, and of avatars of human experience?

To put it briefly, what I am asking comes down to this: is an aesthetics possible in the framework of analytical philosophy? Or does analytical philosophy think that the aesthetic problems are not philosophical problems?

Mr. Urmson: I think that the problem of the relations between language and lived experience (if you mean by this the sort of experience that can be exteriorized in expressions intelligible to a group), or more generally the problem of the relations between experience and communication, has preoccupied a great number of analytic philosophers for a long time. One could cite a whole series of articles, and even books, on this topic. I refer you, for example, to Professor Wisdom's series of articles on "Other Minds," or, once again, to Wittgenstein's *Philosophical Investigations*, in which he discusses the question of the "personal" language which we use to express our intimate experiences. From one point of view, then, one can say that this question of the relations between language and lived experience has been examined attentively by analytic philosophers.

In the second place, one finds in many of these philosophers a constant concern to consider language as a mode of expression, rather than simply as an instrument of conceptual thought or as principally concerned with the description of facts. They would insist, for example, on the differences between an expression such as "I am in pain" and some medical proposition about the state of a patient's nerves or about the beneficial affects of aspirin. For them, the first expression is a way of exteriorizing what you call a "lived experience." The other two are of a wholly different logical order.

About aesthetics, I think that it may fall within the sphere of analytic philosophy, as long as one sticks to the rules of the game. An analytic philosopher tries, according to the criteria set by his own method, to distinguish the circumstances in which we apply expressions which manifest enthusiasm or disapproval. Take for example such expressions as "God, how beautiful!" or "It is simply sublime!," or the classical distinction between the "beautiful" and the "sublime." The only difference that I can see between analytical aesthetics and other parts of analytic philosophy is in the words which are studied: instead of studying words like "true" or "false," we shall be studying words like "beautiful," "sublime," "marvelous," "ugly," "horrible," etc. But, here as elsewhere, we shall be trying to find out in what contexts and in which situations we use one of these words in preference to others.

Insofar as you wish to justify philosophical inquiry of a different sort, which extends into areas beyond the reach of the analytic method (and I think that this is the import of your remarks), all I can say is that analytic philosophy, as it is understood at Oxford, is quite willing to let you try. If you conclude that there are indeed types of philosophical inquiry

which transcend the analytic method, I think that an analytic philosopher would simply say: that is entirely possible. There are important problems which we simply leave alone, and we make no pretense of doing everything. Nor do we try to impose our method on the rest of the world. We only urge that what we, on our side, are doing is well worth doing. Further, we hold that ours is an aspect of philosophy which one puts aside only at considerable risk when one wishes to look at another aspect. I am speaking now, of course, in the name of the characteristic attitudes (as I have tried to define them) of the group of analytic philosophers at Oxford, not for myself.

Mr. Beck: I think that we should close the discussion with one more question — Professor Leroy's.

Mr. Georges Leroy: My question concerns pure methodology. Although one can hardly talk about method without touching upon ultimate problems, I shall leave these alone. To go that far would raise further questions, which I shall save until later.

It is obvious, and here I agree with the linguistic philosophers, that a word has more than one sense, and that its sense is determined by context. Consequently, one can say that a single word corresponds to what we would call different concepts (not just in technical or literary language, but especially in every-day language). Therefore, we can only know what a word means if we know what the phrase containing it means. This is a vitally important point. The meanings of a word which are inferred from knowledge of the meaning of a phrase may vary for a single man, even in a rapid conversation, even in a very short time. Thus we find the same word suddenly expressing very different meanings, and this I think, is why foreign languages are so difficult.

Furthermore, the concepts which correspond to phonemes are concepts which themselves change with the passage of time. As we go through history, we find considerable variations.

Now, despite the great sympathy I feel for the Oxford philosophers, I am embarrassed by this problem. If we can only define the meaning of a word in a long historical perspective, stretching beyond a single generation, must we wait until the analysis of language is finished before we have the right to begin philosophizing? I am well aware, remembering what has just been said, that one can philosophize about other matters, and that analytical philosophers (fortunately, perhaps) do not pretend to include everything. But these reassuring remarks do not diminish my embarrassment. So I ask: just *when* is it legitimate to begin philosophizing?

Mr. Urmson: I quite agree with Professor Leroy, and I admit that there is a real, and serious, difficulty here. Perhaps, however, we can distinguish between what might be called *systematic* evolutions, which are observable in the meaning of a word, on the one hand, and what might be called *aberrant* variations on the other. The first are found in a single period when a single word is employed in several different contexts. The others are seen in historical perspective, as when we see a word shifting little by little away from its primitive meaning into a new context — for example, the evolution of a word like "nice" in English and its present diversity of senses (so that it sometimes means "exact" or "precise" and sometimes something like "good" or "pleasing"). In my view, the latter sort of difference presents no real philosophical difficulty. It is purely and simply a matter of etymology or of lexicography. But, on the other hand, I agree with you that the analysis of language, practiced according to the pure "Oxford method" which I have attempted to define, can never be thought to have been completed. Were it completed for English, we should still have to decide how far its conclusions applied to other languages, such as French, or classical Greek. Now it is obvious that such an extrapolation would encounter enormous difficulties. (It is, notably, quite impossible in the case of Greek.) I should be willing to say that it is impossible to have a proper appreciation of a piece of research in analytical philosophy, conducted according to the principles of this method, if one does not have an intimate knowledge of the conventions of the language and of the technical procedures of the small circle of initiates who practice the method. I grant that this is a very troublesome fact. But, given the present degree of specialization, it may be inevitable.

P. F. STRAWSON

ANALYSIS, SCIENCE, AND METAPHYSICS

It has been said, rightly, that English philosophy between the wars was dominated by the notion of analysis. One might say the same of English and American philosophy after the Second World War, but then one would have to add that the conception of analysis was entirely different from that held earlier. It is true, of course, that even before the Second World War, the word "analysis" was given several different interpretations. Nevertheless, I think that a certain central idea was never far from the minds of all those who praised, or claimed to practice, the analytic method during this earlier period. This was the idea of translation, of an ideal paraphrase as the proper goal of philosophical analysis — even though this goal might itself be a mere ideal. On this conception of analysis, the principal philosophical problems would be resolved if one could translate sentences of ordinary language which contained problematic concepts by means of other sentences — expressions which would exhibit clearly the underly-

A translation of a paper, and the ensuing discussion, presented at the Royaumont Colloquium of 1961, printed in the proceedings of the colloquium (*La philosophie analytique* [Paris: Editions de Minuit, 1962], pp. 105–38). Translated and printed by permission of the author and the publisher. (Copyright 1962 by Les Editions de Minuit.)
Editor's note: Mr. Strawson's paper contains many sentences and paragraphs which occur, in English, in his essay in *The Philosophy of Rudolf Carnap* (Strawson [1]). At these points, I have followed the wording of the latter essay in my translation.

ing complexities of these concepts; or if one could transpose ordinary sentences whose grammatical structure was misleading into a form which would exhibit clearly the true structure of the thoughts they expressed or of the facts they signified. Some among those who held this view thought that the new formal logic offered by *Principia Mathematica* would supply the general structure of the language of paraphrase, the general forms of the clarifying sentences. Some philosophers even thought they knew what the ultimate elements of analysis would turn out to be — what kind of terms would provide the content for these general forms. These primitive terms, they thought, would denote what was immediately presented to the senses — those ephemeral "givens" beloved of British empiricists from the seventeenth century down to the present. Still other philosophers remained skeptical or neutral about these points, while nevertheless accepting the general notion that clarifying paraphrases were, ideally, what analysis should produce.

Toward the end of this earlier period, a sense of disillusion began to be felt by the analysts of this persuasion. On the one hand, Wittgenstein had begun to give lectures of a quite new sort at Cambridge. His ideas, as they spread beyond the small circle of his auditors, made it possible to envisage a more flexible and more fruitful philosophical method. On the other hand, the results of actual attempts to apply the method of analysis were disappointing. The sentences of ordinary language seemed to resist being forced into the molds which had been shaped by men who had preconceived ideas about the proper form or the proper content of the clarifying paraphrases. Even translations which had, at first, seemed obviously successful began to be hedged about with doubts and qualifications, and were often in the end repudiated altogether. In the end, analysts began to feel a pervasive doubt about what they were doing. It seemed that one could only achieve a translation by sacrificing all or part of the meaning of the expression which one was trying to analyze. What was intended as analysis turned out to be falsification; or, if the original meaning was successfully conserved, fidelity was secured only at the cost of circularity.

If translation, as a philosophical method, cannot produce any sound results, it seems clearly necessary to abandon it. But it is possible, in abandoning it, to preserve something of what the analysts had originally intended. This can be done in either of two, apparently opposed, ways. Sentences of ordinary language fulfill our ordinary needs. In general, they leave nothing to be desired in the way of clarity for practical purposes, even though they leave much to be desired from the point of view of *philosophical* clarity. Thus the attempt to replace these sentences with clarifying paraphrases — clarifying in the sense that their form and their content would meet our need for philosophical understanding — was very natural. But since ordinary sentences resisted such translation, a choice had to be made. One could either retain the construction of clarifying paraphrases as one's goal, while admitting that these paraphrases could never have precisely the same meaning as the ordinary sentences they replaced, or else one could retain the goal of explaining the precise meaning of these expressions, while admitting that the construction of paraphrases in an ideal language

would not produce this result. The first choice gives rise to the program of linguistic constructionism, the second to that of description of linguistic usage. If one adopts the most rigorous and most highly developed form of the first program, one will construct a formal system which uses, generally, the apparatus of modern logic and in which the concepts forming the subject-matter of the system are introduced by means of axioms and definitions. The construction of the system will generally be accompanied by extra-systematic remarks in some way relating the concepts of the system to concepts which we already use in an unsystematic way. This is the method of "rational reconstruction"; and indeed the system of elementary logic itself, which provides the general form of the system as a whole, can be regarded as a reconstruction of the set of concepts expressed by the logical constants of daily life. Following the other method seems very different. For it consists in the attempt to describe the complex patterns of logical behavior which the concepts of daily life exhibit. It is not a matter of prescribing the model conduct of model words, but of describing the actual conduct of actual words; not a matter of making rules, but of noting customs. Obviously the first method has certain advantages. The nature and the powers of the apparatus to be used are clear. Its users know in advance what *sort* of thing they are going to make with it. The practitioner of the second method is not so well placed. Unless he is to be content with the production and juxtaposition of particular examples, he needs some metavocabulary in which to describe the features he finds. *Ex hypothesi*, the well-regulated metavocabulary of the first method is inadequate for his purposes. So he has to make his own tools; and, too often, hastily improvised, overweighted with analogy and association, they prove clumsy, lose their edge after one operation and serve only to mutilate where they should dissect.

I wish to examine in more detail these

two apparently opposed methods. I shall compare their merits in respect of that philosophical clarification which they both hope to achieve. Obviously, the result of such a comparison will depend in part on the sense one gives to the notion of "clarification." One could interpret this word in such a way that there was' no interesting question as to which of the two methods would be better for this purpose. Such a result would ensue, for example, from taking "clarification" in the sense which Carnap seems to give it in the first chapter of *Logical Foundations of Probability*. A prescientific concept is clarified in this sense if it is supplanted or succeeded by one which is more *exact* and more *fruitful*. The criterion of fruitfulness, according to Carnap, is that the concept should be useful in the formulation of many logical theorems or empirical scientific laws. The criterion of exactness is that the rules of the use of the concept should be such as to give it a clear place "in a well-connected system of scientific concepts." Such a well-connected system, it seems, is a formal system which incorporates them. If one agrees with Carnap on all these points, then clearly the thesis that clarification can be best achieved by system-construction appears as an understatement.

Even if we abjure this last step, and think of clarification more vaguely as the introduction, for scientific purposes, of scientifically exact and fruitful concepts in place of some of those we use for all the other ordinary and extraordinary purposes of life, the issue between the two methods remains less than exciting. I am not competent to discuss the extent to which theoretical scientists either examine minutely the behavior of words in ordinary language or construct axiom systems. It seems to me extremely improbable that they do much of the first; and I suspect (but may be quite wrong) that logicians exaggerate the extent to which they do, or ought to do, the second. But my incompetence in this area troubles me not at all. For however much or little the constructionist technique is the right means of getting an idea into shape for use in the sciences, it seems *prima facie* evident that to offer formal explanations of key terms of scientific theories to one who seeks philosophical illumination of essential concepts of nonscientific discourse is to do something utterly irrelevant — is a sheer misunderstanding, like offering a text-book on physiology to someone who says (with a sigh) that he wished he understood the workings of the human heart. In the case of many a philosophically troubling concept, indeed, it is hard to know in what direction to look for a scientifically satisfactory concept which stands to it in the required relation of correspondence or similarity. But the general conclusion holds even for those cases where there is a clear correlation. I may mention, for example, Carnap's own example of the clarification of the prescientific concept of warmth by the introduction of the exact and scientifically fruitful concept of temperature. Sensory concepts in general have been a rich source of philosophical perplexity. How are the look, the sound, the feel of a material object related to each other and to the object itself? Does it follow from the fact that the same object can feel warm to one man and cold to another that the object really is neither cold nor warm nor has any such property? These questions can be answered, or the facts and difficulties that lead to our asking them can be made plain; but not by means of formal exercises in the scientic use of the related concepts of temperature, wavelength, and frequency. Indeed the introduction of the scientific concepts may itself produce a further crop of puzzles, arising from an unclarity over the relations between two ways of using language to talk about the physical world, the relations between the quantitative and the sensory vocabularies. This unclarity is another which will scarcely be removed by exhibiting the formal workings of the quantitative concepts.

It is possible, however, to understand

the idea of clarification, and of the contribution which system-construction may make to it, in a different and more philosophical way; in such a way, in fact, that the issue stated at the outset remains open, requires to be argued further. The partisan of constructionism may well concede that introducing exact concepts for scientic purposes is one thing, and clarifying ordinary concepts is another. He may also concede that the latter task is the peculiarly philosophical one. Conceding all this, he may still maintain that the latter task will be best fulfilled by system-construction. He can maintain that attempts to analyze the forms of ordinary discourse are inevitably futile, because of the untidiness, the instability, the disorder, and the complexity of ordinary language. In place of undertaking such an analysis, he may say, let us construct perspicuous models of this language (or at least of some parts of this language) in which all the *essential* logical relations between our ordinary concepts are evident, because they will have been freed from the incidental ambiguities of every-day speech. Such a model of language has the following features. First, it is intrinsically clear, in that its key concepts are related in precise and determinate ways, whereas, *ex hypothesi*, the ordinary concepts to be clarified do not have such precise and determinate relations to each other or to the other ordinary concepts in terms of which we might seek to explain them. Second, at least some of the key concepts of the system are, in important respects, very close to the ordinary concepts which are to be clarified. The system as a whole then appears as a precise and rigid structure to which our ordinary conceptual equipment is a loose and untidy approximation.

The way in which the debate could once more reach an uninteresting deadlock is the following. It could be maintained dogmatically on the one hand that nothing but the mastery of such a system would really *be* understanding in a philosophical sense, of the concepts to be clarified. Or it might be maintained dogmatically on the other hand that since, *ex hypothesi*, the ordinary concepts to be examined do not behave in the well-regulated way in which the model concepts of the system are made to behave, there can be no real understanding of the former except such as may be gained by a detailed consideration of the way they do behave, i.e. by an investigation of the ordinary uses of the linguistic expressions concerned. Here the deadlock is reached by each party refusing to count as *understanding* a condition which is not reached by the method he advocates.

There may be something final about this deadlock. For there may here be something which is in part a matter simply of preference, of choice. Nevertheless, there are considerations which may influence choice. For surely, in deciding what to count as philosophical understanding, it is reasonable to remind ourselves what philosophical problems and unclarities are *like*. Such a reminder I shall briefly attempt later. But I shall partly anticipate it now, in mentioning some general difficulties which arise for the constructionist in the position he is now assumed to occupy.

The constructionist would of course agree that it is necessary to supply an interpretation for the linguistic expressions of his theory. This is not secured merely by the formal relationships between the constructed concepts which the theory exhibits. At some point it is necessary also to explain the meaning of the linguistic expressions for the constructed concepts in terms which do not belong to the theory and the meaning of which is taken as already known. So *some* extra-systematic remarks are essential. This point need not in itself raise any particular difficulty. So long as a small number of extra-systematic points of contact are clearly made, the meaning of the remaining elements follows from their clearly defined relationships within the system to those to which life has been given by the extra-systematic remarks. But if the constructionist claim to achieve clarification is to be vindicated, it is not sufficient, though it is necessary, that the interpretation of the linguistic expressions of his theory should be determined. For the claim to clarify will seem empty, unless the results achieved have some bearing on the typical philosophical problems and difficulties which arise concerning the concepts to be clarified. Now these problems and difficulties (it will be admitted) have their roots in ordinary, unconstructed concepts, in the elusive, deceptive modes of functioning of unformalized linguistic expressions. It is precisely the purpose of the reconstruction (we are now supposing) to solve or dispel problems and difficulties so rooted. But how can this purpose be achieved unless extra-systematic points of contact are made, not just at the one or two points necessary to fix the interpretation of the constructed concepts, but at *every* point where the relevant problems and difficulties concerning the unconstructed concepts arise? That is to say, if the clear mode of functioning of the constructed concepts is to cast light on problems and difficulties rooted in the unclear mode of functioning of the unconstructed concepts, then precisely the ways in which the constructed concepts are connected with and depart from the unconstructed concepts must be plainly shown. And how can *this* result be achieved without accurately describing the modes of functioning of the unconstructed concepts? But this task is precisely the task of describing the logical behavior of the linguistic expressions of natural languages; and may *by itself* achieve the sought-for resolution of the problems and difficulties rooted in the elusive, deceptive mode of functioning of unconstructed concepts. I should not want to deny that in the discharge of this task, the construction of a model object of linguistic comparison may sometimes be of great help. But I do want to deny that the construction and contemplation of such a model object can *take the place* of the discharge of this task; and I want also to suggest that one thinks that it can only if one is led away from

the purpose of achieving philosophical understanding by the fascination of other purposes, such as that of getting on with science.

Moreover, the general usefulness of systems of constructed concepts as objects of comparison with the unconstructed concepts in which our problems are rooted is necessarily limited. For the types or modes of logical behavior which ordinary concepts exhibit are extremely diverse. To detect and distinguish them is a task in which one may well be hindered rather than helped by fixing one's eye too firmly on the limited range of types of logical behavior which the concepts occurring in a formal system can there be shown to display. Such a system can only offer us relations between constructed concepts which have been fixed by stipulative definition. In this respect, system-construction reproduces the limitations and the narrowness of the original conception of analysis. Like it, it simply puts to one side a great number of widely different features of the functioning of our language — features which it is important to observe and describe with precision, if one wishes to resolve philosophical problems. One might put the point metaphorically as follows: living, linguistic beings have an enormous diversity of functions, only some of which can be reproduced by the computer-like machines which the constructionist can build.

It is still, however, too soon for us to say that we have reached a definitive judgment concerning the relative merits of the two methods. It is, in fact, impossible to make such a judgment without attempting a general description of philosophical problems, difficulties, and questions. It is rash to attempt such a general description, but at any rate this much will be broadly agreed: that they are problems, difficulties and questions *about* the concepts we use in various fields, and not problems, difficulties and questions which arise *within* the fields of their use. To say more is to risk the loss of general agreement.

Nevertheless, I think it is possible roughly to distinguish, though not to separate, certain strands or elements in the treatment of this diverse mass of conceptual questions. First, and very centrally, we find the necessity of dealing with paradox and perplexity. For it often happens that someone reflecting on a certain set of concepts finds himself driven to adopt views which seem to others paradoxical or unacceptably strange, or to have consequences which are paradoxical or unacceptably strange. Or — the obverse of this — it may happen that someone so reflecting becomes unable to see how something that he knows very well to be the case can *possibly* be the case. In this situation the critical philosopher must not only restore the conceptual balance which has somehow been upset; he must also diagnose the particular sources of the loss of balance, show just how it has been upset. And these achievements are not independent of each other. It also seems to me possible to say in general what kind of thing the source of conceptual unbalance is. Such unbalance results from a kind of temporary one-sidedness of vision, a kind of selective blindness which cuts out most of the field, but leaves one part of it standing out with a peculiar brilliance. This condition may take many different, though interconnected forms. The producer of philosophical paradox, or the sufferer from philosophical perplexity, is temporarily dominated by one logical mode of operation of expressions, or by one way of using language, or by one logical type or category of objects, or by one sort of explanation, or by one set of cases of the application of a given concept; and attempts to see, to explain, something which is different in terms of, or on analogy with, his favored model. The distortions which result from such attempts are of equally many kinds. To correct the distortions, one must make plain the actual modes of operation of the distorted concepts or types of discourse; and, in doing this, one must make plain the differences between their modes of operation and those of the model concepts or types of discourse; and, in doing this, one must, if one can, make plain the sources of the blinding obsession with the model cases.

This, then, is one strand in the treatment of philosophical problems — one which is in itself quite complex. I call it central, partly because the need for it has in fact provided so strong an impetus to the whole activity. From it can be distinguished, though not separated, certain other strands. One is the attempt to explain, not just how our concepts and types of discourse operate, but why it is that we have such concepts and types of discourse as we do; and what alternatives there might be. This is not a historical enquiry. It attempts to show the natural foundations of our logical, conceptual apparatus, in the way things happen in the world, and in our own natures. A form which propositions exemplifying this strand in philosophy may often take is the following: if things (or we) were different in such-and-such ways, then we might lack such-and-such concepts or types of discourse; or have such-and-such others; or might accord a subordinate place to some which are now central, and a central place to others; or the concepts we have might be different in such-and-such ways. It might reasonably be maintained, or ruled, that full understanding of a concept is not achieved until this kind of enquiry is added to the activities of comparing, contrasting and distinguishing which I mentioned first. Of course speculations of this kind are restricted in certain ways: they are limited by the kinds of experience and the conceptual apparatus we in fact have. But this is only the restriction to intelligibility; it leaves a wide field open to philosophical imagination.

The distinction I used above between the way things happen in the world, and our own natures, is here, though vague, important. For it is a part of our nature that, things other than ourselves being as they are, it is natural for us to have the conceptual apparatus that we do have. But human nature is diverse enough to allow of another, though related, use of philosophical imagination. This consists in imagining ways in which, without things other than ourselves being different from what they are, we might view them through the medium of a different conceptual apparatus. Here, then, is a third strand. Some metaphysics is best, or most charitably, seen as consisting in part in exercises of this sort. Of course, even when it can be so interpreted, it is not *presented* as a conceptual or structural revision by means of which we might see things differently; it is presented as a picture of things as they *really* are, instead of as they delusively seem. And this presentation, with its contrast between esoteric reality and daily delusion, involves and is the consequence of the unconscious distortion of ordinary concepts, i.e. of the ordinary use of linguistic expressions. So metaphysics, though it can sometimes be charitably interpreted in the way I suggest, in fact always involves paradox and perplexities of the kind I first mention; and sometimes embodies no rudimentary vision, but merely rudimentary mistakes.

Still other strands need to be distinguished. That examination of current concepts and types of discourse to which paradox and perplexity so commonly give the initial impulse, can be pursued with no particular therapeutic purpose, but for its own sake. This is not to say that puzzlement is not in question here. One can, without feeling any particular temptation to mistaken assimilations, simply be aware that one does not clearly understand how some type of expression functions, in comparison with others. Or, having noticed, or had one's attention drawn to, a certain logico-linguistic feature appearing in one particular area of discourse, one may simply wish to discover how extensive is the range of this feature, and what other comparable features are to be found. Of course, the resulting enquiries may well pay therapeutic dividends. But this need

not be the purpose for which they are undertaken. Here, then, is a fourth strand.

I think that there is a fifth philosophical aim to which those which I have so far sketched should be subordinated. So far, I have spoken of metaphysics as if its principle aim were the reformation of concepts, and its most frequent achievement their deformation. I have contrasted reforming metaphysics with descriptive analysis. However, we should recognize the existence of another sort of metaphysics, one which shares the descriptive aim of analysis. The descriptive metaphysician resembles the descriptive analyst in that he wishes to make clear the actual behavior of our concepts, rather than to change them. His enterprise differs from that of the analyst only in scope and in level of generality. But this difference is important. An analytical examination of a certain area of human thought — an analysis, say, of the concept of memory, or of cause, or of logical necessity — may, and should, take a great deal for granted, presuppose a great deal. To clarify a particular part of our conceptual apparatus, there is no need to make a profound study of the general structure of that apparatus. But the goal of descriptive metaphysics will consist precisely in the exhibition of that structure. It will try to show how the fundamental categories of our thought hang together and how they relate, in turn, to those formal notions (such as existence, identity, and unity) which range through all categories. Obviously the conclusions which descriptive metaphysics reaches must not conflict with those arrived at by a careful descriptive analysis. Still, it is not evident that the tools and the method of descriptive analysis can suffice by themselves to do the job which descriptive metaphysics attempts.

If these are the tasks of philosophy, what can we now say about the pretensions of the two heirs of the classical program of analysis — the two contrasting methods of philosophical clarification which we have been examining? It seems to me that the roles of these two methods become clear when we consider the first and the fourth objectives of philosophical inquiry which I have distinguished. The description of the modes of functioning of actually employed linguistic expressions is of the essence of the fourth aim; and it is simply the least clouded form of a procedure which is essential to the achievement of the first. Here the arguments put forward above apply. To observe our concepts in action is necessarily the only way of finding out what they can and cannot do. The right kind of attention to the ordinary use of expressions provides a means of refutation of theories founded on mistaken assimilations; it provides a description of the actual functioning of the problematic concepts, to take the place of the mistaken theory; and, finally, it helps, or may help, with the diagnosis of the temptations to the mistakes. This last it may do because the analogies which seduce the philosopher are not, in general, private fantasies; they have their roots in our ordinary thinking, and show themselves in practically harmless, but detectable ways, in ordinary language — both in its syntactical structure and in the buried metaphors which individual words and phrases contain. I have already acknowledged that system-construction may have an ancillary role in achieving these two types of aim, and given reasons for thinking that it must remain ancillary — and limited. Model objects of linguistic comparison may help us to understand the given objects; but it is dogmatism to maintain that the construction of model objects is the best or the only means of achieving such understanding.

In the case of those exercises of philosophical imagination which I have referred to as the second and third strands, the case is somewhat different. To understand the foundation of our concepts in natural facts, and to envisage alternative possibilities, it is not enough to have a sharp eye for linguistic actualities. Nor is system-construction a direct contribution to the

achievement of the first of these two, i.e. to seeing why we talk as we do. But it may be to the second, i.e. to imagining how else we might talk. The constructionist may perhaps be seen as an enlightened reforming metaphysician — one who, perhaps wistfully, envisages the possibility of our situation and our need for communication so changed and simplified that such a well-regulated system of concepts as he supplies is well adapted to both. It is only when the claim to exclusiveness is made on behalf of the constructionist method, and of particular constructions, that one must begin to query the enlightenment. But, again, this claim may be softened to the expression of a preference — which leaves one no more to say.

There remains the fifth strand in the philosophical enterprise. It is obviously interlaced with the others, and cannot be detached from them. Still, it imposes its own demands. It is possible to stick to the scrupulous examination of the actual behavior of words, and to claim that this is the only sure path in descriptive philosophy. But it seems to me that if we do no more than this, then the relations and the structures which we shall discover will not be sufficiently general, or sufficiently far-reaching, to satisfy our urge for full metaphysical understanding. For when we ask ourselves questions about the use of a certain expression, the answers we give ourselves, revealing as they are at a certain level, presuppose, rather than exhibit, the general structural elements which metaphysician wishes to discover. This does not mean that the metaphysician can ignore either the conclusions or the methods of descriptive analysis. On the contrary, these methods and conclusions serve as an indispensable control in the working-out of properly metaphysical solutions. But neither do these methods suffice, of themselves, to arrive at such properly metaphysical conclusions. For myself, I can offer no general recipe for achieving the sort of comprehension I have in mind here. It would indeed be the vainest of dreams to imagine that the structure which descriptive metaphysics wishes to discover could be crystallized in any formal system.

To conclude, then. There is not just one thing which is legitimately required of the philosopher who would increase our conceptual understanding. In particular, it is certainly not *enough* to say that he should describe the functioning of actually employed linguistic expressions. For simply to say this would not be to give any indication of the sort of description he should provide. That indication is given when it is shown how description of the right sort may bear upon our conceptual confusions and problems. Next we see how more may be required of him than the resolution of these confusions with the help of those descriptions; how a more systematic classification and ordering of the types of discourse and concept we employ may be sought; how a fuller understanding of both may be gained by enquiring into their foundation in natural facts; how room may here be found for the envisaging of other possibilities; how he may, in the end, strive for the goal of a descriptive metaphysics. If the philosopher is to do all or only some of these things, it is true that he cannot stop short at the literal description, and illustration, of the behavior of actually used linguistic expressions. Nevertheless, the actual use of linguistic expressions remains his sole and essential point of contact with the reality which he wishes to understand, conceptual reality; for this is the only point from which the actual mode of operation of concepts can be observed. If he severs this vital connection, all his ingenuity and imagination will not save him from lapses into the arid or the absurd.

Editor's note: For comment on the notion of "descriptive metaphysics" which Strawson presents here, see the items cited in footnote 74 of the Introduction. For comment on his criticism of "constructionism" see the article by Maxwell and Feigl reprinted above at pp. 193–200; and also Carnap [7].

· 25b ·

DISCUSSION OF STRAWSON'S
"ANALYSIS, SCIENCE, AND METAPHYSICS"

(Chaired by Jean Wahl)

Mr. Jean Wahl: I will give the floor first to Mr. Taylor, who, I think, has a question on a very particular point.

Mr. Charles Taylor: The question which I should like to ask bears, I think, on the content of your paper rather than simply on its form. I am puzzled about what sort of proposition one would end up with after following out the "fifth strand of the philosophical enterprise" which you have discussed. Would it be simply a sort of abbreviated synthesis of the results obtained along the other four routes (particularly the first and fourth)? Would it be a systematization of the results which one gets from following the second route — namely, a set of reflections on the world and on human nature, taking their point of departure from facts about language? If the latter, would not following out the fifth strand lead one to a sort of conceptual structure? I do not know whether I have followed your train of thought properly, but I would like to know more about the sort of propositions which might emerge along this fifth route.

Mr. Strawson: Perhaps I can answer Mr. Taylor by putting forward one or two examples of what I have in mind. These may be ill-chosen, but if they are sound, they represent what I mean by "descriptive metaphysics."

Let us first take the case of Kant. When he tries to prove that the existence of an objective temporal order (or, more pre-

cisely, that our capacity to dispose phenomena in an objective temporal order) depends necessarily on the use we make of the concept of causality in relating a phenomenon to its cause, he then undertakes an enterprise which, if successful, would establish that a fundamental relation existed between two general concepts — that of an objective temporal order, and that of causality. To establish this, if such a thing could be established, would be a part of descriptive metaphysics as I conceive it.

I can offer another example. If one sets one's face against the empiricist tradition, which tries to reduce everything to the experiences of an individual subject, then one will try to demonstrate that such subjective experiences can only be fitted into an ontology which includes such entities as persons and animals (since these experiences can only be identified if one can identify such entities). This latter thesis, which I personally think is true, is another example of descriptive metaphysics. It relates two very general types of entity — two clearly identifiable categories — and makes manifest the subordination of the one to the other within a general conceptual scheme.

Do these two examples seem sufficient to illustrate what I mean by descriptive metaphysics?

Mr. Taylor: Yes, except that they strike me as simply prolongations of your *second* type of philosophical inquiry. They are very close to the classical forms of ontology.

Mr. Strawson: No doubt. But when I described what I called the second effort of the philosophical imagination, I said that the propositions at which it aimed would have the following form: "If things were different from what they are in such-and-such respects, then our conceptual structure would also differ in certain respects." Now it seems to me that one can cite many cases of such possible differences, and that in these cases we can ask ourselves just how our conceptual structure would be modified. On the other hand, when we reach that higher level on which I have placed descriptive metaphysics (although I concede that it is very difficult to mark off such levels of inquiry from one another), we often encounter the fact that it is almost impossible to describe what an alternative conceptual structure might look like. At this higher level, we attempt something more general and more fundamental than was attempted in the second approach, although obviously closely related to it.

Mr. Leon Apostel: My first question bears upon the following phrase of Mr. Strawson's: "If things were different than they are in certain respects, then we might lack a certain way of speaking . . ." If the world were different, then our language would be different. I am curious to know how one could demonstrate such a proposition. While reflecting on this point, an example has occurred to me. Consider that we are familiar with two languages: L1 and L2. In the first, the verb agrees with the subject. In the second, it agrees with the object. (I am, of course, using "subject" and "object" in the ordinary sense which the grammarian gives them.) Can Mr. Strawson describe a possible world in which L1 would be applicable, and another in which L2 would be applicable? I have tried, in reflecting on this model, to imagine what he might propose. I came up with the following: if we imagine a world where the causes, movers, forces, and agents were extremely diverse and almost completely determined their effects, whereas the matter upon which they acted was homogenous and, so to speak, amorphorus, playing no role in causal interaction, then I can see that a language in which the verb agreed with the subject would be possible, whereas one in which it agreed with the object would be hardly conceivable. Is this the sort of thing Mr. Strawson has in mind? I doubt it, but if not, then I would like to know what would be an illustration of the situation expressed by the phrase I have quoted from his paper.

My second question bears on the notion of "descriptive metaphysics." What is the method of the discipline? Is it, for Mr. Strawson, similar to or different from the inquiries conducted by Benjamin Whorf? You will remember that when Whorf studied certain primitive languages, he claimed that they contained many more modalities than ours, that they had no names for objects, that they placed a much greater emphasis upon action, etc. He inferred from this the existence of an enormous number of modes and degrees of existence, the primacy of becoming over being, and of events over things. Is this the sort of method you envisage for descriptive metaphysics, or is there another?

Mr. Strawson: In the first place, I should say that even if I could form no such picture of the world as you speak of, this would make no difference to the topic under discussion. The question is not really about our being able to say what changes in our vision of the world would produce such-and-such profound modifications in the structure of our language, but rather about being able to say what changes might enter our language as a result of such-and-such profound changes in our vision of the world. However that may be, I think that the first part of your question had a more general import, and that you were really asking me about how one could hope to demonstrate this sort of proposition. I must answer that I do not think there *is* any way of demonstrating that an answer to this sort of question is correct. This is an important point of difference between descriptive metaphysics and analysis as currently practiced, for in the latter we can always provide a demonstration by reference to the current usage of language. Such an appeal is pointless, however, when we want to know what changes of current usage would be brought about by changes in our vision of the world. All I dare to say, on a question as delicate as this, is that one may hope for something like a demonstration — namely, an agreement among those who are particularly aware of, and sensitive to, all the nuances of linguistic expression, about what modifications of language would *probably* be entailed by such changes in our vision of the world. I do not say that such agreement would meet our ideal standards of proof, but I do not think that we are going to get anything better. One sign of the probative value of such agreement seems to be that it is, in fact, relatively easy to achieve on certain points. If you wish, I shall modify the schema for the sort of proposition I would hope might be formulated into the following: "It seems to us extremely probable, in the present circumstances, that our language might adapt itself in such-and-such a way to such-and-such modifications in the way things happen . . ." In this limited form, such propositions seem to me quite plausible, and even demonstrable.

Mr. Apostel: If you don't mind, I should like to add something to suggest why I asked my original question. Propositions from which one can infer certain conclusions concerning unrealized possibilities seem to me to be properly characterized as *laws*. It therefore seems to me that one would first have to lay down the laws which govern the relations between the world of language and the world of things, before one could say anything useful about the possible effects upon one world of a change in the other. If this is so, I think it follows that you would have to construct a formal model of language before you were in a position to put forward any counterfactual proposition.

Mr. Strawson: Yes, but now you are appealing to a certain view about counterfactual conditionals which one can refute by invoking certain propositions which are themselves counter-factual conditionals. (*Laughter from the audience*). The examples which would help to defend this view are probably borrowed from contexts very different from those with which I am concerned. It does not seem proper to extrapolate conclusions drawn from such examples to cover theses of the type we have just been discussing, which seem obviously to belong in a very special context. I would add also that when we are concerned with purely descriptive analyses of languages, we do not appeal to the results of the statistical methods currently practiced in empirical linguistics. Rather, we appeal to our own experience, our own intimate acquaintance with the language which we are studying. This practice seems legitimate as regards the descriptive aspect of linguistic analysis, and I think it may also be applied in descriptive metaphysics. For myself, I see no reason why it should be linked to empirical and statistical methods.

As I have gone along, I have partially anticipated my answer to your second question, for I have admitted that I cannot cite any features which are peculiar to the method of descriptive metaphysics. Still, I have said that the conclusions reached by the descriptive metaphysician cannot conflict with those reached by the other methods practiced within analytic philosophy, and so whatever one can say about these other methods will also apply to descriptive metaphysics. I cannot offer anything more precise than that.

Mr. Wahl: I think that Professor Leroy has a question on a related problem.

Mr. Georges Leroy: I have collected some passages (taken, unfortunately, from the translation of your paper) which may perhaps undermine your position. You can tell me whether in fact they do. First, you say that "We try to uncover the natural foundations of our logical and conceptual apparatus." This will of course, on your view, be achieved by a method which is distinct from a simple historical inquiry. (By "logical" I take it you mean "what concerns language" rather than "what concerns the logical structure of discourse," but we need more precision on this point.) You continue the previous passage by saying ". . . by finding them in the way things happen in the world, and in our own natures." This passage, which is not the only one of its kind, seems to say that language can express, in a rather precise way, not only how things happen in the world, but also how they happen in our own natures. I find confirmation of this interpretation in a passage at the end of your paper where you say that "The actual use of linguistic expressions remains his sole and essential point of contact with the reality which he wishes to understand; conceptual reality." This is the first point which I find troublesome. It becomes still more troublesome when you add "for this is the only point from which the actual mode of operation of concepts can be observed. If he severs this vital connection, all his ingenuity and imagination will not save him from lapses into the arid or the absurd."

I understand from this that you hold that our concepts must always correspond to a certain concrete reality, and that language has no value except insofar as it expresses this reality. Language, then, in its normal usage, as well as the logic which is manifested in this normal usage, proceed directly from the concrete subject — are somehow engendered by life itself. Do we agree on this point? If so, then a question comes to mind at once: Does logic really express the foundation of things, their natural foundation? Does language really express this foundation? If it does, then it is not a descriptive, but an explicative, metaphysics which you are proposing. Such a

metaphysics would describe the foundation of things, and not only the way our language functions. I confess that I find it very difficult to follow you here, for I regard language as expressing hypotheses and inferences about the foundation of things. This is why our language continues to evolve, in order to adapt itself to what we know about things. Here we have two quite different views of the matter, and it seems to me that you tend, at times, to veer toward the second — as when you say "It would indeed be the vainest of dreams to imagine that the structure which descriptive metaphysics wishes to discover could be crystallized in any formal system." I find myself caught in a dilemma here, and I should simply like you to clear up your own position on the topic.

Mr. Strawson: You have raised several points here. In the first place, I should defend the passage which you quoted from the conclusion of my paper by saying that the philosopher's principal task is the understanding of how our thought about things works, and that we cannot find out about these workings except by looking at how we use words. To put it another way, linguistic usage is the only experimental datum which we possess that is relevant to inquiry about the behavior of our concepts. It seems to me to follow that if we want to understand these concepts, we should look to the way in which they are articulately manifested — namely, to language.

You point out that if I adopt the view that our conceptual apparatus depends, in a certain way, on how things happen in the world, then it follows that a description of that apparatus is simultaneously a description of how the world goes. You support this point by citing the passage where I say that part of our job consists precisely in laying bare the foundations of our conceptual structure, and that these foundations will be found by looking to how things happen in the world.

It does not seem to me that there is a real difficulty here. All that we can say about how things happen in the world boils down to a few very general and very commonplace propositions. The relation between how things happen and the nature of our conceptual apparatus only appears clearly when we ask how that apparatus would be affected if the world were to behave differently. Only thus can we get at those particular features of the behavior of things in the world which directly affect the conceptual structures we use. The analyst's first job, nonetheless, remains that of describing the existing conceptual apparatus, and I do not think that from *such* an analysis one can get any interesting new information whatsoever about the nature of things. This admission does not prevent me from saying, as I have, that the behavior of things is the foundation of our conceptual structure. It does not follow from this thesis that language can tell us anything new about the world. I hold to this thesis simply because I think that if things were different, then our language would be different, and this fact seems to me a valid indication, if not a decisive proof, of the interaction in question.

Father H. L. Van Breda: I had at first thought that I would hold off my questions until later, but I am concerned to keep in focus the important point which Professor Leroy has raised concerning the passage in which you say: "The actual use of linguistic expressions remains the philosopher's sole and essential point of contact with the reality he wishes to understand, conceptual reality; for this is the only point from which the actual mode of operation of concepts can be observed."

This thesis, which you have put forward in a very sweeping way, has led me into a certain train of thought. I hope that Mr. Strawson will pardon me for summarizing these reflections. For some years, I have watched the development of the analytic movement in philosophy — not from very near at hand, perhaps, but nonetheless fairly closely. The failure of communication between all (or most) Continental philosophers on the one hand and Anglo-American philosophers on the other is really striking. The sentence I have cited from Mr. Strawson's paper has provided me with an occasion to formulate two or three problems which, I think, are at the bottom of this failure.

I myself, as many of you know, am a representative of the phenomenological movement, rather than of any of the other philosophical traditions which my clerical costume might suggest. For the phenomenologist, or the philosopher who takes his point of departure from the phenomenological movement, the thesis that the sole point of contact with that reality which philosophy wishes to understand is language is entirely inadmissable. To say that the reality we wish to understand is *conceptual* reality is still more objectionable. Here we have a first, and very important, point of difference between the two schools. To the question "What does the philosopher want to understand?" Continental philosophers would firmly reply that it is *not* conceptual reality, but the world in which we live, in all its complexity.

In the second place, you claim that language is the *only* point of contact with reality. I see no good argument for this whatever, especially if I adopt a purely descriptive attitude of the sort which the analytic method recommends. The simple description of my own consciousness, and of all that of which *I am conscious*, shows me that there are a great many ways of being-in-the-world, and thus shows me that I have the ability to understand, to find intelligible, what happens in the world. Such a description in no way suggests that language has the privileged status you claim for it.

Finally, there is a third point of difference which needs emphasis. (I am sorry to restrict myself to pointing out differences between us, but doing so will help us in the ensuing discussion.) For me, the essential philosophical question about language is this: what is language for man? I am not sure I know the answer to this

I cannot be satisfied simply to say, for example, that language in general is that phenomenon which exteriorizes itself in this or that particular language (English, French, etc.). I just do not know what to say. I am still trying to find out what language is. We have already had to drop the traditional view that language is an epiphenomon of the process of comprehension. It seems probable that language is something absolutely essential to comprehension, something at the very heart of consciousness. But I am not willing to take any theses about language for granted, and I leave myself open. I fear (but this is the confession of an adept at phenomenological analysis) that one over-simplifies too much in saying that language is a phenomenon which can more or less be identified with the ensemble of particular languages, or in saying that language is the only path to an understanding of the conceptual world, or in saying that the only goal of philosophy is an understanding of that world.

Mr. Strawson: I think that I can reformulate your point by saying that, for you, philosophy is not a matter of understanding conceptual reality through understanding language (in the sense in which one arrives at this latter understanding by studying observable facts about particular languages), but that its goal is to understand the world.

I think that your second point is entailed by your first, in the sense that if one tries to envisage the world as a whole without direct and precise reference to language one will feel no compulsion or desire to examine our every-day ways of talking about the world. I do not think we can discuss the two questions separately. You have not, however, contested my claim that if what we want to do is to elucidate the conceptual structure which regulates our usual ways of thinking about the world — ways which are revealed in everyday speech — then our essential (if not unique) point of contact is through language, in which our concepts take on an articulate form. I do not think, then, that I have to defend this claim.

The essential issue between us comes up in connection with your first question, about whether the proper end of philosophy is to understand the conceptual structure which the analysis of language reveals, or is rather to undertake that marginal activity which consists in trying to understand the world and our existence in the world.

Father Van Breda: Let us say simply: our *relation with* the world. When you say "our existence in the world" you are adopting a different philosophical jargon.

Mr. Strawson: I have to confess that neither the concept of a relation with the world, nor that of existence in the world, strikes me as very clear. Can't we simply leave all that to the psychologists?

Father Van Breda: I do not believe that that is their job at all.

Mr. Strawson: I should like to be more confident that I grasp what it is that we are supposed to understand. It seems to be neither something which falls within the province of experimental science, nor something to which the methods I described in my paper are relevant. If it is not a conceptual structure, I do not know what it is.

Father Van Breda: You seem at least to be familiar with one of the ways of being-in-the-world — *viz.*, the mode of apprehending the world through the use of concepts. But I am not quite sure I know what your conception of this mode is. You seem quite sure that you know what it is to be with things, to be in touch with them, when speaking about them in conceptual terms. I am still trying to find out what this is. For me, there are still problems about language, and in particular there is the problem of the nature of conceptual language. For you, it seems that apprehension of the world through concepts is the only, or the essential, mode of being-in-the-world. For me, it is only one among a great many others. I might mention, as examples of these others, love, religion, and emotion. Each of these are ways of being with things, of grasping things, and none of them is blind.

Mr. Strawson: I am aware of many ways of standing in relation to things in addition to that particular way which makes use of conceptual structures. But it seems to me that the study of these other relationships belongs elsewhere — in history, the social sciences, scientific research, the practice of the arts and skills which we use in daily life, in the experience of the individual . . .

Father Van Breda: But you have to distinguish what you are doing from what the philologist does! I am putting these questions to you as a *philosopher*. Surely there remains something to do after the historian or the scientist has had his say!

Mr. Strawson: After history has had its say, there will remain problems about, for example, the idea of causality as it is used in the historian's explanations. This is just the sort of problem which leads us to conceptual inquiry, to philosophy as I conceive it. But I don't see what *else* there is for philosophy to do than to conduct inquiry of this type concerning the underlying conceptual schemes, either of particular disciplines or of daily speech.

Father Van Breda: Let me take up the cudgels once again, briefly. To take your example of history, I should say that historical *being* is not a concept. It is a reality. The concept of a historical being is a poor thing in comparison with the reality of that being. What I wish, myself, to try to discover through reflection, and to express, is the totality of that historical being. To be sure, I shall have to express myself using concepts; I have the greatest respect for conceptual thought. But the reality that I shall thus express will always transcend whatever I am able to say. Further, I grasp this reality in my consciousness, apart from my poor concepts. I do not retain all of it when I reduce it to concepts. If I stuck to concepts alone, I should simply impoverish myself. Why, as a philosopher, should I abjure the right to try

to discover something more, by any other method which seems good to me? You will tell me that this "something more" will simply be one more concept, since this is how we think. But despite all that, it will be *that which* I wish to express *in* concepts — not my concept of a historical being, but historical being itself. If I cannot do this, prove to me that I cannot. You have not done so yet.

Mr. Wahl: May I take the floor for a minute? I should like to complement what Father Van Breda has just said. Although I agree with him at bottom, I wish to disagree with part of what he has said, in an attempt to reinterpret Mr. Strawson's remarks.

We are, after all, talking to each other. Thus, at this moment, we are forced back on normal linquistic usage. It is because we trust language to some extent that a conversation like this is possible.

Consider the term "conceptual reality." I should like to ask Mr. Strawson if he intends this term to signify a reality which is purely and strictly conceptual. Does not the term really denote, at bottom, reality itself? Being human, we must, unfortunately, (as Father Van Breda would, I think, agree) see reality more or less in conceptual terms. Thus the passages which Father Van Breda has used to indicate his disagreement with Mr. Strawson may also be used to suggest how they might be brought to agree. Since, alas, we are men, our reality is by necessity conceptual, and therefore we must have confidence in normal linguistic usage (without, however, trusting it entirely).

Father Van Breda: I could easily accept what Professor Wahl has just said, but I fear that this topic takes us far away from anything relating to the goal or the method of analytical philosophy.

Mr. Wahl: But surely the whole question is to find out whether the analysts themselves are not sometimes forced to take positions which they do not reach by applying the methods of analysis. It is quite possible that they are, and if so, then there may be more agreement between them and us than would at first appear.

Mr. Strawson: I think that the term "conceptual reality" is ambiguous, and was an unhappy choice. All that I meant by it was "the facts about our concepts." Given this interpretation, my talk about "conceptual reality" can hardly be construed as an insiduous attempt to reduce reality to concepts.

Mr. Wahl: Out of sheer curiosity, I should like to ask you another question. Once there were two philosophers who collaborated — Russell and Whitehead, when they wrote *Principia Mathematica*. Whitehead attempted a sort of descriptive philosophy. Is his the path you would have us follow? Or rather Nicolai Hartmann's? Or Husserl's? I am not sure which one you have in mind, but there would seem to be many possible paths.

Mr. Strawson: For the descriptive metaphysician to follow?

Mr. Wahl: Yes.

Mr. Strawson: Well, I should think the most illustrious example he could set himself would be Kant.

Mr. Wahl: Or Aristotle? Kant did not describe. Kant looked for conditions.

Mr. Strawson: He looked for conditions, but he described the relations between the fundamental categories of thought.

Mr. Wahl: I should not take up more time. Professor Perelman has asked for the floor.

Mr. Charles Perelman: I should like to take up two sentences which occur near the beginning of your paper: "Sentences of ordinary language fulfill our ordinary needs. In general, they leave nothing to be desired in the way of clarity for practical purposes, even though they leave much to be desired from the point of view of *philosophical* clarity." Later on, you repeat several times that the philosopher ought to concern himself with a specifically philosophical sort of understanding. Unless I am mistaken, you thus adopt an attitude quite different from that of therapeutic positivism. You seem to take philosophical problems to be *real* problems, rather than

assuming that they will somehow be dissolved by the analysis of our every-day use of ordinary language. I take it that an alternative account of analytic philosophy would be that philosophical problems arise from a careless reading of ordinary language, or from a misuse of it, or from its extension beyond its proper domain. If this were the case, the search for philosophical clarity which you propose would hardly be a respectable enterprise. Philosophical problems would be mere pseudo-problems. But if we take philosophical problems seriously, if we do not regard them as simply the fruits of a misuse of language, and if we try to solve them, must we not then be prepared to modify ordinary language in order to provide such solutions? In that case, can we still say, as you did towards the end of your paper, that we are not justified in breaking the links which bind ordinary language to reality?

Let me sum up my point in a dilemma. I may, on the one hand, respect ordinary language, say that philosophers have misused it, and then claim that there are no real philosophical problems — that all so-called philosophical problems are merely results of misunderstanding the language. On the other hand, I may respect the perplexity which philosophers feel, admit that their problems are real, and thus be driven to modify ordinary language in certain respects in order to solve these problems. In the latter case, I cannot be entirely respectful towards ordinary language.

Mr. Strawson: I am not sure why you think that there is a dilemma here. I can quite well say that there are real philosophical problems, and still add that they result, usually if not always, from a misunderstanding, from a mishandling of ordinary language. And I can say that they are not dissolved, but rather are correctly solved, by appealing to a more rigorous analysis of usage. Thus I can manifest a decent respect for ordinary language, while also trying to resolve philosophical problems (treated as quite genuine problems) through analytic methods. I see no absolute opposition between the attitude which respects ordinary language and attempts to dissolve philosophical problems on the one hand, and the attitude which wishes to solve them by modifying language on the other.

Mr. Perelman: I think, then, that what you call "philosophical understanding" boils down to nothing but an understanding of the fact that philosophers have misunderstood ordinary linguistic usage. But in that case the problems are problems arising from misunderstanding — not real problems.

Mr. Strawson: Perhaps we need to distinguish between two sorts of problems. Some problems result from a misunderstanding of ordinary language. Others . . . Of course, the misunderstanding which is in question here cannot be reduced to a simple violation of rules of correct usage. One philosopher may express himself loosely, while another may write with scrupulous care, though still failing to grasp the use he is making of certain expressions. The first may be a better philosopher than the second.

Mr. Perelman: But if the philosopher, who understands ordinary language in practical situations, misuses it when he philosophizes, then on your view, his philosophizing cannot be taken seriously. So we have really come back to what has been called therapeutic positivism. It is a matter of curing a defect of language, not of seriously studying a genuine philosophical issue. Whenever we encounter a philosophical problem, we must set to work to understand our language better, trusting that the problem will then disappear. I need not emphasize once again that if we take this view, "philosophical understanding" is merely the result of a mistake, or of a faulty knowledge of how our language works.

Mr. Strawson: But not *all* philosophical problems stem from theses which philosophers have advanced as result of distortions of ordinary language! Some may

arise from questions which we ask ourselves about a particular array of concepts and about how these concepts work. They do not all take the form of mistakes . . .

Mr. Perelman: If I do not understand how certain concepts work, I do not thereby encounter a philosophical problem, but only a philological one. A philosophical problem arises from encountering a difficulty, a contradiction, not just from simple ignorance.

Mr. Strawson: It does, indeed, often arise out of a contradiction or a paradox. But it may also arise simply out of something which, in the course of our study, provokes our curiosity.

Mr. Perelman: But the instinct of curiosity which directs inquiry is not specifically philosophical. It underlies all intellectual disciplines, not philosophy alone. Personally, I should say that if the use of familiar notions leads me into difficulties, then I have a genuine philosophical problem, and I should proceed to adopt new notions in order to avoid these difficulties. This is why taking philosophy seriously means admitting that philosophers may sometimes change ordinary language in order to solve their problems.

Mr. Wahl: We shall have to close the discussion shortly, but I see that Professor Ayer wishes to speak. We should all be happy that he has chosen to do so.

Mr. A. J. Ayer: I simply wish to make a suggestion which occurred to me as the discussion progressed, and also to put forward a slight reservation about Mr. Strawson's paper.

My suggestion is that you go too far (and needlessly provoke Father Van Breda and his friends) when you put so much stress on the differences between analysis on the facts of language and analysis of the facts which language describes. For after all, these two kinds of analysis come down to the same thing. Take, for example, belief — the fact of believing this or that. One may ask what belief is, or one may ask what one is saying when one says "I believe . . ." For practical purposes, the difference is not great; the only point in emphasizing the "linguistic" aspect so strongly is to avoid confusion between the inquiry philosophers conduct and that conducted in such sciences as ethnology, psychology, or history. In stressing this aspect, however, you have laid a snare into which Father Van Breda and others have fallen only too easily. I think it pointless to set such traps.

I should like to express some reservations, and bring in some further considerations, on another point. To hear you tell it, analytic philosophy sounds like a strange sort of *omnium gatherum*, taking in every sort of study, technique, and preoccupation. And yet, your inventory is incomplete: your five strands do not account for everything that happens in analytic philosophy. In particular, it seems to me that you have left out the epistemological problems which Carnap made so much of and which have given rise to so many discussions and so many lines of inquiry. In the recent history of the discussion of these problems, I do not think that the urge to describe has been particularly important. Rather, a polemical urge has been dominant — the urge to impose one's own point of view, and to answer one's opponents' arguments one by one. This is a very important point, and one which your paper passes over — namely, that analytic philosophers spend their time arguing, refuting each other, and trying to impose their competing descriptions of "underlying conceptual schemes" upon each other. Again, I am not sure whether the sort of discussions which you find in, for example, Ryle's *Concept of Mind*, would fall under any of your five headings. I shall not try to classify these discussions. But I think one should emphasize that they exist, and that a deeper study of the sorts of arguments which are employed in pursuing them would be fruitful.

Mr. Strawson: I think that I am prepared to agree with Mr. Ayer on both points. I certainly had no polemical intention in underlining the distinction between analysis of language and analysis of facts. I would not have wished it to be a distinction at which one could take umbrage.

On your second point, it is of course quite obvious that philosophers never agree. Since the philosopher is concerned, among other things, with the logical relations between concepts which his colleagues are also discussing, it is quite logical and natural that description and argument should go hand-in-hand.

Mr. Gilbert Ryle: You say "among other things." What other things do you have in mind?

Mr. Strawson: I said "among other things" because it seemed to me that concepts which actually function have various facets, and that one can study them in other ways than by noting their logical incompatibility with other concepts.

Mr. Ryle: Such as?

Mr. Strawson: For example, what Professor Austin has called the "performative aspect" of certain concepts does not seem to me to have much to do with the logical aspect of these concepts. (Professor Austin will correct me if I am wrong.) One might also cite the study of presuppositions, which one cannot easily assimilate to the study of relations of logical incompatibility.

Still, it goes without saying that the logical relations between concepts are an important aspect, perhaps the essential aspect, of what we call their "behavior in speech." This is why every description of these concepts will tend to take the form of an argument about the validity (or lack of validity) of these relations. All that one can say by way of opposing description and argument is to say that there are bad descriptions and arguments that do not prove very much.

Mr. Ayer: It seems to me that the part played by description is so slight, and that played by argumentation so great, in certain cases, that your use of "descriptive" is hardly justified. But I do not want to insist too much on this point.

· 26 ·

MAX BLACK

LANGUAGE AND REALITY

Bertrand Russell once said, "The study of grammar, in my opinion, is capable of throwing far more light on philosophical questions than is commonly supposed by philosophers. Although a grammatical distinction cannot be uncritically assumed to correspond to a genuine philosophical difference, yet the one is *prima facie* evidence of the other, and may often be most usefully employed as a source of discovery" (*The Principles of Mathematics*, Cambridge, 1903, p. 42).

The grammatical distinctions that Russell proceeds to use as guides to philosophical discoveries are the familiar ones between nouns, adjectives, and verbs. But he says that he hopes for a "classification, not of words, but of ideas" (*loc. cit.*) and adds, "I shall therefore call adjectives or predicates all notions which are capable of being such, even in a form in which grammar would call them substantives" (*ibid.*). If we are ready to call adjectives nouns, in defiance of grammar, we can hardly expect the grammatical distinction between the two parts of speech to guide us toward what Russell calls a "correct logic" (*ibid.*). If grammar is to teach us anything of philosophical importance, it must be treated with more respect.

Reprinted from *Models and Metaphors* (Ithaca, New York: Cornell University Press, 1962), pp. 1–16, by permission of the author and the publisher. (Copyright 1962 by Cornell University.)

First published in *Proceedings of the American Philosophical Association*, XXXII (1959), 5–17.

My object in this paper is to clarify the character of philosophical inferences from grammar. By "grammar" I shall understand a classification of meaningful units of speech (i.e., "morphology"), together with rules for the correct arrangement of such units in sentences (i.e., "syntax"). The conclusions of the kinds of inferences I have in mind will be propositions commonly called "ontological"; they will be metaphysical statements about "the ultimate nature of reality," like "Relations exist," or "The World is the totality of facts, not of things," or "There exists one and only one substance."

I

In seeking ontological conclusions from linguistic premises, our starting point must be the grammar of some actual language, whether living or dead. From the standpoint of a language's capacity to express what is or what might be the case, it contains much that is superfluous, in grammar as well as in vocabulary. Grammatical propriety requires a German child to be indicated by a neuter expression ("*das Kind*"), a liability from which French children are exempt. If we are willing to speak ungrammatical German or French, so long as the fact-stating resources of the languages are unimpaired, we can dispense with indications of gender. For to be told that the word "*Kind*" is neuter is to be told nothing about children that would have been the case had the German language never existed. The indifference of the English language to the gender of nouns sufficiently demonstrates the superfluity of this particular grammatical feature. For the purpose of eventual metaphysical inference, gender is an accidental, a nonessential, grammatical category.

In order to have any prospects of validity, positive philosophical inferences from grammar must be based upon essential, nonaccidental, grammatical features, that is to say on features whose deletion would impair or render impossible the fact-stating functions of language. The essential grammatical features, if there are any, must therefore be present in all actual or possible languages that have the same fact-stating powers. They must be invariant under all possible transformations of given language that conserve fact-stating resources. The system of all such invariant grammatical features would constitute a universal or philosophical grammar. Metaphysical inferences from grammar must be founded upon the constitution of a hypothetical universal grammar, in abstraction from the idiomatic peculiarities of the grammars of given languages.

There is little reason to suppose that the universal grammar, if there is such a thing, will closely resemble any conventional grammar. Contemporary linguists have made plain the "formal" character of conventional grammatical classifications and the "arbitrariness" of conventional rules of syntax. We shall need something other than grammarians' tools to uncover the universal grammar.

I assume, however, that philosophical grammar will still resemble conventional grammar in consisting of a morphology together with a syntax. I shall suppose throughout that we are considering the prospects of a certain kind of classification, coupled with a system of rules for admissible combinations of the things classified. I shall use the conveniently noncommittal expression, "linguistic features," to refer to the things classified.

Were it possible to construct a philosophical grammar, or any fragment of it, it would be very tempting to say that something would thereby have been revealed about the nature of ultimate reality. For what could be the reason for the presence of some grammatical feaure in all conceivable fact-stating languages except the correspondence of every such language with reality? There is an inclination to say with the author of the *Tractatus* that the essence of language must be "the essence of the World" (*Tractatus*, 5.4711). Or, with a more recent writer, "The universe is not a vain capricious customer of ours. If the shoe fits, this is a good clue to the size of the foot. If a language is adequate to describe it, this indicates something about its structure" (I. M. Copi, in *The Review of Metaphysics*, vol. 4 [1951], p. 436).

Of course, if metaphysical inferences from grammar are not to be circular, the construction of a universal grammar must proceed without prior ontological commitments. We shall need to consider whether the search for a universal grammar can be undertaken from a position of ontological neutrality.

It is obviously easier to show that some linguistic feature does not belong to universal grammar than the reverse; most of the examples I shall consider will have this negative character, that is to say, will be instances in which we argue that some feature of a given language is not essential to the fact-stating powers of the language. The corresponding ontological inference is the negative one that nothing in ultimate reality corresponds to the rejected linguistic feature.

II

In the *Tractatus*, Wittgenstein says, "In the proposition there must be exactly as much distinguishable (*gleich soviel zu unterscheiden*) as in the state of affairs that it represents" (4.04). Let us read this to mean: "In the particular utterance, there must be exactly as many different symbols as there are constituents in the state of affairs represented." Following Wittgenstein, I shall assign two physically similar word-tokens to different symbols, when they have different senses or references.

Let us try to apply this plausible principle of invariance of the number of constituents to a concrete instance. Suppose I am riding in an automobile with somebody who is learning to drive, and I need some pre-arranged signals to tell him to start the car or to stop it. It is natural, and adequate, to use the words "Stop" and "Go"; but, of course, a tap on the shoulder would do just as well. Here we have a system of orders, not statements of fact; but similar considerations will apply in both cases, since the logical structure of the orders will be the same as that of the factual statements specifying the actions performed in response to those orders. An adherent of Wittgenstein's principle of isomorphism might point out that here the two actions to be performed are represented by exactly the same number of distinct symbols, "Stop" and "Go." He might add that it would be logically impossible for the learner-driver to understand the two different orders, unless he were supplied with different and distinct symbols for the two cases. And he might add that every set of symbols that could serve the same purpose would necessarily exhibit the same duality. Whether the instructor spoke German, or Swahili, or anything else, he must necessarily use two symbols: here seems to be a perfect example of an essential feature, necessarily manifested in all the mutually equivalent notations.

But suppose the instructor used a whistle to signal "Start" as well as to signal "Stop." This device would be just as effective as the conventional words, and we need not suppose the whistle blasts to be substitutes for the English sounds: their meanings might have been taught directly, by demonstration and training. Have we not here an exception to Wittgenstein's principle —

one symbol (the blown whistle), but two represented actions?

The retort is obvious: A whistle blown when the car is at rest means one thing ("Go"), but means another ("Stop") when the car is in motion. So the full symbol is whistle-plus-condition-of-car: there are two relevant states of the car, hence two symbols after all. But is this conclusive? Surely it would be just as easy to argue as follows: The whistle is one symbol, not two; but it also represents one action, not two: each time it means a *change-of-state*, whether from motion to rest or vice versa. To be consistent, an advocate of this view must be willing to say that the familiar orders "Stop" and "Go" mean one and the same thing; but a determined searcher for a depth grammar must accept consequences at least as strange as this.

In order to determine whether Wittgenstein's principle applies to the case in hand, we need criteria of identity for actions and criteria of identity for the corresponding symbols. We have to say whether starting the car and stopping it are to count as the same or as different actions; and we have to say whether blowing the whistle is to count as having the same or different meanings on various occasions. There are no definite criteria for identity in these cases. In ordinary life, in a particular setting, we might understand sufficiently well a request to say something different, or to do something different; but here we are not in an ordinary setting. We want to know whether there are *really* two actions and two symbols, and have no way of finding out. We are free to decide whether the symbols are the same or different; the relevant fragment of philosophical grammar must be stipulated. The philosophical questions lack determinate sense and depend for their answers upon how we choose to describe the relevant utterances.

It may be said that this disappointing outcome arises from the artificiality of the example. I shall therefore turn to other cases having greater intrinsic interest.

III

Nowadays, it is often said that the copula, that figures so prominently in traditional logic, is superfluous. Listen to this, for instance: "There might certainly be various relations that the copula stood for, if it stood for any relation at all. But in fact no link is needed to join subject and predicate. . . . The grammatical copula is logically significant only when it serves as a sign of tense" (P. T. Geach, in *Mind*, vol. 59 [1950], p. 464).

But here is a traditionalist speaking: The mode of connection of the subject and the predicate is symbolized in the standard formulation by the word 'is', which is called the 'copula' because it links subject and predicate together; . . . some mode of connection requires symbolization, and this function is performed by the copula" (C. A. Mace, *The Principles of Logic*, London, 1933, pp. 77–78).

The dispute is clearly about philosophical grammar: the question is whether the copula is, or is not, an essential feature of language. On the one side, a strong case can be presented for the dispensability of the copula. There are languages, like Hebrew or Japanese, which manage very well without a copula; and we ourselves do without it in such constructions as "Peter loves Mary," in which the predicate, "Loves Mary," is attached to its subject, "Peter," without benefit of any verbal link. Strongest of all is the argument that we could jettison the copula without in any way impairing the fact-stating resources of our language. Were we to say "Peter happy" as the Chinese are said to do, we would lose nothing in expressive and descriptive power. In any case, *some* words and expressions must be able to "hang together" in a sentence without a symbolic link, for otherwise no completed sentence would be possible. So why not dispense with the copula altogether?

A defender of the copula's significance might reply as follows: "You are right in claiming that we don't need the *word* 'is' or any other word between the subject and the predicate of a sentence. But this is trivial and was never in dispute. Consider the pidgin English sentence 'Peter happy', that you offered as an adequate substitute for the conventional form. What is significant in this sentence is not merely the occurrence of the word-tokens 'Peter' and 'happy', but the *relationship* between them. Separating the two words by others or by a sufficiently wide interval will disintegrate your sentence. It is the relationship of juxtaposition that here performs the function of linking subject and predicate. Similarly, in the conventional form, 'Peter is happy', the union is effected by a relationship generated by writing the three words in correct order and in sufficiently close proximity. What is essential to the copula is not at all deleted by the translation into pidgin English. *Floreat copula!*"

What are we to say of this rebuttal? Its plausibility is undeniable, yet once again nothing compels us to accept it. For one thing, we may feel some reluctance to recognize "juxtaposition" as a genuine relation. Do we really need to *bring* the words into any relationship? Isn't it enough that we use them both in making the statement in question? Here again, consideration of some nonverbal notation might rid us of certain initial prejudices. Could we not, perhaps, use a red disk to mean that Peter is happy, with the disk standing for the man and its color for his condition of felicity? And what then would become of the alleged relationship between subject and predicate? Somebody might still insist, like A. E. Johnson in his *Logic*, that there would have to be a *characterizing relation* between the disk and its color. But anybody who can confidently assert this must already be in a position to analyze reality directly, and has no need of the detour through language.

But indeed, an advocate of the no-copula view can reaffirm his position without invoking a hypothetical notation of qualified objects. *His* analysis of the sentence-fact "Peter happy" might well be in terms of an "object," the word-token

"Peter" qualified by a certain property, that of having the word-token "happy" in immediate proximity. If he conceives of properties as "incomplete," i.e., as having the power to unite with objects without need of intermediaries, he will *see* the linguistic predicate in the same light. For such a neo-Fregean, learning how to *use* a predicate *is* learning how to attach it to subjects in complete statements, and there is no separate rule to be learned about the symbolic significance of the alleged relation of juxtaposition. For such a philosopher, a question about the relationship between subject and predicate of a statement is as otiose as a question about the relationship between a hand and the object it points at. Specification of the hand and the object indicated defines the gesture, without need for further specification; similarly, choice of a subject and an appropriate predicate uniquely determines a statement, without need for a further choice of a relationship between them.

Once again, we have a dispute which is inconclusive and threatens to be undecidable. What turns on the outcome? What difference will it make whether or not we recognize a characterizing relation? Well, a relation is conceived to hold between *terms*, so the traditional recognition of the copula goes with a classification of properties as special kinds of *things*. Admission of a characterizing relation allows questions to be asked about properties, so that predicates or their surrogates are sometimes permitted to function as subjects. The opposite point of view, that treats properties and their representing predicates as incomplete, forbids questions and assertions to be made about properties as subjects. The dispute about the copula, trifling as it may seem at first sight, is a focus of contention for full-blown alternative grammars.

IV

I pass on now to consider whether the ancient distinction between subject and predicate should be regarded as an essential feature of language that belongs to universal grammar.

How do we identify the subject and predicate of a given statement? A contemporary answers as follows: "A predicate is an expression that gives us an assertion about something if we attach it to another expression that stands for what we are making the assertion about" (P. T. Geach, *Mind*, vol. 59 [1950], pp. 461–462).

In order to apply this prescription to a particular instance, we have first to determine what a given assertion is "about." Should the assertion contain an expression standing for what the assertion is about, that expression will be the subject. According to the prescription, the remainder of the sentence will be the attached predicate.

This works well when applied to such a sentence as "Peter is happy," in which there is reference to a person. It is natural to say that a statement using that sentence is about Peter; hence the word "Peter" may be said to be a subject standing for Peter, and the remainder of the sentence, the expression "is happy," counts as the predicate.

But even in this paradigm case of the application of the distinction, an objection can be lodged. It may be plausibly argued that the statement in question is about happiness, no less than about Peter: the assertion, some would say, can be understood as a claim that happiness is instantiated in Peter. If it is permissible to say that the word "happy" stands for happiness, the rule we have adopted would lead us to say that "happy" is the subject and "Peter is" the predicate. The philosopher who formulated the rule I have cited would want to reject this inference.

Or, take the case of the statement "Happiness is desired by all men." Here, it is still more plausible to say that the statement is about happiness, referred to by the word "happiness." But the author of our rule refuses to recognize "happiness" as a subject, preferring to construe the sentence in question as being composed of two predicates.

I do not wish to suggest that a preference for this mode of analysis is willful or capricious; yet I believe there is no rational method for persuading somebody who rejects it. The dispute, like others already reported in this paper, can be resolved only by fiat. It is an error to suppose that we can determine what a statement is "about" by inspection of some extralinguistic realm. No amount of observation or reflection about nonverbal "things" will show whether a given statement is about a person or about a quality. The answer must be sought in language itself.

We know that the statement "Peter is happy" is about Peter, because we recognize "Peter" as a proper name, without knowing whether there is such a person as Peter. The starting point of the intended philosophical distinction between subject and predicate is conventional grammar, relying only upon formal criteria. But conventional grammar leaves us in the lurch as soon as we are asked to decide whether a statement using the word "happiness" is really about happiness.

V

I propose now to test the thesis of the universality of the subject-predicate form, by applying it to the report of a move in chess. The case may be thought to have special peculiarities, but will serve to reveal the chief points in dispute.

A full verbal report of a chess move, such as might be found in nineteenth-century manuals, has the form "The King's pawn moved to the King's fourth square." Here, there is no difficulty in identifying the grammatical subject, i.e., the expression "The King's pawn." Hence, the remainder of the formula, the expression "moved to the King's fourth square" must be the predicate, and the report can be certified as being of the subject-predicate form.

Nowadays, English-speaking chess players commonly use the concise notation,

"*P-K*4." Reading this as a conventional abbreviation of the full English sentence previously cited, it is easy enough to discern a subject and a predicate in this fragment of symbolism: we might say that in "*P-K*4" the "*P*" is the subject, and the rest of the formula the predicate.

But other and equally adequate notations are in common use. In the so-called "Continental notation," a move is specified by giving only co-ordinates of the initial and terminal squares; thus the move already cited would be reported as "*e*2-*e*4." In this version, there is no component homologous with the subject recognized in the other form of report. A last-ditch defender and the omnipresence of the subject-predicate form might still argue that in the formula "*e*2-*e*4" the first complex symbol, "*e*2," indirectly specifies the chessman moved. However, it would be equally correct to treat the initial symbol, "*P*," of the English notation as being really an indirect specification of the square from which the move started. Somebody familiar only with the Continental notation can treat the English notations as having the square-to-square structure of his own paradigm; while a devotee of the English notation can treat the alternative symbolism as a disguised version of his own.

It becomes progressively harder to perceive the subject-predicate form in every conceivable chess notation as alternative notations are imagined. A given chess move might be represented by drawing a line on a square divided into 64 compartments, or by a set of two integers between 1 and 64, or by a single number less than than 4096 ($= 64^2$), or by Morse code, or by suitably modulated electrical waves. Some of these possibilities might be handled by human beings, others might perhaps serve only to inform chess-playing computers; but all alike would have the requisite structure for representing every possible move in a game of chess. All of them, to use Wittgenstein's word, would have the same "multiplicity" (*Tractatus*, 4.04). Now a determination to view all of these equivalent symbolic forms as having the subject-predicate structure would be quixotic in the extreme. Absurd loyalty to a preconception about logical form would be needed in order to view a line drawn on a chessboard as having a subject and a predicate. Long before this point was reached, most of us would prefer to abandon the dogma of the omnipresence of subject-predicate form.

The example may prepare us to expect similar conclusions about languages that are not restricted to the representation of an invented game. We are told, on good authority, that "Chinese, which is fully equipped for every sort of civilized communication, makes no use of the formal categories devised for the Indo-European languages" (W. J. Entwistle, *Aspects of Language*, London, 1953, p. 162). Another writer, after surveying the variety of grammars known to contemporary linguists, concludes that "no grammatical concept seems to be *per se* sacred or universal, far less indispensable" (Mario Pei, *The Story of Language*, New York, 1949, p. 129). In some languages, we are told, "An isolated word is a sentence; a sequence of such sentence words is like a compound sentence . . . [and] the terms verb and noun in such a language are meaningless" (B. L. Whorf, *Language, Thought and Reality*, Boston, 1956, p. 98–99). If Whorf was right, the hope of finding the subject-predicate distinction exemplified in such "polysynthetic" languages is doomed to frustration. For that distinction presupposes a way of distinguishing between nouns and other parts of speech. Yet, "polysynthetic" languages may be just as rich in fact-stating resources as our own relatively analytical English. I conclude that the subject-predicate distinction, valuable as it may be for analyzing Indo-European languages, ought to find no place in a universal philosophical grammar.

VI

The three examples I have discussed sufficiently illustrate the difficulties that beset any serious effort to construct a universal grammar. We are now in a position to diagnose the source of these difficulties. In each case, we were assuming that the logical structure of certain statements ("Stop," "Go," "Peter is happy") must be identical with the structure of the situations or states of affairs represented. The search for what is presumed to be invariant in all statements having the same meaning, that is to say, those representing the same state of affairs, is a search for some way of presenting the common logical structure. In order to do this, we must be able to do at least the following: decide which perceptible features of words or other signs can be treated as nonsignificant, recognize one and the same symbol behind its alternative manifestations (that is to say, recognize when signs mean the same thing), and assign different symbols to the same logical category or type, on the basis of identity of function. In order for the procedure to provide any ground for ontological inference, such recognition, individuation, and classification of symbols must be performed without recourse to ontological premises, or to methods assuming the truth of such premises.

The chief difficulty arose from the need to count nonlinguistic contextual features of statements as significant. So long as we confine ourselves to analysis of conventional verbal statements, in isolation from their settings, traditional grammar provides us with means of segmentation and classification that can subsequently be elaborated and refined in the service of philosophical insight. There is no question but that "Stop" and "Go" are different words; "Peter" is clearly a noun and a grammatical subject in "Peter is happy." But immediately we recognize the nonverbal setting in which the words are pronounced as significant, we face formidable difficulties in identifying, distinguishing, counting and classifying the symbols that interest us. Are the situations in which a car is at rest and in motion to count as the same or as different? Are the actions of stopping and starting a car the same or different? These are not questions to be answered by looking at cars or their drivers. They are questions of philosophical grammar for which there are no decision procedures. We have criteria for deciding whether words are to be treated as the same or different; for rules to this end (superficial rules of grammar) are part of the language we speak and understand. But there are no adequate criteria for deciding whether contextual situations are to be counted as the same or different, for the purpose of determining identities and differences of meaning. It might be thought that we ought to examine the semantical rules governing the sounds and written marks in question. But this maneuver achieves nothing. Were we assured that the rule governing "Stop" must count as different from the rule governing "Go," we would be entitled to conclude that there were indeed two symbols in question. But since the words "Stop" and "Go" or their synonyms will appear in expressions of those semantical rules, individuation of the rules will raise the same troublesome questions. Nor will the case be altered by speaking about "uses" instead of about "rules." For the purposes of philosophical grammar, descriptions in terms of "symbols," "rules," and "uses" are mutually equivalent and generate the same problems. We can choose as we please, and our decisions about the points of philosophical grammar at issue will be determined by the choices we havè made, not by any imposed analysis of the statements inspected.

Similarly in our illustrations of the copula and the subject-predicate form. At the level of surface grammar, there are crude criteria for deciding whether an expression is expendable without loss of meaning. But when we try to push on to a would-be "deeper" level of analysis, we are embarrassed again by lack of criteria. In the relation between "Peter" and "happy" really significant? Is there really a relationship there at all? It all depends upon how you choose to look at the state-

ment. Nothing imposes an answer except the determination of the philosophical analyst to adhere to one mode of logical parsing rather than another. Seen through one pair of grammatical spectacles, there plainly is a significant relation of juxtaposition between subject and predicate; but we can wear another pair of lenses and see nothing but subject and predicate, "hanging in one another like the links of a chain."

When we recognize that the fact-stating functions of language can be adequately performed by nonverbal symbolisms, the problems of detecting invariant logical structure become insuperable. If we represent states of affairs by configurations of physical objects, the task of discerning logical structure demands a capacity to determine the logical structure of certain physical facts. But if we can ever do this, we don't need the detour via language. If we can analyze a fact, we can in principle discover the logical structure of reality without prior recourse to language. On the other hand, if we face some obstacle of principle in dissecting reality, we shall meet the very same difficulties in trying to dissect language. For language, though it represents reality, is also a part of reality.

VII

In the light of the foregoing considerations, the prospects for a universal philosophical grammar seem most unpromising. I believe the hope of finding *the* essential grammar to be as illusory as that of finding the single true co-ordinate system for the representation of space. We can pass from one systematic mode of spatial representation to another by means of rules for transforming co-ordinates, and we can pass from one language to another having the same fact-stating resources by means of rules of translation. But rules for transformation of co-ordinates yield no information about space; and translation rules for sets of languages tell us nothing about the ultimate nature of reality.

It might perhaps be said that common logical structure is shown in an invariant web of entailment relations. It is certainly part of our concept of synonymity that statements of the same meaning shall have parallel consequences: if one statement has an entailment that is not synonymous with some entailment of a second statement, that proves that the two original statements have different meanings. To put the matter differently, we shall not regard two languages as having the same fact-stating resources unless we can trace corresponding patterns of transformation rules in both. But we shall never arrive at a philosophical grammar by this road: correspondence of sets of entailments is compatible with the widest divergences of morphology and of syntax.

If we abandon the vain hope of finding the true philosophical grammar, we may still hope to use its by-products. Schoolroom grammar is coarse-grained for philosophical purposes, and the refinements of latter-day linguists are impressive without being philosophically useful. We shall do well to continue classifying words and expressions according to their uses and functions, inventing whatever labels will help us to remember our discoveries. It is not my intention to deprecate the received grammatical categories of "quality," "relation," "function," "class," and the rest, or the finer classifications invented by contemporaries. I would urge, however, that our attitude to such grammatical sieves should be pragmatic. If reality leaves us free to choose our grammar as convenience and utility dictate, we shall properly regard them as speculative instruments to be sharpened, improved, and, where necessary, discarded when they have served their turn.

To anybody who still feels that there must be an identity of logical form between language and reality, I can only plead that the conception of language as a mirror of reality is radically mistaken. We find out soon enough that the universe is not capricious: the child who learns that fire burns and knife-edges cut knows that there are inexorable limits set upon his desires. Language must conform to the discovered regularities and irregularities of experience. But in order to do so, it is enough that it should be apt for the expression of everything that is or might be the case. To be content with less would be to be satisfied to be inarticulate; to ask for more is to desire the impossible. No roads lead from grammar to metaphysics.

27

JERROLD J. KATZ

THE PHILOSOPHICAL RELEVANCE OF LINGUISTIC THEORY[1]

1. INTRODUCTION

This paper defends the relevance of linguistics to philosophy on the grounds that linguistic theory incorporates solutions to significant philosophical problems. The particular thesis to be defended here is that certain philosophical problems can be represented correctly as questions about the nature of language, and that, so represented, they can be solved on the basis of theoretical constructions that appear in linguistic theory.[2]

Synchronic linguistics involves two distinct but interrelated studies: a study of the diversity in forms of linguistic communication and a study of the limits of such diversity. In the former, linguists investigate what is unique about individual natural languages and formulate such facts in what are called *linguistic descriptions* (or *generative grammars*). In the latter, linguists investigate what is common to all natural languages and formulate these more general facts about language in *linguistic theory*. Linguistic theory, therefore, is a specification of the universals of language. Given this notion of linguistic theory, the thesis of this paper asserts that theoretical constructions initially devised by linguists to enable linguistic theory to systematically state uniformities across natural languages also fulfill the conditions on solutions to certain philosophical problems, owing to the nature of those problems. This thesis should not be interpreted as asserting that the linguist's descriptions of natural languages reveal philosophical insights that somehow must escape philosophers looking at the same languages. This thesis does not concern either a philosopher's or a linguist's account of the facts about a natural language, but rather concerns the more abstract matters that are dealt with in an account of the facts about language in general.

If the defense of this thesis is successful, then linguistics is not incidentally pertinent to philosophy, in the way that philosophy of science bears upon the clarification of methodology and theory construction in linguistics, but is directly relevant in the same way that philosophical theories themselves are. Since I have no *a priori* notions about the *a priori* char-

Reprinted from *The Journal of Philosophy*, LXII (1965), 590–602, by permission of the author and the editor. (Copyright 1965 by The Journal of Philosophy, Inc.)

[1] This paper is a revised and expanded version of my paper "The Relevance of Linguistics to Philosophy," *The Journal of Philosophy*. This work was supported by a grant from the National Institute of Health, No. MH-05120-04, to Harvard University, Center for Cognitive Studies. It was also supported in part by the Joint Services Electronics Program (Contract DA 36-039-AMC-03200(E)); and in part by the U.S. Air Force (Contract AF 19 (628)-2487), National Science Foundation (Grant GP-2495), The National Institutes of Health (Grant MH-04737-05), and the National Aeronautics and Space Administration (Grant Ns G-496).

[2] In the final section of this paper, I will indicate another sort of relevance of linguistic theory to philosophy.

acter of philosophical investigations, I am in no way disturbed by the fact that we might have to know quite a lot about extra-logical matters in order to solve certain philosophical problems.

Within the confines of a paper of this sort it is, of course, impossible to present all the arguments on behalf of this thesis, nor is it possible to formulate those that are presented in their full form. The present paper, then, is best regarded as a presentation of the thesis itself, with a sketch of some of the arguments that can be given for it.

2. The Rationale for Appealing to Linguistics

At the outset, it is appropriate to ask why an appeal to linguistics is necessary; why, that is, we find it necessary to go outside the boundaries of contemporary philosophy to search for the solutions to philosophical problems. The answer is simply that the approaches to the philosophical problems concerned that are available in contemporary philosophy have not dealt successfully with these problems and, moreover, that these approaches contain inherent difficulties which make it quite unlikely that they can deal successfully with them. In other publications, paricularly "What's Wrong with the Philosohy of Language?" and *The Philosophy of Language*,[3] I tried to show in some detail why the two major approaches in contemporary philosophy, Logical Empiricism (Logical Positivism) and Ordinary Language Philosophy, are inherently incapable of providing adequate, well-motivated solutions to the major philosophical problems they tackled. It is neither necessary nor possible to repeat my criticisms here. The general character of the difficulties, however, is this. Logical empiricism confined its efforts to the construction of highly

arbitrary and conceptually impoverished theories about a class of artificial languages whose structure bears little similarity to that of natural languages. Ordinary language philosophy preoccupied itself with unearthing the most minute and detailed facts about the use of English locutions to the almost complete neglect of any concern with theory. Thus, while the former offered us philosophically irrelevant theories, the latter failed to give us any theory. Of course, both approaches prided themselves on their shortcomings, turning their vices into alleged virtues. Logical empiricism prided itself on its exclusive concern with artificial languages, claiming that natural languages are too irregular, amorphous, and vague to provide a basis for the solution to philosophical problems. Ordinary language philosophy prided itself on its avoidance of theory construction, claiming that theories cause the very philosophical perplexities that philosophy seeks to resolve by examination of the use of particular linguistic constructions. But the claim of the logical empiricists was never submitted to empirical investigation, nor, on the other hand, did logical empiricism provide an alternative standard for justifying a theory of artificial languages that might serve as a replacement for the standard of conformity to the facts of language that had been eliminated. Ordinary language philosophers never established that the theories in which they located the source of certain philosophical problems were not just bad theories, and so never seriously asked what a good theory would be able to do toward supplying a conceptual systematization of the facts of language that might offer solutions for the philosophical problems that arise in the course of ordinary, theoretically unsophisticated, uses of language. Accordingly, the solutions that these approaches presented were based either on unmotivated, and hence arbitrary, principles or on particularistic analyses of locutions whose bearing on philosophical problems were neither established nor made fully clear.

[3] J. J. Katz and J. A. Fodor, "What's Wrong with the Philosophy of Language?" *Inquiry*, V (1962), 197–237, and J. J. Katz, *The Philosophy of Language* (New York: Harper & Row, 1966).

This unsatisfactory situation led a number of philosophers — with Quine as the most notable example — to turn some of their attention to empirical linguistics. Though, of course, I endorse this concern, I differ with them on a number of fundamental points. One is the question of what it is in linguistics for which philosophical relevance ought to be claimed, and another is the nature and extent of the relevance of linguistics to philosophy.

3. Linguistic Theory

I have claimed that the part of linguistics that is relevant to philosophy is linguistic theory. In this section, I will try to explain what this part of linguistics is.

As mentioned above, linguistic theory is a specification of the universals of language, the principles of organization and interpretation that are invariant from natural language to natural language. Linguistic theory expresses such invariants in the form of a model of a linguistic description, of which each empirically successful linguistic description must be an instance, exemplifying every aspect of the model. Particular linguistic descriptions account for the diverse ways in which different natural languages realize the abstract structural pattern displayed in the model, while the model itself describes the form of a system of empirical generalizations capable of expressing and organizing the facts about a natural language.

Accordingly, the construction of linguistic theory and linguistic descriptions are strongly interdependent. Linguists can abstract out the common features from a set of linguistic descriptions and so generalize from them to hypotheses about linguistic universals. Alternatively, linguists can facilitate their task of describing a language by using the model provided by linguistic theory as a pattern for their systematization of the facts they uncover in field work. As a consequence, the justification of both linguistic theory and individual linguistic descriptions have a common basis, *viz.* the facts from natural languages on which linguistic descriptions depend for on which linguistic descriptions depend for their empirical support. Since putative linguistic universals are inductively extrapolated generalizations, projected from known regularities cutting across the set of already constructed linguistic descriptions, their empirical adequacy is thus a matter of whether further facts, upon which newly constructed linguistic descriptions will eventually be based, continue to support these generalizations. Thus, the same facts that confirm or disconfirm particular linguistic descriptions also confirm or disconfirm a linguistic theory. Notice, finally, that if the general form of a particular linguistic description can be deduced from linguistic theory, then that linguistic description will be far better confirmed than were it to derive its support solely from the facts about the language it describes, since it will also be supported by a wealth of evidence from many natural languages via the connection through linguistic theory between their linguistic descriptions and this one.

Linguistic theory consists of three subtheories, each corresponding to one of the three components of a linguistic description. The terms "phonological theory," "syntactic theory," and "semantic theory" refer to these subtheories, and "phonological component," "syntactic component," and "semantic component" refer to the corresponding parts of a linguistic description. The phonological, syntactic, and semantic components are rule-formulated descriptions of knowledge that a speaker has acquired in attaining fluency. The first states the rules determining the phonetic structure of speech sounds in a language; the second states the rules determining how speech sounds with a fixed phonetic shape are organized into sentential structures; the third states the rules determining how such sentential structures are interpreted as meaningful messages. At the level of linguistic theory, phonological, syntactic, and semantic theory, jointly, characterize the form of the rules in a linguistic description, specify the theoretical constructs utilized in writing actual rules in appropriate forms, and determine the relations between rules within each component.

Linguistic theory also specifies the relations between these components that weld them into an integrated linguistic description. The fundamental problem to which a linguistic description addresses itself is that of explicating the common system of rules on the basis of which different speakers of the same language can correlate the same speech signal with the same meaningful message. The ability of speakers to transmit their thoughts and ideas to one another through the vehicle of articulated speech sounds presupposes that each speaker has mastered a common system of rules within which each well-formed utterance receives a fixed semantic interpretation. Linguistic communication takes place when the same associations between sounds and meaning are made by different speakers in verbal interaction. Since the linguistic description must formally simulate the sound-meaning correlations made by speakers, its components must be related to one another in such a manner that the representations given by the phonological and syntactic components of the phonetic and syntactic character of a sentence are formally connected with the representation given by the semantic component of its meaning. The model of a linguistic description offered by linguistic theory must show that the various schemes for making such correlations that are found in different natural languages are instances of a general formula which is the same for all natural languages.

On the current model of a linguistic description,[4] this formula is embodied in

[4] Cf. J. J. Katz and P. Postal, *An Integrated Theory of Linguistic Descriptions* (Cambridge: Massachusetts Institute of Technology Press, 1964) and N. Chomsky, *Aspects of the Theory of Syntax* (Cambridge: Massachusetts Institute of Technology Press, 1965).

the following organizational pattern for linguistic descriptions. The syntactic component is the generative source of the linguistic description. It generates abstract formal objects which are the input to the phonological and semantic components. Their outputs, are respectively, phonetic representations and semantic interpretations. Both these components are, therefore, purely interpretive systems. The output of the syntactic component is a syntactic description of each sentence of the language which consists of a set of *phrase markers*, where a phrase marker can be thought of as a labeled bracketing of the constituents of a sentence. The bracketing tells us that the elements enclosed within a single bracket form a constituent and the labeling tells us the syntactic category to which the constituent belongs. Thus, two words, phrases, or clauses are constituents of the same type if and only if they receive the same label. Now, the set of phrase markers which constitutes the syntactic description of a sentence consists of a subset of *underlying phrase markers* and a single *superficial phrase marker*; the number of underlying phrase markers in the syntactic description of a sentence indicates its degree of syntactic ambiguity (so that each underlying phrase marker represents a syntactical unique sentence). An underlying phrase marker describes that aspect of the syntax of a sentence of which its meaning is a function, while a superficial phrase marker describes that aspect which determines its phonetic shape. Accordingly, the rules of the semantic component operate on the underlying phrase markers of a sentence to provide its semantic interpretation, and the rules of the phonological component operate on the superficial phrase marker to provide its phonetic representation. The underlying phrase markers in a syntactic description are related to the superficial phrase marker by virtue of the fact that this same superficial phrase marker is transformationally derived from each of them. That is, transformations are syntactic rules that generate superficial phrase markers from underlying phrase markers. Thus, the set of underlying phrase markers in a given syntactic description is automatically connected with the superficial phrase marker in that description because the latter is obtained from each of the former by a specifiable (but in each case different) sequence of transformations and this superficial phrase marker is not transformationally obtainable from any underlying phrase marker outside this set. Thus, the linguistic description will correlate the phonetic representation of a sentence with its semantic interpretation as desired, the correlation being effected by the tranformations in the syntactic component and the manner in which the phonological and semantic components are organized to operate, respectively, on a superficial phrase marker and the underlying phrase marker from which it was transformationally derived.

4. Advantages of Linguistic Theory as a Starting Point

The advantages of starting with linguistic theory as a basis for the treatment of philosophical problems are strictly complementary to the previously mentioned disadvantages of the logical empiricist and ordinary language philosophy approaches. First, instead of having to content ourselves with philosophical solutions that rest on the arbitrary principles of some artificial language or on an assortment of comments on the use of certain words or expressions from some natural language, if we base our solutions to philosophical problems on linguistic theory we have a straightforward empirical basis on which to justify such solutions in terms of the empirical evidence that provides the support for successful linguistic descriptions. For the justification of the theoretical constructs used in the solutions is provided by the very same evidence that empirically warrants their introduction into linguistic theory. Hence, we avoid the difficulties that stem from the absence of any empirical con-

trols on a solution to a philosophical problem and from the failure to clarify the relation between facts about the uses of words and expressions and the solutions on behalf of which they are adduced. Second, instead of having to resort to oversimplified and largely unexplained concepts from a theory about artificial languages or having no theory at all to appeal to, we can utilize the rich stock of concepts that express the common structure of natural languages, explicitly defined in a formalized theory of linguistic universals, in order to obtain solutions to philosophical problems.

There is a further advantage of this starting point. Basing a solution to a philosophical problem on linguistically universal principles avoids relativizing that solution to one or another particular natural language. Plato and Aristotle wrote in Greek, Descartes in French, Kant in German, and Hume in English. But the philosophical problems about which they wrote were language-independent questions about a common conceptual structure. Accordingly, if it is these problems, rather than some specialized ones having to do exclusively with one language, for which philosophers seek solutions, then we cannot narrow the scope of solutions to philosophical problem. It is just as absurd to say that the solution to a certain philosophical problem is such-and-such in English as it is to say that a broken back is such-and-such a condition among Chinese. By starting with linguistic theory, we can argue from the concepts that underlie language in general to the solution of a philosophical problem, instead of having to argue from concepts that, for all we can say, might underlie only one or another particular language. Furthermore, we can better justify the solution to a philosophical problem because we can adduce far stronger evidence than if we were restricted to the data from one or another particular language (cf. § 3, the concluding remarks of paragraph 3).

5. THE EPISTEMOLOGICAL AND THE PSYCHOLOGICAL

Given that linguistic theory is a formal reconstruction of the universal principles by which speakers relate speech signals and meaningful messages, it is clearly an explication of a facet of a human ability. This makes it in some sense a psychological theory. A philosophical problem, on the other hand, concerns the structure of concepts and the grounds for the validity of cognitive and evaluative principles, which makes it epistemological in the broad sense, not psychological. How, then, can linguistic theory offer solutions to philosophical problems when the "solutions" are apparently not even addressed to the right type of problem?

This criticism rests on a failure to distinguish two senses of the term "psychological." The distinction depends on the difference between a speaker's *linguistic competence*, what he tacitly knows about the structure of his language, and his *linguistic performance*, what he does with this knowledge. A theory in linguistics explicates linguistic competence, not linguistic performance. It seeks to reconstruct the logical structure of the principles that speakers have mastered in attaining fluency. On the other hand, a theory of performance seeks to discover the contribution of each of the factors that interplay to produce natural speech with its various and sundry deviations from ideal linguistic forms. Thus, it must consider such linguistically extraneous factors as memory span, perceptual and motor limitations, lapses of attention, pauses, level of motivation, interest, idiosyncratic and random errors, etc. The linguist, whose aim is to provide a statement of ideal linguistic form unadulterated by the influence of such extraneous factors, can be compared to the logician, whose aim is to provide a statement of ideal implicational form unadulterated by extraneous factors that influence actual inferences men draw.

Hence, there are two senses of "psychological": on one, the subject of a psychological theory is a competence, and in the other, a performance. The criticism cited above applies to a proposed solution for a philosophical problem extracted from a theory that is psychological in the latter sense. But it does not apply to one extracted from a theory in linguistics that is psychological in the former. A theory of performance cannot solve a philosophical problem such as that of formulating an inductive logic that is a valid codification of the principles of nondemonstrative inference in science and daily life. People can be quite consistent in drawing nondemonstrative inferences according to invalid principles, and be inconsistent in their practice of using valid ones. Because a theory of performance must accept such behavior at face value, it has no means of correcting for the acceptance of invalid principles and the rejection of valid ones. In contrast, however, a theory of competence does. Since it regards performance only as evidence for the construction of an idealization, it sifts the facts about behavior, factoring out the distorting influences of variables that are extraneous to the logical structure of the competence. Such a theory has built in a means for correcting itself in cases where invalid principles were accepted or valid ones rejected. Therefore, linguistic theory cannot be criticized as irrelevant to the solution of philosophical problems.

6. GRAMMATICAL FORM AND LOGICAL FORM

But to establish the relevance of linguistic theory, it must be shown to offer solutions to significant philosophical problems. One of the pervasive problems of modern philosophy is that of distinguishing between the grammatical and logical forms of sentences. It has long been recognized that the phonetic or orthographic realization of many sentences is such that no analysis of them in terms of traditional taxonomic grammar can reveal the true conceptual structure of the proposition(s) that they express. Almost invariably, however, this recognition has led twentieth century philosophers — Russell, the early Wittgenstein, Carnap, and Ryle, to mention some notable examples — to seek a philosophical theory about the logical form of propositions. They assumed that grammar had done what it could but that its best is not good enough, so that a philosophical theory of one sort or another is needed to exhibit the conceptual relations unmarked in grammatical analysis.

This assumption is open to a serious challenge, even aside from the fact that such philosophical theories have not achieved much success. From the same cases where grammatical form and logical form do not coincide, one can conclude instead that the traditional taxonomic theory of grammar, on which these philosophers' conception of grammatical form is based, is too limited to reveal the underlying conceptual structure of a sentence. Suitably extended, grammar might well reveal the facts about logical form, too. Philosophers who accepted this assumption simply overlooked the possibility that traditional taxonomic grammar might not be the last word on grammar.

The alternative to a philosophical theory about logical form is thus a linguistic theory about logical form. Support for this alternative has come recently from Chomsky's work on syntactic theory which shows that traditional taxonomic grammar is too limited and revises it accordingly.[5] The feasibility of this alternative rests on whether Chomsky's criticism is directed at just the features of traditional taxonomic grammar that make it incapable of handling logical form and on whether the revision provides the theoretical machinery to handle it.

The traditional taxonomic description of an utterance type is a single labeled bracketing that segments it into continuous phonetic stretches and classifies them as constituents of one, or another sort. Chomsky's basic criticism is that such description cannot mark a variety of syntactic features because it fails to go below the surface structure of sentences. Consider the sentences: (i) "John is easy to leave" and (ii) "John is eager to leave." In a traditional taxonomic description, both receive the same syntactic analysis:

$$((John)_{NP} ((is)([\begin{smallmatrix}easy\\eager\end{smallmatrix}])_A (to\ leave)_V)_{VP})_S$$

This analysis, which, on the terminology introduced in Section 3, is the superficial phrase marker for (i) and (ii), does not mark the logical difference that in (i) "John" is the object of the verb "leave" whereas in (ii) "John" is its subject. Consider, further, a sentence like: (iii) "John knows a kinder person than Bill." The syntactic ambiguity of (iii) cannot be represented in its taxonomic description because a single (superficial) phrase marker cannot explicate the different propositional structures underlying the terms of its ambiguity. Finally, consider a normal imperative such as: (iv) "help him!" Ellipsis, which in such cases absents the subject and future tense auxiliary constituent, cannot be handled by a traditional taxonomic description because it deals only with the phonetically or orthographically realized constituents of a sentence.[6]

These difficulties cannot be remedied by enriching the complexity of superficial phrase markers. More elaborate segmentation and subclassification cannot overcome the inherent inability of this form of description to represent relational information. Rather, the superficial phrase marker, as it stands, has a proper role to play in syntactic description, viz. that of providing the most compact representation of the syntatic information required to determine the phonetic shape of a sentence. What is wrong is that the superficial phrase marker,

[5] Cf. N. Chomsky, *Syntactic Structures* (The Hague: Mouton & Co., 1957) and P. Postal, *Constituent Structure*, Publication Thirty of the Indiana University Research Center in Anthropology, Folklore, and Linguistics (Bloomington, 1964).

[6] For the syntactic motivation behind the claim that there are such phonetically unrealized constitutents in normal imperatives, cf. P. Postal, "Underlying and Superficial Linguistic Structures," *The Harvard Educational Review*, XXXIV (1964).

because it is the only type of description sanctioned by the traditional taxonomic theory of grammar, is made to do work that, in principle, it cannot do so long as it must still play its proper role. To right this wrong, Chomsky introduced the conception of a grammar as a generative, transformational system to supersede the conception of a grammar as a set of segmentation and classification procedures. Within this new conception, Chomsky and others developed the concept of an underlying phrase marker,[7] a form of syntactic description in which semantically significant grammatical relations can be adequately represented and shown to underlie the phonetic form of sentences on the basis of transformational rules that derive superficial phrase markers from appropriate underlying phrase markers by formally specified operations.

The logical difference between (i) and (ii) noted above can be indicated with the underlying phrase markers.[8]

(I) $(((it) ((one)_{NP} ((leaves)_V (John)_{NP})_{VP})_S)_{NP}((is)(easy))_{VP})_S$

(II) $((John)_{NP} ((is)((eager)((John)_{NP} (leaves)_{VP})_S)_A)_{VP})_S$

The grammatical relations *subject of* and *object of* are defined in syntactic theory in terms of subconfigurations of symbols in underlying phrase markers. A simplified version of their definitions is as follows.

Given a configuration of the form $((X)_{NP} (Y)_{VP})_S$ or $((X)_{NP} ((Y)_V (Z)_{NP})_{VP})_S$, *X is the subject of the verb Y and Z is the object of the verb Y*.[9]

---

[7] J. J. Katz and P. Postal, op. cit., and N. Chomsky, *Aspects of the Theory of Syntax*. The notion of an underlying phrase marker used here is the same as Chomsky's notion of a deep phrase marker.

[8] For further discussion, cf. G. A. Miller and N. Chomsky, "Finitary Models of Language Users," *Handbook of Mathematical Psychology*, Volume II, ed. D. R. Luce, R. R. Bush, and E. Galanter (New York: John Wiley & Sons, 1963), pp. 476–80.

[9] Note that this definition reconstructs the intuitive notion that the subject is the noun phrase preceding the verb in a simple sentence and that the object is the noun phrase following it. Restricting the definition to underlying phrase markers makes it possible to have a

By this definition, "John" in (i) is marked as the object of the verb "leaves" because it occupies the Z-position and "leaves" occupies the Y-position in the appropriate subconfiguration of (I), and "John" in (ii) is marked as the subject of "leaves" because it occupies the X-position and "leaves" occupies the Y-position in the appropriate subconfiguration of (II).

Further, since a sentence can be assigned more than one underlying phrase marker in a transformational syntactic component, syntactic ambiguities like those in (iii) can be represented in terms of appropriately different underlying phrase markers transformationally associated with the same superficial phrase marker. Thus, the superficial phrase marker for (iii), *viz.*

$((John)_{NP} ((knows)_V ((a)(kinder) (person)(than)(Bill))_{NP})_{VP})_S$

is associated with two underlying phrase markers both of which have the general form,[10]

$((John)_{NP} ((knows)_V ((a)(. . .)_S(person))_{NP})_{VP})_S$

but where in one . . . is

$(the person)_{NP}((is)(more)(than)((Bill)_{NP} ((is)(kind)_A)_{VP})_S(kind)_A)_{VP}$

while in the other . . . is

$(the person)_{NP}((is)(more)(than)((the) (Bill)_{NP}((knows)_V(the person)_{NP})_{VP})_S (person))_{NP}((is)(kind)_A)_{VP})_S(kind)_A)_{VP}$

The former case underlies the term of the ambiguity on which the person that John knows is kinder than Bill is, and the latter case underlies the term on which the person that John knows is kinder than the person Bill knows.

Finally, in ellipsis phonetically unrealized constituents can be specified in underlying phrase markers and deleted in the transformational derivation of the superficial phrase marker. This enables us to account for their syntactic relations and their semantic contribution without falsely

---

single definition because complex sentences are then handled in terms of the simple sentences from which they are constructed.

[10] For further discussion, cf. C. S. Smith, "A Class of Complex Modifiers in English," *Language*, XXXVII (1961), 342–65.

characterizing the phonetic shape of the sentence, as would be required if we modified the superficial phrase marker to account for them.

But, although it is clear from these examples that the distinction between underlying and superficial syntactic structure is a significant step toward the philosopher's distinction between logical form and grammatical form, even a fully developed transformational syntactic component would not provide all the theoretical machinery necessary to deal adequately with logical form. Philosophers have rightly held that an analysis of the logical form of a sentence should not only tell us about the formal relations between its constituents, but should also tell us about the semantic properties and relations of the proposition(s) expressed by it. In particular, an account of the logical form of a sentence should specify whether it is (1) *semantically anomalous* (i.e. whether it expresses any proposition at all), (2) *semantically ambiguous* (i.e. whether it expresses more than one proposition, and if so, how many), (3) *a paraphrase of a given sentence* (i.e. whether the two sentences express the same proposition), (4) *analytic*, (5) *contradictory*, (6) *synthetic*, (7) *inconsistent with a given sentence*, (8) *entails* or *is entailed by a given sentence*, (9) *a presupposition of a given sentence*, and so on.

The fact that a transformational syntactic component does not suffice, by itself, to determine such semantic properties and relations has brought about the formulation of a conception of a semantic component designed to determine them.[11] This conception is based on the idea that a speaker's ability to produce and understand sentences he has never before spoken

or heard depends on his mastery of principles according to which the meaning of new and unfamiliar sentences can be obtained by a process in which the meaning of syntactically compound constituents is composed out of the meanings of their parts. The semantic component formally reconstructs these compositional principles. It has a *dictionary* that contains an account of the meaning of each syntactically atomic constituent in the language, i.e. representations of the senses of *lexical items*, and a set of *projection rules* that provide the combinatorial machinery for representing the senses of compound constituents on the basis of representations of the senses of the lexical items that make them up. The dictionary is a list of *entries*, each of which consists of a lexical item written in phonological form, a set of syntactic features, and a set of *lexical readings*. A lexical reading, which represents one sense of a lexical item, consists of a set of *semantic markers* and a *selection restriction*.

A semantic marker is a theoretical term representing a class of equivalent concepts. For example, the semantic marker (Physical Object) represents the class of concepts of a material entity whose parts are spatially and temporally contiguous and move in unison each of us has in mind when we distinguish the meanings of words like "chair," "stone," "man," "building," etc., from the meanings of words like "virtue," "togetherness," "shadow," "afterimage," etc. Semantic markers enable us to state empirical generalizations about the senses of words (expressions, and sentences), for, by including the semantic marker (Physical Object) in a lexical reading for each of the words in the former group and excluding it from the lexical readings for words in the latter, we thereby express the generalization that the former words are similar in meaning in this respect but that the latter are not. A selection restriction states a condition — framed in terms of a requirement about the presence or absence of certain semantic markers —

---

[11] J. J. Katz and J. A. Fodor, "The Structure of a Semantic Theory," *Language*, XXXIX (1963), 170–210; reprinted in *The Structure of Language: Readings in the Philosophy of Language*, ed. J. A. Fodor and J. J. Katz (Engelwood Cliffs: Prentice-Hall, Inc., 1964), pp. 479–518; J. J. Katz, "Recent Issues in Semantic Theory," *Foundations of Language, in press.*

under which a reading of a constituent can combine with readings of other constituents to form *derived readings* representing conceptually congruous senses of syntactically compound constituents.

The semantic component operates on underlying phrase markers, converting them into *semantically interpreted underlying phrase markers*, which formally represent all the information about the meaning of the sentences to which they are assigned. Initially, each of the lexical items in an underlying phrase marker receives a subset of the lexical readings that it has in its dictionary entry. Then, the projection rules combine lexical readings from sets assigned to different lexical items to form derived readings, and these are combined to form further derived readings, and so on. Each derived reading is assigned to the compound constituent whose parts are the constituents whose readings were combined to form the derived reading. In this way each constituent in the underlying phrase marker, including the whole sentence, is assigned a set of readings that represents its senses. Thus, a semantically interpreted underlying phrase marker is an underlying phrase marker each of whose brackets is assigned a maximal set of readings (where by "maximal" is meant that the set contains every reading that can be formed by the projection rules without violating a selection restriction).

We are now in a position to define the notions "logical form" and "grammatical form": *The logical form of a sentence is the set of its semantically interpreted underlying phrase markers; the grammatical form of a sentence is its superficial phrase marker with its phonetic representation.* Accordingly, the syntactic and semantic components for a language comprise a theory of logical form for that language, while the syntactic and phonological components for the language comprise a theory of grammatical form for it. Similarly, syntactic theory and semantic theory comprise a theory of logical form in general, while syntactic theory and phonological theory comprise a theory of grammatical form in general.

7. SEMANTIC PROPERTIES AND RELATIONS

However, semantic theory does much more than complete the account of the distinction between logical form and grammatical form. It also provides solutions to the philosophical problems of explicating concepts such as (1) through (9). Definitions of these concepts thus constitute further support for the relevance of the thesis that I am defending.

Restricting our attention to syntactically unambiguous sentences, we can provide a general idea of such definitions. First, a sentence is semantically anomalous just in case the set of readings assigned to it is empty. This explicates the notion that what prevents a sentence from having a meaningful interpretation are conceptual incongruities between senses of its parts that keep these senses from compositionally forming a sense for the whole sentence. Second, a sentence is semantically unique, i.e. expresses exactly one proposition, just in case the set of readings assigned to it contains one member. Third, a sentence is semantically ambiguous just in case the set of readings assigned to it contains n members, for $n > 1$. Fourth, a sentence is a paraphrase of another sentence just in case the set of readings assigned to them have a member in common. Fifth, two sentences are full paraphrases just in case each is assigned the same set of readings. Sixth, a sentence is analytic if there is a reading assigned to it that is derived from a reading for its subject and a reading for its verb phrase such that the latter contains no semantic markers not already in the former.[12] Finally, a sentence entails

---

[12] This is a simplified version of the definition of analyticity given in J. J. Katz, "Analyticity and Contradiction in Natural Language," *The Structure of Language: Readings in the Philosophy of Language*, and in J. J. Katz, *The Philosophy of Language*. This concept of analyticity may be regarded as a linguistically systematized version of Kant's concept of analyticity, with two refinements: one, that Kant's somewhat

another sentence if each semantic marker in the reading for the latter's subject is already contained in the reading for the former's subject and each semantic marker in the reading for the latter's verb phrase is already contained in the reading for the former's verb phrase.[13]

The adequacy of these definitions as solutions to the philosophical problems to which they are addressed is entirely a matter of their empirical justification. Since such definitions are part of semantic theory, which, in turn, is part of linguistic theory, they must be justified on the same evidential basis as any other linguistic universal. Thus, their empirical evaluation consists in verifying the predictions to which they lead about the semantic properties and relations of sentences from natural languages. Given the semantically interpreted underlying phrase marker for a sentence S in a language L and the definition of a semantic property P or relation R, we can deduce a prediction about whether S has P or bears R to some other sentence. This deduction is merely a matter of determining whether or not the semantically interpreted underlying phrase marker(s) of S possess the formal features required by the definition of P or R. Such predictions can be checked against the ways that fluent speakers of L sort sentences in terms of their naive linguistic intuitions. Hence, the justification of these definitions depends on whether such predictions accord with the judgments of fluent speakers about clear cases from L.

To remove from these definitions the

stigma that automatically attaches to definitions of semantic properties and relations since Quine's attack on the analytic-synthetic distinction, I will show how the above definition of analyticity avoids the criticism he leveled against Carnap's explication of analyticity.[14] This case is chosen as our example because of its prominence in the literature, but what I am going to say by way of a defense against Quine's criticism of this concept will apply directly to similar criticisms of any of the other semantic properties and relations.

One of Quine's major criticisms was that Carnap's explication of analyticity, contradiction, and related concepts merely defines one of these concepts in terms of others, whose own definition quickly brings us back to the original one without offering a genuine analysis of any of them. The above definition of analyticity, however, cannot be criticized on grounds of such circularity because it is not the case that any of these related terms, or any others for that matter, were used to define it. The unique feature of the above definitions is that the defining condition in each is stated exclusively in terms of a different set of formal features in semantically interpreted underlying phrase markers. Moreover, no appeal to such definitions is made in the process whereby a semantically interpreted underlying phrase marker obtains the formal features by virtue of which it satisfies such a defining condition. Further, Quine criticizes Carnap for merely labeling sentences as analytic without ever indicating just what is attributed to a sentence so labeled. On Carnap's account, the term "analytic" is just an unexplained label. But, on our account, labeling a sentence as analytic depends on its semantic structure, as determined by its semantically interpreted underlying phrase marker. Thus, labeling a sentence as analytic attributes to it that semantic structure for-

---

vague and restricted notions of subject and predicate are replaced by the formally defined grammatical relations *subject of S* and *verb phrase of S*, and two, that Kant's metaphorical notions of concept and of containment are replaced by the formal analogues of a reading and the inclusion of a set of semantic markers in another set. The semantic properties of contradiction and syntheticity can also be defined, as can inconsistency and other related cases; their definitions, however, involve too many technicalities to be given here.

[13] A conditional sentence is analytic just in case its antecedent entails its consequent.

[14] W. V. Quine, "Two Dogmas of Empiricism," *From a Logical Point of View* (Cambridge: Harvard University Press, 1953).

malized in the definition that introduces "analytic" into linguistic theory. Lastly, the definition of "analytic," as well as that of any of the other semantic properties and relations defined in semantic theory, cannot be criticized for being too particularistic because, as Quine requires, they are formulated for variable S and L. This language–independent generality is guaranteed by the fact that they are given in linguistic theory and that their defining conditions are formulated exclusively in terms of semantically interpreted underlying phrase markers, which are associated with each sentence in any linguistic description.[15]

8. SEMANTIC CATEGORIES

The last philosophical problem whose solution I here want to treat within linguistic theory is that of semantic categories, the most general classes into which the concepts from all fields of knowledge divide. The most influential treatment of semantic categories was certainly Aristotle's. Aristotelian categories claim to be the most abstract classificational divisions under which ideas of any sort can be subsumed. They are the ultimate, unanalyzable, maximally general set of natural kinds that are given in natural languages. Aristotle enumerated ten (perhaps eight) such categories: *substance, quantity, quality, relation, place, time, posture, possession, action,* and *passivity* (with the last two of somewhat questionable status). But he did not explain how he chose these categories nor how he decided that no others belong to the list. The criterion he mentions falls far short of providing a satisfactory principle for categoryhood.

Aristotle's criterion comes to this: each category is the most general answer to a question of the form "What is X?." Thus, *substance* qualifies as a category because

[15] For a more detailed and complete account of how my explication of analyticity avoids Quine's criticisms of Carnap's explication, see J. J. Katz, "Some Remarks on Quine on Analyticity," in *press, The Journal of Philosophy.*

"a substance" is the most general answer to such questions as "What is Socrates?." Likewise, *quality* is a category because "a quality" is the most general answer to such questions as "What is green?." There is, of course, much room for doubt about these answers, but, even if this criterion were fairly successful in picking out cases that we would intuitively regard as among the most abstract classificational divisions in our conceptual system, it would tell us nothing about the nature of the categories it sorted out. Its application relies on intuitive judgments about what are and what are not the most general answers to the test questions, without clarifying either for ourselves or our informants just what makes these judgments appropriate judgments about the concepts concerned. Consequently, assuming that those things that are proper answers to such questions are just those things that are the most general genera for classifying concepts, still, we know no more about the idea of a category than we did before having obtained its extension in this manner. The criterion itself presupposes our intuitive understanding of the notion *maximal generality in the domain of possible concepts* as a condition for its application, but it does not provide any analysis of this notion.

If we can embed the theory of semantic categories into linguistic theory, we can obtain an analysis of this notion and thereby arrive at a clearer understanding of semantic categories. To do this, we have to ask by what means can we distinguish two sets of semantic markers: *first*, the subset of the set of semantic markers appearing in the dictionary of a linguistic description of some particular language whose members represent concepts having the required degree of generality in that language, and, *second*, the subset of the set of universal semantic markers (as given in semantic theory) whose members represent concepts having the required degree of generality for language in general. Thus, we must provide some empirically motivated way for determining the semantic categories of a particular language and the semantic categories of natural language.

As we have characterized the entries for lexical items in the dictionary of a semantic component, lexical readings contain a semantic marker for each independent conceptual component of the sense that they represent. Formulated in this way, almost every lexical reading would exhibit a high degree of redundancy in the manner in which it specifies the semantic information in a sense. For example, the semantic markers (Physical Object) and (Human) that appear in the lexical readings for the words "bachelor," "man," "spinster," "child," etc., are subject to a regularity governing their occurrence with respect to one another in the dictionary, viz. whenever (Human) occurs in a lexical reading, so does (Physical Object). Hence, the occurrence of (Physical Object) in lexical readings that contain (Human) is actually redundant, by virtue of the generalization that the occurrence of (Physical Object) is determined by the occurrence of (Human). However, as we have so far described the dictionary, we have made no provision for the formulation of such generalizations. That is, at present, we have no way to express this regularity in the formalism of semantic theory so that the redundancy of (Physical Object) for these cases is forced on us in order that we be able to fully represent the senses of these words. Without a means for expressing such regularities, linguistic descriptions that are written in accord with semantic theory, as so far formulated, can be correctly criticized for having missed an important generalization about their languages. With a means of representing such regularities, the actual occurrence of the semantic marker (Physical Object) is dispensible because its occurrence in the lexical readings for "bachelor," "man," "spinster, etc., is predictable from the occurrence of (Human) in these lexical readings and the generalization that says that (Human)

never occurs in a lexical reading unless (Physical Object) occurs. Moreover, this case is not an isolated one. Not only is there a broader regularity covering the occurrence of (Physical Object), viz., whenever (Human), (Animal), (Artifact), (Plant), etc., occurs in a lexical reading, so does (Physical Object), but other semantic markers besides (Physical Object) are redundant in the same way, and are similarly predictable from generalizations expressing the appropriate regularities, viz., (Animal) occurs whenever (Mammal) does. Hence, from the viewpoint of the whole dictionary with its thousands of entries, there will be an incredible amount of redundancy in the specification of the senses of lexical items unless we provide some way to eliminate such unnecessary occurrences of semantic markers by finding some formalism to express these lexical generalizations.

The obvious way to make dictionary entries more economical and to provide a means of expressing these regularities is to extend the conception of the dictionary presented in Section 6 so that the dictionary includes rules which state the appropriate generalizations and thereby enable us to exclude redundant semantic markers from lexical readings. In general, these rules will be of the form

$$(M_1) \lor (M_2) \lor \ldots \lor (M_n) \rightarrow (M_k)$$

where (M_k) is distinct from each (M_i), $1 \le i \le n$ and where $\lor$ is the symbol for disjunction. In the case discussed above, we have an example of a rule of this type.

$$(M_1) \lor (M_2) \lor \ldots \lor (\text{Human}) \lor (\text{Animal}) \lor (\text{Artifact}) \lor (\text{Plant}) \lor \ldots \lor (M_n) \rightarrow (\text{Physical Object})$$

Adding this rule to the dictionary enables us to capitalize on the regularity noted above and economize lexical readings that contain one of the semantic markers (M_1), (M_2), . . . , (Human), (Animal), (Artifact), (Plant) . . . , (M_n) by dropping the occurrence of the semantic marker (Physical Object) from those lexical readings. Such rules will comprise a new component of the dictionary, whose list of entries can now contain only lexical readings in maximally reduced form. These rules thus function to compress the readings in dictionary entries, making the dictionary a more economical formulation of the lexical information in the language.

So much for the formalism. The redundancy rules not only simplify the statement of the dictionary and state significant lexical generalizations, they also represent inclusion relations among the concepts represented by semantic markers. For such rules can be interpreted as saying that the concepts represented by the semantic markers on the left-hand side of the arrow are included in, or subsumed under, the concept represented by the semantic marker on the right-hand side. Here, then, is where the application of this formalism to the question of semantic categories comes in. Using the redundancy rules in the dictionary of a linguistic description for a language L, we can formally determine which of the semantic markers in that linguistic description represents the semantic categories of L. *We define a semantic category of* L *to be any concept represented by a semantic marker that occurs on the right-hand side of some rule in the redundancy rules in the dictionary of the linguistic description of* L, *but does not occur on the left-hand side of any rule in that set of redundancy rules.* Thus, to find the semantic categories of a particular language, we simply check over the list of redundancy rules in the linguistic description of L and pick each semantic marker for which there is a rule that says that that marker subsumes other markers, and for which there is no rule that says that that marker is subsumed under other markers. The significance of this definition is two-fold. First, it makes it possible for us to formally determine the semantic categories for a given language with respect to a linguistic description for it. Second, it makes it possible to justify empirical claims to the effect that such-and-such concepts are the semantic categories for a given language. Such justification for a

set of putative semantic categories is a matter of empirically establishing that no simpler formulation of the lexical readings in the dictionary of the language is provided by redundancy rules other than those which, by the above definition of semantic categories of L, yield the set of putative semantic categories in question. This is the same sort of empirical justification appealed to in other branches of science when it is claimed that some theoretical account is best because it employs the simplest laws for describing the phenomena under study.

On the basis of these considerations, we can also formally determine the semantic markers that represent semantic categories of language in general, i.e. the semantic categories for all natural languages as opposed to the semantic categories of some particular natural language. *We define the semantic categories of language to be those concepts represented by the semantic markers belonging to the intersection of the sets of semantic categories for each particular natural language* $L_1, L_2, \ldots, L_n$, *as obtained from the redundancy rules in the dictionaries of the linguistic descriptions for* $L_1, L_2, \ldots, L_n$ *in the manner just described.* That is, a semantic category of language is a concept represented by a semantic marker that is found in each and every set of semantic categories for particular natural languages. The significance of this definition is parallel to that of the previous one. First, it provides us with a formal means to determine the categories of language, and second, it provides us with a clear-cut empirical basis for deciding what is a semantic category of language. The justification for a claim that some concept is a semantic category of language can be given on the basis of the same evidence that warrants the claims that that concept is a semantic category of $L_1, L_2, \ldots, L_n$.

Notice, finally, that the unexplicated notion of maximal generality on which the Aristotelian notion of categories is based is here explicated formally, in terms of membership in the set of semantic markers that comprises the intersection of the sets of semantic markers that are semantic categories for the natural languages, where each of the semantic markers in these latter sets is obtained by the condition that it appears on the right-hand side of a redundancy rule but not on the left-hand side of any.

9. THE SCOPE OF PHILOSOPHICAL RELEVANCE

If the considerations put forth in this paper on behalf of the thesis that linguistic theory is relevant to the solution of philosophical problems are convincing, then it is quite natural to ask to what philosophical problems is linguistic theory *ir*relevant. That there are problems to which linguistic theory is irrelevant need not be questioned, for the philosophy of mathematics and the philosophy of science provide abundant examples. Consequently, it would be highly desirable to have some handy criterion by which to decide whether a philosophical problem is essentially about the underlying conceptual structure of natural languages or about something else. But I find it hard to believe that we can have such a criterion, for not only do philosophical problems not come to us ear-marked as either linguistic or non-linguistic but, even given a fully developed linguistic theory, it would require considerable further inquiry to discover whether some portion of that theory is relevant to some particular philosophical problem and much further argument to establish that the relevance is such that linguistic theory provides an authentic solution for it.

We have so far considered only one sense in which linguistic theory can be relevant to philosophical questions. In conclusion, I would like to consider another way in which it can have philosophical relevance, one that does not depend on the theory offering us the concepts that answer the philosophical question.

The problem of innate ideas, the crux of the controversy between empiricists and rationalists, is a case to which linguistic theory has a significant application in a somewhat different way than the one in which it applies to the problems discussed above.[16] This problem can be recast as the question of whether the acquisition of a natural language can be explained better on the basis of the empiricist hypothesis that the mind starts out as a *tabula rasa*, or on the basis of the rationalist hypothesis that the mind starts out with a rich stock of innately fixed principles which determine the general form of the rules for a natural language. Given that the child obtains his inner representation of the rules of a language from the linguistic data to which he is exposed during his formative years, we may consider the child's mind to be a black box whose input is such linguistic data and whose output is an internalization of the linguistic description of the language. Accordingly, we ask whether the empiricist hypothesis that this internalization is obtained by processing sensory data on the basis of principles of associative learning, or the rationalist hypothesis that this internalization is obtained by a specialization of the innate system of principles when they are activated by appropriate sensory stimulation, is the better account of how the black box converts its input into its output. We have a fairly clear idea of the associative principles with which the empiricist is willing to credit the child's mind prior to experience, but it is by no means clear what are the innately fixed principles concerning the general form of language on the rationalist's account. Here the relevance of linguistic theory is, then, that it provides a statement of the principles required to formulate the rationalist hypothesis in specific terms. The question is, therefore, whether we must assume as rich a conception of innate structure as is given by linguistic theory's account of the universals of language in order to explain language acquisition.

---

[16] For a more complete discussion of the problem of innate ideas, cf. Chapter 5 of my book, *The Philosophy of Language*.

Notice, however, that although this question, which reformulates the problem of innate ideas, can only be raised in an explicit form when linguistic theory supplies the conception of innate structure for the rationalist hypothesis, its answer is not given by linguistic theory. Linguistic theory does not validate the rationalist position in its controversy with the empiricist position, since it is outside the scope of linguistic theory to decide which of these two positions is best supported by the facts about the linguistic information available to the child and about how he copes with them.

This case was introduced not only to show that the relevance of linguistic theory to philosophy goes beyond solving philosophical problems, but also to show that it can be relevant in the specific sense of providing the means by which a philosophical problem can be reformulated in a manner that makes it more susceptible to solution. Whether linguistic theory is relevant to philosophical investigation in still other ways must remain a matter for further philosophical and linguistic inquiry.

Editor's note: For replies to this essay, see the abstracts of the comments read by Neil Wilson and Zeno Vendler at the symposium in which Katz first presented this paper (*Journal of Philosophy*, LXII [1965], 602–08).

Author's note: For replies to the replies of Wilson and Vendler, see my contribution to the forthcoming *Harper Guide to Philosophy*, ed. Arthur Danto (New York: Harper & Row) titled "The Underlying Reality of Language and its Philosophical Import."

28

YEHOSHUA BAR-HILLEL

A PREREQUISITE FOR RATIONAL PHILOSOPHICAL DISCUSSION

Communication between philosophers has been deteriorating during the last decades. Logical empiricists and British linguistic philosophers have been branding large parts of the output of their speculative colleagues as 'nonsense' and 'literally unintelligible'. Speculative metaphysicians, after having recovered from the first shock, either just disregard these declarations, or else declare, on their part, that the standards of intelligibility employed by the critics are arbitrary.

The breakdown of communication is not always as radical as the situation just described might lead one to believe. An analytic philosopher (let us use this term to cover both logical empiricists and linguistic philosophers) might often try to suggest one or more reinterpretations of his colleague's original formulations, thereby making them intelligible to himself. (This, of course, indicates that he does 'understand' the original formulation; thereby his behavior is not made absurd since this kind of understanding is clearly different from the one he professes not to have.) Unfortunately, this conciliatory action seldom does much good. The reinterpretations have a tendency to become either flagrant truisms or flagrant falsities. Even in case they do neither, more often than not the speculative philosopher will reject them as completely missing the point of his intentions, perhaps adding that this failure could have been foreseen, since there is no reason why his deep insights should be formulable in the analytic philosopher's shallow and arbitrarily-restricted language.

One might have expected that another development would arrest and reverse this trend of deteriorating communication. I refer to the well-known fact that the standards of intelligibility of the late twenties and early thirties — 'whatever can be said at all, can be said in ordinary (thing-, observational) language' — have been undergoing a process of continuous liberalization, the history of which has been told many times. In one of the latest attempts at explicating the empiricist's standard of intelligibility,[1] a discourse is regarded as intelligible, not only if it is formulated wholly in observational language, but also if it is formulated in theoretical or mixed language, if only the theoretical terms occurring in it are connected via theoretical postulates and rules of correspondence with the observational terms. True enough, the degree of intelligibility of such discourse is deemed to be inferior to that of a purely observational one. However,

Reprinted from *Logic and Language: Studies Dedicated to Professor Rudolf Carnap* (Dordrecht: D. Reidel Publishing Company, 1962), pp. 1–5, by permission of the author and the publisher. (Copyright 1962 by the D. Reidel Publishing Company.)

[1] R. Carnap, "The methodological character of theoretical concepts," The Foundations of Science and the Concepts of Psychology and Psychoanalysis, *Minnesota Studies in the Philosophy of Science*, Volume I (Minneapolis: University of Minnesota Press, 1956), pp. 38–76.

thereby such discourse is not disqualified nor is one entitled to draw the consequence that it is somehow less important or scientific than fully intelligible observational discourse. Clearly, a treatise in theoretical physics, psychology or linguistics is not the worse off because of the fact that its theoretical terms are only partially and indirectly interpretable.

It is nevertheless rather doubtful whether this liberalization will bring about a reunion in philosophy. Though the analytic philosopher may be willing to regard the specifically metaphysical terms used by his colleague as theoretical terms of which he is quite ready not to require more than partial and indirect interpretation in observational terms, he will continue to ask his colleague to supply him this interpretation, at least in sufficient outline. But the speculative philosopher will quite often refuse to do this, just as he refused to comply with the earlier demand to supply full and direct interpretation by operational definitions. He might even point out that just as the empiricist will now agree that his earlier demands were unjustified, so he will come to realize in due time that his present demands are still unduly restrictive.

This may indeed turn out to be the case. Most analytic philosophers are today aware that the whole conception of an observational language is rather vague, that the line of demarcation between observational and theoretical terms is blurred, elastic and even to a considerable degree arbitrary, and will therefore be rather careful with their use of the epithets 'meaningless', 'nonsensical', or 'unintelligible'. But they will continue refusing to exert themselves overly in order to supply for their own benefit all those theoretical postulates and rules of correspondence, or at least a sufficiently large outline of these, which they regard as necessary in principle for ensuring a modicum of intelligibility. If an analytic philosopher finds that a certain philosophical text is *underinterpreted*, he may or may not attempt to suggest to the reader of this text one or more ways of supplementing the missing links, but if the author refuses to follow suit, the analytic philosopher will still know no more rational reaction than to count himself out. The possibility that he himself twenty years hence, or the next generation of analytic philosophers, might conceivably liberalize the standards of intelligibility still further and then rejoin the metaphysical game, will be more or less cheerfully acknowledged but will not influence the present breakdown of communication.

Is this then the end of the conversation? I am not convinced that it must be so. Though I myself, for instance, as an analytic philosopher, see no way of joining many metaphysical discussions because of the hopelessness of remedying their state of underinterpretedness. I am ready to explain why I regard the language of these discussions as underinterpreted, what are my present standards of intelligibility, why I believe that a discussion that does not comply with them holds little or no promise of being fruitful, etc. And I am ready to listen, and listen attentively, if my colleague will challenge my evaluation, criticize my standards of intelligibility and try to persuade me that the language of this or that speculative philosopher, or of all speculative philosophers, is one which it is worthwhile to adopt, at least for certain purposes. *But I am ready to listen and argue with him only if the (meta-) language, in which he explains to me his reasons for challenging my standards, itself complies with these standards.*

This may sound preposterous, but I don't see how it can be helped. My insistence is due to the fact that the situation is objectively asymmetrical. One cannot expect that the analytic philosopher, while endeavoring to persuade by rational means his speculative colleague of the cognitive poverty of his ways of philosophizing, should himself use speculative discourse for this purpose. This type of discourse is unintelligible to him in any capacity, including that of a metadiscourse. This does not mean that he is unable to intelligently manipulate such discourse for other purposes, should the occasion require it. On the other hand, no similar scruples could prevent the speculative philosopher from using scientific (observational plus theoretical) metalanguage to impress his analytical colleagues with the importance of using metaphysical object-language.

Here then, it seems, the final *conditio sine qua non* of continued philosophical discussion has been reached. Those *speculative philosophers* who are interested in having analytic philosophers discuss their theses couched in metaphysical language *must use a scientific metalanguage as their rational tool of persuasion.* (I shall not discuss here, for obvious reasons, the possible use of extra-rational tools.) The analytic philosopher who is interested in having speculative philosophers stop formulating their theses the way they do, need do nothing beyond stretching his standards of intelligibility to the limit and offering constant reinterpretations in scientific language of the original metaphysical formulations. This includes occasionally reformulating these theses as proposals, comments, exhortations, etc. As I am using the term 'scientific language' now, such languages contain not only declarative sentences but also question sentences, etc.

I am under no illusions as to the effects of my proposal. Even if speculative philosophers should accept it in principle, there is little likelihood that agreement could be reached as to the extent of the *index verborum prohibitorum* for the common philosophical metalanguage. Differences will arise as to which terms of ordinary language are entitled to be considered directly intelligible. As to the theoretical terms, it is only with regard to rigorously-constructed language systems that it is precisely, though not necessarily effectively, determined whether they are or are not empirically significant, relative to the given observational language and after a certain criterion of significance has been

adopted. Since nobody, and certainly not myself, seriously requires that a theoretical term of ordinary language should be admitted into philosophical metadiscourse only after this discourse has been completely formalized, it cannot be assumed that agreement would be reached on the admissibility of all candidates, in anticipation of future formalization. It is notorious that no such agreement has been reached as to the status of, say, certain psychoanalytical terms, and this among methodologists who would all of them be regarded as adherents of analytic philosophy. Similar disagreements exist as to the character of such terms in theoretical semantics as 'class', 'proposition' and the like, which some analytic philosophers simply claim not to understand. Add to this that a given term may doubtless be intelligible, perhaps even straight observational, in some of its uses (meanings) but of doubtful status in other uses (meanings), and this even in the discourse of one and the same author — think of what theologians call 'analogical use', for instance — and the very great difficulties of agreeing upon a common metalanguage in which to discuss the relative merits of the various object-languages used by philosophers should be clear. Nevertheless, I think that an agreement in principle to use for this purpose a language of about the same structure the analytic philosophers believe that the object-language of science has, should have its beneficial impact. One can only wish that prestige considerations ('having to talk the other fellow's language') will not blind the speculative philosophers in this context. I see no rational reason why they should refuse *a priori* to use a scientific metalanguage in order to justify their conviction that the scientific object-language is not adequate for certain philosophical purposes. Should they contend, however, that for intrinsic reasons such a metalanguage is not up to its purpose, then this would now indeed mean either the end of the conversation, or else the whole issue will just be pushed one step higher in the hierarchy of philosophical metalanguages. The simple argument that a scientific metalanguage is unsuitable for the philosopher's use for the *same* reason for which a scientific object-language is unsuitable for this purpose would surely be a rather weak one, as can be shown by innumerable analogies. One can and does show in ordinary non-symbolic (meta-) language that ordinary non-symbolic (object-)language is unsuitable for algebraic purposes. Any contention that a discussion of the relative merits of various proposed notational systems for chemistry should be held in a metalanguage in which these notations are not only mentioned (which they clearly must be) but also used would meet with very strong initial disbelief. Though philosophy is neither chemistry nor algebra, this by itself is not a sufficient reason for rejecting the analogy. My plea is necessarily of a general and vague nature. No recipe follows from what I said. Any single word which the analytical philosopher professes not to understand (sufficiently) in an initial stage of a discussion can be made (sufficiently) intelligible by supplementing a few suitable sentences (though there constantly lurks the danger of *obscurum obscurior* in such situations). However, as to those notorious types of metadiscourse which analytic philosophers tend to regard as definitely underinterpreted *in toto*, it might be simpler to omit them altogether rather than to try giving a sketch of the theory behind them, which would at the best tend to become a very complex and time-consuming affair. But clearly no hard and fast rules of thumb can be expected. Goodwill helps. But unfortunately, though necessary, it is not sufficient.

TEN YEARS AFTER*

The title of Ian Hacking's *Why Does Language Matter to Philosophy?* raises a good question. The question would have found prompt and pat answers thirty, or even ten, years ago. But there has been little consideration of it recently; no one likes any of the old answers, and nobody has thought of any new ones. In the course of the last decade, people who used to accept the description "linguistic philosopher" with equanimity have become inclined to resent and reject it. There is, it is now said, no particular philosophical method called "linguistic"—but it is often added that philosophy of language is at the center of philosophy. In explanation, some view like this of Michael Dummett's is offered:

Because philosophy has, as its first if not its only task, the analysis of meanings, and because, the deeper such analysis goes, the more it is dependent upon a correct general account of meaning, a model for what the understanding of an expression consists in, the theory of meaning, which is the search for such a model, is the foundation of all philosophy, and not epistemology as Descartes misled us into believing.[1]

This explanation, however, raises more questions than it answers. It is true that a couple of generations of Anglo-American philosophers, when asked what they did for a living, might have replied "We analyze meanings." But, since Quine's "Two Dogmas" and Wittgenstein's *Investigations,* philosophers have been increasingly hesitant even to mention meanings, much less formulate a job description in terms of them. Work in philosophy of language in recent years has produced little that helps the metaphilosophically puzzled analyst of meanings to know when he has done his job properly. Indeed, the vigor of that field seems due in some measure to its new-found freedom from such metaphilosophical concerns.

However, this freedom from metaphilosophy has not clarified the objectives of philosophy of language. Back in 1962, Jerry Fodor and Jerrold Katz were already suggesting that philosophy of language had suffered too long from the metaphilosophical presuppositions of positivism and Oxford analysis. Their solution was that it should hereafter conceive of itself as "the philosophy of linguistics, a discipline analogous in every respect to the philosophy of physics, the philosophy of mathematics, the philosophy of psychology, and the like."[2] Such a conception seems to offer no support of Dummett's claim that philosophy of language is "first philosophy." Yet the seeming modesty of their claim is misleading. It did not prevent Fodor and Katz from thinking that the philosophy of language

*"Ten Years After" was first published as a review of Ian Hacking's *Why Does Language Matter to Philosophy?* in *The Journal of Philosophy,* LXXXIV, No. 7 (1977), 416–32. (© Copyright 1977 by The Journal of Philosophy, Inc.) Reprinted by permission.

[1] *Frege: Philosophy of Language* (London: Duckworth, 1973), p. 669.

[2] "Introduction" to *The Structure of Language* (Englewood Cliffs: Prentice-Hall, 1964), p. 18. This piece is a revised version of their "What's Wrong with the Philosophy of Language?," *Inquiry,* v. 3 (Autumn 1962): 197–237. For Katz's later repudiation of this view, see his *The Philosophy of Language* (New York: Harper and Row, 1966), p. 4. Chapter 1 of that book develops a view of philosophy of language as First Philosophy which, as Hugh Wilder has pointed out to me, has difficulty reconciling its priority and universality with its empirical character.

361

could do a lot toward clearing up traditional philosophical problems. They thought this because they thought that Chomskian linguistics had light to shed on these problems; had they not had this confident view they might have been less ready to assign the philosophy of language a parochial role. In the intervening years, however, skepticism about the relevance of linguistics to traditional philosophical problems has increased. Many of the leading research programs in the philosophy of language (e.g., those of Davidson, Kripke, Putnam, and Dummett himself) have come to have less and less to do with the details of work in linguistics. For better or worse, Fodor and Katz's modest proposal did not prosper.

In this situation, philosophers who sympathize with Quine's attack on the notion of meaning and who suspect that the notion of "analysis" is as disreputable as that of "analyticity" have tried to find a Quinean way of stating the importance of language for philosophy without resorting to the notion of "the philosophy of linguistics." Quine himself, in the section on "Semantic Ascent" in *Word and Object*,[3] made a halfhearted stab at this. He said there that one could still put forward the Carnapian claim that philosophical questions were questions of language if one treated language not as a matter of meanings but just as a part of the world in which agreement was more likely to be obtained than elsewhere:

The strategy of semantic ascent [i.e., "moving from talking in certain terms to talking about them"] is that it carries the discussion into a domain where both parties are better agreed on the objects (viz., words) and on the main terms concerning them. Words, or their inscriptions, unlike points, miles, classes, and the rest, are tangible objects of the size so popular in the marketplace, where men of unlike conceptual schemes communicate best. The strategy is one of ascending to a common part of two fundamentally disparate conceptual schemes, the better to discuss the disparate foundations. No wonder it helps in philosophy. (272)

This claim that words, or their inscriptions, are tangible objects about which men of different philosophical persuasions can fairly readily

[3] Cambridge, Mass.: MIT Press, 1960.

agree seems trivial when one thinks of inscriptions and dubious when one thinks of the use of inscriptions. Only the inscriptions themselves are tangible, and it is doubtful whether agreement on the identification and explanation of inscriptions has ever offered any aid to philosophers. As for the uses of those inscriptions, they are not only intangible but presumably *not* a "common part of . . . disparate conceptual schemes." Rather, they are just where disparity comes to a head.

Presumably what Quine has in mind as examples of the success of semantic ascent are the discovery that we need not ask what a sake is because the transcription of "He did it for the sake of his wife" into canonical notation need not include anything like "There is an x such that x is a sake and is his wife's and he did it for x," and, more significant, the discovery that we need not have intensional contexts in canonical notation because (e.g.) we can construe "S believes that p" as "S is in the believing-that-p state" where "believing-that-p" is a single unanalyzable predicate. But this last example, and the principled rejection of this treatment of opacity by such philosophers as Davidson, shows that the criteria for taking a notation as canonical are at least as obscure as the criteria for deciding issues in the philosophy of mind—and one cannot get much more obscure than that. Quine's own refusal to countenance a distinction between languages and theories helps one see why suggestions in the formal mode of speech about how to talk will rarely be less controversial than suggestions in the material mode about what to say. Only an ordinary-language philosopher, who had no canonical notation to recommend, would be in a position to say that language (as the study of "what we would say") was less controversial than metaphysics. But such a philosopher would be in no better a position than Quine to recommend semantic ascent, for inspection of what we would say about X's is no more about the use of the word 'X' than it is about X's themselves. There is point in putting philosophical theses in the form of linguistic recommendations only if one intends to suggest *changing* what we would say; if one wants to leave what we say alone, then there is no reason to be self-consciously linguistic and no reason to distinguish between the essence of X, the concept of X, and the use of the term

"X." In sum: on an ideal-language view, semantic ascent does not help in reaching agreement, whereas on an ordinary-language view it is a pointless detour.

Despite all this, I think we all have some inclination to agree with Quine that semantic ascent does, somehow, "help in philosophy." There is a general belief that philosophers have got clearer about what they are doing since the "linguistic turn." So even if Quine has not explained why the turn was worth taking, it does seem that there is a real phenomenon that does need explaining. Hilary Putnam, who shares Quine's distrust of the notion that philosophers "analyze meanings," has attempted to show that although both positivists and Oxonians have exaggerated the successes produced by the use of linguistic methods, nevertheless "even if we have not discovered 'linguistic solutions' to these problems, we *have* . . . acquired a great deal of new knowledge about them."[4] He offers two grounds for this opinion. The first is an improved version of Dummett's claim that philosophy's primary job is the analysis of meanings.[5] Putnam says that the discovery by Wittgenstein and others that "concepts cannot be identical with mental objects of any kind" (7) was a consideration which "led naturally to the idea that a great deal of philosophy should be reconstructed as about language, even if the authors in question did not think they were talking about language" (9). So, he says, "one reason for upgrading the importance of language in philosophy" was that

concepts and ideas were always thought important; language was unimportant, because it was considered to be merely a system of conventional signs for concepts and ideas (considered as mental entities of some kind . . .). But if having a concept is being able to use signs in particular ways, or if this is even a major part of the story, then all the attention that was traditionally accorded to matters of introspective psychology more prop-

erly belongs to the ways in which we use signs. (14)

This first reason for upgrading language is certainly an accurate description of the rationale with which many linguistic philosophers have provided themselves. But, put thus baldly, it is not obviously a good reason. It would be a good reason only if (a) we agree that concepts and ideas *are* important to philosophy, and if (b) the importance attached to concepts can survive the realization that concepts are not things which stand behind the use of words but are reducible to those uses, and if (c) the constellation of meta-philosophical strategies that revolved around introspectionist psychology could be transferred more or less whole to a study of the use of signs. Unless these lemmata hold, Putnam's argument is as shaky as the following parody of it: "Gods were always thought to be of importance to theology; now that we have discovered that beliefs in gods are internalizations of images of parents, we can see that depth psychology becomes central to theology and that much traditional theology should be reconstrued as about child development."

Putnam's claim that a set of problems which revolved around concepts and ideas can be made to revolve around the use of signs requires something stronger than the discovery that having a concept is being able to use a word. It requires the notion that one can do something to words—analyze them, perhaps—like what we thought we used to do to concepts. When we thought of "meanings" as what replaced concepts, the historical continuity between pre-Kantian essences, Kantian concepts, and the positivists' meanings seemed clear enough. In all three cases, philosophers attempted to separate the necessary truths found by looking to essence, concept, or meaning from the contingent truths that scientists found by looking to the contexts in which instantiations of these essences, concepts, or meanings were embedded. But once we become dubious about the necessary/contingent and structure/content distinctions, it becomes hard to say what methodological continuity links Kant to Wittgenstein or Davidson. To complicate things further, the turn away from mental entities as philosophical data produces doubt about whether Cartesian subjectivism—the turn toward ideas and concepts—was a good

---

[4] *Mind, Language, and Reality* (New York: Cambridge University Press, 1975), p. 2. All subsequent page references to Putnam in the text are to this volume.

[5] The second, which I shall not discuss, is that linguistic philosophy helped us kill off phenomenalism, and thus idealism. I think this claim is misleading; but explaining why would require a full-scale alternative account of the role of idealism in recent philosophy.

idea in the first place.[6] So the assurance that language replaces concepts seems to leave open the question of whether concepts should *ever* have been especially important to philosophy.

Hacking, like Putnam, makes much of the way in which words have come to seem capable of doing the methodological work that concepts seemed to do for seventeenth-century philosophers. But Hacking, unlike Putnam, distinguishes carefully between what he calls "the heyday of meanings"—the pre-Quinean period of analytic philosophy, roughly speaking—and the "heyday of sentences." The former period, he says, originated the notion of philosophical questions as questions of language, but the latter period has made it difficult to preserve this notion. Hacking's book is distinctive among recent metaphilosophical writings by analytic philosophers in that it treats its topic in considerable historical detail. It is written, as is his *The Emergence of Probability,* under the influence of Foucault. Hacking's willingness to grant that the materials as well as the tools of philosophy may change gives his discussion a depth that previous attempts to answer his title question have lacked. In the end, however, I think that he is less radical than his data suggest he should be. Thus, I shall argue, he misses the moral of his own history.

One important virtue of Hacking's book is that he is not tempted to answer his title question by suggesting that old philosophical problems and theories are the result of errors about the nature of language. This sort of view—typified by Austin's remark that "Plato thought all general terms were proper names, and Leibniz that all proper names were general terms"—was briefly exhilarating in the heyday of Oxford philosophy, but now has come to seem jejune. One can argue that false assumptions about language have been strengthened by various philosophical interests and systems, and that these assumptions have in turn lent plausibility to the systems that nurtured them, but it no longer seems plausible to rewrite the history of

European philosophy in terms of various confused theories about meaning. That attempt was one more instance of the phenomenon of philosophers rewriting history so as to make all their predecessors hold half-baked theories about topics of current interest. (Thus, for example, we get a lot of writing these days about Aristotle's views on reference, just as we used to get a lot, a hundred years ago, on Aristotle's treatment of the concrete universals.) It is refreshing to find Hacking saying:

There is a proper sense of "theory of meaning", which I shall now elucidate, in which none of our early empiricists undertook to provide well-worked-out theories of meaning at all. They did make many remarks which can variously be construed as supporting ideational, referential, or behavioural theories of meaning. But what modern philosophers call the theory of meaning did not matter much to them. Language did, avowedly, matter, but not necessarily in the ways that it has mattered of late. (43)

He elucidates the "proper sense" in question as explaining "the essentially public features of language, with whatever it is that is common to you and me, in respect of the word 'violet', which makes it possible for us to talk about the flowers in Knapwell wood" (50). The difference between Locke as paradigmatic philosopher centering philosophy in the theory of ideas and Frege as paradigmatic philosopher centering philosophy in the theory of meaning is explained by Hacking as follows:

Frege, like all his contemporaries, saw that public communication cannot be well explained by what he called private associated ideas. Locke, and *his* contemporaries, did not see this at all clearly. Nor did Locke and his friends care. . . . Locke did not have a theory of public discourse. He had a theory of ideas. That is a theory of mental discourse. . . . When mental discourse was taken for granted, ideas were the interface between the Cartesian *ego* and reality. We have displaced mental discourse by public discourse, and "ideas" have become unintelligible. Something in the domain of public discourse now serves as the interface between the knowing subject and the world. Thus in my opinion the seventeenth-century writers do not help us answer the question "Why does language matter to philosophy?" by what they say about theory of

---

[6] Cf. Hiram Caton, *The Origin of Subjectivity: An Essay on Descartes* (New Haven, Conn.: Yale, 1973), p. 53f.: "The great difference between the Aristotelian and Cartesian methodology is that for Descartes mind is a principle of science." Much of the best contemporary philosophy, both Anglo-Saxon and Continental, is self-consciously Aristotelian in this respect.

meaning. On the contrary, I shall take the *absence of a theory of meaning as part of the data for understanding* why language matters to philosophers today. (52–53)

Thinking of the matter in this way should, it seems to me, suggest the following sort of question: "Given that we no longer take the 'idea' seriously, why need we assume that there is *any* 'interface' between the knowing subject and the world?" Why not say that the relation between the two is as unproblematic as that between the ball and the socket, the dove and the light air it cleaves? Why must there be something "in the domain of public discourse" for philosophers to vex themselves over as they once vexed themselves over "private associated ideas"? Hacking, however, does not raise such doubts. Instead, after the passage just cited, he drops his title question almost completely from sight and gives us five chapters covering "The Heyday of Meanings." These chapters (on Chomsky, Russell, Wittgenstein, Ayer, and Malcolm) run through various of the difficulties encountered when one substitutes meanings for ideas and lead one toward Quinean doubts about the myth of meaning, but offer no clear pointers toward an answer to the title question. We find such pointers only when we reach the final section ("The Heyday of Sentences") and find chapters on Feyerabend and Davidson, whose place in the story is described as follows:

In Part B of this book, which I have called "The Heyday of Meanings," there was always some theory of meaning in the offing. It was regularly assumed that there was something below the level of what is said: there is, in addition, what is meant. Feyerabend is one representative of a new and brazen positivism. There is nothing to language over and above what is said. Here comes the death of meaning. As is often the case when assassins have a common object, they have different motives and different styles. If Feyerabend is the Cassius of the present plot, then Davidson of the next chapter is its Brutus. (128)

The view that "there is nothing to language over and above what is said" suggests once again that we might answer the title question by saying that language *doesn't* particularly matter to philosophy. Reading these two chapters on the

death of meaning leads one to think that Hacking's final chapter (which bears the same title as the book itself) will conclude that although language was bound to matter to philosophy once ideas began to look bad, it now doesn't have to matter any more.

This is not what happens. The final chapter of the book says something much odder and more complicated. Having said in his first chapter that language has always mattered to philosophy, even though the theory of meaning has not, and having promised that he will tell us at the end of the book "why there will be a philosophical labyrinth with language at its center," Hacking startles his reader by beginning his last chapter with the remark "there need not be any true and interesting general answer to my [title] question" (157). He does, however, offer an answer to a more limited question. Here is the final paragraph of the book:

At any rate, I have one answer to the question of why language matters to philosophy now. *It matters for the reason that ideas mattered in seventeenth-century philosophy,* because ideas then, and sentences now, serve as the interface between the knowing subject and what is known. The sentence matters even more if we begin to dispense with the fiction of a knowing subject and regard "discourse" as autonomous. Language matters to philosophy because of what knowledge has become. The topics of this or that school, of "linguistic philosophy", "structuralism", or whatever, will prove ephemeral and will appear as some of the brief recent episodes by which discourse itself has tried to recognize the historical situation in which it finds itself, no longer merely a tool by which experiences are shared, no longer even the interface between the knower and the known, but as that which constitutes human knowledge. (187)

The point seems to be that philosophy will always circle around the question "What is human knowledge?" or "How is human knowledge possible?" and thus will always be asking about either an "interface" or something enough like an interface that it can be recognized as "constituting" knowledge. To draw his conclusion Hacking needs both the claim that "knowledge has become" something different from what it was in the heyday of ideas and some further metaphilosophical premises—premises which would explain why knowledge should be of central philosophical interest even after the veil of ideas has been rent.

I shall first say something about Hacking's claim that knowledge itself has changed since the seventeenth century and then suggest some candidates for the implicit premises he needs to justify the passage I just cited. Hacking wants to say that the period of philosophizing of which Locke and Berkeley were typical, as compared with that represented by Feyerabend or Davidson, has "the same structure but different content" (158). The content has changed because

ideas were once the objects of all philosophizing, and were the link between the Cartesian *ego* and the world external to it. . . . In today's discussions, public discourse has replaced mental discourse. An unquestioned ingredient of all public discourse is the sentence. . . . Quine has said that "the lore of our fathers is a fabric of sentences". The sentences in this fabric of public discourse are an artifact of the knowing subject. Perhaps, as I shall soon suggest, they actually constitute this "knowing subject." At any rate, they are responsible for the representation of reality in a body of knowledge. So sentences appear to have replaced ideas. . . . The very nature of knowledge has changed. Our present situation in philosophy is a consequence of what knowledge has become. . . . A Descartes would no more have thought a theory to be a system of *statements* than a Quine would acknowledge that a theory is a scheme of seventeenth-century *ideas*. (159–60)

Hacking represents the structure within which this change has occurred in a pair of diagrams, showing a quadrilateral of "nodes" connected by arrows: Two of the nodes—"experience" and "reality"—stay the same, but the "Cartesian ego" of the diagram representing seventeenth-century philosophizing is replaced by "the knowing subject" (surmounted with a question mark), and "ideas (mental discourse)" is replaced by "sentences (public discourse)." In the diagrams for both periods, the arrows running from "ideas" and "sentences" to "reality" are marked with a question mark, as is that running from "reality" to "experience." The point seems to be that a continuing structure of philosophizing is given by "the relation between knowledge and reality," so that, though knowledge may

have changed, it still raises problems about "interfacing." Hacking speculates that his second diagram is probably

. . . an anachronism . . . shared by Strawson, Quine, and other individualists, in which our state of knowledge is still mapped on to the philosophical position of the nascent bourgeoisie of the seventeenth century. Knowledge, once possessed by individuals, is now the property of corporations.

And he directs our attention, in his closing pages, to Popper, Althusser, Hegel, and Foucault. But this suggestion of an improved diagram in which the knowing subject is dropped, or replaced by something more Hegelian, does not, he thinks, matter for his answer to his title question. For "the sentence matters even more . . . if we regard discourse as autonomous." (187)

We can get a better sense of what Hacking is up to here if we consider his *The Emergence of Probability,* in which he shows us how even so basic a philosophical notion as that of "evidence" has a datable beginning, emerging out of a period of intellectual ferment. He gives us reason in that book for thinking that it is probably pointless to try to talk about conceptions of the relation between theory and evidence prior to 1600, just as it is pointless to talk about theories of meaning circa 1300 or 1800. The point is that what you can have philosophical views about depends upon what is going on in the rest of the culture. There is no way to isolate topics of such generality ("evidence," "meaning," "truth," "society," "virtue," "science") that reflective intellects of all ages must necessarily have had theories about them. This Foucault-like point can be accepted in full, however, while still leaving one dubious about the claim that knowledge has recently changed in such a way that notions that were applicable once are no longer applicable. We tend to think that Quine's way of looking at knowledge is less problematic than Descartes's, but I do not know how to decide between saying this and saying that they were talking about different phenomena. One can agree that if Descartes were confronted by our culture rather than his own he might see less use for the notion of *cogitatio* than he did, and that if Quine had lived earlier he would have been bothered less by singular terms and more by secondary qualities. But it would be hard to argue that scientific inquiry (or culture generally) is so different from what it was in the days of Kant, or even of Russell, that philosophers are confronted by different data (as a philosopher who took Galileo as a paradigm of our knowledge of nature might be said to be confronted by a different datum for epistemological reflection from that faced by one who took Paracelsus as a model).

However that may be, unless we can get some better way of distinguishing between philosophers' descriptions of what scientists do and what scientists actually do than we have now—a way which will give us a clear-cut distinction between philosophical data and philosophical theories—I think we should not adopt Hacking's "knowledge has changed" formulation. Hacking writes as if philosophical revolutions must be seen as responses to what is going on in some less dubious area of culture, now that Foucault-like considerations have shown that philosophy is not a self-sustaining discipline with a permanent and autonomous problematic. But these are not the only alternatives. Some philosophical revolutions (Hegel's, for example) originate primarily within philosophy and spread to the rest of culture. Other philosophical revolutions are primarily reactive—as Hacking thinks the rise of empiricism was, or as the secularization of moral philosophy was a reaction to the intellectuals' reading novels rather than sermons. The notion of philosophy as "an 'under-labourer' to the best speculative and creative thought of the time" (a phrase which Hacking uses at page 162) needs to make room for the possibility that the best speculative and creative thought is sometimes done by philosophers themselves (as in early nineteenth-century Germany). Foucault's and Hacking's demonstrations of the historical character of philosophical problems need to be complemented by Dewey's and Oakeshott's picture of philosophy as an intermittent voice in a complicated conversation, rather than a discipline that stands in determinate relationships to other disciplines.

Turning now from the questions of whether knowledge has changed to the question of why we should think that philosophy has something special to do with knowledge, we may get some light on Hacking's attitude toward the latter issue by noting a remark in *The Emergence of Probability*.[7] He said there (47) that "the discovery that all names are conventional thunders us into modern philosophy." I take Hacking to be saying here that the discovery that there are no true signs (in the sense in which he describes Paracelsus as thinking that "the [true] names of stars are signs in exactly the way in which the points on a stag's antlers signify the animals' age") gives rise to a set of questions about the truth of statements which make epistemology of interest. This discovery creates an intellectual climate in which the notion of "evidence" both makes sense and is puzzling, and thus one in which (given Descartes's novel use of *cogitatio* to develop a special philosophical notion of "experience") we can make sense of the quadrilaterals that Hacking draws to portray the modern philosophical problematic. But these quadrilaterals are not (as Hacking would agree) particularly useful for understanding what Plato and Aristotle, or the Church Fathers, or the Stoics, were worried about. Nor, as far as I can see, are they of much use for portraying what philosophers have been worrying about lately (with the exception of a few thousand of us parochial and hidebound Anglo-Saxons). So, to return to the queries I raised earlier, Hacking will be in a position to say that the quadrilateral that portrays "public discourse" or "the fabric of sentences" as interface is a description of what philosophy is about now only if he explains why we should still be concerned about skepticism, the gap between theory and evidence, and the like.

The puzzling thing is that Hacking does not attempt an explanation of why philosophy-as-study-of-interfacing should survive the heyday of meanings. His claim that "the sentence matters even more . . . if we regard discourse as autonomous" sidesteps the issue, since sentences do not matter in the way in which meanings were thought to matter—that is, they do not matter as problematic interfaces. To say that they matter more because they now *constitute* human knowledge either means that the objects the sentences are about are now deemed inexistent (which Hacking certainly does not intend) or that the relation between sentence and

---

[7] New York: Cambridge, 1975.

object is not subject to the puzzles to which the relations between ideas and meanings and their objects were subject. The latter seems to me the right move for Hacking to make, but making it would lead him to deny that language *does* matter to philosophy. He is not willing to do this, and so he seems to me to fall between two stools—saying on the one hand that epistemology is pretty well over with and urging on the other that something *like* epistemology ("philosophy of language"?) will remain central to philosophy.

To see this ambivalence from another perspective, consider Hacking's attitude toward Dummett. He views Dummett's book on Frege's philosophy of language as an attempt to revive meaning after the friends of sentences have killed it off (cf. 180), and he might well view Dummett's premise, that philosophy's "first task" is "analysis of meanings," as just a ritual incantation for raising the dead. Still, he seems to want to adopt Dummett's conclusion—that at the middle of the philosophical labyrinth there will be questions about "what the understanding of an expression consists in." It is difficult, however, to feel that we need such a model when the expression in question is a sentence. We may, for Davidsonian reasons, want an account of how we manage to understand indirect quotations, sentences with adverbs, and a lot of other cases in which we do not see how the mastery of parts of the sentence can produce a mastery of the sentence as a whole.[8] But this is not a question about the relation between language and the world, nor does it call for a general model of "understanding expressions." To have such a general model we should have to have something that answered the question "How does 'Snow is white' manage to represent the fact that snow is white?"—something more enlightening than simply correlating "snow" with snow and "white" with white. A truth theory for English would indeed be enlightening about more complex sentences, but it is hard to see how it could be enlightening about *representation in general*—the "tie between language and the world" as opposed to the tie between small bits of language and

larger bits of language.[9] A Davidsonian truth theory can answer the questions "How can we get from knowledge of how to use a small number of short strings of phonemes to a knowledge of how to construct a potentially infinite number of such strings of a potentially infinite length?" and "What must we quantify over to understand the inferential relationships of English?" But these questions are, respectively, parallel to "How can we get from simple to complex ideas?" and "What kinds of ideas do we have?" Nothing in Davidson looks much like a parallel to "How do we know that any of our ideas have anything to do with reality?"[10] It was the latter question, and the epistemological skepticism made possible by thinking of ideas as a veil between the subject and the object, which made ideas-as-interface a topic for philosophical reflection in the seventeenth and eighteenth centuries. But unless we can come to see *sentences* as a veil, and thus raise the question "How do we know that any sentence can represent anything?" it will be hard to get exercised about sentences-as-interface.

To sum up this point, one cannot be Davidsonian about language and still think of language as an interface, nor as itself having an interface with what it "represents." For the behaviorism that Davidson shares with Quine, with or without the Hegelian modifications that Hacking suggests (some of which Sellars and Rosenberg have already adumbrated), makes language into something people do, rather than something standing between them and something else. It can, to be sure, also be viewed as a system of representations—but then so can

---

[8] Cf. the concluding paragraphs of Donald Davidson, "Truth and Meaning," *Synthese,* XVII, 3 (September 1967): 304–23.

[9] See Davidson's distinction between "uncovering the logical grammar or form of sentences (which is in the province of a theory of meaning as I construe it) and the analysis of individual words or expressions (which are treated as primitive by the theory)," "Truth and Meaning," p. 316. The latter task is the one which inspired most of the philosophers who took "the linguistic turn."

[10] Note Davidson's rejection of "the third, and perhaps the last, dogma of empiricism"—the distinction between scheme and content—in "The Very Idea of a Conceptual Scheme," *Proceedings of the American Philosophical Association,* XLVII (1973–74): 11. See also his scorn for those who think that " 'Snow is white' iff . . . " expresses "a relation between sentences and what they are about" "True to the Facts," *Journal of Philosophy,* LXVI, 21 (Nov. 6, 1969): 748–64, p. 761.

anything—the rings in trees or the grooves on phonograph records.[11] We cannot see representation and knowledge as posing philosophical problems unless we can reinvent something like the seventeenth-century gap between two kinds of reality, and thus reinvent an interface. Hacking's own suggestion in the last words of his book: that discourse is "no longer even the interface between the knower and that known, but . . . constitutes human knowledge" throws away the ladder he has climbed up. If there is no longer an interface, then, if language now matters to philosophy, it is *not* "for the reason that ideas mattered in seventeenth-century philosophy," for ideas *were* an interface.

I would suggest, therefore, that Hacking is not being historical enough and thus not being radical enough. There are all sorts of reasons (connected with the Reformation, the New Science, and various other overdetermining factors) which could have motivated the concern with epistemological skepticism and the problem of justifying our beliefs which is characteristic of the seventeenth and eighteenth centuries. As the methods and results of modern science have come to replace the religious outlook in the common consciousness, skepticism has become more and more the parochial concern of the professional philosopher. Hacking's picture of the philosophical problematic that survives the heyday of ideas suggests that skepticism is a permanent and important possibility for thought, and that there is a permanent problem of how to cross some interface or other—if not the veil of

[11] For an explanation of how language can be seen bifocally, as system of representations and as social practice, without engendering interface problems, see David Lewis, "Languages and Language," in Keith Gunderson, ed., *Language, Mind and Knowledge, Minnesota Studies in the Philosophy of Language,* vol. VII (Minneapolis: Univ. of Minnesota Press, 1975), pp. 3–35, and Robert Brandom, "Truth and Assertibility," *Journal of Philosophy,* LXXIII, 6 (March 25, 1976): 137–49. The latter paper, it seems to me, effectively dissolves the issue that Dummett (op. cit., p. 671) calls "the fundamental question of metaphysics . . . the dispute between realism and idealism" when it is seen as Dummett sees it, "as a dispute between a theory in which the notions of truth and falsity play the central roles, as in Frege's theory, and one in which these roles are taken by the quite different notions of verification and falsification."

ideas, then something else which gives the skeptic a chance to suggest that we don't know as much as we think. But once we adopt something like the Neurath-Quine picture of knowledge, something which leads pretty shortly to Feyerabend's "brazen positivism," we are not going to make sense of epistemological skepticism. Unless we can develop some new form of skepticism, problems about the relation between language and reality are not going to seem particularly philosophical, or, at least, will not seem continuous with the old epistemological problematic. If one is to see sentences as filling a place once filled by ideas, then one has to explain why it is *representation in general,* not just the representation of the physical by the mental or the public by the private, which is philosophically problematic.

Despite Hacking's recognition that representation became crucial to philosophy only a few hundred years back, the final pages of his book seem to depend on the tacit assumption that philosophy just *is* the "study of representing." This premise seems to me widely shared, though rarely articulated. In the heyday of meanings it *did* seem as if we could be skeptical about how language got in contact with the world, and could produce plausible answers. The *Tractatus,* for example, is dominated by the conviction that, if one can only explain how language manages to represent, then "all the problems of philosophy are solved." In the light of the *Investigations,* however, it is hard to reconstruct the problems that Wittgenstein thought he had solved in the *Tractatus,* and it is significant that Wittgenstein diagnosed the source of his earlier concerns as the same picture that had held philosophers captive in the heyday of ideas: the picture of certain privileged representations having a natural, rather than a conventional, relation to what they represent. If philosophy of language as foundational philosophy is to make sense, then we have to reconstruct the problematic of the *Tractatus* in a way that disproves Wittgenstein's diagnosis. We have to show that some question of the form "How is it possible that language should represent?" makes as much sense as the seventeenth-century question "How is it possible that the contents of my mind should be known by me to represent something outside my mind?," not just that it is the closest analogue formulable in current philosophical jargon. We have to say that the concern with skepticism that loomed up in the seventeenth century was even more overdetermined than we had realized: that some permanent problem about representation was being shadowed forth by the transitory intellectual crises of those times.

The reason why skepticism is so hard to formulate for language is that asking how languages manage to represent reality seems a bit like asking how it is possible for wrenches to wrench. That is what we *made* them to do, we are tempted to answer. So it is easier to understand biological or sociological questions about how we managed to make the particular language we have made, or how we teach it to our young, than transcendental questions about how anything *could* do what we have made language do. That is why Davidsonian questions about the logical form of action sentences do not have the resonance of Tractarian questions about the logical forms of any possible sentence. We know what would count as answering Davidson's questions, and we do not feel in suspense about our activity of attributing responsibility for actions until the question is answered. Nor are we tempted to wonder whether the "ontology of English" gradually disclosed by successive answers to Davidsonian questions is the *right* ontology. Wittgenstein came to think the former sort of resonance a result of hollowness rather than depth. If we want to use Hacking's parallel quadrilateral structures to illuminate the contemporary philosophical scene, we shall have to give *Tractatus*-like questions a new depth.

Hacking ends by wavering between two answers to his title question—the one in which sentences are construed as the interface between knower and known, and a more daring Hegelian conception in which discourse becomes "autonomous," constitutes human knowledge rather than serves as an interface for it, and in which we think of human inquiry as "a process without a subject." (This last phrase is Althusser's description of Hegel's contribution to philosophy, quoted approvingly by Hacking.) If we adopt the second sort of answer, in which the various quadrilateral diagrams Hacking offers are replaced by a simple confrontation of a squirming mass of sentences with the world they are about, then we certainly have a reason for thinking language *important,* but not a reason for thinking it important to *philosophy.* Or, to put it another way, we have a reason for thinking that philosophy is going to have to be something very different from anything we have known since Descartes. We also have reason for doubting that we know enough about what it will be like to be confident about what will matter to it. If the notion of representation goes, as philosophers like Derrida want it to, then philosophy cannot be conceived of as centering around the study of representation. What it might be, and what else it might center around, are hardly clear. But it is possible that it might not have a center, that it might not have an architectonic structure at all. It may be that what Hacking calls the death of meaning at the hands of Quine, Wittgenstein, Davidson, and Feyerabend brings with it the death of philosophy as a discipline with a method of its own. If there are no meanings to analyze, if there is just a wriggling mass of intertwined sentences, if there are no reductionisms to advocate as the result of analyzing meanings, then perhaps there are *no* central or foundational questions in philosophy. There may remain only philosophy as kibitzing—philosophy in the style of Aristotle, Dewey, and the later Wittgenstein. If we make a virtue of necessity by embracing this alternative, we can answer the question "Why Does Language Matter to Philosophy?" by saying "because everything does, but it does not matter more than anything else."

—Richard M. Rorty

TWENTY-FIVE YEARS AFTER

I wrote "Metaphilosophical Difficulties of Linguistic Philosophy" in 1965. In 1975 I took up some of the same topics in a review of Ian Hacking's *Why Does Language Matter to Philosophy?*—the piece which is translated above under the title "Ten Years After." It is now 1990, and I have taken the occasion of the translation of these two earlier essays into Spanish to reread them.

What I find most striking about my 1965 essay is how seriously I took the phenomenon of the "linguistic turn," how portentous it then seemed to me. I am startled, embarrassed, and amused to reread the following passage:

Linguistic philosophy, over the last thirty years, has succeeded in putting the entire philosophical tradition, from Parmenides through Descartes and Hume to Bradley and Whitehead, on the defensive. It has done so by a careful and thorough scrutiny of the ways in which traditional philosophers have used language in the formulation of their problems. This achievement is sufficient to place this period among the great ages of the history of philosophy.

That last sentence now strikes me as merely the attempt of a thirty-three-year-old philosopher to convince himself that he had had the luck to be born at the right time—to persuade himself that the disciplinary matrix in which he happened to find himself (philosophy as taught in most English-speaking universities in the 1960s) was more than just one more philosophical school, one more tempest in an academic teapot.

It now seems to me to have been little more than that. The controversies which I discussed with such earnestness in 1965 already seemed quaint in 1975. By now they seem positively antique. The most eminent of the philosophers now teaching at Oxford, Bernard Williams, writes of "'linguistic analysis', that now distant philosophical style . . ."[1] The slogan that "the problems of philosophy are problems of language" now strikes me as confused, for two reasons. The first is that I am no longer inclined to view "the problems of philosophy" as naming a natural kind—no longer inclined to think of "philosophy" as (in the words I quoted from Stuart Hampshire at the end of my 1965 essay) "one of man's recognizable activities." The second is that I am no longer inclined to think that there is such a thing as "language" in any sense which makes it possible to speak of "problems of language." In what follows, I shall briefly discuss each of these two reasons.

The only natural kind which might usefully be designated by the term "the problems of philosophy" is, I think, the set of interlinked problems posed by representationalist theories of knowledge—the problems connected with what Hacking called "interfacing." These are problems about the relation between mind and reality, or language and reality, viewed as the relation between a medium of representation and what is purportedly represented. In my review of Hacking, I suggested that the Quine-Davidson assault on the distinctions between analytic and synthetic judgments, conceptual questions and empirical questions, language and fact, had made it difficult to formulate such problems—difficult to think of the relation be-

[1] Williams, "The Need to Be Sceptical," *Times Literary Supplement*, February 16–22, 1990, 163.

371

tween sentences and the world as a representational one.[2] But at that time (1975) I had not yet realized how radical Davidson's attack on traditional conceptions of language was—even though Davidson had by then published his remarkable paper "On the Very Idea of a Conceptual Scheme."[3]

In that seminal paper, Davidson urged that we give up the "dualism of scheme and world," and thus the idea that different languages represent the world from different perspectives. In later papers, he has made his attack on representationalism more explicit—saying, for example:

Beliefs are true or false, but they represent nothing. It is good to be rid of representations, and with them the correspondence theory of truth, for it is thinking that there are representations that engenders thoughts of relativism.[4]

If one gives up thinking that there are representations, then one will have little interest in the relation between mind and the world or language and the world. So one will lack interest in either the old disputes between realists and idealists or the contemporary quarrels within analytic philosophy about "realism" and "antirealism." For the latter quarrels presuppose that bits of the world "make sentences true," and that these sentences in turn represent those bits. Without these presuppositions, we would not be interested in trying to distinguish between those true sentences which correspond to "facts of the matter" and those which do not (the distinction around which realist-vs.-antirealist controversies revolve).[5]

[2] In this piece, however, I was still representationalist enough to say that "we *made* languages to represent reality." This was a mistake. I should not have said that the notion of language representing reality was unproblematic, but rather that it was unnecessary.
[3] This essay was published in *Proceedings and Addresses of the American Philosophical Association* 47 (1974), and reprinted in Davidson's *Inquiries into Truth and Interpretation* (Oxford, Clarendon Press, 1984).
[4] Davidson, "The Myth of the Subjective," in *Relativism: Interpretation and Confrontation,* ed. Michael Krausz (Notre Dame: University of Notre Dame Press, 1989), 165–66.
[5] I discuss the relations between representationalism and the realist-vs.-antirealist controversies which dominate contemporary analytic philosophy in more detail in the Introduction to my *Objectivity, Relativ-*

Davidson shows us how to give up the notion of "truth-makers" as well as the notion of representation.[6] He has shown how to escape from one of the pictures which, as Wittgenstein put it, "hold us captive"—where "us" means "most philosophers from Descartes to the present." But the problems produced by the notion that true sentences are representations of reality and are made true by reality cannot be identified with "the problems of philosophy." They are, at best, the majority of the problems of philosophy discussed by the nineteenth-century philosophy textbooks. There are lots of thinkers—e.g., Plato, Aristotle, Vico, Hegel, Marx, Nietzsche, Heidegger—who have discussed lots of problems which can be only tenuously and tangentially connected with representationalist problems. There is, I think, no way to bring all these thinkers together with Descartes, Kant, and Frege into a common enterprise called "philosophy"—a "recognizable human activity" with a continuous history.

If there was ever any truth in the slogan "the problems of philosophy are problems of language" it was that the particular problems *about representation* which philosophers have discussed were pseudo-problems, created by a bad description of human knowledge, one that turned out to be optional and replaceable. I argued in my *Philosophy and the Mirror of Nature* (1979) that these problems were characteristic of post-Cartesian rather than of pre-Cartesian philosophy, and that it was only after Kant that they achieved sufficient prominence to be taken as central to an autonomous academic discipline called "philosophy." Though Heidegger is certainly right that the Greeks paved the way for Descartes, nevertheless what Heidegger calls "the transformation of man into a *subiectum*" is a distinctively Cartesian accomplishment, and only with that transformation do problems of representation come to seem central.

I should now want to argue that the philos-

ism and Truth (Cambridge: Cambridge University Press, 1990), and also in my Introduction to Joseph Murphy, *Pragmatism: From Peirce to Davidson* (Boulder: Westview Press, 1990).
[6] I try to spell out the way in which he has done this in various essays included in *Objectivity, Relativism and Truth,* in particular in "Non-Reductive Physicalism" and "Pragmatism, Davidson and Truth."

ophers of the twentieth century —Dewey, Heidegger, and Wittgenstein above all, but also Quine, Sellars, and Davidson— have shown us how to avoid representationalism. But they did so not by "dissolving" old problems, not by showing that they rested upon "conceptual confusions" or upon a "misunderstanding of language," but rather by suggesting a new way of describing knowledge and inquiry. The only sense in which this suggestion was "linguistic" is the sense in which the change from a Ptolemaic-Aristotelian cosmology to a Copernican-Newtonian one was a change in "language." This sense is very attenuated, for in both cases one could as easily speak of a change in theory as of a change in language. (Indeed, it is central to Davidson's position that it does not matter which of the two one says—that it is a matter of indifference whether one speaks of "a better theory" or of "a more perspicuous language.")

The idea that philosophical problems can be dissolved by detecting the "logic of our language" already seemed to me, in 1965, untenable. But I was still, alas, attached to the idea that there was something called "linguistic method in philosophy." I now find it impossible to isolate such a method—to specify a procedure of inquiry (a "logical" or "linguistic" as opposed to a "phenomenological" or "ontological" procedure) which distinguishes late Wittgenstein from early Heidegger, or Davidson's *Inquiries into Truth and Interpretation* from Dewey's *Experience and Nature*. Nevertheless, I should claim that Davidson largely succeeds where Dewey largely failed—succeeds in the attempt to replace a representationalist picture of knowledge and inquiry with a nonrepresentationalist one.

So, insofar as the linguistic turn made a distinctive contribution to philosophy I think that it was not a metaphilosophical one at all. Its contribution was, instead, to have helped shift from talk about experience as a medium of representation to talk of language as such a medium—a shift which, as it turned out, made it easier to set aside the notion of representation itself. Dewey's attempt to set aside the problematic of realism and idealism had involved him in an obscure and dubious attempt to see "experience" and "nature" as two descriptions of the same events and in the idea that "experience become true." But philosophers like Davidson, who speak of sentences instead of experiences, have an easier time.

The term "experience," as used by philosophers such as Kant and Dewey, was, like Locke's term "idea," ambiguous between "sense-impression" and "belief." The term "sentence," used by philosophers in the Fregean tradition, lacks this ambiguity. Once the philosophy of language was freed from what Quine and Davidson call "the dogmas of empiricism" with which Russell, Carnap, and Ayer (though not Frege) had entangled it, sentences were no longer thought of as expressions of experience nor as representations of extra-experiential reality. Rather, they were thought of as strings of marks and noises used by human beings in the development and pursuit of social practices—practices which enabled people to achieve their ends, ends which do not include "representing reality as it is in itself."[7]

Developing this picture of the role which sentences and sentential attitudes play in human life leads Davidson to say that

We have erased the boundary between knowing a language and knowing our way around in the world generally.
. . . there is no such thing as a language, not if a language is anything like what many philosophers and linguists have supposed. . . . We must give up the idea of a clearly defined shared structure to which language-users appeal and then apply to cases. . . . We should give up the attempt to illuminate how we communicate by appeal to conventions.[8]

Davidson here brings to its logical conclusion the naturalism, the holism, and the antidualism characteristic of both Dewey and Quine. He gives up the idea of "a language" as a structured medium of representation, capable of standing in determinate relations to a distinct entity

---

[7] On the relation between representationalist and social-practice theories of truth and knowledge, see Robert Brandom, "Truth and Assertibility," *Journal of Philosophy* 73 (1976), and "Heidegger's Categories in *Being and Time*," *The Monist* 66 (1983), as well as my "Representation, Social Practise, and Truth," *Philosophical Studies* 54 (1988) (reprinted in my *Objectivity, Relativism and Truth*).

[8] Davidson, "A Nice Derangement of Epitaphs," in *Truth and Interpretation: Perspective on the Philosophy of Donald Davidson*, ed. Ernest LePore (Oxford, Blackwell, 1986), 445–46.

called "the world." He thereby shows that the basic idea of linguistic philosophy as I defined it in 1965—the idea that philosophy could be advanced by studying a topic called "language" or "our language"—was deeply flawed, deeply implicated in a *non*-naturalistic picture of human knowledge and inquiry, one which still incorporated a "scheme-content" distinction, the distinction which Davidson calls the "third, and perhaps the last, dogma of empiricism."

This completes my sketch of my reasons for believing that neither "philosophy" nor "language" names anything unified, continuous, or structured, and thus of why I should now resist talk of "the problems of philosophy" or of "linguistic problems." I am often accused of being an "end of philosophy" thinker, and I should like to take this occasion to reemphasize (as I tried to do on the final page of *Philosophy and the Mirror of Nature*) that philosophy is just not the sort of thing that can have an end—it is too vague and amorphous a term to bear the weight of predications like "beginning" or "end." What does have a beginning, and may now be coming to an end, is three hundred years' worth of attempts to bridge the gap which the Cartesian, representationalist picture of knowledge and inquiry led us to imagine existed.

I said in my review of Hacking:

It may be that what Hacking calls the death of meaning at the hands of Quine, Wittgenstein, Davidson and Feyerabend brings with it the death of philosophy as a discipline with a method of its own.

I still believe something like this. Though I do not think that philosophy can end, centuries-old philosophical research programs can end, and have in the past. (Think of Thomism.) So might the idea that philosophy is a special field of inquiry distinguished by a special method. The end of this latter idea would, as far as I can see, do culture no harm. If "philosophy" comes to be viewed as continuous with science (as Quine wishes it to be) on the one hand and as continuous with poetry (as Heidegger and Derrida often suggest it is) on the other, then our descendants will be less concerned with questions about "the method of philosophy" or about "the nature of philosophical problems." The fifty-year history of linguistic philosophy, a history which is now behind us, suggests that such questions are likely to prove unprofitable.[9]

—Richard M. Rorty

[9] To say that linguistic philosophy is now behind us is of course not to say that analytic philosophy is behind us, but only to say that most of those who call themselves "analytic philosophers" would now reject the epithet "linguistic philosophers" and would not describe themselves as "applying linguistic methods." Analytic philosophy is now the name not of the application of such methods to philosophical problems, but simply of the particular set of problems being discussed by philosophy professors in certain parts of the world. These problems, at the moment, center around problems of "realism" and "antirealism"—a fact which we Davidsonians, of course, deplore. What they will center around a decade from now, I should not wish to predict. Since analytic philosophers are typically trained to pay little attention to the history of thought, and since their own sense of the function and cultural role of their discipline therefore lacks an anchor to windward, the direction of their inquiries tends to shift from decade to decade.

A BIBLIOGRAPHY

OF WRITINGS IN ENGLISH ON LINGUISTIC

METHOD IN PHILOSOPHY AND RELATED ISSUES

1930–1965

COMPILED BY JEROME NEU AND RICHARD RORTY

The title of this bibliography is not an exact description. A few items published earlier than 1930, and a few items in languages other than English, are included. Furthermore, the phrase "related issues" has been broadly construed, in order to include important discussions of, for example, analyticity and ontological commitment, even when these discussions do not explicitly bear on problems of philosophical method. Discussions of phenomenological and other philosophical methods have been included in cases in which useful comparisons with linguistic methods are made. No attempt has been made to include items which provide case studies of the practice of linguistic methods.

The compilers have attempted to provide sufficient cross-references to enable the user of the bibliography to work his way down the chains of reply, rebuttal, surrebuttal, etc., which make up some of the debates on the more important issues. It is not pretended, however, that every appropriate cross-reference has been included. Where a cross-reference contains "etc." (as in See: Langford [3], etc.), the "etc." refers to the cross-references listed under the item in question.

It may be helpful to list here certain entries which provide rather full cross-referencing, and which may be used as capsule bibliographies of certain topics. The reader interested in the "paradox of analysis" should consult the entry for Langford [3]; in the "paradigm-case argument," Watkins [3]; in

the slogan that "ordinary language is correct language," Malcolm [5]; in the notion of "categories," Ryle [1]; in the problem of analyticity, Quine [7]; in the verifiability criterion of empirical meaningfulness, Hempel [1]; in Austin's metaphilosophical views, Austin [1]; in Wittgenstein's metaphilosophical views, Wittgenstein [1].

An asterisk indicates items which are reprinted, in whole or in part, in this volume.

The reader who finds this bibliography useful may wish to consult the following: the very extensive bibliography on positivism and linguistic philosophy in *Logical Positivism*, ed. A. J. Ayer (New York: Free Press, 1959), 381–446; Copi and Beard's bibliography of secondary material on Wittgenstein's *Tractatus* in their *Essays on Wittgenstein's Tractatus* (London: Routledge Kegan Paul, 1966), 393–405; Pitcher's bibliography of secondary material on Wittgenstein's later philosophy in his *Wittgenstein: The Philosophical Investigations: A Collection of Critical Essays* (New York: Doubleday, 1966), 497–510; Roland Hall's "Analytic-Synthetic — A Bibliography" in *Philosophical Quarterly* XVI (1966), 178–81.

ABBREVIATIONS

Periodicals

A	*Analysis*
AJ	*Australasian Journal of Psychology and Philosophy* (sometimes

called simply *Australasian Journal of Philosophy*)

APQ *American Philosophical Quarterly*

BJPS *British Journal for the Philosophy of Science*

I *Inquiry*

IPQ *International Philosophical Quarterly*

JP *Journal of Philosophy*

JSL *Journal of Symbolic Logic*

M *Mind*

ME *Methodos*

MO *Monist*

P *Philosophy*

PPR *Philosophy and Phenomenological Research*

PQ *Philosophical Quarterly*

PR *Philosophical Review*

PS *Philosophy of Science*

PSt *Philosophical Studies*

PAPA *Proceedings of the American Philosophical Association*

PAS *Proceedings of the Aristotelian Society*

PAS, SV *Proceedings of the Aristotelian Society, Supplementary Volume*

RIP *Revue Internationale de Philosophie*

RM *Review of Metaphysics*

Anthologies

APW AMERICAN PHILOSOPHERS AT WORK, ed. Sidney Hook (New York: Criterion Books, 1956).

CAP CLASSICS OF ANALYTIC PHILOSOPHY, ed. Robert R. Ammerman (New York: McGraw-Hill, 1965).

CNE CLARITY IS NOT ENOUGH, ed. H. D. Lewis (New York: Humanities Press, 1963).

ECA ESSAYS IN CONCEPTUAL ANALYSIS, ed. A. N. Flew (London: Macmillan, 1960).

LL (I) LOGIC AND LANGUAGE, First Series, ed. A. N. Flew (Oxford: Blackwell, 1951).

LL (II) LOGIC AND LANGUAGE, Second Series, ed. A. N. Flew (Oxford: Blackwell, 1953).

MIP A MODERN INTRODUCTION TO PHILOSOPHY, ed. Paul Edwards and Arthur Pap (Revised edition: New York: Free Press, 1965).

NM THE NATURE OF METAPHYSICS, ed. D. F. Pears (London: Macmillan, 1957).

OL ORDINARY LANGUAGE, ed. V. C. Chappell (Englewood Cliffs, N.J.: Prentice-Hall, 1964).

PA PHILOSOPHICAL ANALYSIS, ed. Max Black (Englewood Cliffs: Prentice-Hall, 1950).

POL PHILOSOPHY AND ORDINARY LANGUAGE, ed. Charles Caton (Urbana: University of Illinois Press, 1963).

REV THE REVOLUTION IN PHILOSOPHY, by A. J. Ayer *et al.* (London: Macmillan, 1956).

RPA READINGS IN PHILOSOPHICAL ANALYSIS, ed. Herbert Feigl and Wilfrid Sellars (New York: Appleton-Century-Crofts, 1949).

RPM READINGS IN THE PHILOSOPHY OF MATHEMATICS, ed. Paul Benacerraf and Hilary Putnam (Englewood Cliffs, N.J.: Prentice-Hall, 1964).

SPL SEMANTICS AND THE PHILOSOPHY OF LANGUAGE, ed. Leonard Linsky (Urbana: University of Illinois Press, 1952).

Bibliography

Adams, E. M. [1] "The Nature of the Sense-Datum Theory," *M*, LXVII (1958), 216–26.

Adler, Mortimer J. [1] *The Conditions of Philosophy: Its Checkered Past, Its Present Disorder, and Its Future Promise,* (New York: Atheneum, 1965).

——— [2] "The Next Twenty-Five Years in Philosophy," *The New Scholasticism,* XXV (1951), 81–110.

Aiken, H. [1] "The Fate of Philosophy in the Twentieth Century," *The Kenyon Review,* XXIV (1962), 233–52.

Albritton, Rogers. [1] "On Wittgenstein's Use of the Term 'Criterion'," *JP*, LVI (1959), 845–57. (Symposium on "Criteria" with M. Scriven.) *See:* Garver [1]; Malcolm [9]; Putnam [2]; Richman [1]; Scriven [2]; Wellman [1]; Wolgast [1].

Aldrich, V. C. [1] "The Informal Logic of the Employment of Expressions," *PR*, LXIII (1954), 380–400.

—— [2] "The Spirit of the New Positivism," *JP*, XXXVII (1940), 431–37.

Alexander, H. G. [1] "Language and Metaphysical Truth," *JP*, XXXIV (1937), 645–52.

—— [2] "More about the Paradigm-Case Argument," *A*, XVIII (1959), 117–20. *See*: Watkins [3], etc.

Alston, W. P. [1] "Are Positivists Metaphysicians?" *PR*, LXIII (1954), 43–57.

—— [2] "Ontological Commitments," *PSt*, IX (1958), 8–17. *Included in: RPM. See*: Quine [5].

—— [3] "Philosophical Analysis and Structural Linguistics," *JP*, LIX (1962), 709–20. *See*: Katz [1], etc.; Wells [1].

—— [4] "Pragmatism and the Verifiability Theory of Meaning," *PSt*, VI (1955), 65–71. *See*: Hempel [1], etc.

Ambrose (Lazerowitz), Alice. [1] "Austin's *Philosophical Papers*," *P*, XXXVIII (1963), 201–16.

—— [2] "Everett J. Nelson on 'The Relation of Logic to Metaphysics'," *PR*, LVIII (1949), 12–15. *See*: Hall [5]; Nagel [3]; Nelson [2].

*—— [3] "Linguistic Approaches to Philosophical Problems," *JP*, XLIX (1952), 289–301. *See*: Chisholm [1]; Nowell-Smith [2].

—— [4] "Moore's 'Proof of an External World'," in *The Philosophy of G. E. Moore*, ed. P. A. Schilpp (New York: Tudor, Second Edition, 1952), 395–417. *See*: Moore [3].

—— [5] "The Problem of Linguistic Inadequacy," in *PA*, 14–35. *See*: Bar-Hillel [1].

Anderson, Alan Ross. [1] "Church on Ontological Commitment," *JP*, LVI (1959), 448–52. *See*. Church [2]; Kaminsky [1].

Anonymous. [1] "An Original Philosopher," *Times Literary Supplement*, (February 9, 1962), 81–83. (Review of J. L. Austin, *Philosophical Papers* and *Sense and Sensibilia*). *See*: Austin [1].

Anonymous. [2] "The Post-Linguistic Thaw: Getting Logical Conclusions Out of the System," *Times Literary Supplement*, LX (September 9, 1960).

Anscombe, G. E. M. [1] "Modern Moral Philosophy," *P*, XXXIII (1958), 1–19.

Aqvist, Lennart. [1] "Comments on the Paradox of Analysis," *I*, V (1962), 260–64. *See*: Langford [3], etc.

Armstrong, A. MacC. [1] "Philosophy and Common Sense," *PPR*, XXII (1962), 354–59. *See*: Armstrong [2]; Robinson [1].

—— [2] "Reply to Professor Robinson," *PPR*, XXIII (1963), 437.

Austin, J. L. [1] *Philosophical Papers*, ed. J. O. Urmson and G. J. Warnock (London: Oxford University Press, 1961). *See*: Ambrose [1]; Anonymous [1]; Brown [1]; Cavell [1]; Chisholm [2]; Hampshire [6]; Urmson [2], etc.; Urmson and Warnock [1]; Warnock [3] (ch. XII) and [4]; B. Williams [1]; P. Wilson [1].

—— [2] "A Plea for Excuses," *PAS*, LVII (1956–57), 1–29. *Included in: CAP*; Austin [1]; *OL*; Gustafson (ed.), *Essays in Philosophical Psychology. See*: Isaacs [1]; Shapere [1]; Tennessen [1].

—— [3] *Sense and Sensibilia*, ed. G. J. Warnock (Oxford: Clarendon Press, 1962), 55–61. *See*: Firth [1]; Lazerowitz [1].

Ayer, A. J. [1] "The Claims of Philosophy," *Polemic*, No. 7 (1947), 18–33.

—— [2] "Demonstration of the Impossibility of Metaphysics," *M*, XLIII (1934), 335–45. *Included in: MIP. See*: Ayer [15]; Sidgwick [2]; Stace [2].

—— [3] "Does Philosophy Analyze Common Sense?" *PAS*, *SV* XVI (1937), 162–76. *See*: Duncan-Jones [2], etc.; Stebbing [9].

—— [4] "Editor's Introduction," in Ayer [7], 3–28.

—— [5] "The Genesis of Metaphysics," *A*, I (1934), 55–58. *Included in*: Macdonald (ed.), *Philosophy and Analysis. See*: Mace [2] and [4].

—— [6] *Language, Truth and Logic* (London: Gollancz, 1936, 2nd ed. 1946). *See*: Charlesworth [1] (ch. IV); Hempel [1], etc.; Joad [1]; Malcolm [1]; Stebbing [4]; Weinberg [1]; Wisdom [11] (p. 229–47).

—— [7] (ed.) *Logical Positivism* (Glencoe: Free Press, 1959).

—— [8] "Logical Positivism — A Debate," in *MIP*, 586–618. *See*: Copleston [3].

—— [9] "On What There Is," *PAS*, *SV*

XXV (1951), 137–48. *Included in*: Ayer, *Philosophical Essays*. *See*: Geach [2]; Quine [5] and [6].

——— [10] "Phenomenology and Linguistic Analysis," *PAS, SV* XXXIII (1959), 111–24. *See*: Schmitt [1]; Taylor [2].

——— [11] "Philosophical Scepticism," in *Contemporary British Philosophy* (Third Series), ed. H. D. Lewis (London: George Allen and Unwin, 1956), 45–62.

——— [12] "Philosophie et Langage Ordinaire," *Dialectica*, XII (1958), 99–129.

——— [13] "Philosophy and Language," in his *The Concept of a Person and Other Essays* (New York: St. Martin's Press, 1963), 1–35. *Included in*: *CNE*.

——— [14] "Philosophy and Science," *Soviet Studies in Philosophy*, I (1962), 14–19. Also in *Ratio*, V (1963), 156–67. *See*: Gellner [2]; Kedrov [1]; Kuznetsov [1].

——— [15] "Principle of Verifiability," *M*, XLV (1936), 199–203. (Reply to Stace) *See*: Ayer [2]; Sidgwick [2]; Stace [2].

——— [16] et al., *The Revolution in Philosophy* (London: Macmillan, 1956).

——— [17] "To See the World Rightly," *Twentieth Century*, CLIV (1953), 202–8. (Review of Wisdom [11]; and of H. J. Blackman, *Six Existentialist Thinkers*.)

——— [18] "The Vienna Circle," in *REV*, 70–87.

——— [19] "What Can Logic Do for Philosophy" *PAS, SV* XXII (1948), 167–78. *See*: Kneale [2]; Popper [3].

Baier, K. [1] "The Ordinary Use of Words," *PAS*, LII (1951–52), 47–70.

Baker, A. J. [1] "Category Mistakes," *AJ*, XXXIV (1956), 13–26. *See*: Ryle [1], etc.

Bambrough, Renford. [1] "Principia Metaphysica," *P*, XXXIX (1964), 97–109.

Bar-Hillel, Y. [1] "Analysis of 'Correct' Language," *M*, LV (1946), 328–40. *See*: Ambrose [5].

——— [2] "Comments on Logical Form," *PSt*, II (1951), 26–29. *See*: Wittgenstein [2], etc.

——— [3] "Husserl's Conception of a Purely Logical Grammar," *PPR*, XVII (1957), 362–69.

*——— [4] "A Prerequisite for Rational Philosophical Discussion," *Synthese*, XII (1960), 328–32. *Included in*: *Logic Language: Studies Dedicated to Professor Rudolf Carnap*.

——— [5] "Remarks on Carnap's *Logical Syntax of Language*," in *The Philosophy of Rudolf Carnap*, ed. P. A. Schilpp (LaSalle: Open Court, 1963), 519–43. *See*: Carnap [7].

Barnes, W. H. F. [1] "Is Philosophy Possible? . . . A Study of Logical Positivism," *P*, XXII (1947), 25–48.

——— [2] "Meaning and Verifiability," *P*, XIV (1939), 410–21. *See*: Hempel [1], etc.

——— [3] *The Philosophic Predicament* (London: A. and C. Black, 1950).

Barzin, Marcel. [1] "L'Empiricisme Logique," *RIP*, IV (1950), 84–94.

Basson, A. H. and D. J. O'Connor. [1] "Language and Philosophy: Some Suggestions for an Empirical Approach," *P*, XXII (1947), 49–65. *Also in*: *ME*, V (1953), 203–21.

Baylis, C. A. [1] "How to Make Our Ideas Clearer," *JP*, XXXVII (1940), 225–32.

Beardsley, M. [1] "Categories," *RM*, VIII (1954), 3–29. *See*: Ryle [1], etc.

*Beck, Leslie. [1] (ed.) *La Philosophie Analytique* (Paris: Editions de Minuit, 1962). *See* Strawson [1]; Urmson [1].

Bednarowski, W. [1] "Philosophical Argument," *PAS, SV* XXXIX (1965), 19–46. *See*: Tucker [1].

Benacerraf, Paul. [1] "Comments on 'Meaning and Speech Acts'," in *Knowledge and Experience*, ed. C. D. Rollins (Pittsburgh: University of Pittsburgh Press, 1963), 43–49. *See*: Searle [1].

Bennett, J. [1] "Analytic-Synthetic," *PAS*, LIX (1958–59), 163–88. *See*: Quine [7], etc.

——— [2] "A Myth about Logical Necessity," *A*, XXI (1961), 59–63.

Berenda, C. W. [1] "A Five-Fold Skepticism in Logical Empiricism," *PS*, XVII (1950), 123–32.

Bergmann, Gustav. [1] "The Glory and the Misery of Ludwig Wittgenstein," *Rivista di Filosofia*, 1961. *Included in*: Bergman [3].

——— [2] "Ineffability, Ontology, and Method," *PR*, LXIX (1960), 18–40. *Included in*: Bergmann [3].

———— [3] *Logic and Reality* (Madison: The University of Wisconsin Press, 1964).

*———— [4] "Logical Positivism, Language, and the Reconstruction of Metaphysics," *Rivista Critica di Storia della Filosofia*, 1953. *Included in*: Bergmann [6].

———— [5] *Meaning and Existence* (Madison: The University of Wisconsin Press, 1960).

———— [6] *The Metaphysics of Logical Positivism* (New York and London: Longmans, Green, 1954).

———— [7] "Pure Semantics, Sentences, and Propositions as Developed in R. Carnap's *Introduction to Semantics*," *M*, LIII (1944), 238–57. *See*: Carnap [3].

———— [8] "The Revolt Against Logical Atomism (I & II)," *PQ*, VII (1957), 323–39; VIII (1958), 1–13. (Discussion of Urmson [3].) *Included in*: Bergmann [5].

———— [9] "Sense Data, Linguistic Conventions and Existence," *PS, XIV* (1947), 152–63. (Reply to A. J. Ayer, "The Terminology of Sense-Data," *M*, 1945). *Included in*: Bergmann [6].

———— [10] "Strawson's Ontology," *JP*, LVII (1960), 601–22. (Review of Strawson [2].) *Included in*: Bergmann [3].

———— [11] "Two Cornerstones of Empiricism," *Synthese*, VIII (1950–51), 435–52. (Reply to Quine [7]). *Included in*: Bergmann [6].

*———— [12] "Two Criteria for an Ideal Language," *PS*, XVI (1949), 71–74. *See*: Copi [3] and [5].

———— [13] "Two Types of Linguistic Philosophy," *RM*, V (1952), 417–38. *Included in*: Bergmann [6].

Berlin, Isaiah. [1] "Logical Translation," *PAS*, L (1949–50), 157–88.

———— [2] "Philosophy and Beliefs," *Twentieth Century*, CLVII (1955), 495–521. (Symposium with Hampshire, Murdoch, and Quinton.)

Bernstein, R. J. [1] "Wittgenstein's Three Languages," *RM*, XV (1961), 278–98.

Beth, E. W. [1] "Carnap's Views on the Advantages of Constructed Systems over Natural Languages in the Philosophy of Science," in *The Philosophy of Rudolf Carnap*, ed. P. A. Schilpp (LaSalle:

Open Court, 1963), 469–502. *See*: Carnap [7].

———— [2] "The Relationship Between Formalized Languages and Natural Language," *Synthese*, XV (1963), 1–16.

Black, Max. [1] "How Can Analysis Be Informative?" *PPR*, VI (1946), 628–31. *See*: Langford [1], [3], etc.

———— [2] "Introduction," in *PA*, 1–13.

———— [3] "Is Analysis a Useful Method in Philosophy?" *PAS, SV* XIII (1934), 53–64. *See*: Cornforth [2]; Wisdom [2].

*———— [4] "Language and Reality," *PAPA*, XXXII (1959), 5–17. *Included in*: Black, *Models and Metaphors* (Ithaca: Cornell University Press, 1962); *CNE*.

———— [5] "Linguistic Method in Philosophy," *PPR*, VIII (1948), 635–49. *Included in*: Black, *Language and Philosophy* (Ithaca: Cornell University Press, 1949).

———— [6] "Linguistic Relativity: The Views of Benjamin Lee Whorf," *PR*, LXVIII (1959), 228–38. *Included in*: Black, *Models and Metaphors*. *See*: Whorf [1], etc.

———— [7] Logic and Semantics," in *Philosophical Studies: Essays in Memory of L. Susan Stebbing*, (London, 1948.) *Included* (as "Carnap on Logic and Semantics") *in*: Black, *Problems of Analysis* (Ithaca: Cornell University Press, 1954).

———— [8] "On Speaking with the Vulgar," *PR*, LVIII (1949) 616–21. *See*: Malcolm [2], etc.

———— [9] "The 'Paradox of Analysis'," *M*, LIII (1944), 263–67. *See*: Langford [3], etc.

———— [10] "The 'Paradox of Analysis Again: A Reply," *M*, LIV (1945), 272–73. *See*: White [1] and [6].

———— [11] "Philosophical Analysis," *PAS*, XXXIII (1932–33), 237–58. *See*: Stebbing [6].

———— [12] *"The Philosophy of G. E. Moore.* Ed. P. A. Schilpp," *JP*, XL (1943), 682–95.

———— [13] "The Principle of Verifiability," *A*, II (1934), 1–6. *See*: Hempel [1], etc.

———— [14] "Relations between Logical Positivism and the Cambridge School of

Analysis," *Erkenntnis* (*Journal of Unified Science*), VIII (1939), 24–35.

*——— [15] "Russell's Philosophy of Language," in *The Philosophy of Bertrand Russell*, ed. P. A. Schilpp (Evanston: Northwestern University, 1944), 227–55. *Included in*: Black, *Language and Philosophy*. *See*: Russell [11].

——— [16] "Some Problems Connected with Language," *PAS*, XXXIX (1938–39), 43–68. *Included* (as "Wittgenstein's *Tractatus*") *in*: Black, *Language and Philosophy*.

Blackstone, William T. [1] "Are Meta-ethical Theories Normatively Neutral?" *AJ*, XXXIX (1961), 65–74.

——— [2] "On Justifying a Meta-ethical Theory," *AJ*, XLI (1963), 57–66.

——— [3] "On the Logical Status of Meta-ethical Theories," *Theoria*, XXVIII (1962), 298–303. *See*: Wheatley [2].

Blake, Ralph M. [1] "Can Speculative Philosophy Be Defended?" *PR*, LII (1943), 127–34. *See*: Murphy [1]; Stace [1].

Blanshard, Brand. [1] "The Philosophy of Analysis," *Proceedings of the British Academy*, XXXVIII (1952), 39–69. *Included in*: CNE.

——— [2] *Reason and Analysis* (The Paul Carus Lectures: Twelfth Series), (LaSalle: Open Court; London: Allen and Unwin, 1962). *See*: Rorty [3].

Blumberg, Albert E. [1] "Demonstration and Inference in the Sciences and Philosophy," *MO*, XLII (1932), 577–84.

——— [2] "The Nature of Philosophic Analysis," *PS*, II (1935), 1–8.

Blumberg, A. E. and H. Feigl. [1] "Logical Positivism," *JP*, XXVIII (1931), 281–96.

Bochenski, I. M. [1] *Contemporary European Philosophy* (Berkeley: University of California Press, 1956).

Bogholt, C. M. [1] "Professor Ducasse's Disposal of Naturalism," *PR*, L (1941), 622–28. *See*: Ducasse [6].

Boodin, J. E. [1] "Fictions in Science and Philosophy (I & II)," *JP*, XL (1943), 673–82, 701–16.

Bosanquet, B. [1] "Science and Philosophy," *PAS*, XV (1914–15), 1–21.

Bouwsma, O. K. [1] *Philosophical Essays* (Lincoln: University of Nebraska Press, 1965).

Braithwaite, R. B. [1] "Reducibility," *PAS*, SV XXVI (1952), 121–38. *See*: Thomson [1]; Warnock [6].

——— [2] "Universals and the 'Method of Analysis'," *PAS*, SV VI (1926), 27–38. *See*: Joseph [1]; Ramsey [2].

——— [3] "Verbal Ambiguity and Philosophical Analysis," *PAS*, XXVIII 1927–28), 135–54. *See*: Moore [1], etc.

Broad, C. D. [1] "Critical and Speculative Philosophy," in *Contemporary British Philosophy* (First Series), ed. J. H. Muirhead (New York: Macmillan, 1924), 75–100. *See*: Körner [2] and [5]; Murphy [3].

——— [2] "The Local Historical Background of Contemporary Cambridge Philosophy," in *British Philosophy in the Mid-Century*, ed. C. A. Mace (London: George Allen and Unwin; New York: Macmillan, 1957), 13–61. *See*: Warnock [3].

——— [3] "Philosophy (I & II)," *I*, (1958), 99–129. *Included in*: CNE.

——— [4] "A Reply to My Critics: (I) Nature, Subdivisions, and Methods of Philosophy," in *The Philosophy of C. D. Broad*, ed. P.A. Schilpp (New York: Tudor, 1959), 711–18. (Reply to Körner [2].)

——— [5] "Some Methods of Speculative Philosophy," *PAS*, SV XXI (1947), 1–32.

Bronstein, Daniel J. [1] "What Is Logical Syntax?" *A*, II (1936), 49–56. *See*: Macdonald [1].

Bronstein, Eugene D. [1] "Miss Stebbing's Directional Analysis and Basic Facts," *A*, II (1934), 10–14. *See*: Stebbing [1].

Brown, N. J. [1] "Judgment and the Structure of Language," *PAS*, LII (1951–52), 23–46.

Brown, Robert. [1] "*Philosophical Papers and Sense and Sensibilia*. By J. L. Austin," *AJ*, XL (1962), 347–65.

——— [2] "Meaning and Rules of Use," *M*, LXXI (1962), 494–511.

Brunner, M. Fernand and M. Joseph Moreau et al. [1] "Limites et Criteres de la Connaissance Metaphysique," *Dialectica*, XV (1961), 263–96.

Brutian, G. A. [1] "The Philosophical Bearings of the Theory of Linguistic Relativity," *Soviet Studies in Philosophy*, II (1963–64), 31–38. *See*: Whorf [1], etc.

Buchdahl, Gerd. [1] "Science and Metaphysics," in *NM*, 61–82.

Burtt, E. A. [1] "Descriptive Metaphysics," *M*, LXXII (1963), 18–39. *See*: Strawson [2].

——— [2] "The Problem of Philosophic Method," *PR*, LV (1946), 505–33.

——— [3] "The Status of 'World Hypotheses'," *PR*, LII (1943), 590–601. (Review of Pepper [7].) *See*: Pepper [5].

——— [4] "What is Metaphysics?" *PR*, LIV (1945), 533–57.

Butchvarov, Panayot. [1] "Knowledge of Meanings and Knowledge of the World," *P*, XXXIX (1964), 145–60.

——— [2] "Meaning-as-Use and Meaning-as-Correspondence," *P*, XXXV (1960), 314–25.

——— [3] "On an Alleged Mistake of Logical Atomism," *A*, XIX (1959), 132–37. *See*: Shoemaker [1].

Butler, Ronald J. [1] "Language Strata and Alternative Logics," *AJ*, XXXIII (1955), 77–87. *See*: Waismann [3].

Cameron, J. M. [1] *"Words and Things.* By Ernest Gellner," *Philosophical Studies* (Maynooth), IX (1959), 138–51.

Campbell, C. A. [1] "Commonsense Propositions and Philosophical Paradoxes," *PAS*, XLV (1944–45), 1–25. *Included in*: *CNE*. *See*: Campbell [2]; Edwards [1]; Malcolm [5], etc.

——— [2] "Mr. Edwards on 'Ordinary Language and Absolute Certainty'," *PSt*, I (1950), 60–63. (Reply to P. Edwards [1].)

Carmichael, P. A. [1] "First Philosophy First," *PR*, LVI (1947), 293–305.

——— [2] "Professor Copi Concerning Analysis," *PSt*, V (1954), 73–74. (Reply to Copi [1]). *See*: Copi [2]; Scriven [1].

Carnap, Rudolf. [1] "The Elimination of Metaphysics Through Logical Analysis of Language," tr. A. Pap, in *Logical Positivism*, ed. A. J. Ayer (Glencoe: Free Press, 1959), 60–81. (Originally published as "Uberwindung der Metaphysik durch Logische Analyse der Sprache," *Erkenntnis*, II (1932). *See*: Frank [1].

*——— [2] "Empiricism, Semantics, and Ontology," *RIP*, IV (1950), 20–40. *Included in*: *RPM*; Carnap, *Meaning and Necessity*; *SPL*; *Readings in Philosophy of Science*, ed. P. P. Wiener. *See*: Cornman [2]; Martin [1]; Mays [1]; Quine [4]; Rorty [1], Ryle [7]; White [8] (ch. V).

——— [3] "Hall and Bergmann on Semantics," *M*, LIV (1945), 148–55. *See*: Bergmann [7]; Hall [2].

——— [4] *The Logical Syntax of Language* (London: Kegan Paul, 1937). *See*: Bar-Hillel [5]; Oakeley [1]; Wick [2].

——— [5] "Meaning and Synonymy in Natural Languages," *PS*, VI (1955), 33–47. *Included in*: Carnap, *Meaning and Necessity*; *APW*. *See*: Goodman [1] and [2]; Katz and Fodor [2] (sect. 20); Quine [1] (ch. III); Quine, *Word and Object* (Cambridge: M.I.T. Press, 1960).

*——— [6] "On the Character of Philosophic Problems," tr. W. M. Malisoff, *PS*, I (1934), 5–19.

——— [7] "Philosophical Problems" and "Replies and Systematic Expositions," in *The Philosophy of Rudolf Carnap*, ed. Paul Arthur Schilpp (LaSalle: Open Court; London: Cambridge University Press, 1963), 44–84; 867–86; 900–5; 923–47. *See*: Bar-Hillel [5]; Beth [1]; Frank [1]; Goodman [4]; P. Henle [2]; Popper [1]; Strawson [1].

——— [8] *Philosophy and Logical Syntax* (London: Kegan Paul, 1935). *See*: Ducasse [7] (ch. VII); Stebbing [8].

——— [9] "A Reply to Leonard Linsky on 'Intentional Isomorphism and the Paradox of Analysis'," *PS*, XVI (1949), 347–50. (Reply to Linsky [4].)

——— [10] *The Unity of Science* (London: Kegan Paul, 1934).

Carney, James D. [1] "Is Wittgenstein Impaled on Miss Hervey's Dilemma?" *P*, XXXVIII (1963), 167–70. *See*: Hervey [1] and [2]; Wittgenstein [1], etc.

——— [2] "Malcolm and Moore's Rebuttals," *M*, LXXI (1962), 353–63. *See*: Malcolm [3], etc.

Cartwright, Richard L. [1] "Ontology and the Theory of Meaning," *PS*, XXI (1954), 316–25. *See*: Quine [1]; Robbins [1].

Caton, Charles E. [1] (ed.) *Philosophy and Ordinary Language* (Urbana: University of Illinois Press, 1963).

——— [2] " 'What-For' Questions and the Use of Sentences," *A*, XVII (1957), 87–92. *See*: Ryle [8], etc.; A. R. White [4].

*Cavell, Stanley. [1] "Austin at Criticism," *PR*, LXXIV (1965), 204–19. *See*: Hampshire [6]; Urmson and Warnock [1].

——— [2] "The Availability of Wittgenstein's Later Philosophy," *PR*, LXXI (1962), 67–93. *See*: Pole [2].

——— [3] "Existentialism and Analytic Philosophy," *Daedalus*, (1964), 946–74. *See*: Cerf [1].

——— [4] "Must We Mean What We Say?" *I*, I (1958), 172–212. *Included in*: *OL*. *See*: Mates [2], etc.

Ceccato, Silvio. [1] "Discussion of 'Language and Metaphysics'," *ME*, IX (1957), 51. (Reply to Feibleman [3].)

Cerf, Walter. [1] "Logical Positivism and Existentialism," *PS*, XVIII (1951), 327–38. *See*: Cavell [3].

Chappell, V. C. [1] "Malcolm on Moore," *M*, LXX (1961), 417–25. *See*: Malcolm [3], etc.

——— [2] (ed.) *Ordinary Language* (Englewood Cliffs: Prentice-Hall, 1964).

Charlesworth, Max. [1] *Philosophy and Linguistic Analysis* (Pittsburgh: Duquesne University Press, 1959).

Chaudhury, P. J. [1] "The Nature and Place of Metaphysics," *The Indian Journal of Philosophy*, II (1960), 118–25. *See*: Hoffman [1].

Chihara, C. S. and J. A. Fodor. [1] "Operationalism and Ordinary Language: A Critique of Wittgenstein," *APQ*, II (1965), 281–95.

Child, Arthur. [1] "On the Theory of Categories," *PPR*, VII (1946), 316–35. *See*: Ryle [1], etc.

*Chisholm, R. M. [1] "Comments on the 'Proposal Theory' of Philosophy," *JP*, XLIX (1952), 301–6. *See*: Ambrose [3].

——— [2] "J. L. Austin's *Philosophical Papers*," *M*, LXIII (1964), 1–26.

*——— [3] "Philosophers and Ordinary Language," *PR*, LX (1951), 317–28. *See*: Malcolm [5], etc., and [7].

Chomsky, Noam and Israel Scheffler [1] "What Is Said to Be?" *PAS*, LIX (1958–59), 71–82. *See*: Quine [6], etc.

Church, A. [1] "On the Paradox of Analysis," *JSL*, XI (1946), 132–33. (Critique of Black [9] and [10] and of White [6].) *See*: Langford [3], etc.

——— [2] "Ontological Commitment," *JP*,

LV (1958), 1008–14. *See*: Anderson [1]; Carnap [2], etc.; Kaminsky [1]; Quine [5].

Clarke, B. L. [1] "The Contribution of Logical Positivism," *ME*, XV (1963), 73–88.

Cleobury, F. H. [1] "Post-Kantian Idealism and Modern Analysis," *M*, LXI (1952), 359–65.

Cobitz, J. L. [1] "The Appeal to Ordinary Language," *A*, XI (1950), 9–11. *See*: Malcolm [5], etc.

——— [2] "Metaphysics as Wish Fulfillment," *PR*, LXVII (1958), 76–84. (Review of Lazerowitz [9].)

Cohen, F. S. [1] "The Relativity of Philosophical Systems and the Method of Systematic Relativism," *JP*, XXXVI (1939), 57–72. *See*: Burtt [2].

Cohen, L. Jonathan. [1] "Are Philosophical Theses Relative to Language?" *A*, IX (1949), 72–77.

——— [2] "On the Use of 'The Use Of'," *P*, XXX (1955), 7–14. *See*: Ryle [8], etc.

Cole, Richard. [1] "On the Possible Impossibility of Metaphysics," *PSt*, XIV (1963), 43–48. *See*: Hanson [1], etc.

Collingwood, R. G. [1] *An Essay on Metaphysics* (Oxford: Clarendon Press, 1940). *See*: Dingle [1]; Dykstra [1]; Llewelyn [1]; Stebbing [2].

——— [2] *An Essay on Philosophical Method* (Oxford: Clarendon Press, 1933). *See*: Ducasse [5] and [7] (ch. III); Harris [1].

Compton, John J. [1] "Hare, Husserl, and Philosophic Discovery," *Dialogue*, III (1964), 42–51. *See*: Hare [1].

Coombe-Tennant, A. H. S. [1] "Mr. Wisdom on Philosophical Analysis," *M*, XLV (1936), 432–49. *See*: Wisdom [2], [3], and [8].

Copi, Irving M. [1] "Analytical Philosophy and Analytical Propositions," *PSt*, IV (1953), 87–93. *See*: Carmichael [2]; Copi [2]; Scriven [1].

——— [2] "Further Remarks on Definition and Analysis," *PSt*, VII (1956), 19–24. (Reply to Scriven [1] and to Carmichael [2].)

*——— [3] "Language Analysis and Metaphysical Inquiry," *PS*, XVI (1949), 65–70. *See*: Bergmann [12]; Copi [5].

——— [4] "Philosophy and Language,"

RM, IV (1951), 427–37.
*——— [5] "Reply to Professor Bergmann," *PS*, XVI (1949), 74.
Copleston, F. C. [1] *Contemporary Philosophy* (London: Burns and Oates, 1956).
——— [2] "The Flight from Metaphysics," *The Month*, (1948), 150–65.
——— [3] "Logical Positivism — A Debate," in *MIP*, 586–618. *See*: Ayer [8].
——— [4] "Philosophical Knowledge," in *Contemporary British Philosophy* (Third Series), ed. H. D. Lewis (London: George Allen and Unwin, 1956), 117–40.
——— [5] "The Possibility of Metaphysics," *PAS*, L (1949–50), 65–82.
——— [6] "Some Reflections on Logical Positivism," *The Dublin Review*, No. 448 (1950), 71–86.
Corbett, J. P. [1] "Innovation and Philosophy," *M*, LXVIII (1959), 289–308. *See*: Hampshire [2].
Coreth, Emerich. [1] "The Problem and Method of Metaphysics," *IPQ*, III (1963), 403–17.
Cornforth, Maurice. [1] *In Defence of Philosophy against Positivism and Pragmatism* (London: Lawrence and Wishart, 1950). (New York: International Publishers, 1952.) *See*: Nowell-Smith [1].
——— [2] "Is Analysis a Useful Method in Philosophy?" *PAS*, *SV* XIII (1934), 90–118. *See*: Black [3]; Wisdom [2].
——— [3] *Marxism and the Linguistic Philosophy* (London: Lawrence and Wishart, 1965).
*Cornman, James W. [1] "Language and Ontology," *AJ*, XLI (1963), 291–305.
——— [2] "Linguistic Frameworks and Metaphysical Questions," *I*, VII (1964), 129–42. *See*: Carnap [2].
*——— [3] "Uses of Language and Philosophical Problems," *PSt*, XV (1964), 11–17.
Coulson, John. [1] "Philosophy and Integrity," *The Downside Review*, LXXIX (1961), 122–27. (On Gellner [5]; and on Malcolm, *Ludwig Wittgenstein*.)
Crawshay-Williams, Rupert. [1] *Methods and Criteria of Reasoning: An Inquiry into the Structure of Controversy* (New York: Humanities Press, 1957).
Crockett, Campbell. [1] "An Attack upon Revelation in Semantics," *JP*, LVI

(1959), 103–11. *See*: H. Tennessen [1].
Cross, R. C. [1] "Category Differences," *PAS*, LIX (1958–59), 255–70. *See*: Ryle [1], etc.
Cunningham, G. W. [1] "On the Meaningfulness of Vague Language," *PR*, LVIII (1949), 541–62.
Daly, C. B. [1] "Logical Positivism, Metaphysics and Ethics," *The Irish Theological Quarterly*, (1956), 111–50.
——— [2] "Metaphysics and the Limits of Language," in *Prospects for Metaphysics*, ed. I. Ramsey (London: Allen and Unwin, 1961), 178–205.
——— [3] "New Light on Wittgenstein, I and II," *Philosophical Studies* (Maynooth), X (1960), 5–49; and XI (1961–62), 28–62.
Davis, John W. [1] "Is Philosophy a Sickness or a Therapy?" *The Antioch Review*, XXIII (1963), 5–23.
Daya, K. [1] "Some Considerations on Morris Lazerowitz's *The Structure of Metaphysics*," *M*, LXVII (1958), 236–43.
DeGeorge, R. T. [1] "The Uneasy Revival of Metaphysics," *RM*, XVI (1962), 68–81.
DeLaguna, Grace A. [1] "Speculative Philosophy," *PR*, LX (1951), 3–19.
Dewey, J. [1] "Ethical Subject-Matter and Language," *JP*, XLII (1945), 701–12. (On C. L. Stevenson, *Ethics and Language*.)
——— [2] "Experience and Philosophic Method," in his *Experience and Nature* (Paul Carus Lectures: First Series), (LaSalle: Open Court, 2nd ed., 1929), 1–36.
——— [3] *Reconstruction in Philosophy* (New York: Henry Holt, 1920).
Dickie, J. S. [1] "What Are the Limits of Metaphysics?" in *Prospects for Metaphysics*, ed. I. Ramsey (London: Allen and Unwin, 1961), 50–63.
Dingle, Reginald J. [1] "Metaphysics: History or Science?" *Nineteenth Century*, CXXVIII (1940), 289–94. *See*: Collingwood [1].
Dommeyer, Frederick C. [1] "A Critical Examination of C. J. Ducasse's Metaphilosophy," *PPR*, XXI (1961), 439–52. *See*: Ducasse [9].
Doney, Willis. [1] "*Words and Things*. By Ernest Gellner," *PR*, LXXI (1962), 252–57.

Downes, Chauncey. [1] "On Husserl's Approach to Necessary Truth," *MO*, XLIX (1965), 87–106.

Dubs, Homer H. [1] "Language and Philosophy," *PR*, LXVII (1958), 395. (Reply to Vendler [2].)

Ducasse, C. J. [1] "Concerning the Status of So-Called 'Pseudo-Object' Sentences," *JP*, XXXVII (1940), 309–24. *See*: Carnap [8].

———— [2] "Correctness *vs.* Occurrence of Appraisals," *JP*, XXXIX (1942), 118–23. (Reply to Hall [4].)

———— [3] "Is Scientific Verification Possible in Philosophy?" *PS*, II (1935), 121–27.

———— [4] "The Method of Knowledge in Philosophy," *University of California Publications in Philosophy*, XVI (1946), 143–58. *Included in*: *APW*.

———— [5] "Mr. Collingwood on Philosophical Method," *JP*, XXXIII (1936), 95–106. (Review of Collingwood [2].)

———— [6] "Philosophy and Natural Science," *PR*, XLIX (1940), 121–41. *See*: Bogholt [1].

———— [7] *Philosophy as a Science* (New York: Oskar Piest, 1941). *See*: Hall [4].

———— [8] "Philosophy Can Become a Science," *RIP*, XIII (1959), 3–16. *See*: Granger [1]; Guzzo [1]; Mehlberg [1]; Poirier [1]; Schaerer [1].

———— [9] "Some Comments on Professor Dommeyer's Criticisms," *PPR*, XXI (1961), 552–55. (Reply to Dommeyer [1].)

———— [10] "The Subject-Matter Distinctive of Philosophy," *PPR*, VI (1946), 417–21. (Reply to Ledden [2].)

———— [11] "Verification, Verifiability, and Meaningfulness," *JP*, XXXIII (1936), 230–36. *See*: Hempel [1], etc.

Dummett, M. [1] "Constructionalism," *PR*, LXVI (1957), 47–65. (Examination of *The Structure of Appearance* by N. Goodman.)

———— [2] "Oxford Philosophy," *Black-friars*, XLI (1960), 74–81. (Review of Gellner [5].)

Duncan-Jones, A. E. [1] "Are All Philosophical Questions Questions of Language?" *PAS*, *SV* XXII (1948), 49–62. *See*: Hampshire [1]; Körner [1].

———— [2] "Does Philosophy Analyze Common Sense?" *PAS*, *SV* XVI (1937), 139–61. *See*: Ayer [3]; Duncan-Jones [3]; Lewy [1]; Stebbing [9].

———— [3] "Lewy's Remarks on Analysis," *A*, V (1937), 5–12. (Reply to Lewy [1].)

Dykstra, V. H. [1] "Philosophers and Presuppositions," *M*, LXIX (1960), 63–68. *See*: Collingwood [1].

Edel, Abraham. [1] "Interpretation and the Selection of Categories," *University of California Publications in Philosophy*, XXV (1950), 57–95.

———— [2] *Method in Ethical Theory* (Indianapolis: Bobbs-Merrill, 1963).

Edwards, Paul. [1] "Ordinary Language and Absolute Certainty," *PSt*, I (1950), 8–16. *See*: Campbell [1] and [2], etc.

Ekstein, Rudolf. [1] "The Philosophical Refutation," *JP*, XXXVIII (1941), 57–67.

Emmet, D. M. [1] "Can Philosophical Theories Transcend Experience?" *PAS*, *SV* XX (1946), 198–209. *See*: Laird [1]; Whiteley [1].

———— [2] "The Choice of a World Outlook," *P*, XXIII (1948), 208–26.

———— [3] *The Nature of Metaphysical Thinking* (London: Macmillan, 1946).

———— [4] "The Use of Analogy in Metaphysics," *PAS*, XLI (1940–41), 27–46.

Engel, Morris S. [1] "Isomorphism and Linguistic Waste," *M*, LXXIV (1965), 28–45.

Epstein, Joseph. [1] "Quine's Gambit Accepted," *JP*, LV (1958), 673–83. *See*: Quine [5] and [6], etc.

Erickson, R. W. [1] "The Metaphysics of a Logical Empiricist," *PS*, VIII (1941), 320–28.

Eslick, Leonard J. [1] "Grammatical and Logical Form," *The New Scholasticism*, XIII (1939), 233–44.

Evans, J. L. [1] "On Meaning and Verification," *M*, LXII (1953), 1–19. *See*: Hempel [1], etc.; A. R. White [3].

Eveling, H. S. and G. O. M. Leith [1] "When to Use the Paradigm-Case Argument," *A*, XVIII (1958), 150–52. (Reply to Watkins [3].)

Ewing, A. C. [1] "Is Metaphysics Impossible?" *A*, VIII (1948), 33–38.

———— [2] "Meaninglessness," *M*, XLVI

(1937), 347–64. *Included in: MIT.*
See: Hempel [1], etc.
——— [3] "The Necessity of Metaphysics,"
in *Contemporary British Philosophy*
(Third Series), ed. H. D. Lewis (London: George Allen and Unwin, 1956),
141–64.
——— [4] "Philosophical Analysis in
Ethics," *PSt*, I (1950), 74–80.
——— [5] "Pseudo-Solutions," *PAS*, LVII
(1956–57), 31–52. *See*: Malcolm [5],
etc.
——— [6] "Two Kinds of Analysis," *A*,
II (1935), 60–64.
Farber, Marvin. [1] "Concerning 'Freedom
from Presuppositions'," *PPR*, VII
(1947), 367–68.
——— [2] "The Ideal of a Presuppositionless Philosophy," in *Philosophical Essays in Memory of Edmund Husserl*,
ed. M. Farber (Cambridge: Harvard
University Press, 1940), 44–64.
——— [3] *Phenomenology as a Method
and as a Philosophical Discipline* (University of Buffalo, 1928).
——— [4] "Reflections on the Nature and
Method of Philosophy," in *Structure,
Method, and Meaning: Essays in Hon-
or of Henry M. Sheffer*, ed. P. Henle
et al. (New York: Liberal Arts, 1951),
183–206.
Farrell, B. A. [1] "An Appraisal of Therapeutic Positivism," *M*, LV (1946), 25–
48 and 133–50. *See*: Findlay [2].
Feibleman, J. K. [1] "A Defense of Ontology," *JP*, XLVI (1949), 41–51.
——— [2] *Inside the Great Mirror: A
Critical Examination of Russell, Wittgenstein, and Their Followers* (The
Hague: Martinus Nijhoff, 1958).
——— [3] "Language and Metaphysics,"
ME, IX (1957), 31–50. *See*: Ceccato [1].
——— [4] "The Metaphysics of Logical
Positivism," *RM*, V (1951), 55–82.
Feigl, Herbert. [1] "Logical Empiricism," in
Twentieth Century Philosophy, ed. D.
D. Runes (New York: Philosophical
Library, 1943), 371–416. *Included in:
RPA.*
——— [2] "De Principiis Non Disputan-
dum . . . ?" in *PA*, 113–47.
——— [3] "The Power of Positivistic
Thinking," *PAPA*, XXXVI (1963),
21–41.
——— [4] "Scientific Method Without

Metaphysical Presuppositions," *PSt*, V
(1954), 17–29.
Feigl, H. and A. E. Blumberg. [1] "Logical
Positivism," *JP*, XXVIII (1931), 281–
96.
*Feigl, H. and G. Maxwell. [1] "Why Or-
dinary Language Needs Reforming,"
JP, LVIII (1961), 488–98. *See*:
Bouwsma [1]; Thompson [4].
Feuer, L. S. [1] "The Paradox of Verifiabil-
ity," *PPR*, XII (1951), 24–41. *See*:
Hempel [1], etc.
Feyerabend, P. K. [1] "An Attempt at a
Realistic Interpretation of Experience,"
PAS, LVIII (1957–58), 143–70. *See*:
Harré [1].
——— [2] "Explanation, Reduction, and
Empiricism," in *Minnesota Studies in
the Philosophy of Science* (Volume
III), ed. H. Feigl and G. Maxwell
(Minneapolis: University of Minnesota
Press, 1962), 28–97.
——— [3] "A Note on the Paradox of
Analysis," *PSt*, VII (1956), 92–96. *See*:
Langford [3], etc.
——— [4] "Wittgenstein's *Philosophical In-
vestigations*," *PR*, LXIV (1955), 449–
83.
Findlay, J. N. [1] "E. Gellner: *Words and
Things*," *The Indian Journal of Phi-
losophy*, III (1961), 130–38. *See*:
Gourlie [1].
——— [2] "Some Reactions to Recent
Cambridge Philosophy (I & II)," *AJ*,
XVIII (1940), 193–211; XIX (1941),
1–13. *Included in*: Findlay, *Language,
Mind and Value. See*: Farrell [1].
——— [3] "Use, Usage and Meaning,"
PAS, SV XXXV (1961), 231–42. *In-
cluded in: CNE. See*: Ryle [15].
——— [4] "Wittgenstein's *Philosophical
Investigations*," *RIP*, VII (1953), 201–
16. *Included in*: Findlay, *Language,
Mind and Value.*
Firth, Roderick. [1] "Austin and the Argu-
ment from Illusion," *PR*, LXXIII
(1964), 372–82. *See*: Austin [3].
Fisher, Mark. [1] "Category-Absurdities,"
PPR, XXIV (1963), 260–67. *See*:
Ryle [1], etc.
Fitch, F. B. [1] "Self-Reference in Philosophy," *M*, LV (1946), 64–73.
——— [2] "Universal Metalanguages for
Philosophy," *RM*, XVII (1964), 396–
402.

Flew, A. G. N. [1] "Farewell to the Paradigm-Case Argument: A Comment," A, XVIII (1957), 34–40. See: Watkins [3], etc.

―――― [2] "Introduction," in LL (I), 1–10.

―――― [3] "Introduction," in LL (II), 1–10.

―――― [4] "Philosophy and Language," PQ, V (1955), 21–36. Included in: ECA. See: Heath [1]; Urmson, [3]; Watkins [3], etc.

Fodor, J. A. [1] "Of Words and Uses," I, IV (1961), 190–208. See: Ryle [8], etc.

―――― [2] "On Knowing What We Would Say," PR, LXXIII (1964), 198–212. See: Fodor and Katz [1].

―――― [3] "What Do You Mean," JP, LVII (1960), 499–506.

Fodor, J. A. and C. S. Chihara. [1] "Operationalism and Ordinary Language: A Critique of Wittgenstein," APQ, II (1965), 281–95.

Fodor, Jerry A. and J. J. Katz. [1] "The Availability of What We Say," PR, LXXII (1963), 57–71. (Reply to Cavell [2] and [4].) See: Mates [2], etc.

―――― [2] (eds.) The Structure of Language: Readings on the Philosophy of Language (Englewood Cliffs: Prentice-Hall, 1964).

―――― [3] "What's Wrong with the Philosophy of Language?" I, V (1962), 197–237. Included (in part) in: "Introduction" to Fodor and Katz [2].

Foster, M. B. [1] " 'We' in Modern Philosophy," in Faith and Logic, ed. B. Mitchell (London: Allen and Unwin, 1957), 194–220.

―――― [2] Mystery and Philosophy (London: SCM Press, 1957), Chapter 1. "Mystery and the Philosophy of Analysis."

Frank, Philipp. [1] "The Pragmatic Components in Carnap's 'Elimination of Metaphysics'," in The Philosophy of Rudolph Carnap, ed. P. A. Schilpp (LaSalle: Open Court, 1963), 159–64. See: Carnap [7].

Frankel, Charles. [1] "On the Nature of Proof in Philosophy," RIP, VIII (1954), 109–23. See: Johnstone [4]; Morpurgo-Tagliabue [1]; Ryle [11].

―――― et al. [2] "Discussion of 'La Preuve en Philosophie'," RIP, VIII (1954), 158–69.

Frick, Ivan E. [1] "A Study in Comparisons: Alfred North Whitehead and the 'Ordinary Language' Philosophers," The Indian Journal of Philosophy, IV (1964), 69–84.

Gahringer, R. E. [1] "Analytic Propositions and Philosophical Truths," JP, LX (1963), 481–502.

Gale, Richard M. [1] "Studies in Metaphilosophy. By Morris Lazerowitz," PQ, XV (1965), 363–69.

Gale, Richard M., C. Douglas McGee, and Frank A. Tillman. [1] "Ryle on 'Use,' 'Usage,' and 'Utility'," PSt, XV (1964), 57–60. See: Ryle [8], etc.

Gallie, W. B. [1] "Essentially-Contested Concepts," PAS, LVI (1955–56), 167–99. Included in: Black (ed.), The Importance of Language.

―――― [2] "The Limitations of Analytical Philosophy," A, IX (1949), 35–44.

Gamertsfelder, Walter S. [1] "Current Skepticism of Metaphysics," MO, XLIII (1933), 105–18.

Garver, Newton. [1] "Wittgenstein on Criteria," in Knowledge and Experience, ed. C. D. Rollins (Pittsburgh: University of Pittsburgh Press, 1963), 55–71. See: Albritton [1], etc.

Gasking, D. A. T. [1] "The Philosophy of John Wisdom (I & II)," AJ, XXXII (1954), 136–56, 185–212.

G(asking), D. A. T. and A. C. J(ackson). [1] "Ludwig Wittgenstein," AJ, XXIX (1951), 73–80. See: Wittgenstein [1], etc.

*Geach, P. T. [1] "Ascriptivism," PR, LXIX (1960), 221–25.

―――― [2] "On What There Is," PAS, SV XXV (1951), 125–36. See: Ayer [9]; Quine [5] and [6].

Gellner, E. A. [1] "Analysis and Ontology," PQ, I (1951), 408–15.

―――― [2] "Ayer's Epistle to the Russians," Ratio, V (1963), 168–80. See: Ayer [14], etc.

―――― [3] "Logical Positivism and After or The Spurious Fox," Universities Quarterly, XI (1957), 348–64. See: Gellner [4]; Toulmin [1] and [2].

―――― [4] "Professor Toulmin's Return to Aristotle," Universities Quarterly, XI (1957), 368–72. (Reply to Toulmin [1].)

―――― [5] Words and Things: A Critical

Account of Linguistic Philosophy and a Study In Ideology (Boston: Beacon Press, 1960; London: Gollancz, 1959). *See*: Cameron [1]; Coulson [1]; Doney [1]; Dummett [2]; Findlay [1]; Gourlie [1]; Mehta [1]; Nuchelmans [1]; Pole [4].

———— [6] "The Crisis in the Humanities and the Mainstream of Philosophy," in *Crisis in the Humanities*, ed J. H. Plumb (Baltimore: Penguin Books, 1964), 45–81.

———— [7] "Reflexions on Linguistic Philosophy," *The Listener* (August 8 and 15, 1957), 205–7, 237–41.

Gendlin, Eugene T. [1] "What Are the Grounds of Explication?: A Basic Problem in Linguistic Analysis and in Phenomenology," *MO*, XLIX (1965), 137–64.

George, F. H. [1] "Language, Philosophy and Empirical Science," *Synthese*, XI (1959), 63–71.

Gerber, W. [1] "The Significance of Disagreement among Philosophers," *The Hibbert Journal*, LVII (1959), 368–74.

Gewirth, A. [1] "Meta-ethics and Normative Ethics," *M*, LXIX (1960), 187–205.

———— [2] "Positive 'Ethics' and Normative 'Science'," *PR*, LXIX (1960), 311–30.

Ginsburg, E. B. [1] "On the Logical Positivism of the Viennese Circle," *JP*, XXIX (1932), 121–29.

Glicksman, M. [1] "Relativism and Philosophic Methods," *PR*, XLVI (1937), 649–56.

Goddard, L. [1] *Philosophy and Argument. By Henry W. Johnstone, Jr.*," *AJ*, XXXVIII (1960), 279–82.

Goodman, Nelson. [1] "On Likeness of Meaning," *A*, X (1949), 1–7. *Included in*: Macdonald (ed.), *Philosophy and Analysis. See*: Carnap [5], etc.

———— [2] "On Some Differences about Meaning," *A*, XIII (1953), 90–96. *Included in*: Macdonald (ed.), *Philosophy and Analysis. See*: Carnap [5], etc.

———— [3] *Philosophical Analysis. By J. O. Urmson*," *M*, LXVII (1958), 107–9. *See*: Bergmann [8]; Urmson [3].

———— [4] "The Significance of *Der logische Aufbau der Welt*," in *The Philosophy of Rudolf Carnap*, ed. P. A. Schilpp (LaSalle: Open Court, 1963),

545–58. *Included* (as "The Revision of Philosophy") *in*: *APW*.

Gourlie, John. [1] "Findlay on *Words and Things*," *The Indian Journal of Philosophy*, IV (1964), 56–61. (Reply to Findlay [1].)

Grabau, Richard F. [1] "Philosophy of Science and the Revival of Classical Ontology: A Reply," *JP*, LIV (1957), 131–37. (Reply to Sontag [1].) *See*: Sontag [2].

Granger, G. [1] "Sur la Connaissance Philosophique," *RIP*, XIII (1959), 96–111. *See*: Ducasse [8]; Guzzo [1]; Mehlberg [1]; Poirier [1]; Schaerer [1].

Grant, C. K. [1] "On Using Language," *PQ*, VI (1956), 327–43.

———— [2] "Polar Concepts and Metaphysical Arguments," *PAS*, LVI (1955–56), 83–108. *Included in*: *CNE*.

Grave, S. A. [1] "Are the Analyses of Moral Concepts Morally Neutral?" *JP*, LV (1958), 455–60.

———— [2] *Philosophical Reasoning. By John Passmore*," *AJ*, XL (1962), 366–77.

Greenman, Martin A. [1] "Existence and the Limits of Analysis," *PPR*, XV (1955), 551–57.

Grice, H. P. and P. F. Strawson. [1] "In Defense of a Dogma," *PR*, LXV (1956), 141–58. (Reply to Quine [7].) *Included in*: *CAP*.

Grice, H. P., D. F. Pears, and P. F. Strawson. [2] "Metaphysics," in *NM*, 1–22.

Gruender, D. [1] "Wittgenstein on Explanation and Description," *JP*, LIX (1962), 523–30.

Grynpas, Jerome. [1] "Remarques sur le probleme de la Critique Philosophique en Philosophie," *RIP*, XV (1961).

Gullväg, Ingemund. [1] "Skepticism and Absurdity," *I*, VII (1964), 163–90.

Guzzo, Augusto. [1] "Puo la Filosofia Essere una Scienza?" *RIP*, XIII (1959), 17–32. *See*: Ducasse [8]; Granger [1]; Mehlberg [1]; Poirier [1]; Schaerer [1].

Hahn, L. E. [1] "Metaphysical Interpretation," *PR*, (1952), 176–87.

———— [2] "Philosophy as Comprehensive Vision," *PPR*, XXII (1961), 16–25.

———— [3] "What is the Starting Point of Metaphysics?" *PPR*, XVIII (1958), 293–311.

Hall, Everett W. [1] *Categorial Analysis:*

Selected Essays, ed. E. M. Adams (Chapel Hill: North Carolina, 1964).

———— [2] "The Extra-Linguistic Reference of Language," *M*, LII and LIII (1943, 1944), 230–46 and 25–47. *Included in*: Hall [1]. *See*: Carnap [3].

———— [3] "Ghosts and Categorial Mistakes," *PSt*, VII (1956), 1–6. *Included in*: Hall [1]. *See*: Ryle [2]

———— [4] "Is Philosophy a Science?" *JP*, XXXIX (1942), 113–18. *See*: Ducasse [2] and [7].

———— [5] "The Metaphysics of Logic," *PR*, LVIII (1949), 16–25. *Included in*: Hall [1]. *See*: Ambrose [2]; Nagel [3]; Nelson [2].

———— [6] "Of What Use Is Metaphysics?" *JP*, XXXIII (1936), 236–45. *See*: Pepper [3].

———— [7] *Philosophical Systems: A Categorial Analysis* (Chicago: University of Chicago Press, 1960). *See*: Rorty [4].

Hall, R. [1] "Conceptual Reform — One Task of Philosophy," *PAS*, LXI (1960–61), 169–88. *See*: Hampshire [5].

Haldén, Sören [1] *The Logic of Nonsense* (Uppsala: Uppsala Universitets Årskrift, 1949).

Hallie, P. P. [1] "Wittgenstein's Grammatical-Empirical Distinction," *JP*, LX (1963), 565–78.

Hamlyn, D. W. [1] "Categories, Formal Concepts and Metaphysics," *P*, XXXIV (1959), 111–24.

*Hampshire, Stuart. [1] "Are All Philosophical Questions Questions of Language?" *PAS*, SV XXII (1948), 31–48. *See*: Duncan-Jones [1]; Körner [1].

———— [2] "Changing Methods in Philosophy," *P*, XXVI (1951), 142–45. *See*: Corbett [1].

———— [3] *The Concept of Mind.* By Gilbert Ryle," *M*, LIX (1950), 237–55.

———— [4] "Fallacies in Moral Philosophy," *M*, LVIII (1949), 466–82. *See*: M. White [8] (ch. XIII).

*———— [5] "The Interpretation of Language: Words and Concepts," in *British Philosophy in the Mid-Century*, ed. C. A. Mace (London: Allen and Unwin; New York, Macmillan, 1957), 267–79. *See*: R. Hall [1].

*———— [6] "J. L. Austin," *PAS*, LX (1959–60, i–xiv. *See*: Austin [1], etc.; Cavell [1]; Urmson and Warnock [1].

———— [7] "J. L. Austin and Philosophy" (abstract), *JP*, LXII (1965), 511–13. *See*: Urmson [2], etc.

———— [8] "Logical Form," *PAS*, XLVIII (1947–48), 37–58. *See*: Wittgenstein [2], etc.

———— [9] "Logical Necessity," *P*, XXIII (1948), 332–45.

———— [10] "Metaphysical Systems," in *NM*, 23–38.

———— [11] "The Nature of Metaphysics," in *Spinoza* (Baltimore: Penguin Books, 1951), 210–26.

———— [12] "Philosophy and Beliefs," Twentieth Century, CLVII (1955), 495–521. (Symposium with Berlin, Murdoch, and Quinton.)

———— [13] "The Progress of Philosophy," *Polemic*, No. 5 (1946), 22–32.

———— [14] *Thought and Action*, (New York: Viking, 1960; London: Chatto and Windus, 1959).

———— [15] "Friedrich Waismann, 1896–1959," *Proceedings of the British Academy*, XLVI (1960), 309–17.

Handy, Rollo. [1] "Doubts about Ordinary Language in Ethics," *I*, III (1960), 270–77.

Hanson, Norwood Russell. [1] "On the Impossibility of Any Future Metaphysics," *PSt*, XI (1960), 86–96. *See*: Cole [1]; Lehrer [1]; Weiss [2].

———— [2] "Philosophy and Philology," *The Indian Journal of Philosophy*, III (1961), 44–47.

Hardie, W. F. R. [1] "Ordinary Language and Perception," *PQ*, V (1955), 97–108. *Included in*: CNE.

*Hare, R. M. [1] "Philosophical Discoveries," *M*, LXIX (1960), 145–62. *Included* (in part, under the title "Are Discoveries About Uses of Words Empirical?") *in*: *JP*, LIV (1957). *See*: Compton [1]; Henle [1]; Körner [5].

———— [2] "A School for Philosophers," *Ratio*, II (1960), 107–20. *See*: Tomlin [1].

Harré, R. [1] "Notes on P. K. Feyerabend's Criticism of Positivism," *BJPS*, X (1959), 43–48. *See*: Feyerabend [1].

———— [2] "Tautologies and the Paradigm-Case Argument," *A*, XVIII (1958), 94–96. *See*: Watkins [3], etc.

Harris, Errol E. [1] "Collingwood on Eternal Problems," *PQ*, I (1951), 228–41. *See*: Collingwood [1] and [2].

—— [?] "Misleading Analyses," *PQ*, III (1953), 289–300. *Included in*: *CNE*.

Harrison, Bernard, [1] "Category Mistakes and Rules of Language," *M*, LXXIV (1965), 309–25. *See*: Ryle [1], etc.

Hart, H. L. A. [1] "A Logician's Fairy Tale," *PR*, LX (1951), 198–212. *See*: Strawson [6].

Hartland-Swann, J. [1] "On the State of Modern Philosophy," *P*, XXVII (1952), 76–79.

Hartman, Robert S. [1] "The Logical Difference between Philosophy and Science," *PPR*, XXIII (1963), 353–79.

Hartnack, Justus. [1] "Philosophical Analysis and Its Functions," *Theoria*, XXVI (1960), 224–28. *See*: Storheim [1]; Wedberg [1].

—— [2] *Wittgenstein and Modern Philosophy* (London: Methuen, 1965).

Hartshorne, Charles. [1] "Anthropomorphic Tendencies in Positivism," *PS*, VIII (1941), 184–203.

—— [2] "Metaphysical Statements as Nonrestrictive and Existential," *RM*, XII (1958), 35–47.

—— [3] "Metaphysics for Positivists," *PS*, II (1935), 287–303.

—— [4] *The Structure of Metaphysics*: A Criticism of Lazerowitz's Theory," *PPR*, XIX (1958), 226–40.

Hawkins, D. J. B. [1] "Towards the Restoration of Metaphysics," in *Prospect for Metaphysics*, ed. I. Ramsey (London: Allen and Unwin, 1961), 111–20.

—— [2] *Wittgenstein and the Cult of Language* (Aquinas Society of London, Aquinas Paper No. 27, London: Blackfriars, 1957).

Heath, P. L. [1] "The Appeal to Ordinary Language," *PQ*, II (1952), 1–12. *Included in*: *CNE*. *See*: Flew [4]; Malcolm [5], etc.

—— [2] "Wittgenstein Investigated," *PQ*, VI (1956), 66–71. (Review of L. Wittgenstein [1])

Heidegger, Martin. [1] *What Is Philosophy?* tr. W. Kluback and J. T. Wilde (New York: Twayne, 1958).

Heinemann, F. H. "Is Philosophy Finished?" *The Hibbert Journal*, LVII (1959), 279–85.

Hempel, Carl G. [1] "Problems and Changes in the Empiricist Criterion of Meaning," *RIP*, IV (1950), 41–63. *Included in*:

CAP; *SPL*. *See*: Alston [4]; Ayer [2], [6], [15], etc.; Barnes [2]; Black [13]; Ducasse [11]; Evans [1]; Ewing [2]; Feuer [1]; Henle [2]; Lazerowitz [7] and [8]; Macdonald [4]; J. O. Nelson [3]; Passmore [3] (ch. V); Ruja [1]; Russell [8]; Ryle [7] and [16]; Rynin [1]; Schlick [2]; Waismann [4] (ch. XVI) and [5]; Warnock [3] (ch. IV) and [7]; A. R. White [3]; J. O. Wisdom [2]; Wisdom [6]; Zimmerman [1].

—— [2] "Empiricist Criteria of Cognitive Significance: Problems and Changes," in Hempel, *Aspects of Scientific Explanation* (New York: Free Press, 1965).

*Henle, P. [1] "Do We Discover Our Uses of Words?" *JP*, LIV (1957), 750–58. *See*: Hare [1].

—— [2] "Meaning and Verifiability," in *The Philosophy of Rudolf Carnap*, ed. P. A. Schilpp (LaSalle: Open Court, 1963), 165–81. *See*: Carnap [7].

Henle, Robert J. [1] *Method in Metaphysics* (Milwaukee: Marquette, 1951).

Henson, Richard G. [1] "What We Say," *APQ*, II (1965), 52–62. (Reply to Fodor and Katz [1].) *See*: Mates [2], etc.

Hervey, Helen. [1] "The Problem of the Model Language Game in Wittgenstein's Later Philosophy," *P*, XXXVI (1961), 333–51. *See*: Carney [1]; Hervey [2]; Sellars [7]; H. R. Smart [1]; Wittgenstein [1], etc.

—— [2] "A Reply to Dr. Carney's Challenge," *P*, XXXVIII (1963), 170–75. (Reply to Carney [1].)

Hillman, D. J. [1] "On Grammars and Category Mistakes," *M*, LXXII (1963), 224–34. *See*: Ryle [1], etc.

Hocking, William Ernest. [1] "Metaphysics: Its Function, Consequences, and Criteria," *JP*, XLIII (1946), 365–78. *See*: Lamprecht [1]; Randall [1].

Hoffman, Robert. [1] "Linguistic Oddness, Modality, and Metaphysical Statements," *The Indian Journal of Philosophy*, III (1961), 48–54. (Reply to Chaudhury [1].)

Hofstadter, A. [1] "A Conception of Empirical Metaphysics," *JP*, XLV (1948), 421–35.

—— [2] "Professor Ryle's Category-Mistakes," *JP*, XLVIII (1951), 257–70. *See*: Ryle [2].

—— [3] "The Question of Categories,"

JP, XLVIII (1951), 173–85. *See*: Ryle [1], etc.

Holloway, John. [1] "The 'New Philosophy of Language' in England," *The Hudson Review*, IV (1951), 448–57.

Holmes, Arthur F. [1] "Martian Unicorns or Blue Cats? An Essay on Philosophical Method," *PPR*, XXIV (1963), 135–42.

———— [2] "Moore's Appeal to Common Sense," *JP*, LVIII (1961), 197–207. *See*: Moore [1], etc.

Holmes, Roger W. [1] "The Problem of Philosophy in the Twentieth Century," *The Antioch Review*, XXII (1962), 287–96.

Hook, S. [1] "Scientific Knowledge and Philosophical 'Knowledge'," *The Partisan Review*, XXIV (1957), 215–34.

Horgby, I. [1] "The Double Awareness in Heidegger and Wittgenstein," *I*, II (1959), 235–64.

Houlgate, Laurence D. [1] "The Paradigm-Case Argument and 'Possible Doubt'," *I*, V (1962), 318–24. *See*: Watkins [3], etc.

Howard, R. J. [1] "Ryle's Idea of Philosophy," *The New Scholasticism*, XXXVII (1963), 141–63. *See*: Ryle [1], [2], and [3].

Hudson, H. [1] "The Value of Metaphysics," *AJ*, XXI (1943), 1–9.

Hutten, E. H. [1] "Natural and Scientific Language," *P*, XXIX (1954), 27–43.

Isaacs, Nathan. [1] "What do Linguistic Philosophers Assume?" *PAS*, LX (1959–60), 211–30.

Jenkins, Iredell. [1] "Logical Positivism, Critical Idealism, and the Concept of Man," *JP*, XLVII (1950), 677–95.

Joad, C. E. M. [1] *A Critique of Logical Positivism* (London: Victor Gollancz, 1950).

Joergensen, Joergen. [1] *The Development of Logical Empiricism* (Chicago: University of Chicago Press, 1951).

———— [2] "Some Remarks Concerning Languages, Calculuses, and Logic," *Synthese*, XII (1960), 338–49. *Included in*: *Logic and Language: Studies Dedicated to Professor Rudolf Carnap*.

Johnstone, Henry W., Jr. [1] "Argument and Truth in Philosophy," *PPR*, XVIII (1957), 228–36.

———— [2] "Argumentation and Inconsistency," *RIP*, XV (1961), 353–65.

———— [3] "Can Philosophical Arguments be Valid?" *Bucknell Review*, XI (1963), 89–98.

———— [4] "The Logical Powerfulness of Philosophical Arguments," *M*, LXIV (1955), 539–41. *See*: Ryle [11], etc.

———— [5] "The Methods of Philosophical Polemic," *ME*, V (1953), 131–40.

———— [6] "The Nature of Philosophical Controversy," *JP*, LI (1954), 294–300.

———— [7] "A New Theory of Philosophical Argumentation," *PPR*, XV (1954), 244–52. (On Perelman and Olbrechts-Tyteca [1].) *See*: Perelman [5].

———— [8] *Philosophy and Argument* (University Park: Pennsylvania State University Press, 1959). *See*: Goddard [1]; Perelman [1]; Rorty [4].

———— [9] "Philosophy and *Argumentum ad Hominem*," *JP*, XLIX (1952), 489–98.

———— [10] "Some Aspects of Philosophical Disagreement," *Dialectica*, VIII (1954), 245–57.

———— [11] ed., *What Is Philosophy?* (New York: Macmillan, 1965).

Johnstone, Henry W., Jr. and Maurice Natanson, eds. [1] *Philosophy, Rhetoric, and Argumentation* (University Park: Pennsylvania State University Press, 1965).

Joseph, H. W. B. [1] "Universals and the 'Method of Analysis'," *PAS*, *SV* VI (1926), 1–16. *See*: Braithwaite [2]; Ramsey [2].

Juhos, von Bela. [1] "The Application of Logistic Analysis to Philosophical Problems," *ME*, III (1951), 106–17.

———— [2] "Answer to Mr. Vaccarino," *ME*, III (1951), 120–22. *See*: Vaccarino [1].

Kalish, D. [1] "Logical Form," *M*, LXI (1952), 57–71. *See*: Russell [4]; Wittgenstein [2], etc.

Kaminsky, Jack. [1] "Church on Ontological Commitment," *JP*, LVI (1959), 452–58. (Reply to Church [2].) *See*: Anderson [1].

———— [2] "Metaphysics and the Problem of Synonymity," *PPR*, XIV (1953), 49–61.

———— [3] "Ontology and Language," *PPR*, XXIII (1962), 176–91.

Kattsoff, L. O. [1] "Lazerowitz's Verbalism," *PSt*, IX (1958), 17–20. (Reply to M. Lazerowitz [4].)

*Katz, Jerrold J. [1] "The Relevance of Linguistics to Philosophy," *JP*, LXII (1965), 590–602. *See*: Alston [3]; Vendler [1]; Wells [1]; N. L. Wilson [1]. (Expanded form reprinted as "The Philosophical Relevance of Linguistic Theory" in this volume.)

Katz, J. J. and Jerry A. Fodor. [1] "The Availability of What We Say," *PR*, LXXII (1963), 57–71. *See*: Mates [2], etc.

———— [2] (eds.) *The Structure of Language: Readings in the Philosophy of Language* (Englewood Cliffs: Prentice-Hall, 1964).

———— [3] "What's Wrong with the Philosophy of Language?" *I*, V (1962), 197–237. *Included* (in part) *in*: "Introduction" to Katz and Fodor [2].

Kaufmann, Walter [1] *Critique of Religion and Philosophy* (New York: Harper, 1958), chap. II ("Positivism and Existentialism").

Kedrov, B. M. [1] "Philosophy as a General Science," *Soviet Studies in Philosophy*, I (1962), 3–24. (Reply to Ayer [14].)

Kennick, W. E. [1] "Metaphysical Presuppositions," *JP*, LII (1955), 769–80.

Kent, William. [1] "Classifications of Philosophies," *JP*, L (1953), 569–77.

Khatchadourian, Haig. [1] "Vagueness, Meaning, and Absurdity," *APQ*, II (1965), 119–29.

King-Farlow, J. [1] "Metaphysics and Regimented Language," *RM*, XV (1962), 508–17.

King-Farlow, J. and J. M. Rothstein. [1] "Paradigm Cases and the Injustice to Thrasymachus," *PQ*, XIV (1964), 15–22. *See*: Watkins [3], etc.

Klemke, E. D. [1] "Mr. Warnock on Moore's Conception of Philosophy," *PSt*, XIII (1962), 81–84. *See*: Moore [1] and [3], etc.; Warnock [3] (ch. II).

Kneale, M. [1] "Logical and Metaphysical Necessity," *PAS*, XXXVIII (1937–38), 253–68.

Kneale, W. C. [1] "Gottlob Frege and Mathematical Logic," in *REV*, 26–40.

———— [2] "What Can Logic Do for Philosophy?" *PAS*, *SV* XXII (1948), 155–66. *See*: Ayer [19]; Popper [3].

Knox, T. M. [1] "Two Conceptions of Philosophy," *P*, XXXVI (1961), 289–308.

Körner, S. [1] "Are All Philosophical Questions, Questions of Language?" *PAS*, *SV* XXII (1948), 63–78. *See*: Duncan-Jones [1]; Hampshire [1].

———— [2] "Broad on Philosophical Method," in *The Philosophy of C. D. Broad*, ed. P. A. Schilpp (New York: Tudor, 1959), 95–114. *See*: Broad [4] and [5].

———— [3] "The Meaning of Some Metaphysical Propositions," *M*, LVII (1948), 275–93.

———— [4] "Mr. Watkins on Metaphysics," *M*, LXVIII (1959), 548–49. *See*: Watkins [1], [2], and [6].

———— [5] "Some Remarks on Philosophical Analysis," *JP*, LIV (1957), 758–66. *See*: Hare [1] etc.

———— [6] "Some Types of Philosophical Thinking," in *British Philosophy in the Mid-Century*, ed. C. A. Mace (London: Allen and Unwin; New York: Macmillan, 1957), 115–31.

Koestenbaum, Peter [1] "The Phenomenology of Metaphysics: The Nature of Philosophical Differences," *PPR*, XIX (1958), 183–97.

Kraft, V. [1] *The Vienna Circle* (New York: Philosophical Library, 1952).

Kreisel, G. [1] "Wittgenstein's Theory and Practice of Philosophy," *BJPS*, XI (1960), 238–51. *See*: Wittgenstein [1], etc.

Kuntz, Paul G. [1] "Order in Language, Phenomena, and Reality: Notes on Linguistic Analysis, Phenomenology, and Metaphysics," *MO*, XLIX (1965), 107–36.

Kurtz, Paul W. [1] "Has Mr. Flew Abandoned 'The Logic of Ordinary Use'?" *PSt*, IX (1958), 73–78.

Kuznetsov, I. V. [1] "But Philosophy *Is* a Science," *Soviet Studies in Philosophy*, I (1962), 20–36. (Reply to Ayer [14].)

Laird, J. [1] "Can Philosophical Theories Transcend Experience?" *PAS*, *SV* XX (1946), 228–32. *See*: Emmet [1]; Whiteley [1].

———— [2] "Positivism, Empiricism and Metaphysics," *PAS*, XXXIX (1938–39), 207–24.

Lamprecht, Sterling P. [1] "Metaphysics: Its Function, Consequences, and Criteria," *JP*, XLIII (1946), 393–401. *See*: Hocking [1]; Randall [1].

Landesman, C. [1] "Does Language Embody a Philosophical Point of View?" *RM*,

XIV (1961), 617–36. *See*: Whorf [1], etc.; Swanson [1].

Langford, C. H. [1] "Critique of Max Black. The 'Paradox of Analysis'," *JSL*, IX (1944), 104–5. *See*: Black [1] and [9]; Langford [3], etc.

———— [2] "The Nature of Formal Analysis," *M*, LVIII (1949), 210–14.

———— [3] "The Notion of Analysis in Moore's Philosophy," in *The Philosophy of G. E. Moore*, ed. P. A. Schilpp (New York: Tudor Publishing Company, Second Edition, 1952), 319–42. *See*: Aqvist [1]; Black [1], [9], [10]; Church [1]; Copi [1], etc.; Feyerabend [3]; Hare [1], etc.; Langford [1]; Linsky [4], etc.; Moore [3]; Pap [4] (ch. 10) and [5]; Sellars [2], [4], and [5]; M. White [1], [3], [6], and [7].

———— [4] "Usage," *JP*, LXI (1964), 181–86.

Lazerowitz, Alice Ambrose. See Ambrose, Alice.

Lazerowitz, Morris. [1] "Austin's *Sense and Sensibilia*," *P*, XXXVIII (1963), 242–52.

———— [2] "Meaninglessness and Conventional Use," *A*, V (1938), 33–42. (Reply to Wisdom [9].)

———— [3] "Moore and Philosophical Analysis," *P*, XXXIII (1958), 193–220. *Included in*: Lazerowitz [10]. *See*: Moore [1] and [3]; Wasserstrom [1].

———— [4] "Moore's Paradox," *The Philosophy of G. E. Moore*, ed. P. A. Schilpp (New York: Tudor, 1952). *See*: Kattsoff [1]; Moore [3], etc.

———— [5] "The Nature of Metaphysics," in Lazerowitz [9], 23–79.

———— [6] "The Positivistic Use of 'Nonsense'," *M*, LV (1946), 247–55. *Included in*: Lazerowitz [9].

———— [7] "The Principle of Verifiability," *M*, XLVI (1937), 372–78. *See*: Hempel [1], etc.

———— [8] "Strong and Weak Verification, I and II," *M*, XLVIII (1939), 202–13; LIX (1950), 345–57. *Included in*: Lazerowitz [9].

———— [9] *The Structure of Metaphysics* (London: Routledge and Kegan Paul; New York: Humanities Press, 1955). *See*: Cobitz [2]; Daya [1]; Hartshorne [4].

———— [10] *Studies in Metaphilosophy*

(London: Routledge and Kegan Paul; New York: Hun____:s Press, 1964). *See*: Gale [1]; Watkins [8].

Ledden, J. E. [1] "The Nature of Philosophical Problems," *PPR*, IX (1948), 251–68.

———— [2] "Questions Concerning the Metaphilosophy of C. J. Ducasse," *PPR*, VI (1946), 410–17. *See*: Ducasse [10].

Lehrer, Keith. [1] "A Note on the Impossibility of Any Future Metaphysics," *PSt*, XIII (1962), 49–51. (Reply to Hanson [1].)

Leith, G. O. M. and H. S. Eveling. [1] "When to Use the Paradigm-Case Argument," *A*, XVIII (1958), 150–52. *See*: Watkins [3], etc.

Lejewski, Czeslaw. [1] "Logic and Existence," *BJPS*, V (1954), 104–19. *See*: Prior [1].

Leonard, Henry S. [1] "Logical Positivism and Speculative Philosophy," in *Philosophical Essays for Alfred North Whitehead* (London and New York: Longmans, Green, 1936), 125–52.

Levi, Albert William. [1] "Wittgenstein as Dialectician," *JP*, LXI (1964), 127–39.

Levison, A. D. [1] "Waismann on Proof and Philosophic Argument," *M*, LXXIII (1964), 111–16. (Reply to Waismann [2].)

Lewis, Charles J. [1] "Logical Positivism and Metaphysics," *The New Scholasticism*, XVI (1942), 242–56.

Lewis, H. D. [1] (ed.) *Clarity is Not Enough; Essays in Criticism of Linguistic Philosophy* (New York: Humanities, 1963).

Lewy, Casimir. [1] "Some Remarks on Analysis," *A*, V (1937), 1–5. (Reply to Duncan-Jones [2].) *See*: Duncan-Jones [3].

Lieb, I. C. [1] "Wittgenstein's Investigations," *RM*, VIII (1954), 125–43. (Review of *Philosophical Investigations*.)

Linsky, Leonard. [1] "Deception," *I*, VI (1963), 157–69.

———— [2] "On Understanding Philosophical Writings," *PPR*, XV (1954), 222–29.

———— [3] (ed.) *Semantics and the Philosophy of Language* (Urbana: University of Illinois, 1952).

———— [4] "Some Notes on Carnap's Concept of Intensional Isomorphism and the Paradox of Analysis," *PS*, XVI (1949), 343–47. *See*: Carnap [9]; Langford [3], etc.

Llewelyn, John E. [1] "Collingwood's Doctrine of Absolute Presuppositions," *PQ*, XI (1961), 49–60. *See*: Collingwood [1].

Lodge, R. C. [1] "Synthesis or Comparison," *JP*, XXXV (1938), 432–40. *See*: Burtt [2].

Lowe, Victor. [1] "Categorial Analysis, Metaphysics, and C. I. Lewis," *JP*, LV (1958), 862–71.

——— [2] "Empirical Method in Metaphysics," *JP*, XLIV (1947), 225–33.

Lucas, John B. [1] "On Not Worshipping Facts," *PQ*, (1958), 144–56.

McCloskey, H. J. [1] "The Philosophy of Linguistic Analysis and the Problem of Universals," *PPR*, XXIV (1964), 329–38.

Macdonald, M. [1] "Language and Reference," *A*, IV (1936), 33–41. *See*: D. J. Bronstein [1].

——— [2] "Linguistic Philosophy and Perception," *P*, XXVIII (1953), 311–24. *See*: Spinney [1].

——— [3] "The Philosopher's Use of Analogy," *PAS*, XXXVIII (1937–38), 291–312. *Included in*: *LL* (I). *See*: Passmore [5].

——— [4] "Verification and Understanding," *PAS*, XXXIV (1933–34), 143–56. *See*: Hempel [1], etc.

McGee, C. Douglas. [1] "Fun, Games and Natural Language," *AJ*, LXII (1964), 335–44.

McGill, V. J. [1] "Some Queries Concerning Moore's Method," in *The Philosophy of G. E. Moore* (Second Edition), ed. P. A. Schilpp (New York: Tudor Publishing Company, 1952), 481–514. *See*: Moore [3].

McGlynn, James V. [1] "Philosophy and Analysis (I & II)," *The Downside Review*, LXXVIII (1959–60), 25–35, 93–107.

McGreal, Ian Philip. [1] "An Analysis of Philosophical Method," *MO*, XLVIII (1964), 513–32.

McKeon, Richard. [1] "Dialogue and Controversy in Philosophy," *PPR*, XVII (1956), 143–63.

——— [2] "Flight from Certainty and the Quest for Precision," *RM*, XVIII (1964), 234–53.

——— [3] *Freedom and History: The Semantics of Philosophical Controversies and Ideological Conflicts* (New York: Noonday Press, 1952).

——— [4] "Philosophy and Method," *JP*, XLVIII (1951), 653–82.

Mackie, John. [1] "The Logical Status of Grammar Rules," *AJ*, XXVII (1949), 197–216.

McKinney, J. P. [1] "Philosophical Implications of Logical Analysis," *The Hibbert Journal*, LV (1957), 249–59. (On Russell [9].)

Mackinnon, D. M. [1] "What is a Metaphysical Statement?" *PAS*, XLI (1940–41), 1–26.

McMullin, Ernan. [1] "The Analytic Approach to Philosophy," *Proceedings of the American Catholic Philosophical Association*, XXXIV (1960), 50–79.

Macmurray, J. [1] "Some Reflections on the Analysis of Language," *PQ*, I (1951), 319–37.

McPherson, Thomas. [1] "Grammaticism," *AJ*, XXXI (1953), 206–11. (Reply to Passmore [5].)

——— [2] "Philosophy and Language," *The Church Quarterly Review*, CLVI (1955), 158–69.

Mace, C. A. [1] "The Logic of Elucidation," in *Philosophical Studies — Essays in Memory of L. Susan Stebbing*, 1948.

——— [2] "Metaphysics and Emotive Language," *A*, II (1934), 6–10. *See*: Ayer [5]; Mace [4].

——— [3] "Must Philosophers Disagree?" *PAS*, *SV* XII (1933), 131–37. *See*: Schiller [1]; Stocks [1].

——— [4] "Representation and Expression," *A*, I (1934), 33–38. *Included in*: M. Macdonald (ed.), *Philosophy and Analysis*. *See*: Ayer [5]; Mace [2].

Malcolm, N. [1] "Are Necessary Propositions Really Verbal?" *M*, XLIX (1940), 189–203.

——— [2] "Defending Common Sense," *PR*, LVIII (1949), 201–20. *See*: Black [8]; Malcolm [3]–[7], etc.; Moore [1] and [3], etc.; Rollins [1]; Woozley [1].

——— [3] "*G. E. Moore: A Critical Exposition*. By Alan R. White," *M*, LXIX (1960), 92–98. *See*: Carney [2]; Chappell [1]; Malcolm [5], etc.; Odegard [1].

———— [4] "George Edward Moore," *Knowledge and Certainty* (Englewood Cliffs: Prentice-Hall, 1963), 163–83.

*———— [5] "Moore and Ordinary Language," in *The Philosophy of G. E. Moore*. ed. P. A. Schilpp (New York: Tudor, Second Edition, 1952), 343–68. *Included in*: *OL*. *See*: Campbell [1], etc.; Chappell [1]; Chisholm [3]; Cobitz [1]; Ewing [5]; Heath [1]; Malcolm [2] and [3], etc.; Moore [3], etc.; O'Connor [1]; Tennessen [4]; Weitz [4]; Wiener [1].

———— [6] "Moore's Use of 'Know'," *M*, LXII (1953), 241–47. (Reply to Rollins [1].) *See*: Malcolm [2], etc.

———— [7] "Philosophy and Ordinary Language" (mistakenly titled "Philosophy for Philosophers"), *PR*, LX (1951), 329–40. (Reply to Chisholm [3].)

———— [8] "Understanding Austin" (abstract), *JP*, LXII (1965), 508–9. *See*: Urmson [2], etc.

———— [9] "Wittgenstein's *Philosophical Investigations*," *PR*, LXIII (1954), 530–59. *Included in*: Chappell (ed.), *The Philosophy of Mind*; Malcolm, *Knowledge and Certainty*. *See*: Albritton [1], etc.; Chihara and Fodor [1].

Margolis, Joseph. [1] "Individuals and the Ways of Philosophy," *PQ*, XIII (1963), 33–38.

Marsh, R. C. [1] "The Function of Criticism in Philosophy," *PAS*, LIII (1952–53), 135–50.

Martin, Oliver. [1] *Metaphysics and Ideology* (Milwaukee: Marquette University Press, 1959).

Martin, R. M. [1] "Category-Words and Linguistic Frameworks," *Kant-Studien*, LIV (1963), 176–80. *See*: Carnap [2].

———— [2] "Existential Quantification and the 'Regimentation' of Ordinary Language," *M*, LXXI (1962), 525–92.

Masterman, Margaret. [1] "What *Is* Philosophy Nowadays?" *Theology*, LIV (1951), 15–21.

Mates, B. [1] "Analytic Sentences," *PR*, LX (1951), 525–34. *See*: Naess [3]; Quine [7], etc.

———— [2] "On the Verification of Statements about Ordinary Language," *I*, I (1958), 161–71. *Included in*: *OL*. *See*: Cavell [4]; Fodor [2]; Fodor and Katz [1]; Henson [1]; Tennesson [7] and [8].

*Maxwell, G. and H. Feigl. [1] "Why Ordinary Language Needs Reforming," *JP*, LVIII (1961), 488–98. *See*: Bouwsma [1]; Thompson [4].

Mays, W. [1] "Carnap on Logic and Language," *PAS*, LXII (1961–62), 21–38. *See*: Quine [7], etc.

———— [2] "Linguistic Rules and Language Habits," *PAS*, *SV* XXIX (1955), 165–84. *See*: Midgley [2].

Mehlberg, Henry. [1] "Can Science Absorb Philosophy?" *RIP*, XIII (1959), 61–87. *See*: Ducasse [8]; Granger [1]; Guzzo [1]; Poirier [1]; Schaerer [1].

Mehta, Ved. [1] "A Battle against the Bewitchment of Our Intelligence," *The New Yorker*, XXXVIII (1961), 59–159. *Included in*: Mehta, *The Fly and the Fly Bottle*. (On reactions to Gellner [5].)

Mei, Tsu-Lin. [1] "Chinese Grammar and the Linguistic Movement in Philosophy," *RM*, XIV (1961), 463–92.

———— [2] "The Logic of Depth Grammar," *PPR*, XXIV (1963), 97–105.

———— [3] "Subject and Predicate, A Grammatical Preliminary," *PR*, LXX (1961), 153–75. *See*: R. Price [1].

Mele, Jacob. [1] "Dialogue on the Hypothetical Character of Logical Analysis," *I*, I (1958), 72–84.

Midgley, G. C. J. [1] "Linguistic Rules," *PAS*, LIX (1958–59), 271–90.

———— [2] "Linguistic Rules and Language Habits," *PAS*, *SV* XXXIX (1955), 185–91. *See*: Mays [2].

Miller, H. [1] "Some Major Confusions of Contemporary Positivism," *JP*, XXXII (1935), 515–20.

Miller, J. F., III. [1] "Wittgenstein's Weltanschauung," *Philosophical Studies* (Maynooth), XIII (1964), 127–40.

Miller, Robert G. [1] "Linguistic Analysis and Metaphysics," *Proceedings of the American Catholic Philosophical Association*, XXXIV (1960), 80–109.

Mohanty, Jitendranath. [1] "On Moore's Defence of Common Sense," *The Indian Journal of Philosophy*, II (1960), 40–49. *See*: Moore [1], etc.

Moody, Ernest A. [1] "The Age of Analysis," *PAPA*, XXXVII (1964), 53–67.

Moore, G. E. [1] "A Defense of Common

Sense," in *Contemporary British Philosophy* (Second Series), ed. J. H. Muirhead (London: Allen & Unwin; New York: Macmillan, 1925), 193–223. *Included in: CAP*; Moore, *Philosophical Papers. See:* Braithwaite [3]; Charlesworth [1] (ch. I); Holmes [2]; Klemke [1]; Malcolm [2]–[7], etc.; Mohanty [1]; Murphy [2] and [3]; Nagel [1]; Paul [1]; Warnock [3] (ch. II); A. R. White [1] and [2].

———— [2] "The Justification of Analysis," *A*, I (1934), 28–30.

———— [3] "A Reply to my Critics: III. Philosophic Method," in *The Philosophy of G. E. Moore*, ed. P. A. Schilpp (New York: Tudor, Second Edition, 1952), 660–77. *See:* Ambrose [4]; Black [12]; Langford [2], [3], and [4], etc.; Lazerowitz [3] and [4]; McGill [1]; Malcolm [5], etc.; Moore [1], etc.; Murphy [2]; Stebbing [7]; M. G. White [2]; Wisdom [7].

———— [4] "What Is Philosophy?" in his *Some Main Problems of Philosophy* (London: Allen and Unwin; New York: Macmillan, 1953), 1–27.

Mora, José Ferrater. [1] "Wittgenstein, A Symbol of Troubled Times," *PPR*, XIV (1953), 89–96.

Morgan, Douglas N. [1] "Philosophers in Spite of Themselves," *Ethics*, LXII (1951), 55–60. (Review of *LL* (I).)

Morpurgo-Tagliabue, G. [1] "La Preuve au Point de Vue Philosophique," *RIP*, VIII (1954), 124–49. *See:* Frankel [1]; Johnstone [4]; Ryle [11].

Morris, C. W. [1] *Logical Positivism, Pragmatism, and Scientific Empiricism* (Paris: Hermann, 1937).

Müller, Gustav E. [1] *Dialectic. A Way into and within Philosophy* (New York: Bookman, 1953).

———— [2] "Dialectic — the Logic of Philosophy," *Dialectica*, XIII (1959), 235–61.

Munson, Thomas N. [1] "Wittgenstein's Phenomenology," *PPR*, XXIII (1962), 37–50.

Murdoch, I. [1] "Philosophy and Beliefs," *Twentieth Century*, CLVII (1955), 495–521. (Symposium with Berlin, Hampshire, and Quinton.)

Mure, G. R. G. [1] *Retreat from Truth* (Oxford; Blackwell, 1958). *See:* Passmore [2].

Murphy, Arthur E. [1] "Can Speculative Philosophy Be Defended?" *PR*, LII (1943), 135–43. *See:* Blake [1]; Stace [1].

———— [2] "Moore's 'Defence of a Common Sense'," in *The Philosophy of G. E. Moore*, ed. P. A. Schilpp (New York: Tudor, Second Edition, 1952), 299–317. *See:* Moore [3], etc.

———— [3] "Two Versions of Critical Philosophy," *PAS*, XXXVIII (1937–38), 143–60. *See:* Broad [1]; Burtt [2]; Moore [1], etc.; Stebbing [9].

———— [4] "Whitehead and the Method of Speculative Philosophy," in *The Philosophy of Alfred North Whitehead*, ed. P. A. Schilpp (New York: Tudor, Second Edition, 1951), 351–80.

Myers, Gerald E. [1] "Metaphysics and Extended Meaning," *AJ*, XLII (1964), 211–15.

Naess, Arne. [1] *Interpretation and Preciseness: A Contribution to the Theory of Communication* (Oslo: Skrifter Norske Vid. Akademi, 1953).

———— [2] "Synonymity and Empirical Research," *ME*, VII (1956), 3–22. *See:* Carnap [5], etc.

———— [3] "Synonymity as Revealed by Intuition," *PR*, LXVI (1957), 87–93. (Reply to Mates [1].)

———— [4] "Toward a Theory of Interpretation and Preciseness," *Theoria*, XV (1949), 220–41. *Included in: SPL*.

Nagel, Ernest. [1] "The Debt We Owe to G. E. Moore," *JP*, LVII (1960), 810–16.

———— [2] "Impressions and Appraisals of Analytic Philosophy in Europe (I & II)," *JP*, XXXIII (1936), 5–24, 29–53. *Included in:* Nagel, *Logic Without Metaphysics*.

———— [3] "In Defense of Logic without Metaphysics," *PR*, LVIII (1949), 26–34. *Included in:* Nagel, *Logic Without Metaphysics. See:* Ambrose [2]; Hall [5]; Nelson [2].

———— [4] "Logic without Ontology," in *Naturalism and the Human Spirit*, ed. Y. Krikorian (New York: Columbia University Press, 1944). *Included in: RPA*; Nagel, *Logic Without Metaphysics; RPM*.

Narskii, I. S. [1] "The Concept of Formal

Analysis and Dialectics," *Soviet Studies in Philosophy*, II (1964), 45–56. *See*: Cornforth [3].

Natanson, M. [1] "Rhetoric and Philosophical Argumentation," *Quarterly Journal of Speech*, XLVIII (1962), 24–30. *Included in*: Natanson and Johnstone [1].

Natanson, Maurice and Henry W. Johnstone, Jr., [1] (eds.) *Philosophy, Rhetoric, and Argumentation* (University Park: Pennsylvania State University Press, 1965).

Nelson, Everett J. [1] "Categorial Interpretation of Experience," *PPR*, XIII (1952), 84–95.

——— [2] "The Relation of Logic to Metaphysics," *PR*, LVIII (1949), 1–11. *See*: Ambrose [2]; Hall [5]; Nagel [3].

Nelson, J. O. [1] "On Sommer's Reinstatement of Russell's Ontological Program," *PR*, LXXIII (1964), 517–21. (Reply to Sommers [2].) *See*: Sommers [3].

——— [3] "On the Impossibility of Theories of Meaning," *JP*, LX (1963), 296–303.

Nidditch, P. H. [1] "A Note on Logic and Linguistic Ambiguities," *A*, XII (1952), 122–24.

Nielson, H. A. [1] "Wittgenstein on Language," *Philosophical Studies* (Maynooth), VIII (1958), 115–21.

Norburn, Greville. [1] "The Philosophical Quest and the Logical Positivists," *The Church Quarterly Review*, CLI (1950), 141–54.

Novak, Michael. [1] "An Empirically Controlled Metaphysics," *IPQ*, IV (1964), 265–82.

Nowell-Smith, P. H. [1] "*In Defence of Philosophy*. By Maurice Cornforth." *P*, XXVII (1952), 178–83.

——— [2] "Philosophical Theories," *PAS*, XLVIII (1947–48), 165–86. *See*: Ambrose [3], etc.

Nuchelmans, Gabriël. [1] "Mr. Gellner's Attack on Linguistic Philosophy," *Synthese*, XIII (1961), 88–97. (Review of Gellner [5].)

Oakeley, H. D. [1] "Epistemology and the Logical Syntax of Language," *M*, XLIX (1940), 427–44. *See*: Carnap [4].

O'Connor, D. J. [1] "Philosophy and Ordinary Language," *JP*, XLVIII (1951), 797–808. *See*: Malcolm [5], etc.

O'Conner, D. J. and A. H. Basson. [1] "Lan-

guage and Philosophy: Some Suggestions for an Empirical Approach," *P*, XXII (1947), 49–65. Also in: *ME*, V (1953), 203–21.

Odegard, Douglas. [1] "The Correct Use of a Sentence," *A*, XXIV (1964), 63–67. (Reply to Malcolm [3].)

Olbrechts-Tyteca, L. and C. Perelman. [1] *Rhétorique et Philosophie: pour une Théorie de l'Argumentation en Philosophie* (Paris: Presses Universitaires de France, 1952). *See*: Johnstone [7].

Orr, Sydney Sparkes. [1] "Some Reflections on the Cambridge Approach to Philosophy (I & II)," *AJ*, XXIV (1946), 34–76, 129–67. *See*: Farrell [1]; Findlay [2]; Wisdom [6].

Pap, Arthur. [1] "Logical Nonsense," *PPR*, IX (1948), 269–83.

——— [2] "The Philosophical Analysis of Natural Language," *ME*, I (1949), 344–69.

——— [3] "Semantic Analysis and Psycho-Physical Dualism," *M*, (1952), 209–21.

——— [4] *Semantics and Necessary Truth: An Inquiry into the Foundations of Analytic Philosophy* (New Haven: Yale University Press, 1958).

——— [5] "Synonymy, Identity of Concepts and the Paradox of Analysis," *ME*, VII (1955), 115–28. *See*: Langford [3], etc.

——— [6] "Types and Meaninglessness," *M*, LXIX (1960), 41–54. *See*: Sommers [2], etc.

Pasch, Alan [1] *Experience and the Analytic* (Chicago: University of Chicago Press, 1959).

Passmore, J. A. [1] "Logical Positivism (I, II, & III)," *AJ*, XXI (1943), 65–92; XXII (1944), 129–53; XXVI (1948), 1–19.

——— [2] "The Meeting of Extremes in Contemporary Philosophy," *PR*, LXIX (1960), 363–75. (Review of Mure [1] and M. White [8].)

*——— [3] *Philosophical Reasoning* (London: Duckworth; New York: Charles Scribner's Sons, 1961). *See*: Grave [2]. (Chapter 6 is reprinted in the present volume.)

——— [4] "Professor Ryle's Use of 'Use' and 'Usage'," *PR*, LXIII (1954), 58–64. (Reply to Ryle [8].)

——— [5] "Reflections on *Logic and Lan-

guago," *AJ*, XXX (1952), 153–76. *See*:
McPherson [1].

—— [6] "Wittgenstein and Ordinary Language Philosophy," in his *A Hundred Years of Philosophy* (London: Duckworth, 1957), 425–58.

Paul, G. A. [1] "G. E. Moore: Analysis. Common Usage, and Common Sense," in *REV*, 56–69.

—— [2] "Wittgenstein," in *RP*, 88–96.

Pears, D. F. [1] "Logical Atomism: Russell and Wittgenstein," in *REV*, 41–55.

—— [2] (ed.) *The Nature of Metaphysics* (London: Macmillan, 1957).

—— [3] "Universals," *PQ*, I (1951), 218–27. *Included in*: LL (II). *See*: Joseph [1], etc.; McCloskey [1].

Pears, D. F., H. P. Grice and P. F. Strawson. [1] "Metaphysics," in *NM*, 1–22.

Pepper, S. C. [1] "Categories," *University of California Publications in Philosophy*, XIII (1930), 73–98. *See*: Ryle [1], etc.

—— [2]. "Metaphysical Method," *PR*, LII (1943), 252–69. *Included in*: *APW*.

—— [3] "On the Cognitive Value of World Hypotheses," *JP*, XXXIII (1936), 575–77. (Reply to E. W. Hall [6].)

—— [4] "The Root Metaphor Theory of Metaphysics," *JP*, XXXII (1935), 365–74.

—— [5] "The Status of 'World Hypotheses': A Rejoinder," *PR*, LII (1943), 602–04. (Reply to Burtt [3].)

—— [6] "What Are Categories For?" *JP*, XLIV (1947), 546–66.

—— [7] *World Hypotheses: A Study in Evidence* (Berkeley and Los Angeles: University of California, 1942), *See*: Burtt [2] and [3].

Perelman, Ch. [1] "A Propos de Henry W. Johnstone, Jr., *Philosophy and Argument*," *RIP*, XIV (1960), 96–100.

—— [2] "On Self-Evidence in Metaphysics," *IPQ*, IV (1964), 5–19.

—— [3] "Philosophies Premieres et Philosophie Regressive," *Dialectica*, III 1949), 175–91. *Included in*: Perelman and Olbrechts-Tyteca [1].

—— [4] "Pragmatic Arguments," *P*, XXXIV (1959), 18–27.

—— [5] "Reply to Henry W. Johnstone, Jr." *PPR*, XVI (1955), 245–47. (Reply to Johnstone [7].)

—— [6] "Science et Philosophie," *RIP*, XVII (1963), 133–40.

Perelman, Ch. and L. Olbrechts-Tyteca. [1] *Rhétorique et Philosophie: pour une Théorie de l'Argumentation en Philosophie* (Paris: Presses Universitaires de France, 1952). *See*: Johnstone [7].

Pitcher, George: [1] *The Philosophy of Wittgenstein* (Englewood Cliffs: Prentice-Hall, 1964), ch. 8 ("Puzzlement and Philosophy") and ch. 11 ("Philosophy"). *See*: Wittgenstein [1], etc.

Plochmann, G. K. [1] "Metaphysical Truth and the Diversity of Systems," *RM*, LV (1961), 51–66.

Poirier, Rene. [1] "La Philosophie Peut-Elle Etre une Science?" *RIP*, XIII (1959), 33–60. *See*: Ducasse [8]; Granger [1]; Guzzo [1]; Mehlberg [1]; Schaerer [1].

Pole, David. [1] "'Languages' and Aspects of Things," *PQ*, XII (1962), 306–15.

—— [2] *The Later Philosophy of Wittgenstein* (London: Athlone Press, 1958). *See*: Cavell [2].

—— [3] "Logical Rigidity and License," *PAS*, LV (1954–55), 133–56.

—— [4] "Words and Mr. Gellner," *Twentieth Century*, CLXVII (1960), 49–55. *See*: Gellner [5].

Popper, Karl R. [1] "The Demarcation Between Science and Metaphysics," in *The Philosophy of Rudolf Carnap*, ed. P. A. Schilpp (LaSalle: Open Court, 1963), 183–226. *Included in*: Popper, *Conjectures and Refutations*. *See*: Carnap [7].

—— [2] "The Nature of Philosophical Problems and Their Roots in Science," *BJPS*, III (1952), 124–56. *Included in*: Popper, *Conjectures and Refutations*.

—— [3] "What Can Logic Do for Philosophy?" *PAS*, *SV* XXII (1948), 141–54. *See*: Ayer [19]; Kneale [2].

Price, H. H. [1] "The Appeal to Common Sense (I & II)," *P*, V (1930), 24–35, 191–202.

—— [2] "British Philosophy between the Wars," *Horizon*, XIX (1949), 54–74.

—— [3] "Clarity Is Not Enough," *PAS*, *SV* XIX (1945), 1–31. *Included in*: *CNE*.

—— [4] "Logical Positivism and Theology," *P*, X (1935), 313–31.

Price, Robert. [1] "Descriptive Metaphysics, Chinese, and the Oxford Common Room," *M*, LXXIII (1964), 106–10. *See*: Mei [1] and [3].

Prior, A. N. [1] "English and Ontology,"

BJPS, VI (1955), 64–65. (Reply to Lejewski [1].)

Puccetti, Roland. [1] "Are Metaphysical Statements Confirmable?" *BJPS*, XIII (1962), 52–53. *See*: Watkins [7].

Putnam, H. [1] "The Analytic and the Synthetic," *Minnesota Studies in the Philosophy of Science*, III, ed. Feigl and Maxwell (Minneapolis: University of Minnesota Press, 1962), 358–97. *See*: Quine [7], etc.

—— [2] "Dreaming and 'Depth Grammar'," in *Analytical Philosophy*, First Series, ed. R. J. Butler (Oxford: Basil Blackwell, 1962), 211–35. (On N. Malcolm, *Dreaming*.)

—— [3] "Psychological Concepts, Explication, and Ordinary Language," *JP*, LIV (1957), 94–100.

Quine, W. V. [1] *From a Logical Point of View* (Cambridge: Harvard, 1953). *See*: Cartwright [1]; Strawson [5]; Warnock [5].

—— [2] "J. L. Austin: Comment" (abstract), *JP*, LXII (1965), 509–10. *See*: Urmson [2], etc.

—— [3] "Mr. Strawson on Logical Theory," *M*, LXII (1953), 433–51. (Review of Strawson [4].)

—— [4] "On Carnap's Views on Ontology," *PSt*, II (1951), 65–72. (Reply to Carnap [2].)

—— [5] "On What There Is," *RM*, II (1948), 21–38. *Included in*: Quine [1]; *RPM*; *SPL*. *See*: Alston [2]; Church [2].

—— [6] "On What There Is," *PAS, SV* XXV (1951), 149–60. (Symposium with P. T. Geach and A. J. Ayer.) See: Ayer [9]; Scheffler and Chomsky [1]; Epstein [1]; Geach [2].

—— [7] "Two Dogmas of Empiricism," *PR*, LX (1951), 20–43. *Included in*: *RPM*; *CNE*; Quine [1]; *CAP*. *See*: Bennett [1]; Bergmann [11]; Goodman [1], [2]; Grice and Strawson [1]; Malcolm [1]; Mates [1]; Pap [4]; Putnam [1]; Rynin [2]; Waismann [1]; Weitz [3]; M. G. White [2], [8] (Part II).

Quinton, A. [1] "Contemporary British Philosophy," in *A Critical History of Western Philosophy*, ed. D. J. O'Connor (The Free Press of Glencoe; London: Collier-Macmillan, 1964), 530–56.

—— [2] "Linguistic Analysis" in *Philoso-*

phy in the Mid-Century, ed. R. Klibansky (Firenze, 1958).

—— [3] "Philosophy and Beliefs," *Twentieth Century*, CLVII (1955), 495–521. (Symposium with S. Hampshire, I. Murdoch, and I. Berlin.)

—— [4] "Final Discussion," in *NM*, 142–64. (Symposium with Ryle and Warnock.)

Ramsey, F. P. [1] "Philosophy," in his *The Foundations of Mathematics*, ed. R. B. Braithwaite (London: Routledge and Kegan Paul, 1931), 263–69. *Included in*: Ayer [7].

—— [2] "Universals and the 'Method of Analysis'," *PAS, SV* VI (1926), 17–26. *See*: Braithwaite [2]; Joseph [1]; McCloskey [1].

Randall, J. Herman, Jr. [1] "Metaphysics: Its Function, Consequences, and Criteria," *JP*, XLIII (1946), 401–12. *See*: Hocking [1]; Lamprecht [1].

Rankin, K. W. [1] "Linguistic Analysis and the Justification of Induction," *PQ*, V (1955), 316–28.

Ray, Punya Sloka. [1] "Language and Philosophy," *The Indian Journal of Philosophy*, II (1960), 50–64.

Reichenbach, H. [1] "Logistic Empiricism in Germany and the Present State of Its Problems," *JP*, XXXIII (1936), 141–60.

—— [2] "Rationalism and Empiricism: An Inquiry into the Roots of Philosophical Error," *PR*, LVII (1948), 330–46.

—— [3] *The Rise of Scientific Philosophy* (Berkeley and Los Angeles: University of California Press; London: Cambridge University Press, 1951).

Rescher, Nicholas. [1] "Discourse on a Method," *ME*, XI (1959), 81–89.

—— [2] "Logical Analysis in Historical Application," *ME*, XI (1959), 187–94.

—— [3] "Translation as a Tool of Philosophical Analysis," *JP*, LIII (1956), 219–24.

Richman, Robert J. [1] "Concepts without Criteria," *Theoria*, XXXI (1965), 65–85. *See*: Albritton [1], etc.

—— [2] "On the Argument of the Paradigm Case," *AJ*, XXXIX (1961), 75–81. *See*: Richman [3]; Urmson [3]; Watkins [3], etc.; C. Williams [1].

—— [3] "Still More on the Argument of

the Paradigm Case," *AJ*, XL (1962), 204–7.

Rickman, H. P. [1] "Metaphysics as the Creation of Meaning," *The Hibbert Journal*, LII (1954), 166–74.

Ritchie, A. D. [1] "Errors of Logical Positivism," *P*, XII (1937), 47–60.

Robbins, Beverly. [1] "Ontology and the Hierarchy of Languages," *PR*, LXVII (1958), 531–37. *See*: Cartwright [1].

Robinson, Daniel S. [1] "Mr. Armstrong on Philosophy and Common Sense," *PPR*, XXIII (1963), 433–36. (Reply to Armstrong [1].) *See*: Armstrong [2].

Rogers, D. W. [1] "Philosophic Method," *PR*, LVI (1947), 656–69.

Rogers, R. [1] "Mathematical and Philosophical Analyses," *PS*, XXXI (1964), 255–64.

Rollins, C. D. [1] "Ordinary Language and Procrustean Beds," *M*, LX (1951), 223–32. *See*: Malcolm [2] and [6], etc.

Rorty, Richard M. [1] "The Limits of Reductionism," in *Experience, Existence, and The Good*, ed. I. C. Lieb (Carbondale: Southern Illinois University Press, 1961), 100–16. *See*: Carnap [2], etc.

―――― [2] "Realism, Categories, and the 'Linguistic Turn'," *IPQ*, II (1962), 307–22.

―――― [3] "*Reason and Analysis*. By Brand Blanshard," *JP*, LX (1963), 551–57.

―――― [4] "Recent Metaphilosophy," *RM*, XV (1961), 299–318. (Review of Hall [7] and Johnstone [8].)

Rosen, S. [1] "Wisdom: The End of Philosophy," *RM*, XVI (1962), 181–211.

Rothstein, J. M. and J. King-Farlow. [1] "Paradigm Cases and the Injustice to Thrasymachus," *PQ*, XIV (1964), 15–22. *See*: Watkins [3], etc.

Rudner, Richard. [1] "Counter-Intuitivity and the Method of Analysis," *PSt*, I (1950), 83–89.

Ruja, Harry. [1] "The Present Status of the Verifiability Criterion," *PPR*, XXII (1961), 216–22. *See*: Hempel [1], etc.

Russell, Bertrand. [1] "The Cult of 'Common Usage'," *BJPS*, III (1953), 303–7.

―――― [2] "Language and Metaphysics," in his *An Inquiry into Meaning and Truth* (London: George Allen and Unwin, 1940), 341–47.

―――― [3] "Logic and Ontology," *JP*, LIV (1957), 225–30. (Reply to Warnock [5].)

―――― [4] "Logic as the Essence of Philosophy," in his *Our Knowledge of the External World* (Chicago and London: Open Court, 1914), 33–59. *See*: Kalish [1].

―――― [5] "Logical Positivism," *Polemic*, (1946), 6–13.

―――― [6] "Logical Positivism," *RIP*, IV (1950), 3–19. *Included in*: R. C. Marsh (ed.), *Logic and Knowledge*, and in part in Russell, *Human Knowledge: Its Scope and Limits*.

―――― [7] "On Scientific Method in Philosophy," in his *Mysticism and Logic* (London: Longmans, Green, 1921), 97–124. *See*: Ducasse [7] (ch. V).

―――― [8] "On Verification," *PAS*, XXXVIII (1937–38), 1–20. *See*: Hempel [1], etc.

―――― [9] "*Philosophical Analysis*," *The Hibbert Journal*, LIV (1956), 319–29. (Review of Urmson [3].) *See*: McKinney [1].

―――― [10] "The Philosophy of Logical Atomism: VIII. Excursus into Metaphysics: What There Is," *MO*, XXIX (1919), 364–80. *Included in*: Marsh (ed.), *Logic and Knowledge*. *See*: Charlesworth [1] (ch. II); Urmson [2]; Warnock [3] (ch. III).

―――― [11] "Reply to Criticisms," in *The Philosophy of Bertrand Russell*, ed. P. A. Schilpp (Evanston: Northwestern University, 1944), 684–86, 691–95, 695–96. *See*: Black [15]; Weitz [1].

Ryle, G. [1] "Categories," *PAS*, XXXVIII (1937–38), 189–206. *Included in*: *LL* (II). *See*: Baker [1]; Cross [1]; Fisher [1]; Harrison [1], Hillman [1]; Hofstadter [2] and [3]; Passmore [3] (ch. VII); Pole [1]; Ryle [2]; Smart [1]; Sommers [2]; Thompson [3]; Waismann [3].

―――― [2] *The Concept of Mind* (London: Hutchinson; New York: Barnes & Noble, 1949). *See*: Hampshire [3]; Hall [3]; Hartnack [2] (ch. V); Hofstadter [2]; Lewis [1] (ch. XIII and XIV); Warnock [2] (ch. VII).

―――― [3] *Dilemmas* (Cambridge: Cambridge University Press, 1954). *See*: Howard [1].

————— [4] "Final Discussion," in *NM*, 142–64. (Symposium with Quinton and Warnock.)

————— [5] "Introduction," in *REV*, 1–11.

————— [6] "Ludwig Wittgenstein," *A*, XII (1951), 1–9.

————— [7] *Meaning and Necessity*. By Rudolf Carnap," *P*, XXIV (1949), 69–76. *See*: Carnap [2]; Hempel [1], etc.

————— [8] "Ordinary Language," *PR*, LXII (1953), 167–86. *Included in*: *POL* and *OL*. *See*: Caton [2]; Cohen [2]; Gale [1]; Grant [1]; Passmore [4]; Tennessen [4]; A. R. White [4].

————— [9] "La Phénomenologie contre the Concept of Mind" in Beck [1], 65–84.

————— [10] "Philosophical Arguments," in *Logical Positivism*, ed. A. J. Ayer (Glencoe: Free Press, 1959), 327–44. (An inaugural lecture, published separately [Oxford: Clarendon Press, 1946].) *See*: Howard [1].

————— [11] "Proofs in Philosophy," *RIP*, VIII (1954), 150–57. (Symposium on "La Preuve en Philosophie" with C. Frankel and G. Morpurgo-Tagliabue.)

*————— [12] "Systematically Misleading Expressions," *PAS*, XXXII (1931–32), 139–70. *Included in*: *LL* (I). *See*: Bar-Hillel [5]; Bergmann [13]; Harris [2]; Passmore [5]; Shapere [1].

————— [13] "Taking Sides in Philosophy," *P*, XII (1937), 317–32.

————— [14] "The Theory of Meaning," in *British Philosophy in the Mid-Century*, ed. C. A. Mace (London: George Allen & Unwin, 1957), 239–64. *Included in*: *POL*.

————— [15] "Use, Usage and Meaning," *PAS*, *SV* XXXV (1961), 223–30. *See*: Findlay [3].

————— [16] "The Verification Principle," *RIP*, V (1951), 243–50. *See*: Hempel [1], etc.

Rynin, David. [1] "Vindication of L*g*c*l P*s*t*v*sm," *PAPA*, XXX (1957), 45–67. *See*: Hempel [1], etc.

————— [2] "The Dogma of Logical Pragmatism," *M*, LXV (1956), 379–91. (Discussion of Quine [7].)

Sacksteder, William. [1] "Inference and Philosophic Typologies," *MO*, XLVIII (1964), 567–601.

Schaerer, Rene. [1] "La Philosophie Peut-Elle Etre une Science?" *RIP*, XIII (1959), 88–95. *See*: Ducasse [8]; Granger [1]; Guzzo [1]; Mehlberg [1]; Poirier [1].

Scheffler, Israel. [1] "Prospects of a Modest Empiricism, I & II," *RM*, X (1957), 383–400, 602–25.

Scheffler, Israel and Noam Chomsky. [1] "What Is Said to Be?" *PAS*, LIX (1958–59), 71–82. *See*: Quine [6], etc.

Schiller, F. C. S. [1] "Must Philosophers Disagree?" *PAS*, *SV* XII (1933), 118–30. *Included in*: Schiller, *Must Philosophers Disagree? See*: Mace [3]; Stocks [1].

Schilpp, Paul Arthur. [1] "The Abdication of Philosophy," *PAPA*, XXXII (1959), 19–39.

————— [2] "Is 'Standpointless Philosophy' Possible?" *PR*, XLIV (1935), 227–53.

*Schlick, M. [1] "The Future of Philosophy," *College of the Pacific Publications in Philosophy*, I (1932), 45–62. *Included in*: Schlick, *Gesammelte Aufsätze* and D. Bronstein, Y. Krikorian and P. Weiner, *Basic Problems in Philosophy*.

————— [2] "Meaning and Verification," *PR*, XLV (1936), 339–69. *Included in*: *RPA*; Schlick, *Gesammelte Aufsätze*. *See*: Hempel [1], etc.

————— [3] "The Turning Point in Philosophy," tr. D. Rynin, in *Logical Positivism*, ed. A. J. Ayer (Glencoe: Free Press, 1959), 53–59. (Originally published as "Die Wende Der Philosophie," *Erkenntnis*, I (1930–31). *Included in*: Schlick, *Gesammelte Aufsätze*.

Schmidt, Paul F. [1] "Self-Referential Justification," *PSt*, VIII (1957), 49–54.

Schmitt, Richard. [1] "Phenomenology and Analysis," *PPR*, XXIII (1962), 101–10. *See*: Ayer [10], etc.

————— [2] "Phenomenology and Metaphysics," *JP*, LIX (1962), 421–28.

Schwayder, David. [1] "Some Remarks on 'Synonymity' and the Language of Semanticists," *PSt*, V (1954), 1–5.

Scriven, Michael [1] "Definitions in Analytical Philosophy," *PSt*, V (1954), 36–40. (Reply to Copi [1].) *See*: Copi [2]; Carmichael [2].

————— [2] "The Logic of Criteria," *JP*, LVI (1959), 857–68. *See*: Albritton [1], etc.

Searle, J. R. [1] "Meaning and Speech Acts,"

PR, LXXI (1962), 423–32. Included in C. D. Rollins (ed.), *Knowledge and Experience*. *See*: Benacerraf [1].

Sellars, Roy Wood. [1] "Positivism and Materialism," *PPR*, VII (1946), 12–40.

Sellars, Wilfrid. [1] "Empiricism and the Philosophy of Mind," in *Minnesota Studies in the Philosophy of Science*, I, ed. H. Feigl and M. Scriven (Minneapolis: University of Minnesota Press, 1956), 253–329. *Included in*: Sellars, *Science, Perception and Reality*.

——— [2] "Gestalt Qualities and the Paradox of Analysis," *PSt*, I (1950), 92–94. *See*: Langford [3], etc.

——— [3] "Grammar and Existence: A Preface to Ontology," *M*, LXIX (1960), 499–533. *Included in*: Sellars, *Science, Perception and Reality*.

——— [4] "The Identity of Linguistic Expressions and the Paradox of Analysis," *PSt*, I (1950), 24–31. *See*: Langford [3], etc.

——— [5] "The Paradox of Analysis: a Neo-Fregean Approach," *A*, XXIII (1963–64), 84–98. *See*: Langford [3], etc.

——— [6] "Philosophy and the Scientific Image of Man," in his *Science, Perception and Reality* (London: Routledge & Kegan Paul, 1963), 1–40.

——— [7] "Some Reflections on Language Games," *PS*, XXI (1954), 204–28. Included in Sellars, *Science, Perception and Reality*. *See*: Hervey [1], etc.

*Shapere, Dudley. [1] "Philosophy and the Analysis of Language," *I*, III (1960), 29–48. *See*: Austin [2]; Ryle [12]; Wittgenstein [1], etc.

Shoemaker, Sydney. [1] "Logical Atomism and Language," *A*, XX (1960), 49–52. (Reply to Butchvarov [3].)

Shorter, J. M. [1] "Causality, and a Method of Analysis," in *Analytical Philosophy* (Second Series), ed. R. J. Butler (Oxford: Basil Blackwell, 1965), 145–57.

——— [2] "Facts, Logical Atomism and Reducibility," *AJ*, XL (1962), 283–302.

Sidgwick, Alfred. [1] "Verbalistic Tendencies," *M*, XLIII (1934), 409–23.

——— [2] "Verifiability and Meaning," *M*, XLV (1936), 61–66. *See*: Ayer [2] and [15]; Stace [2].

Sinha, D. [1] "Phenomenology and Positivism," *PPR*, XXIII (1963), 562–77.

Smart, H. R. [1] "Language-Games," *PQ*, VII (1957), 224–35. *See*: Hervey [1], etc.

——— [2] *Philosophy and Its History* (LaSalle: Open Court, 1962).

Smart, J. J. C. [1] "A Note on Categories," *BJPS*, IV (1953), 227–28. *See*: Ryle [1], etc.

——— [2] "Plausible Reasoning in Philosophy," *M*, LXVI (1957), 75–78.

——— [3] "The Province of Philosophy," in his *Philosophy and Scientific Realism* (London: Routledge, 1963), 1–15.

Smith, James W. [1] *A Theme for Reason* (Princeton: Princeton University Press, 1957).

Smullyan, A. F. [1] "The Variety of Philosophic Idioms," *JP*, XLV (1948), 350–56.

Sommers, Fred. [1] "The Ordinary Language Tree," *M*, LXVIII (1959), 160–85.

——— [2] "Types and Ontology," *PR*, LXXII (1963), 327–63. *See*: J. O. Nelson [1].

——— [3] "A Program for Coherence," *PR*, LXXIII (1964), 522–27. (Reply to Nelson [1].)

Sontag, Frederick. [1] "Philosophy of Science and the Revival of Classical Ontology," *JP*, LII (1956), 597–607. *See*: Grabau [1]; Sontag [2].

——— [2] "Ontology and the Philosophy of Science: A Reply," *JP*, LV (1958), 337–39. (Reply to Grabau [1].)

Spinney, G. H. [1] "On the Contrast between Scientific and Philosophic Hypotheses," *P*, XXX (1955), 15–32. (Reply to Macdonald [2].)

Stace, W. T. [1] "Can Speculative Philosophy Be Defended?" *PR*, LII (1943), 116–26. *See*: Blake [1]; Murphy [1].

——— [2] "Metaphysics and Meaning," *M*, XLIV (1935), 417–38. *Included in*: *MIP*. *See*: Ayer [2] and [15]; Sidgwick [2].

——— [3] "Positivism," *M*, LIII (1944), 215–37. *See*: Wisdom [4].

Stebbing, L. Susan. [1] "Directional Analysis and Basic Facts," *A*, II (1934), 33–36. (Reply to E. D. Bronstein [1].)

——— [2] *"An Essay on Metaphysics.* By

R. G. Collingwood," *M*, L (1941), 184–90.

———— [3] "Language and Misleading Questions," *The Journal of Unified Science (Erkenntnis)*, VIII (1939), 1–6.

———— [4] "*Language, Truth and Logic* by A. J. Ayer," *M*, XLV (1936), 355–64.

———— [5] "Logical Positivism and Analysis," *Proceedings of the British Academy*, XIX (1933), 53–87.

———— [6] "The Method of Analysis in Metaphysics," *PAS*, XXXIII (1932–33), 65–94. *See*: Black [11].

———— [7] "Moore's Influence," in *The Philosophy of G. E. Moore* ed. P. A. Schilpp (New York: Tudor Publishing Company, Second Edition, 1952), 515–32. *See*: Moore [3].

———— [8] "R. Carnap: *Logische Syntax der Sprache* and Other Works," *M*, XLIV (1935), 499–511.

———— [9] "Some Puzzles About Analysis," *PAS*, XXXIX (1938–39), 69–84. *See*: Ayer [3]; Black [16]; Duncan-Jones [2]; Murphy [3]; Wisdom [9].

Stedman, R. E. [1] "A Defence of Speculative Philosophy," *PAS*, XXXVIII (1937–38), 113–42.

Stevenson, C. L. [1] "Persuasive Definitions," *M*, XLVII (1938), 331–50. *Included in*: *APW*; Stevenson, *Facts and Values*.

———— [2] "Some Relations between Philosophy and the Study of Language," *A*, VIII (1947), 1–9. *Included in*: Stevenson, *Facts and Values*.

Stigen, Anfinn. [1] "What Does Mr. Tennessen Mean, and What Should I Say?" *I*, III (1960), 180–84. (Reply to Tennessen [8].) *See*: Tennessen [7].

Stocks, J. L. [1] "Must Philosophers Disagree?" *PAS, SV* XII (1933), 138–49. *See*: Mace [3]; Schiller [1].

Storer, Thomas. [1] "An Analysis of Logical Positivism," *ME*, III (1951), 245–72.

———— [2] "Linguistic Isomorphisms," *PS*, XIX (1952), 77–85.

———— [3] "The Philosophical Relevance of a Behavioristic Semiotic," *PS*, XV (1948), 316–30. (Review of C. Morris, *Signs, Language and Behavior*.)

Storheim, Eivind. [1] "Empirical Semantics in Oslo," *Theoria*, XXVI (1960), 236–40. *See*: Hartnack [1]; Wedberg [1].

*Strawson, P. F. [1] "Carnap's Views on Constructed Systems *vs.* Natural Languages in Analytic Philosophy," in *The Philosophy of Rudolf Carnap*, ed. P. A. Schilpp (LaSalle: Open Court, 1963), 503–18. *See*: Carnap [7]. (Partially identical with his "Analyse, Science, et Métaphysique" in Beck [1]; translated as "Analysis, Science, and Metaphysics" in this volume.)

———— [2] *Individuals: An Essay in Descriptive Metaphysics* (London: Methuen, 1959). *See*: Bergmann [10]; Burtt [1]; Zabeeh [1].

———— [3] "Construction and Analysis," in *REV*, 97–110. *See*: Feigl and Maxwell [1]; Warnock [1].

———— [4] *Introduction to Logical Theory* (London: Methuen, 1952). *See*: Quine [3].

———— [5] "A Logician's Landscape," *P*, XXX (1955), 229–37. (On Quine [1].)

———— [6] "On Referring," *M*, LIX (1950), 320–44. *Included in*: *CAP; POL; ECA*. *See*: Hart [1]; Hartnack [2] (ch. V); Weitz [4].

———— [7] "*Philosophical Investigations*. By Ludwig Wittgenstein," *M*, LXIII (1954), 70–99.

Strawson, P. F. and H. P. Grice. [1] "In Defense of a Dogma," *PR*, LXV (1956), 141–58. *Included in*: *CAP*. *See*: Quine [7], etc.

Strawson, P. F., H. P. Grice and D. F. Pears. [1] "Metaphysics," in *NM*, 1–22.

Stroll, Avrum. [1] "Is Everyday Language Inconsistent?" *M*, LXIII (1954), 219–25.

———— [2] "When Is an Analysis of Ordinary Discourse Correct?" in his *The Emotive Theory of Ethics, University of California Publications in Philosophy*, XXVIII (1954), 78–87.

Supek, Ivan. [1] "Escape of Philosophy into Linguistic Depths," *Dialectica*, XIV (1960), 80–92.

Swanson, J. W. [1] "Landesman on Linguistic Relativity," *RM*, XV (1961), 336–39. (Reply to Landesman [1].)

———— [2] "Linguistic Relativity and Translation," *PPR*, XXII (1961), 185–92.

Sweet, Albert M. [1] "A Semantic Explication of Metaphysical Analogy," *PPR*, XXIII (1963), 595–604.

Taylor, Charles. [1] "Ontology," *P*, XXXIV (1959), 125–41.

—— [2] "Phenomenology and Linguistic Analysis," *PAS*, *SV* XXXIII (1959), 93–110. *See*: Ayer [10]; Schmitt [1].

Tennessen, Herman. [1] "The Fight against Revelation in Semantical Studies," *Synthese*, VIII (1950–51), 225–34. *See*: Crockett [1].

—— [2] *Language Analysis and Empirical Semantics* (University of Alberta).

—— [3] "Logical Oddities and Locutional Scarcities," *Synthese*, XI (1959), 369–88.

—— [4] "Ordinary Language *In Memoriam*," *I*, VIII (1965), 225–48.

—— [5] "Permissible and Impermissible Locutions," *Synthese*, XII (1960), 495–508. *Included in*: *Logic and Language: Studies Dedicated to Professor Rudolf Carnap*.

—— [6] *Revelation and Logical Analysis* (Oslo, 1955).

—— [7] "Vindication of the Humpty Dumpty Attitude towards Language," *I*, III (1960), 185–98. (Reply to Stigen [1].) *See*: Tennessen [8]; Weiler [1].

—— [8] "What Should We Say?" *I*, II (1959), 265–90. *See*: Mates [2], etc.; Stigen [1].

—— [9] "Whereof One Has Been Silent, Thereof One May Have to Speak," *JP*, LVIII (1961), 263–74.

Terrell, D. B. [1] "What You Will, or The Limits of Analysis," *PSt*, III (1952), 33–38.

Thomas, L. E. [1] "Philosophic Doubt," *M*, LXIV (1955), 333–41.

Thomas, Sid B., Jr. [1] "Is the Appeal to Ordinary Usage Ever Relevant in Philosophical Argument?" *MO*, XLVIII (1964), 533–46.

Thompson, Manley. [1] "Metaphysics," in *Philosophy* (a volume in the Princeton Studies on *Humanistic Scholarship in America*), by R. M. Chisholm, et. al. (Englewood Cliffs: Prentice–Hall, 1964), 125–232.

—— [2] "On Category Differences," *PR*, LXV (1957), 486–508. *See*: Ryle [1], etc.

—— [3] "Reduction Sentences and Metaphysics," *PR*, L (1941), 610–15.

*—— [4] "When Is Ordinary Language Reformed?" *JP*, LVIII (1961), 498–504. (Reply to Maxwell and Feigl [1].)

Thomson, J. F. [1] "Reducibility," *PAS*, *SV* XXVI (1952), 87–104. *See*: Braithwaite [1]; Warnock [6].

Tillman, Frank A. [1] "Explication and Ordinary Language Analysis," *PPR*, XXV (1965), 375–83.

Todd, William. [1] "Infinite Analysis," *PSt*, XIII (1962), 24–27.

Tomlin, E. W. F. [1] "Mr. Hare's Paper: A Rejoinder," *Ratio*, III (1960), 1–8. (Reply to Hare [2].)

Toms, Eric. [1] "Exposition and Explanation," *P*, XXV (1950), 253–65.

Toulmin, Stephen. [1] "Logical Positivism and After, or Back to Aristotle," *Universities Quarterly*, XI (1957), 335–47. *See*: Gellner [3] and [4]; Toulmin [2].

—— [2] "Mr. Gellner's Spurious Fox," *Universities Quarterly*, XI (1957), 365–67. (Reply to Gellner [3].)

—— [3] *The Uses of Argument* (New York: Cambridge University Press, 1958.)

Tucker, John. [1] "Philosophical Argument," *PAS*, *SV* XXXIX (1965), 47–64. *See*: Bednarowski [1].

Turnbull, Robert G. [1] "Linguistic Analysis, Phenomenology, and the Problems of Philosophy: An Essay in Metaphilosophy," *MO*, XLIX (1965), 44–69.

*Urmson, J. O. [1] "Histoire de l'Analyse" in Beck [1]; translated as "History of Analysis" in this volume.

*—— [2] "J. L. Austin," *JP*, LXII (1965), 499–508. *See*: Austin [1], etc.; Hampshire [7]; Malcolm [8]; Quine [2].

—— [3] *Philosophical Analysis: Its Development Between the Two World Wars* (Oxford: Clarendon Press, 1956). *See*: Bergmann [8]; Goodman [3]; McKinney [1]; Russell [9]; Watling [1].

—— [4] "Some Questions Concerning Validity," *RIP*, VII (1953), 217–29. *Included in*: *ECA*. *See*: Watkins [3], etc.

*Urmson, J. O. and G. J. Warnock. [1] "J. L. Austin," *M*, LXX (1961), 256–57.

(Reply to Hampshire [6].) *See*: Cavell [1].

Uygur, Nermi. [1] "What is a Philosophical Question?" *M*, LXXIII (1964), 64–83.

Vaccarino, G. [1] "Discussion of 'The Application of Logistic Analysis to Philosophical Problems'," *ME*, III (1951), 117–20. (Reply to Juhos [1].)

Veatch, Henry. [1] *Philosophical Analysis. Ed. Max Black,*" *The Thomist*, XV (1952), 169–73.

Vendler, Zeno. [1] "Comments on 'The Relevance of Linguistics to Philosophy'" (abstract), *JP*, LXII (1965), 602–5. *See*: Katz [1]; N. L. Wilson [1].

——— [2] "Reply to Professor Dubs," *PR*, LXVII (1958), 395–96. (Reply to Dubs [1].)

Von Bertalanffy, L. [1] "An Essay on the Relativity of Categories," *PS*, XXII (1955), 243–63. *See*: Whorf [1], etc.

Waismann, F. [1] "Analytic–Synthetic, I–VI," *A*. I: X (1949), 25–40; II: XI (1950), 25–38; III: XI (1951), 49–61; IV: XI (1951), 115–24; V: XIII (1952), 1–14; VI: XIII (1953), 73–89. *See*: Quine [7], etc.

——— [2] "How I See Philosophy," in *Contemporary British Philosophy* ed. H. D. Lewis (London: George Allen and Unwin, Third Series, 1956), 445–90. *Included in*: Ayer [7]. See Hampshire [14]; Levison [1]; Passmore [3].

——— [3] "Language Strata," in *Logic and Language*, ed. A. G. N. Flew (Oxford: Basil Blackwell, Second Series, 1953), 11–31. *See*: Butler [1]; Rorty [2].

——— [4] *The Principles of Linguistic Philosophy* (London: Macmillan, 1965).

——— [5] "Verifiability," *PAS, SV* XIX (1945), 119–50. *Included in*: *LL* (I). *See*: Hempel [1], etc.

——— [6] "Was ist Logische Analyse?" *The Journal of Unified Science* (*Erkenntnis*), VIII (1940), 265–89.

Wang, Hao. [1] "On Formalization," *M*, LXIV (1955), 226–38.

Warnock, G. J. [1] "Analysis and Imagination," in *REV*, 111–26. *See*: Strawson [3]; Wild [1].

——— [2] "Criticisms of Metaphysics," in *NM*, 124–41.

——— [3] *English Philosophy Since 1900* (London: Oxford University Press, 1958). *See*: Klemke [1]; Whiteley [3].

——— [4] "John Langshaw Austin, 1911–1960," *Proceedings of the British Academy*, XLIX (1963), 345–63. *See*: Austin [1], etc.

——— [5] "Metaphysics in Logic," *PAS*, LI (1950–51), 197–222. *Included in*: *ECA*. *See*: Quine [1]; B. Russell [3].

——— [6] "Reducibility," *PAS, SV* XXVI (1952), 105–20. *See*: Braithwaite [1]; Thomson [1].

——— [7] "Verification and the Use of Language," *RIP*, V (1951), 307–22. *See*: Hempel [1], etc.; Weitz [4].

*Warnock, G. J. and J. O. Urmson. [1] "J. L. Austin," *M*, LXX (1961), 256–57. *See*: Hampshire [5], etc.

Warnock, Mary. [1] "Final Discussion," in *NM*, 142–64. (Symposium with Quinton and Ryle.)

Wasserstrom, Richard. [1] "Hume and Philosophical Analysis: A Reply to Professor Lazerowitz," *P*, XXXV (1960), 151–53. (Reply to Lazerowitz [3].)

Watkins, J. W. N. [1] "Between Analytic and Empirical," *P*, XXXII (1957), 112–31. *See*: Körner [4]; Watkins [2] and [6].

——— [2] "Confirmable and Influential Metaphysics," *M*, LXVII (1958), 344–65.

——— [3] "Farewell to the Paradigm-Case Argument," *A*, XVIII (1957), 25–33. *See*: Alexander [2]; Eveling and Leith [1]; Flew [1] and [4]; Gellner [5] (ch. II); Harré [2]; Houlgate [1]; King-Farlow and Rothstein [1]; Passmore [3] (ch. VI); Richman [2] and [3]; Urmson [4]; Watkins [4]; Williams [1].

——— [4] "A Reply to Professor Flew's Comment," *ibid.*, 41–42.

——— [5] "A Modern Samson in the Philosopher's Temple: Morton White's New Book," *Ratio*, I (1957), 68–84. (On White [8].)

——— [6] "Reply to Professor Körner," *M*, LXIX (1960), 406–7. (Reply to Körner [4].)

——— [7] "Reply to Professor Puccetti," *BJPS*, XIII (1962), 53–54. (Reply to Puccetti [1].)

——— [8] "Word-Magic and the Trivialization of Philosophy," *Ratio*, VII (1965). (Review of Lazerowitz [10].)

Watling, John. [1] "About J. O. Urmson's *Philosophical Analysis: Its Development between the Two World Wars*," *RIP*, X (1956), 340–46.

Wedberg, Anders. [1] "Philosophical Analysis: Types and Aims," *Theoria*, XXVI (1960), 228–36. *See*: Hartnack [1]; Storheim [1].

Weiler, Gershon. [1] "Is Humpty Dumpty Vindicated?" *I*, III (1960), 278–81. (Reply to Tennessen [7].)

Weinberg, J. [1] *A Critical Examination of Logical Positivism* (London: Kegan Paul, 1936).

Weiss, Paul. [1] *Modes of Being* (Carbondale: Southern Illinois University Press, 1958), ch. 5 ("The Adequacy of a Philosophy").

————— [2] "Twenty-Two Reasons for Continuing as Before," *PSt*, XIII (1962), 65–68. (Reply to Hanson [1].)

Weitz, Morris. [1] "Analysis and Real Definition," *PSt*, I (1950), 1–8.

————— [2] "Analysis and the Unity of Russell's Philosophy," in *The Philosophy of Bertrand Russell*, ed. P. A. Schilpp (Evanston: Northwestern University, 1944), 55–121. *See*: Russell [11].

————— [3] "Analytic Statements," *M*, LXIII (1954), 487–94. *See*: Quine [7], etc.

————— [4] "Oxford Philosophy," *PR*, LXII (1953), 187–233. *See*: Charlesworth [1] (ch. VI).

————— [5] "Philosophy and the Abuse of Language," *JP*, XLIV (1947), 533–46. *See*: Malcolm [5], etc.; Wiener [1].

Wellman, Carl. [1] "Wittgenstein's Conception of a Criterion," *PR*, LXXI (1962), 433–47. *See*: Albritton [1], etc.

Wells, Rulon. [1] "What Has Linguistics Done for Philosophy?" *JP*, LIX (1962), 697–708. *See*: Alston [3]; Katz [1], etc.

Werkmeister, William Henry. [1] "Seven Theses of Logical Positivism Critically Examined," *PR*, XLVI (1937), 276–97 and 357–76.

Wheatley, Jon. [1] "How to Give a Word a Meaning," *Theoria*, XXX (1964), 119–36.

————— [2] "The Logical Status of Metaethical Theories," *Theoria*, XXVI (1960), 71–82. *See*: Blackstone [3].

————— [3] "Some Notes on John Wisdom's Position," *M*, LXX (1961), 351–61.

————— [4] "Tomatoes and Vegetables," *Theoria*, XXVIII (1962), 312–15.

White, Alan R. [1] *G. E. Moore: A Critical Exposition* (Oxford: Basil Blackwell, 1958). *See*: Malcolm [3], etc.

————— [2] "Moore's Appeal to Common Sense," *P*, XXXIII (1958), 221–39. *See*: Moore [1], etc.

————— [3] "A Note on Meaning and Verification," *M*, LXIII (1954), 66–69. (Reply to Evans [1].) *See*: Hempel [1], etc.

————— [4] "The Use of Sentences," *A*, XVII (1956), 1–4. (Reply to Ryle [8].) *See*: Caton [2].

White, M. G. [1] "Analysis and Identity: A Rejoinder," *M*, LIV (1945), 357–61. (Reply to Black [10].) *See*: White [6], etc.

————— [2] "The Analytic and the Synthetic: An Untenable Dualism," in *John Dewey: Philosopher of Science and Freedom*, ed. S. Hook (New York: Dial, 1950), 316–30. *Included in*: *SPL*. *See*: Quine [7], etc.

————— [3] "Critique of C. H. Langford on 'The Notion of Analysis in Moore's Philosophy' and Moore's Reply," *JSL*, VIII (1943), 149–51. *See*: Langford [3]; Moore [3], etc.

————— [4] "A Finitistic Approach to Philosophical Theses," *PR*, LX (1951), 299–316.

————— [5] "New Horizons in Philosophy," *The Saturday Evening Post*, CCXXXIII (1960), 24–25.

————— [6] "A Note on the 'Paradox of Analysis'," *M*, LIV (1945), 71–72. (Reply to Black [9].) *See*: Black [10]; Langford [3], etc.; White [1].

————— [7] "On the Church-Frege Solution of the Paradox of Analysis," *PPR*, IX (1948), 305–8. *See*: Langford [3], etc.

————— [8] *Toward Reunion in Philosophy* (Cambridge: Harvard University Press, 1956). *See*: Passmore [2]; Watkins [5].

Whiteley, C. H. [1] "Can Philosophical Theories Transcend Experience?" *PAS*, SV XX (1946), 210–27. *See*: Emmet [1]; Laird [1].

————— [2] "Metaphysics and Science," *PQ*, IX (1959), 244–49.

————— [3] "Mr. Warnock on Ordinary

Language," *M*, LXVIII (1959), 396–98. *See*: Warnock [3] (ch. XII).

Whittier, Duane H. [1] "Basic Assumption and Argument in Philosophy," *MO*, XLVIII (1964), 486–500.

Whorf, B. L. [1] *Language, Thought, and Reality: Selected Writings of Benjamin Lee Whorf*, ed. J. B. Carroll (Cambridge: M.I.T. and New York: Wiley, 1956). *See*: Black [6]; Brutian [1]; Landesman [1]; Swanson [1]; Von Bertalanffy [1].

Wick, W. A. [1] "Moral Problems, Moral Philosophy, and Meta-ethics; Some Further Dogmas of Empiricism," *PR*, LXII (1953), 3–22.

——— [2] "On the Identification of Philosophy with Logical Analysis," *PR*, LI (1942), 508–13.

——— [3] "The Political Philosophy of Logical Empiricism," *PSt*, II (1951), 49–57.

Wiener, P. P. [1] "Philosophical, Scientific, and Ordinary Language," *JP*, XLV (1948), 260–67. (Reply to Weitz [5].)

——— [2] "Some Metaphysical Assumptions and Problems of Neo-Positivism," *JP*, XXXII (1935), 175–81.

Wild, John. [1] "Is There a World of Ordinary Language?" *PR*, LXVII (1958), 460–76. *See*: Warnock [1].

Williams, Bernard. [1] "J. L. Austin's Philosophy," *The Oxford Magazine*, n.s. III (1962), 115–18. *See*: Austin [1], etc.

——— [2] "Metaphysical Arguments," in *NM*, 39–60.

Williams, C. J. F. [1] "More on the Argument of the Paradigm Case," *AJ*, XXXIX (1961), 276–78. (Reply to Richman [2].) *See*: Richman [3].

Wilson, N. L. [1] "Comments on 'The Relevance of Linguistics to Philosophy',," (abstract) *JP*, LXII (1965), 605–6. *See*: Katz [1]; Vendler [1].

Wilson, Patrick. [1] "Austin on Knowing," *I*, III (1960), 49–60. *See*: Austin [1], etc.

Winch, Peter. [1] "Contemporary British Philosophy and Its Critics," *Universities Quarterly*, X (1955), 24–37.

Wisdom, J. O. [1] "Esotericism," *P*, XXXIV (1959), 338–54.

——— [2] "Metamorphoses of the Verifiability Theory of Meaning," *M*, LXXII (1963), 335–47. *See*: Hempel [1], etc.

——— [3] *The Metamorphosis of Philosophy* (Cairo: Al-Maaref Press, 1947).

——— [4] "Positivism," *M*, LIV (1945), 65–70. *See*: Stace [3].

Wisdom, John. [1] "A Feature of Wittgenstein's Technique," *PAS*, *SV* XXXV (1961), 1–14. *Included in*: Wisdom [8].

——— [2] "Is Analysis a Useful Method in Philosophy?" *PAS*, *SV* XIII (1934), 65–89. *Included in*: Wisdom [11]. *See*: Black [3]; Cornforth [2].

——— [3] "Logical Constructions," *M*, I: XL (1931), 188–216; II: XL (1931), 460–75; III: XLI (1932), 441–64; IV: XLII (1933), 43–66; V: XLII (1933), 186–202.

——— [4] "The Metamorphosis of Metaphysics," *Proceedings of the British Academy*, XLVII (1961), 37–59. *Included in*: Wisdom [8].

——— [5] "Metaphysics," *PAS*, LI (1950–51), i-xxiv. *Included in*: Wisdom, *Other Minds*.

——— [6] "Metaphysics and Verification," *M*, XLVII (1938), 452–98. *Included in*: Wisdom [11]. *See*: Hempel [1], etc.; Orr [1]; Stebbing [9].

——— [7] "Moore's Technique," in *The Philosophy of G. E. Moore*, ed. P. A. Schilpp (New York: Tudor Publishing Company, Second Edition, 1952), 419–50. *Included in*: Wisdom [11]. *See*: Moore [3], etc.

——— [8] *Paradox and Discovery* (Oxford: Blackwell, 1965).

*——— [9] "Philosophical Perplexity," *PAS*, XXXVII (1936–37), 71–88. *Included in*: Wisdom [11]. *See*: Lazerowitz [2]; Stebbing [9].

——— [10] "Philosophy and Psycho-Analysis," *Polemic*, No. 4 (1946), 37–48. *Included in*: *CAP*; Wisdom [11].

——— [11] *Philosophy and Psycho-Analysis* (Oxford: Blackwell, 1953). *See*: Ayer [17]; Charlesworth [1] (ch. V); Coombe-Tennant [1]; Gasking [1]; Wheatley [3].

——— [12] "Philosophy, Anxiety and Novelty," *M*, LIII (1944), 170–76. *Included in*: Wisdom [11].

——— [13] "Philosophy, Metaphysics, and Psycho-Analysis," in Wisdom [11].

Wittgenstein, Ludwig. [1] *Philosophical Investigations.* (New York: Macmillan; Oxford: Blackwell, 1953). *See:* Albritton [1], etc. (on 'Criterion'); Bergmann [1]; Bouwsma [1]; Cavell [2]; Charlesworth [1] (ch. III); Daly [3]; Farrell [1]; Feyerabend [4]; Findlay [2] and [4]; Fodor and Chihara [1]; Gruender [1]; Gasking and Jackson [1]; Hallie [1]; Hartnack [2]; Heath [2]; Hervey [1], etc.; Horgby [1]; Kreisel [1]; Levi [1]; Lieb [1]; Malcolm [9]; Miller [1]; Mora, [1]; Munson [1]; Nielson [1]; Passmore [6]; Paul [2]; Pitcher [1]; Pole [2]; Ryle [6]; Strawson [7]; Warnock [3] (VI); Wisdom [1]; Wolter [1].

—— [2] "Some Remarks on Logical Form," *PAS, SV* IX (1929), 162–71. *See:* Bar-Hillel [2]; Eslick [1]; Hampshire [8]; Kalish [1].

—— [3] *The Tractatus Logico-Philosophicus,* trans. D. F. Pears and B. F. McGuinness (London: Routledge, 1961). *See:* Bernstein [1]; Black [16]; Urmson [2]; Wittgenstein [1], etc.

Wolfson, W. [1] "What Is Philosophy?" *JP,* LV (1958), 322–36.

Wolgast, Elizabeth H. [1] "Wittgenstein and Criteria," *I,* VII (1964), 348–66. *See:* Albritton [1], etc.

Wollheim, R. A. [1] "F. H. Bradley," in *REV,* 12–25.

—— [2] "Modern Philosophy and Unreason," *PQ,* XXVI (1955), 246–57.

Wolter, Allan B. [1] "The Unspeakable Philosophy of the Late Wittgenstein," *Proceedings of the American Catholic Philosophical Association,* XXXIV (1960), 168–93.

Wood, O. P. [1] "The Force of Linguistic Rules," *PAS,* LI (1950–51), 313–28.

Woozley, A. D. [1] "Ordinary Language and Common Sense," *M,* LXII (1953), 301–12. *See:* Malcolm [2], etc.

Xenakis, Jason. [1] "Ordinary Language and Ordinary Belief," PSt, V (1954), 40–46.

—— [2] "Ordinary-Language Philosophy: Language, Logic and Philosophy," *Synthese,* XI (1959), 294–306.

Yalden-Thomson, D. C. [1] "Remarks about Philosophical Refutations," *MO,* XLVIII (1964), 501–12.

Yolton, John W. [1] "Philosophical and Scientific Explanation," *JP,* LV (1958), 133–43.

Zabeeh, Farhang. [1] "Metaphysics or Descriptive Semantics," *ME,* XIV (1962), 3–10. *See:* Strawson [2].

—— [2] "Oxford and Metaphysics: A New Page in Contemporary Philosophy," *IPQ,* III (1963), 307–20.

Ziff, Paul. [1] "About Ungrammaticalness," *M,* LXXIII (1964), 204–14.

—— [2] *Semantic Analysis* (Ithaca: Cornell, 1960). *See:* Fodor and Katz [2].

Zimmerman, Marvin. [1] "The Status of the Verifiability Principle," *PPR,* XXII (1962), 334–43. *See:* Hempel [1], etc.